2021
湖北统计年鉴
HUBEI STATISTICAL YEARBOOK

湖　北　省　统　计　局
国家统计局湖北调查总队　编

Compiled by
Hubei Provincial Bureau of Statistics
Survey Office of the National Bureau of Statistics in Hubei

（总第37期　NO.37）

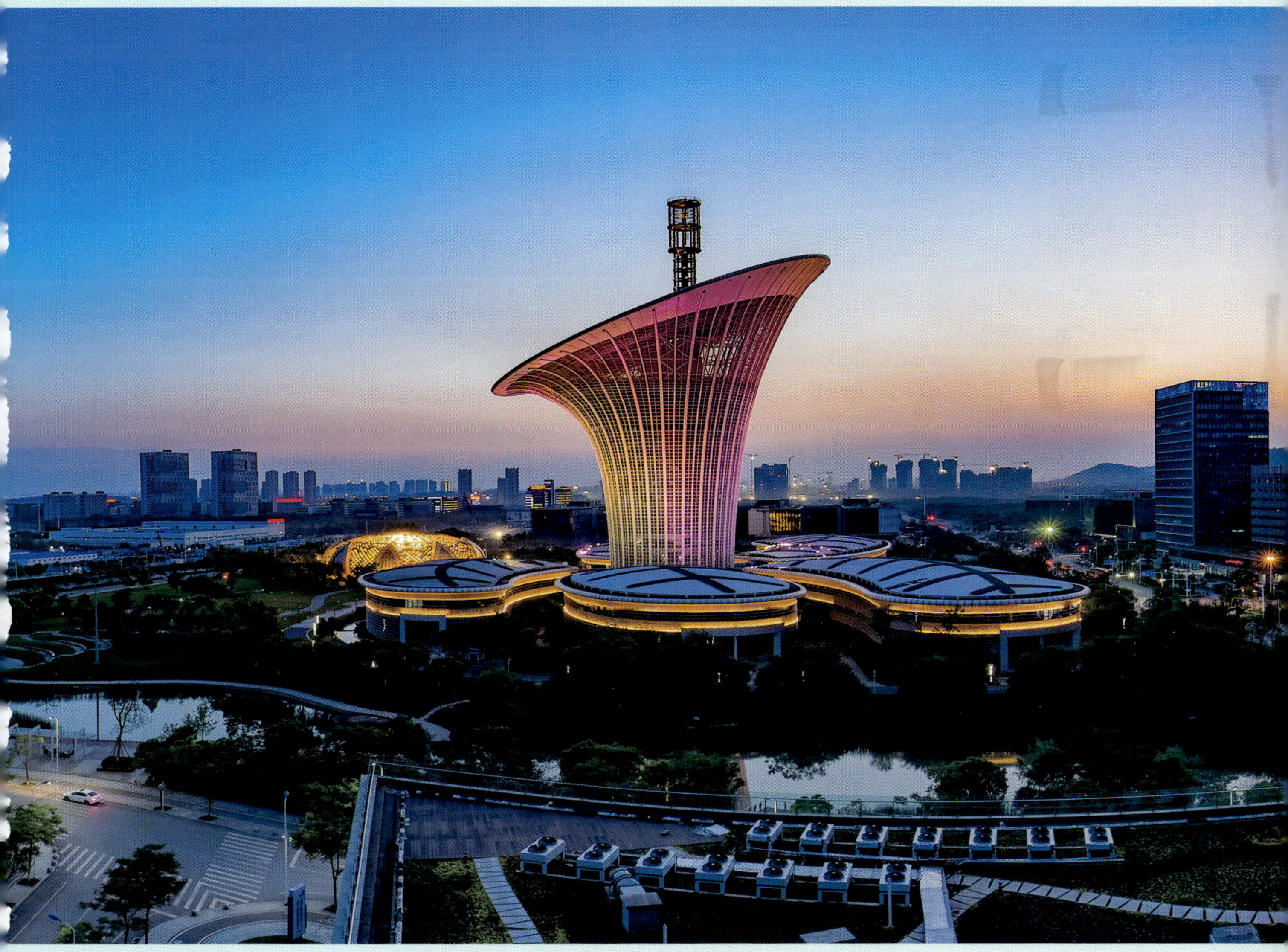

地区生产总值（亿元）

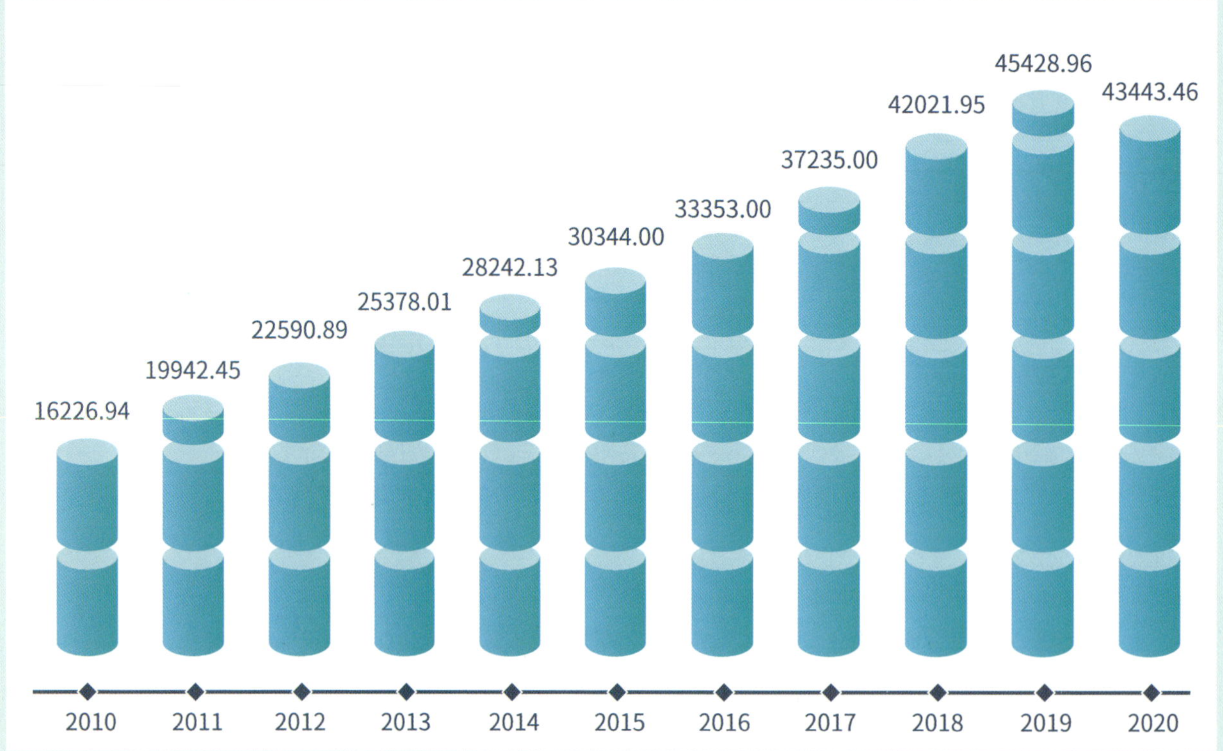

地区生产总值增速（%）

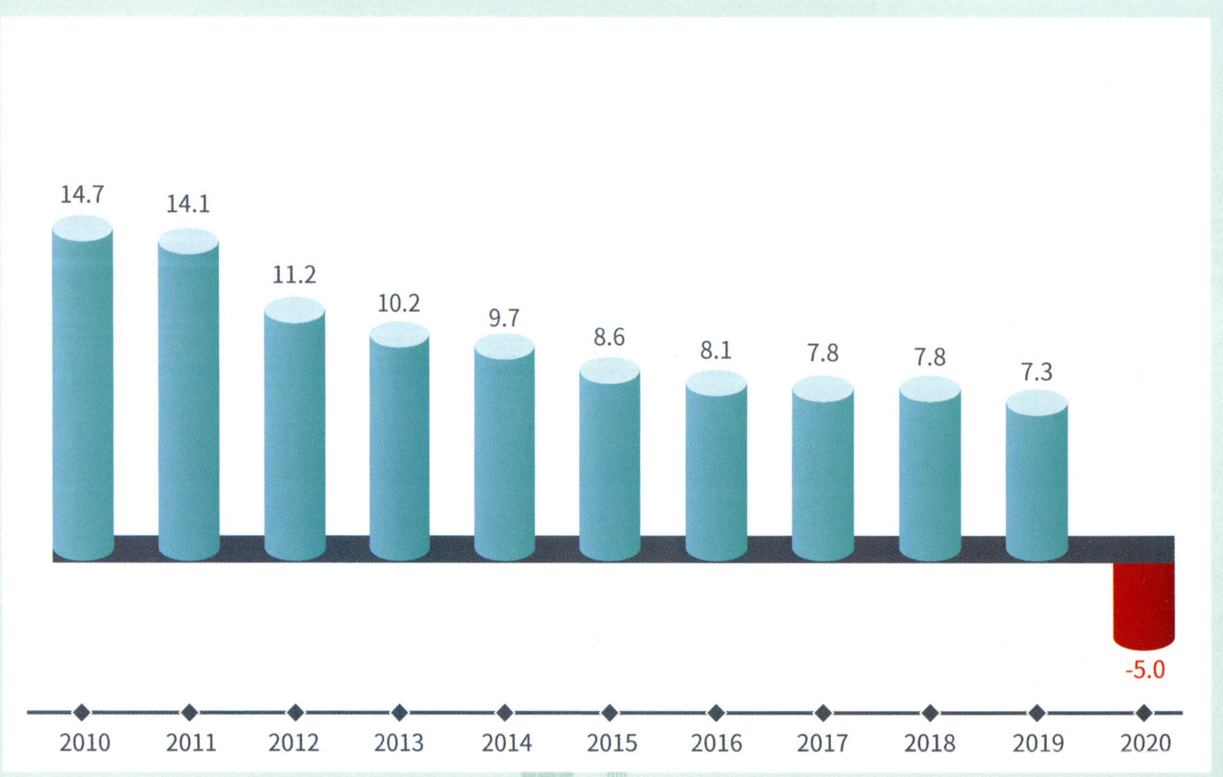

人均生产总值(元)

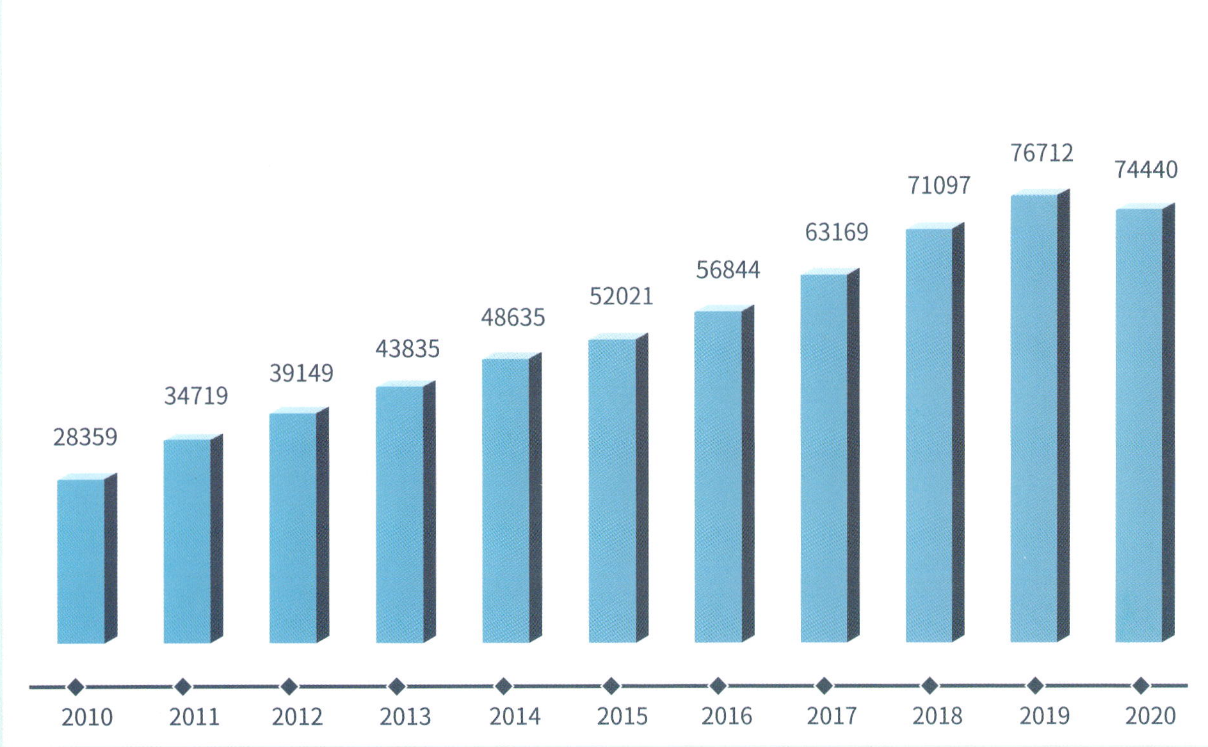

常住人口(万人)

城镇化率(%)

49.70
51.78
53.23
54.51
55.73
57.18
58.57
59.88
61.00
61.83
62.89
2010
2011
2012
2013
2014
2015
2016
2017
2018
2019
2020

财政收支(亿元)

地方一般公共预算收入
地方一般公共预算支出
2501.40
1011.23
3214.74
1526.91
3759.79
1823.05
4371.65
2191.22
4934.15
2566.90
6132.84
3005.53
6422.98
3102.06
6831.74
3248.44
7258.27
3307.08
7970.21
3388.57
8439.04
2511.52
2010
2011
2012
2013
2014
2015
2016
2017
2018
2019
2020

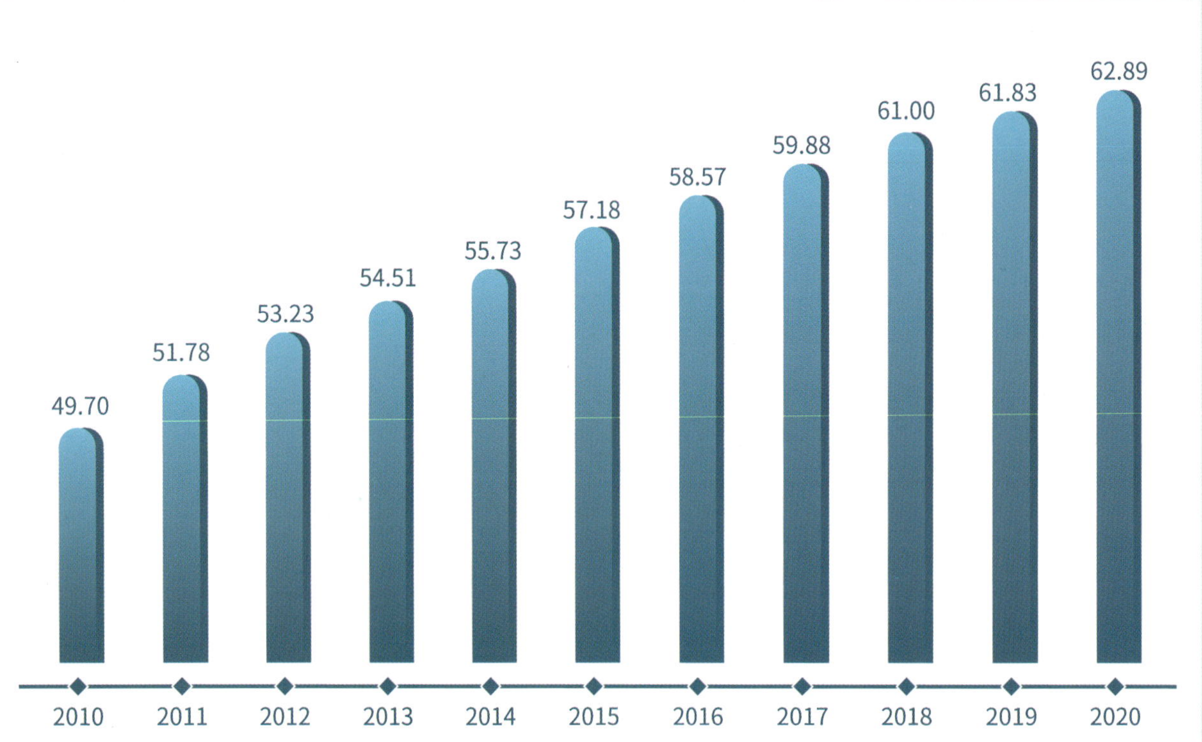

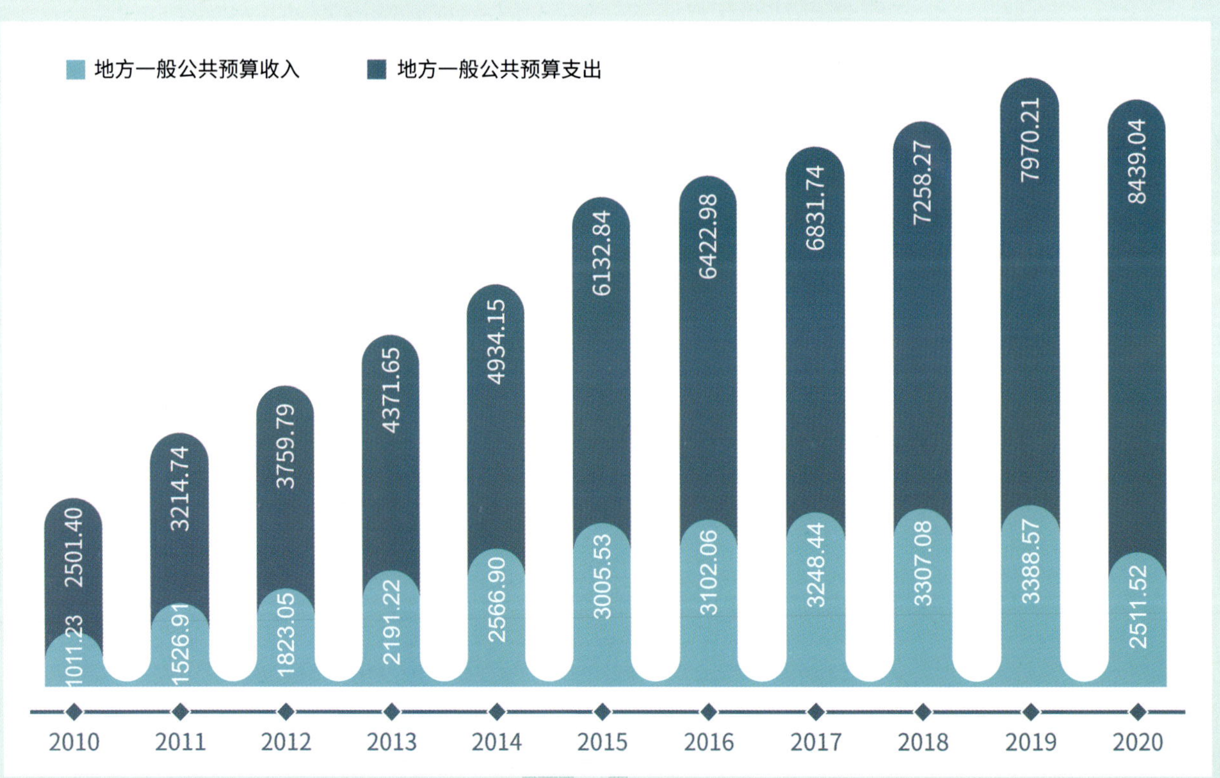

规模以上工业增加值增速（%）

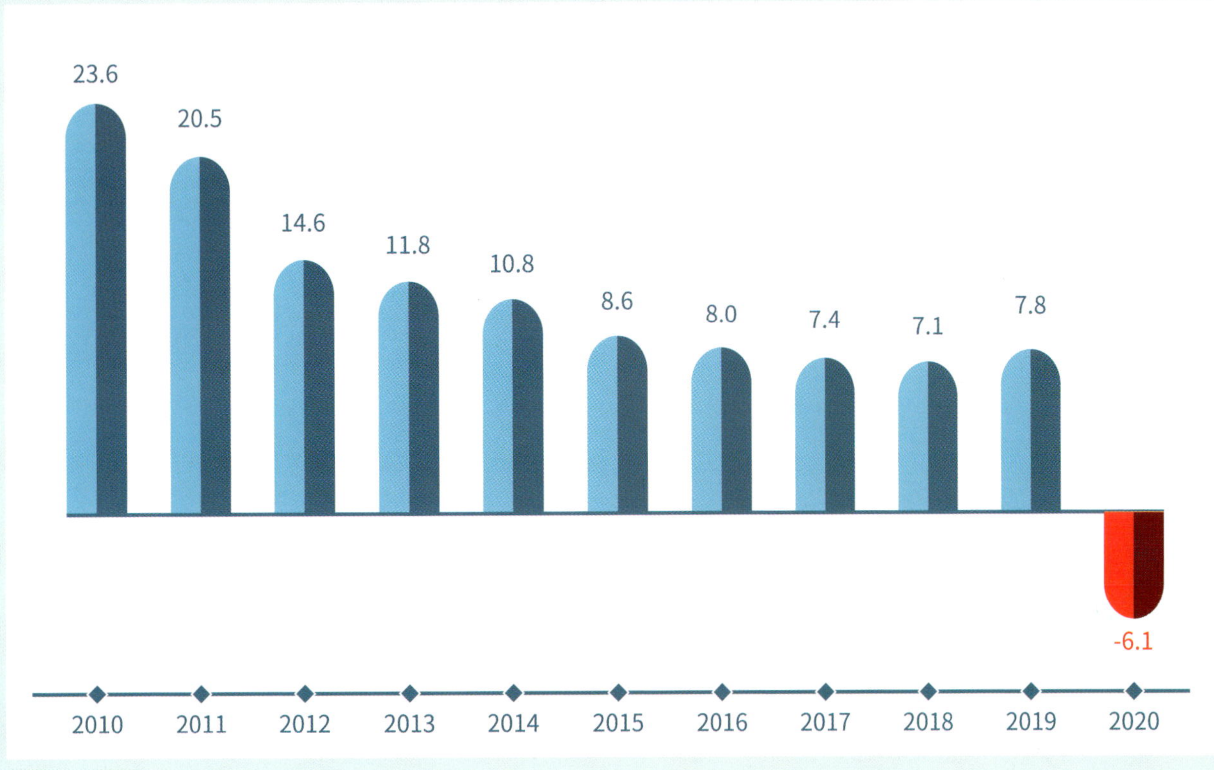

三次产业结构（%）

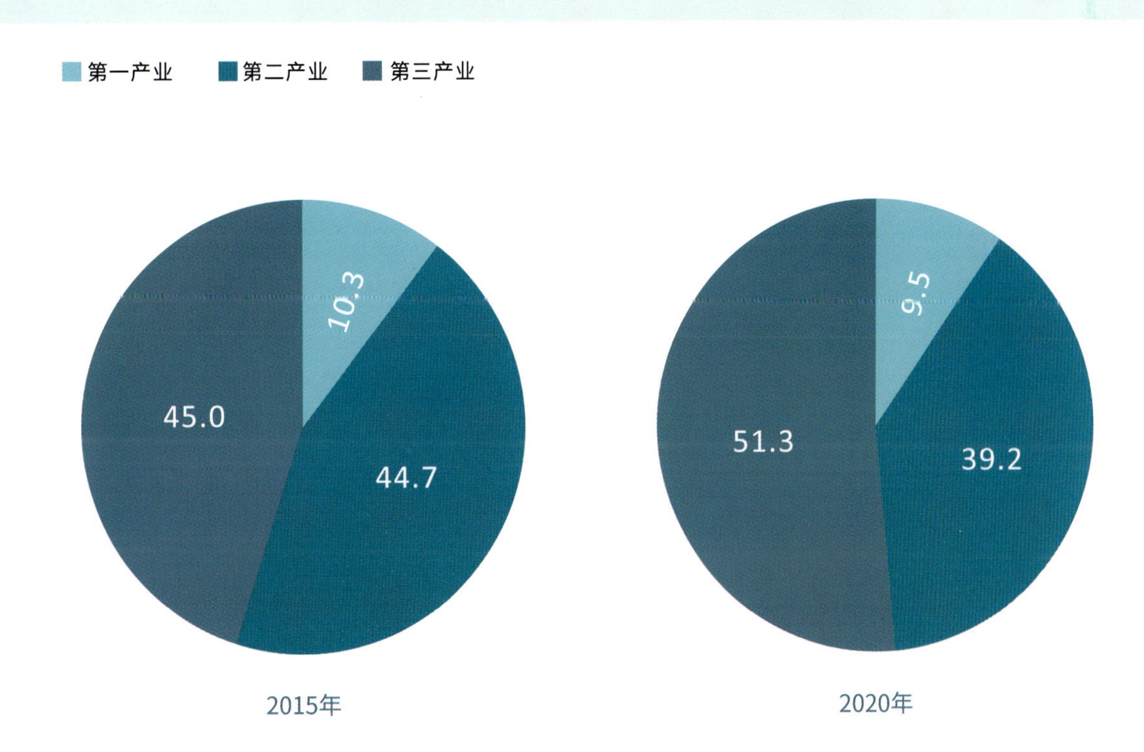

高新技术产业增加值（亿元）

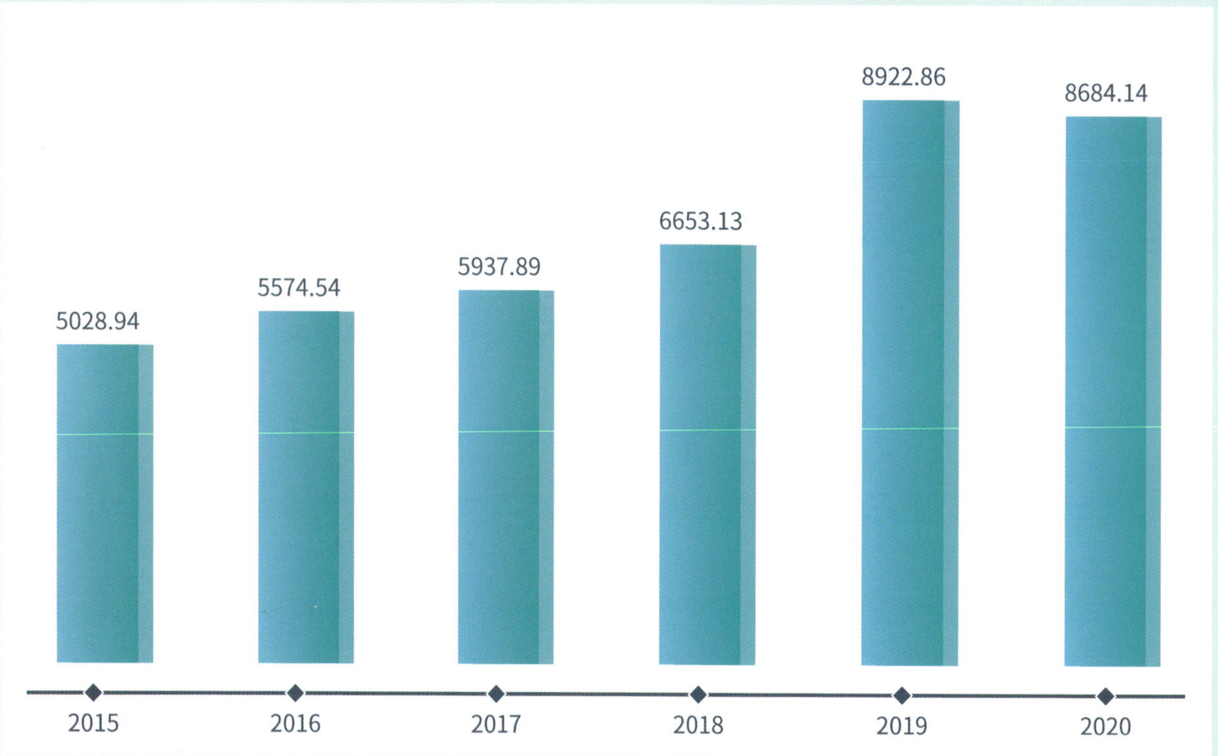

社会消费品零售总额（亿元）

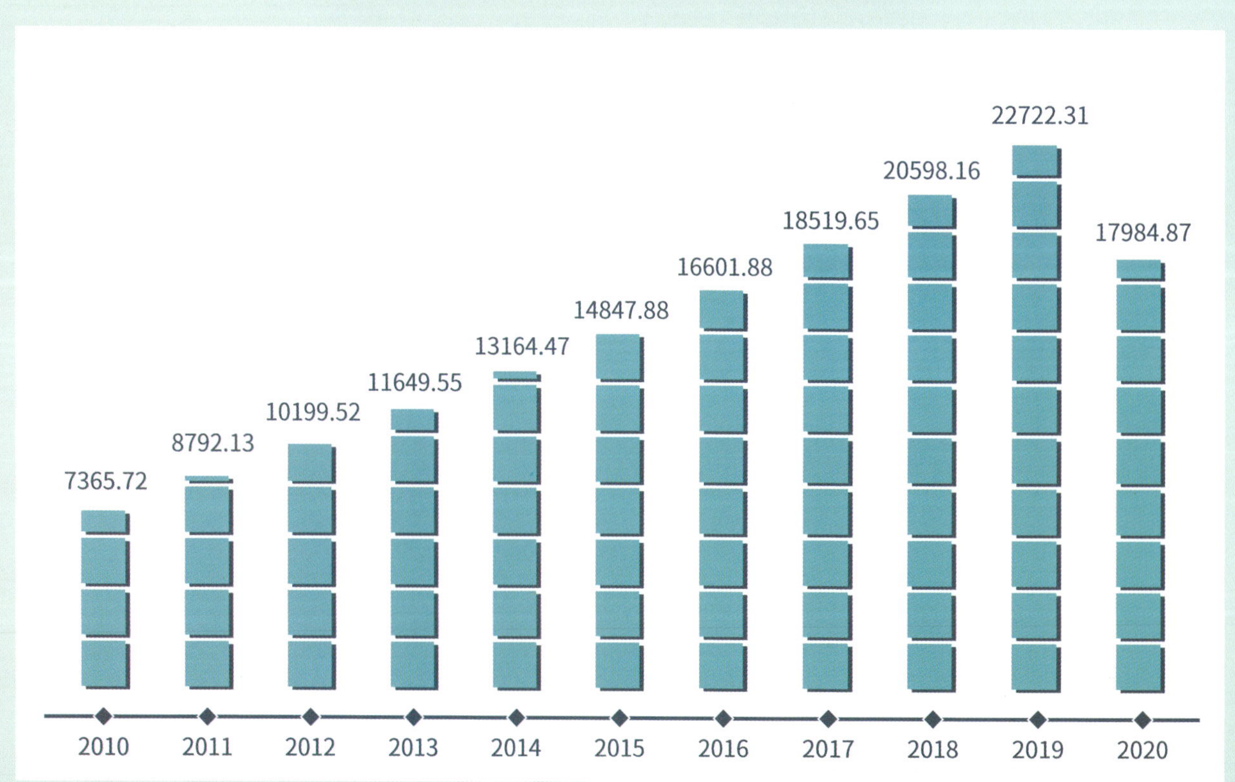

《湖北统计年鉴—2021》

编委会和编辑工作人员

Hubei Statistical Yearbook 2021

EDITORIAL BOARD AND STAFF

编 者 说 明

一、《湖北统计年鉴—2021》是一本信息密集的资料工具书。通过大量数据,全面地记载和反映了湖北省2020年经济、社会、科技、文化等方面的发展情况。具有信息量大、权威性强、适用性广等特点。

二、本年鉴分为首卷和统计资料。卷首为特载《2020年湖北省国民经济和社会发展统计公报》。统计资料分为24个章节,即:综合、人口、就业和工资、固定资产投资、对外经济贸易和旅游、能源、财政和金融、价格、人民生活、城市概况、资源和环境、农业、工业、建筑业、服务业、交通运输和邮电、国内贸易、科技和教育、卫生和社会服务、文化和体育、公共管理及其他、长江经济带、县域经济主要指标、附录。为方便读者使用,各篇章篇末附有《主要统计指标解释》。

三、与《湖北统计年鉴—2020》相比较,本年鉴在内容和篇章结构上增加了服务业。参照执行了国家统计局《省级统计年鉴指标体系目录》,采用了最新的国民经济行业分类标准和指标口径,并对英文注释和指标解释进行了全面修订。2021年湖北统计年鉴大量选用第四次全国经济普查和第七次全国人口普查数据。

四、本年鉴对过去发表的统计资料重新予以审核,凡与本年鉴资料有出入的,均以本年鉴为准。本年鉴中统计公报的数据为初步数,若与年鉴数据不一致,请以年鉴数据为准。本年鉴中部分数据合计数或相对数由于单位取舍不同而产生的计算误差,均未作机械调整。年鉴表中的“空格”表示该项统计指标数据不足本表最小单位数、数据不详或无该项数据;“#”表示其中的主要项。

五、年鉴中指标的使用要结合文中的指标解释,以及注解合理使用,以免发生错误。

六、《湖北统计年鉴》公开出版以来,受到国内外读者的爱护与支持,对本年鉴的内容和编辑工作提出了许多宝贵意见,为此,我们特表谢意。由于水平有限,编辑工作中难免有疏误之处,竭诚欢迎读者批评指正。

EDITOR'S NOTES

Ⅰ. *Hubei Statistical Yearbook 2021* is an information–intensive data reference book. In a comprehensive manner, it records and reflects the economic, social, technological and cultural developments among other aspects in Hubei Province in 2020, featuring a large amount of information, authority, wide applicability and so on.

Ⅱ. The yearbook includes a special issue and statistical data. The special issue is 2020 Statistics Bulletin of the National Economic and Social Development of Hubei Province. The statistical data contains the following 24 chapters:1.General Survey; 2.Population; 3.Employment and Wages; 4.Investment in Fixed Assets; 5.International Trade and Economic Cooperation & Tourism; 6.Energy; 7.Government Finance and Banking; 8.Prices; 9.People's Livlihoods; 10.City Overview; 11.Resources and Environment; 12.Agriculture; 13.Industry; 14.Construction; 15.Service; 16.Transportation, Postal and Telecommunication Services; 17.Domestics Trade; 18.Science, Technology and Education; 19.Public Health and Social Services; 20. Culture and Sports; 21.Public Management and Other; 22.Yangtze River Economic Zone; 23.Main Economic Indicators of Counties; 24.Major Indicators by Region. To facilitate readers, at the end of each chapter, Explanatory Notes on Main Statistical Indicators are included.

Ⅲ. Compared with *Hubei Statistical Yearbook 2020*, the mainly supplement in content and chapter structure is service. *Hubei Statistical Yearbook 2021* refers to the implementation of the Provincial Statistics Index System Directory. The yearbook adopts the latest industrial categorization standards and indicator range, while the English notes and the interpretation of indicators have been revised thoroughly. In 2021, the yearbook adopts data of the Fourth National Economic Census and the Seventh National Population Census.

Ⅳ. The yearbook adopts the updated statistical data based on the review of the past publications. Should any discrepancy arise, the yearbook shall prevail. Data of the statistical communique in the yearbook are the initial count. If that is not consistent with data of the yearbook, the latter shall prevail. Statistical discrepancies due to rounding are not adjusted in the yearbook. In the yearbook, blank space indicates that the figure is not large enough to be measured with the smallest unit in the table, or date are unknown or are not available, "#" indicates a major breakdown of the total.

Ⅴ. For any use of the indicators in the yearbook, please refer to the explanatory notes and annotations, so as to avoid mistakes.

Ⅵ. Since publication, *Hubei Statistical Yearbook* has received concern and support from domestic and foreign readers, who also offer a number of valuable suggestions concerning the content and editorial work, for which we hereby express our gratitude. It is undeniable that editing work is subject to human errs, and we thereby sincerely welcome criticisms and corrections from readers.

目　　录
CONTENTS

特 载
Specifically Stated

1 综 合
General Survey

2 人　口

Population

3 就业和工资

Employment and Wages

4 固定资产投资

Investment in Fixed Assets

5 对外经济贸易和旅游

International Trade and Economic Cooperation & Tourism

6 能 源

Energy

7 财政和金融

Government Finance and Banking

8 价 格

Prices

9 人民生活

People's Livelihoods

10 城市概况

City Overview

11 资源和环境

Resources and Environment

12 农 业

Agriculture

13 工 业

Industry

14 建筑业

Construction

15 服务业

Service

16 交通运输和邮电

Transport, Postal and Telecommunication Services

17 国内贸易

Domestics Trade

18 科技和教育

Science, Technology and Education

19 卫生和社会服务

Public Health and Social Services

20 文化和体育

Culture and Sports

21 公共管理及其他

Public Management and Other

特　　载

Specifically Stated

2020年湖北省国民经济和社会发展统计公报

湖 北 省 统 计 局
国家统计局湖北调查总队

2020年是新中国成立以来湖北历史上极不平凡、极不容易、极其难忘的一年。在以习近平同志为核心的党中央坚强领导下，全省上下众志成城、万众一心、攻坚克难，全力打好战疫、战洪、战贫三场硬仗，稳住了经济基本盘，兜住了民生底线，守牢了社会稳定底线，夺取了统筹疫情防控和经济社会发展的“双胜利”，全年经济在巨大的困难挑战面前实现复苏向好发展，交出了一份让全省人民引以为豪的英雄答卷。

一、综合

2020年，全省完成生产总值43443.46亿元，比上年下降5.0%。其中，第一产业完成增加值4131.91亿元，按不变价计算与上年持平；第二产业完成增加值17023.90亿元，下降7.4%；第三产业完成增加值22287.65亿元，下降3.8%。三次产业结构由2019年的8.4:41.2:50.4调整为9.5:39.2:51.3。在第三产业中，金融业、其他服务业增加值分别增长6.3%和3.2%。交通运输仓储和邮政业、批发和零售业、住宿和餐饮业、房地产业增加值分别下降16.5%、12.1%、23.7%、8.7%。

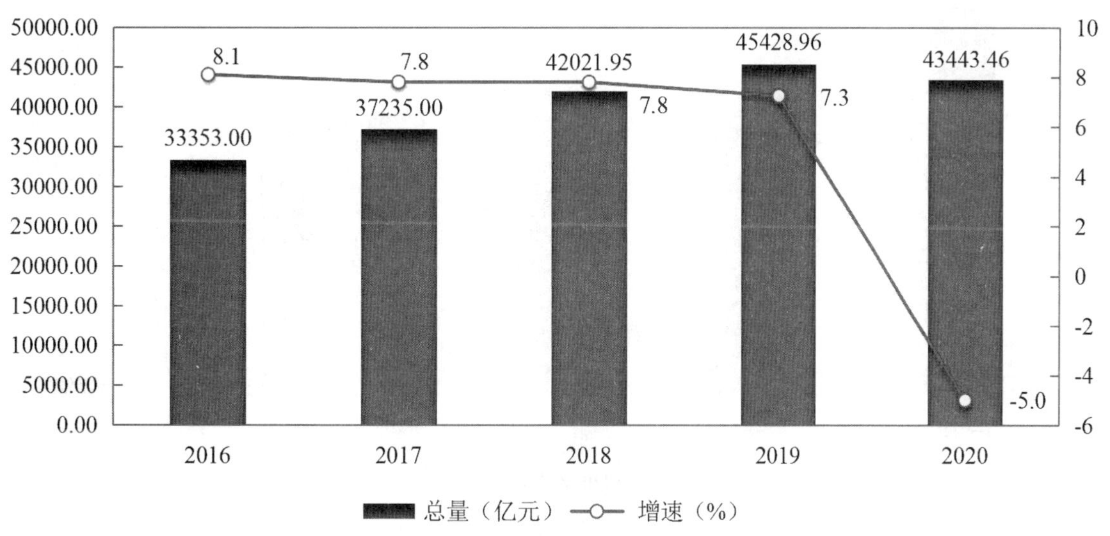

图1 2016–2020年湖北地区生产总值及其增速

价格运行保持平稳。全省居民消费价格上涨2.7%，涨幅比上年回落0.4个百分点。其中，城市上涨2.5%，农村上涨3.5%。分类别看，八大类商品及服务价格“五涨三降”。其中，食品烟酒价格上涨9.3%，衣着价格下降0.3%，居住价格下降0.8%，生活用品及服务价格上涨0.1%，交通和通信价格下降3.5%，教育文化和娱乐价格上涨0.9%，医疗保健价格上涨2.2%，其他用品和服务价格上涨4.8%。全省工业生产者出厂价格下降0.9%，工业生产者购进价格下降1.6%。

市场主体不断发展。全省新登记市场主体73.10万户，其中，新登记私营企业22.62万户，新登记个体工商户49.13万户。

就业形势基本稳定。全省城镇新增就业75.18万人，超额完成全年目标任务。年末全省城镇登记失业率为3.35%。

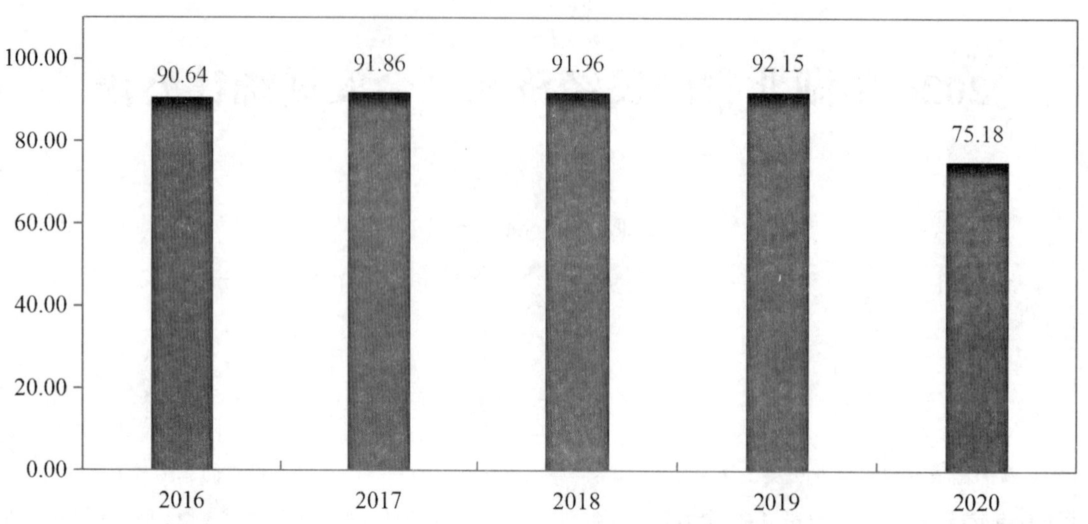

图 2　2016–2020 年湖北城镇新增就业人数

劳动生产率保持平稳。全省全员劳动生产率预计为 12.19 万元/人，比上年下降 5.2%。

脱贫攻坚成效明显。按照每人每年 2300 元(2010 年不变价)的国家贫困线标准，5.8 万剩余贫困人口全部脱贫，贫困县全部摘帽，绝对贫困历史性消除。全年贫困地区农村居民人均可支配收入 13075 元，比上年增长 1.6%。

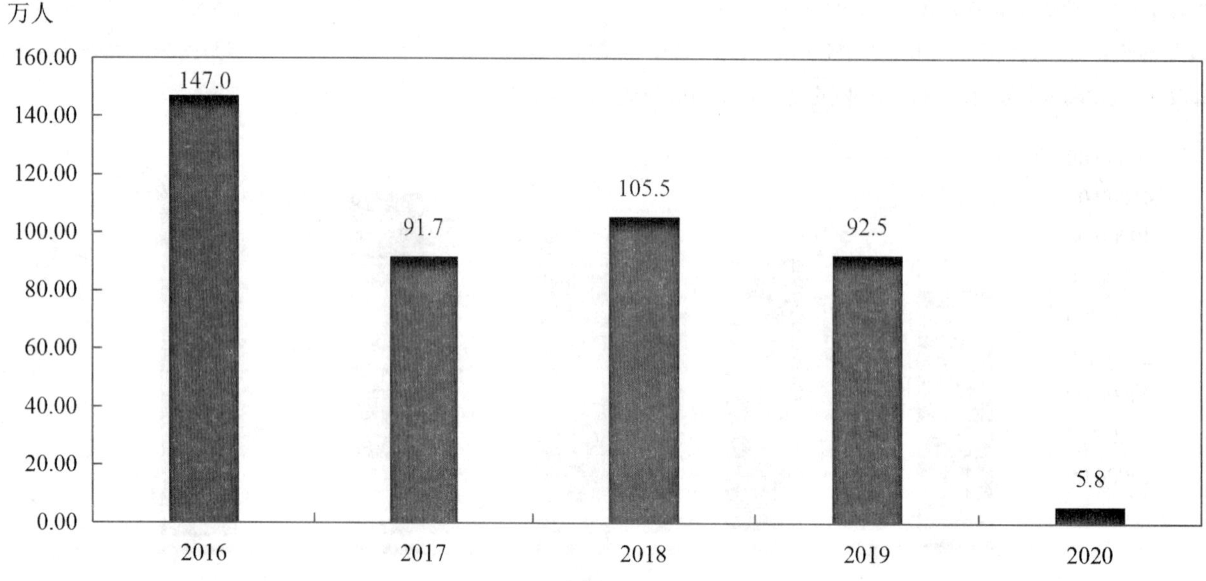

图 3　2016–2020 年末湖北减贫人口数

二、农业

全年全省农林牧渔业增加值 4358.69 亿元，按可比价格计算，比上年增长 0.3%。

粮食产能保持稳定。全省粮食总产量 2727.43 万吨，增长 0.1%，连续 8 年稳定在 500 亿斤以上；种植面积 4645.27 千公顷，增长 0.8%。

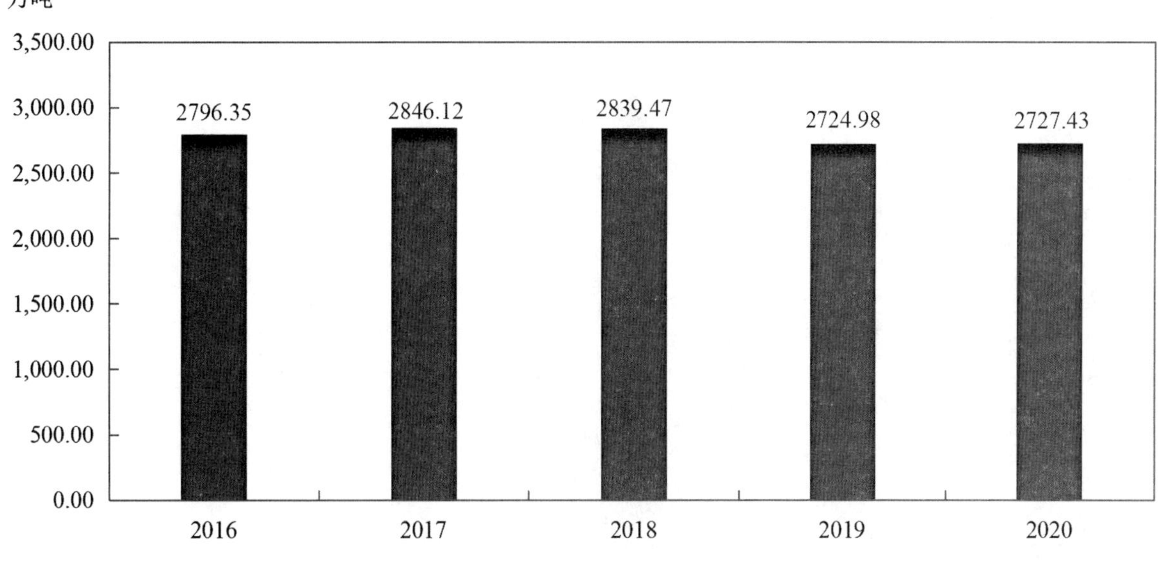

图 4 2016-2020 年湖北粮食产量

特色优势经济作物保持增长。油料产量 344.45 万吨，增长 9.7%；茶叶产量 36.08 万吨，增长 2.4%；园林水果产量 716.38 万吨，增长 8.4%。

畜类生产有所下降，禽类养殖保持稳定。生猪出栏 2631.12 万头，下降 17.5%；牛出栏 101.96 万头，下降 6.9%；羊出栏 532.68 万只，下降 13.5%；家禽出笼 59325.84 万只，下降 0.1%；禽蛋产量 193.09 万吨，增长 8.0%。

水产品生产形势趋稳，渔业生产基本持平。水产品总产量 467.88 万吨，微降 0.4%。

表 1 2020 年全省主要农产品产量

单位：万吨

产品名称	产量	比上年增长(%)
粮食	2727.43	0.1
棉花	10.79	-24.9
油料	344.45	9.7
# 油菜籽	241.06	14.1
茶叶	36.08	2.4
园林水果(不含果用瓜)	716.38	8.4
蔬菜及食用菌	4119.37	0.8

三、工业和建筑业

年末全省规模以上工业企业达到 15769 家。全年全省规模以上工业增加值下降 6.1%。分经济类型看，国有及国有控股企业下降 1.6%；集体企业下降 12.4%；股份合作企业下降 31.9%；股份制企业下降 6.2%；外商及港澳台投资企业下降 6.7%；其他经济类型企业下降 9.3%。轻工业下降 7.2%；重工业下降 5.6%。分门类看，采矿业下降 16.0%，制造业下降 6.2%，电力、热力、燃气及水生产和供应业下降 2.5%。

高技术制造业增加值增长 4.1%，增速快于规模以上工业 10.2 个百分点，占规模以上工业增加值的比重达 10.2%。其中，计算机、通信和其他电子设备制造业增长 4.4%。

全年规模以上工业销售产值下降 7.7%，产品销售率为 97.3%，出口交货值下降 0.4%。全年规模以上工业企业实现利润 2519.0 亿元，下降 8.3%。

表 2 2020 年全省规上工业主要产品产量及其增速

产品名称	单位	产量	比上年增长(%)
白酒(折 65 度,商品量)	万千升	35.9	-42.9
啤酒	万千升	97.5	-11.8
卷烟	亿支	1330.5	4.5
布	亿米	43.1	-17.7
硫酸(折 100%)	万吨	1330.5	5.7
农用氮、磷、钾化学肥料(折纯)	万吨	482.1	-8.9
化学药品原药	万吨	18.3	-6.2
中成药	万吨	23.1	-22.7
发电量	亿千瓦小时	2911.35	0.5
#水电	亿千瓦小时	1574.53	19.0
水泥	万吨	10108.7	-12.8
平板玻璃	万重量箱	9584.5	-7.5
生铁	万吨	2727.4	-4.9
粗钢	万吨	3557.2	-1.5
钢材	万吨	3653.0	-2.2
十种有色金属	万吨	80.6	-6.1
#精炼铜	万吨	51.2	-4.5
工业机器人	套	9857.0	-5.5
汽车	万辆	209.4	-6.0
#新能源汽车	万辆	3.2	-48.4
发电机组	万千瓦	114.7	-4.7
锂离子电池	亿只	11.2	2.9
房间空气调节器	万台	1760.3	-18.0
微型计算机设备	万台	1720.0	35.4
显示器	万台	1457.3	-4.1
移动通信手持机	万台	2667.0	-32.0

建筑业稳步发展。全年全省具有总承包和专业承包资质建筑企业完成总产值 16136.10 亿元,下降 5.0%;全年新签合同额 22055.89 亿元,增长 9.1%。

四、固定资产投资

全省完成固定资产投资(不含农户)下降 18.8%。按产业划分,一、二、三次产业投资分别下降 28.2%、23.8%、15.4%。分领域看,基础设施投资、工业投资和房地产开发投资分别下降 22.8%、23.9%和 4.4%。高技术制造业投资下降 9.4%,其中医药制造业、计算机及办公设备制造业投资分别增长 20.4%、14.7%。补短板强功能建设加快推进,电信、广播电视和卫星传输服务业投资增长 16.8%,卫生投资增长 65.8%,航空运输业投资增长 1.29 倍。

商品房销售面积 6587.83 万平方米,下降 23.4%;实现商品房销售额 6087.90 亿元,下降 21.5%。

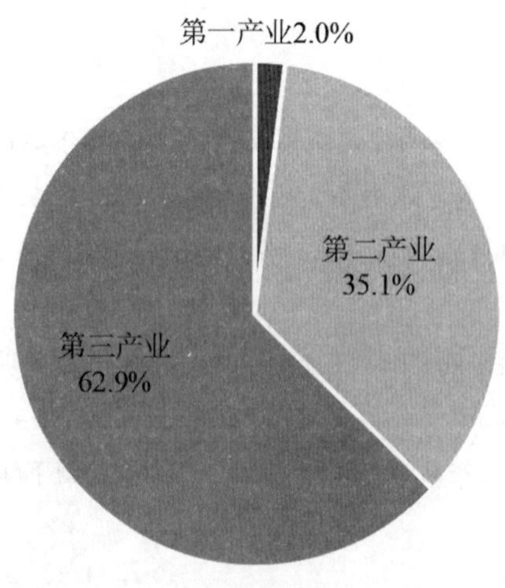

图 5 2020 年湖北三次产业投资占固定资产投资(不含农户)比重

全省亿元以上新开工项目3649个，下降7.7%，亿元以上项目完成投资额下降21.2%。

五、国内贸易

全年全省实现社会消费品零售总额17984.87亿元，下降20.8%。分城乡看，城镇实现零售额15284.69亿元，下降20.9%；乡村实现零售额2700.18亿元，下降20.8%。其中，限额以上企业(单位)实现消费品零售额6592.93亿元，下降14.2%。

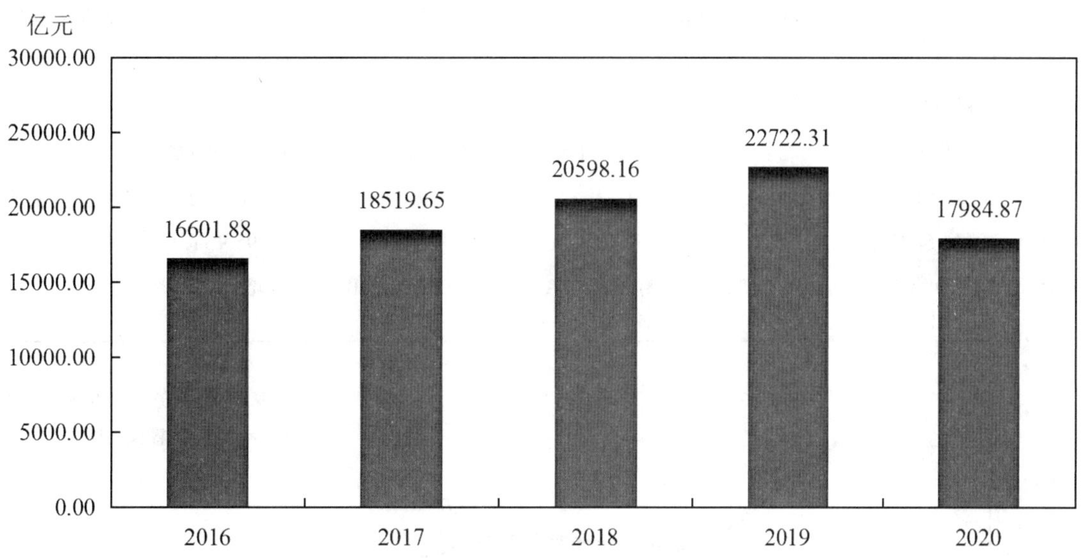

图6 2016-2020年湖北社会消费品零售总额

2020年，全省网上零售额达到2866.6亿元，增长1.6%，其中实物商品网上零售额2448.9亿元，增长4.6%，占社会消费品零售总额的比重为13.6%，比上年提高1.8个百分点。

六、对外经济

全年全省实现货物进出口总额4294.1亿元，增长8.8%，其中，进口1592.1亿元，增长9.1%；出口2702.0亿元，增长8.7%。2020年欧盟替代东盟跃升为湖北省第一大贸易伙伴，双边贸易值595.2亿元，增长17.1%。

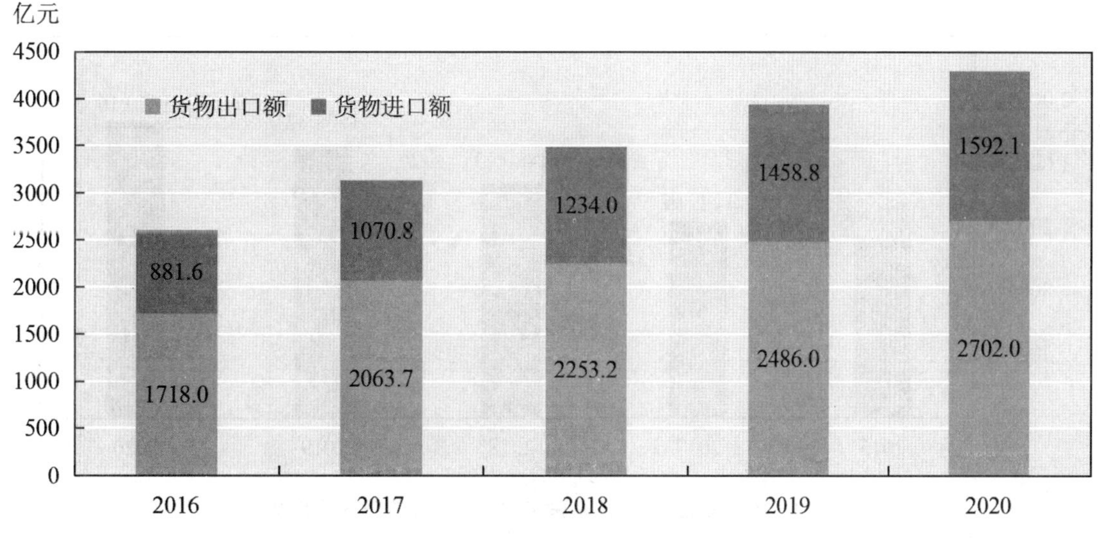

图7 2016-2020年湖北货物进出口总额

新批外商直接投资项目296个。全年实际使用外资103.52亿美元，下降19.8%。欧亚部分国家在湖北投资逆势增长，德国、荷兰、新加坡投资分别增长92.5%、27.3%、16.0%。全年高技术产业(制造业)实际使用外资1.07亿美元(商务部口径)，下降

16.9%。

全年对外非金融类直接投资额 20.0 亿美元，增长 2.0%。对外承包工程完成营业额 64.15 亿美元，下降 3.0%。对外劳务合作派出各类劳务人员 12484 人次，增长 8.4%。

七、交通运输和邮电通信

年末全省公路总里程达 289960.44 公里，增长 0.3%；高速公路里程达 7229.81 公里，增长 5.4%。全年全省完成货物周转量 5295.68 亿吨公里，下降 13.9%；旅客周转量 612.42 亿人公里，下降 55.8%；港口完成货物吞吐量 3.80 亿吨，增长 23.9%。港口集装箱吞吐量 229 万标准箱，增长 9.8%。

全省邮政业务总量 471.77 亿元，增长 2.9%。其中，快递业务量 17.85 亿件，快递业务收入 178.69 亿元。全省电信业务总量 4204.91 亿元，增长 24.9%。长途光缆线路长度达到 3.21 万公里；移动电话交换机容量达 9043.50 万户；固定电话用户 481.61 万户；移动电话用户达到 5681.07 万户；全省电话普及率为 104.0 部/百人，移动电话普及率为 95.9 部/百人；固定互联网宽带接入用户 1870.16 万户，比上年增加 161.84 万户；移动互联网用户接入流量 50.67 亿 GB，比上年增长 32.4%。

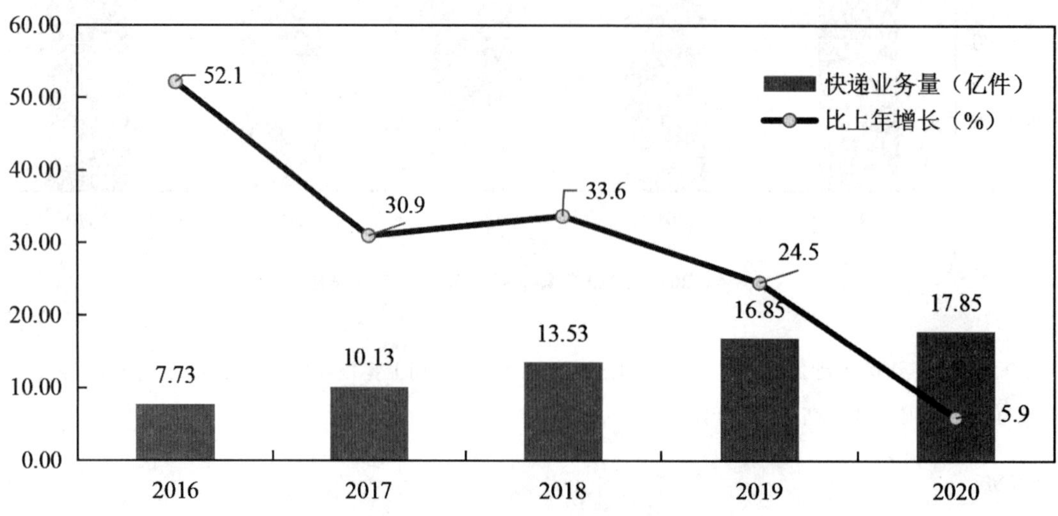

图 8　2016–2020 年湖北快递业务量及其增长速度

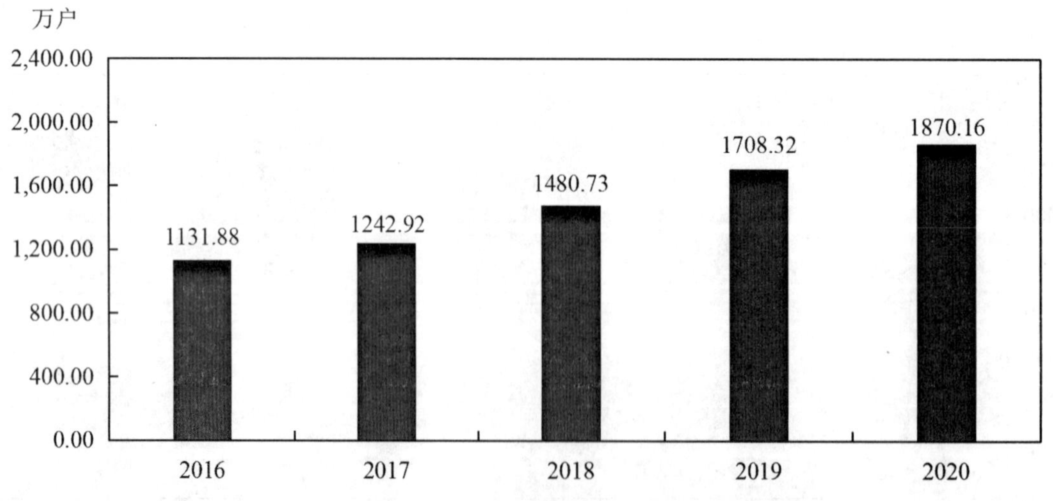

图 9　2016–2020 年湖北年末固定互联网宽带接入用户数

八、财政和金融

全年全省完成财政总收入 4580.89 亿元，下降 20.8%。其中，地方一般公共预算收入 2511.52 亿元，下降 25.9%。在地方一般公共预算收入中，税收收入 1923.4 亿元，下降 24.0%。地方一般公共预算支出 8439.04 亿元，增长 5.9%。

年末全省金融机构本外币各项存款余额 67159.32 亿元，增长 10.9%，比年初增加 6621.87 亿元。其中，住户存款 34144.37 亿元，增加 4170.57 亿元。金融机构人民币各项贷款余额 59872.13 亿元，增长 14.6%，比年初增加 7629.53 亿元。其中，住户贷款 18706.43 亿元，增加 2121.43 亿元；非金融企业及机关团体贷款 40165.08 亿元，增加 5613.34 亿元。

全年实现保费收入 1854.38 亿元，增长 7.3%。其中，财产险保费收入 370.25 亿元，下降 6.9%；人身险保费收入 1484.14 亿元，增长 11.5%。支付各类赔款及给付 518.15 亿元，增长 1.2%，其中，财产险赔付支出 218.15 亿元，增长 3.7%；人身险赔付支出 300.01 亿元，下降 0.6%。

九、教育和科学技术

2020 年，全省普通高等教育本专科招生 51.40 万人，在校生 161.69 万人，毕业生 40.18 万人；研究生招生 6.66 万人，在校研究生 17.88 万人，毕业生 4.53 万人；各类中等职业教育招生 15.23 万人，在校生 42.03 万人，毕业生 11.78 万人；普通高中招生 31.32 万人，在校生 89.19 万人，毕业生 27.41 万人；普通初中在校生 170.83 万人，小学在校生 380.85 万人，幼儿园在园幼儿 178.43 万人。

科学研究和技术开发取得新的成果。全年共登记重大科技成果 1553 项。其中，基础理论成果 54 项，应用技术成果 1447 项，软科学成果 52 项。全年共签订技术合同 39749 项，技术合同成交金额 1686.95 亿元，合同金额增长 16.4%。

2020 年末，全省共建有 246 家省级工程研究中心（工程实验室）、589 家省级企业技术中心。

全省共有国家级检验检测中心 33 个；累计有 15376 家企业通过 ISO9000 体系认证；企业获得强制性认证证书 10288 张。法定计量技术机构有 107 个，强制检定计量器具 151.54 万台件。

全省天气雷达观测站点 16 个，卫星云图接收站点 18 个。地震遥测台网 3 个，地震台站 52 个。

十、文化旅游、卫生和体育

2020 年末，全省共有国有艺术表演团体 87 个，群艺馆、文化馆 125 个，公共图书馆 115 个，博物馆 230 个。电影放映管理机构 103 个，放映单位 1797 个。广播电台 1 座，电视台 1 座，广播电视台 82 座，有线电视用户 1203 万户。广播节目综合人口覆盖率为 99.86%，电视节目综合人口覆盖率为 99.82%。全年出版全国性和省级报纸 5.7 亿份，各类期刊 0.7 亿册，图书 2.8 亿册。全年规模以上文化及相关产业企业营业收入 3930.7 亿元，下降 1.2%。

全年共接待游客 43729.64 万人次，下降 27.8%，旅游总收入 4379.49 亿元，下降 36.8%。

全省共有医疗卫生机构 35447 家，其中医院 1048 家，基层医疗卫生机构 33853 家，专业公共卫生机构 479 家；全省共有卫生计生人员 53.81 万人，其中执业（助理）医师 15.97 万人，注册护士 20.01 万人；全省共有医疗卫生机构床位 41.18 万张，其中医院床位 29.65 万张，社区卫生服务机构床位 1.63 万张，卫生院床位 8.16 万张。全年总诊疗人次 29457.34 万人次，出院人数 1027.45 万人。

全年全省运动健儿在国际比赛中共获得冠军 18 项次、亚军 7 项次、季军 7 项次；奥运会项目最高水平比赛冠军 19 项次、亚军 18 项次、季军 17 项次；在各类全国比赛中，获冠军 124 项次、亚军 92 项次、第三名 88 项次；全运会项目全国最高水平比赛中冠军 19 项次、亚军 18 项次、第三名 17 项次。全年销售体育彩票 82.8 亿元。

十一、居民生活和社会保障

全省城镇居民人均可支配收入 36706 元，下降 2.4%；农村居民人均可支配收入 16306 元，下降 0.5%。城镇居民人均消费支出 22885 元，下降 13.4%；农村居民人均消费支出 14473 元，下降 5.6%。

社会保障进一步加强。年末全省参加城镇职工基本养老保险 1746.09 万人，其中，在职职工 1149.62 万人，离退休人员 596.47 万人；参加城乡居民基本养老保险 2368.86 万人；参加职工基本医疗保险 1136.93 万人；参加城乡居民基本医疗保险 4446.05 万人；参加工伤保险 752.43 万人；参加生育保险 645.88 万人；参加失业保险人数 651.31 万人，年末领取失业保险金人数 14.05 万人。

全年全省城镇居民最低生活保障对象 30.7 万人，农村居民最低生活保障人数 144.6 万人，国家抚恤、补助各类优抚对象 37.27 万人。社会福利事业不断发展。年末全省养老机构 1831 家，城乡社区养老服务设施覆盖率分别达到 97%和 67%。全年销售社会福利彩票52.5亿元。

十二、节能降耗、资源环境

全省继续大力推进节能降耗工作，单位GDP能耗继续保持下降态势，年初确定的1%的下降目标顺利完成。

全省国有建设用地供应总量2.72万公顷，比上年下降13.79%。水资源总量1903.3亿立方米，增长210%。万元地区生产总值用水量76立方米，上升2.7%。万元工业增加值用水量56立方米，下降3.4%。

全省完成造林面积24.86万公顷，其中人工造林面积11.05万公顷，占全部造林面积的44.45%。森林抚育面积38.47万公顷。截至年底，全省国家级自然保护区22个。

全省主要河流的179个地表水水质监测断面中，水质优良为Ⅰ~Ⅲ类的占93.9%，水质较差为Ⅳ类、Ⅴ类的占6.1%，无水质污染严重为劣Ⅴ类的水质监测断面。全省主要湖泊、水库的32个水域中，水质优良为Ⅰ~Ⅲ类水域占62.5%，水质较差为IV类、Ⅴ类的占37.5%，无劣Ⅴ类水域。

在省内监测的13个地级及以上城市中，空气质量达标的城市占38.5%，未达标的城市占61.5%。细颗粒物(PM2.5)未达标城市年平均浓度40微克/立方米，比上年下降11.1%。

全省平均气温为16.8℃，比常年上升0.4℃。

注：1.本公报所列数据为统计快报数。

2.2020年开展第七次全国人口普查，相关数据预计将于2021年5月发布，公报中不再单独发布人口相关数据。

资料来源：本公报中城镇新增就业、城镇登记失业率、养老保险、工伤保险、失业保险等数据来自省人力社保厅；减贫人口数据来自省扶贫办；渔业数据来自省水产局；货物进出口数据来自武汉海关；实际使用外资、对外直接投资、对外承包工程、对外劳务合作等数据来自省商务厅；旅游总收入、旅游总人数、公共图书馆、文化馆、博物馆、艺术表演团体等数据来自省文化和旅游厅；货物周转量、旅客周转量、公路总里程、高速公路里程、港口货物吞吐量、集装箱吞吐量等数据来自中国铁路总公司、省交通运输厅、南航湖北分公司、东航武汉公司、国航湖北分公司；邮政业务量、快递业务量、快递业务收入等数据来自省邮政管理局；电信业务总量、长途光缆线路、电话用户、互联网用户、电话普及率等数据来自省通信管理局；财政数据来自省财政厅；金融数据来自人民银行武汉分行；保费数据来自省银保监局；教育数据来自省教育厅；卫生机构、床位、人员等数据来自省卫健委；广播电视数据来自省广电局；电影、出版数据来自省委宣传部；体育、体育彩票等数据来自省体育局；低保、社会服务、福利彩票等数据来自省民政厅；国家抚恤、补助优抚对象数据来自省退役军人事务厅；医疗保险、生育保险数据来自省医保局；省级工程研究中心和省级企业技术中心数据来自省发改委；重大科技成果、技术合同等数据来自省科技厅；市场主体、国家级检验检测中心、通过ISO9000体系认证企业数、法定计量技术机构数等数据来自省市场监管局；地震数据来自省地震局；建设用地数据来自省自然资源厅；水资源、水土流失治理面积等数据来自省水利厅；森林资源、自然保护区等数据来自省林业局；生态环境、环境监测等数据来自省生态环境厅；气象数据来自省气象局。价格、粮食、畜禽、城乡居民收支、贫困地区农村居民人均可支配收入等数据来自国家统计局湖北调查总队；其它数据均来自省统计局。

2020 Statistics Bulletin of the National Economic and Social Development of Hubei Province

Hubei Provincial Bureau of Statistics
Survey Office of the National Bureau of Statistics in Hubei

2020 was an extremely extraordinary, extremely difficult and extremely unforgettable year in Hubei's history since the founding of the People's Republic of China. Under the strong leadership of the Party Central Committee with Comrade Xi Jinping as the core, the whole province united together to overcome difficulties and fight hard battles against the COVID-19 epidemics, floods, and poverty. The province has stabilized the basic economic fundamentals, held the bottom line of people's livelihood, secured the bottom line of social stability, and won the "double victories" of coordinating the COVID-19 epidemic prevention and control and the economic and social development. The economy throughout the year achieved a recovery trend in the face of huge difficulties and challenges. Hubei had handed over a heroic answer sheet that the people of the whole province are proud of.

Ⅰ. General

In 2020, the province saw a GDP of 4,344.346 billion yuan, a decrease of 5.0% from the previous year. The primary industry saw the added value of 413.191 billion yuan, which was basically the same as the previous year at constant prices; the secondary industry saw the added value of 1702.390 billion yuan, a decrease of 7.4%; the tertiary industry saw the added value of 2,228.765 billion yuan, a decrease of 3.8%. The structure of the three industries was adjusted from 8.4:41.2:50.4 in 2019 to 9.5:39.2:51.3. In the tertiary industry, the added value of the financial industry and other service industries increased by 6.3% and 3.2%, respectively. The added value of transportation, storage and postal industry, wholesale and retail industry, accommodation and catering industry, and real estate industry decreased by 16.5%, 12.1%, 23.7%, and 8.7%, respectively.

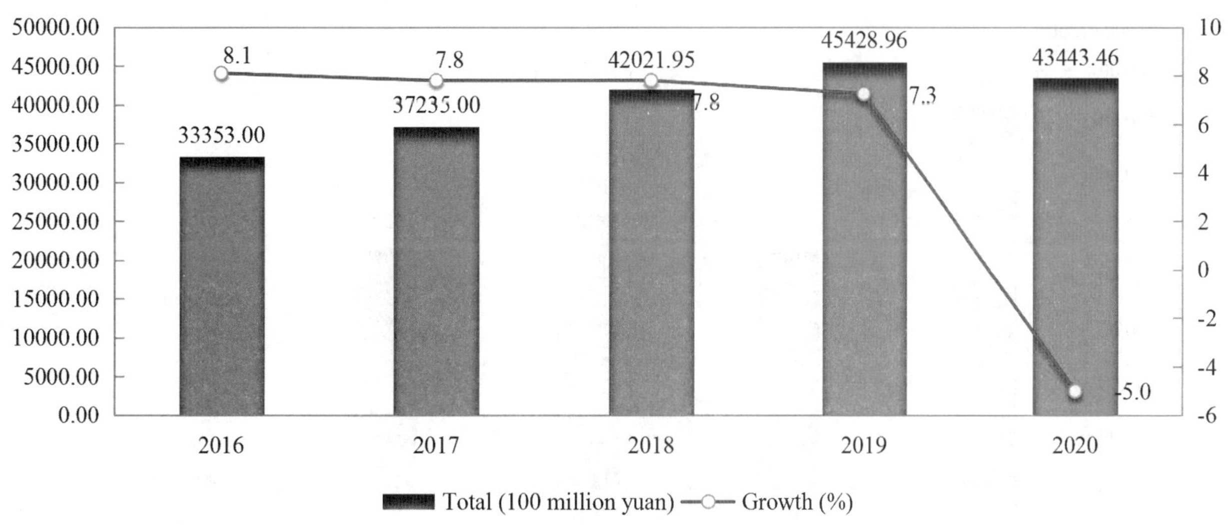

Figure 1 Hubei GDP and Growth Rates from 2016–2020

The price level remained basically stable. The consumer prices in Hubei rose by 2.7%, 0.4% less than that of the previous year. Within this category, urban consumer price increased by 2.5%, and rural 3.5%. By categories, among the eight categories of commodity, five saw price rises and three saw price falls. Specifically, the prices of food, tobacco and wine rose by 9.3%, clothing fell by 0.3%, residence fell by 0.8%, articles of daily use and services rose by 0.1%, traffic and communication fell by 3.5%, education, culture and entertainment rose by 0.9%, medical care rose by 2.2%, and other articles for use and services rose by 4.8%. In Hubei, the producer price for industrial producers fell by 0.9% and the purchase price for industrial producers fell by 1.6%.

Market entities kept development. The whole province saw 731,000 newly registered market entities, including 226,200 newly registered private enterprises and 491,300 newly registered individual businesses.

Employment remained stable. A total of 751,800 new urban jobs were created, exceeding the annual target. The registered urban unemployment rate was 3.35% at the end of the year.

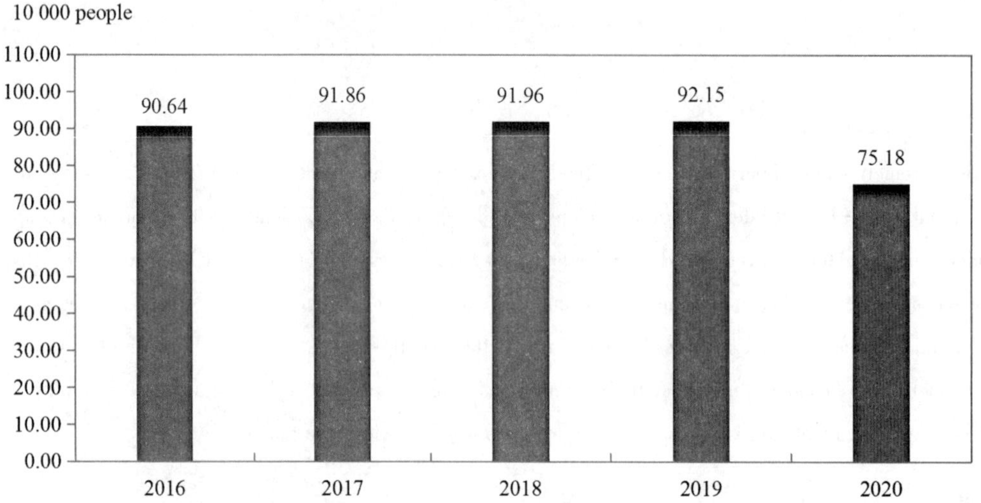

Figure 2 New Urban Jobs of Hubei for 2016–2020

Labor productivity remained steady. The overall labor productivity of the whole province was 121,900 yuan/person, a decrease of 5.2% compared with the previous year.

Significant progress has been made in the decisive efforts to poverty alleviation. According to the national poverty line of 2,300 yuan per person per year (at constant price as 2010), the remaining 58,000 poor people were all lifted out of poverty, and all poverty-stricken counties were removed from poverty. Absolute poverty had been eliminated on a historic basis. The per capita disposable income of rural residents in poor areas was 13,075 yuan, up 1.6% over the previous year.

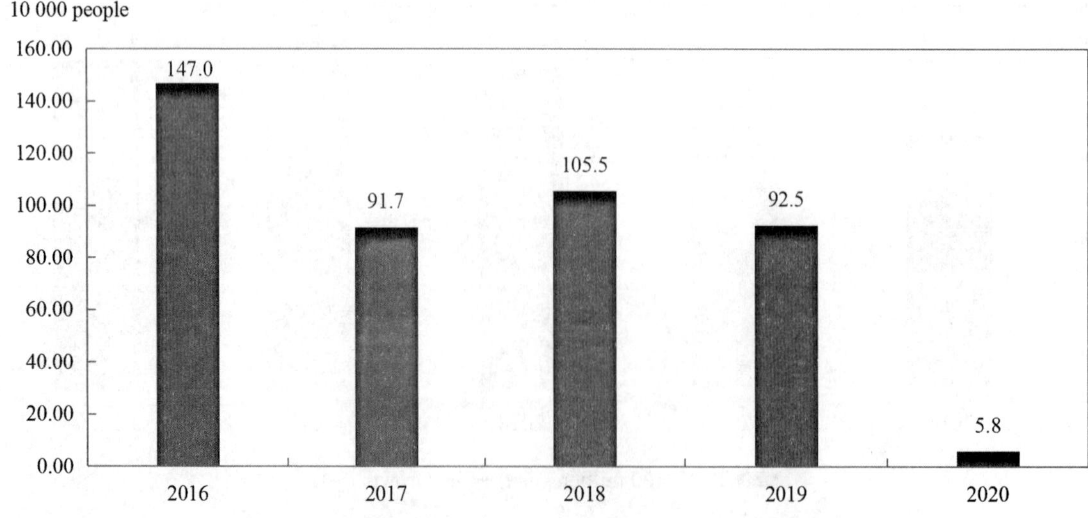

Figure 3 Poverty Alleviated Population of Hubei for 2016–2020

Ⅱ. Agriculture

The added value of agriculture, forestry, animal husbandry and fishery was 435.869 billion yuan, an increase of 0.3% over the previous year, calculated at comparable prices.

Grain production capacity remained stable. The total grain output of the province was 27.2743 million tons, up 0.1%, maintaining an output of above 25 million tons (50 billion jin) for 8 consecutive years. The planted area was 4645.27 thousand hectares, up 0.8%.

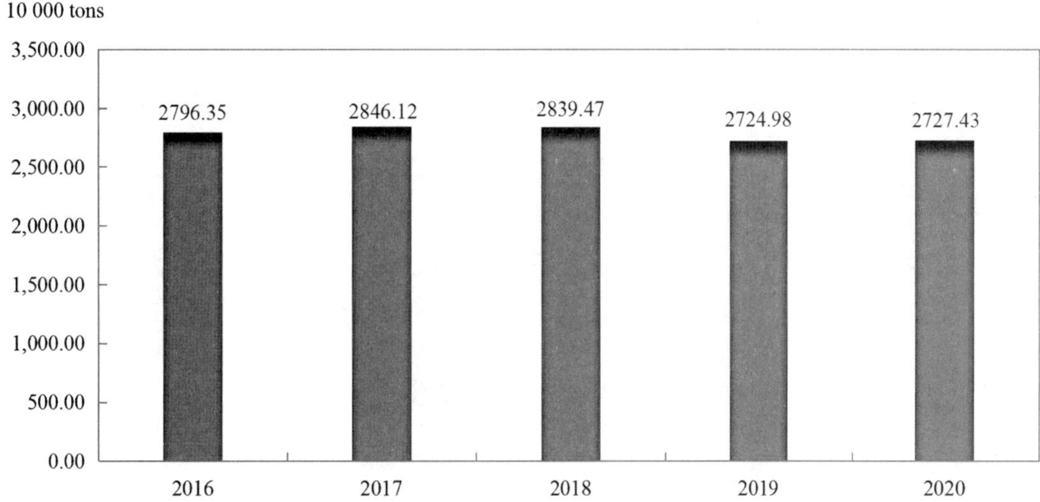

Figure 4 Grain Output of Hubei for 2016–2020

Economic crops with distinctive advantages maintained growth. The output of oil plants was 3,444,500 tons, an increase of 9.7%; the output of tea was 360,800 tons, an increase of 2.4%; the output of garden fruits was 7,163,800 tons, an increase of 8.4%.

Livestock production declined, and poultry breeding remained stable. The slaughter of pigs was 26,311,200, a decrease of 17.5%; the slaughter of cattle was 1,019,600, a decrease of 6.9%; the slaughter of sheep was 5,326,800, a decrease of 13.5%; the slaughter of poultry was 593.2584 million, a decrease of 0.1%; the output of poultry eggs was 1,930,900 tons, an increase of 8.0%.

The production of aquatic products remained stable, and fishery production remained basically the same. The total output of aquatic products was 4,678,800 tons, a slight decrease of 0.4%.

Table 1 Output of Main Agricultural Products of Hubei in 2020

Unit: 10 000 tons

Product	Output	YoY Growth Rate (%)
Grain	2727.43	0.1
Cotton	10.79	-24.9
Oil	344.45	9.7
#Rapeseed	241.06	14.1
Tea	36.08	2.4
Garden fruits (excluding melons)	716.38	8.4
Vegetables and edible fungi	4119.37	0.8

Ⅲ. Industry and Construction

By the end of the year, the number of industrial enterprises above designated size of the whole province reached 15769. The added value of industrial enterprises above designated size of the whole province decreased by 6.1% in the whole year. By category of economy, state-owned and state-controlled enterprises fell by 1.6%; collectively-owned enterprises fell by 12.4%; joint-stock cooperative enterprises decreased by 31.9%; joint-stock enterprises fell by 6.2%; enterprises invested by foreign investors or investors from

Hong Kong, Macao and Taiwan fell by 6.7%; enterprises under other economic categories fell by 9.3%. Light industry fell by 7.2%; heavy industry fell by 5.6%. By sector, mining fell by 16.0%, manufacturing by 6.2% and electricity, heat, gas and water production and supply by 2.5%.

The added value of high-tech manufacturing sector increased by 4.1%, 10.2% faster than that of industries above designated size, and accounting for 10.2% of the total added value of industries above designated size. Among them, manufacturing of computers, communications and other electronic equipment grew by 4.4%.

Throughout the year, the output value of industries above designated size decreased by 7.7%, the product sales rate was 97.3% and the export delivery value decreased by 0.4%. The profits of industrial enterprises above designated size reached 251.9 billion yuan, down by 8.3 %.

Table 2 Output of Major Products of Industries above Designated Size of Hubei and its Growth in 2020

Product	Unit	Output	YoY Growth Rate (%)
Liquor (65°, amount of goods)	10 000 kiloliters	35.9	-42.9
Beer	10 000 kiloliters	97.5	-11.8
Cigarette	100 million	1330.5	4.5
Cloth	100 million meters	43.1	-17.7
Sulfuric acid (100%)	10 000 tons	1330.5	5.7
Agricultural nitrogen, phosphorus and potassium chemical fertilizer (pure)	10 000 tons	482.1	-8.9
Chemical ingredients	10 000 tons	18.3	-6.2
Chinese patent medicine	10 000 tons	23.1	-22.7
Power generation	100 million kwh	2911.35	0.5
#Water and electricity	100 million kwh	1574.53	19.0
Cement	10 000 tons	10108.7	-12.8
Plate glass	10 000 weight cases	9584.5	-7.5
Pig iron	10 000 tons	2727.4	-4.9
Crude steel	10 000 tons	3557.2	-1.5
Steel products	10 000 tons	3653.0	-2.2
Ten kinds of non-ferrous metals	10 000 tons	80.6	-6.1
#Refined copper	10 000 tons	51.2	-4.5
Industrial robot	set	9857.0	-5.5
Automobile	10 000 sets	209.4	-6.0
#New Energy Vehicle	10 000 sets	3.2	-48.4
Generator set	10 000 kw	114.7	-4.7
Lithium ion battery	100 million PCS	11.2	2.9
Room air conditioner	10 000 sets	1760.3	-18.0
Microcomputer equipment device	10 000 sets	1720.0	35.4
Displayer	10 000 sets	1457.3	-4.1
Mobile communication handset	10 000 sets	2667.0	-32.0

The construction industry developed steadily. Throughout the year, the province's construction enterprises with general contracting and professional contracting qualifications saw a total output of 1,613.61 billion yuan, a decrease of 5.0%; the value of newly signed contracts for the year was 2,205.589 billion yuan, an increase of 9.1%.

Ⅳ. Fixed Assets Investment

The province's completed investment in fixed assets (excluding rural households) fell by 18.8%. Divided by industry, investment in the primary, secondary and tertiary industries fell by 28.2%, 23.8%, and 15.4%, respectively. In terms of sectors, infrastructure investment, industrial investment and real estate development investment fell by 22.8%, 23.9% and 4.4%, respectively. Investment in high-tech manufacturing fell by 9.4%, of which investment in pharmaceutical manufacturing, computer and office equipment manufac-

turing increased by 20.4% and 14.7%, respectively. The construction for strengthening weak points and strengthening functions was accelerated. Investment in telecommunications, radio and television and satellite transmission services increased by 16.8%, investment in health increased by 65.8%, and investment in air transportation increased by 1.29 times.

The sold area of commercial housing was 65,878,300 square meters, a decrease of 23.4%; the sales of commercial housing reached 608.79 billion yuan, a decrease of 21.5%.

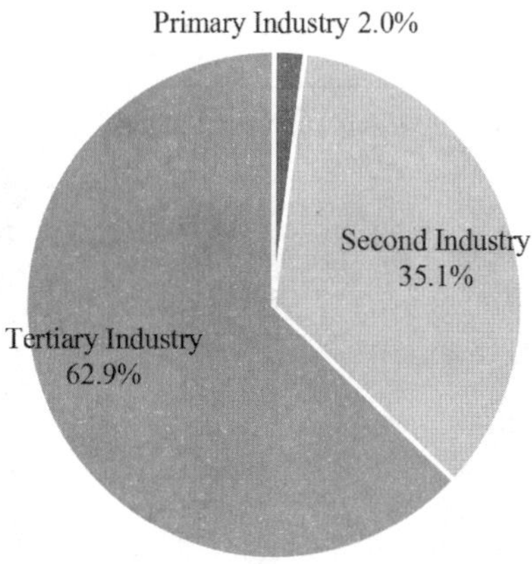

Figure 5 Proportions of Investments in Hubei's Three Industries to Fixed Asset Investment (Excluding Rural Households) in 2020

There were 3649 newly started projects in the province with a value of more than 100 million yuan, a decrease of 7.7%, and the completed investment in projects with a value of more than 100 million yuan decreased by 21.2%.

V. Domestic Trade

The province's total annual retail sales of consumer goods reached 1,798.487 billion yuan, a decrease of 20.8%. In terms of urban and rural areas, urban retail sales reached 1,528.469 billion yuan, a decrease of 20.9%; rural retail sales reached 270.018 billion yuan, a decrease of 20.8%. Among them, the retail sales of consumer goods by enterprises (institutions) above designated size reached 659.293 billion yuan, down 14.2%.

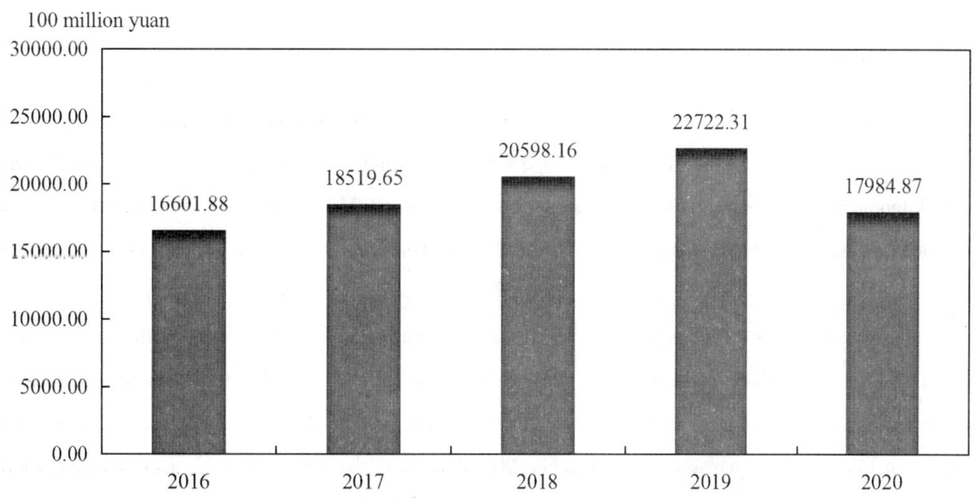

Figure 6 Total Retail Sales of Consumer Goods in Hubei for 2016–2020

In 2020, the province's online retail sales reached 286.66 billion yuan, an increase of 1.6%, of which online retail sales of physical goods were 244.89 billion yuan, an increase of 4.6%, accounting for 13.6% of the total retail sales of consumer goods, an increase of 1.8% over the previous year.

Ⅵ. Foreign Trade

In the whole year, the province's total value of imports and exports of goods reached 429.41 billion yuan, an increase of 8.8%, of which the value of imports was 159.21 billion yuan, an increase of 9.1%; the value of exports was 270.2 billion yuan, an increase of 8.7%. In 2020, the EU replaced ASEAN to be the largest trading partner of Hubei, with a bilateral trade value of 59.52 billion yuan, an increase of 17.1%.

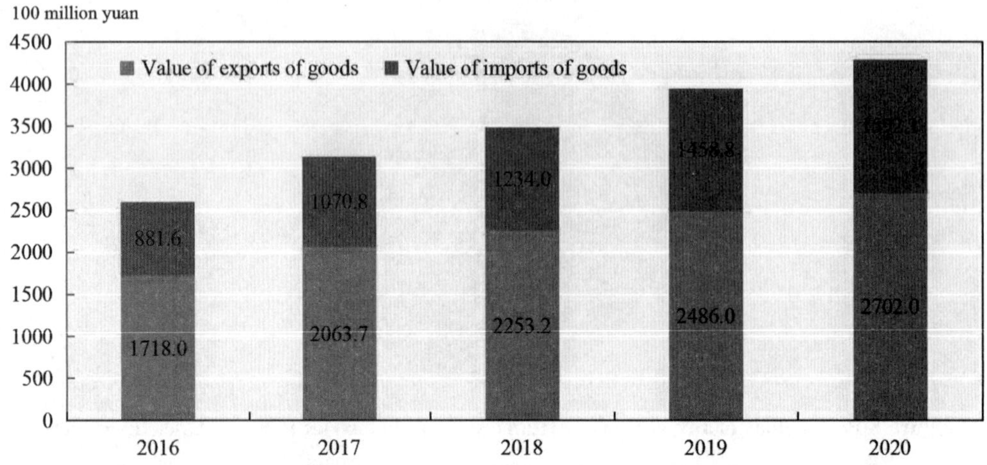

Figure 7 Total Value of Imports and Exports of Goods of Hubei for 2016–2020

296 foreign direct investment projects were newly approved. The actual use of foreign capital in the whole year was 10.352 billion US dollars, a decrease of 19.8%. Investment in Hubei from some countries in Europe and Asia grew against the trend: investments from Germany, the Netherlands, and Singapore increased by 92.5%, 27.3%, and 16.0%, respectively. The actual use of foreign capital in the high-tech industry (manufacturing industry) for the whole year was US$107 million (data from the Ministry of Commerce), a decrease of 16.9%.

The annual foreign non-financial direct investment amounted to US$2.0 billion, an increase of 2.0%. The turnover of foreign contracted projects was US$6.415 billion, down 3.0%. 12,484 laborers of various types were dispatched for foreign labor service cooperation, an increase of 8.4%.

Ⅶ. Transport, Post and Telecommunications

By the end of the year, the total highway mileage of the province reached 289,960.44 kilometers, an increase of 0.3%; the expressway mileage reached 7,229.81 kilometers, an increase of 5.4%. In the whole year, the province's completed cargo turnover was 529.568 billion ton-kilometers, a decrease of 13.9%; passenger turnover was 61.242 billion person-kilometers, a decrease of 55.8%; the ports' cargo throughput was 380 million tons, an increase of 23.9%. The ports' container throughput was 2.29 million TEUs, an increase of 9.8%.

The province's total postal business volume was 47.177 billion yuan, an increase of 2.9%. Among them, the express delivery saw a business volume of 1.785 billion pieces, and a business income of 17.869 billion yuan. The total telecommunications business volume of the province was 420.491 billion yuan, an increase of 24.9%. The length of the long-distance optical cable line reached 32,100 kilometers; the mobile phone exchange capacity reached 90.435 million; the fixed telephone users reached 4.8161 million; the mobile phone users reached 56.8107 million; the telephone penetration rate in the province was 104.0 units per 100 people, and the mobile phone penetration rate was 95.9 units per 100 people; there were 18.7016 million fixed Internet broadband access users, an increase of 1.6184 million over the previous year; mobile Internet user access traffic reached 5.067 billion GB, an increase of 32.4% over the previous year.

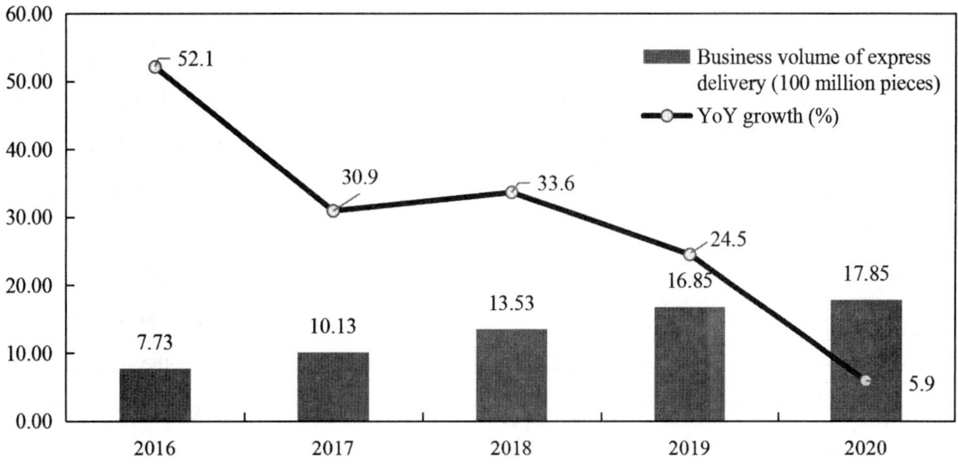

Figure 8 Business Volume of Express Delivery in Hubei and Its Growth Rate for 2016–2020

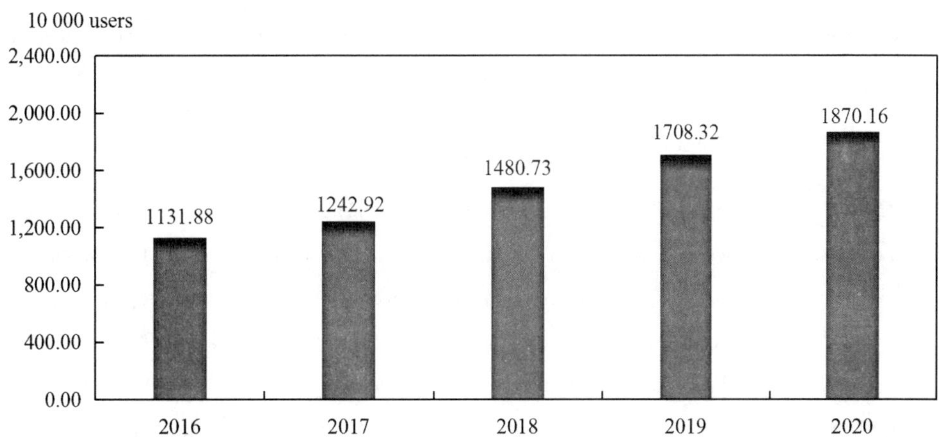

Figure 9 Number of Fixed Internet Broadband Access Users in Hubei by the End of 2016–2020

Ⅷ. Government Revenue & Finance

In the whole year, the province's total fiscal revenue was 458.089 billion yuan, a decrease of 20.8%. Among them, local general public budget revenue was 251.152 billion yuan, a decrease of 25.9%. Among the local general public budget revenue, tax revenue was 192.34 billion yuan, a decrease of 24.0%. Local general public budget expenditures were 843.904 billion yuan, an increase of 5.9%.

At the end of the year, RMB and foreign currency deposit balance in financial institutions of Hubei was 6,715.932 billion yuan, an increase of 10.9%, or an increase of 662.187 billion yuan over the beginning of the year. Among them, household deposits were 3,414.437 billion yuan, an increase of 417.057 billion yuan. The balance of various RMB loans of financial institutions was 5,987.213 billion yuan, an increase of 14.6%, or an increase of 762.953 billion yuan over the beginning of the year. Among them, loans to household were 1,870.643 billion yuan, an increase of 212.143 billion yuan; loans to non-financial enterprises and government agencies and organizations were 4,016.508 billion yuan, an increase of 561.334 billion yuan.

The annual premium income was 185.438 billion yuan, an increase of 7.3%. Among them, property insurance premium income was 37.025 billion yuan, a decrease of 6.9%; personal insurance premium income was 148.414 billion yuan, an increase of 11.5%. Payment of various compensations and benefits was 51.815 billion yuan, an increase of 1.2%. Among them, property insurance compensation expenditures were 21.815 billion yuan, an increase of 3.7%; personal insurance compensation expenditures were 30.001 billion yuan, a decrease of 0.6%.

Ⅸ. Education, Science and Technology

In 2020, the province saw the enrollment of 514,000 students into post-secondary education, totaling 1.6169 million students and 401,800 graduates. Graduate colleges admitted 66,600 students, totaling 178,800 graduate students and 45,300 graduates. Specialized secondary schools of various kinds enrolled 152,300 students, totaling 420,300 students and 117,800 graduates. Senior high schools enrolled 313,200 students, with 891,900 students and 274,100 graduates. 1.7083 million students studied in junior high schools, 3.8085 million students in primary schools and 1.7843 million children in kindergartens.

New achievements were made in scientific research and technological development. A total of 1,553 major scientific and technological achievements were registered, including 54 basic theories, 1,447 applied technologies and 52 results in soft science. A total of 39,749 technology contracts were signed, involving 168.695 billion yuan, an increase of 16.4% over the previous year.

By the year-end of 2020, the province has established 246 provincial-level engineering research centers (engineering laboratories) and 589 provincial-level enterprise technology centers.

The province boasts 33 national-level inspection and testing centers; a total of 15,376 companies have passed ISO9000 system certification; 10,288 compulsory certification certificates have been obtained. There were 107 statutory measurement technology institutions, and 1.5154 million sets of compulsory inspection and measurement instruments.

The province has 16 weather radar observation sites, 18 satellite cloud image receiving sites, 3 seismic telemetry stations and 52 seismic stations.

Ⅹ. Culture, Tourism, Public Health and Sports

By the end of 2020, the province had 87 state-owned art troupes, 125 mass art and cultural centers, 115 public libraries and 230 museums. There were 103 film projection management organizations and 1,797 projection units, 1 radio station, 1 television station, 82 radio and television stations, and 12.03 million cable TV subscribers. The comprehensive population coverage rate of radio programs was 99.86%, and the comprehensive population coverage rate of television programs was 99.82%. In the whole year, 570 million copies of national and provincial newspapers, 70 million copies of various periodicals, and 280 million copies of books were published. The annual operating income of cultural and related industrial enterprises above designated size was 393.07 billion yuan, down 1.2%.

In the whole year, a total of 437.2964 million tourists (person-times) were received, a decrease of 27.8%, and the total tourism revenue was 437.949 billion yuan, a decrease of 36.8%.

There were 35,447 medical and health institutions in the province, including 1,048 hospitals, 33,853 primary medical and health institutions, and 479 professional public health institutions. There were 538,100 health and family planning personnel in the province, including 159,700 practicing (assistant) physicians and 200,100 registered nurses; the province had a total of 411,800 beds in medical and health institutions, including 296,500 beds in hospitals, 16,300 beds in community health service institutions, and 81,600 beds in health centers. In the whole year, the total number of consultations and treatments was 294.5734 million, and the number of discharged patients was 10.2745 million.

Throughout the year, the province's athletes won 18 championships, 7 runner-up events, and 7 second runner-up events in international competitions; 19 championships, 18 runner-up events and 17 second runner-up events in the highest level of Olympic events; 124 championships, 92 runner-up events, and 88 second runner-up events in domestic competitions; and 19 championships, 18 runner-up events, and 17 second runner-up events in the National Games. The annual sports lottery sales totaled 8.28 billion yuan.

Ⅺ. Residents' Livelihood and Social Security

The per capita disposable income of urban residents in the province was 36,706 yuan, a decrease of 2.4%; the per capita disposable income of rural residents was 16,306 yuan, a decrease of 0.5%. The per capita consumption expenditure of urban residents was 22,885 yuan, a decrease of 13.4%; the per capita consumption expenditure of rural residents was 14,473 yuan, a decrease of 5.6%.

Social security was further strengthened. By the end of the year, 17.4609 million people have participated in the basic endowment insurance for urban workers, including 11.4962 million employees and 5.9647 million retirees. 23.6886 million people have participated in the basic endowment insurance for urban and rural residents; 11.3693 million people have participated in the basic medical insurance for urban workers; 44.4605 million people have participated in the basic medical insurance for urban and rural residents; 7.5243 million people were covered by work-related injury insurance, and 6.4588 million people by maternity insurance; 6.5131 million people by unemployment insurance and 140,500 received unemployment insurance compensation by the end of the year.

Throughout the year, 307,000 urban residents and 1.446 million rural residents received the minimum living allowances, and the entitled group of 372,700 people has received special pensions and subsidies by the state. Social welfare programs continued developing. By the end of the year, there were 1831 elderly care institutions in the province, and the coverage of elderly care service facilities in urban and rural communities reached 97% and 67%, respectively. The annual sales of social welfare lottery tickets amounted to 5.25 billion yuan.

XII. Energy Saving and Consumption Reduction, Resources and Environment

The province continued rolling out efforts to conserve energy and cut consumption. As a result, energy consumption per unit of GDP continued declining, and the target of 1% reduction set at the beginning of the year has been successfully achieved.

The total supply of state-owned construction land in the province was 27,200 hectares, a decrease of 13.79% over the previous year. The total amount of water resources was 190.33 billion cubic meters, an increase of 210%. Water consumption per 10,000 yuan of GDP was 76 cubic meters, an increase of 2.7%. Water consumption per 10,000 yuan of industrial added value was 56 cubic meters, down 3.4%.

The province completed afforestation of 248,600 hectares, including 110,500 hectares of artificial afforestation area, accounting for 44.45% of the total afforestation area. The forest tending area was 384,700 hectares. By the end of the year, there were 22 national nature reserves in the province.

Among the 179 surface water quality monitoring sections of the main rivers in the province, 93.9% had good water quality at Grade I~III, 6.1% had poor water quality at Grade IV and Grade V, and there was no water quality monitoring section that was seriously polluted to inferior to Grade V. Among the 32 waters of the province's main lakes and reservoirs, 62.5% had the water quality of Grade I to III, 37.5% had poor water quality of Grade IV and Grade V, and none had the water quality inferior to Grade V.

Among the 13 cities at prefecture-level and above monitored in the province, 38.5% of cities met air quality standards, and 61.5% of cities failed to meet air quality standards. The annual average concentration of fine particulate matter (PM2.5) in cities that did not meet the standards was 40 micrograms/m3, down 11.1% over the previous year.

The average temperature of the province was 16.8 ℃, 0.4℃ higher than the previous year.

Note:1. The data in this Bulletin are statistical express data.

2. The relevant data of the seventh national census carried out in 2020 is expected to be released in May 2021, and population-related data will no longer be released separately in the Bulletin.

Source:The data on new urban employment, urban registered unemployment rate, endowment insurance, work-related injury insurance, and unemployment insurance in this Bulletin are from the Provincial Department of Human Resources and Social Security; data on poverty alleviation are from the Provincial Office of Poverty Alleviation; fishery data from the Provincial Fisheries Bureau; import and export data from Wuhan Customs; data on actual use of foreign capital, foreign direct investment, foreign contracted projects, and foreign labor cooperation are from the Provincial Department of Commerce; data on total tourism revenue, total number of tourists, public libraries, cultural centers, museums, and art performance groups are from the Provincial Department of Culture and Tourism; data on cargo turnover, passenger turnover, total highway mileage, expressway mileage, port cargo throughput, container throughput, etc. are from China Railway Corporation, the Provincial Department of Transport, China Southern Airlines Hubei Branch, China Eastern Airlines Wuhan Company, Air China Hubei branch; data such as postal business volume, express business volume, and express business revenue are from the Provincial Postal Administration; data on total telecommunications business volume, long-distance optical cable lines, telephone users, Internet users, and telephone penetration rates are from the Provincial Communications Administration; government finance data are from the Provincial Department of Finance; financial data are from Wuhan Branch of the People's Bank of China; insurance premium data are from China Banking and Insurance Regulatory Commission Hubei Office; education data are from the Provincial Department of Education; data on health institutions, beds, and personnel are from the Provincial Health Commission; radio and television data comes from the Provincial Radio and Television Bureau; Movies and publication data come from the Propaganda Department of the Provincial Party Committee; data on sports, sports lottery, etc. come from the Provincial Sports Bureau; data on subsistence allowances, social services, welfare lotteries, etc. come from the Provincial Civil Affairs Department; data on national pensions, subsidies and preferential treatment come from the Provincial Veteran Affairs Department; medical insurance and maternity insurance data are from the Provincial Medical Insurance Bureau; data on provincial engineering research centers and provincial enterprise technology centers are from the Provincial Development and Reform Commission; data on major scientific and technological achievements, technical contracts and so on are from the Provincial Science and Technology Department; data on the number of market entities, national inspection and testing centers, enterprises that have passed ISO9000 system certification and statutory metrology technical institutions are from the Provincial Administration for Market Regulation; seismic data are from the Provincial Earthquake Agency; data on construction land are from the Provincial Department of Natural Resources; data on water resources and soil erosion control areas are from the Provincial Department of Water Resources; data on forest resources and nature reserves are from the Provincial Forestry Bureau; data on ecological environment and environmental monitoring are from the Provincial Department of Ecology and Environment; meteorological data are from the Provincial Meteorological Bureau. Data on prices, food, livestock, income and expenditure of urban and rural residents, and per capita disposable income of rural residents in poverty-stricken areas are from the Survey Office of the National Bureau of Statistics in Hubei; other data are from Hubei Provincial Bureau of Statistics.

资料整理人员：程文懿　周 真　王喜锋
　　　　　　　闵胜男　金 花　刘 颖

综 合
General Survey

从数字看 2020 年的湖北
Statistic about Hubei in 2020

湖 北 的 地 位
Position of Hubei in the Country

地区生产总值 43443.46 亿元	Gross Domestic Production: 4344.346 billion yuan	占全国的 4.28%
#第三产业 22287.65 亿元	Tertiary Industry: 2228.765 billion yuan	占全国的 4.02%
人均地区生产总值 74440 元	Per Capita Regional GDP: 74440 yuan	相当于全国的 103.39%
社会消费品零售总额 17984.87 亿元	Total Retail Sales of Social Consumption: 1798.487 billion yuan	占全国的 4.59%
进出口总额 620.83 亿美元	Total Imports and Exports: 62.083 billion US dollars	占全国的 1.34%
#出口总额 390.61 亿美元	Total Exports: 39.061 billion US dollars	占全国的 1.51%
实际外商直接投资 103.52 亿美元	Actual Foreign Direct Investment: 10.352 billion US dollars	占全国的 7.17%
粮食产量 2727.43 万吨	Grain: 27.2743 million tons	占全国的 4.07%
钢产量 3649.11 万吨	Rolled Steel: 36.4911 million tons	占全国的 2.75%
发电量 2911.35 亿千瓦小时	Electricity: 291.135 billion kwh	占全国的 3.74%
城镇居民人均可支配收入 36706 元	Per Capita Disposable Income of Urban Residents: 36706 yuan	相当于全国的 83.74%
农村居民人均可支配收入 16306 元	Per Capita Net Incomes of Rural Residents:16306 yuan	相当于全国的 95.18%

湖 北 的 人 口
Population of Hubei

常住人口	Population of Permanent Residents	5775.26 万人
从业人员	Employment	3261 万人
#在岗职工人数	Staff and Workers	1023.41 万人
出生人口	Birth Population	48.32 万人
死亡人口	Death Population	44.76 万人
城镇人口	Urban Population	3632.04 万人
乡村人口	Rural Population	2143.22 万人
人口密度	Density of Population	311 人/平方公里

湖 北 的 经 济 发 展
Economic Development of Hubei

		1979–2020 年平均增长(%)
地区生产总值	Regional Gross Production	10.0
第一产业	Primary Industry	4.5
第二产业	Second Industry	11.6
第三产业	Tertiary Industry	11.9
财政收入	Government Revenue	11.0
货物运输量	Cargo Transport Volume	6.8
社会消费品零售总额	Total Retail Sales of Social Consumption	14.6
出口总额	Total Exports	14.0

湖 北 的 一 天
One Day in Hubei

地区生产总值	Gross Domestic Product	118.70 亿元
第一产业	Primary Industry	11.29 亿元
第二产业	Second Industry	46.51 亿元
第三产业	Tertiary Industry	60.90 亿元
地方公共财政收入	Local Government Public Finance Income	6.86 亿元
货物运输量	Freight Traffic	438.33 万吨
竣工房屋面积	Floor Space of Building Completed	72.57 万平方米
社会消费品零售总额	Total Retail Sales of Social Consumption	49.14 亿元
出口总额	Total Exports	10672.35 万美元
出版报纸	Newspapers Published	156.27 万份
邮寄函件	Letters and Correspondents Delivered	8.47 万件

1-1 土地面积与行政区划
Land Area and Administrative Division

项 目	Item	2000	2005	2010	2015	2018	2019	2020
常住人口 (万人)	Population of the Whole Province (10 000 persons)	5646	5710	5724	5850	5917	5927	5775
土地面积（万平方公里）	Land Area (10 000 sq.km)			18.59	18.59	18.59	18.59	18.59
耕地面积 （千公顷）	Cultivated Area (1 000 hectares)			5312.30	5255.00	5235.40		
行政区划	Adinimisrtative Division							
省辖市 （个）	Municipality (unit)	12	12	12	12	12	12	12
自治州 （个）	Autonomous (unit)	1	1	1	1	1	1	1
林区 （个）	Forest Zone (unit)	1	1	1	1	1	1	1
县级市 （个）	City (unit)	24	24	24	24	25	25	26
省辖行政单位 （个）	Adinimistrative Units under the Jurisdiction of Province (unit)	3	3	3	3	3	3	3
县 （个）	County (unit)	41	39	40	39	38	38	37
乡政府 （个）	Local Government (unit)	476	217	201	168	163	162	161
镇政府 （个）	Township Government (unit)	853	737	742	761	762	760	761
办事处 （个）	Office (unit)	145	163	211	304	310	327	329
村民委员会 （个）	Village Community (unit)	32400	26678	26018	25343	23571	23202	22532
村民小组 （个）	Village Groups (unit)	259250	212587	209598	208546	205059	203005	208002

注：耕地面积数据来源于自然资源部门。
Note: Statistics of cultivated area sources from the Department of Natural Resources of Hubei Province.

1-2 市、州行政区划
Administrative Division of Cities and Prefectures

单位:个 (2020 年底)(by the End of 2020) (unit)

地 区	Region	县级市 Cities	县 Counties	区 Districts	乡政府 Village Government	镇政府 Township Government	村民委员会 Village Community	村民小组 Village Groups
全 省	**Total**	**26**	**37**	**39**	**161**	**761**	**22532**	**208002**
武汉市	Wuhan			13	3	1	1742	16345
黄石市	Huangshi	1	1	4	1	27	785	8310
十堰市	Shiyan	1	4	3	34	72	1801	10381
荆州市	Jingzhou	4	2	2	12	88	1486	17472
宜昌市	Yichang	3	5	5	19	67	1321	8399
襄阳市	Xiangyang	3	3	3	4	74	2265	15400
鄂州市	Ezhou			3	3	18	305	3784
荆门市	Jingmen	2	1	2	2	48	1346	10321
孝感市	Xiaogan	3	3	1	23	72	1983	22364
黄冈市	Huanggang	2	7	1	16	99	3879	37899
咸宁市	Xianning	1	4	1	12	52	884	10177
恩施自治州	Enshi	2	6		29	54	2304	23245
随州市	Suizhou	1	1	1		37	848	9290
仙桃市	Xiantao	1				15	654	4733
天门市	Tianmen	1			1	21	528	6567
潜江市	Qianjiang	1				10	334	2984
神农架林区	Shennongjia				2	6	67	331

注:乡政府、镇政府、村民委员会、村民小组数只涉及农村生产经营单位数。
Note:The number of village government, township government, village community and village groups only refers to the number of units run by village production peration.

1-3 全省法人和产业活动单位数(2020年)
Number of Legal Entities and Industrial Activity Units of Hubei(2020)

单位:个 (unit)

指标名称	Item	法人单位数 Corporation Units	规模、资质或限额以上单位 Unit of Scale, Qualification or Above	产业活动单位数 Number of Economic Activities Units
总计	**Total**	**1183265**	**41965**	**1304976**
一、按地区分组	**Grouped by Region**	**1183265**	**41965**	**1304976**
武汉市	Wuhan	383631	11905	411277
黄石市	Huangshi	49718	1860	54763
十堰市	Shiyan	63957	2320	73255
宜昌市	Yichang	91037	4055	100833
襄阳市	Xiangyang	108729	4098	117318
鄂州市	Ezhou	23182	886	25494
荆门市	Jingmen	50300	2240	56298
孝感市	Xiaogan	59076	2163	68720
荆州市	Jingzhou	73774	2964	81517
黄冈市	Huanggang	78486	2871	90378
咸宁市	Xianning	48866	2030	53524
随州市	Suizhou	30918	1391	34906
恩施自治州	Enshi	66736	1149	76302
仙桃市	Xiantao	20106	871	21682
潜江市	Qianjiang	13600	469	15464
天门市	Tianmen	18355	626	19945
神农架林区	Shennongjia	2794	67	3300
二、按国民经济行业门类分组	**Grouped by Sector**	**1183265**	**41965**	**1304976**
农、林、牧、渔业	Farming, Forestry, Animal Husbandary and Fishery	83408		84287
采矿业	Mining	2977	366	3179
制造业	Manufacturing	114737	14805	117239
电力、热力、燃气及水生产和供应业	Power, Gas and Water Production and Supply	5826	462	8441
建筑业	Construction	102993	4875	110561
批发和零售业	Transportaation, Storage and Post	314974	8600	348059
交通运输、仓储和邮政业	Information Transmission, Computer Service and Software	30590	1336	38174
住宿和餐饮业	Wholesale and Retail Sale	19944	2306	24320
信息传输、软件和信息技术服务业	Hotel and Catering	64252	673	69711
金融业	Banking	3305		14322
房地产业	Real Estate	39805	4786	45080
租赁和商务服务业	Leasing and Commerical Service	146105	1276	155747
科学研究和技术服务业	Scietific Research, Polytechnical Service and Geological Prospecting	71496	887	77400
水利、环境和公共设施管理业	Water Conservancy, Environment and Public Facility Management	11806	209	13106
居民服务、修理和其他服务业	Resident Service and Others	23830	270	25399
教育	Education	30650	239	33766
卫生和社会工作	Health Care, Social Security and Social Welfare	13404	272	20483
文化、体育和娱乐业	Culture, Sports and Recreation	26551	603	27878
公共管理、社会保障和社会组织	Public Management and Social Organization	76612		87824

1-3 续表 1 continued

单位:个 (unit)

指标名称	Item	法人单位数 Corporation Units	规模、资质或限额以上单位 Unit of Scale, Qualification or Above	产业活动单位数 Number of Economic Activities Units
总计	**Total**	**1183265**	**41965**	**1304976**
三、按登记注册类型分组	**Grouped by Type of Registration**	**1183265**	**41965**	**1304976**
内资	Inner Funded	1179070	40735	1294098
国有	State-owned	62386	793	84013
集体	Collective-owned	10235	171	14708
股份合作	Share Holding Cooperative	480	33	680
联营	Joint Funded	1192	22	1412
国有联营	State Join-owned	78	9	126
集体联营	Collective Joint-owned	621	4	724
国有与集体联营	State-owned and Collective Joint-owned	69	5	83
其他联营	Other Joint-owned	424	4	479
有限责任公司	Co. Ltd	49919	9697	67063
国有独资公司	State-owned Solely Funded Co.	1897	596	4641
其他有限责任公司	Other Co. Ltd	48022	9101	62422
股份有限公司	Share Holding Co.Ltd.	3475	1060	14992
私营	Private-owned Enterprises	909026	28660	961654
私营独资	Private Solely Funded Enterprises	82428	960	84367
私营合伙	Private Partnership Enterprises	11212	164	11594
私营有限责任公司	Private Co. Ltd	810889	26327	859119
私营股份有限公司	Private Share Holding Co.Ltd.	4497	1209	6574
其他内资	Others	142357	299	149576
港澳台商投资	Hongkong, Macao and Taiwan Funded Enterprises	1811	518	4165
与港澳台商合资经营	Joint Venture with Hongkong, Macao and Taiwan	614	162	656
与港澳台商合作经营	Cooperate with Hongkong, Macao and Taiwan Funded	24	7	29
港澳台商独资	Enterprises Solely Funded by Hongkong, Macao and Taiwan	1131	322	3371
港澳台商投资股份有限公司	Share Holding Co.Ltd. with Hongkong, Macao and Taiwan Investment	24	16	57
其他港、澳、台商投资	Other Hongkong, Macao and Taiwan Investment	18	11	52
外商投资	Foreign Funded Enterprises	2384	712	6713
中外合资经营	Sino - Foreign Joint Funded Enterprises	807	302	944
中外合作经营	Sino - Foreign Cooperative Funded Enterprises	17	6	23
外资企业	Foreign Solely Funded Enterprises	1358	363	4705
外商投资股份有限公司	Foreign Funded Share Holding Co.Ltd.	142	19	933
其他外商投资	Other Foreign Investment	60	22	108
四、按机构类型分组	**Grouped by Type**	**1183265**	**41965**	**1304976**
企业	Enterprise	968729	41595	1065147
事业单位	Public Institution	42109	36	55817
机关	Government Agency	10381		15420
社会团体	Mass Organization	15574		15613
民办非企业单位	Private Non Enterprise Unit	21978	199	21825
基金会	Foundation	163		163
居委会	Neighborhood Committee	5234		5393
村委会	Village Committee	25429		25648
农民专业合作社	Farmer Specialized Cooperative	86887	115	87243
其他组织机构	Others	6781	20	12707

注:规模、资质或限额以上单位不包括投资专业法人单位。
Note: Entities above the scale, qualifications or quota do not include professional investment legal entities.

1-4 国民经济和社会发展总量与速度指标

指 标	Item	总量指标 Aggregate Data					
		1978	1990	2000	2010	2019	2020
人口与就业	**Population and Employment**						
人口 （万人）	**Population (10 000 persons)**						
年末人口	Population at Year-end	4574.91	5439.29	5646.00	5723.77	5927.00	5775.26
城镇人口	Urban	690.23	1551.51	2285.11	2844.95	3615.47	3632.04
乡村人口	Rural	3884.68	3887.78	3360.89	2878.82	2311.53	2143.22
就业 （万人）	**Employment (10 000 persons)**						
就业人数	Employment	1910.40	3040.40	3384.90	3375.00	3375.00	3261.00
职工人数	Staff and Workers	457.34	698.55	677.96	685.21	1089.16	1023.41
#国有单位	State-owned Units	371.56	524.12	506.11	277.60	221.51	215.32
宏观经济	**Marcoeconomy**						
国民核算 （亿元）	**National Accounting (100 million yuan)**						
地区生产总值	Gross Domestic Products	151.00	824.38	3545.39	16114.59	45828.31	43443.46
第一产业	Primary Industry	61.11	289.45	662.30	2147.00	3809.09	4131.91
第二产业	Second Industry	63.71	313.39	1437.38	7869.02	19098.62	17023.90
第三产业	Tertiary Industry	26.18	221.54	1445.71	6098.57	22920.60	22287.65
支出法地区生产总值	Gross Domestic Expenditures						
#最终消费	Final Consumption Expenditures	81.70	535.49	2030.07	7363.80		
居民消费	Resident Consumption	74.70	434.62	1594.08	5136.78		
政府消费	Government Consumption Expenditures	7.00	100.87	436.00	2227.02		
资本形成总额	Gross Capital Formation	43.13	261.95	1882.47	8684.17		
固定资本形成	Fixed Capital Formation	31.40	147.13	1451.85	8373.40		
存货增加	Changes in Stock	11.72	114.82	430.62	310.77		
固定资产投资 （亿元）	**Investment in Fixed Assets (100 million yuan)**						
固定资产投资总额	Total Investment in Fixed Assets	33.58	144.44	1421.55	10802.69		
#国有单位	State-owned Units	33.19	100.35	857.01	3768.95		
集体单位	Collective-owned Units	0.39	15.59	128.32	602.80		
财政 （亿元）	**Public Finance (100 million yuan)**						
地方一般公共预算收入	Local Public Financial Revenue	31.38	77.85	214.35	1011.23	3388.57	2511.52
地方一般公共预算支出	Local Public Financial Expenditures	29.98	84.82	368.77	2501.40	7970.21	8439.04
物价 （上年=100）	**Price (preceding year = 100)**						
商品零售价格总指数	General Retail Price Index	100.5	102.9	97.8	103.1	102.6	102.2
居民消费价格指数	General Consumer Price Index	100.3	104.2	99.0	102.9	103.1	102.7
利用外资 （亿美元）	**Utilization of Foreign Capital (100 million dollars)**						
实际外商直接投资	Actual Foreign Direct Investment		0.29	9.44	40.50	129.07	141.69
产业	**Industry**						
农业	**Agriculture**						
农林牧渔业总产值 （亿元）	Gross Output Value of Farming, Forestry, Animal Husbandry and Fishery (100 million yuan)	84.46	402.23	1125.64	3407.64	6681.85	7303.64
主要农产品产量（万吨）	Output of Major Farm Products (10 000 tons)						
粮食	Grain	1725.60	2475.03	2218.49	2304.26	2724.98	2727.43
棉花	Cotton	36.67	51.73	30.43	47.41	14.36	10.79
油料	Oil-Bearing Crops	23.71	95.75	269.98	302.28	313.95	344.45
糖料	Sugar Crops	8.73	34.66	101.66	28.37	27.90	28.15
蚕茧	Silkworm Cocoons	0.47	0.79	1.22	0.68	0.38	0.11
肉类产量	Output of Meat	64.00	146.85	271.19	383.48	349.20	307.44
水产品	Aquatic Products	11.00	70.98	234.34	353.00	469.54	467.93

注：1.人口数除 1982 年、1990 年、2000 年、2010 年、2020 年是以人口普查为基数推算外，1982 年及以后为人口抽样调查推算数。
2.2000 年以前数据是总人口数，2001 年以后数据为常住人口数。
3.2017 年地区生产总值数据根据第三次农业普查数据进行调整，历史数据未调整。
4.从 2016 年，固定资产投资总额对 2015 年基数进行调整，且不再包含农户投资。
5.根据第三次全国农业普查结果对农业相关数据进行了修订，其中水产数据修订到 2012 年，产值、增加值、粮食、畜牧、经济作物数据修订到 2007 年。

Aggregate Indicators on National Economic and Social Development and Growth Rates

速度指标 Indices of Growth Rates								
2020年比下列各年增长(%) Increases					年平均增长(%) Average Annual Growth Rate			
1978	1990	2000	2010	2019	1979~2020	1991~2020	2001~2020	2011~2020
26.2	6.2	2.3	0.9	-2.6	0.6	0.2	0.1	0.1
426.2	134.1	58.9	27.7	0.5	4.0	2.9	2.3	2.5
-44.8	-44.9	-36.2	-25.6	-7.3	-1.4	-2.0	-2.2	-2.9
70.7	7.3	-3.7	-3.4	-3.4	1.3	0.2	0.2	0.3
123.8	46.5	51.0	49.4	-6.0	1.9	1.3	2.1	4.1
-42.1	-58.9	-57.5	-22.4	-2.8	-1.3	-2.9	-4.2	-2.5
5395.7	1763.2	563.3	113.2	-5.0	10.0	10.2	9.9	7.9
539.6	234.9	127.4	43.0	0.0	4.5	4.1	4.2	3.6
10083.8	2876.2	725.2	115.1	-7.4	11.6	12.0	11.1	8.0
10991.4	2394.8	628.2	131.0	-3.8	11.9	11.3	10.4	8.7
7903.6	3126.1	1071.7	148.4	-25.9	11.0	12.3	13.1	9.5
28048.9	9849.4	2188.4	237.4	5.9	14.4	16.6	16.9	12.9
1.7	-0.7	4.5	-0.9	-0.4	0.0	0.0	0.2	-0.1
2.4	-1.4	3.7	-0.2	-0.4	0.1	0.0	0.2	0.0
	48758.7	1401.0	249.9	9.8		22.9	14.5	13.3
8547.5	1715.8	548.8	114.3	9.3	11.2	10.1	9.8	7.9
58.1	10.2	22.9	18.4	0.1	1.1	0.3	1.0	1.7
-70.6	-79.1	-64.5	-77.2	-24.9	-2.9	-5.1	-5.1	-13.8
1352.8	259.7	27.6	14.0	9.7	6.6	4.4	1.2	1.3
222.5	-18.8	-72.3	-0.8	0.9	2.8	-0.7	-6.2	-0.1
-76.8	-86.2	-91.1	-84.0	-71.3	-3.4	-6.4	-11.4	-16.7
380.4	109.4	13.4	-19.8	-12.0	3.8	2.5	0.6	-2.2
4153.9	559.2	99.7	32.6	-0.3	9.3	6.5	3.5	2.9

Note: a)Data of 1982,1990,2000,2010 and 2020 are based on population census, and data of other years are based on sampling survey.
b)Data before 2000 refer to total population. Data after 2001 refer to permanent residents.
c)The GDP data for 2017 were adjusted according to the data of the third agricultural census, and historical data were not adjusted.
d)Since 2016,the basic number of 2015 is adjusted and famer investment is no longer included in the social fixed assets investment.
e)According to the results of the third national agricultural census, the relevant agricultural data were revised, including aquatic product data to 2012, output value, added value, grain, animal husbandry, cash crop data to 2007.

1-4 续表 1 continued

指 标	Item	总量指标 Aggregate Data					
		1978	1990	2000	2010	2019	2020
工业	**Industry**						
主要工业产品产量 (万吨)	Output of Major Industrial Products (10 000 tons)						
粗 钢	Steel	307.97	629.25	895.92	2498.67	3594.73	3621.83
成品钢材	Rolled-Steel	184.63	533.07	811.10	2894.72	3769.26	3649.11
发电量 (亿千瓦小时)	Electricity (100 million kwh)	91.64	340.39	538.11	2028.67	2896.40	2911.35
原煤	Coal	644.01	924.26	389.34	1291.71	38.53	40.27
农用氮、磷、钾化学肥料(折纯)	Chemical Furtilizers	27.62	132.07	221.11	899.08	558.32	482.10
化学农药原药(折有效成分100%)	Chemical Pesicide	2.97	1.07	5.18	19.71	18.48	14.91
水泥	Cement	328.65	987.00	2460.92	8982.87	11622.84	9886.77
化学纤维	Chemical Fiber	0.48	2.48	9.82	11.66	26.52	32.54
布 (亿米)	Cloth (100 million meter)	6.70	14.09	17.15	46.38	57.15	41.92
汽车 (万辆)	Automobile (10 000 units)	0.80	11.38	19.57	172.29	223.97	210.53
建筑业	**Construction**						
建筑业企业职工平均人数 (万人)	Average Number of Employed Persons (10 000 persons)	25.94	41.88	82.76	170.71	251.25	214.55
建筑业总产值 (亿元)	Gross Output Value (100 million yuan)	11.11	49.30	454.35	4344.39	16979.59	16136.10
施工房屋面积 (万平方米)	Floor Space of Building Under Construction (10 000 sq.m)	596.00	1684.90	6256.50	25046.72	92042.23	85268.18
竣工房屋面积 (万平方米)	Floor Space of Building Completed (10 000 sq.m)	297.40	785.90	3150.10	12813.44	33907.92	26559.53
交通运输	**Transportation**						
货运量 (万吨)	Freight Traffic (10 000 tons)	10199.08	10916.10	40949.00	97006.94	188143.00	160427.50
# 铁路	Railway	3513.00	3901.00	6558.00	10145.00	5480.00	5362.70
公路	Highway	3556.00	2941.00	27863.00	71020.00	143549.00	114345.95
水运	Waterway	3130.00	3784.00	6270.00	15832.00	39105.00	40713.70
客运量 (万人)	Passenger Capacity (10 000 persons)	12009.20	32145.93	31593.00	105415.50	88926.43	30900.20
# 铁路	Railway	2854.00	2107.00	3469.00	7281.30	17216.06	8148.04
公路	Highway	7429.00	27333.00	27184.00	96873.00	69584.36	21730.86
水运	Waterway	1722.00	2693.00	679.00	375.80	631.63	232.90
港口货物吞吐量 (万吨)	Volume of Freight Handled at Seaports (10 000 tons)			4113.46	18782.67	30660.74	37976.00
邮电通信业	**Postal Telecommunication Services**						
邮电业务总量 (亿元)	Total Business Revenue (100 million yuan)	0.56	4.80	116.60	1028.09	3824.44	4676.68
函件 (亿件)	Number of Letters Delivered (100 million pieces)	1.18	2.39	3.62	1.00	0.65	0.31
年末移动电话用户 (万户)	Number of Local Telephone Users (10 000 units)				3454.70	5688.02	5681.07
国际互联网用户 (万户)	Internet Users (10 000 units)				459.40	1708.32	1870.16
国内商业	**Domestic Commerce**						
社会消费品零售总额 (亿元)	Total Retail Sales of Consumer Goods (100 million yuan)	59.84	326.36	1789.35	7013.90	22722.31	17984.87
对外经济贸易和旅游	**Foreign Trade and Tourism**						
进出口总额 (亿美元)	Total Imports and Exports (100 million dollars)	1.73	11.90	32.10	259.07	571.28	620.83
进口	Imports	0.14	1.18	12.79	114.65	211.49	230.23
出口	Exports	1.59	10.72	19.31	144.42	359.80	390.61
入境旅游人数 (万人次)	Number of Tourists Received (10 000 person-times)	1.01	15.57	45.08	181.74	450.02	35.21
金融保险	**Banking and Insurance**						
金融机构存款 (亿元)	Deposits of Banking System (100 million yuan)	42.16	406.56	3037.22	21568.31	59747.70	66355.69
金融机构贷款 (亿元)	Loans of Banking System (100 million yuan)	96.78	732.77	3147.77	14136.58	50663.96	58478.81
国内保险保费收入 (亿元)	Domestic Premium (100 million yuan)		6.19	60.53	500.33	1728.57	1854.38

注:2017 年因铁路运输调整统计方法,货运量和客运量相关数据与前期不可比。

速度指标 Indices of Growth Rates								
2020年比下列各年增长(%) Increases					年平均增长(%) Average Annual Growth Rate			
1978	1990	2000	2010	2019	1979~2020	1991~2020	2001~2020	2011~2020
1076.0	475.6	304.3	45.0	0.8	6.0	6.0	7.2	3.8
1876.4	584.5	349.9	26.1	−3.2	7.4	6.6	7.8	2.3
3076.9	755.3	441.0	43.5	0.5	8.6	7.4	8.8	3.7
−93.7	−95.6	−89.7	−96.9	4.5	−6.4	−9.9	−10.7	−29.3
1645.5	265.0	118.0	−46.4	−13.7	7.0	4.4	4.0	−6.0
402.2	1293.8	187.9	−24.3	−19.3	3.9	9.2	5.4	−2.7
2908.3	901.7	301.8	10.1	−14.9	8.4	8.0	7.2	1.0
6679.1	1212.1	231.4	179.1	22.7	10.6	9.0	6.2	10.8
525.7	197.5	144.4	−9.6	−26.6	4.5	3.7	4.6	−1.0
26216.9	1750.0	975.8	22.2	−6.0	14.2	10.2	12.6	2.0
727.1	412.3	159.2	25.7	−14.6	5.2	5.6	4.9	2.3
145139.4	32630.4	3451.5	271.4	−5.0	18.9	21.3	19.5	14.0
14206.7	4960.7	1262.9	240.4	−7.4	12.5	14.0	14.0	13.0
8830.6	3279.5	743.1	107.3	−21.7	11.3	12.5	11.2	7.6
1473.0	1369.6	291.8	65.4	−14.7	6.8	9.4	7.1	5.2
52.7	37.5	−18.2	−47.1	−2.1	1.0	1.1	−1.0	−6.2
3115.6	3788.0	310.4	61.0	−20.3	8.6	13.0	7.3	4.9
1200.8	975.9	549.3	157.2	4.1	6.3	8.2	9.8	9.9
157.3	−3.9	−2.2	−70.7	−65.3	2.3	−0.1	−0.1	−11.5
185.5	286.7	134.9	11.9	−52.7	2.5	4.6	4.4	1.1
192.5	−20.5	−20.1	−77.6	−68.8	2.6	−0.8	−1.1	−13.9
−86.5	−91.4	−65.7	−38.0	−63.1	−4.7	−7.8	−5.2	−4.7
		823.2	102.2	23.9			11.8	7.3
835021.4	97330.8	3910.9	354.9	22.3	24.0	25.8	20.3	16.4
−73.7	−87.0	−91.4	−69.0	−52.3	−3.1	−6.6	−11.6	−11.1
			64.4	−0.1				5.1
			307.1	9.5				15.1
29954.9	5410.7	905.1	156.4	−20.8	14.6	14.3	12.2	9.9
35786.4	5117.1	1834.1	139.6	8.7	15.0	14.1	16.0	9.1
164347.4	19410.7	1700.1	100.8	8.9	19.3	19.2	15.5	7.2
24466.5	3543.7	1922.8	170.5	8.6	14.0	12.7	16.2	10.5
3386.3	126.2	−21.9	−80.6	−92.2	8.8	2.8	−1.2	−15.1
157290.2	16221.3	2084.8	207.7	11.1	19.2	18.5	16.7	11.9
60324.5	7880.5	1757.8	313.7	15.4	16.5	15.7	15.7	15.3
	29857.7	2963.6	270.6	7.3		20.9	18.7	14.0

Note: Due to the statistics method of railway transportation has been adjusted, the data related to freight traffic and passenger traffic in 2017 can not be compared with the previous.

1-4 续表 2 continued

指标	Item	1978	1990	2000	2010	2019	2020
		总量指标 Aggregate Data					
教育、科技、文化	**Education, Science and Technology, and Culture**						
教育	**Education**						
高等学校本专科在校学生 (万人)	Students Enrollment in Institutions of Higher Eduction (10 000 persons)	4.94	13.04	34.66	129.69	149.81	161.37
中等职业学校在校学生 (万人)	Students Enrollment in Specialized Secondary Schools (10 000 persons)	5.36	1458.00	27.86	90.38	39.19	42.03
普通中学在校学生 (万人)	Students Enrollment in Regular Secondary Schools (10 000 persons)	372.38	211.56	350.93	341.83	250.59	260.00
小学在校学生 (万人)	Students Enrollment in Primary Schools (10 000 persons)	765.73	623.06	667.74	365.55	376.48	380.85
文化	**Culture**						
图书出版量 (亿册)	Books Published (100 million copies)	1.62	4.02	2.88	2.75	3.17	2.96
杂志出版量 (亿册)	Magazines Issued (100 million copies)	0.09	0.73	2.20	3.01	1.05	0.71
报纸出版量 (亿份)	Newspaper Issued (100 million copies)	1.97	6.24	13.42	18.17	7.37	5.72
家庭、生活、环境	**Family, People´s Livelihood and Environment**						
家庭	**Family**						
城镇居民平均每户家庭人口 (人)	Average Household size in Urban Areas (person)	4.32	3.47	3.14	2.93	3.01	3.03
农村居民平均每户常住人口 (人)	Average Household size in Rural Areas (person)	6.02	4.67	4.11	3.98	3.08	3.10
居住	**Housing**						
城镇居民人均住房建筑面积 (平方米)	Per Capita Net Floor Space of Urban Residents (sq.m)		9.80	13.90	33.20	46.30	43.08
农村居民人均住房面积 (平方米)	Per Capita Net Floor Space of Rural Residents (sq.m)		25.73	30.11	40.99	58.68	57.79
生活	**People´s Livelihood**						
城镇居民人均可支配收入 (元)	Per Capita Annual Disposbale Income of Urban Residents (yuan)	325.00	1427.20	5524.50	16058.00	37601.36	36705.74
农村居民人均可支配收入 (元)	Per Capita Annual Disposbale Income of Rural Residents (yuan)	110.52	670.80	2268.50	5832.00	16390.86	16305.91
居民储蓄存款余额 (亿元)	Saving Deposit (100 million yuan)	6.96	244.38	1908.80	9851.00	29804.55	33968.87
工资	**Wages**						
工资总额 (亿元)	Total Wages of Staff and Workers (100 million yuan)	25.89	131.24	405.34	1870.51	6944.45	7130.27
职工平均工资 (元)	Average Wages of Staff and Workers (yuan)	581	1903	7565	28092	64661	71110
卫生	**Health Care**						
卫生机构数 (个)	Number of Health Care Organizations (unit)	5940	10472	11065	34269	35479	35445
#医院	Hospitals	1817	2024	2041	602	1034	1048
床位数 (万张)	Number of Hospital Beds (10 000 units)	11.52	16.34	14.96	20.04	40.65	41.14
#医院	Hospitals	10.34	13.16	12.99	13.50	29.12	29.66
卫生技术人员数 (万人)	Number of Medical Technical Personels (10 000 persons)	14.06	20.92	23.88	25.58	41.95	42.90
#执业(助理)医师	Licensed(assitant) Doctors	5.82	8.68	10.30	9.95	15.50	16.00
环境	**Environment**						
污染治理项目本年完成投资 (亿元)	Investment for the Pollusion Treatment Projects Completed (100 million yuan)		1.81	8.52	27.74	13.39	
本年施工污染治理项目数 (个)	Number of Pullution Treatment Project Under Construction (unit)		1545	851	226	179	
工业废水排放量 (亿吨)	Volume of Industrial Waste Water Discharged (100 million tons)		16.23	10.67	9.46	5.71	

注：卫生机构数从2009年起包含村卫生室数量。

速度指标 Indices of Growth Rates								
2020年比下列各年增长(%) Increases					年平均增长(%) Average Annual Growth Rate			
1978	1990	2000	2010	2019	1979~2020	1991~2020	2001~2020	2011~2020
3166.6	1137.5	365.6	24.4	7.7	8.7	8.7	8.0	2.2
684.2	−97.1	50.9	−53.5	7.3	5.0	−11.1	2.1	−7.4
−30.2	22.9	−25.9	−23.9	3.8	−0.9	0.7	−1.5	−2.7
−50.3	−38.9	−43.0	4.2	1.2	−1.6	−1.6	−2.8	0.4
82.5	−26.5	2.6	7.5	−6.7	1.4	−1.0	0.1	0.7
683.5	−3.4	−67.9	−76.6	−32.8	5.0	−0.1	−5.5	−13.5
190.3	−8.3	−57.4	−68.5	−22.4	2.6	−0.3	−4.2	−10.9
−29.8	−12.7	−3.5	3.4	0.7	−0.8	−0.5	−0.2	0.3
−48.5	−33.6	−24.6	−22.1	0.6	−1.6	−1.4	−1.4	−2.5
	339.6	209.9	29.8	−7.0		5.1	5.8	2.6
	124.6	91.9	41.0	−1.5		2.7	3.3	3.5
11194.1	2471.9	564.4	128.6	−2.4	11.9	11.4	9.9	8.6
14653.8	2330.8	618.8	179.6	−0.5	12.6	11.2	10.4	10.8
487958.5	13800.0	1679.6	244.8	14.0	22.4	17.9	15.5	13.2
27440.6	5333.0	1659.1	281.2	2.7	14.3	14.2	15.4	14.3
12139.2	3636.7	840.0	153.1	10.0	12.1	12.8	11.9	9.7
496.7	238.5	220.3	3.4	−0.1	4.3	4.1	6.0	0.3
−42.3	−48.2	−48.7	74.1	1.4	−1.3	−2.2	−3.3	5.7
257.1	151.8	175.0	105.3	1.2	3.1	3.1	5.2	7.5
186.8	125.4	128.3	119.7	1.9	2.5	2.7	4.2	8.2
205.1	105.1	79.6	67.7	2.3	2.7	2.4	3.0	5.3
174.9	84.3	55.3	60.8	3.2	2.4	2.1	2.2	4.9

Note: The number of health institutions has included the number of village clinics since 2009.

1-5 国民经济和社会发展结构指标
Composition Indicators on National Economic and Social Development

单位:% (%)

指 标	Item	1978	2000	2005	2010	2018	2019	2020
人口与就业	**Population and Employment**							
人口	**Population**							
城乡结构	Urban and Rural Structure							
城镇	Urban	14.6	40.5	43.2	49.7	60.3	61.0	62.9
乡村	Rural	85.4	59.5	56.8	50.3	39.7	39.0	37.1
性别结构	Sexual Structure							
男	Male	51.3	52.1	51.8	51.4	50.8	50.8	51.4
女	Female	48.7	47.9	48.2	48.6	49.2	49.2	48.6
就业	**Employment**							
产业结构	Industrial Structure							
第一产业	Primary Industry	77.0	48.0	47.7	46.4	34.0	32.8	27.5
第二产业	Second Industry	14.1	20.8	20.5	20.7	23.4	23.7	26.3
第三产业	Tertiary Industry	8.9	31.2	31.8	32.9	42.6	43.5	46.2
经济类型结构	Structrues by Ownership							
城镇单位从业人员	Staff and Workers Employed in Urban Units							
国有单位	State-owned	81.2	74.7	62.1	40.4	37.8	36.3	21.3
城镇集体单位	Collective-owned	18.8	14.3	8.0	3.1	1.7	1.7	0.7
其他单位	Others		11.0	29.9	56.5	60.5	62.0	78.0
宏观经济	**Macroeconomy**							
国民核算	**National Accounting**							
地区生产总值产业结构	Industrial Structure							
第一产业	Primary Industry	40.5	18.7	16.3	13.3	9.0	8.3	9.5
第二产业	Second Industry	42.2	40.5	43.4	48.8	43.4	41.7	39.2
第三产业	Tertiary Industry	17.3	40.8	40.3	37.9	47.6	50.0	51.3
地区生产总值支出结构	Domestic Expenditures							
最终消费	Total Consumption	54.0	54.0	54.6	45.7			
居民消费	Residents Consumption	49.4	42.4	42.0	31.9			
政府消费	Government Consumption Expenditures	4.6	11.6	12.6	13.8			
资本形成总额	Gross Capital Formation	28.5	50.1	45.3	53.9			
固定资本	Fixed Capital Formation	20.8	38.6	43.2	52.0			
存货增加	Changes in Stock	7.7	11.5	2.1	1.9			
净出口	Net Exports	17.4	-4.0	0.0	0.4			
投资	**Investment**							
经济类型结构	Structrues by Ownership							
国有经济	State-owned	98.8	60.3	38.7	34.9	20.6	19.5	17.7
集体经济	Collective-owned	1.2	9.0	2.8	5.6	0.4	0.4	0.2
其他	Others		30.7	58.5	59.5	79.0	80.1	82.1
资金来源结构	Structure of Funded Sources							
国家预算资金	State Budget	77.2	10.0	9.0	8.0	6.1	5.4	6.3
国内贷款	Domestic Loans	0.4	17.2	16.7	16.4	11.3	10.5	11.1
利用外资	Foreign Investment		2.0	2.5	1.4	0.2	0.4	0.6
自筹资金	Fundraising	18.0	54.9	52.7	62.1	61.2	62.4	61.3
其他投资	Others	4.3	15.9	19.1	12.2	21.2	21.3	20.7

1-5 续表 1 continued

指 标	Item	1978	2000	2005	2010	2018	2019	2020
财政	**Finance**							
地方公共支出结构	Local Public Financial Expenditure Structure							
#一般公共服务	General Public Service				12.6	10.2	10.0	9.2
教育	Education				14.7	14.7	14.4	14.1
社会保障和就业	Social Security and Employment				14.7	16.1	15.9	16.8
利用外资	**Foreign Investment**							
实际外商直接投资结构	Actual Foreign Direct Investment							
合资经营企业	Joint Venture		63.4	40.8	35.3	33.7	38.7	28.9
合作经营企业	Cooperation		3.0	4.8	1.6	0.5	1.1	0.4
外资企业	Sole Proprietorship Business		33.6	34.5	63.1	60.6	55.1	69.3
外商投资股份制企业	Joint-stock Enterprises with Foreign Investment			0.9		3.8	2.6	1.2
产业经济	**Industrial Economy**							
农业	**Agriculture**							
农林牧渔业产值结构	Agricultural Output Value Structure							
农业	Agriculture	77.3	54.7	52.5	55.3	48.9	48.7	47.8
林业	Forestry	4.9	3.6	2.1	1.9	3.8	3.9	3.4
牧业	Animal Husbandry	12.8	30.1	30.7	25.9	22.3	22.8	25.5
渔业	Fishery	0.8	11.6	13.3	13.5	17.8	17.2	15.8
农林牧渔服务业	Agriculture, Animal Husbandry and Fishery Service			1.4	3.4	7.2	7.4	7.5
工业	**Industry**							
工业产值按经济类型分	Industrial Output by Type							
#国有企业	State-owned Enterprises	77.3	35.3	25.3	21.0	3.0	3.4	3.9
集体企业	Collective Enterprises	22.7	18.4	1.8	0.9	0.2	0.2	0.1
港澳台商投资企业	Hong Kong, Macao And Taiwan Invested Enterprises		4.2	4.3	5.1	4.2	4.4	4.0
外商投资企业	Foreign-invested Enterprises		6.8	18.3	15.0	11.6	11.4	12.8
工业产值按轻重分	Industrial Output Divided by Weight							
轻工业	Light Industry	47.1	38.4	24.8	27.5	34.6	34.4	33.6
重工业	Heavy Industry	52.9	61.6	75.2	72.5	65.4	65.6	66.4
建筑业	**Building Industry**							
建筑业总产值结构	Gross Output Value Structure							
国有经济	State-owned Economy	88.6	58.6	57.6	52.6	44.5	47.5	54.3
地方	Local	42.8	23.5	19.9	9.5	8.0	10.1	21.1
中央	Central	45.6	35.1	37.7	43.1	36.6	37.4	43.8
其它经济	Other Economic		14.3	37.3	45.9	55.5	52.5	35.1
运输业	**Transport**							
货运量结构	Cargo Structures							
铁路	Railway	34.4	16.0	16.9	10.5	2.0	2.9	3.3
公路	Highway	34.9	68.0	66.5	73.2	80.1	76.3	71.3
水运	Water Transport	30.7	15.3	15.8	16.3	17.9	20.8	25.4

1-5 续表 2 continued

指 标	Item	1978	2000	2005	2018	2019	2020
国内商业	**Domestic Trade**						
社会消费品零售总额结构	Total Retail Sales of Consumer Goods						
商品零售额	Retail Sales				89.8	87.6	87.8
餐饮收入额	Food and Beverage Revenue				10.2	12.4	12.2
对外经济贸易和国际旅游	**Foreign Trade and Tourism**						
进出口总额	Total Imports and Exports						
#出口	Exports	8.1	39.8	51.1	64.6	63.0	62.9
进口	Imports	91.9	60.2	48.9	35.4	37.0	37.1
海外旅游人数结构	Structure of Tourists						
外国人	Foreigners	47.3	79.3	75.9	75.8	77.8	
港澳台同胞	Compatriots from Hongkong, Macao and Taiwan	52.7	20.7	24.1	24.2	22.2	
教育、科技、文化	**Education, Science and Technology, and Culture**						
教育	**Education**						
在校学生结构	Structure of Students Enrollment						
大学生	College and University Students	0.4	3.3	10.4	19.1	19.2	20.1
中学生	Secondary School Students	32.6	33.3	45.7	32.1	32.3	32.4
小学生	Primary School Students	67.0	63.4	43.9	48.8	48.5	47.5
专任教师结构	Full-time Teacher by Type						
大学	College and Universities	2.9	11.9	17.5	17.3	17.3	17.7
中学	Secondary Schools	39.6	38.9	44.5	40.5	40.5	40.5
小学	Primary Schools	57.5	49.2	38.0	42.2	42.2	41.8
科技	**Science and Technology**						
R&D 经费支出结构	Expenditure on R&D						
基础研究	Basic Research			4.6	3.7	4.5	4.5
应用研究	Applied Research			20.0	13.2	12.5	12.2
实验发展	Expenditure Development			71.3	83.1	83.0	83.3
生活、环境	**People´s Livelihood and Environment**						
生活	**People´s Livelihood**						
城镇居民消费结构	Consumption Structutre of Urban Residents						
食品	Food		38.3	39.0	28.1	27.8	31.1
衣着	Clothing		11.4	12.0	7.3	7.1	6.4
居住	Residence		14.1	10.2	22.5	22.4	25.2
其他	Others		36.2	38.8	42.2	42.7	37.3
农村居民消费结构	Consumption Structutre of Rural Residents						
食品	Food	70.8	53.2	49.1	28.2	27.2	29.7
衣着	Clothing	12.0	4.8	5.1	5.6	5.4	5.4
居住	Residence	8.9	11.5	12.8	21.2	21.3	22.1
其他	Others	8.3	30.5	33.0	45.0	46.1	42.8

注:2020 年因受新冠疫情影响,文化和旅游部未布置开展入境游客花费抽样调查工作,故相关数据缺失。

Note: In 2020, due to the impact of the "COVID-19", the Ministry of Culture and Tourism did not arrange to carry out a sample survey on the expenses of inbound tourists, so the relevant data are missing.

1-6 湖北国民经济占全国的比重(2020)
Proportion of Hubei´s National Economy in China (2020)

指 标		Item		全国 Country	湖北 Hubei	湖北占全国的比重(%) Percentage to the Country
土地面积	(万平方公里)	Ground space	(10 000 sq.km.)	960.00	18.59	1.94
年末常住人口	(万人)	Population	(10 000 persons)	141178	5775	4.09
地区生产总值	(亿元)	Gross Domestic Product	(100 million yuan)	1015986.20	43443.46	4.28
第一产业		Primary Industry		77754.10	4131.91	5.31
第二产业		Second Industry		384255.30	17023.90	4.43
第三产业		Tertiary Industry		553976.80	22287.65	4.02
人均地区生产总值	(元)	GDP Per Capita	(yuan)	72000	74440	相当于全国 103.39%
投资	(亿元)	Investment	(100 million yuan)			
#房地产开发		Development of Real Estate		141442.95	4888.87	3.46
地方公共财政收入	(亿元)	Local Public Financial Revenue	(100 million yuan)	100123.84	2511.52	2.51
社会消费品零售总额	(亿元)	Total Retail Sales of Social Consumption	(100 million yuan)	391980.60	17984.87	4.59
进出口总额	(亿美元)	Total Imports and Exports	(100 million dollars)	46462.57	620.83	1.34
#出口		Exports		25906.46	390.61	1.51
实际外商直接投资	(亿美元)	Actual Foreign Direct Investment	(100 million dollars)	1443.70	103.52	7.17
普通高等学校本专科在校生	(万人)	Students Enrollment in Institutions of Higher Eductioan	(10 000 persons)	3285.29	161.37	4.91
卫生机构床位数	(万张)	Number of Hospital Beds	(10 000 units)	911.30	41.14	4.51
卫生技术人员	(万人)	Number of Medical Technical Personnels	(10 000 persons)	1067.10	42.90	4.02
#执业(助理)医师		Professional (assistant) Doctors		408.20	16.00	3.92
在岗职工平均工资	(元)	Average Wages of Employee		97379	71110	相当于全国 73.02%
城镇居民人均可支配收入	(元)	Per Capita Disposable Income of Urban Residents	(yuan)	43834	36706	相当于全国 83.74%
农村居民人均可支配收入	(元)	Per Capita Net Incomes of Rural Residents	(yuan)	17131	16306	相当于全国 95.18%
工农业主要产品产量	(万吨)	Output of Major Products in Argriculture and Industry	(10 000 tons)			
粮食		Grain		66949.0	2727.4	4.07
棉花		Cotton		591.0	10.8	1.83
油料		Oil-bearing Crops		3586.4	344.5	9.60
粗钢		Crude Steel		106476.7	3621.8	3.40
钢材		Steel		132489.2	3649.1	2.75
发电量	(亿千瓦小时)	Electricity	(100 million kwh)	77790.6	2911.4	3.74
原煤		Coal		390157.7	40.3	0.01
农用氮、磷、钾化学肥料(折纯)		Agricultural Nitrogen, Phosphorus and Potassium Fertilizer		5496.0	482.1	8.77
水泥		Cement		239483.7	9886.8	4.13
生铁		Pig Iron		88752.4	2727.4	3.07
布	(亿米)	Cloth	(100 million meters)	460.3	41.9	9.11
汽车	(万辆)	Moter Vehicles	(10 000 units)	2532.5	210.5	8.31

注:全国数据来源于中国统计摘要。
Note: The national data comes from *China Statistical Abstract*.

1-7 全省人均国民经济主要指标

指标	Item	1990	2000
地区生产总值 (元)	Gross Domestic Product (yuan)	1541.00	6293.00
第一产业	Primary Industry	541.00	1164.00
第二产业	Second Industry	586.00	2525.00
第三产业	Tertiary Industry	414.00	2540.00
地方公共财政预算收入(元)	Government Revenue (yuan)	145.54	376.61
地方财政支出 (元)	Government Expenditure (yuan)	158.57	1647.93
社会消费品零售额 (元)	Total Retail Sales of Consumer Goods (yuan)	610.00	3144.00
进出口总额 (美元)	Total Imports and Exports (US.dollars)	22.24	56.40
#出口 (美元)	Exports (US.dollars)	20.04	33.93
农村居民可支配收入 (元)	Net Income of Rural Residents (yuan)	671.00	2268.00
城镇居民可支配收入 (元)	Disposable Income of Urban Residents (yuan)	1427.00	5524.00
居民储蓄存款 (元)	Outstanding Amount of Saving Deposits of Urabn And Rural Residents (yuan)	455.00	3209.00
在校大学生数 (人/万人)	Number of Students Enrollment in Institutions of Higher Education (person/10 000 persons)	24.38	60.89
医院病床数 (张/万人)	Hospital Beds (bed/10 000 persons)	24.60	22.42
卫生技术人员数 (人/万人)	Number of Medical Technical Personnels (person/10 000 persons)	39.11	41.96
#执业(助理)医师	Professional (assitant) Doctors	16.22	17.40
主要工农业产品产量(千克)	Output of Major Industrial and Agricultural Products (kg)		
粮食	Grain	467.10	372.92
棉花	Cotton	9.76	5.12
油料	Oil-Bearing Crops	18.07	45.38
钢材	Steel	100.60	136.34
原煤	Coal	174.43	64.45
发电量 (千瓦小时)	Electricity (kwh)	639.62	904.54

注:2010 年之后农产品产量根据第三次农业普查数据进行调整。

Major Per Capita Indicators of Hubei´s

2005	2010	2015	2018	2019	2020
11554.00	28163.01	51224.05	66615.70	77386.54	74440.47
1897.00	3752.25	5673.61	6003.06	6432.10	7080.04
4926.00	13752.46	23575.28	28917.76	32250.28	29170.50
4607.00	10658.30	21975.16	31694.88	38704.15	38189.94
658.36	1767.30	5151.97	5596.21	5722.00	4303.49
1368.21	4371.64	10446.47	12282.38	13458.64	14460.31
5197.00	11743.40	24003.84	31023.94	38369.32	30817.12
159.40	452.77	781.42	893.52	964.68	1063.80
78.02	252.40	500.78	576.85	607.56	669.31
3099.00	5832.27	11843.89	14977.82	16390.86	16305.91
8786.00	16058.37	27051.47	34454.63	37601.36	36705.74
7929.00	17211.00	33539.49	44531.00	50328.52	58205.74
177.54	226.66	241.48	242.99	252.97	276.51
17.00	23.59	42.27	47.63	49.13	50.82
37.69	44.71	63.01	69.51	70.78	73.51
14.90	17.39	23.20	69.51	26.15	27.42
382.00	402.71	499.64	480.49	460.15	467.35
6.26	8.25	5.16	2.53	2.42	1.85
51.50	52.83	54.29	51.19	53.01	59.02
278.04	505.90	586.45	623.05	635.95	625.28
83.80	225.75	130.00	9.89	6.51	6.90
2204.00	3545.46	3944.98	4660.34	4890.92	4988.61

Note: Production of agricultural products after 2010 is adjusted according to the data of the third agricultural census.

1-8 湖北的一天
One Day in Hubei

指 标	Item	2000	2005	2010	2015	2019	2020
每天创造的财富	**Daily Production**						
地区生产总值 (亿元)	Gross Domestic Products (100 million yuan)	9.71	17.86	44.15	81.87	125.56	118.70
第一产业	Primary Industry	1.81	2.96	5.88	9.07	10.44	11.29
第二产业	Second Industry	3.94	7.70	21.56	37.68	52.32	46.51
第三产业	Tertiary Industry	3.96	7.20	16.71	35.12	62.8	60.90
地方公共财政预算收入 (亿元)	Government Revenue (100 million yuan)	0.59	1.03	2.77	8.23	9.28	6.86
粮食 (万吨)	Grain (10 000 tons)	6.08	5.97	6.31	7.99	7.47	7.45
肉类产量 (吨)	Meat (ton)	7429.86	9387.12	10506.30	12155.07	9567.12	8400.00
水产品 (吨)	Aquatic Products (ton)	6420.27	8713.15	9671.23	12487.67	12864.11	12784.93
粗钢 (万吨)	Steel (10 000 tons)	2.45	4.31	6.85	8.00	9.85	9.90
成品钢材 (万吨)	Rolled-steel (10 000 tons)	2.22	4.34	7.93	9.37	10.33	9.97
发电量 (亿千瓦小时)	Electricity (100 million kwh)	1.47	3.44	5.56	6.31	7.94	7.95
水泥 (万吨)	Cement (10 000 tons)	6.74	12.36	24.61	30.93	31.84	27.01
布 (万米)	Cloth (10 000 meters)	470.00	573.00	1270.69	2187.67	1565.78	1145.40
每天消费量	**Daily Consumption**						
最终消费 (亿元)	Final Consumption (100 million yuan)	5.56	9.99	20.25	37.81		
居民消费 (亿元)	Resident Consumption (100 million yuan)	4.37	7.63	14.07	27.86		
政府消费 (亿元)	Government Consumption Expenditure (100 million yuan)	1.19	2.36	6.17	9.95		
城镇居民每人消费性支出 (元)	Per Capita Living Expenditure of Urban Residents (yuan)	12.69	18.46	31.37	49.84	72.39	62.53
#食品消费	Food Consumption	4.86	7.19	12.14	10.68	11.38	19.43
农村居民每人生活消费支出 (元)	Per Capita Living Expenditure of Rural Residents (yuan)	4.26	6.66	11.21	26.86	41.99	39.54
#食品消费 (亿元)	Food Consumption (100 million yuan)	2.27	3.27	4.83	8.09	11.41	11.76
社会消费品零售总额 (亿元)	Total Retail Sales of Consumer Goods (100 million yuan)	4.90	8.12	18.41	38.37	62.25	49.14
每天其他经济活动	**Other Daily Economic Acitivities**						
货物运输量 (万吨)	Freight Traffic (10 000 tons)	112.19	136.78	265.77	439.43	515.46	438.33
旅客运输量 (万人)	Passenger Traffic (10 000 persons)	86.56	195.61	288.81	286.83	243.63	84.43
竣工房屋面积 (万平方米)	Floor Space of Housing Completed (10 000 sq.m)	8.63	18.90	35.11	73.49	92.90	72.57
出版报纸 (万份)	Newspapers Published (10 000 pieces)	367.67	536.16	497.80	423.39	201.89	156.27
函件 (万件)	Letters Delivered (10 000 pieces)	99.00	41.64	27.40	18.63	17.89	8.47
进出口总额 (万美元)	Total Imports and Exports (10 000 USD)	879.45	2490.96	7097.81	12489.32	15651.64	16962.69
#出口	Exports	529.04	1219.18	3956.71	8003.84	9875.53	10672.35
实际外商直接投资 (万美元)	Actual Foreign Direct Investment (10 000 USD)	258.63	598.63	1109.59	2451.51	3536.29	2828.39
每天人口变动和婚姻	**Daily Population Changes and Marriages**						
出生人数 (人)	Birth (person)	1582	1441	1625	1716	1841	1320
死亡人数 (人)	Death (person)	979	940	944	932	1149	1223
结婚对数 (对)	Marriage (couple)	969	1080	1564	1570	1067	862
离婚对数 (对)	Divorce (couple)	58	146	244	396	516	472

1-9 地区生产总值
Gross Domestic Product

本表按当年价格计算 (At current price)

年 份 Year	地区生产总值(亿元) Total Output (100 million yuan)	第一产业 Primary Industry	第二产业 Secondary Industry	工 业 Industry	建筑业 Contruction	第三产业 Tertiary Industry	# 金融业 Banking	# 房地产业 Real Estate	人均地区生产总值(元) Per Capita GDP (yuan)	人均地区生产总值(美元) Per Capita GDP (USD)
1952	24.51	13.90	3.82	3.17	0.66	6.79			90.13	34.44
1955	34.05	18.14	7.43	6.25	1.20	8.48			117.88	47.88
1957	48.86	24.33	11.56	9.03	2.56	12.97			162.17	65.87
1962	52.13	29.30	10.60	9.10	1.53	12.23			161.47	65.59
1965	72.43	37.74	21.10	17.36	3.80	13.59			209.26	85.00
1970	88.15	44.41	26.82	21.79	5.11	16.92			221.78	90.09
1975	120.10	53.71	45.36	32.68	12.80	21.03			274.30	139.50
1978	151.00	61.11	63.52	52.17	11.54	26.37	4.54	1.42	332.03	210.53
1980	199.38	71.22	91.39	75.63	16.04	36.77	5.51	2.83	427.98	279.67
1985	396.26	144.44	173.78	152.88	21.47	78.04	10.71	4.61	808.11	275.19
1986	442.04	163.61	187.35	164.93	23.03	91.08	13.68	5.97	885.96	256.59
1987	517.77	183.99	223.79	197.66	26.87	109.99	17.09	7.39	1018.42	273.61
1988	626.52	214.66	270.34	244.17	27.08	141.52	20.82	8.88	1215.93	326.68
1989	717.08	239.07	299.43	276.47	23.99	178.58	28.14	9.18	1373.22	364.72
1990	824.38	289.45	312.33	284.15	29.24	222.60	33.77	11.36	1541.17	322.20
1991	913.38	279.30	358.64	327.50	32.36	275.44	40.30	13.61	1668.03	313.34
1992	1088.39	303.00	443.11	402.59	42.02	342.28	48.07	17.22	1962.45	355.86
1993	1325.83	346.39	535.83	475.44	62.16	443.61	52.22	25.63	2360.53	409.67
1994	1700.92	501.44	655.47	580.80	76.83	544.01	56.83	37.85	2991.34	347.07
1995	2109.38	619.77	777.64	680.92	99.26	711.97	60.86	42.07	3671.40	439.64
1996	2499.77	716.34	920.68	805.53	118.15	862.75	65.37	62.23	4310.99	811.22
1997	2856.47	767.92	1068.40	929.91	141.95	1020.15	69.68	69.65	4883.80	589.13
1998	3114.02	778.22	1195.20	1041.20	157.88	1140.60	74.14	81.78	5287.04	638.60
1999	3229.29	653.99	1310.20	1139.52	174.92	1265.10	78.81	85.01	5452.46	658.65
2000	3545.39	662.30	1432.75	1243.24	194.14	1450.34	81.49	99.40	6121.17	739.41
2001	3880.53	692.17	1569.33	1360.10	214.29	1619.03	88.48	122.49	6865.76	829.50
2002	4212.82	707.00	1704.41	1473.00	236.89	1801.41	96.95	145.17	7436.58	898.46
2003	4757.45	798.35	1949.76	1682.16	273.86	2009.34	107.31	176.80	8378.00	1012.20
2004	5546.78	1008.87	2273.53	1955.61	325.21	2264.38	115.85	199.62	9745.73	1177.48
2005	6469.66	1069.81	2758.83	2410.42	357.39	2641.02	118.52	235.26	11342.32	1384.61
2006	7531.80	1125.52	3270.80	2863.47	418.00	3135.48	161.79	333.55	13210.21	1691.73
2007	9451.39	1331.44	4128.89	3597.37	544.92	3991.06	316.57	495.05	16593.03	2206.08
2008	11497.46	1716.03	5066.19	4406.90	675.70	4715.24	364.38	661.46	20153.30	2902.09
2009	13192.14	1717.32	6035.52	5212.66	842.27	5439.30	439.41	713.42	23081.34	3376.39
2010	16226.94	2043.20	7748.26	6750.66	1022.73	6435.48	508.50	766.12	28359.43	4189.30
2011	19942.45	2469.20	9766.13	8551.19	1246.78	7707.12	602.70	893.63	34718.75	5375.42
2012	22590.89	2674.82	11152.55	9771.03	1417.91	8763.52	769.06	1014.77	39148.93	6201.81
2013	25378.01	2883.73	11846.30	10227.36	1657.03	10647.98	1033.11	1484.94	43834.55	7078.31
2014	28242.13	3001.59	13007.91	11174.22	1875.40	12232.63	1196.39	1698.70	48634.63	7917.34
2015	30344.00	3109.93	13569.49	11677.26	1957.78	13664.58	1588.78	1879.93	52021.26	8352.27
2016	33353.00	3406.46	14527.01	12480.47	2109.18	15419.53	1975.11	2231.70	56843.63	8557.82
2017	37235.00	3528.96	15713.86	13431.59	2342.51	17992.18	2255.19	2794.30	63169.06	9355.88
2018	42021.95	3548.17	17573.87	14849.55	2781.41	20899.91	2554.00	3320.08	71097.12	10743.97
2019	45428.96	3809.41	18723.05	15707.64	3073.13	22896.50	2783.57	3455.34	76712.19	11120.13
2020	43443.46	4131.91	17023.90	14249.78	2827.95	22287.65	3027.37	3308.51	74440.47	10793.48

注:1.2020 年为快报数。2.2011 年以来人均地区生产总值根据人口数进行了修订。

Notes: a)The data for 2020 are express data. b)Since 2011, the per capita gross regional product has been revised based on the population.

1-10 地区生产总值指数(上年=100)
Indices of Gross Domestic Product (preceding year=100)

按可比价计算，上年=100 (In comparable price, preceding year=100)

年 份 Year	地区生产总值(%) Total Output (%)	第一产业 Primary Industry	第二产业 Secondary Industry	工业 Industry	建筑业 Contruction	第三产业 Tertiary Industry	#金融业 Banking	#房地产业 Real Estate	人均地区生产总值(%) Per Capita GDP(%)
1953	114.0	107.4	129.4	141.0	93.3	122.7			111.6
1955	127.1	135.5	104.9	100.2	139.2	127.1			124.8
1957	107.4	106.4	115.3	109.5	146.0	102.6			104.7
1962	100.9	112.3	84.0	92.7	50.5	94.0			99.0
1965	118.1	111.5	132.5	124.5	196.4	114.9			115.5
1970	126.9	112.2	161.2	151.2	222.0	111.3			123.4
1975	111.4	94.5	139.0	135.2	152.5	116.0			110.0
1978	113.5	103.4	128.4	131.9	112.2	107.4			112.1
1980	106.4	86.9	123.5	126.7	107.0	111.0	97.4	160.6	105.1
1985	116.2	108.3	124.7	124.7	124.3	79.8	112.4	112.3	115.1
1986	105.5	103.3	105.2	103.9	116.8	155.2	120.5	122.2	103.7
1987	108.4	103.1	111.3	112.9	99.0	110.7	114.5	113.4	106.4
1988	107.8	94.9	113.7	115.1	101.5	114.3	107.0	105.6	106.4
1989	104.5	105.2	102.1	104.2	81.3	109.3	121.8	93.2	103.1
1990	105.0	107.5	99.0	99.5	92.8	114.8	108.9	109.7	102.5
1991	106.6	95.1	111.1	111.6	106.1	115.4	114.4	114.7	104.1
1992	114.1	108.2	116.6	117.5	107.5	116.9	111.5	117.8	112.7
1993	113.0	105.8	116.7	116.1	123.3	115.2	112.0	119.4	111.6
1994	113.7	107.1	119.0	119.2	117.6	112.4	107.7	127.3	112.3
1995	113.2	108.9	116.3	116.0	118.5	112.5	107.3	121.0	112.0
1996	111.6	104.5	115.8	115.7	116.6	111.3	107.3	116.5	110.6
1997	111.9	106.9	113.4	113.5	112.3	113.5	103.4	110.3	110.9
1998	108.6	99.4	111.1	110.9	113.9	111.5	107.0	117.9	107.8
1999	107.8	101.9	108.3	108.3	107.5	111.0	103.7	106.1	107.2
2000	108.6	102.5	109.1	109.0	110.7	111.5	105.6	116.8	111.0
2001	108.9	102.5	109.9	110.2	108.5	110.8	107.4	122.1	111.6
2002	109.2	102.0	110.1	110.0	110.5	111.4	108.4	114.5	108.9
2003	109.7	105.8	110.1	110.1	110.6	110.8	110.1	119.0	109.4
2004	110.8	107.6	113.5	113.5	113.4	109.4	105.2	113.2	110.5
2005	112.1	104.1	115.0	115.9	109.6	112.2	104.1	108.5	111.9
2006	113.3	105.1	116.1	116.5	113.7	113.6	135.1	129.4	113.3
2007	114.6	104.7	116.3	115.4	122.9	116.4	166.8	131.6	114.7
2008	113.4	106.0	116.7	117.0	114.8	112.5	110.8	117.4	113.3
2009	113.7	105.2	116.9	115.7	124.6	112.9	122.5	114.6	113.5
2010	114.7	104.6	119.8	121.0	112.6	111.8	110.0	109.7	114.6
2011	114.1	104.4	117.9	119.1	109.9	112.6	112.8	104.4	113.7
2012	111.2	104.7	113.4	113.6	111.4	110.4	126.1	105.0	110.7
2013	110.2	105.3	110.6	110.9	111.6	111.1	115.3	109.9	109.8
2014	109.7	104.8	110.2	110.2	110.9	110.3	114.7	106.6	109.4
2015	108.6	104.5	108.3	108.6	106.1	110.1	130.7	106.5	108.1
2016	108.1	103.9	107.8	107.7	107.8	109.5	123.6	108.1	107.5
2017	107.8	103.6	107.1	107.2	106.2	109.5	109.0	113.3	107.4
2018	107.8	102.9	106.8	107.1	104.2	109.9	105.0	106.3	107.6
2019	107.3	102.4	106.7	106.8	105.8	108.7	107.1	102.5	107.0
2020	95.0	100.0	92.6	92.6	92.1	96.2	106.3	91.3	96.4

注：1.2020 年为快报数。2.2011 年以来人均地区生产总值根据人口数进行了修订。
Note: a)The data for 2020 are express data. b)Since 2011, the per capita gross regional product has been revised based on the population.

1-11 地区生产总值指数(1952 年=100)

Indices of Gross Domestic Product (year of 1952=100)

按可比价计算,1952=100 (In comparable price, 1952 = 100)

年份 Year	地区生产总值(%) Total Output (%)	第一产业 Primary Industry	第二产业 Secondary Industry	工业 Industry	建筑业 Contruction	第三产业 Tertiary Industry	#金融业 Banking	#房地产业 Real Estate	人均地区生产总值(%) Per Capita GDP (%)
1953	114.0	107.4	129.4	141.0	93.3	122.7			111.6
1955	121.6	115.7	152.3	168.4	102.2	118.2			114.4
1957	169.5	143.7	280.1	295.2	233.2	172.0			153.0
1962	141.6	129.9	223.7	257.9	116.2	124.2			119.2
1965	205.6	161.3	490.0	538.8	339.3	161.1			161.5
1970	242.8	158.4	705.8	745.7	581.7	202.1			166.1
1975	320.1	185.0	1126.0	1165.0	998.6	258.7			198.8
1978	398.9	204.4	1615.6	1857.3	928.0	313.6			238.5
1980	490.6	211.1	2256.6	2637.9	1175.6	398.2	110.8	179.8	286.4
1985	869.8	341.6	4108.2	5129.6	1386.7	565.8	186.6	253.4	482.4
1986	917.7	352.8	4321.8	5329.7	1619.7	878.2	224.8	309.7	500.2
1987	994.7	363.8	4810.2	6017.2	1603.5	972.1	257.4	351.2	532.1
1988	1072.3	345.2	5469.2	6925.8	1627.6	1111.1	275.4	370.8	565.9
1989	1120.6	363.2	5584.0	7216.7	1323.2	1214.5	335.4	345.6	583.6
1990	1176.6	390.4	5528.2	7180.6	1227.9	1394.2	365.3	379.2	598.2
1991	1254.3	371.3	6141.8	8013.5	1302.9	1608.9	417.9	434.9	622.9
1992	1431.1	401.7	7161.3	9415.9	1400.6	1880.8	466.0	512.3	701.7
1993	1617.2	425.0	8357.3	10931.8	1726.9	2166.7	521.9	611.7	783.1
1994	1838.7	455.2	9945.2	13030.7	2030.8	2435.4	562.1	778.7	879.4
1995	2081.5	495.7	11566.2	15115.7	2406.5	2739.8	603.1	942.2	985.0
1996	2322.9	518.0	13393.7	17488.8	2806.0	3049.4	647.1	1097.7	1089.4
1997	2599.3	553.7	15188.5	19849.8	3151.2	3461.1	669.1	1210.7	1208.1
1998	2822.9	550.4	16874.4	22013.4	3589.2	3859.1	716.0	1427.4	1302.4
1999	3043.1	560.9	18274.9	23840.6	3858.4	4283.6	742.5	1514.5	1396.1
2000	3304.8	574.9	19938.0	25986.2	4271.2	4776.2	784.0	1769.0	1549.7
2001	3598.9	589.3	21911.8	28636.8	4634.3	5292.1	842.1	2159.9	1729.5
2002	3930.0	601.1	24124.9	31500.5	5120.9	5895.4	912.8	2473.1	1883.4
2003	4311.2	635.9	26561.5	34682.0	5663.7	6532.1	1005.0	2943.0	2060.4
2004	4776.8	684.3	30147.3	39364.1	6422.6	7146.1	1057.2	3331.4	2276.8
2005	5354.8	712.3	34669.4	45623.0	7039.2	8017.9	1100.6	3614.6	2547.7
2006	6067.0	748.6	40251.2	53150.8	8003.5	9108.3	1486.9	4677.3	2886.6
2007	6952.7	783.8	46812.2	61336.0	9836.3	10602.1	2480.1	6155.3	3310.9
2008	7884.4	830.8	54629.8	71763.2	11292.1	11927.4	2748.0	7226.4	3751.2
2009	8964.6	874.1	63862.3	83030.0	14070.0	13466.0	3366.3	8281.4	4257.7
2010	10282.4	914.3	76507.0	100466.3	15842.8	15055.0	3702.9	9084.7	4879.3
2011	11732.2	954.5	90201.7	119655.3	17411.2	16951.9	4176.9	9484.4	5547.7
2012	13046.2	999.3	102288.8	135928.5	19396.1	18714.9	5267.0	9958.7	6141.4
2013	14376.9	1052.3	113131.4	150744.7	21646.1	20792.3	6072.9	10944.6	6743.2
2014	15771.4	1102.8	124670.8	166120.6	24005.5	22933.9	6965.6	11666.9	7377.1
2015	17127.8	1152.5	135018.4	180407.0	25469.8	25250.2	9104.0	12425.3	7974.6
2016	18515.1	1197.4	145549.9	194298.3	27456.5	27649.0	11252.6	13431.7	8572.7
2017	19959.3	1240.5	155883.9	208287.8	29158.8	30275.7	12265.3	15218.1	9207.1
2018	21516.2	1276.5	166484.0	223076.2	30383.4	33272.9	12878.6	16176.9	9906.8
2019	23076.1	1307.4	177677.7	238350.2	32145.7	36156.4	13793.0	16576.7	10600.3
2020	21922.3	1307.4	164529.6	220712.3	29606.2	34782.5	14661.9	15134.5	10218.7

注:金融业、房地产业指数以 1978 年为 100。
Note: The index of financial industry and real estate industry was 100 in 1978.

1-12 地区生产总值构成
Composition of Gross Domestic Product

本表按当年价格计算 (At current prices)

年 份 Year	地区生产总 值(%) Total Output (%)	第一产业 Primary Industry	第二产业 Secondary Industry	工 业 Industry	建筑业 Contruction	第三产业 Tertiary Industry	# 金融业 Banking	# 房地产业 Real Estate
1952	100	56.7	15.6	12.9	2.7	27.7		
1955	100	53.3	21.8	18.4	3.5	24.9		
1957	100	49.8	23.7	18.5	5.2	26.5		
1962	100	56.2	20.3	17.5	2.9	23.5		
1965	100	52.1	29.1	24.0	5.2	18.8		
1970	100	50.4	30.4	24.7	5.8	19.2		
1975	100	44.7	37.8	27.2	10.7	17.5		
1978	100	40.5	42.1	34.5	7.6	17.4	3.0	0.9
1980	100	35.7	45.8	37.9	8.0	18.5	2.8	1.4
1985	100	36.4	43.9	38.6	5.4	19.7	2.7	1.2
1986	100	37.0	42.4	37.3	5.2	20.6	3.1	1.4
1987	100	35.5	43.2	38.2	5.2	21.3	3.3	1.4
1988	100	34.3	43.1	39.0	4.3	22.6	3.3	1.4
1989	100	33.3	41.8	38.6	3.3	24.9	3.9	1.3
1990	100	35.1	37.9	34.5	3.5	27.0	4.1	1.4
1991	100	30.6	39.3	35.9	3.5	30.1	4.4	1.5
1992	100	27.8	40.7	37.0	3.9	31.5	4.4	1.6
1993	100	26.1	40.4	35.9	4.7	33.5	3.9	1.9
1994	100	29.5	38.5	34.1	4.5	32.0	3.3	2.2
1995	100	29.4	36.9	32.3	4.7	33.7	2.9	2.0
1996	100	28.7	36.8	32.2	4.7	34.5	2.6	2.5
1997	100	26.9	37.4	32.6	5.0	35.7	2.4	2.4
1998	100	25.0	38.4	33.4	5.1	36.6	2.4	2.6
1999	100	20.2	40.6	35.3	5.4	39.2	2.4	2.6
2000	100	18.7	40.4	35.1	5.5	40.9	2.3	2.8
2001	100	17.8	40.5	35.0	5.5	41.7	2.3	3.2
2002	100	16.8	40.4	35.0	5.6	42.8	2.3	3.4
2003	100	16.8	41.0	35.4	5.8	42.2	2.3	3.7
2004	100	18.2	41.0	35.3	5.9	40.8	2.1	3.6
2005	100	16.5	42.7	37.3	5.5	40.8	1.8	3.6
2006	100	15.0	43.4	38.0	5.5	41.6	2.1	4.4
2007	100	14.1	43.7	38.1	5.8	42.2	3.3	5.2
2008	100	14.9	44.1	38.3	5.9	41.0	3.2	5.8
2009	100	13.0	45.8	39.5	6.4	41.2	3.3	5.4
2010	100	12.6	47.7	41.6	6.3	39.7	3.1	4.7
2011	100	12.4	49.0	42.9	6.3	38.6	3.0	4.5
2012	100	11.8	49.4	43.3	6.3	38.8	3.4	4.5
2013	100	11.4	46.7	40.3	6.5	41.9	4.1	5.9
2014	100	10.6	46.1	39.6	6.6	43.3	4.2	6.0
2015	100	10.3	44.7	38.5	6.5	45.0	5.2	6.2
2016	100	10.2	43.6	37.4	6.3	46.2	5.9	6.7
2017	100	9.5	42.2	36.1	6.3	48.3	6.1	7.5
2018	100	8.5	41.8	35.3	6.6	49.7	6.1	7.9
2019	100	8.4	41.2	34.6	6.8	50.4	6.1	7.6
2020	100	9.5	39.2	32.8	6.5	51.3	7.0	7.6

注:1.2020 年为快报数。2.2011 年以来人均地区生产总值根据人口数进行了修订。
Note: a)The data for 2020 are express data. b)Since 2011, the per capita gross regional product has been revised based on the population.

1-13 三次产业贡献率

Share of the Contributions of the Three Strata of Industry to the Increase of the GDP

单位:% 本表按可比价格计算 (In comparable price) (%)

年 份 Year	地区生产总值 Gross Domestic Product	第一产业 Primary Industry	第二产业 Secondary Industry	#工业 Industry	第三产业 Tertiary Industry
1992	100	18.2	46.5	44.8	35.3
1993	100	13.2	51.7	45.9	35.1
1994	100	14.4	57.9	53.4	27.7
1995	100	17.7	53.7	48.6	28.6
1996	100	9.8	60.9	55.5	29.3
1997	100	13.7	52.4	48.3	33.9
1998	100	-1.6	61.0	54.5	40.6
1999	100	5.0	51.1	47.1	43.9
2000	100	5.7	51.5	46.3	42.8
2001	100	5.2	45.1	40.0	49.7
2002	100	3.8	44.6	38.5	51.6
2003	100	9.8	42.9	37.0	47.3
2004	100	11.1	51.4	44.7	37.5
2005	100	5.2	52.4	48.0	42.4
2006	100	6.4	51.8	46.3	41.8
2007	100	5.0	49.0	40.4	46.0
2008	100	6.3	55.0	48.7	38.7
2009	100	5.0	56.2	45.6	38.8
2010	100	3.8	63.3	57.8	32.9
2011	100	3.9	60.6	56.4	35.5
2012	100	4.8	59.0	52.9	36.2
2013	100	5.6	52.3	47.5	42.1
2014	100	5.1	53.1	46.8	41.8
2015	100	5.2	48.8	44.8	46.0
2016	100	4.9	42.8	36.5	52.3
2017	100	4.5	40.5	35.4	55.0
2018	100	3.6	38.3	34.7	58.1
2019	100	3.0	40.7	35.8	56.3
2020	100				

1–14 三次产业拉动率
Contribution of the Three Strata of Industry to GDP Growth

单位：百分点　　本表按可比价格计算(In comparable price)　　(percentage point)

年 份 Year	地区生产总值 Gross Domestic Product	第一产业 Primary Industry	第二产业 Secondary Industry	# 工业 Industry	第三产业 Tertiary Industry
1992	14.1	2.5	6.8	6.5	4.8
1993	13.0	1.7	6.7	6.0	4.6
1994	13.7	2.0	7.9	7.3	3.8
1995	13.2	2.3	7.1	6.4	3.8
1996	11.6	1.1	7.1	6.4	3.4
1997	11.9	1.6	6.2	5.7	4.1
1998	8.6	-0.1	5.2	4.7	3.5
1999	7.8	0.4	4.0	3.7	3.4
2000	8.6	0.5	4.4	4.0	3.7
2001	8.9	0.5	4.0	3.6	4.4
2002	9.2	0.4	4.1	3.5	4.7
2003	9.7	1.0	4.2	3.6	4.5
2004	10.8	1.2	5.6	4.8	4.0
2005	12.1	0.6	6.3	5.8	5.2
2006	13.3	0.8	6.9	6.2	5.6
2007	14.6	0.7	7.2	5.9	6.7
2008	13.4	0.8	7.4	6.5	5.2
2009	13.7	0.7	7.7	6.2	5.3
2010	14.7	0.6	9.3	8.5	4.8
2011	14.1	0.6	8.5	8.0	5.0
2012	11.2	0.5	6.6	5.9	4.1
2013	10.2	0.6	5.3	4.8	4.3
2014	9.7	0.5	5.2	4.5	4.0
2015	8.6	0.4	4.2	3.8	4.0
2016	8.1	0.4	3.5	3.0	4.2
2017	7.8	0.4	3.2	2.8	4.2
2018	7.8	0.3	3.0	2.7	4.5
2019	7.3	0.2	3.0	2.6	4.1
2020	-5.0				

1-15 市、州生产总值(2020)
Gross Domestic Product of Cities and Prefectures (2020)

单位:亿元 (100 million yuan)

地 区	Regions	地区生产总值 Gross Domestic Product	第一产业 Primary Industry	第二产业 Secondary Industry	第三产业 Tertiary Industry
武汉市	Wuhan	15616.06	402.18	5557.47	9656.41
黄石市	Huangshi	1641.32	115.79	797.80	727.73
十堰市	Shiyan	1915.07	190.25	793.18	931.64
宜昌市	Yichang	4261.42	459.68	1828.46	1973.28
襄阳市	Xiangyang	4601.97	513.01	2104.13	1984.83
鄂州市	Ezhou	1005.23	99.20	435.03	471.00
荆门市	Jingmen	1906.41	251.49	848.97	805.95
孝感市	Xiaogan	2193.55	343.14	860.66	989.75
荆州市	Jingzhou	2369.04	453.02	806.24	1109.78
黄冈市	Huanggang	2169.55	438.29	749.83	981.43
咸宁市	Xianning	1524.67	217.49	628.72	678.46
随州市	Suizhou	1096.72	173.37	477.31	446.04
恩施自治州	Enshi	1117.70	202.39	252.28	663.03
仙桃市	Xiantao	827.91	96.50	358.02	373.39
潜江市	Qianjiang	765.23	83.45	367.81	313.97
天门市	Tianmen	617.49	90.25	273.85	253.39
神农架林区	Shennongjia	30.73	2.41	9.13	19.19

1-16 市、州生产总值指数(2020)
Indices of Gross Domestic Product of Cities and Prefectures (2020)

(上年=100,单位:%) (preceding year = 100,%)

地 区	Regions	地区生产总值 Gross Domestic Product	第一产业 Primary Industry	第二产业 Secondary Industry	第三产业 Tertiary Industry
武汉市	Wuhan	95.3	96.2	92.7	96.9
黄石市	Huangshi	94.1	100.5	92.1	95.7
十堰市	Shiyan	95.1	100.7	93.2	96.1
宜昌市	Yichang	95.3	102.3	92.4	97.1
襄阳市	Xiangyang	94.7	102.3	92.7	95.5
鄂州市	Ezhou	90.2	97.2	83.0	97.6
荆门市	Jingmen	95.0	101.1	92.2	96.6
孝感市	Xiaogan	95.5	101.4	91.6	97.8
荆州市	Jingzhou	94.1	100.2	90.0	95.4
黄冈市	Huanggang	93.4	99.6	90.6	93.3
咸宁市	Xianning	95.1	100.0	91.7	97.3
随州市	Suizhou	94.7	103.0	91.6	95.7
恩施自治州	Enshi	95.8	100.6	91.9	96.3
仙桃市	Xiantao	95.7	98.6	93.1	98.1
潜江市	Qianjiang	95.4	100.1	94.2	95.7
天门市	Tianmen	94.4	98.2	92.5	95.4
神农架林区	Shennongjia	93.1	99.5	95.2	91.2

1-17 市、州民营经济增加值
Value Added of Private Economy (2020)

地　区	Regions	增加值(亿元) Value-Added (100 million yuan)		占 GDP 比重(%) Percentage(%)	
		2019	2020	2019	2020
全　省	**Total**	**24820.54**	**22944.65**	**54.6**	**52.8**
武汉市	Wuhan	6963.61	6294.31	42.9	40.3
黄石市	Huangshi	1017.36	935.54	57.6	57.0
十堰市	Shiyan	1048.81	933.42	52.1	48.7
宜昌市	Yichang	2825.89	2623.99	63.3	61.6
襄阳市	Xiangyang	2544.85	2411.44	52.9	52.4
鄂州市	Ezhou	799.21	673.31	70.1	67.0
荆门市	Jingmen	1276.77	1181.81	62.8	62.0
孝感市	Xiaogan	1500.84	1399.49	65.2	63.8
荆州市	Jingzhou	1289.23	1205.17	51.2	50.9
黄冈市	Huanggang	1693.97	1517.74	72.9	70.0
咸宁市	Xianning	1058.84	983.30	66.4	64.5
随州市	Suizhou	786.58	713.16	67.7	65.0
恩施自治州	Enshi	510.35	481.24	44.0	43.1
仙桃市	Xiantao	632.16	591.96	72.8	71.5
潜江市	Qianjiang	601.75	549.40	74.0	71.8
天门市	Tianmen	472.86	437.12	72.7	70.8
神农架林区	Shennongjia	15.65	12.23	47.6	39.8

主要统计指标解释

平均增长速度 计算平均增长速度有两种方法：一种是习惯上经常使用的“水平法”，又称几何平均法，是以间隔期最后一年的水平同基期水平对比来计算平均每年增长(或下降)速度；另一种是“累计法”，又称代数平均法或方程法，是以间隔期内各年水平的总和同基期水平对比来计算平均每年增长(或下降)速度。在一般正常情况下，两种方法计算的平均每年增长速度比较接近；但在经济发展不平衡、出现大起大落时，两种方法计算的结果差别较大。

国民经济行业分类 自2012年定期报表开始使用新的《国民经济行业分类》(GB/T4754-2011)。该分类是由国家统计局组织修订，国家质量监督检验检疫总局和中国国家标准化管理委员会于2011年4月29日发布。这次修订是在2002年分类标准的基础上，参照联合国《全部经济活动的国际标准产业分类》(ISIC/Rev.4)进行的。修订后的《国民经济行业分类》(GB/T4754-2012) 共有门类20个，大类96个，中类432个，小类1094个

企业(单位)登记注册类型 是以在工商行政管理机关登记注册的各类企业为划分对象，以工商行政管理部门对企业登记注册的类型为依据，将企业登记注册类型分为内资企业、港澳台商投资企业和外商投资企业三大类。内资企业包括国有企业、集体企业、股份合作企业、联营企业、有限责任公司、股份有限公司、私营公司和其他企业；港澳台商投资企业和外商投资企业分别包括合资经营企业、合作经营企业、独资经营企业和股份有限公司。对不在工商行政管理部门进行登记注册的行政机关、事业单位和社会团体，主要按其经费来源和管理方式进行划分。

国有企业 指企业全部资产归国家所有，并按《中华人民共和国企业法人登记管理条例》规定登记注册的非公司制的经济组织。不包括有限责任公司中的国有独资公司。

集体企业 指企业资产归集体所有，并按《中华人民共和国企业法人登记管理条例》规定登记注册的经济组织。

股份合作企业 指以合作制为基础，由企业职工共同出资入股，吸收一定比例的社会资产投资组建，实行自主经营，自负盈亏，共同劳动，民主管理，按劳分配与按股分红相结合的一种集体经济组织。

联营企业 指两个及两个以上相同或不同所有制性质的企业法人或事业单位法人，按自愿、平等、互利的原则，共同投资组成的经济组织。联营企业包括国有联营企业、集体联营企业、国有与集体联营企业和其他联营企业。

有限责任公司 指根据《中华人民共和国公司登记管理条例》规定登记注册，由两个以上、五十个以下的股东共同出资，每个股东以其所认缴的出资额对公司承担有限责任，公司以其全部资产对其债务承担责任的经济组织。有限责任公司包括国有独资公司以及其他有限责任公司。

股份有限公司 指根据《中华人民共和国公司登记管理条例》规定登记注册，其全部注册资本由等额股份构成并通过发行股票筹集资本，股东以其认购的股份对公司承担有限责任，公司以其全部资产对其债务承担责任的经济组织。

私营企业 指由自然人投资设立或由自然人控股，以雇佣劳动为基础的营利性经济组织。包括按照《公司法》、《合伙企业法》、《私营企业暂行条例》规定登记注册的私营有限责任公司、私营股份有限公司、私营合伙企业和私营独资企业。

其他企业 指上述企业之外的其他内资经济组织。

与港澳台商合资经营企业 指港澳台地区投资者与内地企业依照《中华人民共和国中外合资经营企业法》及有关法律的规定，按合同规定的比例投资设立、分享利润和分担风险的企业。

与港澳台商合作经营企业 指港澳台地区投资者与内地企业依照《中华人民共和国中外合作经营企业法》及有关法律的规定，依照合作合同的约定进行投资或提供条件设立、分配利润和分担风险的企业。

港澳台商独资经营企业 指依照《中华人民共和国外资企业法》及有关法律的规定，在内地由港澳台地区投资者全额投资设立的企业。

港澳台商投资股份有限公司 指根据国家有关规定，经原外经贸部依法批准设立，其中港、澳、台商的股本占公司注册资本的比例达25%以上的股份有限公司。凡其中港、澳、台商的股本占公司注册资本的比例小于25%的，属于内资企业中的股份有限公司。

中外合资经营企业 指外国企业或外国人与中国内地企业依照《中华人民共和国中外合资经营企业法》及有关法律的规定，按合同规定的比例投资设立、分享利润和分担风险的企业。

中外合作经营企业 指外国企业或外国人与中国内地

企业依照《中华人民共和国中外合作经营企业法》及有关法律的规定,依照合作合同的约定进行投资或提供条件设立、分配利润和分担风险的企业。

外资企业 指依照《中华人民共和国外资企业法》及有关法律的规定，在中国内地由外国投资者全额投资设立的企业。

外商投资股份有限公司 指根据国家有关规定，经原外经贸部依法批准设立，其中外资的股本占公司注册资本的比例达25%以上的股份有限公司。凡其中外资股本占公司注册资本的比例小于25%的，属于内资企业中的股份有限公司。

行政机关、事业单位和社会团体 参照企业登记注册类型,主要按其经费来源和管理方式划分。具体规定如下：

(1)行政机关:包括国家机关和政党机关,原则上均列为"国有"。但有特殊规定的,如供销社等,则列为"集体"。

(2)事业单位:包括经国家机构编制部门和有关业务主管部门批准成立的各类事业单位，不包括实行企业化管理的事业单位。事业单位的划分办法如下：

①由国家财政预算拨款或列入财政预算外资金管理以及经费主要来源于国有主管部门或国有上级单位的事业单位,列为"国有"。

②经费主要来源于集体单位的事业单位,列为"集体"。

③公民个人(或个人合伙)开办的事业单位,列为"私营"。

④上述以外的其他事业单位,如果其经费来源不明确,按管理方式进行归类。

(3)社会团体:包括经民政部门批准成立以及未纳入社会团体管理条例范围的工会、妇联等各类社会团体。社会团体的划分办法如下：

①未纳入民政部社会团体管理条例范围的工会、妇联、共青团、青联、工商联、科协、侨联等社会团体,国家拨款设立的基金会或基金管理组织以及经费主要来源于国有业务主管部门或国有上级单位的社会团体,列为"国有"。

②经费主要来源于集体单位的社会团体,列为"集体"。

③公民个人(或个人合伙)开办的社会团体,划为"私营"。

④上述以外的其他社会团体,如果其经费来源不明确,改按管理方式进行归类。

地区生产总值(GDP) 指按市场价格计算的一个地区所有常住单位在一定时期内生产活动的最终成果。地区生产总值有三种表现形态，即价值形态、收入形态和产品形态。从价值形态看,它是所有常住单位在一定时期内生产的全部货物和服务价值超过同期投入的全部非固定资产货物和服务价值的差额,即所有常住单位的增加值之和;从收入形态看，它是所有常住单位在一定时期内创造并分配给常住单位和非常住单位的初次收入之和;从产品形态看,它是所有常住单位在一定时期内最终使用的货物和服务价值减去货物和服务流进价值。在实际核算中,地区生产总值有三种计算方法,即生产法、收入法和支出法。三种方法分别从不同的方面反映地区生产总值及其构成。

国民总收入(GNI) 即国民生产总值,指一个国家(或地区）所有常住单位在一定时期内收入初次分配的最终结果。一国常住单位从事生产活动所创造的增加值在初次分配中主要分配给该国的常住单位，但也有一部分以生产税及进口税(扣除生产和进口补贴)、劳动者报酬和财产收入等形式分配给非常住单位;同时,国外生产所创造的增加值也有一部分以生产税及进口税（扣除生产和进口补贴)、劳动者报酬和财产收入等形式分配给该国的常住单位，从而产生了国民总收入的概念。它等于国内生产总值加上来自国外的净要素收入。与国内生产总值不同,国民总收入是个收入概念,而国内生产总值是个生产概念。

三次产业 三产业的划分是世界上较为常用的产业结构分类,但各国的划分不尽一致。我国的三次产业划分是：

第一产业是指农、林、牧、渔业。

第二产业是指采矿业,制造业,电力、煤气及水的生产和供应业,建筑业。

第三产业是指除第一、二产业以外的其他行业。

劳动者报酬 指劳动者因从事生产活动所获得的全部报酬。包括劳动者获得的各种形式的工资、奖金和津贴,既包括货币形式的,也包括实物形式的,还包括劳动者所享受的公费医疗和医药卫生费、上下班交通补贴、单位支付的社会保险费、住房公积金等。对于个体经济来说,其所有者所获得的劳动报酬和经营利润不易区分，这两部分统一作为劳动者报酬处理。

生产税净额 指生产税减生产补贴后的余额。生产税指政府对生产单位从事生产、销售和经营活动以及因从事生产活动使用某些生产要素(如固定资产、土地、劳动力)所征收的各种税、附加费和规费。生产补贴与生产税相反,指政府对生产单位的单方面转移支出,因此视为负生产税,包括政策亏损补贴、价格补贴等。

固定资产折旧 指一定时期内为弥补固定资产损耗按照规定的固定资产折旧率提取的固定资产折旧，或按国民经济核算统一规定的折旧率虚拟计算的固定资产折旧。它反映了固定资产在当期生产中的转移价值。各类企业和企业化管理的事业单位的固定资产折旧是指实际计提的折旧费;不计提折旧的政府机关、非企业化管理的事业单位和居民住房的固定资产折旧是按照统一规定的折旧率和固定资产原值计算的虚拟折旧。原则上,固定资产折旧应按固定资产当期的重置价值计算，但是目前我国尚不具备对全社会固定资产进行重估价的基础，所以暂时只能采用上述办法。

营业盈余 指常住单位创造的增加值扣除劳动者报酬、生产税净额和固定资产折旧后的余额。它相当于企业的营业利润加上生产补贴，但要扣除从利润中开支的工资和福利等。

支出法地区生产总值 是从最终使用的角度反映一个地区一定时期内生产活动最终成果的一种方法，包括最终消费支出、资本形成总额及货物和服务净流出三部分。计算公式为：

支出法国内生产总值=
最终消费支出+资本形成总额+货物和服务净流出

最终消费支出 指常住单位为满足物质、文化和精神生活的需要，从本国经济领土和国外购买的货物和服务的支出。它不包括非常住单位在本国经济领土内的消费支出。最终消费支出分为居民消费支出和政府消费支出。

居民消费支出 指常住住户在一定时期内对于货物和服务的全部最终消费支出。居民消费支出除了直接以货币形式购买的货物和服务的消费支出外，还包括以其他方式获得的货物和服务的消费支出，即所谓的虚拟消费支出。居民虚拟消费支出包括如下几种类型：单位以实物报酬及实物转移的形式提供给劳动者的货物和服务；住户生产并由本住户消费了的货物和服务，其中的服务仅指住户的自有住房服务和付酬的家庭雇员提供的家庭和个人服务；金融机构提供的金融媒介服务；保险公司提供的保险服务。

政府消费支出 指政府部门为全社会提供的公共服务的消费支出和免费或以较低的价格向居民住户提供的货物和服务的净支出，前者等于政府服务的产出价值减去政府单位所获得的经营收入的价值，后者等于政府部门免费或以较低价格向居民住户提供的货物和服务的市场价值减去向住户收取的价值。

资本形成总额 指常住单位在一定时期内获得减去处置的固定资产和存货的净额，包括固定资本形成总额和存货增加两部分。

固定资本形成总额 指生产者在一定时期内获得的固定资产减处置的固定资产的价值总额。固定资产是通过生产活动生产出来的，且其使用年限在一年以上、单位价值在规定标准以上的资产，不包括自然资产。可分为有形固定资本形成总额和无形固定资本形成总额。有形固定资本形成总额包括一定时期内完成的建筑工程、安装工程和设备工器具购置(减处置)价值，以及土地改良、新增役、种、奶、毛、娱乐用牲畜和新增经济林木价值。无形固定资本形成总额包括矿藏的勘探、计算机软件等获得减处置。

存货增加 指常住单位在一定时期内存货实物量变动的市场价值，即期末价值减期初价值的差额，再扣除当期由于价格变动而产生的持有收益。存货增加可以是正值，也可以是负值，正值表示存货上升，负值表示存货下降。存货包括生产单位购进的原材料、燃料和储备物资等存货，以及生产单位生产的产成品、在制品和半成品等存货。

货物和服务净流出 指货物和服务流出减货物和服务流进的差额。流出包括常住单位向非常住单位出售或无偿转让的各种货物和服务的价值；流进包括常住单位从非常住单位购买或无偿得到的各种货物和服务的价值。由于服务活动的提供与使用同时发生，一般把常住单位从非常住单位得到的服务作为流进，非常住单位从常住单位得到的服务作为流出。

Explanatory Notes on Main Statistical Indicators

Average Annual Growth Rate Two methods for calculating average annual growth rate are applied, one is often called level approach, or the method of calculating geometric average, which is derived by comparing the level of the last year of the interval with that of the beginning year; the other is called accumulative approach or algebraic average or equation method, which is derived by the summation of the actual figure of each year in the interval divided by the figure in the base year. Usually the results calculated by the two methods are fairly close, but they differed sharply when uneven economic development occurred with striking fluctuations in growth.

Industrial Classification of the National Economy The new Industrial Classification of the National Economy (GB/T 4754–2011) is introduced starting from the compilation of 2012 annual statistics. The revision, based on the 2002 classification, was organized by the National Bureau of Statistics taking into consideration of the International Standards of the Industrial Classification of All Economic Activities (ISIC/Rev.4) of the United Nations. The new Classification was promulgated by the National Administration of Quality Supervision, Inspection and Quarantine and the Standardization Administration of the People´s Republic of China on April 29, 2011. The revised version of the Industrial Classification of the National Economy (GB/T 4754–2012) is composed of 20 sections, 96 divisions, 432 groups and 1094 classes.

Registration Status of Enterprises Enterprises are classified into 3 categories, namely domestic–funded enterprises, enterprises with investment from Hong Kong, Macau and Taiwan, and enterprises with foreign investment, in the light of the registration status of an enterprise in industrial and commercial administration agencies. Domestic–funded enterprises include state–owned enterprises, collective–owned enterprises, cooperative enterprises, joint ownership enterprises, limited liability corporations, share–holding corporations Ltd., private enterprises and other enterprises. Included in the enterprises with investment from Hong Kong, Macau and Taiwan and enterprises with foreign investment are joint–venture enterprises, cooperative enterprises, sole investment enterprises and share–holding corporations Ltd. For government agencies, institutions and social organizations which are not requested to be registered in industrial and commercial administration agencies, they are classified mainly by their sources of funds and way of management.

State–owned Enterprises refer to non–corporation economic units where the entire assets are owned by the state and which have registered in accordance with the Regulation of the People's Republic of China on the Management of Registration of Corporate Enterprises. Excluded from this category are sole state–funded corporations in the limited liability corporations.

Collective–owned Enterprises refer to economic units where the assets are owned collectively and which have registered in accordance with the Regulation of the People's Republic of China on the Management of Registration of Corporate Enterprises.

Cooperative Enterprises refer to a form of collective economic units (enterprises) where capitals come mainly from employees as their shares, with certain proportion of capital from the outside, where production is organized on the basis of independent operation, independent accounting for profits and losses, joint work, democratic management, and a distribution system that integrates remuneration according to work with dividend according to capital share.

Joint Ownership Enterprises refer to economic units established by two or more corporate enterprises or corporate institutions of the same or different ownership, through joint investment on the basis of equality, voluntary participation and mutual benefits. They include state joint ownership enterprises, collective joint ownership enterprises, joint state–collective enterprises, other joint ownership enterprises.

Limited Liability Corporations refer to economic units established with investment from 2–50 investors and registered in accordance with the Regulation of the People's Republic of China on the Management of Registration of Corporations, each investor bearing limited liability to the corporation depending on its share of investment, and the corporation bearing liability to its debt to the maximum of its total assets. Limited liability corporations include exclusive state–funded limited liability corporations and other limited liability corporations.

Share-holding Corporations Ltd. refer to economic units registered in accordance with the Regulation of the People's Republic of China on the Management of Registration of Corporations, with total registered capitals divided into equal shares and raised through issuing stocks. Each investor bears limited liability to the corporation depending on the holding of shares, and the corporation bears liability to its debt to the maximum of its total assets.

Private Enterprises refer to profit-making economic units invested and established by natural persons, or controlled by natural persons using employed labour. Included in this category are private limited liability corporations, private share-holding corporations Ltd., private partnership enterprises and private-funded enterprises registered in accordance with the Corporation Law, Partnership Enterprises Law and Interim Regulations on Private Enterprises .

Other Domestic-funded Enterprises refer to domestic-funded economic units other than those mentioned above.

Cooperative Enterprises with Funds from Hong Kong Macau and Taiwan established by investors from Hong Kong, Macau and Taiwan with enterprises in the mainland of China in accordance with the Law of the People's Republic of China on Sino-foreign Cooperative Enterprises and other relevant laws, where the investment or provision of facilities, and the share of profits and risks is stipulated in the cooperative contract.

Enterprises with Sole (exclusive) Investment from Hong Kong, Macau and Taiwan refer to enterprises established in the mainland of China with exclusive investment from investors from Hong Kong, Macau and Taiwan in accordance with the Law of the People's Republic of China on Foreign-Funded Enterprises and other relevant laws.

Share-holding Corporations Ltd. with Investment from Hong Kong, Macau and Taiwan refer to share-holding corporations Ltd. established with the approval from the former Ministry of Foreign Trade and Economic Relations in line with relevant state regulations, where the share of investment from Hong Kong, Macau or Taiwan businessmen exceeds 25% of the total registered capital of the corporation. In case the share of investment from Hong Kong, Macau or Taiwan is less than 25% of the total registered capital, the enterprise is to be classified as domestic-funded share-holding corporation Ltd.

Joint-venture Enterprises with Foreign Investment refer to enterprises jointly established by foreign enterprises or foreigners with enterprises in the mainland of China in accordance with the Law of the People's Republic of China on Sino-foreign Joint Venture Enterprises and other relevant laws, where the share of investment, profits and risks is stipulated in the contract.

Cooperation Enterprises with Foreign Investment refer to enterprises jointly established by foreign enterprises or foreigners with enterprises in the mainland of China in accordance with the Law of the People's Republic of China on Sino-foreign Cooperative Enterprises and other relevant laws, where the investment or provision of facilities, and the share of profits and risks is stipulated in the cooperative contract.

Enterprises with Sole (exclusive) Foreign Investment refer to enterprises established in the mainland of China with exclusive investment from foreign investors in accordance with the Law of the People's Republic of China on Foreign-Funded Enterprises and other relevant laws.

Share-holding Corporations Ltd. with Foreign Investment refer to share-holding corporations Ltd. established with the approval from the Ministry of Foreign Trade and Economic Relations in line with relevant state regulations, where the share of investment from foreign investors exceeds 25% of the total registered capital of the corporation. In case the share of foreign investment is less than 25% of the total registered capital, the enterprise is to be classified as domestic-funded share-holding corporation Ltd.

Government Agencies, Institutions and Social Organizations are classified into following categories by source of funds and way of management taking reference of the registration status of enterprises:

(1) Government agencies: include state and party agencies, classified in principle as state-owned. There are exceptions, such as supply and marketing cooperatives which are classified as collective-owned.

(2) Institutions: include institutions of various types established with the approval by organization and staffing departments of the government, but exclude institutions where enterprise management system is introduced. Institutions are further classified as follows:

(a) Institutions whose main budget is listed in the government budget appropriations or extra-budget funds, or allocated from the budget of their competent government agencies. Such institutions are classified as state-owned.

(b) Institutions whose budget mainly comes from collective units. Such institutions are classified as collective-owned.

(c) Institutions other than those mentioned above whose source of budget is not clear. Such institutions are classified by way of management.

(3) Social organizations: include social organizations established with the approval from the Ministry of Civil Affairs, and organizations that are not covered by social organization management regulations such as trade unions, women's federations etc.. Social organizations are further classified as follows:

(a) Social organizations that are not covered by social organization management regulations of the Ministry of Civil Affairs such as trade unions, women's federations, communist youth leagues, youth associations, industrial and commerce associations, scientists associations, overseas Chinese associations, etc., foundations and fund management organizations established with funds from the state, and social organizations whose funds mainly come from the budget of their competent government agencies. Such institutions are classified as state-owned.

(b) Social organizations whose budget mainly comes from collective units. Such institutions are classified as collective-owned.

(c) Social organizations established by individual or a group of citizens, which are classified as private.

(d) Social organizations other than those mentioned above whose source of budget is not clear. Such organizations are classified by way of management.

Gross Domestic Product (GDP) refers to the final products at market prices produced by all resident units in a country (or a region) during a certain period of time. Gross domestic product is expressed in three different forms, i.e. value, income, and products respectively. GDP in its value form refers to the total value of all goods and services produced by all resident units during a certain period of time, minus the total value of input of goods and services of the nature of non-fixed assets; in other term, it is the sum of the value-added of all resident units. GDP in the form of income includes the income created by all resident units and distributed to resident and non-resident units. GDP in the form of products refers to the value of all goods and services for final consumption by all resident units minus the net exports of goods and services during a given period of time. In the practice of national accounting, gross domestic product is calculated with three approaches, i.e. production approach, income approach and expenditure approach, which reflect gross domestic product and its composition from different aspects.

Gross National Income (GNI) also known as gross national product, refers to the final result of the primary distribution of the income created by all the resident units of a country (or a region) during a certain period of time. The value-added created by the resident units of a country engaged in production activities is distributed, during the primary distribution, mainly to the resident units of that country, while part of it is distributed to the non-resident units in the form of production tax and import duties (minus subsidies to production and import), remuneration for the labourers and property income. At the meantime, a part of the value-added created abroad is distributed to the resident units of the country in the form of production tax and import duties (minus subsidies to production and import), remuneration for the labourers and property income. The concept of gross national income is thus developed, which equals to the gross domestic product plus the net factor income from abroad. Unlike the gross domestic product which is a concept of production, the gross national income is a concept of income.

Three Industries Classification of economic activities into three branches of industries is a common practice in the world, although the grouping varies to some extent form country to country. In China economic activities are categorized into following industries:

Primary industry: refers to agriculture, forestry, animal husbandry and fishery.

Secondary industry: refers to mining and quarrying, manufacturing, production and supply of electricity, water and gas, and construction.

Tertiary industry: refers to all other economic activities not included in primary or secondary industry.

Labourers Remuneration refers to the whole payment of various forms earned by the labourers from the productive activities they are engaged in. It includes wages, bonuses and allowances the labourers earned in monetary form and in kind. It also includes the free medical services provided to the labourers and the medicine expenses, traffic subsidies and social insurance, housing fund paid by the employers. As the individual economy is concerned, since the labourers remuneration is not easily distinguished from the operating profit, both are treated as labourers remuneration.

Net Taxes on Production refers to the difference of the taxes on production minus the subsidies on production. The taxes on production refers to the various taxes, extra charges and fees levied on the production units on their production, sale and business activities as well as on the use of some factors of production, such as fixed assets, land and labour force in the production activities they are engaged in. In contrast to the taxes on production, the subsidies on production refer to the unilateral government transfer to the production units and are therefore regarded as negative taxes on production. They include subsidies on the loss due to implementation of government policies, price subsidies, etc.

Depreciation of Fixed Assets refers to the depreciation of fixed assets of a given period, drawn in accordance with the stipulated depreciation rate for the purpose of compensating the wear loss of the fixed assets or the depreciation of fixed assets calculated in a fictitious way in accordance with the stipulated unified depreciation rate in the national economic accounting system. It reflects the value of transfer of the fixed assets in the production of the current period. The depreciation of fixed assets in various enterprises and institutions managed as enterprises refers to the depreciation expenses actually drawn. In government agencies and institutions not managed as enterprises which do not draw the depreciation expenses, as well as for the houses of residents, the depreciation of fixed assets is the imputed depreciation, which is calculated in accordance with the stipulated unified depreciation rate. In principle, the depreciation of fixed assets should be calculated on the basis of the re-purchased value of the fixed assets. However, there is no actual condition to re-evaluate all the fixed assets in China. Therefore, the above-mentioned methods are temporarily adopted at present.

Operating Surplus refers to the balance of the value added created by the resident units deducting the labourers remuneration, net taxes on production and the depreciation of fixed assets. It is equivalent to the business profit of the enterprises plus subsidies on production, but the wages and welfare expenses paid from the profits should be deducted.

GDP by Expenditure Approach refers to the method of measuring the final results of production activities of a country (region) during a given period from the perspective of final use. It includes final consumption expenditure, total capital formation and net export of goods and services, i.e.:

GDP by expenditure approach = final consumption expenditure + total capital formation + net export of goods and services

Final Consumption Expenditure refers to the total expenditure of resident units for purchases of goods and services from domestic economic territory and abroad to meet the requirements of material, cultural and spiritual life. It excludes the expenditure of non-resident units on consumption in the economic territory of the country. The final consumption expenditure is broken down into household consumption expenditure and government consumption expenditure.

Households Consumption Expenditure refers to the total expenditure of resident households on the final consumption of goods and services. In addition to the consumption of goods and services bought by the households directly with money, the households consumption expenditure also includes expenditure on goods and services obtained by the households in other ways, i.e. the so-called imputed consumption expenditure, which includes the following: (a) the goods and services provided to the households by the employer in the form of payment in kind and transfer in kind; (b) goods and services produced and consumed by the households themselves, in which the services refer only to the owner-occupied housing and domestic and individual services provided by the paid household workers; (c) financial intermediate services provided by financial institutions; (d) insurance services provided by insurance companies.

Government Consumption Expenditure refers to the expenditure on the consumption of the public services provided by the government to the whole society and the net expenditure on the goods and services provided by the government to the households free of charge or at low prices. The former equals to the output value of the government services minus the value of operating income obtained by the government departments. The latter equals to the market value of the goods and services provided by the government free of charge or at low prices to the households minus the value received by the government from the households.

Total Capital Formation refers to the fixed assets acquired minus those disposed of and the net value of inventory, including the total fixed capital formation and the increase in inventory.

Total Fixed Capital Formation refers to the value of fixed assets acquired minus those disposed of during a given period. Fixed assets are the assets produced through production activities with specified unit value which could be used for over one year, excluding natural assets. Total fixed capital formation can be categorized into total tangible capital formation and total intangible capital formation. The total tangible capital formation include the value of the construction projects, installation projects completed and the equipment, apparatus and instruments purchased as well as the value of land improved, the value of draught animals, breeding stock, animals for milk, wool and for recreational purpose, and the newly increased forest with economic value during a given period. The total intangible capital formation includes the prospecting of minerals, the acquisition of computer software minus the disposal of them.

Increase in Inventory refers to the market value of the change in inventory of resident units during a given period, i.e. the difference of value between the beginning and the end of the period minus the current gains due to the change in prices. The increase in inventory can be positive or negative. A positive value indicates the increase in inventory while a negative value indicates the decrease in stock. The inventory includes the raw materials, fuels and reserve materials purchased by the production units as well as the inventory of finished products, semi-finished products, work-in-progress, etc.

Outflow of Goods and Services refers to the difference of the exports of goods and services minus the imports of goods and services. The imports include the value of various goods and services sold or gratuitously transferred by the resident units to the non-resident units. The imports include the value of various goods and services purchased or gratuitously acquired by the resident units from the non-resident units. Because the provision of services and the use of them happen simultaneously, the acquisition of services by the resident units from abroad is usually treated as import while the acquisition of services by non-resident units in this country is usually treated as export. The export and import of goods are calculated at FOB.

2 人 口 Population

资料整理人员:刘　通　　邓丽嫚

2-1 人口数
Population

单位:万人 (年底数)(number at year-end) (10 000 persons)

年份 Year	户籍人口 Total Population	男 Male	女 Female	常住人口 Population of Permnant Residents	男 Male	女 Female
1952	2745.0	1414.6	1330.4			
1957	3062.4	1579.7	1482.7			
1965	3504.5	1793.3	1711.2			
1975	4408.2	2261.7	2146.5			
1980	4684.5	2401.8	2282.7			
1985	4931.0	2540.0	2391.0	4980.8	2566.3	2414.5
1986	4989.0	2573.4	2415.6	5047.8	2603.3	2444.5
1987	5058.1	2608.7	2449.4	5120.3	2640.3	2480.0
1988	5144.2	2652.1	2492.1	5184.9	2673.1	2511.8
1989	5223.9	2694.6	2529.3	5258.8	2712.5	2546.3
1990	5373.5	2771.5	2602.0	5439.3	2805.5	2633.8
1991	5446.8	2805.4	2641.4	5512.3	2839.1	2673.2
1992	5513.6	2841.2	2672.4	5579.9	2862.3	2717.6
1993	5590.5	2880.9	2709.6	5653.5	2913.3	2740.2
1994	5656.8	2915.6	2741.2	5718.8	2947.5	2771.3
1995	5727.1	2952.1	2775.0	5772.1	2959.6	2812.5
1996	5776.3	2979.5	2796.8	5825.1	3004.8	2820.3
1997	5838.8	3014.0	2824.8	5872.6	3016.6	2856.0
1998	5890.6	3039.9	2850.7	5907.2	3032.6	2874.6
1999	5942.5	3061.8	2880.7	5938.0	3031.9	2906.1
2000	5936.0	3066.1	2869.9	5646.0	2939.3	2706.7
2001	5956.6	3073.2	2883.4	5658.0	2919.1	2738.9
2002	5978.2	3086.2	2892.0	5672.0	2928.1	2743.9
2003	6000.5	3109.9	2890.6	5685.0	2946.3	2738.7
2004	6001.3	3107.8	2893.5	5698.0	2950.7	2747.3
2005	5984.1	3102.4	2881.7	5710.0	2960.2	2749.8
2006	6038.3	3129.6	2908.7	5693.0	2950.6	2742.4
2007	6084.9	3154.0	2930.9	5699.0	2953.9	2745.1
2008	6110.8	3167.5	2943.3	5711.0	2960.2	2750.8
2009	6141.9	3185.5	2956.4	5720.0	2966.6	2753.4
2010	6176.0	3202.0	2974.0	5723.8	2939.3	2784.5
2011	6164.1	3194.0	2970.1	5760.0	2957.0	2803.0
2012	6165.4	3194.0	2971.4	5781.0	2964.9	2816.1
2013	6170.6	3199.5	2971.1	5798.0	2971.5	2826.5
2014	6162.3	3198.1	2964.2	5816.0	2980.3	2835.7
2015	6138.9	3190.1	2948.8	5850.0	2983.7	2866.3
2016	6156.8	3200.4	2956.3	5885.0	2997.2	2887.8
2017	6141.8	3191.1	2950.7	5904.0	2997.8	2906.2
2018	6172.9	3206.5	2966.4	5917.0	3004.4	2912.6
2019	6177.8	3208.7	2969.1	5927.0	3009.5	2917.5
2020	6160.1	3199.2	2960.9	5775.3	2969.5	2805.8

注:1982、1990、2000、2010、2020年数据为当年人口普查时点数据,其余年份数据为年度人口抽样调查推算数据(下相关表同)。因2020年开展第七次全国人口普查,根据普查结果对2010-2019年数据进行修正。

Note: The date of 1982, 1990, 2000, 2010 and 2020 are the population census time point date of that year, the date of other years are the estimated date of annual population sampling survey (the same as the relevant table below). The 2010-2019 date was revised based on the results of the seventh national population census in 2020.

2-2 人口城乡构成
Composition of Urban and Rural Population

单位:万人 (年底数)(number at year-end) (10 000 persons)

年份 Year	总人口 Total Population	城镇人口 Urban Population	乡村人口 Rural Population
1952	2745.00	271.41	2416.17
1957	3062.41	411.69	2650.72
1965	3504.54	485.06	3019.48
1975	4408.15	626.22	3781.93
1980	4684.45	786.49	3897.96
1985	4980.81	1464.65	3516.16
1986	5047.83	1187.23	3860.60
1987	5120.27	1288.61	3831.66
1988	5184.94	1389.99	3794.95
1989	5258.83	1491.37	3767.46
1990	5439.29	1551.51	3887.78
1991	5512.33	1433.06	4079.27
1992	5579.85	1637.68	3942.17
1993	5653.48	1731.66	3921.82
1994	5718.81	1604.13	4114.68
1995	5772.07	1800.89	3971.18
1996	5825.13	1965.40	3859.73
1997	5872.60	1834.60	4038.00
1998	5907.23	1884.41	4022.82
1999	5938.03	1990.17	3947.86
2000	5646.00	2285.11	3360.89
2001	5658.00	2308.50	3349.50
2002	5672.00	2348.20	3323.80
2003	5685.00	2387.70	3297.30
2004	5698.00	2427.30	3270.70
2005	5710.00	2466.70	3243.30
2006	5693.00	2493.50	3199.50
2007	5699.00	2524.70	3174.30
2008	5711.00	2581.40	3129.60
2009	5720.00	2631.20	3088.80
2010	5723.77	2844.51	2879.26
2011	5760.00	2982.53	2777.47
2012	5781.00	3077.23	2703.77
2013	5798.00	3160.49	2637.51
2014	5816.00	3241.26	2574.74
2015	5850.00	3345.03	2504.97
2016	5885.00	3446.84	2438.16
2017	5904.00	3535.32	2368.68
2018	5917.00	3609.37	2307.63
2019	5927.00	3664.66	2262.34
2020	5775.26	3632.04	2143.22

注:1981年及以前数据为户籍统计数;1982、1990、2000、2010、2020年数据为当年人口普查时点数据;其余年份数据为年度人口抽样调查推算数据(下相关表同)。因2020年开展第七次全国人口普查,根据普查结果对2010-2019年数据进行修正。

Note: The data of 1981 and before are the household registration statistics; the data of 1982, 1990, 2000, 2010 and 2020 are the population census time point data of that year; the data of other years are the estimated data of annual population sampling survey (the same as the relevant table below). The 2010-2019 data was revised based on the results of the seventh national population census in 2020.

2-3 全省人口自然变动
Natural Change of Population

年 份 Year	人口变动数(万人) Number of Population Changed (10 000 persons)			变动系数(‰) Growth Rates		
	出生数 Number of Birth	死亡数 Number of Death	自然增长数 Number of Nature Growth	出生率 Birth Rate	死亡率 Death Rate	自然增长率 Natural Growth Rate
1965	121.48	34.75	86.73	35.10	10.04	25.06
1975	90.80	34.52	56.28	20.74	7.88	12.86
1980	94.84	32.59	62.25	20.36	7.00	13.36
1985	97.83	37.37	60.46	19.95	7.62	12.33
1986	107.09	39.45	67.64	21.01	7.74	13.27
1987	108.56	36.12	72.44	21.43	7.13	14.30
1988	97.62	32.95	64.67	19.08	6.44	12.64
1989	110.13	36.24	73.89	21.09	6.94	14.15
1990	114.40	38.66	75.74	21.60	7.30	14.30
1991	113.34	40.30	73.04	20.70	7.36	13.34
1992	105.60	38.08	67.52	19.05	6.87	12.18
1993	112.55	38.92	73.63	20.04	6.93	13.11
1994	103.31	37.98	65.33	18.17	6.68	11.49
1995	92.96	39.70	53.26	16.18	6.91	9.27
1996	93.24	40.18	53.06	16.08	6.93	9.15
1997	86.62	39.13	47.49	14.81	6.69	8.12
1998	74.09	39.46	34.63	12.58	6.70	5.88
1999	68.52	37.73	30.79	11.57	6.37	5.20
2000	57.76	35.75	22.01	9.71	6.01	3.70
2001	50.84	36.27	14.57	8.51	6.07	2.44
2002	50.10	36.90	13.20	8.38	6.17	2.21
2003	49.50	35.60	13.90	8.26	5.94	2.32
2004	50.66	36.23	14.43	8.43	6.03	2.40
2005	52.60	34.30	18.30	8.74	5.69	3.05
2006	54.80	35.90	18.90	9.08	5.95	3.13
2007	55.69	36.12	19.57	9.19	5.96	3.23
2008	55.98	39.51	16.47	9.21	6.50	2.71
2009	57.80	36.58	21.22	9.48	6.00	3.48
2010	59.30	34.46	24.84	10.36	6.02	4.34
2011	59.67	34.52	25.15	10.39	6.01	4.38
2012	63.45	35.30	28.15	11.00	6.12	4.88
2013	64.14	35.60	28.54	11.08	6.15	4.93
2014	68.88	40.42	28.46	11.86	6.96	4.90
2015	62.65	34.01	28.64	10.74	5.83	4.91
2016	70.65	40.90	29.75	12.04	6.97	5.07
2017	74.26	41.31	32.95	12.60	7.01	5.59
2018	68.28	41.42	26.86	11.54	7.00	4.54
2019	67.21	41.93	25.29	11.35	7.08	4.27
2020	48.32	44.76	3.56	8.28	7.67	0.61

2-4 全省市、州、县年底人口数(2020)

Population of Cities, Prefectures and Counties of Hubei at Year-end(2020)

单位:万人 (10 000 persons)

地 区	Region	户籍人口 Total Population	常住人口 Population of Permnant Residents	地 区	Region	户籍人口 Total Population	常住人口 Population of Permnant Residents
全省	**Province**	**6160.05**	**5775.26**	丹江口市	Danjiangkou	45.70	40.99
武汉市	**Wuhan**	**916.19**	**1244.77**	**宜昌市**	**Yichang**	**389.90**	**389.64**
江岸区	Jiang´an	79.72	96.53	西陵区	Xiling	39.76	53.03
江汉区	Jianghan	51.58	64.79	伍家岗区	Wujiagang	20.29	33.63
硚口区	Qiaokou	54.19	66.67	点军区	Dianjun	10.43	10.16
汉阳区	Hanyang	74.49	83.73	猇亭区	Xiaoting	5.04	6.87
武昌区	Wuchang	109.87	110.22	夷陵区	Yiling	52.62	55.03
青山区	Qingshan	45.72	43.18	远安县	Yuan´an	18.90	17.67
洪山区	Hongshan	127.69	255.44	兴山县	Xingshan	16.25	14.39
东西湖区	Dongxihu	36.81	84.58	秭归县	Zigui	36.68	30.96
汉南区	Hannan	11.66	14.51	长阳县	Changyang	38.36	31.57
蔡甸区	Caidian	47.09	93.08	五峰县	Wufeng	19.48	16.10
江夏区	Jiangxia	65.29	130.85	宜都市	Yidu	38.42	35.74
黄陂区	Huangpi	116.06	115.16	当阳市	Dangyang	46.33	41.75
新洲区	Xinzhou	96.00	86.04	枝江市	Zhijiang	47.36	42.74
黄石市	**Huangshi**	**273.49**	**246.91**	**襄阳市**	**Xiangyang**	**588.91**	**526.10**
黄石港区	Huangshigang	20.86	24.16	襄城区	Xiangcheng	46.54	47.56
西塞山区	Xisai mountainous	19.97	19.72	樊城区	Fancheng	81.50	92.08
下陆区	Xialu	16.21	21.52	襄州区	Xiangzhou	100.30	92.32
铁山区	Tieshan	4.66	4.19	南漳县	Nanzhang	56.72	45.57
大冶市	Daye	99.88	87.12	谷城县	Gucheng	59.31	48.33
阳新县	Yangxin	111.91	90.20	保康县	Baokang	26.48	22.36
十堰市	**Shiyan**	**341.48**	**320.90**	老河口市	Laohekou	50.85	42.05
茅箭区	Maojian	30.16	60.15	枣阳市	Zaoyang	111.59	88.88
张湾区	Zhangwan	25.67	43.19	宜城市	Yicheng	55.62	46.94
郧阳区	Yunyang	62.04	39.52	**鄂州市**	**Ezhou**	**111.74**	**107.94**
郧西县	Yunxi	51.04	37.10	梁子湖区	Liangzihu	19.20	12.68
竹山县	Zhushan	44.96	34.61	华容区	Huarong	26.96	25.68
竹溪县	Zhuxi	35.01	28.36	鄂城区	Ercheng	65.58	69.57
房县	Fang	46.89	36.98				

2-4 续表 Continued

单位:万人 (10 000 persons)

地 区	Region	户籍人口 Total Population	常住人口 Population of Permnant Residents	地 区	Region	户籍人口 Total Population	常住人口 Population of Permnant Residents
荆门市	**Jingmen**	**288.91**	**259.69**	蕲春县	Hanchun	100.41	79.21
东宝区	Dongbao	35.27	35.69	黄梅县	Huangmei	102.71	78.78
掇刀区	Zhuodao	29.54	43.05	麻城市	Macheng	114.94	89.37
京山市	Jingshan	62.05	54.48	武穴市	Wuxue	81.97	67.63
沙洋县	Shayang	58.68	39.57	**咸宁市**	**Xianning**	**305.26**	**265.83**
钟祥市	Zhongxiang	103.38	86.89	咸安区	Xian′an	63.11	65.76
孝感市	**Xiaogan**	**508.77**	**427.04**	嘉鱼县	Jiayu	36.40	28.56
孝南区	Xiaonan	94.99	98.85	通城县	Tongcheng	52.67	42.63
孝昌县	Xiaochang	66.05	48.34	崇阳县	Congyang	51.22	42.71
大悟县	Dawu	61.66	48.62	通山县	Tongshan	48.87	39.13
云梦县	Yunmeng	56.55	43.41	赤壁市	Chibi	52.99	47.04
应城市	Yingcheng	63.24	47.66	**随州市**	**Suizhou**	**247.04**	**204.79**
安陆市	Anlu	60.50	49.84	曾都区	Zengdu	66.10	69.95
汉川市	Hanchuan	105.78	90.33	随县	Sui	91.32	63.75
荆州市	**Jingzhou**	**632.63**	**523.12**	广水市	Guangshui	89.62	71.09
沙市区	Shashi	52.74	67.28	**恩施自治州**	**Enshi Prefecture**	**402.22**	**345.61**
荆州区	Jingzhou	54.57	56.34	恩施市	Enshi	81.68	83.68
公安县	Gong′an	97.54	74.71	利川市	Jianli	91.95	75.07
监利市	Jianli	155.59	112.08	建始县	Jianshi	50.79	41.16
江陵县	Jianglin	38.71	30.04	巴东县	Badong	48.44	39.54
石首市	Shishou	61.00	47.37	宣恩县	Xuan′en	35.71	28.50
洪湖市	Honghu	90.92	69.82	咸丰县	Xianfeng	38.52	31.88
松滋市	Songzi	81.57	65.48	来凤县	Laifeng	33.47	28.33
黄冈市	**Huanggang**	**734.46**	**588.27**	鹤峰县	Hefeng	21.67	17.47
黄州区	Huangzhou	35.50	45.69	**直管县级行政区**	**Jurisdictional**	**419.03**	**324.64**
团风县	Tuanfeng	36.32	26.62	仙桃市	Xiantao	152.70	113.47
红安县	Hong′an	64.26	51.02	潜江市	Qianjiang	99.59	88.65
罗田县	Luotian	58.97	47.32	天门市	Tianmen	158.89	115.86
英山县	Yingshan	39.51	31.02	神农架林区	Shennongjian	7.85	6.66
浠水县	Xishui	99.88	71.63				

主要统计指标解释

人口数 指一定时点、一定地区范围内有生命的个人总和。

年度统计的年末人口数指每年 12 月 31 日 24 时的人口数。

城镇人口和乡村人口 城镇人口是指居住在城镇范围内的全部常住人口；乡村人口是除上述人口以外的全部人口。

出生率(又称粗出生率) 指在一定时期内(通常为一年)一定地区的出生人数与同期内平均人数(或期中人数)之比,用千分率表示。本资料中的出生率指年出生率,其计算公式为：

$$出生率=\frac{年出生人数}{年平均人数}\times 1000‰$$

式中:出生人数指活产婴儿,即胎儿脱离母体时(不管怀孕月数),有过呼吸或其他生命现象。年平均人数指年初、年底人口数的平均数,也可用年中人口数代替。

死亡率(又称粗死亡率) 指在一定时期内(通常为一年)一定地区的死亡人数与同期内平均人数(或期中人数)之比,用千分率表示。本资料中的死亡率指年死亡率,其计算公式为：

$$死亡率=\frac{年死亡人数}{年平均人数}\times 1000‰$$

人口自然增长率 指在一定时期内(通常为一年)人口自然增加数（出生人数减死亡人数）与该时期内平均人数(或期中人数)之比,用千分率表示。计算公式为：

$$人口自然增长率=\frac{本年出生人数-本年死亡人数}{年平均人数}\times 1000‰$$

$$=人口出生率-人口死亡率$$

Explanatory Notes on Main Statistical Indicators

Total Population refers to the total number of people alive at a certain point of time within a given area.

The annual statistics on total population is taken at midnight, the 3lst of December.

Urban Population and Rural Population Urban population refer to all people residing in cities and towns, while rural population refer to population other than urban population.

Birth Rate (or Crude Birth Rate) refers to the ratio of the number of births to the average population (or mid-period population) during a certain period of time (usually a year), expressed in ‰. Birth rate in the chapter refers to annual birth rate. The following formula is used:

Birth Rate = (Number of Births/Average Number of Population)×1000‰

Number of births in the formula refers to live births, i.e. when a baby has breathed or showed any vital phenomena regardless of the length of pregnancy.

Annual average number of population is the average of the number of population at the beginning of the year and that at the end of the year. Sometimes it is substituted by the mid-year population.

Death Rate (or Crude Death Rate) refers to the ratio of the number of deaths to the average population (or mid-period population) during a certain period of time (usually a year), expressed in ‰. Death rate in the chapter refers to annual death rate. The following formula is used:

Death Rate= (Number of Deaths/Annual Average Number of Population)×1000‰

Natural Growth Rate of Population refers to the ratio of natural increase in population (number of births minus number of deaths) in a certain period of time (usually a year) to the average population (or mid-period population) of the same period, expressed in ‰. The following formula is applied:

Natural Growth Rate of Population = [(Number of Births-Number of Deaths)/Average Number of Population]×1000‰

Natural Growth Rate of Population = Birth Rate-Death Rate

3

就业和工资

Employment and Wages

资料整理人员：刘　通　　邓丽嫚

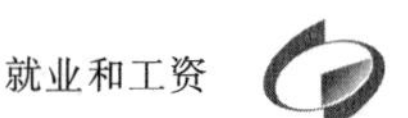

3-1 全社会从业人员
Total Employed Persons for the Whole Society

单位：万人 (10 000 persons)

年 份 Year	合 计 Total	按城乡分 Grouped by Areas		按产业分 Grouped by Industries		
		城 镇 Urban	乡 村 Rural	第一产业 Primary Industry	第二产业 Secondary Industry	第三产业 Tertiary Industry
1952	1020.30	141.60	878.70			
1965	1404.20	222.70	1181.60			
1970	1618.50	278.00	1340.80			
1975	1802.50	381.70	1420.80			
1978	1910.40	458.00	1452.30	1470.60	269.00	170.80
1980	1986.90	507.20	1479.70	1453.70	286.30	247.00
1985	2238.10	637.60	1600.50	1383.30	485.40	369.50
1990	3040.40	890.80	2149.60	1859.80	628.50	552.10
1991	3082.70	909.40	2173.30	1897.40	623.00	562.30
1992	3118.60	923.10	2195.50	1869.00	650.90	598.70
1993	3157.60	940.90	2216.70	1818.80	684.60	654.20
1994	3196.90	980.10	2216.80	1760.50	717.10	719.30
1995	3232.50	1015.00	2217.50	1697.00	743.50	792.00
1996	3275.50	1050.80	2224.70	1677.10	746.80	851.60
1997	3311.20	1070.50	2240.70	1663.20	752.00	896.00
1998	3328.20	1093.60	2234.60	1612.50	705.60	1010.10
1999	3358.10	1110.50	2247.60	1612.60	697.80	1047.70
2000	3384.90	1123.80	2261.10	1625.10	702.40	1057.40
2001	3414.50	1148.70	2265.80	1639.00	706.80	1068.70
2002	3443.00	1177.00	2266.00	1652.60	704.10	1086.30
2003	3476.00	1211.00	2265.00	1661.50	712.60	1101.90
2004	3507.00	1245.00	2262.00	1672.90	720.30	1113.80
2005	3537.00	1271.00	2266.00	1687.30	725.00	1124.70
2006	3564.00	1297.00	2267.00	1694.70	732.40	1136.90
2007	3584.00	1322.00	2262.00	1697.00	740.10	1146.90
2008	3607.00	1337.00	2270.00	1707.91	730.42	1168.67
2009	3622.00	1357.00	2265.00	1702.30	736.60	1183.10
2010	3375.00	1280.19	2094.81	1565.83	698.80	1110.37
2011	3387.00	1303.33	2083.67	1547.86	711.27	1127.87
2012	3398.00	1318.46	2079.54	1510.44	720.34	1167.23
2013	3404.00	1325.83	2078.17	1458.59	731.88	1213.53
2014	3408.00	1328.63	2079.37	1374.29	771.06	1262.65
2015	3398.00	1797.47	1600.53	1304.21	774.72	1319.07
2016	3385.00	1932.42	1452.58	1246.66	779.86	1358.47
2017	3379.00	1952.52	1426.48	1196.22	785.31	1397.46
2018	3377.00	1969.60	1407.40	1147.05	792.37	1437.58
2019	3375.00	1988.09	1386.91	1107.24	799.99	1467.76
2020	3261.00	1872.00	1389.00	897.00	857.00	1507.00

注：因 2020 年开展第七次全国人口普查，根据普查结果对 2010–2019 年数据进行修正。
Note: The 2010–2019 data was revised based on the results of the seventh national population census in 2020.

3-2 分行业城镇单位从业人员数(2020)
Number of Employed Persons in Urban Units by Sector(2020)

单位:人 (person)

行业	Sector	城镇全部单位 All the Units In Urban Area	国有经济单位 State Owned Units	城镇集体单位 Urban Collective Owned Units	其他经济单位 Other Units	城镇私营单位 Urban Private Units
总计	**Total**	**10667683**	**2276147**	**77539**	**3958023**	**4355974**
农、林、牧、渔业	Farming, Forest, Herd, Ishery	42990	15256	433	3573	23728
采矿业	Mining and Quarrying	44030	1064	654	25139	17173
制造业	Manufacturing	2592022	32042	3168	1264517	1292295
电力、燃气及水的生产和供应业	Power, Gas and Water Production and Supply	158782	86098	2312	56943	13429
建筑业	Construction	1952851	44823	17295	980546	910187
批发和零售业	Wholesale and Retail Sale	851355	25477	8122	280985	536771
交通运输、仓储和邮政业	Transportation, Storage and Post	419995	54755	4597	232354	128289
住宿和餐饮业	Hotel and Catering	206168	3644	1361	84751	116412
信息传输、软件和信息技术服务业	Information Transmission, Software and Computer Services	269778	10754	82	153168	105774
金融业	Banking	271492	10709		226960	33823
房地产业	Real Estate	436741	8392	1884	176952	249513
租赁和商务服务业	Leasing and Commerical Services	671757	43752	4641	147278	476086
科学研究、技术服务业	Scietific Research, Polytechnical	324079	64951	2099	104185	152844
水利、环境和公共设施管理业	Water Conservance, Environment and Public Facilities Management	111369	57986	2865	26514	24004
居民服务、修理和其他服务业	Resident Service and Others	101085	7215	957	12805	80108
教育	Education	857847	621412	16316	114800	105319
卫生和社会工作	Health, Social Security and	485947	393706	7799	40639	43803
文化、体育和娱乐业	Culture, Sports and Entertainment	107572	36601	917	23639	46415
公共管理、社会保障和社会组织	Public Management, Social Security and Social Organization	761819	757510	2036	2273	

注:城镇全部单位统计范围含城镇私营单位(后表未经特别注明均同此口径)。

Note: All Statistics of Units in Urban Areas of 2010 including all the private run unit. (The following tables if without specific notes are considered the same standard with this one.)

3-3 分行业在岗职工人数(2020)
Number of Staff and Workers by Sector(2020)

单位:人 (person)

行业	Sector	城镇全部单位 All the Units In Urban Area	国有经济单位 State Owned Units	城镇集体单位 Urban Collective Owned Units	其他经济单位 Other Units	城镇私营单位 Urban Private Units
总计	**Total**	**10234100**	**2153173**	**73261**	**3651692**	**4355974**
农、林、牧、渔业	Farming, Forest, Herd, Fishery	40133	12511	413	3480	23728
采矿业	Mining and Quarrying	40896	1059	649	22015	17173
制造业	Manufacturing	2568094	29876	3143	1242780	1292295
电力、燃气及水的生产和供应业	Power, Gas and Water Production and Supply	156423	84911	2255	55829	13429
建筑业	Construction	1808691	37432	16377	844695	910187
批发和零售业	Wholesale and Retail Sale	838029	24427	7956	268875	536771
交通运输、仓储和邮政业	Transportation, Storage and Post	409899	53432	4488	223689	128289
住宿和餐饮业	Hotel and Catering	188179	3189	1294	67284	116412
信息传输、软件和信息技术服务业	Information Transmission, Software and Computer Services	267278	10355	81	151068	105774
金融业	Banking	193760	10514		149423	33823
房地产业	Real Estate	431203	7597	1757	172336	249513
租赁和商务服务业	Leasing and Commerical Services	658181	39280	4072	138743	476086
科学研究、技术服务业	Scietific Research, polytechnical	316040	61860	1936	99400	152844
水利、环境和公共设施管理业	Water Conservance, Environment and Public Facilities Management	102183	50550	2310	25318	24004
居民服务、修理和其他服务业	Resident Service and Others	98860	6090	898	11764	80108
教育	Education	824823	593801	15390	110313	105319
卫生和社会工作	Health, Social Security and	469695	378730	7468	39694	43803
文化、体育和娱乐业	Culture, Sports and Entertainment	104978	34896	874	22793	46415
公共管理、社会保障和社会组织	Public Management, Social Security and Social Organization	716755	712664	1897	2194	

3-4 分行业在岗女职工人数(2020)
Number of Female Staff and Workers by Sector(2020)

单位:人 (person)

行业	Sector	城镇全部单位(不含私营单位) All the Units In Urban Area	国有经济单位 State Owned Units	城镇集体单位 Urban Collective Owned Units	其他经济单位 Other Units
总计	**Total**	**2405603**	**1002867**	**34724**	**1368013**
农、林、牧、渔业	Farming, Forest, Herd, Fishery	6962	5716	136	1110
采矿业	Mining and Quarrying	5844	159	191	5494
制造业	Manufacturing	472817	8842	1306	462668
电力、燃气及水的生产和供应业	Power, Gas and Water Production and Supply	42163	23306	742	18114
建筑业	Construction	133224	6724	2262	124237
批发和零售业	Wholesale and Retail Sale	175319	8721	6185	160414
交通运输、仓储和邮政业	Transportation, Storage and Post	74025	19045	1327	53653
住宿和餐饮业	Hotel and Catering	56962	2401	847	53713
信息传输、软件和信息技术服务业	Information Transmission, Software and Computer Services	63393	4969	30	58394
金融业	Banking	135169	4791		130378
房地产业	Real Estate	79520	3113	724	75682
租赁和商务服务业	Leasing and Commerical Services	70275	16280	2096	51899
科学研究、技术服务业	Scietific Research, Polytechnical	49443	20107	540	28796
水利、环境和公共设施管理业	Water Conservance, Environment and Public Facilities Management	34141	21805	1439	10897
居民服务、修理和其他服务业	Resident Service and Others	10542	2782	466	7294
教育	Education	422606	329137	10455	83014
卫生和社会工作	Health, Social Security and	297640	263733	4922	28986
文化、体育和娱乐业	Culture, Sports and Entertainment	29355	16597	391	12367
公共管理、社会保障和社会组织	Public Management ,Social Security and Social Organization	246204	244637	664	902

3-5 城镇登记失业人数及失业率
Number of Registered Unemployed Persons and Unemployment Rate in Urban Area

单位：万人 (10 000 persons)

年份 Year	年末城镇登记失业人数 The Number of Unemployeed in Urban Areas by the End of Year	年末城镇登记失业率(%) Year End Unemployment Registered Rate (%)
1978	20.03	4.19
1980	15.54	2.97
1990	12.66	1.72
1991	14.20	1.88
1992	16.89	2.17
1993	17.96	2.20
1994	21.06	2.90
1995	24.45	3.10
1996	28.25	3.50
1997	29.83	3.50
1998	31.33	3.30
1999	33.10	3.30
2000	36.64	3.50
2001	42.15	4.00
2002	44.66	4.30
2003	49.34	4.30
2004	49.37	4.20
2005	52.60	4.33
2006	52.56	4.22
2007	46.72	4.21
2008	55.07	4.20
2009	55.25	4.21
2010	55.65	4.18
2011	55.11	4.10
2012	42.26	3.83
2013	40.26	3.49
2014	37.88	3.10
2015	33.43	2.64
2016	32.91	2.41
2017	37.07	2.59
2018	36.14	2.55
2019	37.63	2.44
2020	55.29	3.35

3-6 职工平均工资及指数

年 份 Year	平均货币工资(元) Average Money Wages (yuan)					指数(上年=100) Indices (preceding year=100)	
	合计 Total	国有经济单位 State Owned Units	城镇集体经济单位 Urban Collective Owned	其他经济单位 Other Units	城镇私营单位 Urban Private Units	货币工资 Money Wages	国有经济单位 State Owned Units
1978	581	592	532			104.5	104.5
1980	719	744	619			116.0	115.9
1990	1903	2045	1467	2259		111.7	107.6
1992	2370	2532	1837	2575		113.9	114.4
1993	2933	3141	2183	3248		123.8	124.1
1994	4050	4348	2845	4352		138.1	138.4
1995	4685	4991	3308	5093		115.7	114.8
1996	5099	5411	3590	5754		108.8	108.4
1997	5401	5741	3731	5740		105.9	106.1
1998	6436	6783	4748	6166		108.7	109.1
1999	6991	7381	5001	6681		108.6	108.8
2000	7565	7989	5090	7327		108.2	108.2
2001	8619	9133	5677	8035		113.9	114.3
2002	9611	10403	6534	8180		111.5	113.9
2003	10692	11806	7137	8698		111.2	113.5
2004	11855	13096	7608	10270		110.9	110.9
2005	13330	14774	8663	11572		112.4	112.8
2006	15172	17078	9848	13098		113.8	115.6
2007	17397	21971	12921	16829		114.7	128.7
2008	19597	24756	14840	20293		112.6	112.7
2009	23709	30032	19181	23528	15615	121.0	121.3
2010	28092	35981	24429	28799	18626	118.5	119.8
2011	32050	40345	26988	34354	20788	114.1	112.1
2012	35179	43438	33551	38675	23037	109.8	107.7
2013	38720	46126	34181	43975	25898	110.1	106.2
2014	43217	55071	37599	48163	28534	111.6	119.4
2015	47320	60615	41152	52060	31051	109.5	110.1
2016	51415	68983	44154	56461	34167	108.7	113.8
2017	55903	78423	49064	61286	37142	108.7	113.7
2018	60561	85712	52514	70512	40126	108.3	109.3
2019	64661	91665	55560	76157	43536	106.8	106.9
2020	71110	101253	57686	80277	48295	110.0	110.5

注:1998 年以后为在岗职工平均工资。2007 年以后统计范围含城镇全部私营单位。

Average Wages and Indices of Staff and Workers

指数(上年=100) Indices (preceding year=100)							
城镇集体经济单位 Urban Collective Owned	其他经济单位 Other Units	城镇私营单位 Urban Private Units	实际工资 Real Wages	国有经济单位 State Owned Units	城镇集体经济单位 Urban Collective Owned	其他经济单位 Other Units	城镇私营单位 Urban Private Units
106.4			104.2	103.9	106.1		
116.4			108.6	108.5	109.0		
107.1	107.1		107.8	108.3	104.4	103.9	
110.5	109.0		103.1	103.5	100.0	98.7	
118.8	126.1		106.6	106.8	102.3	108.6	
130.3	134.0		108.7	109.0	102.6	105.5	
116.3	117.0		96.3	95.6	96.8	97.4	
108.5	113.0		95.1	94.0	95.3	99.9	
103.9	99.8		97.6	96.6	95.9	96.6	
109.2	99.1		110.2	110.2	110.8	100.5	
105.3	108.4		110.0	111.0	107.4	110.6	
101.8	109.7		109.3	109.3	102.7	110.8	
111.5	109.7		113.6	114.0	111.2	109.3	
115.1	101.8		112.0	114.4	115.6	102.2	
109.2	106.3		108.8	111.1	106.8	104.0	
106.6	118.1		105.7	105.7	101.6	112.6	
113.9	112.7		109.2	109.6	110.7	109.5	
113.7	113.2		112.0	113.8	111.9	111.4	
131.2	128.5		109.4	122.8	125.2	122.6	
114.9	120.6		106.0	106.0	108.0	113.4	
129.3	115.9		121.8	122.2	130.2	116.8	
127.4	122.4	119.3	115.1	116.4	123.8	119.0	115.9
110.5	119.3	111.6	107.8	106.0	104.4	112.8	105.5
124.3	112.6	110.8	106.7	104.6	120.8	109.4	107.7
101.9	113.7	112.4	107.1	103.3	99.1	110.6	109.4
110.0	109.5	110.2	109.4	117.1	107.8	107.4	108.0
109.4	108.1	108.8	107.9	108.4	107.8	106.5	107.2
107.3	108.5	110.0	106.3	111.4	105.0	106.1	107.7
111.1	108.5	108.7	107.1	112.0	109.5	106.9	107.1
107.0	115.1	108.0	106.4	107.4	105.1	113.2	106.1
105.8	108.0	108.5	103.7	103.8	102.7	104.9	105.4
103.8	105.4	110.9	107.3	107.8	101.1	102.7	108.2

Note: Data after 1998 refers to average wages and indices of employed staff and workers. Statistics of 2007 involves all the private run units in urban areas.

3-7 分行业在岗职工平均工资(2020)
Average Wages of Staff and Worker on the Job by Sector(2020)

单位:元 (yuan)

行业	Sector	城镇全部单位 All the Units In Urban Area	国有经济单位 State Owned Units	城镇集体单位 Urban Collective Owned Units	其他经济单位 Other Units	城镇私营单位 Urban Private Units
总计	**Total**	**71110**	**101253**	**57686**	**80277**	**48295**
农、林、牧、渔业	Farming, Forest, Herd, Fishery	38940	49070	40752	47506	37183
采矿业	Mining and Quarrying	61322	85024	40726	106299	41533
制造业	Manufacturing	56870	93982	50861	75040	49213
电力、燃气及水的生产和供应业	Power, Gas and Water Production and Supply	108837	130708	46774	117987	48762
建筑业	Construction	61591	73156	42236	72674	51115
批发和零售业	Wholesale and Retail Sale	51614	118639	40908	63577	42464
交通运输、仓储和邮政业	Transportation, Storage and Post	79421	82645	53334	95486	50136
住宿和餐饮业	Hotel and Catering	41017	45384	38665	47925	38387
信息传输、软件和信息技术服务业	Information Transmission, Software and Computer Services	111229	108550	53864	115737	57821
金融业	Banking	124276	121578		135022	76929
房地产业	Real Estate	59291	89665	49761	73045	48848
租赁和商务服务业	Leasing and Commerical Services	53348	66819	65967	71643	46757
科学研究、技术服务业	Scietific Research, Polytechnical	105309	106181	72113	139280	54724
水利、环境和公共设施管理业	Water Conservance, Environment and Public Facilities Management	69433	81507	52328	75778	38554
居民服务、修理和其他服务业	Resident Service and Others	44506	87316	54631	46975	40724
教育	Education	88048	102682	73897	56855	38450
卫生和社会工作	Health, Social Security and	104477	105877	72293	70134	53206
文化、体育和娱乐业	Culture, Sports and Entertainment	63725	98260	110774	77802	46427
公共管理、社会保障和社会组织	Public Management, Social Security and Social Organization	108039	109316	76888	81866	

主要统计指标解释

经济活动人口 指在16周岁及以上，有劳动能力，参加或要求参加社会经济活动的人口。包括就业人员和失业人员。

就业人员 指在16周岁及以上，从事一定社会劳动并取得劳动报酬或经营收入的人员。这一指标反映了一定时期内全部劳动力资源的实际利用情况，是研究我国基本国情国力的重要指标。

单位就业人员 指报告期末最后一日24时在各类单位工作，并取得工资或其他形式劳动报酬的人员数。该指标为时点指标，不包括最后一日当天及以前已经与单位解除劳动合同关系的人员，是在岗职工、劳务派遣人员及其他从业人员之和。从业人员不包括：

1.离开本单位仍保留劳动关系，并定期领取生活费的人员；

2.在本单位实习的各类在校学生；

3.本单位因劳务外包而使用的人员。

在岗职工 指在本单位工作且与本单位签订劳动合同，并由单位支付各项工资和社会保险、住房公积金的人员，以及上述人员中由于学习、病伤、产假等原因暂未工作仍由单位支付工资的人员。在岗职工还包括：

1.应订立劳动合同而未订立劳动合同人员（如使用的农村户籍人员）；

2.处于试用期人员；

3.编制外招用的人员，如临时人员；

4.派往外单位工作，但工资仍由本单位发放的人员（如挂职锻炼、外派工作等情况）。

在岗职工平均工资 指单位在岗职工在一定时期内平均每人所得的货币工资。它表明一定时期在岗职工工资收入的高低程度，是反映在岗职工工资水平的主要指标。计算公式为：

$$平均工资=\frac{报告期实际支付的全部在岗职工工资总额}{报告期全部在岗职工平均人数}$$

平均工资指数 指报告期在岗职工平均工资与基期平均工资的比率，是反映不同时期在岗职工货币工资水平变动情况的相对数。计算公式为：

$$平均工资指数=\frac{报告期在岗职工平均工资}{基期在岗职工平均工资}\times100\%$$

平均实际工资指数 在岗职工平均实际工资指扣除物价变动因素后的在岗职工平均工资。在岗职工平均实际工资指数是反映实际工资变动情况的相对数，表明职工实际工资水平提高或降低的程度。计算公式为：

$$平均实际工资指数=\frac{报告期职工平均工资指数}{报告期城镇居民消费价格指数}\times100\%$$

城镇登记失业人员 指有非农业户口，在一定的劳动年龄内（16周岁至退休年龄），有劳动能力，无业而要求就业，并在当地就业服务机构进行求职登记的人员。

城镇登记失业率 城镇登记失业人员与城镇单位就业人员（扣除使用的农村劳动力、聘用的离退休人员、港澳台及外方人员）、城镇单位中的不在岗职工、城镇私营业主、个体户主、城镇私营企业和个体就业人员、城镇登记失业人员之和的比。

$$城镇登记失业率=\frac{城镇登记失业人数}{\begin{gathered}（城镇单位就业人员-\\使用的农村劳动力-\\聘用的离退休人员-\\聘用的港澳台及外方人员）\end{gathered}}\times100\%$$

Explanatory Notes on Main Statistical Indicators

Economically Active Population refers to the population aged 16 and over who are capable to work, are participating in or willing to participate in economic activities, including employed persons and unemployed persons.

Employed Persons refer to the persons aged 16 and over who are engaged in social working and receive remuneration payment or earn business income. This indicator reflects the actual utilization of total labour force during a certain period of time and is often used for the research on China's economic situation and national power.

Persons Employed in Various Units refer to all the persons working in government agencies of various levels, political and party organizations, social organizations, enterprises and institutions, and receiving wages or other forms of payment. They include fully-employed staff and workers, re-employed retirees, teachers in schools run by the local people, foreigners and Chinese compatriots from Hong Kong, Macao, and Taiwan working in various units, part-time employees, employees of other units working temporarily at current posts, and employees holding the second job, but exclude staff and workers who have left their working units while keeping their labour contract (employment relation) unchanged. This indicator reflects the total number of laborers actually engaged in production or other operations in various units.

Staff and Workers refer to persons working in,and receive payment from units of state ownership,collective ownership,joint ownership, share holding ownership, foreign ownership, and ownership by entrepreneurs from Hong Kong, Macao, and Taiwan, and other types of ownership and their affiliated units. They do not include 1) persons employed in township enterprises, 2) persons employed in private enterprises, 3) urban self-employed persons, 4) retirees, 5) re-employed retirees, 6) teachers in the schools run by the local people, 7) foreigners and persons from Hong Kong, Macao and Taiwan who work in urban units, and 8) other persons not to be included by relevant regulations. (Data of 1998 and afterward refer to fully employed staff and workers. Other related statistics such as total wage bill and average wage are adjusted since 1998 accordingly).

Average Wage refers to the average wage in money terms per person during a certain period of time for staff and workers in enterprises, institutions, and government agencies, which reflects the general level of wage income during a certain period of time and is calculated as follows:

Average Wage = Total Wages of Staff and Workers at Reference Time /Average Number of Staff and Workers at Reference Time.

Average Wage Indices refers to the ratio of average wage of staff and workers in the report period to that in the base period, which reflects the change of wage of staff and workers at the different period. It is calculated as follows:

Average Wage Indices = Average Wage of Staff and Workers at Reference Time / Average Wage of Staff and Workers at Base Period x 100%

Average Real Wage Indices average real wage of staff and workers refers to the average wage of staff and workers after removing the effects of the price changes and average real wage indices of staff and workers refers to the change of real wage, which reflects the relative increasing or decreasing level of real wage of staff and workers, which is calculated as follows:

Average Real Wage Indices = Average Wage Indices of Staff and Workers at the Reference Time / Urban Consumer Price Indices at Reference Time × 100%

Registered Urban Unemployed Persons refer to the persons with non-agricultural household registration at certain working ages (16-50 years for male and 16-45 years for females), who are capable of work, unemployed and willing to work, and have been registered at the local employment service agencies to apply for a job.

Registered Urban Unemployment Rate refers to the ratio of the number of the registered unemployed persons to the sum of the number of persons employed in various units (minus the rural labour force, retirees, and Hong Kong, Macao, Taiwan or foreign employees they employ) laid-off workers in urban units, owners and employees in urban private enterprises, urban self-employed individuals and the registered urban unemployed persons. The formula is as follows:

Registered urban unemployment rate = number of registered urban unemployed persons ÷(number of persons employed in urban units – rural labour force employed retirees employed – Hong Kong, Macao, Taiwan or foreign employees employ + laid–off workers + owners and employees in urban private enterprises + self–employed individuals in urban areas + registered urban unemployed persons) × 100%.

4

固定资产投资

Investment in Fixed Assets

资料整理人员:肖　悦　　张　萍

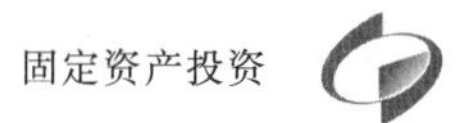

固定资产投资

Investment in Fixed Assets

2020

固定资产投资	Urban Investment	-18.80 %
#房地产开发	Real Estate Development	-4.40 %

2009-2020 年固定资产投资增速(%)

Growth Rate of Investment in Fixed Assets During 2009-2020 (%)

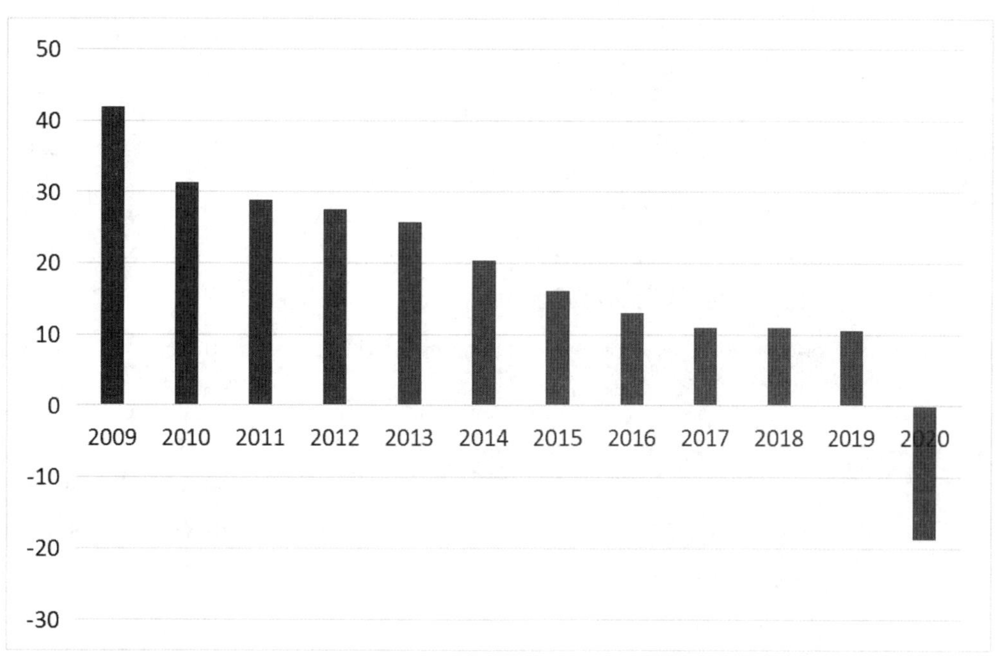

附:固定资产投资完成额构成(%)

Attachment: Composition of the Completed Investment in Fixed Assets (%)

		2009	2010	2011	2012	2013	2014	2015	2016	2017	2018	2019	2020
国有投资	State-Owned	38.1	34.9	29.1	25.8	24.4	23.3	23.9	27.2	28.9	20.6	19.5	17.7
集体投资	Collective-Owned	5.0	5.6	5.1	4.4	4.0	3.3	2.6	2.3	1.6	0.4	0.4	0.2
私营个体投资	Individuals	21.6	23.2	25.6	28.6	32.6	34.8	35.6	31.8	31.9	33.7	31.9	34.0
外商港澳台商投资	Foreign, HK, Macao and Taiwan	4.9	4.2	4.5	4.1	3.1	2.7	2.9	2.7	3.0	3.2	3.9	3.5
其他	Others	30.4	32.1	35.7	37.1	35.9	35.9	35.0	36.0	34.6	42.1	44.3	44.6

注:从 2011 年起固定资产投资统计口径调整为计划总投资 500 万元及以上项目,取消城镇农村公布口径,其他年份未做相应调整。2016 年对 2015 年基数进行了调整。从 2016 年起,固定资产投资不包含农户投资。

Note: Since 2011, the fixed assets investment accounts for investment over 5 million yuan, canceling town and countryside. Other years´ statistics do not correspond to this adjustment. The basic number of 2015 is adjusted in 2016. Since 2016, farmer investment isn´t induded in the fixed assets investment.

4-1 固定资产投资主要指标

指 标	Item	1990	2000	2005	2008
投资总额 (亿元)	**Total Investment (100 million yuan)**	**144.44**	**1421.55**	**2834.75**	**5798.56**
按经济类型分	**Grouped by Ownership**				
国有经济	State-owned Units	100.35	857.01	1095.71	2273.83
集体经济	Collective-owned Units	15.59	128.32	79.47	253.32
#农村	Rural Area	9.59	98.95	26.55	65.02
私营个体经济	Individuals	28.50	221.43	554.27	1201.53
#农村	Rural Area	23.62	106.65	135.95	190.19
联营经济	Joint-ownership Economic Units		3.94	19.56	15.05
股份制经济	Share Holding Co.Ltd.		86.29	232.34	462.81
有限责任公司	Limited Liability Corporations		53.33	557.21	1109.43
港澳台投资经济	Economic Units Funded by Hongkong, Macao and Taiwan		36.57	92.68	160.62
外商投资经济	Foreign Funded Enterprise Units		23.90	116.23	178.60
其他经济	Others		10.76	87.28	143.37
按资金来源分	**Grouped by Source of Finance**				
国家预算内资金	State Budgetary Apporpriations	11.38	141.48	255.76	570.17
国内贷款	Domestic Loans	22.22	243.90	474.21	894.57
利用外资	Foreign Investment	4.79	28.28	71.34	57.02
自筹资金	Fund Raising	92.96	781.50	1492.66	3677.00
其他资金来源	Others	13.09	226.39	540.78	599.80
按构成分	**Grouped by Usage of Funds**				
建筑安装工程	Construction Installation	92.64	814.66	1696.80	3568.96
设备工器具购置	Purchase of Equipments and Instruments	41.02	371.56	642.86	1245.73
其他费用	Others	10.78	235.33	495.09	983.87
按产业分	**Grouped by Industry**				
#住宅	Residential Housing	39.61	290.24	510.04	901.26
第一产业	Primary Industry	12.16	103.05	92.88	231.25
第二产业	Second Industry	67.41	521.58	1086.34	2344.36
第三产业	Tertiary Industry	64.87	796.92	1655.53	3222.95
房屋建筑面积 (万平方米)	**Floor Space of Building (10 000 sq.m)**				
施工面积	Floor Space Under Construction	5103.48	9920.42	12572.00	16417.07
#住宅	Residential Housing	3507.53	6831.02	8401.20	9896.66
竣工面积	Floor Space Completed	4169.12	7508.96	7863.85	7551.82
#住宅	Residential Housing	3058.40	5417.38	5627.67	4679.96
商品房销售面积 (万平方米)	**Floor Space of Commercial (10 000 sq.m)**	**130.53**	**612.05**	**1708.02**	**1941.62**

注:2006年投资总额(城镇投资)不含城镇工矿区私人建房投资(下同)。由于方法制度调整,按可比口径计算,2005年扣除城镇工矿区私人建房投资基数应为2788.92亿元;从2011年起固定资产投资统计口径调整为计划总投资500万元及以上项目,取消城镇农村公布口径,其他年份未做相应调整。从2017年起,三次产业采用新的划分标准。

Major Indicators of Investment in Fixed Assets

2009	2010	2011	2014	2015	2016	2017
8211.85	**10802.69**	**12935.02**	**25001.77**	**29191.06**	**29503.88**	**31872.57**
3124.90	3768.95	3764.22	5829.79	6983.99	8021.33	9199.68
411.18	602.80	660.59	820.75	754.53	677.42	524.02
77.50	99.23	137.69	117.04	143.42		
1771.61	2510.61	3307.47	8708.83	10386.49	9386.11	10168.42
240.48	301.05	365.51	698.73	940.57		
11.32	19.89	22.49	11.84	13.38	64.03	36.84
659.79	896.87	987.66	1238.81	1125.37	983.55	986.38
1648.26	2221.99	3056.98	6026.42	6634.45	8614.44	8621.09
202.38	207.81	253.89	343.93	393.90	443.65	484.72
200.79	245.92	328.55	333.45	459.38	344.86	479.99
181.62	327.85	553.17	1687.95	2439.57	968.49	1371.45
711.98	868.46	663.18	1107.45	1339.03	1829.24	2326.38
1432.98	1768.79	1707.46	2874.92	2907.66	3068.40	3078.89
68.33	147.03	189.26	78.99	46.86	59.01	65.59
4956.65	6703.61	8800.61	18732.35	22470.65	20623.21	21408.69
1041.91	1314.80	1574.51	2208.06	2426.86	3924.02	4993.03
5025.62	6701.91	8056.53	18185.42	21826.03	22876.58	23772.98
1753.28	2308.73	2812.91	4292.85	4845.70	4124.21	4891.02
1432.95	1792.05	2065.58	2523.50	2519.33	2503.08	3208.57
1127.28	1417.95	1750.16	3461.65	3853.52	3434.85	3555.18
321.59	393.00	440.91	799.35	997.94	889.94	912.24
3097.68	4169.92	5526.40	10733.09	12146.51	12224.54	13236.47
4792.58	6239.77	6967.71	13469.32	16046.61	16389.40	17723.86
20142.81	25284.83	31388.88	58064.39	58095.72	44198.73	42087.64
11762.06	14486.90	16337.96	27199.41	29006.34	24286.60	23849.67
9772.28	11802.18	14585.68	21175.37	22992.18	8878.64	7172.55
5556.71	6785.61	7375.38	8702.01	9381.09	3582.22	3094.58
2718.30	**3508.61**	**4187.62**	**5601.98**	**6244.55**	**7427.16**	**8155.21**

Note: In 2006 the investment (town investment) does not contain town private house industrial investment.(same below) Because of method adjustment, according to comparable caliber, 2005′s investment base should be 278.892 billion yuan deducting industrial town private house. Since 2011, the fixed assets investment accounts for investment over 5 million yuan, canceling town and countryside. Other years′ statistics do not correspond to this adjustment. Since 2017, the division of three industries emploies a new standard.

4-2 固定资产投资额
Investment in Fixed Assets

单位:亿元 (100 million yuan)

年 份 Year	投资额 Investment	#房地产开发 Real Estate Development	#国有经济 State Owned Units	#集体经济 Collective Owned Units	#私营个体 Individuals
"六五"时期	**315.82**		**207.57**	**49.41**	**58.84**
1985	102.91		61.66	17.44	23.81
"七五"时期	**680.12**	**5.94**	**435.32**	**94.17**	**150.64**
1986	111.44		66.42	15.89	29.13
1987	140.08		85.32	22.31	32.46
1988	160.46		102.21	24.60	33.64
1989	123.70		81.02	15.78	26.91
1990	144.44	5.94	100.35	15.59	28.50
"八五"时期	**2211.67**	**254.77**	**1497.69**	**190.04**	**261.87**
1991	168.19	7.88	119.07	19.49	29.63
1992	240.73	12.55	182.86	22.52	35.35
1993	383.18	37.01	275.84	30.62	40.37
1994	593.07	76.20	401.16	44.83	56.62
1995	826.50	121.13	518.76	72.58	99.90
"九五"时期	**6022.80**	**634.60**	**3425.23**	**573.74**	**943.77**
1996	984.38	118.40	593.32	96.50	124.78
1997	1083.60	126.47	567.60	107.12	160.56
1998	1231.10	131.23	661.94	116.92	194.52
1999	1302.17	123.87	745.36	124.88	242.48
2000	1421.55	134.63	857.01	128.32	221.43
"十五"时期	**10321.69**	**1354.15**	**4817.55**	**541.41**	**1806.78**
2001	1551.75	151.24	918.21	126.41	249.59
2002	1695.22	178.64	963.18	121.42	263.00
2003	1883.59	239.04	888.72	109.05	303.90
2004	2356.38	337.28	951.73	105.06	436.02
2005	2834.75	447.95	1095.71	79.47	554.27
"十一五"时期	**32919.93**	**4999.84**	**12449.99**	**1533.63**	**7020.48**
2006	3572.69	564.76	1473.70	110.67	636.25
2007	4534.14	723.73	1808.61	155.66	900.48
2008	5798.56	892.67	2273.83	253.32	1201.53
2009	8211.85	1200.44	3124.90	411.18	1771.61
2010	10802.69	1618.24	3768.95	602.80	2510.61
"十二五"时期	**104385.93**	**16124.98**	**25912.37**	**3796.30**	**33879.07**
2011	12935.02	2066.48	3764.22	660.59	3307.47
2012	16504.17	2539.46	4265.95	733.92	4712.60
2013	20753.91	3286.02	5068.42	826.51	6763.68
2014	25001.77	3983.79	5829.79	820.75	8708.83
2015	29191.06	4249.23	6983.99	754.53	10386.49
"十三五"时期					
2016	29503.88	4296.38	8021.33	677.42	9386.11
2017	31872.57	4574.89	9199.68	524.02	10168.42

注:房地产开发投资统计制度从1990年开始建立。从2011年起固定资产投资统计口径调整为计划总投资500万元及以上项目,取消城镇农村公布口径,其他年份未做相应调整。

Note: The statistical system of real estate development investment is established in 1990. Since 2011, the fixed assets investment accounts for investment over 5 million yuan, canceling town and countryside. Other years′ statistics do not correspond to this adjustment.

4-3 按登记注册类型分固定资产投资增幅
Growth Rate of Investment in Fixed Assets by Registration Status

单位:%

指 标	Item	2017	2018	2019	2020
总计	**Total**	**11.0**	**11.0**	**10.6**	**-18.8**
内资企业	**Domestic Funded Enterprises**	**10.6**	**11.5**	**9.8**	**-18.5**
国有企业	State-owned Enterprises	10.3	12.9	4.4	-26.1
集体企业	Collective-owned Enterprises	-5.5	-30.9	-3.5	-65.3
股份合作企业	Share Holding Cooperative Enterprises	-39.9	-63.0	-34.2	-27.9
联营企业	Joint Owned Enterprise	-41.5	-21.6	-6.3	-41.2
国有联营	State Joint Ownership	127.0	54.0	15.4	-65.9
集体联营	Collective Joint Ownership	-61.7	-25.5	22.9	228.0
国有与集体联营	Joint State-Collective	33.8	21.6	-97.1	700.0
其他联营企业	Other Joint Owned Enterprise	-63.5	-48.3	29.0	-100.0
有限责任公司	Co. Ltd	10.5	6.4	18.9	-15.5
国有独资公司	Solely State Funded Co.	50.3	-2.4	16.8	-12.4
其他有限责任公司	Other Co. Ltd	3.6	8.9	19.5	-16.2
股份有限公司	Share Holding Co.Ltd.	3.7	11.5	-0.2	-24.4
私营企业	Private-owned Enterprises	11.0	22.8	4.8	-13.5
其他企业	Others	42.6	-20.1	10.1	-52.5
港、澳、台商投资企业	**Hongkong, Macao and Taiwan Funded**	**10.1**	**-1.4**	**43.4**	**-34.3**
合资经营企业	Joint Funded Enterprises	31.8	18.5	58.6	28.4
合作经营企业	Cooperative Operation Enterprises	-74.1	0.3	-33.5	6.9
独资经营企业	Solely Funded Enterprises	1.3	3.3	48.6	-36.4
股份有限公司	Share Holding Co.Ltd.	344.7	84.0	-48.6	-48.8
外商投资企业	**Foreign Invested Enterprises**	**40.3**	**-0.6**	**24.2**	**-18.9**
合资经营企业	Joint Funded Enterprises	25.1	-29.8	39.4	-31.8
合作经营企业	Cooperative Operation Enterprises				-2.0
独资企业	Solely Funded Enterprises	122.8	58.3	2.9	-1.9
股份有限公司	Share Holding Co.Ltd.	35.9	21.7	2.4	-48.0
个体经营	**Individual Investment**	**50.8**	**27.2**	**2.0**	**-17.3**
个体户	Individual Self-Employed	55.1	19.1	18.8	-16.2
个人合伙	Individual Pattenership	34.0	79.2	-70.1	-35.7

注:从 2011 年起固定资产投资统计口径调整为计划总投资 500 万元及以上项目,取消城镇农村公布口径,其他年份未做相应调整。

Note: Since 2011, the fixed assets investment accounts for investment over 5 million yuan, canceling town and countryside. Other years' statistics do not correspond to this adjustment.

4-4 按构成分固定资产投资增幅(2020)
Growth Rate of Investment in Fixed Assets by Composition of Investment(2020)

单位:%

行 业	Sector	全部投资 Investment	建筑安装工程 Construction and Installation	设备工器具购置 Purchases of Equipments and Instruments	其 他 Others
总计	**Total**	**-18.8**	**-18.9**	**-22.3**	**-14.2**
农、林、牧、渔业	**Farming, Forestry, Animal Husbandry and Fishery**	**-26.7**	**-22.6**	**-36.7**	**-46.9**
农业	Farming	-45.1	-40.3	-57.1	-67.3
林业	Forestry	-34.5	-28.4	-81.3	-35.6
畜牧业	Animal Husbandry	50.8	54.0	74.3	-2.4
渔业	Fishery	-67.2	-65.4	-75.9	-70.5
农、林、牧、渔专业及辅助性活动	Professional and Support for Agriculture, Forestry, Animal Husbandry and Fishery	-16.2	-10.9	-41.5	-36.5
采矿业	**Mining**	**-11.3**	**-7.4**	**-29.2**	**11.6**
制造业	**Manufacturing**	**-24.5**	**-24.9**	**-21.4**	**-36.6**
农副食品加工业	Processing of Food from Agriculture Products	-31.1	-24.5	-44.8	-52.1
食品制造业	Manufacture of Foods	-20.5	-24.3	-12.6	4.8
酒、饮料和精制茶制造业	Manufacture of Liquor, Beverages and Refined Tea	-31.8	-35.0	-18.0	-57.6
烟草制品业	Manufacture of Tobacco	263.3	300.6	248.9	-35.4
纺织业	Manufacture of Textile	-36.0	-33.7	-38.3	-48.0
纺织服装、服饰业	Manufacture of Textile, Wearing Apparel and Accessaries	-44.4	-42.8	-53.5	-29.6
皮革、毛皮、羽毛及其制品和制鞋业	Manufacture of Leather, Fur, Feather and Related Products and Footwear	-54.5	-69.5	-0.3	-75.0
木材加工和木、竹、藤、棕、草制品业	Processing of Timber, Manufacture of Wood, Bamboo, Rattan, Palm and Straw Products	-30.0	-24.0	-36.0	-64.0
家具制造业	Manufacture of Furniture	-29.6	-29.1	-29.2	-39.9
造纸和纸制品业	Manufacture of Paper and Paper Products	-48.7	-49.7	-43.9	-66.4
印刷和记录媒介复制业	Printing and Reproduction of Recording Media	-23.3	-21.5	-28.8	-17.1
文教、工美、体育和娱乐用品制造业	Manufacture of Articles for Culture, Education, Arts and Crafts Sport and Entertainment Activities	-37.2	-42.7	-21.1	-14.5
石油、煤炭及其他燃料加工业	Processing of Petroleum, Coal and Other Fuels	-13.3	-25.7	6.4	51.3
化学原料和化学制品制造业	Manufacture of Raw Chemical Materials and Chemical Products	-27.1	-17.7	-40.4	-40.0
医药制造业	Manufacture of Medicines	20.4	17.5	30.5	6.7
化学纤维制造业	Manufacture of Chemical Fibres	-8.9	12.6	-38.4	-25.7
橡胶和塑料制品业	Manufacture of Rubber and Plastic Products	-7.4	-1.0	-22.3	15.5
非金属矿物制品业	Manufacture of Non-metallic Mineral Products	-21.9	-18.1	-35.7	9.7
黑色金属冶炼和压延加工业	Smelting and Pressing of Ferrous Metals	10.6	11.0	0.8	203.6
有色金属冶炼和压延加工业	Smelting and Pressing of Non-ferrous Metals	6.4	24.5	-26.2	-19.5
金属制品业	Manufacture of Metal Products	-35.7	-34.4	-36.2	-49.1
通用设备制造业	Manufacture of General Purpose Machinery	-28.9	-24.2	-35.4	-53.2
专用设备制造业	Manufacture of Special Purpose Machinery	-38.8	-44.8	-14.3	-42.6
汽车制造业	Manufacture of Automobiles	-30.3	-36.0	-21.3	-11.5
铁路、船舶、航空航天和其他运输设备制造业	Manufacture of Railway, Ship, Aerospace and Other Transport Equipment	-31.0	-13.8	-19.9	-98.2
电气机械和器材制造业	Manufacture of Electrical Machinery and Apparatus	-27.2	-25.6	-32.5	-20.6
计算机、通信和其他电子设备制造业	Manufacture of Computers, Communication and Other Electronic Equipment	-5.0	-21.3	13.4	-54.4
仪器仪表制造业	Manufacture of Measuring Instruments and Machinery	-36.4	-33.9	-32.1	-76.9
其他制造业	Other Manufacture	-41.8	-28.4	-92.9	7.3
废弃资源综合利用业	Utilization of Waste Resources	-9.6	2.9	-32.7	-36.4
金属制品、机械和设备修理业	Repairing Service of Metal Products, Mechanical Equipment	-79.8	-76.8	-83.9	-94.5
电力、热力、燃气及水生产和供应业	**Production and Supply of Electricity, Heat, Gas and Water**	**-19.9**	**-28.5**	**7.8**	**4.1**
电力、热力生产和供应业	Production and Supply of Electric Power and and Heat Power	-3.5	-17.5	28.6	13.1
燃气生产和供应业	Production and Supply of Gas	-24.9	-16.0	-68.6	9.1
水的生产和供应业	Production and Supply of Water	-43.4	-43.1	-52.2	-26.7

注:从2011年起固定资产投资统计口径调整为计划总投资500万元及以上项目,取消城镇农村公布口径,其他年份未做相应调整。从2018年起执行新的国民经济行业代码(GB/T4754-2017)。

Note: Since 2011, the fixed assets investment accounts for investment over 5 million yuan, canceling town and countryside. Other years' statistics do not correspond to this adjustment.Since 2018, a new national economy industry code(GB/T4754-2017)is implemented.

4-4 续表 continued

单位:%

行 业	Sector	全部投资 Investment	建筑安装工程 Construction and Installation	设备工器具购置 Purchases of Equipments and Instruments	其 他 Others
建筑业	**Construction**	**-3.7**	**7.4**	**-8.1**	
交通运输、仓储和邮政业	**Transport, Storage and Post**	**-8.9**	**-9.3**	**-26.3**	**1.3**
铁路运输业	Railway Transport	-20.1	-14.0	-48.8	-20.2
道路运输业	Road Transport	-10.2	-9.7	-51.9	-3.5
水上运输业	Water Transport	-29.8	-37.5	6.4	27.6
航空运输业	Air Transport	128.7	56.5	479.1	536.8
管道运输业	Transport via Pipelines	241.7	47.9		
多式联运和运输代理业	Intermodality and Forwarding Agency	-64.5	-57.5	-98.4	-94.6
装卸搬运和仓储业	Loading, Unloading and Storage	-5.2	-7.7	26.1	-20.1
邮政业	Post	76.2	158.4	540.4	-93.7
信息传输、软件和信息技术服务业	**Information Transmission, Software and Information Technology Service**	**-33.5**	**-44.1**	**-11.1**	**32.4**
电信、广播电视和卫星传输服务	Telecom, Radio and Tv and Satellite Transmission Service	16.8	6.0	27.2	103.7
互联网和相关服务	Internet and Related Service	-53.9	-60.8	-37.3	63.0
软件和信息技术服务业	Software and Information Technology	-66.7	-67.9	-64.6	-54.6
批发和零售业	**Wholesale and Retail Trades**	**-35.3**	**-33.0**	**-59.1**	**-26.0**
住宿和餐饮业	**Hotels and Catering Services**	**-21.3**	**-21.8**	**-26.7**	**-11.6**
金融业	**Financial Intermediation**	**-12.0**	**-11.5**		**-99.8**
房地产业	**Real Estate**	**-9.6**	**-8.7**	**-37.1**	**-9.7**
租赁和商务服务业	**Leasing and Commercial Services**	**6.5**	**9.4**	**9.9**	**-20.3**
租赁业	Leasing	-47.0	-53.1	-5.7	-86.3
商务服务业	Business Services	7.4	10.5	10.5	-20.3
科学研究和技术服务业	**Scientific Research and Technical Services**	**-28.5**	**-27.2**	**-35.2**	**-40.0**
水利、环境和公共设施管理业	**Management of Water Conservancy, Environment and Public Facilities**	**-30.8**	**-31.4**	**-44.6**	**-13.9**
水利管理业	Management of Water Conservancy	-31.6	-33.6	-25.8	2.2
生态保护和环境治理业	Ecological Protection and Environment Treatment	-22.4	-17.1	-44.4	-52.2
公共设施管理业	Management of Public Facilities	-31.8	-32.8	-46.6	-8.4
土地管理业	Management of Land	0.1	9.9	-34.4	-98.9
居民服务、修理和其他服务业	**Service to Households, Repair and Others Services**	**-15.9**	**-10.8**	**-37.6**	**-32.4**
教育	**Education**	**-11.2**	**-12.3**	**-46.7**	**65.0**
卫生和社会工作	**Health Care and Social Service**	**49.5**	**39.5**	**92.5**	**86.7**
卫生	Health	65.8	54.3	103.1	133.1
社会工作	Social Service	5.5	1.8	29.4	21.6
文化、体育和娱乐业	**Culture, Sports and Entertainment**	**-20.5**	**-16.5**	**-33.7**	**-44.7**
广播、电视、电影和影视录音制作业	Radio, Television, Motion Picture and Videotape Programme	-69.3	-72.9	-7.5	-99.5
文化艺术业	Culture and Art Activities	-32.1	-31.3	-70.1	9.3
体育	Sports Activities	-42.7	-40.8	-27.7	-75.7
娱乐业	Entertainment	-15.5	-10.1	-30.6	-44.2
公共管理、社会保障和社会组织	**Public Management, Social Security and Social Organization**	**-28.2**	**-19.9**	**-56.1**	**-6.6**

4-5 按建设性质分固定资产投资增幅(2020)
Growth Rate of Investment in Fixed Assets by Type of Construction(2020)

单位:%

行 业	Sector	全部投资 Investment	新 建 New Construction	扩 建 Expension	改建和技术改 造 Reconstruction and Technical Transformation
总计	**Total**	**-18.8**	**-19.8**	**-27.0**	**-28.6**
农、林、牧、渔业	**Farming, Forestry, Animal Husbandry and Fishery**	**-26.7**	**-24.6**	**-45.7**	**-26.7**
农业	Farming	-45.1	-41.8	-76.5	-47.0
林业	Forestry	-34.5	-32.4	-56.8	-7.2
畜牧业	Animal Husbandry	50.8	64.7	-29.2	-9.3
渔业	Fishery	-67.2	-67.2	-63.7	-82.1
农、林、牧、渔专业及辅助性活动	Professional and Support for Agriculture, Forestry, Animal Husbandry and Fishery	-16.2	-26.1	88.1	1.1
采矿业	**Mining**	**-11.3**	**20.2**	**-18.1**	**-19.7**
制造业	**Manufacturing**	**-24.5**	**-19.0**	**-28.3**	**-31.6**
农副食品加工业	Processing of Food from Agriculture Products	-31.1	-14.9	-46.6	-44.7
食品制造业	Manufacture of Foods	-20.5	-0.1	-4.3	-38.4
酒、饮料和精制茶制造业	Manufacture of Liquor, Beverages and Refined Tea	-31.8	-18.8	-54.1	-32.5
烟草制品业	Manufacture of Tobacco	263.3	207.6		175.6
纺织业	Manufacture of Textile	-36.0	-39.1	-23.2	-46.3
纺织服装、服饰业	Manufacture of Textile, Wearing Apparel and Accessaries	-44.4	-32.8	-40.8	-75.0
皮革、毛皮、羽毛及其制品和制鞋业	Manufacture of Leather, Fur, Feather and Related Products and Footwear	-54.5	-52.0	-55.8	-59.1
木材加工和木、竹、藤、棕、草制品业	Processing of Timber, Manufacture of Wood, Bamboo, Rattan, Palm and Straw Products	-30.0	-21.1	-27.3	-48.0
家具制造业	Manufacture of Furniture	-29.6	-16.5	-53.4	-54.3
造纸和纸制品业	Manufacture of Paper and Paper Products	-48.7	-49.0	-63.1	-41.6
印刷和记录媒介复制业	Printing and Reproduction of Recording Media	-23.3	-63.8	79.6	-17.3
文教、工美、体育和娱乐用品制造业	Manufacture of Articles for Culture, Education, Arts and Crafts Sport and Entertainment Activities	-37.2	-18.1	-76.7	-36.1
石油、煤炭及其他燃料加工业	Processing of Petroleum, Coal and Other Fuels	-13.3	-38.4	-56.1	16.0
化学原料和化学制品制造业	Manufacture of Raw Chemical Materials and Chemical Products	-27.1	-18.8	-41.5	-31.4
医药制造业	Manufacture of Medicines	20.4	14.4	7.7	40.1
化学纤维制造业	Manufacture of Chemical Fibres	-8.9	20.4	-49.6	-48.1
橡胶和塑料制品业	Manufacture of Rubber and Plastic Products	-7.4	21.5	-20.7	-19.8
非金属矿物制品业	Manufacture of Non-metallic Mineral Products	-21.9	-13.7	-24.8	-30.2
黑色金属冶炼和压延加工业	Smelting and Pressing of Ferrous Metals	10.6	7.1	-48.6	15.6
有色金属冶炼和压延加工业	Smelting and Pressing of Non-ferrous Metals	6.4	40.4	-61.8	-15.7
金属制品业	Manufacture of Metal Products	-35.7	-31.3	-52.1	-35.6
通用设备制造业	Manufacture of General Purpose Machinery	-28.9	-30.4	-11.0	-34.9
专用设备制造业	Manufacture of Special Purpose Machinery	-38.8	-16.2	-29.1	-62.3
汽车制造业	Manufacture of Automobiles	-30.3	-31.1	-23.4	-31.6
铁路、船舶、航空航天和其他运输设备制造业	Manufacture of Railway, Ship, Aerospace and Other Transport Equipment	-31.0	-14.6	-16.8	-58.5
电气机械和器材制造业	Manufacture of Electrical Machinery and Apparatus	-27.2	-18.6	-61.8	-27.1
计算机、通信和其他电子设备制造业	Manufacture of Computers, Communication and Other Electronic Equipment	-5.0	-18.9	56.1	47.9
仪器仪表制造业	Manufacture of Measuring Instruments and Machinery	-36.4	-26.0	-26.9	-64.7
其他制造业	Other Manufacture	-41.8	26.2	-88.8	-36.3
废弃资源综合利用业	Utilization of Waste Resources	-9.6	27.3	-13.9	-54.3
金属制品、机械和设备修理业	Repairing Service of Metal Products, Mechanical Equipment	-79.8	-72.9	-100.0	-85.8
电力、热力、燃气及水生产和供应业	**Production and Supply of Electricity, Heat, Gas and Water**	**-19.9**	**-21.1**	**-5.8**	**-30.8**
电力、热力生产和供应业	Production and Supply of Electric Power and and Heat Power	-3.5	-9.2	34.2	-9.7
燃气生产和供应业	Production and Supply of Gas	-24.9	16.0	-51.6	-81.6
水的生产和供应业	Production and Supply of Water	-43.4	-43.7	-50.7	-36.2

4-5 续表 continued

单位:%

行 业	Sector	全部投资 Investment	新 建 New Construction	扩 建 Expension	改建和技术改 造 Reconstruction and Technical Transformation
建筑业	**Construction**	**-3.7**	**-17.3**		
交通运输、仓储和邮政业	**Transport, Storage and Post**	**-8.9**	**-9.4**	**-5.3**	**2.9**
铁路运输业	Railway Transport	-20.1	-20.8		90.6
道路运输业	Road Transport	-10.2	-11.7	-0.8	8.9
水上运输业	Water Transport	-29.8	-28.6	-34.4	-94.6
航空运输业	Air Transport	128.7	282.3	-53.9	-100.0
管道运输业	Transport via Pipelines	241.7	233.9		
多式联运和运输代理业	Intermodality and Forwarding Agency	-64.5	-63.2	-100.0	
装卸搬运和仓储业	Loading, Unloading and Storage	-5.2	-2.4	11.8	-78.0
邮政业	Post	76.2	87.5		50.1
信息传输、软件和信息技术服务业	**Information Transmission, Software and Information Technology Service**	**-33.5**	**-35.8**	**498.5**	**-4.7**
电信、广播电视和卫星传输服务	Telecom, Radio and Tv and Satellite Transmission Service	16.8	9.0	1860.0	10447.0
互联网和相关服务	Internet and Related Service	-53.9	-52.6	21.4	-30.6
软件和信息技术服务业	Software and Information Technology	-66.7	-70.5	-16.3	215.6
批发和零售业	**Wholesale and Retail Trades**	**-35.3**	**-34.8**	**-44.6**	**-31.0**
住宿和餐饮业	**Hotels and Catering Services**	**-21.3**	**-21.0**	**-37.2**	**-14.7**
金融业	**Financial Intermediation**	**-12.0**	**-11.1**		**-87.8**
房地产业	**Real Estate**	**-9.6**	**-30.7**	**-6.1**	**-1.6**
租赁和商务服务业	**Leasing and Commercial Services**	**6.5**	**5.8**	**8.3**	**30.7**
租赁业	Leasing	-47.0	-47.6	-100.0	
商务服务业	Business Services	7.4	6.7	12.2	30.7
科学研究和技术服务业	**Scientific Research and Technical Services**	**-28.5**	**-29.1**	**60.4**	**-29.6**
水利、环境和公共设施管理业	**Management of Water Conservancy, Environment and Public Facilities**	**-30.8**	**-29.6**	**-46.6**	**-24.0**
水利管理业	Management of Water Conservancy	-31.6	-32.3	-48.2	-12.6
生态保护和环境治理业	Ecological Protection and Environment Treatment	-22.4	-27.3	-3.4	5.7
公共设施管理业	Management of Public Facilities	-31.8	-29.6	-47.8	-34.7
土地管理业	Management of Land	0.1	16.0	-100.0	-100.0
居民服务、修理和其他服务业	**Service to Households, Repair and Others Services**	**-15.9**	**-11.7**	**-9.4**	**-32.7**
教育	**Education**	**-11.2**	**-9.2**	**-9.7**	**-55.6**
卫生和社会工作	**Health Care and Social Service**	**49.5**	**47.8**	**83.2**	**-13.0**
卫生	Health	65.8	67.2	94.6	-2.4
社会工作	Social Service	5.5	7.0	25.0	-63.2
文化、体育和娱乐业	**Culture, Sports and Entertainment**	**-20.5**	**-16.7**	**-51.1**	**-29.8**
广播、电视、电影和影视录音制作业	Radio, Television, Motion Picture and Videotape Programme	-69.3	-71.5	9.5	-80.6
文化艺术业	Culture and Art Activities	-32.1	-31.8	-51.5	9.2
体育	Sports Activities	-42.7	-38.0	-98.6	-43.5
娱乐业	Entertainment	-15.5	-11.3	-45.9	-30.6
公共管理、社会保障和社会组织	**Public Management, Social Security and Social Organization**	**-28.2**	**-10.7**	**-81.1**	**-58.7**

4-6 按行业分施工投产项目个数(2020)
Number of Projects under Construction and Put into Production by Sector (2020)

行业	Sector	施工项目(个) Number of Projects under Construction (unit)	#新开工 Newly Started	全部建成投产项目(个) Completion and Put into Production of All Projects (unit)	项目建成投产率(%) Rate of Completion and Put into Production (%)
总计	**Total**	**19047**	**8841**	**8324**	**43.7**
农、林、牧、渔业	**Farming, Forestry, Animal Husbandry and Fishery**	**970**	**512**	**501**	**51.6**
农业	Farming	374	169	219	58.6
林业	Forestry	44	12	23	52.3
畜牧业	Animal Husbandry	311	220	140	45.0
渔业	Fishery	77	30	38	49.4
农、林、牧、渔专业及辅助性活动	Professional and Support for Agriculture, Forestry, Animal Husbandry and Fishery	164	81	81	49.4
采矿业	**Mining**	**183**	**92**	**87**	**47.5**
制造业	**Manufacturing**	**8101**	**3973**	**3855**	**47.6**
农副食品加工业	Processing of Food from Agriculture Products	670	342	362	54.0
食品制造业	Manufacture of Foods	189	89	98	51.9
酒、饮料和精制茶制造业	Manufacture of Liquor, Beverages and Refined Tea	279	152	127	45.5
烟草制品业	Manufacture of Tobacco	14	8	5	35.7
纺织业	Manufacture of Textile	371	209	202	54.4
纺织服装、服饰业	Manufacture of Textile, Wearing Apparel and Accessaries	201	99	111	55.2
皮革、毛皮、羽毛及其制品和制鞋业	Manufacture of Leather, Fur, Feather and Related Products and Footwear	38	22	18	47.4
木材加工和木、竹、藤、棕、草制品业	Processing of Timber, Manufacture of Wood, Bamboo, Rattan, Palm and Straw Products	141	73	77	54.6
家具制造业	Manufacture of Furniture	134	47	73	54.5
造纸和纸制品业	Manufacture of Paper and Paper Products	93	47	38	40.9
印刷和记录媒介复制业	Printing and Reproduction of Recording Media	94	47	47	50.0
文教、工美、体育和娱乐用品制造业	Manufacture of Articles for Culture, Education, Arts and Crafts Sport and Entertainment Activities	61	32	30	49.2
石油、煤炭及其他燃料加工业	Processing of Petroleum, Coal and Other Fuels	56	28	19	33.9
化学原料和化学制品制造业	Manufacture of Raw Chemical Materials and Chemical Products	610	292	278	45.6
医药制造业	Manufacture of Medicines	455	257	211	46.4
化学纤维制造业	Manufacture of Chemical Fibres	21	11	9	42.9
橡胶和塑料制品业	Manufacture of Rubber and Plastic Products	317	164	150	47.3
非金属矿物制品业	Manufacture of Non-metallic Mineral Products	1021	536	491	48.1
黑色金属冶炼和压延加工业	Smelting and Pressing of Ferrous Metals	132	63	45	34.1
有色金属冶炼和压延加工业	Smelting and Pressing of Non-ferrous Metals	93	31	47	50.5
金属制品业	Manufacture of Metal Products	425	197	210	49.4
通用设备制造业	Manufacture of General Purpose Machinery	384	190	182	47.4
专用设备制造业	Manufacture of Special Purpose Machinery	416	215	190	45.7
汽车制造业	Manufacture of Automobiles	764	333	343	44.9
铁路、船舶、航空航天和其他运输设备制造业	Manufacture of Railway, Ship, Aerospace and Other Transport Equipment	73	36	34	46.6
电气机械和器材制造业	Manufacture of Electrical Machinery and Apparatus	387	164	168	43.4
计算机、通信和其他电子设备制造业	Manufacture of Computers, Communication and Other Electronic Equipment	415	160	176	42.4
仪器仪表制造业	Manufacture of Measuring Instruments and Machinery	48	18	20	41.7
其他制造业	Other Manufacture	21	12	10	47.6
废弃资源综合利用业	Utilization of Waste Resources	172	97	79	45.9
金属制品、机械和设备修理业	Repairing Service of Metal Products, Mechanical Equipment	6	2	5	83.3
电力、热力、燃气及水生产和供应业	**Production and Supply of Electricity, Heat, Gas and Water**	**691**	**298**	**276**	**39.9**
电力、热力生产和供应业	Production and Supply of Electric Power and and Heat Power	298	117	119	39.9
燃气生产和供应业	Production and Supply of Gas	61	24	21	34.4
水的生产和供应业	Production and Supply of Water	332	157	136	41.0

4-6 续表 continued

行 业	Sector	施工项目(个) Number of Projects under Construction (unit)	#新开工 Newly Started	全部建成投产项目(个) Completion and Put into Production of All Projects (unit)	项目建成投产率(%) Rate of Completion and Put into Production (%)
建筑业	**Construction**	**7**	**3**	**7**	**100.0**
交通运输、仓储和邮政业	**Transport, Storage and Post**	**1826**	**695**	**711**	**38.9**
铁路运输业	Railway Transport	37	7	8	21.6
道路运输业	Road Transport	1493	577	584	39.1
水上运输业	Water Transport	46	10	13	28.3
航空运输业	Air Transport	15	2	3	20.0
管道运输业	Transport via Pipelines	6	5		
多式联运和运输代理业	Intermodality and Forwarding Agency	12	4	9	75.0
装卸搬运和仓储业	Loading, Unloading and Storage	203	85	88	43.3
邮政业	Post	14	5	6	42.9
信息传输、软件和信息技术服务业	**Information Transmission, Software and Information Technology Service**	**99**	**52**	**34**	**34.3**
电信、广播电视和卫星传输服务	Telecom, Radio and Tv and Satellite Transmission Service	40	23	12	30.0
互联网和相关服务	Internet and Related Service	42	19	14	33.3
软件和信息技术服务业	Software and Information Technology	17	10	8	47.1
批发和零售业	**Wholesale and Retail Trades**	**300**	**150**	**143**	**47.7**
住宿和餐饮业	**Hotels and Catering Services**	**201**	**99**	**91**	**45.3**
金融业	**Financial Intermediation**	**9**	**2**	**9**	**100.0**
房地产业	**Real Estate**	**761**	**275**	**269**	**35.3**
租赁和商务服务业	**Leasing and Commercial Services**	**275**	**149**	**76**	**27.6**
租赁业	Leasing	4	2	3	75.0
商务服务业	Business Services	271	147	71	26.2
科学研究和技术服务业	**Scientific Research and Technical Services**	**138**	**55**	**44**	**31.9**
水利、环境和公共设施管理业	**Management of Water Conservancy, Environment and Public Facilities**	**3205**	**1373**	**1262**	**39.4**
水利管理业	Management of Water Conservancy	449	162	191	42.5
生态保护和环境治理业	Ecological Protection and Environment Treatment	298	120	119	39.9
公共设施管理业	Management of Public Facilities	2446	1089	944	38.6
土地管理业	Management of Land	12	2	8	66.7
居民服务、修理和其他服务业	**Service to Households, Repair and Others Services**	**90**	**50**	**44**	**48.9**
教育	**Education**	**629**	**308**	**246**	**39.1**
卫生和社会工作	**Health Care and Social Service**	**535**	**319**	**226**	**42.2**
卫生	Health	435	282	187	43.0
社会工作	Social Service	100	37	39	39.0
文化、体育和娱乐业	**Culture, Sports and Entertainment**	**832**	**350**	**356**	**42.8**
广播、电视、电影和影视录音制作业	Radio, Television, Motion Picture and Videotape Programme	12	4	6	50.0
文化艺术业	Culture and Art Activities	102	40	33	32.4
体育	Sports Activities	62	23	25	40.3
娱乐业	Entertainment	655	283	292	44.6
公共管理、社会保障和社会组织	**Public Management, Social Security and Social Organization**	**195**	**86**	**87**	**44.6**

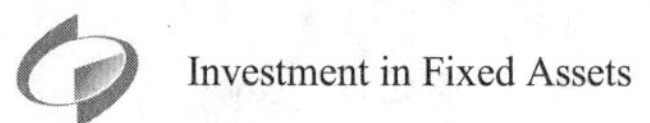

4-7 按国民经济行业分的固定资产投资增幅
Growth Rate of Investment in Fixed Assets by National Economic Sector

单位:%

行 业	Sector	2019	2020
总计	**Total**	**10.6**	**-18.8**
农、林、牧、渔业	**Farming, Forestry, Animal Husbandry and Fishery**	**17.0**	**-26.7**
农业	Farming	23.2	-45.1
林业	Forestry	6.6	-34.5
畜牧业	Animal Husbandry	8.1	50.8
渔业	Fishery	23.2	-67.2
农、林、牧、渔专业及辅助性活动	Professional and Support for Agriculture, Forestry, Animal Husbandry and Fishery	7.3	-16.2
采矿业	**Mining**	**0.3**	**-11.3**
制造业	**Manufacturing**	**10.0**	**-24.5**
农副食品加工业	Processing of Food from Agriculture Products	-0.5	-31.1
食品制造业	Manufacture of Foods	-16.9	-20.5
酒、饮料和精制茶制造业	Manufacture of Liquor, Beverages and Refined Tea	-0.2	-31.8
烟草制品业	Manufacture of Tobacco	-18.2	263.3
纺织业	Manufacture of Textile	16.9	-36.0
纺织服装、服饰业	Manufacture of Textile, Wearing Apparel and Accessaries	38.8	-44.4
皮革、毛皮、羽毛及其制品和制鞋业	Manufacture of Leather, Fur, Feather and Related Products and Footwear	-13.9	-54.5
木材加工和木、竹、藤、棕、草制品业	Processing of Timber, Manufacture of Wood, Bamboo, Rattan, Palm and Straw Products	26.8	-30.0
家具制造业	Manufacture of Furniture	34.3	-29.6
造纸和纸制品业	Manufacture of Paper and Paper Products	0.6	-48.7
印刷和记录媒介复制业	Printing and Reproduction of Recording Media	-8.4	-23.3
文教、工美、体育和娱乐用品制造业	Manufacture of Articles for Culture, Education, Arts and Crafts Sport and Entertainment Activities	-15.9	-37.2
石油、煤炭及其他燃料加工业	Processing of Petroleum, Coal and Other Fuels	-17.2	-13.3
化学原料和化学制品制造业	Manufacture of Raw Chemical Materials and Chemical Products	18.1	-27.1
医药制造业	Manufacture of Medicines	-10.3	20.4
化学纤维制造业	Manufacture of Chemical Fibres	40.4	-8.9
橡胶和塑料制品业	Manufacture of Rubber and Plastic Products	10.7	-7.4
非金属矿物制品业	Manufacture of Non-metallic Mineral Products	11.8	-21.9
黑色金属冶炼和压延加工业	Smelting and Pressing of Ferrous Metals	18.6	10.6
有色金属冶炼和压延加工业	Smelting and Pressing of Non-ferrous Metals	10.0	6.4
金属制品业	Manufacture of Metal Products	29.4	-35.7
通用设备制造业	Manufacture of General Purpose Machinery	14.9	-28.9
专用设备制造业	Manufacture of Special Purpose Machinery	0.2	-38.8
汽车制造业	Manufacture of Automobiles	3.4	-30.3
铁路、船舶、航空航天和其他运输设备制造业	Manufacture of Railway, Ship, Aerospace and Other Transport Equipment	9.8	-31.0
电气机械和器材制造业	Manufacture of Electrical Machinery and Apparatus	-18.6	-27.2
计算机、通信和其他电子设备制造业	Manufacture of Computers, Communication and Other Electronic Equipment	38.6	-5.0
仪器仪表制造业	Manufacture of Measuring Instruments and Machinery	40.1	-36.4
其他制造业	Other Manufacture	66.2	-41.8
废弃资源综合利用业	Utilization of Waste Resources	55.5	-9.6
金属制品、机械和设备修理业	Repairing Service of Metal Products, Mechanical Equipment	106.2	-79.8
电力、热力、燃气及水生产和供应业	**Production and Supply of Electricity, Heat, Gas and Water**	**-7.2**	**-19.9**
电力、热力生产和供应业	Production and Supply of Electric Power and and Heat Power	0.3	-3.5
燃气生产和供应业	Production and Supply of Gas	-7.0	-24.9
水的生产和供应业	Production and Supply of Water	-16.5	-43.4

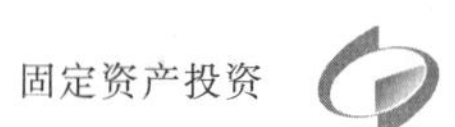

4-7 续表 continued

单位:%

行 业	Sector	2019	2020
建筑业	**Construction**	**-97.5**	**-3.7**
交通运输、仓储和邮政业	**Transport, Storage and Post**	**5.4**	**-8.9**
铁路运输业	Railway Transport	-29.4	-20.1
道路运输业	Road Transport	12.6	-10.2
水上运输业	Water Transport	-19.1	-29.8
航空运输业	Air Transport	158.6	128.7
管道运输业	Transport via Pipelines	-26.5	241.7
多式联运和运输代理业	Intermodality and Forwarding Agency	-19.8	-64.5
装卸搬运和仓储业	Loading, Unloading and Storage	-11.4	-5.2
邮政业	Post	5168.3	76.2
信息传输、软件和信息技术服务业	**Information Transmission, Software and Information Technology Service**	**58.6**	**-33.5**
电信、广播电视和卫星传输服务	Telecom, Radio and Tv and Satellite Transmission Service	24.6	16.8
互联网和相关服务	Internet and Related Service	126.2	-53.9
软件和信息技术服务业	Software and Information Technology	12.4	-66.7
批发和零售业	**Wholesale and Retail Trades**	**-6.5**	**-35.3**
住宿和餐饮业	**Hotels and Catering Services**	**15.2**	**-21.3**
金融业	**Financial Intermediation**	**-16.1**	**-12.0**
房地产业	**Real Estate**	**8.1**	**-9.6**
租赁和商务服务业	**Leasing and Commercial Services**	**14.2**	**6.5**
租赁业	Leasing	-21.8	-47.0
商务服务业	Business Services	15.0	7.4
科学研究和技术服务业	**Scientific Research and Technical Services**	**27.5**	**-28.5**
水利、环境和公共设施管理业	**Management of Water Conservancy, Environment and Public Facilities**	**18.0**	**-30.8**
水利管理业	Management of Water Conservancy	13.6	-31.6
生态保护和环境治理业	Ecological Protection and Environment Treatment	44.4	-22.4
公共设施管理业	Management of Public Facilities	16.4	-31.8
土地管理业	Management of Land	-15.8	0.1
居民服务、修理和其他服务业	**Service to Households, Repair and Others Services**	**-12.1**	**-15.9**
教育	**Education**	**61.4**	**-11.2**
卫生和社会工作	**Health Care and Social Service**	**-2.1**	**49.5**
卫生	Health	-7.4	65.8
社会工作	Social Service	15.6	5.5
文化、体育和娱乐业	**Culture, Sports and Entertainment**	**69.6**	**-20.5**
广播、电视、电影和影视录音制作业	Radio, Television, Motion Picture and Videotape Programme	24.8	-69.3
文化艺术业	Culture and Art Activities	7.3	-32.1
体育	Sports Activities	-13.4	-42.7
娱乐业	Entertainment	109.5	-15.5
公共管理、社会保障和社会组织	**Public Management, Social Security and Social Organization**	**-27.4**	**-28.2**

4-8 按资金来源和构成分固定资产投资
Investment in Fixed Assets by Funds Source and Composition

年份 Year	按资金来源分 Grouped by Source of Finance					按构成分 Grouped by Use of Funds		
	国家预算内资金 State Budgetary Appropriations	国内贷款 Domestic Loans	利用外资 Foreign Investment	自筹资金 Fund Raising	其他资金来源 Others	建筑安装工程 Construction Installation	设备工器具购置 Purchases of Equipment and Instruments	其他费用 Others
投资额(亿元) Investment (100 million yuan)								
1990	11.38	22.22	4.79	92.96	13.09	92.64	41.02	10.78
1995	58.40	173.47	88.71	422.92	83.00	454.40	248.51	123.59
1998	85.18	225.95	33.86	703.44	182.66	695.55	323.47	212.08
1999	108.18	207.61	36.57	730.92	218.89	771.24	329.26	201.67
2000	141.48	243.90	28.28	781.50	226.39	814.66	371.56	235.33
2001	174.03	241.96	29.89	874.60	231.27	890.60	419.20	241.95
2002	200.95	280.11	63.22	717.24	433.69	974.73	418.55	301.94
2003	150.20	291.60	57.41	786.40	597.98	1059.98	463.23	360.38
2004	197.03	383.78	64.74	1182.36	528.47	1409.25	537.25	409.88
2005	255.76	474.21	71.34	1492.66	540.78	1696.80	642.86	495.09
2006	378.79	708.39	79.32	1902.71	503.48	2252.72	717.10	602.87
2007	472.98	790.84	88.37	2470.28	711.66	2857.31	896.36	780.47
2008	570.17	894.57	57.02	3677.00	599.80	3568.96	1245.73	983.87
2009	711.93	1432.89	68.32	4956.88	1041.83	5025.62	1753.28	1432.95
2010	868.46	1768.79	147.03	6703.61	1314.80	6701.91	2308.73	1792.05
2011	663.18	1707.46	189.26	8800.61	1574.51	8056.52	2812.91	2065.59
2012	784.27	1964.14	131.64	11812.15	1811.96	11054.16	3162.99	2287.02
2013	886.58	2720.19	66.82	14823.15	2257.17	14312.25	3856.68	2584.98
2014	1107.45	2874.92	78.99	18732.35	2208.06	18185.42	4292.85	2523.50
2015	1339.03	2907.66	46.86	22470.65	2426.86	21826.03	4845.70	2519.33
2016	1829.24	3068.40	59.01	20623.21	3924.02	22876.58	4124.21	2503.08
2017	2326.38	3078.89	65.59	21408.69	4993.03	23772.98	4891.02	3208.57
构成(%) Composition (%)								
1990	7.9	15.4	3.3	64.4	9.0	64.1	28.4	7.5
1995	7.1	21.0	10.7	51.2	10.0	58.6	30.3	11.1
1998	6.9	18.4	2.8	57.1	14.8	70.2	18.4	11.4
1999	8.3	15.9	2.8	56.1	16.9	63.4	26.5	10.1
2000	10.0	17.2	2.0	55.0	15.8	64.3	23.9	11.8
2001	11.2	15.6	1.9	56.4	14.9	64.8	24.3	10.9
2002	11.9	16.5	3.7	42.3	25.6	64.4	23.6	12.1
2003	8.0	15.5	3.0	41.8	31.7	60.9	23.4	15.7
2004	8.4	16.3	2.7	50.2	22.4	63.9	20.8	15.3
2005	9.0	16.7	2.5	52.7	19.1	59.9	22.7	17.4
2006	10.6	19.8	2.2	53.3	14.1	63.1	20.1	16.8
2007	12.6	19.7	1.3	81.1	13.2	78.7	27.5	21.7
2008	9.8	15.4	1.0	63.4	10.4	61.5	21.5	17.0
2009	8.7	17.4	0.8	60.4	12.7	61.2	21.4	17.4
2010	8.1	16.4	1.4	62.1	12.0	62.0	21.4	16.6
2011	5.1	13.2	1.5	68.0	12.2	62.3	21.7	16.0
2012	4.8	11.9	0.8	71.6	11.0	67.0	19.2	13.9
2013	4.3	13.1	0.3	71.4	10.9	69.0	18.6	12.4
2014	4.4	11.5	0.3	74.9	8.9	72.7	17.2	10.1
2015	4.6	10.0	0.2	77.0	8.3	74.8	16.6	8.6
2016	6.2	10.4	0.2	69.9	13.3	77.5	14.0	8.5
2017	7.3	9.7	0.2	67.2	15.7	74.6	15.3	10.1
2018	6.1	11.3	0.2	61.2	21.2	74.2	13.8	12.0
2019	5.4	10.5	0.4	62.4	21.3	74.3	14.0	11.7
2020	6.3	11.1	0.6	61.3	20.7	74.3	13.4	12.3

注：从2011年起固定资产投资统计口径调整为计划总投资500万元及以上项目，取消城镇农村公布口径，其他年份未做相应调整。

Note: Since 2011, the fixed assets investment statistical adjustment plan for a total investment of 5 million yuan RMB and the above project, cancel the town and countryside, other years did not do corresponding adjustment.

4-9 按国民经济行业分的改建和技术改造投资增幅
Growth Rate of Investment in Reconstruction and Technological Transformation by National Economic Sector

单位:%

行 业	Sector	2019	2020
总计	**Total**	**12.4**	**-28.6**
农、林、牧、渔业	**Farming, Forestry, Animal Husbandry and Fishery**	**-35.3**	**-26.7**
农业	Farming	-16.5	-47.0
林业	Forestry	-29.0	-7.2
畜牧业	Animal Husbandry	-18.6	-9.3
渔业	Fishery	-73.9	-82.1
农、林、牧、渔专业及辅助性活动	Professional and Support for Agriculture, Forestry, Animal Husbandry and Fishery	-35.8	1.1
采矿业	**Mining**	**32.3**	**-19.7**
制造业	**Manufacturing**	**14.9**	**-31.6**
农副食品加工业	Processing of Food from Agriculture Products	6.8	-44.7
食品制造业	Manufacture of Foods	11.4	-38.4
酒、饮料和精制茶制造业	Manufacture of Liquor, Beverages and Refined Tea	3.4	-32.5
烟草制品业	Manufacture of Tobacco	-47.1	175.6
纺织业	Manufacture of Textile	5.7	-46.3
纺织服装、服饰业	Manufacture of Textile, Wearing Apparel and Accessaries	9.1	-75.0
皮革、毛皮、羽毛及其制品和制鞋业	Manufacture of Leather, Fur, Feather and Related Products and Footwear	-25.8	-59.1
木材加工和木、竹、藤、棕、草制品业	Processing of Timber, Manufacture of Wood, Bamboo, Rattan, Palm and Straw Products	89.6	-48.0
家具制造业	Manufacture of Furniture	49.6	-54.3
造纸和纸制品业	Manufacture of Paper and Paper Products	-0.9	-41.6
印刷和记录媒介复制业	Printing and Reproduction of Recording Media	-21.9	-17.3
文教、工美、体育和娱乐用品制造业	Manufacture of Articles for Culture, Education, Arts and Crafts Sport and Entertainment Activities	-57.3	-36.1
石油、煤炭及其他燃料加工业	Processing of Petroleum, Coal and Other Fuels	8.5	16.0
化学原料和化学制品制造业	Manufacture of Raw Chemical Materials and Chemical Products	10.2	-31.4
医药制造业	Manufacture of Medicines	-16.2	40.1
化学纤维制造业	Manufacture of Chemical Fibres	-35.1	-48.1
橡胶和塑料制品业	Manufacture of Rubber and Plastic Products	28.8	-19.8
非金属矿物制品业	Manufacture of Non-metallic Mineral Products	21.5	-30.2
黑色金属冶炼和压延加工业	Smelting and Pressing of Ferrous Metals	159.0	15.6
有色金属冶炼和压延加工业	Smelting and Pressing of Non-ferrous Metals	-11.3	-15.7
金属制品业	Manufacture of Metal Products	25.6	-35.6
通用设备制造业	Manufacture of General Purpose Machinery	5.7	-34.9
专用设备制造业	Manufacture of Special Purpose Machinery	61.7	-62.3
汽车制造业	Manufacture of Automobiles	14.4	-31.6
铁路、船舶、航空航天和其他运输设备制造业	Manufacture of Railway, Ship, Aerospace and Other Transport Equipment	77.9	-58.5
电气机械和器材制造业	Manufacture of Electrical Machinery and Apparatus	-12.4	-27.1
计算机、通信和其他电子设备制造业	Manufacture of Computers, Communication and Other Electronic Equipment	11.3	47.9
仪器仪表制造业	Manufacture of Measuring Instruments and Machinery	28.4	-64.7
其他制造业	Other Manufacture	15.6	-36.3
废弃资源综合利用业	Utilization of Waste Resources	47.4	-54.3
金属制品、机械和设备修理业	Repairing Service of Metal Products, Mechanical Equipment	-14.3	-85.8
电力、热力、燃气及水生产和供应业	**Production and Supply of Electricity, Heat, Gas and Water**	**-28.5**	**-30.8**
电力、热力生产和供应业	Production and Supply of Electric Power and and Heat Power	-8.9	-9.7
燃气生产和供应业	Production and Supply of Gas	40.5	-81.6
水的生产和供应业	Production and Supply of Water	-54.2	-36.2

4-9 续表 continued

单位:%

行 业	Sector	2019	2020
建筑业	**Construction**	**-100.0**	
交通运输、仓储和邮政业	**Transport, Storage and Post**	**-14.3**	**2.9**
铁路运输业	Railway Transport	-95.0	90.6
道路运输业	Road Transport	-5.2	8.9
水上运输业	Water Transport	-86.8	-94.6
航空运输业	Air Transport	338.0	-100.0
管道运输业	Transport via Pipelines		
多式联运和运输代理业	Intermodality and Forwarding Agency	-100.0	
装卸搬运和仓储业	Loading, Unloading and Storage	-51.4	-78.0
邮政业	Post		50.1
信息传输、软件和信息技术服务业	**Information Transmission, Software and Information Technology Service**	**-7.2**	**-4.7**
电信、广播电视和卫星传输服务	Telecom, Radio and Tv and Satellite Transmission Service	-98.9	
互联网和相关服务	Internet and Related Service	10.1	-30.6
软件和信息技术服务业	Software and Information Technology	-25.7	215.6
批发和零售业	**Wholesale and Retail Trades**	**-53.1**	**-31.0**
住宿和餐饮业	**Hotels and Catering Services**	**32.9**	**-14.7**
金融业	**Financial Intermediation**	**14.1**	**-87.8**
房地产业	**Real Estate**	**-29.6**	**-1.6**
租赁和商务服务业	**Leasing and Commercial Services**	**0.6**	**30.7**
租赁业	Leasing		
商务服务业	Business Services	0.6	30.7
科学研究和技术服务业	**Scientific Research and Technical Services**	**615.8**	**-29.6**
水利、环境和公共设施管理业	**Management of Water Conservancy, Environment and Public Facilities**	**51.0**	**-24.0**
水利管理业	Management of Water Conservancy	-6.5	-12.6
生态保护和环境治理业	Ecological Protection and Environment Treatment	247.6	5.7
公共设施管理业	Management of Public Facilities	43.8	-34.7
土地管理业	Management of Land	10.7	-100.0
居民服务、修理和其他服务业	**Service to Households, Repair and Others Services**	**26.4**	**-32.7**
教育	**Education**	**-37.4**	**-55.6**
卫生和社会工作	**Health Care and Social Service**	**-19.0**	**-13.0**
卫生	Health	-17.5	-2.4
社会工作	Social Service	-25.7	-63.2
文化、体育和娱乐业	**Culture, Sports and Entertainment**	**23.8**	**-29.8**
广播、电视、电影和影视录音制作业	Radio, Television, Motion Picture and Videotape Programme	-36.2	-80.6
文化艺术业	Culture and Art Activities	-77.1	9.2
体育	Sports Activities	-27.0	-43.5
娱乐业	Entertainment	135.8	-30.6
公共管理、社会保障和社会组织	**Public Management, Social Security and Social Organization**	**35.9**	**-58.7**

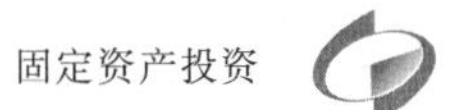

4-10 房地产开发投资主要指标
Major Indicators of Investment in Real Estate Development

指标	Item	1990	1995	2000	2005	2010
企业个数 （个）	**Number of Enterprises (unit)**	**129**	**571**	**1052**	**1990**	**3556**
内资	Inner Funded	129	404	848	1782	3395
#国有	State-owned	129	292	380	228	187
集体	Collective-owned		51	105	74	66
港澳台投资	Funded by Enterprises from Hongkong, Macao and Taiwan		68	149	129	106
外商投资	Foreign Funded		99	55	79	55
投资完成额 （亿元）	**Investment Completed This Year (100 million yuan)**	**5.94**	**121.13**	**134.63**	**447.95**	**1618.24**
按构成分	Grouped by Use of Funds					
#建筑安装工程	Construction Projects	5.45	89.56	99.59	315.15	1059.26
设备工器具购置	Installation Projects		4.47	2.83	4.68	29.07
按工程用途分	Grouped by Use of Projects					
#住宅	Residential Houses	4.70	61.78	93.15	317.65	1040.25
#经济适用房屋	Economical Houses		7.44	23.53	13.49	40.33
资金来源	Grouped by Source of Finance	5.94	138.88	117.88	513.44	2219.50
国内贷款	Domestic Loans	1.21	39.01	18.08	100.41	415.43
利用外资	Foreign Investments		16.35	1.15	1.82	97.29
自筹投资	Fund Raising	3.72	41.26	47.27	186.95	784.39
其他投资	Others	1.01	42.26	51.38	224.26	922.40
房屋建筑面积 （万平方米）	**Floor Space of Building (10 000 sq.m)**					
施工面积	Floor Space Under Construction	390.11	2049.30	2102.86	4804.35	11589.44
#住宅	Residential Buildings	325.82	1299.03	1673.84	4012.13	9172.43
竣工面积	Floor Spaace Completed	183.91	518.88	843.55	1627.03	2541.21
#住宅	Residential Buildings	156.77	427.19	733.27	1411.67	2129.33
土地开发及购置 （万平方米）	**Land Development and Purchase (10 000 sq.m)**					
本年土地开发面积	Area of Land Development This Year		903.00	469.28	941.26	
本年土地购置面积	Area of Land Purchased This Year		719.00	838.12	1530.64	1422.06
商品房销售情况	**Selling of Commercial Houses**					
房屋销售面积 （万平方米）	Floor Psace of Selling Houses (10 000 sq.m)	130.53	240.00	612.05	1708.02	3508.61
#住宅	Residential Buildings	112.67	211.00	571.04	1549.19	3236.88
#经济适用房	Economic Houses		40.00	172.99	111.31	99.48
商品房销售额 （亿元）	Sales Value of Commercial House (100 million yuan)	6.93	31.00	83.74	386.57	1313.20
#住宅	Residential Buildings				335.19	1134.94

注：本表资金来源均为资金到位数；从2010年起本年土地开发面积指标取消；从2011年起经济适用房分组指标取消。

Note: The source of capital in this table are the number of achieved funds; From 2010 the land development indicators of this year had been canceled. From 2011 the group index of affordable housing had been canceled.

4-10 续表 continued

指 标	Item	2016	2017	2018	2019	2020
企业个数 （个）	**Number of Enterprises (unit)**	4280	4039	4300	4275	4186
内资	Inner Funded	4173	3936	4195	4180	4090
#国有	State-owned	74	61	41	43	52
集体	Collective-owned	15	11	11	9	6
港澳台投资	Funded by Enterprises from Hongkong, Macao and Taiwan	83	76	72	64	60
外商投资	Foreign Funded	24	27	33	31	36
投资完成额 （亿元）	**Investment Completed This Year (100 million yuan)**	4296.38	4574.89	4676.12	5111.73	4888.87
按构成分	Grouped by Use of Funds					
#建筑安装工程	Construction Projects	3377.98	3232.22	3122.66	3457.7	3349.54
设备工器具购置	Installation Projects	75.45	102.53	72.23	94.99	69.19
按工程用途分	Grouped by Use of Projects					
#住宅	Residential Houses	3012.35	3235.42	3453.66	3954.72	3715.43
#经济适用房屋	Economical Houses					
资金来源	Grouped by Source of Finance	5696.35	6438.19	7388.38	6824.77	5947.60
国内贷款	Domestic Loans	1031.66	976.97	1150.01	1065.73	766.43
利用外资	Foreign Investments	0.80	1.15	0.00	10.33	2.11
自筹投资	Fund Raising	2175.22	2257.39	2520.42	2094.25	2039.31
其他投资	Others	2488.67	3202.68	276.81	212.21	260.67
房屋建筑面积 （万平方米）	**Floor Space of Building (10 000 sq.m)**					
施工面积	Floor Space Under Construction	29879.88	30510.48	31281.35	33825.07	35419.40
#住宅	Residential Buildings	21803.01	22479.79	23362.74	25540.84	26598.05
竣工面积	Floor Spaace Completed	3127.49	3219.72	2770.46	2558.60	2646.83
#住宅	Residential Buildings	2348.38	2433.72	2088.15	2019.29	2166.11
土地开发及购置 （万平方米）	**Land Development and Purchase (10 000 sq.m)**					
本年土地开发面积	Area of Land Development This Year					
本年土地购置面积	Area of Land Purchased This Year	648.64	676.44	956.58	784.90	710.80
商品房销售情况	**Selling of Commercial Houses**					
房屋销售面积 （万平方米）	Floor Psace of Selling Houses (10 000 sq.m)	7427.16	8155.21	8858.35	8602.04	6587.83
#住宅	Residential Buildings	6789.21	7363.67	8094.76	7967.09	5960.08
#经济适用房	Economic Houses					
商品房销售额 （亿元）	Sales Value of Commercial House (100 million yuan)	4994.05	6258.92	7525.89	7751.79	6087.90
#住宅	Residential Buildings	4383.81	5380.31	6585.94	6903.70	5447.32

4-11 按登记注册类型分房地产开发投资(2020)
Investment in Real Estate Development by Registration Status(2020)

单位:亿元 (100 million yuan)

项 目	Item	总 计 Total	内 资 Inner Funded	国 有 State-owned	集 体 Collective-owned	港澳台商投资 Hongkong, Macao and Taiwan Funded	外商投资 Foreign Investment
企业个数 (个)	**Number of Enterprises (unit)**	**4186**	**4090**	**52**	**6**	**60**	**36**
#亏损企业个数	Loss-Making Enterprises	2126	2073	46	1	32	21
本年完成投资	**Investment Completed This Year**	**4888.87**	**4667.16**	**104.04**	**3.44**	**141.40**	**80.31**
按构成分	**Grouped by Use of Funds**						
建筑工程	Construction Projects	3054.68	2912.89	50.41	2.24	83.11	58.68
安装工程	Installation Projects	294.86	289.78	5.79	0.52	4.75	0.33
设备工器具购置	Purchase of Equipment, Tools and Instruments	69.19	68.52	0.67	0.41	0.64	0.03
其他费用	Other Funds	1470.14	1395.98	47.16	0.27	52.90	21.26
#土地购置费	Purchase of Land	1150.41	1100.12	36.83		37.06	13.22
按构成用途分	**Grouped by Use of Projects**						
住宅	Residential Buildings	3715.43	3565.56	68.20	0.69	87.14	62.73
#经济适用房	Economical Houses						
别墅、高档公寓	Villa, Top Grade Flat						
办公楼	Office Building	271.57	250.88	8.94	0.01	12.60	8.10
商业营业用房	Business Buildings	447.22	410.90	7.01	2.33	27.53	8.79
其他	Others	454.65	439.83	19.89	0.40	14.13	0.70
本年新增固定资产	**Newly Increased Fixed Assets This Year**	**1241.83**	**1236.86**	**5.93**		**4.97**	
资金来源	**Finance Sources**	**5947.60**	**5705.40**	**138.25**	**3.15**	**141.92**	**100.28**
国内贷款	Domestic Loans	766.43	737.81	10.57		15.99	12.63
利用外资	Foreign Investments	2.11	1.71	0.02			0.40
自筹资金	Fund Raising	2039.31	1986.88	83.17	1.02	35.92	16.51
定金及预收款	Deposit and Pre Payment	1951.19	1841.66	42.10	0.57	54.41	55.13
个人按揭贷款	Individual Mortgage Loans	927.88	881.30	2.27	0.97	30.96	15.62
其他到位资金	Others	260.67	256.03	0.12	0.59	4.64	
土地开发 (万平方米)	**Land Development (10 000 sq.m)**						
待开发土地面积	Area of Land to be Developed	2416.43	2351.19	6.95		48.78	16.46
本年购置土地面积	Area of Land Purchased This Year	710.80	710.80	7.52			
本年土地成交价款	Value of Land Transaction	475.74	475.74	2.14			

注:本表资金来源均为资金到位数,从2010年起土地开发投资额和本年土地开发面积指标取消。

Note: The sources of capital in this table are the number of achieved funds. From 2010, the indicators of investment and area of land development had been canceled.

4-12 市、州固定资产投资增幅
Growth Rate of Investment in Fixed Assets of Cities and Prefectures

单位:%

市、州	Cities and Prefectures	2012	2013	2014	2015	2016	2017	2018	2019	2020
全 省	**Total**	**27.6**	**25.8**	**20.4**	**16.2**	**13.1**	**11.0**	**11.0**	**10.6**	**-18.8**
武汉市	Wuhan	20.1	19.1	16.5	10.3	-2.8	11.0	10.6	9.8	-11.8
黄石市	Huangshi	25.2	28.7	21.3	17.6	10.2	14.0	11.1	12.6	-18.4
十堰市	Shiyan	34.5	30.5	21.9	17.8	18.0	16.6	11.7	11.8	-21.1
宜昌市	Yichang	34.3	29.4	22.1	18.2	18.8	-19.1	11.3	12.1	-20.5
襄阳市	Xiangyang	40.1	29.9	22.5	19.3	18.7	15.3	11.5	12.1	-20.6
鄂州市	Ezhou	34.6	28.1	21.1	17.3	17.0	15.3	10.8	12.2	-17.2
荆门市	Jingmen	35.7	28.5	21.6	18.0	18.9	16.9	11.5	12.0	-21.3
孝感市	Xiaogan	35.7	29.3	22.0	18.8	17.3	7.5	11.4	12.3	-20.8
荆州市	Jingzhou	36.1	29.3	22.0	18.0	18.0	11.5	11.0	11.7	-22.4
黄冈市	Huanggang	34.9	28.8	21.4	18.1	13.4	8.1	11.0	11.3	-21.9
咸宁市	Xianning	34.6	28.9	20.5	17.5	17.6	16.5	11.3	11.7	-21.7
随州市	Suizhou	34.9	28.4	22.3	18.1	17.7	16.3	11.2	11.3	-23.3
恩施自治州	Enshi	29.7	25.4	20.5	17.3	17.0	15.5	11.2	11.0	-22.1
仙桃市	Xiantao	36.2	30.1	22.1	18.9	18.8	16.9	11.9	11.4	-37.2
潜江市	Qianjiang	36.0	29.3	21.8	17.9	16.3	16.7	11.3	12.4	-23.3
天门市	Tianmen	36.1	30.3	21.5	17.9	17.8	16.4	11.3	4.3	-26.8
神农架林区	Shennongjia	27.2	28.1	20.7	16.9	15.3	9.2	10.2	10.2	-25.8

注:2006年固资资产(城镇投资)不含城镇工矿区私人建房投资(下同)。由于方法制度调整,按可比口径计算,2005年扣除城镇工矿区私人建房投资基数应为2788.92亿元,各市、州固资资产未做调整。从2011年起固定资产投资统计口径调整为计划总投资500万元及以上项目,取消城镇农村公布口径,其他年份未做相应调整。

Note: In 2006 the investment (town investment) does not contain town private house industrial investment (the same below). Because method system adjustment, the comparable caliber calculation, 2005 deduct industrial town private house should be 278.892 billion yuan investment base; Since 2011, the fixed assets investment statistical adjustment plan for a total investment of 5 million yuan RMB and the above project, cancel the town and countryside, other years did not corresponding adjustment.

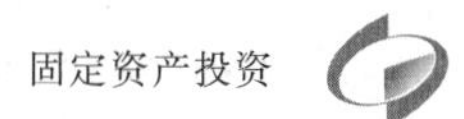

4-13 市、州民间固定资产投资增幅
Growth Rate of Non-governmental Investment of Fixed Assets of Cities and Prefectures

单位:%

市、州	Cities and Prefectures	2019	2020
全 省	**Total**	**11.6**	**-21.3**
武汉市	Wuhan	8.0	-18.8
黄石市	Huangshi	12.7	-19.8
十堰市	Shiyan	17.4	-5.9
宜昌市	Yichang	17.1	-19.9
襄阳市	Xiangyang	10.3	-24.7
鄂州市	Ezhou	6.9	-26.8
荆门市	Jingmen	13.2	-17.2
孝感市	Xiaogan	9.0	-22.2
荆州市	Jingzhou	10.0	-27.8
黄冈市	Huanggang	11.7	-20.6
咸宁市	Xianning	19.6	-21.5
随州市	Suizhou	10.3	-28.7
恩施自治州	Enshi	23.4	-8.2
仙桃市	Xiantao	7.4	-51.1
潜江市	Qianjiang	15.2	-29.5
天门市	Tianmen	3.8	-27.3
神农架林区	Shennongjia	0.0	-46.2

4-14 市、州基础设施投资增幅
Growth Rate of Infrastructure Investment of Cities and Prefectures

单位:%

市、州	Cities and Prefectures	2020
全 省	**Total**	**-22.8**
武汉市	Wuhan	-16.7
黄石市	Huangshi	-27.6
十堰市	Shiyan	-35.0
宜昌市	Yichang	-26.9
襄阳市	Xiangyang	-19.0
鄂州市	Ezhou	29.0
荆门市	Jingmen	-35.3
孝感市	Xiaogan	-10.1
荆州市	Jingzhou	-30.7
黄冈市	Huanggang	-23.3
咸宁市	Xianning	-32.2
随州市	Suizhou	-27.0
恩施自治州	Enshi	-39.8
仙桃市	Xiantao	13.0
潜江市	Qianjiang	-13.7
天门市	Tianmen	-45.3
神农架林区	Shennongjia	-35.0

4-15 市、州工业投资增幅
Growth Rate of Industrial Investment in Fixed Assets of Cities and Prefectures

单位：%

市、州	Cities and Prefectures	2019	2020
全　省	**Total**	**8.1**	**-23.9**
武汉市	Wuhan	16.3	-20.4
黄石市	Huangshi	6.8	-21.1
十堰市	Shiyan	10.3	-6.6
宜昌市	Yichang	10.0	-21.9
襄阳市	Xiangyang	4.0	-30.3
鄂州市	Ezhou	-9.8	-49.8
荆门市	Jingmen	12.2	-22.1
孝感市	Xiaogan	10.0	-31.4
荆州市	Jingzhou	-0.2	-27.4
黄冈市	Huanggang	5.2	-20.4
咸宁市	Xianning	10.7	-23.6
随州市	Suizhou	8.6	-29.8
恩施自治州	Enshi	11.4	-6.0
仙桃市	Xiantao	11.1	-49.4
潜江市	Qianjiang	-7.7	-25.3
天门市	Tianmen	-5.5	-11.6
神农架林区	Shennongjia	-34.3	-39.1

4-16 市州改建和技术改造投资增幅
Growth Rate of Investment in Reconstruction and Technological Transformation of Cities and Prefectures

单位：%

市、州	Cities and Prefectures	2019	2020
全　省	**Total**	**12.4**	**-28.6**
武汉市	Wuhan	44.6	-27.2
黄石市	Huangshi	21.0	-43.4
十堰市	Shiyan	7.4	-30.2
宜昌市	Yichang	26.4	-28.3
襄阳市	Xiangyang	18.0	-15.8
鄂州市	Ezhou	10.2	-72.5
荆门市	Jingmen	-4.0	-26.5
孝感市	Xiaogan	-15.7	-24.5
荆州市	Jingzhou	15.9	-27.4
黄冈市	Huanggang	-20.4	-13.0
咸宁市	Xianning	39.8	-10.4
随州市	Suizhou	-5.8	-50.8
恩施自治州	Enshi	30.3	-7.2
仙桃市	Xiantao	-21.4	-62.9
潜江市	Qianjiang	-9.2	-38.1
天门市	Tianmen	-2.7	-13.3
神农架林区	Shennongjia	-1.9	-42.2

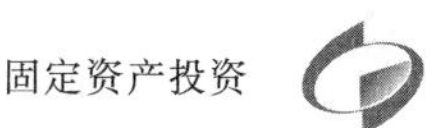

4-17 市、州房地产开发投资
Investment in Real Estate Development of Cities and Prefectures

单位:亿元 (100 million yuan)

市、州	Cities and Prefectures	2012	2013	2014	2015	2016	2017	2018	2019	2020
全 省	**Total**	**2539.46**	**3286.02**	**3983.79**	**4249.23**	**4296.38**	**4574.89**	**4676.12**	**5111.73**	**4888.87**
武汉市	Wuhan	1574.86	1905.60	2353.63	2581.79	2517.44	2686.34	2780.13	2966.21	2777.15
黄石市	Huangshi	56.04	84.68	115.77	130.14	132.37	156.29	149.13	170.57	141.85
十堰市	Shiyan	76.64	101.11	90.80	83.01	87.28	66.50	76.95	95.34	109.07
宜昌市	Yichang	176.59	203.18	194.60	241.89	244.18	197.85	256.30	263.63	242.97
襄阳市	Xiangyang	186.19	301.94	330.94	334.58	340.76	336.49	287.36	263.53	283.77
鄂州市	Ezhou	11.65	22.78	20.39	21.09	22.88	29.23	36.71	59.41	80.77
荆门市	Jingmen	64.31	87.79	123.98	118.11	100.39	94.36	111.64	140.37	163.33
孝感市	Xiaogan	74.95	111.13	136.35	171.58	160.02	175.66	181.36	198.18	174.15
荆州市	Jingzhou	54.89	76.79	134.17	113.33	151.53	238.12	194.51	270.68	270.97
黄冈市	Huanggang	78.57	132.73	174.27	200.05	265.73	284.33	238.66	268.16	242.97
咸宁市	Xianning	84.96	112.06	109.14	59.94	56.99	62.74	65.92	54.42	69.33
随州市	Suizhou	19.79	29.23	33.98	28.77	24.05	38.04	39.95	57.67	58.17
恩施自治州	Enshi	40.28	57.06	91.54	100.99	130.75	131.50	142.70	171.94	174.01
仙桃市	Xiantao	15.66	26.62	24.80	22.66	19.23	35.87	39.72	44.15	31.77
潜江市	Qianjiang	9.15	18.11	22.58	15.60	21.06	23.25	30.61	34.00	36.54
天门市	Tianmen	14.93	15.24	26.84	25.68	21.73	18.34	43.56	52.70	31.51
神农架林区	Shennongjia							0.91	0.77	0.54

4-18 按构成分的固定资产投资
Investment in Fixed Assets by Composition of Investment

单位:亿元 (100 million yuan)

年 份	全 省			# 地方		
In copies	建筑安装工程 Building Installation	设备工具器具购置 Equipment Tools, Equipment Purchase	其他费用 Other Expenses	建筑安装工程 Building Installation	设备工具器具购置 Equipment Tools, Equipment Purchase	其他费用 Expenses Other
1978	20.30	9.98	3.30	9.89	4.51	0.48
1980	23.85	9.76	1.89	14.01	4.55	0.97
"六五"时期	**216.19**	**83.11**	**16.52**	**155.63**	**59.71**	**7.43**
1985	67.53	28.67	6.71	54.64	23.00	3.39
"七五"时期	**434.43**	**195.59**	**50.10**	**352.24**	**152.75**	**32.96**
1990	92.64	41.02	10.78	73.58	29.31	7.11
"八五"时期	**1300.95**	**606.68**	**304.04**	**972.09**	**429.78**	**178.69**
1991	108.07	45.11	15.01	86.74	33.68	10.64
1992	149.34	68.03	23.36	119.61	51.46	15.94
1993	227.25	98.91	57.02	174.02	74.17	39.83
1994	361.89	146.12	85.06	261.27	99.72	49.60
1995	454.40	248.51	123.59	330.45	170.75	62.68
"九五"时期	**3392.01**	**1596.34**	**1034.45**	**2593.68**	**1108.81**	**598.32**
1996	510.52	307.89	165.97	392.06	218.14	82.28
1997	600.04	264.16	219.40	405.69	171.97	201.38
1998	695.55	323.47	212.08	556.36	230.59	101.48
1999	771.24	329.26	201.67	594.41	248.78	94.54
2000	814.66	371.56	235.33	645.16	239.33	118.64
"十五"时期	**6031.36**	**2481.09**	**1809.24**	**5317.08**	**1883.69**	**1216.75**
2001	890.60	419.20	241.95	739.97	276.93	124.89
2002	974.73	418.55	301.94	829.11	303.57	155.49
2003	1059.98	463.23	360.38	945.58	363.78	243.47
2004	1409.25	537.25	409.88	1282.71	416.98	307.87
2005	1696.80	642.86	495.09	1519.71	522.43	385.03
"十一五"时期	**20406.53**	**6921.20**	**5592.20**	**18649.08**	**5890.61**	**4859.93**
2006	2252.72	717.10	602.87	1918.63	601.90	477.07
2007	2857.31	896.36	780.47	2492.24	756.58	660.27
2008	3568.97	1245.73	983.86	3226.13	971.37	819.50
2009	5025.62	1753.28	1432.95	4683.30	1472.52	1243.52
2010	6701.91	2308.73	1792.05	6328.78	2088.24	1659.57
"十二五"时期	**73434.38**	**18971.13**	**11980.42**	**71272.16**	**18040.47**	**11545.96**
2011	8056.52	2812.91	2065.59	7626.28	2520.40	1950.61
2012	11054.16	3162.99	2287.02	10609.45	2942.10	2192.00
2013	14312.25	3856.68	2584.98	13934.73	3702.30	2508.97
2014	18185.42	4292.85	2523.50	17765.47	4160.35	2425.92
2015	21826.03	4845.70	2519.33	21336.23	4715.32	2468.46
"十三五"时期						
2016	22876.58	4124.21	2503.08	22349.47	3980.74	2421.55
2017	23772.98	4891.02	3208.57	23194.42	4678.76	3083.96

4-19 按三次产业划分的固定资产投资
Investment in Fixed Assets by Three Strata of Industry

单位:亿元 (100 million yuan)

年 份 In copies	全 省			# 地方		
	第一产业 Primary Industry	第二产业 Second Industry	第三产业 Third Industry	第一产业 Primary Industry	第二产业 Second Industry	第三产业 Third Industry
1978	2.24	25.28	6.06	2.24	8.80	3.85
1980	2.11	22.75	10.64	2.03	9.98	7.52
"六五"时期	**24.77**	**155.02**	**136.03**	**24.05**	**83.83**	**114.89**
1985	8.37	47.42	47.12	8.09	31.48	41.46
"七五"时期	**49.76**	**335.53**	**294.83**	**47.24**	**245.00**	**245.71**
1990	12.16	67.41	64.87	11.61	46.30	52.09
"八五"时期	**78.98**	**1074.06**	**1058.63**	**73.97**	**674.84**	**831.75**
1991	12.48	77.95	77.76	12.12	55.25	63.69
1992	12.42	121.00	107.31	11.04	87.18	88.79
1993	11.89	170.93	200.36	10.10	114.05	163.87
1994	14.97	302.49	275.61	14.38	173.32	222.89
1995	27.22	401.69	397.59	26.11	220.95	316.82
"九五"时期	**272.08**	**2298.38**	**3452.34**	**271.69**	**1265.99**	**2763.13**
1996	29.76	451.28	503.34	29.73	272.79	389.96
1997	41.02	436.04	606.54	41.02	269.87	468.15
1998	59.48	450.16	721.46	59.48	234.94	594.01
1999	71.22	439.32	791.63	71.22	227.20	639.31
2000	70.60	521.58	829.37	70.24	261.19	671.70
"十五"时期	**416.79**	**3952.90**	**5969.82**	**414.74**	**2724.92**	**5277.86**
2001	77.48	590.01	902.08	77.33	323.55	740.91
2002	80.08	648.81	966.33	79.02	375.77	833.38
2003	88.80	714.81	1079.98	88.35	489.49	974.99
2004	77.55	912.93	1365.90	77.16	684.54	1245.86
2005	92.88	1086.34	1655.53	92.88	851.57	1482.72
"十一五"时期	**1202.88**	**12641.78**	**19075.27**	**1197.58**	**10748.83**	**17471.71**
2006	107.64	1317.12	2147.93	107.56	1044.17	1845.87
2007	149.40	1710.74	2674.00	148.72	1395.28	2365.09
2008	231.25	2346.32	3220.99	230.95	1859.42	2926.62
2009	321.59	3097.68	4792.58	319.58	2656.02	4442.25
2010	393.00	4169.92	6239.77	390.77	3793.94	5891.88
"十二五"时期	**3354.26**	**44874.29**	**56157.36**	**3351.93**	**43109.22**	**54397.45**
2011	440.91	5526.40	6967.71	440.51	5032.88	6623.90
2012	525.45	7281.04	8697.68	525.13	6891.67	8326.75
2013	590.61	9187.25	10976.04	589.28	8883.83	10672.89
2014	799.35	10733.09	13469.32	799.07	10432.00	13120.68
2015	997.94	12146.51	16046.61	997.94	11868.84	15653.23
"十三五"时期						
2016	889.94	12224.54	16389.40	885.93	11929.18	15936.64
2017	912.24	13236.47	17723.86	911.18	12831.31	17214.65

主要统计指标解释

全社会固定资产投资 是以货币形式表现的在一定时期内全社会建造和购置固定资产的工作量以及与此有关的费用的总称。该指标是反映固定资产投资规模、结构和发展速度的综合性指标,又是观察工程进度和考核投资效果的重要依据。全社会固定资产投资按登记注册类型可分为国有、集体、个体、联营、股份制、外商、港澳台商、其他等。

固定资产投资 指各种登记注册类型的企业、事业、行政单位及个体户进行的计划总投资500万元及500万元以上的建设项目投资、房地产开发投资、城镇和工矿区私人建房投资。

城镇和工矿区私人建房投资 包括市、县城、城关镇、工矿区所辖范围内的全部私人建房,不论其房主是否系本地的常住户口均应包括。

农村投资 包括在农村区域范围内进行固定资产投资活动的企业、事业、行政单位及农村个人投资。

固定资产投资的资金来源 根据固定资产投资的资金来源不同,分为国家预算内资金、国内贷款、利用外资、自筹资金和其他资金。

(1)国家预算内资金:分为财政拨款和财政安排的贷款两部分。包括中央财政的基本建设基金(分经营性基金和非经营性基金两部分)、专项支出(如煤代油专项等)、收回再贷、贴息资金,财政安排的挖潜改造和新产品试制支出、城建支出、商业部门简易建筑支出、不发达地区发展基金等资金中用于固定资产投资的资金;地方财政中由国家统筹安排的资金等。

(2)国内贷款:指报告期固定资产投资单位向银行及非银行金融机构借入的用于固定资产投资的各种国内借款,包括银行利用自有资金及吸收的存款发放的贷款、上级主管部门拨入的国内贷款、国家专项贷款(包括煤代油贷款、劳改煤矿专项贷款等)、地方财政专项资金安排的贷款、国内储备贷款、周转贷款等。

(3)利用外资:指报告期收到的用于固定资产建造和购置的国外资金(包括设备、材料、技术在内)。包括对外借款(外国政府、国际金融组织贷款、出口信贷、外国银行商业贷款、对外发行债券和股票)、外商直接投资及外商其他投资。不包括我国自有外汇资金(国家外汇、地方外汇、留成外汇、调剂外汇和中国银行自有资金发行的外汇贷款等)。计算利用外资时,需要折算成人民币,折算中所使用的外汇汇率按现汇计算,即按使用外汇时的汇率计算。

(4)自筹资金:指固定资产投资单位报告期收到的,由各地区、各部门及企、事业单位筹集用于固定资产投资的预算外资金,包括中央各部门、各级地方和企、事业单位的自筹资金。

(5)其他资金:指在报告期收到的除以上各种资金之外其他用于固定资产投资的资金,包括企业或金融机构通过发行各种债券筹集到的资金、群众集资、个人资金、无偿捐赠的资金及其他单位拨入的资金等。

固定资产投资按国民经济行业分 根据建设项目建成投产后的主要产品或主要用途及社会经济活动性质来确定国民经济行业。一般情况下,一个建设项目或一个企业、事业单位只能属于一种国民经济行业。

固定资产投资按隶属关系分 是按建设单位或企业、事业、行政单位的主管上级机关确定的。

(1)中央:是指中共中央、人大常委会和国务院各部、委、局、总公司以及直属机构直接领导的建设项目和企业、事业、行政单位。这些单位的固定资产投资计划由国务院各部门直接编制和下达,建设中所需物资、主要设备以及建设中的问题都由中央有关部门安排和解决。

(2)地方:是由省(自治区、直辖市)、地区(州、盟、省辖市)、县(旗、县级市)三级政府及业务主管部门直接领导和管理的建设项目、企业、事业、行政单位。地方项目还包括不隶属以上各级政府及主管部门的建设项目和企业、事业单位,如外商投资企业和无主管部门的企业等。

固定资产投资按建设性质分 根据整个建设项目情况来确定。建设项目的性质一般分为新建、扩建、改建和技术改造、迁建、恢复。房地产开发单位、农村投资、城镇工矿区私人建房投资不划分建设性质。

(1)新建:一般指从无到有"平地起家"开始建设的企业、事业和行政单位或建设项目。现有企业、事业、行政单位一般不属于新建。但如有的单位原有基础很小,经过建设后新增的固定资产价值超过该企、事业、行政单位原有固定资产价值(原值)三倍以上的也应作为新建。

(2)扩建:指在厂内或其他地点,为扩大原有产品的生产能力(或效益)或增加新的产品生产能力,而增建主要的生产车间(或主要工程)、分厂、独立的生产线。行政、事业单位在原单位增建业务用房(如学校增建教学用房、医院增建

门诊部、病房等)也作为扩建。

现有企、事业单位为扩大原有主要产品生产能力或增加新的产品生产能力,增建一个或几个主要生产车间(或主要工程)、分厂,同时进行一些更新改造工程的,也应作为扩建。

(3)改建和技术改造:指现有企业、事业单位,对原有设施进行技术改造或更新(包括相应配套的辅助性生产、生活福利设施)的建设项目。现有企业、事业单位为适应市场变化的需要,而改变企业的主要产品种类(如军工企业转产民用品等)的建设项目,应作为改建。原有产品生产作业线由于各工序(车间)之间能力不平衡,为填平补齐充分发挥原有生产能力而增建不增加本企业主要产品设计能力的车间,也应作为改建。技术改造是指企业、事业单位在现有基础上,用先进的技术代替落后的技术,用先进的工艺和装备代替落后的工艺和装备,以改变企业落后的技术经济面貌,实现以内涵为主的扩大再生产,达到提高产品质量、促进产品更新换代、节约能源、降低消耗、扩大生产规模、全面提高社会经济效益的目的。技术改造具体包括以下内容:机器设备和工具的更新改造;生产工艺改革、节约能源和原材料的改造;厂房建筑和公共设施的改造;劳动条件和生产环境的改造等。

固定资产投资按构成分 固定资产投资活动按其工作内容和实现方式分为建筑安装工程,设备、工具、器具购置,其他费用三个部分。

(1)建筑安装工程(建筑安装工作量):指各种房屋、建筑物的建造工程和各种设备、装置的安装工程。包括各种房屋建造工程;各种用途设备基础和各种工业窑炉的砌筑工程及金属结构工程;为施工而进行的各种准备工作和临时工程以及完工后的清理工作等;铁路、道路的铺设,矿井的开凿及石油管道的架设等;水利工程;防空地下建筑等特殊工程;列入房屋工程预算内的暖气、卫生、通风、照明、煤气等设备的价值及装设油饰工程;列入建筑工程预算内的各种管道(蒸汽、压缩空气、石油、给排水等管道)、电力、电讯电缆导线等的敷设工程;以及各种机械设备的安装工程;为测定安装工程质量,对设备进行的试运工作;房地产开发单位进行的商品房屋开发建设工程、土地开发工程。

在安装工程中,不包括被安装设备本身的价值。

(2)设备、工具、器具购置:指建设单位或企、事业单位购置或自制的,达到固定资产标准的设备、工具、器具的价值。新建单位及扩建单位的新建车间,按照设计或计划要求购置或自制的全部设备、工具、器具,不论是否达到固定资产标准均计入"设备、工具、器具购置"中。

(3)其他费用:指在固定资产建造和购置过程中发生的,除上述几项内容以外的各种应分摊计入固定资产的费用。

施工项目 指报告期内进行过建筑或安装施工活动的项目。凡是报告期内施过工的建设项目,不论施工时间长短,均作为施工项目统计。施工项目个数可以反映一定时期固定资产投资的实际规模,与同期全部建成投产项目个数相比,可以从建设速度的角度反映固定资产投资的效果。根据建设项目施工活动的不同性质,施工项目又分为:本年正式施工项目、本年收尾项目和以前年度全部停缓建项目。

全部建成投产项目 工业项目指设计文件规定形成生产能力的主体工程及其相应配套的辅助设施全部建成,经负荷试运转,证明具备生产设计规定合格产品的条件,并经过验收鉴定合格或达到竣工验收标准,与生产性工程配套的生活福利设施可以满足近期正常生产的需要,正式移交生产的建设项目。非工业项目指设计文件规定的主体工程和相应的配套工程全部建成,能够发挥设计规定的全部效益,经验收鉴定合格或达到竣工验收标准,正式移交使用的建设项目。

新增生产能力(或工程效益) 指通过固定资产投资活动而增加的设计能力(或工程效益),该指标是以实物形态表现的反映固定资产投资成果的指标,也是考核投资经济效果的重要依据之一。

房屋建筑面积 指房屋建筑物勒脚以上外墙外围的水平截面面积,包括房屋建筑物的有效面积和结构面积。该指标是从实物形态上反映建设规模和建设成果的重要指标之一,也是检查工程形象进度、计算工程造价、分析投资效果、研究施工任务和建筑材料之间平衡情况的重要依据。

住宅建筑面积 指施工和竣工房屋建筑面积中供居住用的房屋建筑面积。

施工面积 指报告期内施工的全部房屋建筑面积。包括本期新开工的面积和上期开工跨入本期继续施工的房屋面积,以及上期已停建在本期恢复施工的房屋面积。本期竣工和本期施工后又停缓建的房屋,其建筑面积仍计入本期房屋施工面积中。

竣工面积 指在报告期内房屋建筑按照设计要求已经全部完工,达到住人和使用条件,经验收鉴定合格(或达到竣工验收标准),正式移交使用单位的各栋房屋建筑面积的总和。

房屋建筑面积竣工率 指一定时期内房屋竣工面积占同期房屋施工面积的比率。是从房屋建筑施工速度的角度反映投资效果的指标。

新增固定资产 指报告期内已经完成建造和购置过程,并已交付生产或使用单位的固定资产价值。该指标是表示固定资产投资成果的价值指标,也是反映建设进度,计算固定资产投资效果的重要指标。

项目建设投产率 指一定时期内全部建成投产项目个数与同期施工项目个数的比率。该指标是从建设单位建设速度的角度反映投资效果的指标。

固定资产交付使用率 指一定时期新增固定资产与同期完成投资额的比率。该指标是反映固定资产动用速度,衡量建设过程中宏观投资效果的综合指标。由于新增固定资产是较长时期内形成的结果,而投资额则是当年完成的,因此,该指标一般适宜于反映较长时期内固定资产的动用情况。

商品房销售面积 指报告期内出售商品房屋的合同总面积（即双方签署的正式买卖合同中所确定的建筑面积）。由现房销售建筑面积和期房销售建筑面积两部分组成。

商品房销售额 指报告期内出售商品房屋的合同总价款(即双方签署的正式买卖合同中所确定的合同总价)。该指标与商品房销售面积同口径，由现房销售额和期房销售额两部分组成。

 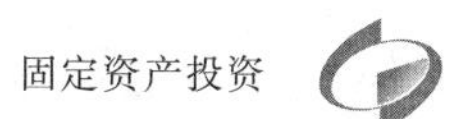

Explanatory Notes on Main Statistical Indicators

Total Investment in Fixed Assets in the Whole Country refers to the volume of activities in construction and purchases of fixed assets and related fees, expressed in monetary terms. It is a comprehensive indicator which shows the size, structure and growth of the investment in fixed assets, providing basis for observing the progress of construction projects and evaluating results of investment. Total investment in fixed assets in the whole country includes, by type of ownership, the investment by the state–owned units, collective units, individuals, joint ownership units, share–holding units, as well as investment by businessmen from foreign countries and from Hong Kong, Macao and Taiwan, and by other units.

Investment in Fixed Assets refers to construction projects involving a total planned investment of 500,000 yuan and over by enterprises and institutions of various types of ownership, by administrative units and by individuals, investment in real estate development, and housing investment by individuals in urban areas and in industrial and mining areas.

Investment in Housing Construction in Urban Areas and in Industrial and Mining Areas refers to all private housing construction under the jurisdiction of cities, county towns and industrial and mining areas, no matter whether the owner of the house is registered as the permanent resident in the locality or not.

Investment in Rural Areas refers to investment in fixed assets by enterprises, institutions and individuals in rural areas.

Sources of Funds for Investment in Fixed Assets include fund from state budget, domestic loans, foreign investment, self–raised funds, and others depending on the source of investment.

(1) Fund from state budget consists of budgetary appropriation and loans from state budget. More specifically, it includes, from the budget of the central government, capital construction fund (operation fund and non–operational fund), special expenses (e.g. expenses on substituting petroleum with coal), loans from repayment, discount fund, expenses on innovation and trial production of new products, expenses on urban construction, expenses on temporary construction by trade departments, development fund for less developed areas, as well as local budgetary fund transferred from the central budget.

(2) Domestic loans refer to loans of various forms borrowed by investing units from banks and non–bank financial institutions during the reference period for the purpose of investment in fixed assets, including loans issued by banks from their self–owned funds and deposit, loans appropriated by higher responsible authorities, special loans by government (including loan for substituting petroleum with coal, special loan for reform–through–labour coal mines), loans arranged by local government from special funds, domestic reserve loan, and working loan, etc..

(3) Foreign Investment refers to foreign funds received during the reference period for the construction and purchase of investment in fixed assets (covering equipment, materials and technology), including foreign borrowings (loans from foreign governments and international financial institutions, export credit, commercial loans from foreign banks, issue of bonds and stocks overseas), foreign direct investment and other foreign investment. Excluded in this category are capitals in foreign exchanges owned by China (foreign exchanges owned by the central and local governments, foreign exchanges retained by enterprises, foreign exchanges by enterprises through regulating mechanism, loans in foreign exchanges issued by the Bank of China with its own fund, etc.). In calculating the utilization of foreign capitals, foreign currencies are converted into Chinese Renminbi applying the current exchange rate when the foreign capitals are actually used.

(4) Self–raised funds refer to extra–budgetary funds for investment in fixed assets received by investing units from central government ministries, local governments, enterprises and institutions, including their self–raised funds.

(5) Others refer to funds for investment in fixed assets received from the sources other than those listed above, including capitals raised through issuing bonds by enterprises or financial institutions, funds raised from individuals and through donations, and funds transferred from other units.

Investment in Fixed Assets by Sector The classification of construction projects by sector is determined by the major products or the purpose of the projects when they are put into production or use, and by the nature of their social economic activities. In general, one project or one enterprise or institution can only be classified into one sector.

Investment in Fixed Assets by Jurisdiction of Management refers to the classification of investment by the competent authorities under which investment is made by construction units, enterprises, institutions or administrative units.

(1) Central investment refers to the investment in projects or by enterprises, institutions or administrative units which are under the direct leadership and management of the CPC Central Committee, the NPC Standing Committee, the State Council and of the national commissions, ministries, agencies and state-owned large corporations. Various ministries and departments of the State Council prepare and implement plans for investment in fixed assets by those departments, and arrange and ensure the supply of materials and key equipment required for the projects.

(2) Local investment refers to the investment in projects or by enterprises, institutions or administrative units which are under the direct leadership and management of departments under the provincial, prefecture and county governments. Also included are projects by foreign-invested enterprises and enterprises without competent managing authorities.

Investment in Fixed Assets by Type of Construction The construction projects in general can be classified, by the type of construction, into new construction, expansion, reconstruction and technical transformation, moving and restoration. However, investment by type of construction is not applied to investment by real-estate development units, investment in rural areas and investment in housing by urban individuals.

(1) New construction in general refers to newly constructed enterprises, institutions, administrative agencies or independent projects from scratch. Construction in the existing enterprises, institutions or agencies is not considered as new construction. In case the assets of the existing unit is quite small, and the value of newly added fixed assets exceeds the original value of assets by three times, the expansion will be considered as new construction.

(2) Expansion refers to construction of new major production workshop, branch factory or independent production line within a factory or in other locations, for the purpose of increasing the production capacity (or improving efficiency) of the original products. Newly constructed houses for the operation of institutions and administrative organizations (such as the newly constructed buildings for teaching in schools, buildings for clinics or wards in hospitals, etc.) are also classified as expansion.

Also included in the expansion are investments by existing enterprises or institutions in building major production line (s) or branch factories along with some work on innovation, for the purpose of expending the production capacity of original products or producing new products.

(3) Reconstruction refers to construction projects by existing enterprises or institutions in innovation or technical transformation of the old facilities (including auxiliary production equipment and welfare facilities). Also considered as reconstruction is the construction of new workshops by the existing enterprises or institutions to change the variety of products to meet the market demand (such as the production of civil products by defence industries), or to bring the designed production capacity into full play through a more balanced production process on production lines. Technical transformation refers to replacement of old technology or equipment by new technology or equipment, in order to expand the reproduction through improvement of technology contents in production, to improve product quality, to promote new products, to save energy and reduce consumption and to improve overall social-economic efficiency. Contents of technical transformation include: updating of machinery, equipment and tools; reforming production process by using energy or materials saving technology; construction of factory workshops and transformation of public facilities; improvement of working conditions and environment, etc.

Investment in Fixed Assets by Structure By their contents, investment activities are classified into 3 categories, i.e. construction and installation, purchase of equipment and instrument, and other expenses.

(1) Construction and installation (work volume of construction and installation) refers to the construction of various houses and buildings and installation of various kinds of equipment and instruments. They include construction of various houses; equipment foundations, industrial kilns and stoves, and metal structure work; preparation works for project construction, and clearing up works post project construction; pavement of railways and roads, drilling of mines and putting up of oil pipes; construction of projects of water conservancy; construction of underground air-raid shelters and construction of other special projects; value of equipment for heating, sanitation, ventilation, lighting, gas, painting, etc. that are covered by the budget of housing projects; laying out of various pipelines (for steam, compressed air, petroleum, tap water and sewage) and lines for electric power and for communications; installation of various machinery equipment,

testing operation for pre-testing the quality of installation projects, and land and other development work conducted by real estate developers for commercial housing. The value of equipment installed is not included in the value of installation projects.

(2) Purchase of equipment and instruments refers to the total value of equipment, tools, and instruments purchased or self-produced which come up to standards for fixed assets by the construction units or investing enterprises or institutions. Equipment, tools and instruments purchased or self-produced for new workshops by newly established or expanded units are categorized as "purchase of equipment and instruments" no matter whether they come up to the standards for fixed assets.

(3) Other expenses refer to expenses occurring during the construction or purchase of fixed assets other than those mentioned above.

Projects under Construction refer to projects with construction and installation activities undertaken in the reference period. All projects that have construction activities undertaken during the reference period are reported as projects under construction irrespective of the length of construction work. The number of projects under construction can reflect the actual size of investment in fixed assets during a given period, and when compared with the number of projects completed and put into use during the same period, it demonstrates the results of investment in fixed assets. Depending on the nature of construction activities, projects under construction can also be classified into projects under construction in current year, winding-up projects in current year and stopped or suspended projects in previous years (with preservation work in current year).

Projects Completed and Put into Use Industrial projects refer to the major projects and accessory facilities completed which result in forming production capacity and have been checked and accepted while the living and welfare facilities have been completed and can ensure normal production and formally put into production. Non-industrial projects refer to the major projects and accessory facilities completed which possess the designed capacity and have been checked, accepted and formally put into production.

Newly Increased Production Capacity (or Project Efficiency) refers to the increase of designed capacity (or project efficiency) through investment in fixed assets, which reflects the accomplishment of investment in fixed assets in kind and serves as important basis for evaluating the economic efficiency of investment.

Floor Space of Buildings under Construction refers to total floor space of the horizontal section of outer walls above the plinth of the building, including the effective area and the area occupied by the structure. This indicator is one of the important indicators in physical terms to reflect the scale and accomplishment of the construction industry, and important basis for monitoring the progress, calculating the cost, analyzing the efficiency and studying the supply of building materials in relation with the construction projects.

Floor Space of Residential Buildings refers to the floor space of the residential buildings among the total space of buildings under construction or completed.

Floor Space under Construction refers to total floor space of all buildings under construction during the reference period, including floor space of newly started buildings during the reference period, floor space of construction extended from the previous period to the current period, and floor space of construction suspended during the previous period and resumed in the current period. Floor space of construction completed in the current period, and floor space of construction started and then suspended in the current period are also included in the floor space under construction of the current year.

Floor Space of Buildings Completed refers to the floor space of all buildings completed in the reference period, which have been appraised and accepted (or come up to the designed standards) and have been transferred to the owners for use.

Completion Rate of Floor Space of Buildings refers to the ratio of the floor space of buildings completed in certain period of time to the floor space of buildings under construction in the same period. This indicator reflects the investment result from the perspective of the speed of construction.

Newly Increased Fixed Assets refer to the newly increased value of fixed assets, constructed or purchased, that have been transferred to the investors. This is an indicator that demonstrates the results of investment in fixed assets in monetary terms, and an important indicator to reflect the speed of construction and to calculate the efficiency of investment.

Rate of Construction Projects Completed and Put into Use refers to the ratio of the number of construction projects completed and put into use in certain period of time to the number of projects under construction in the same period. This reflects the investment efficiency from the perspective of the speed of projects construction.

Rate of Projects of Fixed Assets Completed and Put into Operation refers to the ratio of the newly increased fixed assets to the total investment made in the same period. This is a comprehensive indicator reflecting the speed of the employment of fixed assets and the investment efficiency at the macro-level. As the newly increase fixed assets is the result of a long period while the investment is completed in the current year, this indicator is expected to be used to reflect the employment of fixed assets over a long period of time.

Area of Commercial Housing Sold refers to total contracted area of commercial housing (i.e. area of floor space as designated in the formal contracts signed by both sides) during the reference time. It constitutes floor space of completed housing and floor space of future housing.

Value of Commercial Housing Sold refer to total value of contracts (i.e. value of sales/purchase for selling/purchase of commercial housing as designated in the contracts signed by both sides) during the reference time. It has the same coverage as the area of commercial housing sold, constituting completed housing and floor space of future housing.

5

对外经济贸易和旅游

International Trade and Economic Cooperation & Tourism

资料整理人员:王　芳

5-1 对外经济主要指标
Major Indicators of International Trade and Economic Cooperation

单位:万美元 (USD 10 000)

指 标	Item	1995	2000	2005	2010	2015	2018	2019	2020
进出口总额	**Total Imports and Exports**	**340920**	**320249**	**905475**	**2593211**	**4560531**	**5280245**	**5712847**	**6208343**
进口总额	Total Imports	142484	127369	462607	1149031	1638490	1871372	2114883	2302264
出口总额	Total Exports	198435	192880	442868	1444180	2922041	3408873	3597964	3906079
合同外商直接投资项目(个)	**Contracted Projets of Foreign Direct Investment (uint)**	**881**	**331**	**520**	**306**	**274**	**418**	**446**	**296**
合同外商直接投资	**Contracted Value of Foreign Direct Investment**	**108847**	**106583**	**211023**	**278627**	**416112**	**1481727**	**1624612**	**1416901**
实际外商直接投资	**Actual Value of Foreign Direct Investment**	**62253**	**94368**	**218475**	**405015**	**894801**	**1194095**	**1290746**	**1035189**
对外经济合作	**Economic Cooperation with Foreign Countries & Regions**								
合同金额	Contracted Value	7300	36706	35953	776945				
#对外承包工程	Contracted Projects			27952	765547	1145362	1488185	1663154	1789911
对外劳务合作	Labor Services			5568	11398				
完成营业额	Value of Tornover Fulfilled	4100	15815	31843	327164				
#对外承包工程	Contracted Projects			28852	319979	523369	643554	661042	641470
对外劳务合作	Labor Services			2601	7186				

5-2 对外贸易进出口总额
Total Imports and Exports of International Trade

单位:万美元 (USD 10 000)

年 份 Year	合 计 Total	进 口 Imports	出 口 Exports
1992	174533	58696	115837
1995	340920	142484	198435
1996	286287	133684	152603
1997	320668	128583	192084
1998	283189	112478	170711
1999	268107	116729	151378
2000	320249	127369	192880
2001	357720	178041	179679
2002	395314	185488	209826
2003	510930	245393	265537
2004	676581	338361	338219
2005	905475	462607	442868
2006	1176219	550157	626063
2007	1489647	669593	820054
2008	2070567	899676	1170891
2009	1725102	727222	997880
2010	2593211	1149031	1444180
2011	3358693	1405233	1953460
2012	3196409	1256525	1939884
2013	3638928	1355160	2283768
2014	4306401	1641821	2664580
2015	4560531	1638490	2922041
2016	3939760	1332470	2607290
2017	4630863	1580938	3049925
2018	5280245	1871372	3408873
2019	5712847	2114883	3597964
2020	6208343	2302264	3906079

注:根据海关统计有关文件规定2008年年终数据部分调整。
Note: According to the provisions of the relevant documents to customs statistics data portion of the 2008 year-end adjustments.

5-3 按贸易方式和经济类型分的进出口总额

单位:万美元

项 目	Item	2000		2005	
		进 口 Imports	出 口 Exports	进 口 Imports	出 口 Exports
总计	**Total**	**127369**	**192880**	**462607**	**442868**
按贸易方式分	**Grouped by Type of Trade**				
一般贸易	General Trade	91576	138907	340768	350354
来料加工装配贸易	Processing and Assembling Trade	20136	13265	15428	22381
进料加工贸易	Raw Material Input Processing Trade	32803	14154	54328	71920
来料加工装配进口的设备	Processing and Assembling Import Equipment Provided With Material	6		18	
外商作为投资进口的设备	Goods as Invested for Import Equipments	8602		45087	
租赁贸易	Leasing Trade			114	
出料加工贸易	Raw Material Output Processing Trade				
易货贸易	Repalce Goods with Goods				
保税仓库进出境货物	Import and Export Goods of Protcetive Tariff Storage	105		8028	33
按经济类型分	**Grouped by Ownership**				
#国有企业	State-Owned Enterprises	64805	140826	221963	213955
集体企业	Collective-Owned Enterprises	1255	9124	5719	20033
外商投资企业	Foreign-funded Enterprises	61691	42901	190170	130579
民营企业	Private-Owned Enterprises	111	240	45839	80397

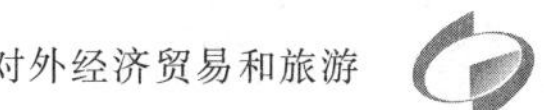

Total Imports and Exports by Type of Trade and Ownership

(USD 10 000)

2010		2015		2018		2019		2020	
进 口 Imports	出 口 Exports	进 口 Imports	出 口 Exports	进 口 Imports	出 口 Exports	进 口 Imports	出 口 Exports	进 口 Imports	出 口 Exports
1149031	**1444180**	**1638490**	**2922041**	**1871372**	**3408873**	**2114883**	**3597964**	**2302264**	**3906079**
841306	829994	1088411	1961768	1445928	2605974	1620005	2829499	1747817	2936983
28304	32269	11584	53984	15420	69122	12830	62977	11582	44800
210483	518911	487467	744388	245421	543998	255398	525648	207566	493193
348		29		320		62		39	
43809		8312		10820		5015		3961	
5	144		10	2051	133	1986	32	120	3803
320	212	913	607	1259	963	1137	773	1296	838
								0.6	
20511	16794	16030	16982	73606	30460	66714	30066	114669	64753
513134	472230	401246	574791	575181	609771	791391	493809	823189	453911
4021	16161	1398	18099	2902	19531	2731	16251	1884	16106
534565	569501	556216	674909	637159	725349	610226	738358	556134	667317
93032	386177	679603	1653454	654283	2048247	703447	2331576	917617	2762543

5-4 进出口商品主要国别和地区
Imports and Exports Value by Countries and Regions

单位：万美元 (USD 10 000)

国家（地区）	Countries (Regions)	2019 进出口 Imports and Exports	2019 进口 Imports	2019 出口 Exports	2020 进出口 Imports and Exports	2020 进口 Imports	2020 出口 Exports
亚　洲	**Asia**	**3065133**	**1210382**	**1854751**	**3227206**	**1415405**	**1811801**
#香港	Hongkong	362591	2097	360494	439453	1632	437821
日本	Japan	491288	375261	116027	538754	410282	128472
韩国	Korea, Rep.	341507	218231	123276	426220	292969	133251
台湾省	Taiwan Province	277656	189381	88275	374126	286265	87861
印度	India	202698	24095	178603	167916	25731	142185
越南	Vietnam	208442	63360	145083	166225	47421	118804
泰国	Thailand	136041	51710	84331	147379	49389	97991
马来西亚	Malaysia	164160	40638	123522	165999	44988	121010
新加坡	Singapore	164911	68976	95935	136090	69858	66233
非　洲	**Africa**	**273474**	**142076**	**131399**	**257165**	**128995**	**128170**
欧　洲	**European**	**928659**	**279697**	**648962**	**1117684**	**274326**	**843358**
#德国	Germany	192698	100946	91752	219466	85667	133799
法国	France	84964	22928	62037	132000	21817	110183
荷兰	Netherland	119796	37666	82130	109626	36979	72648
英国	England	77305	16305	61000	146345	25903	120441
北美洲	**North America**	**739986**	**191570**	**548416**	**917970**	**210577**	**707393**
#美国	United States of America	674413	170831	503582	824709	191942	632767
墨西哥	Mexico	80096	11981	68115	85070	15278	69792
大洋洲	**Occeania**	**185824**	**115298**	**70526**	**177473**	**100619**	**76854**
#澳大利亚	Australia	151664	101862	49802	159015	94421	64594
附：东南亚国家联盟	**Association of Southeast-Asia Nations**	**849962**	**249385**	**600577**	**802298**	**238509**	**563789**
欧洲联盟	**European Union**	**813381**	**258166**	**555215**	**859298**	**217751**	**641547**
亚太经济合作组织	**Asia-Pacific Economic Cooperation**	**3630053**	**1582658**	**2047395**	**4062497**	**1792248**	**2270249**

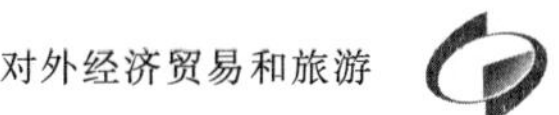

5-5 合同外商直接投资项目
Number of Foreign Direct Investment´s Contracted Projects

单位:个 (unit)

指　标	Item	1990	1995	2000	2005	2010	2015	2017	2018	2019	2020
合计	**Total**	**99**	**881**	**331**	**520**	**306**	**274**	**272**	**418**	**446**	**296**
合资经营企业	Equity Joint Venture	17	577	156	203	108	101	127	192	191	90
合作经营企业	Contractual Joint Venture	75	44	16	29	5	4	3	1	3	0
外资企业	Wholly Foreign-owned Enterprise	7	260	158	285	193	168	134	224	250	190
外商投资股份制企业	FDI Shareholding Inc.			1	3		1	3	1	2	2
合伙企业	Partnership							5			12

5-6 合同外商直接投资金额
Value of Foreign Direct Investment´s Contracted Projects

单位:万美元 (USD 10 000)

指　标	Item	1990	1995	2000	2005	2010	2015	2017	2018	2019	2020
合计	**Total**	**3947**	**108847**	**106583**	**211023**	**278627**	**416112**	**860726**	**1481727**	**1624612**	**1416901**
合资经营企业	Equity Joint Venture	1364	68923	27936	51010	132679	78912	235632	965332	526689	932837
合作经营企业	Contractual Joint Venture	2464	7899	48711	24480	3319	11078	144791	29597	71190	3563
外资企业	Wholly Foreign -owned Enterprise	119	32025	29936	132897	235498	313337	321903	477066	716197	460196
外商投资股份制企业	FDI Shareholding Inc.				2636	33519	12785	3528	9732	310536	51
合伙企业	Partnership							154872			13855

5-7 实际外商直接投资金额
Actual Value of Foreign Direct Investment

单位:万美元 (USD 10 000)

指　标	Item	1990	1995	2000	2004	2005	2010
合计	**Total**	**2900**	**62253**	**94368**	**207126**	**218475**	**405015**
合资经营企业	Equity Joint Venture	2492	40259	59879	130048	65472	132679
合作经营企业	Contractual Joint Venture	85	5012	2789	11741	5089	3319
外资企业	Wholly Foreign-owned Enterprise	323	16982	31700	62155	75305	235498
外商投资股份制企业	FDI Shareholding Inc.					2739	33519
合伙企业	Partnership						

5-7 续表 continued

单位:万美元 (USD 10 000)

指　标	Item	2014	2015	2016	2017	2018	2019	2020
合计	**Total**	**792792**	**894801**	**1012889**	**1099392**	**1194095**	**1290746**	**1035189**
合资经营企业	Equity Joint Venture	300982	329123	359083	410416	402894	499461	298821
合作经营企业	Contractual Joint Venture	759	4261	7480	15178	5529	14738	3868
外资企业	Wholly Foreign-owned Enterprise	440949	548452	548867	621377	723081	711424	717431
外商投资股份制企业	FDI Shareholding Inc.	35969	9325	56625	28789	44838	33459	12668
合伙企业	Partnership				243			2401

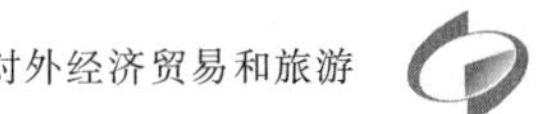

5-8 按行业分外商直接投资(2020)
Foreign Direct Investment Grouped by Sector(2020)

行 业	Item	项目(个) Number of Projects (unit)	合同外资(万美元) Contracted Foreign Capital (USD 10 000)	实际使用外资(万美元) Foreign Capital Actually Used (USD 10 000)
总计	**Total**	**296**	**1416901**	**1035189**
农、林、牧、渔业	Agriculture, Forestry, Animal Husbandry and Fishery	5	728	2721
采矿业	Mining			
制造业	Manufactruring	39	864268	505133
电力、燃气及水的生产和供应业	Production and Supply of Electricity, Heat, Gas and Water	8	68735	36158
建筑业	Construction	5	23136	15428
交通运输、仓储和邮政业	Transport, Storage and Post	5	18406	39997
信息传输、软件和信息技术服务业	Information Transmision, Software and Information Technology	23	28722	61247
批发和零售业	Wholesale and Retail Trades	49	68004	90039
住宿和餐饮业	Hotels and Catering Services	7	302	468
金融业	Financial Intermediation	4	5887	1679
房地产业	Real Estate	9	10364	101807
租赁和商务服务业	Leasing and Business Services	45	137415	125047
科学研究和技术服务业	Scientific Research and Technical Services	81	150069	41304
水利、环境和公共设施管理业	Management of Water Conservancy, Environment and Public Facilities	2	435	6767
居民服务、修理和其他服务业	Sevice to Households, Repair and Other Services	2	305	
教育	Education	1	1	
卫生和社会工作	Health and Social Security	1	35438	1454
文化、体育和娱乐业	Culture, Sports and Entertainment	10	4686	5940

5-9 年末登记外商投资企业行业分布情况(2020)
Industry Distribution of Registered Foreign-invested Enterprises at Year-end(2020)

单位:个 (unit)

行 业	Item	企业存量数 Number of Enterprises Stock
总计	**Total**	**15511**
农、林、牧、渔业	Agriculture, Forestry, Animal Husbandry and Fishery	428
采矿业	Mining	140
制造业	Manufactruring	8919
电力、燃气及水的生产和供应业	Production and Supply of Electricity, Heat, Gas and Water	218
建筑业	Construction	663
交通运输、仓储和邮政业	Transport, Storage and Post	237
信息传输、软件和信息技术服务业	Information Transmision, Software and Information Technology	285
批发和零售业	Wholesale and Retail Trades	676
住宿和餐饮业	Hotels and Catering Services	338
金融业	Financial Intermediation	85
房地产业	Real Estate	1272
租赁和商务服务业	Leasing and Business Services	668
科学研究和技术服务业	Scientific Research and Technical Services	385
水利、环境和公共设施管理业	Management of Water Conservancy, Environment and Public Facilities	77
居民服务、修理和其他服务业	Sevice to Households, Repair and Other Services	967
教育	Education	43
卫生和社会工作	Health and Social Security	28
文化、体育和娱乐业	Culture, Sports and Entertainment	82

5-10 对外承包工程和劳务合作
Contracted Projects and Labor Services Cooperation with Foreign Countries or Regions

年 份 Year	Item	合同金额(万美元) Contracted Value (USD 10 000)	实际完成营业额(万美元) Value of Turnover Fulfilled (USD 10 000)	年末在外人数(人) Number of Persons Working Abroad at Year-end (person)
对外承包工程	**Contracted Projects**			
2003		17900	28552	1759
2004		28027	25334	2199
2005		27952	28852	2365
2006		56930	36266	2671
2007		183749	54416	5950
2008		318872	142456	9145
2009		526671	256368	10546
2010		765547	319978	17655
2011		631308	406741	13961
2012		726900	456194	16404
2013		1021254	520733	20801
2014		1269954	579636	31957
2015		1145362	523369	16406
2016		1263523	511109	20274
2017		1486979	707516	13830
2018		1488185	643554	10594
2019		1663154	661042	11520
2020		1789911	641470	12484
对外劳务合作	**Labor Cooperation**			
2003		823	1783	3136
2004		1565	1597	3583
2005		5568	2601	5143
2006		6331	4379	7602
2007		6520	5340	8704
2008		6016	6856	6239
2009		6208	6988	4602
2010		11398	7186	4717
2011		7965	8261	3425
2012		11045	9669	8258
2013		12286	18194	8296
对外设计咨询	**Design Consulting**			
2002		541	267	42
2003		507	650	28
2004		475	1517	72
2005		390	2433	91
2006		983	452	90
2007		5423	2511	461
2008		6531	2804	22

注:2009 年起“对外设计咨询”指标数并入“对外承包工程”中;“年末在外人数(人)”修订为“劳务外派人数(人)”。

Note: From 2009, “Design and Consultation” index number combined into the “International Contractors”; “outer (person) at the end of the year” to “manning (person)”.

5-11 湖北旅游主要指标
Major Indicators of Hubei´s Tourism

年 份 Year	旅游总收入(亿元) Total Earnings of Tourism (100 million yuan)	国内旅游收入(亿元) Earnings from Domestic Tourism (100 million yuan)	国内游客(万人次) Number of Domestic Tourists (10 000 person-times)	外汇收入(万美元) Foreign Exchange Earnings (USD 10 000)	入境游客(万人次) Number of Overseas Vistor Arrivals (10 000 person-times)
1982				299.60	2.00
1983				355.30	2.40
1984				731.30	5.40
1985				1008.60	8.50
1986	3.47	2.50	1262.00	1166.00	10.50
1987	3.67	2.40	1184.00	1545.00	12.20
1988	3.56	2.40	1208.00	1411.80	11.30
1989	3.99	3.10	1034.00	1085.50	8.20
1990	4.56	2.70	890.00	2263.20	15.60
1991	5.83	3.90	984.00	2350.00	17.00
1992	9.03	5.40	1071.00	4432.20	26.30
1993	13.26	9.50	1350.00	4588.90	23.10
1994	18.09	13.00	1500.00	6211.40	24.70
1995	24.00	18.00	1700.00	7316.90	27.10
1996	163.28	153.00	3152.00	12545.60	36.90
1997	193.92	180.00	3600.00	16977.50	58.00
1998	217.24	210.00	4044.00	8831.40	29.60
1999	247.11	238.50	4659.00	10498.50	30.50
2000	282.26	270.30	5478.00	14572.10	45.10
2001	353.66	337.20	6064.00	20075.20	66.80
2002	407.48	384.20	6670.00	28390.90	102.40
2003	342.77	331.60	5684.00	13626.90	40.50
2004	410.00	394.20	6849.00	19240.40	61.20
2005	473.15	450.80	7630.00	27636.30	82.60
2006	539.74	514.24	8459.78	32000.38	105.57
2007	640.87	609.40	10135.00	41264.00	131.81
2008	744.19	713.43	11678.00	44255.31	118.75
2009	1004.48	969.63	15065.18	51020.22	133.46
2010	1460.53	1409.48	20946.00	75116.49	181.74
2011	1992.89	1931.80	27154.87	94018.00	213.52
2012	2629.54	2553.55	34230.00	120296.72	264.72
2013	3205.61	3130.13	40621.04	121892.18	267.96
2014	3752.11	3675.98	46900.00	123851.30	277.07
2015	4308.76	4206.02	50668.24	167190.01	311.76
2016	4879.24	4764.18	56930.83	187238.97	337.56
2017	5514.90	5372.79	63499.86	210473.63	368.14
2018	6178.00	6021.42	53556.28	237968.93	405.11
2019	6927.38	6743.99	60143.70	265415.75	450.02
2020	4379.49	4365.89	43694.43	20755.51	35.21

注:按照文化和旅游部统计督查整改意见,对2018年度旅游总收入、国内旅游收入、国内旅游人数进行了调整。

Note: According to the opinions of the Ministry of Culture and Tourism, Total Earnings of Tourism, Earnings from Domestic Tourism and Number of Domestic Tourists in 2018 were adjusted.

5-12 接待入境旅游人数
Number of Entrance Tourists

单位:人次 (person-times)

年份 Year	总计 Total	外国人 Foreigners	港澳台同胞 Compatroits from Hongkong, Macao and Taiwan	#港澳同胞 Compatroits from Hongkong, Macao	#台湾同胞 Compatroits from Taiwan
1982	19775	15126	4649		
1983	24200	18903	5297		
1984	53800	40496	13304		
1985	84598	68103	16495		
1986	105300	83570	21730		
1987	122390	82029	40361		
1988	113051	78206	34845	19725	15120
1989	81781	49511	32270	13908	18362
1990	155734	36374	119360	11560	107800
1991	170121	53055	117066	12645	104421
1992	263401	72691	190323	14054	176269
1993	230883	84552	146331	28460	117871
1994	247212	133343	113869	56417	57452
1995	270890	172869	98021	42785	55236
1996	368877	243595	125282	58949	66333
1997	580223	359700	220523	64466	156057
1998	295643	209402	86241	30337	55904
1999	305408	224748	80660	30935	49725
2000	450805	357352	93453	42928	53162
2001	667818	542737	125081	48417	76664
2002	1024312	755718	268594	49113	219481
2003	405214	323151	82063	40294	41769
2004	611859	501873	109986	57086	52900
2005	825700	626805	198895	107141	91754
2006	1055752	857028	198724	110246	88478
2007	1318179	1077189	240990	140384	100606
2008	1187549	926625	260924	152631	108293
2009	1334634	1017620	317014	182616	134398
2010	1817416	1385457	431959	241430	190529
2011	2135247	1601129	534118	291487	242631
2012	2647163	1929571	717592	410921	306671
2013	2679623	2047316	632307	365184	267123
2014	2770689	2132562	638127	363810	274317
2015	3117592	2397892	719700	377115	342585
2016	3375628	2546454	829174	390797	438377
2017	3681433	2779487	901946	427834	474112
2018	4051128	3070321	980807	438550	542257
2019	4500182	3499353	1000829	415709	585120
2020	352119				

注:2020年因受新冠疫情影响,文化和旅游部未布置开展入境游客花费抽样调查工作,故相关数据缺失。
Note: In 2020, due to the impact of the New Crown Epidemic, the Ministry of Culture and Tourism did not arrange to carry out a sample survey on the expenses of inbound tourists, so the relevant data are missing.

5-13 入境旅游外汇收入
Foreign Exchange Earnings from Inbound Tourism

年 份 Year	外汇收入(万美元) Foreign Exchange Earnings (USD 10 000)	发展指数(1978 年为 100) Development Index (year1978=100)	同比 Comparision Percentage (±%)	人均天花费(美元) Expenditures Per Capita a day (USD)
1982	299.64	129.85	82.00	
1983	355.30	153.98	18.58	
1984	731.30	316.92	105.83	
1985	1008.58	327.69	37.92	
1986	1166.00	505.31	15.61	
1987	1545.00	669.56	32.50	
1988	1411.75	611.81	-8.62	
1989	1085.45	470.40	-23.11	
1990	2263.18	980.79	108.50	
1991	2350.00	1018.42	3.84	
1992	4432.16	1920.76	88.60	
1993	4588.88	1988.68	3.54	
1994	6211.42	2691.84	35.36	125.10
1995	7316.86	3170.90	17.80	155.70
1996	12545.60	5436.88	71.46	167.04
1997	16977.51	7357.53	35.33	168.52
1998	8831.43	3827.27	-47.98	162.87
1999	10498.49	4549.72	18.88	166.31
2000	14572.13	6315.12	38.80	166.58
2001	20075.16	8699.96	37.76	164.25
2002	28390.95	12303.77	41.42	160.57
2003	13626.93	5905.50	-52.00	160.57
2004	19240.41	8338.21	51.00	169.92
2005	27636.30	11976.73	43.64	170.14
2006	32000.38	13867.99	15.79	177.16
2007	41264.00	17882.56	28.95	181.68
2008	44255.31	19178.90	7.25	197.56
2009	51020.22	22110.60	15.29	193.43
2010	75116.49	32553.20	47.23	192.84
2011	94018.00	40744.53	25.16	195.36
2012	120296.72	52132.92	27.95	193.04
2013	121892.18	52824.35	1.33	194.44
2014	123851.30	53675.70	1.61	192.34
2015	167190.01	72458.19	34.99	214.30
2016	187238.97	81143.65	11.99	198.95
2017	210473.63	91212.84	12.41	209.34
2018	237968.93	103124.63	13.06	233.10
2019	265415.75	115023.07	11.50	211.63
2020	20755.51	8994.80	-92.18	

注:2020 年因受新冠疫情影响,文化和旅游部未布置开展入境游客花费抽样调查工作,故相关数据缺失。

Note: In 2020, due to the impact of the "COVID-19", the Ministry of Culture and Tourism did not arrange to carry out a sample survey on the expenses of inbound tourists, so the relevant data are missing.

5-14 接待入境旅游者天数
Number of Days Receiving Inbound Tourists

单位:人天 (person-day)

年 份 Year	总 计 Total	外国人 Foreigners	港澳台同胞 Compatroits from Hongkong, Macao and Taiwan	# 港澳同胞 Compatroits from Hongkong, Macao	# 台湾同胞 Compatroits from Taiwan
1981	22946	15282	7664		
1982	29016	24188	4828		
1983	29830	25298	4532		
1984	107600	37806	69794		
1985	143815	115774	28041		
1986	186379	139677	46702		
1987	167035	115219	51816		
1988	190486	132301	58185	35505	22680
1989	127891	79217	48674	20862	27812
1990	178737	49487	129250	11960	117290
1991	235595	74913	160682	17450	143232
1992	351591	101878	249713	18973	230740
1993	324350	142240	182110	49959	132151
1994	472467	231716	240751	117889	122862
1995	501038	317246	183792	86910	96882
1996	729968	477152	252816	131993	120823
1997	949661	591127	358534	111291	247243
1998	513569	366348	147221	61491	85730
1999	622037	478486	143551	57765	85786
2000	852455	676130	176325	81432	94893
2001	1208938	891787	317151	93376	223775
2002	1712230	1232818	479412	86427	392985
2003	799824	603001	196823	98230	98593
2004	1069442	849071	220371	118234	102137
2005	1513678	1135995	377683	194122	183561
2006	1824387	1502277	322110	176901	145209
2007	2342786	1926484	416302	233946	182356
2008	2217172	1734211	482961	243638	239323
2009	2640362	2025972	614390	338898	275492
2010	3750746	2868024	882722	481484	401238
2011	4596252	3494098	1102154	581193	520961
2012	5934359	4424239	1510060	822210	687850
2013	6009111	4581165	1427946	802642	625304
2014	6370867	4926991	1443876	805502	638374
2015	7248536	5634388	1614448	833216	781232
2016	8026469	6119616	1901053	906834	994219
2017	9267815	7198608	2069207	985599	1083608
2018	10209040	7931912	2277128	1008464	1268664
2019	11319394	8818976	2500418	1045213	1455205
2020					

注:1.2000 年国家不再设“华侨”指标,“华侨”人数含在“外国人”中。

2.2020 年因受新冠疫情影响,文化和旅游部未布置开展入境游客花费抽样调查工作,故相关数据缺失。

Note: a)The item of “overseas Chinese” is cancled by state since 2000, The number of “Overseas Chinese” is included in the number of “Foreigner”.

b)In 2020, due to the impact of the “COVID-19”, the Ministry of Culture and Tourism did not arrange to carry out a sample survey on the expenses of inbound tourists, so the relevant data are missing.

5-15 湖北国内旅游接待人数及收入
Number of Domestic Tourist Received and Earnings in Hubei

年 份 Year	接待人数(万人次) Number of Tourists Received (10 000 person-times)	同比(±%) Comparision Percentage (±%)	旅游收入(亿元) Earnings (100 million yuan)	同比(±%) Comparision Percentage (±%)	人均花费(元) Expenditures Per Capita (yuan) 全国 The Whole Nation	 湖北 Hubei
1987	1184	-6.2	2.37	-6.0		
1988	1208	2.0	2.42	2.1		
1989	1034	-14.4	3.10	28.1		
1990	890	-13.9	2.67	-13.9		
1991	984	10.6	3.93	47.2		
1992	1071	8.8	5.36	36.4		
1993	1350	26.1	9.50	77.2		
1994	1500	11.1	13.00	36.8		
1995	1700	13.3	18.00	38.5		
1996	3152	85.4	152.95		256	485
1997	3600	14.2	180.00	17.7	328	500
1998	4044	12.3	210.03	16.7	344	519
1999	4659	15.2	238.50	13.6	394	511
2000	5478	17.6	270.31	13.3	427	493
2001	6064	10.7	337.18	24.7	450	556
2002	6670	10.0	384.24	14.0	441	576
2003	5684	-14.8	331.60	-13.7	395	583
2004	6849	20.5	394.22	18.9	550	576
2005	7630	11.4	450.76	14.3	436	591
2006	8460	10.9	514.24	14.1	447	607
2007	10135	19.8	609.40	18.5	482	601
2008	11678	15.2	713.43	17.1	511	610
2009	15065	29.0	969.63	35.9	535	644
2010	20946	39.0	1409.48	45.4	598	673
2011	27155	29.6	1931.80	37.1	731	711
2012	34230	26.1	2553.55	32.2	766	746
2013	40621	18.6	3130.13	22.6	806	771
2014	46900	15.5	3752.11	17.1	839	782
2015	50668	12.7	4206.02	14.3	857	830
2016	56931	12.4	4764.18	13.3	888	837
2017	63500	11.5	5372.79	12.8		846
2018	53556	13.8	6021.42	15.2		1124
2019	60144	12.3	6743.99	12.0		1121
2020	43694	-26.4	4365.89	-35.3		999

注:按照文化和旅游部统计督查整改意见,对2018年度接待人数、旅游收入进行了调整。
Note: According to the opinions of the Ministry of Culture and Tourism, Number of Tourists Received and Earnings in 2018 were adjusted.

5-16 湖北旅游总收入
Total Earnings of Tourism in Hubei

年份 Year	旅游总收入 Total Earnings of Tourism	
	绝对额(亿元) (100 million yuan)	同比(±%) Comparision Percentage (±%)
1997	193.92	18.8
1998	217.27	12.0
1999	247.11	13.7
2000	282.26	14.2
2001	353.64	24.9
2002	407.52	15.2
2003	342.77	-15.9
2004	410.00	19.6
2005	473.15	15.4
2006	539.74	14.1
2007	640.87	18.7
2008	744.19	16.1
2009	1004.48	35.0
2010	1460.53	45.4
2011	1992.89	36.5
2012	2629.54	32.0
2013	3205.61	21.9
2014	3752.11	17.1
2015	4308.76	14.8
2016	4888.51	13.5
2017	5514.90	12.8
2018	6178.00	12.0
2019	6927.38	12.1
2020	4379.49	-36.8

注：按照文化和旅游部统计督查整改意见，对2018年度旅游总收入进行了调整。
Note: According to the opinions of the Ministry of Culture and Tourism, Total Earnings of Tourism in 2018 was adjusted.

主要统计指标解释

货物进出口总额 指实际进出我国关境的货物总金额。包括对外贸易实际进出口货物,来料加工装配进出口货物,国家间、联合国及国际组织无偿援助物资和赠送品,华侨、港澳台同胞和外籍华人捐赠品,租赁期满归承租人所有的租赁货物,进料加工进出口货物,边境地方贸易及边境地区小额贸易进出口货物,中外合资企业、中外合作经营企业、外商独资经营企业进出口货物和公用物品,到、离岸价格在规定限额以上的进出口货样和广告品(无商业价值、无使用价值和免费提供出口的除外),从保税仓库提取在中国境内销售的进口货物,以及其他进出口货物。该指标可以观察一个国家在对外贸易方面的总规模。我国规定出口货物按离岸价格统计,进口货物按到岸价格统计。

商品收发货人所在地进、出口额 指所在地海关注册登记的有进出口经营权的企业实际进、出口额。

商品目的地进口额和商品货源地出口额 目的地进口额指进口货物的消费、使用或最终抵运地的实际进口额;货源地出口额指出口货物的产地或原始发货地的实际出口额。

外商直接投资 指外国企业和经济组织或个人(包括华侨、港澳台胞以及我国在境外注册的企业)按我国有关政策、法规,用现汇、实物、技术等在我国境内开办外商独资企业、与我国境内的企业或经济组织共同举办中外合资经营企业、合作经营企业或合作开发资源的投资(包括外商投资收益的再投资),以及经政府有关部门批准的项目投资总额内企业从境外借入的资金。

对外承包工程 根据《对外承包工程管理条例》,对外承包工程是指中国的企业或者其他单位承包境外建设工程项目的活动。

对外劳务合作 指组织劳务人员赴其他国家或地区为国外的企业或机构工作的经营性活动。

入境游客 指报告期内来中国(大陆)观光、度假、探亲访友、就医疗养、购物、参加会议或从事经济、文化、体育、宗教活动的外国人、港澳台同胞等游客(即入境旅游人数)。统计时,入境游客按每入境一次统计1人次。入境旅游人数包括入境过夜游客和入境一日游游客。

国内游客 指报告期内在中国(大陆)观光游览、度假、探亲访友、就医疗养、购物、参加会议或从事经济、文化、体育、宗教活动的中国(大陆)居民人数,其出游的目的不是通过所从事的活动谋取报酬。统计时,国内游客按每出游一次统计1人次。

国内旅游收入 指国内游客在国内旅行、游览过程中用于交通、参观游览、住宿、餐饮、购物、娱乐等全部花费。

国际旅游(外汇)收入 指入境旅游的外国人、华侨、港澳同胞和台湾同胞在中国大陆旅游过程中发生的一切旅游支出,其对于国家来说就是国际旅游(外汇)收入。

Explanatory Notes on Main Statistical Indicators

Total Import and Export at Goods refer to the real value of commodities imported into and exported across the border of China. They include the actual imports and exports through foreign trade, imported and exported goods under the processing and assembling trades and materials, supplies and gifts as aid given gratis between governments and by the United Nations and other international organizations, and contributions donated by overseas Chinese, compatriots in Hong Kong and Macao and Chinese with foreign citizenship, leasing commodities owned by tenant at the expiration of leasing period, the imported and exported commodities processed with imported materials, commodities trading in border areas, the imported and exported commodities and articles for public use of the Sino-foreign joint ventures, cooperative enterprises and ventures with sole foreign investment. Also included are import or export of samples and advertising goods for which CIF or FOB value are beyond the permitted ceiling (excluding goods of no trading or use value and free commodities for export), imported goods sold in China from bonded warehouses and other imported or exported goods. The indicator of the total imports and exports at customs can be used to observe the total size of external trade in a country. In accordance with the stipulation of the Chinese government, imports are calculated at CIF, while exports are calculated at FOB.

Import or Export Value by Location of China' s Foreign Trade Managing Units refers to actual value of imports and exports carried out by corporations which have been registered by the local Customs house and are vested with right to run import export business.

Import Value of Commodities by the Places of their Destination and Export Value of Commodities by the Places of their Origin in China The former indicator refers to the value of import commodities of the places of their consumption, utilization or the places of their final destination. The latter indicator refers to the value of export commodities of the places of their origin or the places of the commodities dispatched.

Foreign Direct Investment refers to the investments inside China by foreign enterprises and economic organizations or individuals (including overseas Chinese, compatriots from Hong Kong, Macao and Taiwan, and Chinese enterprises registered abroad), following the relevant policies and laws of China, for the establishment of ventures exclusively with foreign own investment, Sino-foreign joint ventures and cooperative enterprises or for co-operative exploration of resources with enterprises or economic organizations in China. It includes the re investment of the foreign entrepreneurs with the profits gained from the investment and the funds that enterprises borrow from abroad in the total investment of projects which are approved by the relevant department of the government.

Overseas Contracted Projects refer to activities of contracting overseas contruction projects by Chinese enterprises or any other units, which are stipulated in the Regulations on Administration of Foreign Contracted Project.

Overseas Labour Services refer to operational activities of organizing labour force to go abroad providing services to foreign enterprises or agencies.

Overseas Vistor Arrivals refer to the number of tourists of foreigners, Chinese compatriots from Hong Kong,Macao and Taiwan who come to China (mainland) within the reference period for sight-seeing, vacation, visiting relatives, medical treatment,shopping, attending conference, or to engage in economic, cultural, sports and religious activities (namely the number of overseas visitor arrivals). In compiling statistics, each arrival is counted as one person-time. The number of overseas visitor arrivals includes inbound overnight tourists and one-day tourists.

Number of Domestic Tourists refers to the number of Chinese (mainland) residents who travel within China (mainland) for sight-seeing, vacation, visiting relatives, medical treatment, shopping, attending conference, or to engage in economic, cultural, sports and religious activities. In compiling statistics, each time of travelling is counted as one person-time.

Income from Domestic Tourism refer to expenditure of domestic tourists on transportation, sighting, accommodation, food,shopping and entertainment while they travel.

Foreign Exchange Earnings from International

Tourism refer to the total expenditures of foreigners, overseas Chinese, Chinese compatriots from Hong Kong, Macao and Taiwan during their stay in the mainland of China, which are earnings of foreign exchange from international tourism from the point of view from China.

资料整理人员:苏 畅 高 媛

6-1 工业能源生产量
Output of Industrial Energy Production

产品		Item		2017	2018	2019	2020
原煤	(万吨)	Coal	(10 000 tons)	311.59	58.46	38.53	40.27
原油	(万吨)	Crude Oil	(10 000 tons)	55.50	54.25	53.62	53.50
天然气	(亿立方米)	Natural Gas	(100 million cu.m)	1.27	5.09	4.89	1.01
水电	(亿千瓦时)	Water and Electricity	(100 million kw/h)	1459.22	1430.89	1330.27	1574.53

注:原煤、原油、天然气以及水电产量为规模以上工业生产量。
Note: Raw coal, crude oil, natural gas and hydropower output are the above scale industrial production.

6-2 规模以上工业能源消费量
Energy Consumption of Industry above Designated Size

产品		Item		2017	2018	2019	2020
能源消费量合计	**(万吨标准煤)**	**Total**	**(10 000 tons standardized coal)**	**14159.66**	**14074.61**	**15019.74**	**13468.37**
原煤	(万吨)	Coal	(10 000 tons)	7116.78	7704.97	8718.65	7421.00
洗精煤	(万吨)	Cleaned Coal	(10 000 tons)	1250.16	1251.52	1162.50	1118.70
其他洗煤	(万吨)	Other Washed Coal	(10 000 tons)	16.12	22.31	20.77	19.73
煤制品	(万吨)	Moulded Coal	(10 000 tons)	11.52	8.72	12.51	12.98
焦炭	(万吨)	Coke	(10 000 tons)	1062.32	1131.70	1115.52	1114.11
其他焦化产品	(万吨)	Other Coked Products	(10 000 tons)	0.73	0.50	0.26	0.00
焦炉煤气	(亿立方米)	Coke-oven Gas	(100 million cu.m)	36.23	32.92	30.35	27.44
高炉煤气	(亿立方米)	Bblast Furnace Gas	(100 million cu.m)	352.79	358.70	357.85	333.98
其他煤气	(亿立方米)	Other Gases	(100 million cu.m)	24.63	23.46	25.37	26.23
天然气	(亿立方米)	Natural Gas	(100 million cu.m)	28.20	33.73	36.27	31.27
原油	(万吨)	Crude Oil	(10 000 tons)	1427.76	1419.60	1515.43	1273.84
汽油	(万吨)	Gasoline	(10 000 tons)	8.00	7.08	6.16	4.60
煤油	(万吨)	Kerasene	(10 000 tons)	1.02	0.61	0.74	0.49
柴油	(万吨)	Diesel Oil	(10 000 tons)	44.35	43.23	42.99	37.98
燃料油	(万吨)	Fuel Oil	(10 000 tons)	3.29	3.08	6.43	3.20
液化石油气	(万吨)	LPG	(10 000 tons)	34.37	36.59	38.12	27.99
炼厂干气	(万吨)	Dry Gas	(10 000 tons)	41.84	37.99	38.54	72.24
其他石油制品	(万吨)	Other Petroleum Products	(10 000 tons)	684.37	238.24	254.19	172.59
热力	(万百万千焦)	Heat	(10 billion kilo-joule)	8875.93	9206.97	9668.64	9673.38
电力	(亿千瓦时)	Electricity	(100 million kw/h)	1290.62	1298.95	1350.86	1251.51
其他燃料	(万吨标准煤)	Other Fuels	(10 000 tons standardized coal)	22.00	20.93	19.65	12.46

注:1.能源消费量包括加工转换投入量,且为当量值。
2.2020 年起能源消费量仅为工业生产消费量合计。
Note: a)The conversion of energy consumption, including processing input, and when the money is.
b)Starting from 2020, energy consumption is the total consumption in industrial production only.

6-3 规模以上工业分行业能源消费量(2020)
Energy Consumption of Industry above Designated Size by Sector(2020)

行 业	Item	原煤消费量(万吨) Coal Consumption (10 000 tons)	汽油消费量(万吨) Gasoline Consumption (10 000 tons)	柴油消费量(万吨) Diesel Consumption (10 000 tons)	电力消费量(亿千瓦时) Electricity Consumption (100 million kw/h)
总消费量	**Total Consumption**	**7421.00**	**4.60**	**37.98**	**1251.51**
采矿业	**Mining**	**26.77**	**0.22**	**3.70**	**21.85**
煤炭开采和洗选业	Mining and Washing of Coal	5.62	0.00	0.01	0.12
石油和天然气开采业	Extraction of Petroleum and Natural Gas	0.00	0.08	0.45	2.90
黑色金属矿采选业	Mining and Processing of Ferrous Metal Ores	2.42	0.00	0.15	5.67
有色金属矿采选业	Mining and Processing of Non-Ferrous Metal Ores	0.00	0.00	0.03	1.87
非金属矿采选业	Mining and Processing of Non-metal Ores	10.43	0.13	2.87	10.43
开采辅助活动	Mining Auxiliary	0.00	0.01	0.00	0.27
其他采矿业	Mining of Other Ores	8.29	0.00	0.18	0.60
制造业	**Manufacturing**	**2893.47**	**4.22**	**33.19**	**1031.84**
农副食品加工业	Processing of Food from Agricultural Products	10.08	0.22	2.23	31.48
食品制造业	Manufacture of Foods	30.18	0.06	0.14	13.41
酒、饮料和精制茶制造业	Manufacture of Wine, Beverages and Tea	7.83	0.13	0.16	10.02
烟草制品业	Manufacture of Tobacco	0.00	0.00	0.02	1.20
纺织业	Manufacture of Textile	3.50	0.05	0.26	51.18
纺织服装、服饰业	Manufacture of Textile Wearing Apparel	0.67	0.04	0.04	3.62
皮革、毛皮、羽毛及其制品和制鞋业	Manufacture of Leather, Fur, Feather and Related and Footware	0.03	0.02	0.00	1.89
木材加工和木、竹、藤、棕、草制品业	Processing of Timber, Manufacture of Wood, Bamboo, Rattan, Palm, and Straw Products	0.80	0.07	0.14	8.47
家具制造业	Manufacture of Furniture	0.01	0.01	0.12	1.89
造纸和纸制品业	Manufacture of Paper and Paper Products	124.75	0.03	1.64	27.71
印刷和记录媒介复制业	Printing and Reproduction of Recording Media	6.80	0.08	0.27	10.79
文教、工美、体育和娱乐用品制造业	Manufacture of Articles for Culture, Education, Art, Sport and Entertainment	2.91	0.02	0.21	15.68
石油加工、炼焦和核燃料加工业	Processing of Petroleum, Coking and Nuclear Fuel	8.83	0.00	0.01	15.23
化学原料和化学制品制造业	Manufacture of Raw Chemical Materials and Chemical Products	1187.16	0.13	1.65	221.62
医药制造业	Manufacture of Medicines	54.18	0.06	0.62	30.00
化学纤维制造业	Manufacture of Chemical Fibres	14.14	0.00	0.01	2.54
橡胶和塑料制品业	Manufacture of Rubber and Plastics	4.98	0.57	0.30	20.84
非金属矿物制品业	Manufacture of Non-metal Mineral Products	890.53	0.20	9.34	124.13
黑色金属冶炼和压延加工业	Smelting an Processing of Ferrous Metals	493.22	0.01	0.73	187.85
有色金属冶炼和压延加工业	Smelting an Processing of Non-ferrous Metals	41.05	0.02	0.55	26.99
金属制品业	Manufacture of Metal Products	5.21	0.17	1.34	29.65
通用设备制造业	Manufacture of General Purpose Machinery	0.29	0.28	2.42	15.50
专用设备制造业	Manufacture of Special Purpose Machinery	0.14	0.30	8.46	12.01
汽车制造业	Manufacture of Automobile	1.08	1.17	1.44	71.90
铁路、船舶、航空航天和其他运输设备制造业	Manufacture of Realway, Ship, Aircraft and Other Transport Equipment	0.56	0.04	0.14	2.49
电气机械和器材制造业	Manufacture of Electrical Machinery and Equipment	0.01	0.18	0.23	26.77
计算机、通信和其他电子设备制造业	Manufacture of Computers, Communication Equipment and Other Electronic Equipment	0.05	0.16	0.04	58.63
仪器仪表制造业	Manufacture of Measuring Instruments	0.00	0.16	0.02	1.35
其他制造业	Manufacture of Other Products	0.00	0.02	0.01	0.61
废弃资源综合利用业	Recycling and Disposal of Waste	4.47	0.00	0.20	5.98
金属制品、机械和设备修理业	Repairing of Metal Products and Mechanical Equipment	0.00	0.02	0.47	0.40
电力、燃气及水生产和供应业	**Electric Power, Gas and Water Production and Supply**	**4500.75**	**0.16**	**1.09**	**197.81**
电力、热力生产和供应业	Production and Supply of Electric Power and Heat Power	4500.75	0.05	1.08	179.97
燃气生产和供应业	Production and Supply of Gas	0.00	0.03	0.00	7.26
水的生产和供应业	Production and Supply of Water	0.00	0.08	0.01	10.58

6-4 全社会综合能源平衡表(等价值)
Overall Energy Balance Sheet for the Whole Society (Equivalence Value)

单位:万吨标准煤 (10 000 tons standardized coal)

项 目	Item	2017	2018	2019	2020
一、可供量	**Quantity Available**	**16180**	**16682**	**17316**	**16251**
一次能源生产量	Primary Energy Production	5341	5331	4892	5653
外省(区、市)调入量	Engery Moblized from other Province	13571	14045	14879	13224
进口量	Import Volume	20	114	262	223
本省(区、市)调出量(-)	Engery Moblized to other Province	2675	2665	2588	2989
出口量(-)	Output Volume	45	67	51	51
年初年末库存差额	Storage Balance Difference Between the Beginning and the End of the Year	-31	-75	-78	191
年初库存量	Storage Volume at the Beginning of the Year	804	834	911	997
年末库存量(-)	Storage Volume by the End of the Year	835	909	989	806
二、消费量	**Consumption**	**16180**	**16682**	**17316**	**16251**
消费量分组一	Consumption Group 1.	16180	16682	17316	16251
1.农、林、牧、渔业	Agriculture, Forestry, Animal Husbandary, Fishing	415	426	452	476
2.工业	Industry	9533	9488	9574	8925
3.建筑业	Construction	382	395	424	422
4.交通运输、仓储和邮政业	Transport Communication, Storage, Post Service	1959	2003	2220	1869
5.批发、零售业和住宿、餐饮业	Wholesale, Retail Sale, Hotel and Catering Industry	805	876	909	839
6.其他	Others	865	1015	1093	1071
7.生活消费	Living Consumption	2222	2480	2644	2649
消费量分组二	Consumption Group 2.	16180	16682	17316	16251
1.终端消费	Terminal Consumption	16123	16665	17321	16340
#工业	Industry	9476	9472	9580	9013
2.加工转换损失	Loss in Processing	-287	-361	-391	-407
火力发电损失	Loss in Thermal Power Generation				0
供热损失	Loss in Heating	166	139	123	141
洗选煤损失	Loss in Coal Seperation	1		2	1
炼焦损失	Loss in Coke Making	34	37	34	37
炼油及煤制油损失	Loss in Oil Refining	48	54	41	30
制气损失	Loss in Gas Drying				5
天然气液化损失	Loss in Natural Gas Liquefaction	4	5	1	1
煤制品加工损失	Loss in Coal Products Processing		0		
回收能	Recuperated Energy	-541	-597	-591	-621
3.损失量	Loss in Processing	344	378	386	318
三、平衡差额	**Balance**				

注:根据第四次全国经济普查结果对2018及之前年度数据进行了修订。
Note: Based on the results of the fourth national economic census, the data of 2018 and previous years are revised.

6-5 全社会煤炭平衡表
Coal Balance Sheet for the Whole Society

单位:万吨 (10 000 tons)

项　目	Item	2017	2018	2019	2020
一、可供量	**Quantity Available**	**10721**	**11100**	**11768**	**10371**
生产量	Production Capacity	315	119	41	40
外省(区、市)调入量	Engery Moblized from other Province	10385	11007	11716	10144
进口量	Import Volume	28	20	51	20
本省(区、市)调出量(-)	Engery Moblized to other Province				
出口量(-)	Output Volume				
年初年末库存差额	Storage Balance Difference Between the Beginning and the End of the Year	-7	-47	-40	167
年初库存量	Storage Volume at the Beginning of the Year	610	617	664	703
年末库存量(-)	Storage Volume by the End of the Year	617	664	703	537
二、消费量	**Consumption**	**10721**	**11100**	**11768**	**10371**
消费量分组一	Consumption Group 1.	10721	11100	11768	10371
1.农、林、牧、渔业	Agriculture, Forestry, Animal Husbandary, Fishing	206	196	190	182
2.工业	Industry	9360	9791	10493	9179
3.建筑业	Construction	46	36	35	32
4.交通运输、仓储和邮政业	Transport Communication, Storage, Post Service	49	44	45	13
5.批发、零售业和住宿、餐饮业	Wholesale, Retail Sale, Hotel and Catering Industry	257	253	246	239
6.其他	Others	270	264	258	249
7.生活消费	Living Consumption	534	516	501	477
消费量分组二	Consumption Group 2.	10721	11100	11768	10371
1.终端消费	Terminal Consumption	5257	4802	4618	4323
#工业	Industry	3895	3493	3344	3131
2.用于加工转换	Coal Used for Processing	5464	6299	7150	6048
火力发电	Thermal Power Generation	3724	4510	5356	4245
供热	Heating	485	537	591	574
洗煤损耗	Loss in Washing Coal	5		41	1
炼焦	Coke Making	1250	1252	1163	1119
炼油及煤制油	Oil Refining and Coal Preparation				
制气	Air Drying				110
型煤加工损耗	Loss in Standardlized Coal Processing				
3.损失量	Loss				
三、平衡差额	**Balance**				

注:根据第四次全国经济普查结果对2018及之前年度数据进行了修订。
Note: Based on the results of the fourth national economic census, the data of 2018 and previous years are revised.

6-6 全社会石油平衡表
Petroleum Balance Sheet for the Whole Society

单位:万吨 (10 000 tons)

项 目	Item	2017	2018	2019	2020
一、可供量	**Quantity Available**	**2601**	**2707**	**2927**	**2679**
生产量	Production Capacity	56	54	54	54
外省(区、市)调入量	Engery Moblized from other Province	2605	2670	2783	2473
进口量	Import Volume		68	169	147
本省(区、市)调出量(-)	Engery Moblized to other Province	16	14	31	50
出口量(-)	Output Volume	32	47	36	36
年初年末库存差额	Storage Balance Difference Between the Beginning and the End of the Year	-12	-26	-12	47
年初库存量	Storage Volume at the Beginning of the Year	211	223	248	260
年末库存量(-)	Storage Volume by the End of the Year	223	248	260	213
二、消费量	**Consumption**	**2601**	**2707**	**2927**	**2679**
消费量分组一	Consumption Group 1.	2601	2707	2927	2679
1.农、林、牧、渔业	Agriculture, Forestry, Animal Husbandary, Fishing	107	111	120	120
2.工业	Industry	595	612	628	543
3.建筑业	Construction	177	182	195	208
4.交通运输、仓储和邮政业	Transport Communication, Storage, Post Service	1146	1159	1288	1101
5.批发、零售业和住宿、餐饮业	Wholesale, Retail Sale, Hotel and Catering Industry	127	137	147	157
6.其他	Others	106	145	159	158
7.生活消费	Living Consumption	343	360	388	391
消费量分组二	Consumption Group 2.	2601	2707	2927	2679
1.终端消费	Terminal Consumption	2554	2676	2895	2629
# 工业	Industry	547	581	597	493
2.加工转换损失	Coal Used for Processing	47	31	31	50
火力发电	Thermal Power Generation	3	3	3	6
供热	Heating	4	4	5	7
炼油损耗	Loss in Oil Refining	40	24	24	36
制气	Gas Making				
3.损失量	Loss				
三、平衡差额	**Balance**				

注:根据第四次全国经济普查结果对2018及之前年度数据进行了修订。
Note: Based on the results of the fourth national economic census, the data of 2018 and previous years are revised.

6-7 全社会电力平衡表
Electricity Balance Sheet for the Whole Society

单位:亿千瓦时 (100 million kw/h)

项 目	Item	2017	2018	2019	2020
一、可供量	**Quantity Available**	**2021**	**2166**	**2323**	**2184**
生产量	Production Capacity	2606	2830	2958	3016
火电	Thermal Power Generation	1043	1239	1470	1222
水电、核电、风电及其它	Hydroelectricity Generation, Nuclearpower Generation, Windpower Generation and others	1563	1591	1488	1794
外省(区、市)调入量	Engery Moblized from other Province	282	204	205	143
进口量	Import Volume				
本省(区、市)调出量(-)	Engery Moblized to other Province	868	867	840	974
出口量(-)	Output Volume				
二、消费量	**Consumption**	**2021**	**2166**	**2323**	**2184**
消费量分组一	Consumption Group 1.	2021	2166	2323	2184
1.农、林、牧、渔业	Agriculture, Forestry, Animal Husbandary, Fishing	30	33	40	42
2.工业	Industry	1321	1349	1421	1310
3.建筑业	Construction	32	37	40	35
4.交通运输、仓储和邮政业	Transport Communication, Storage, Post Service	54	62	69	60
5.批发、零售业和住宿、餐饮业	Wholesale, Retail Sale, Hotel and Catering Industry	98	110	115	101
6.其他	Others	149	180	202	197
7.生活消费	Living Consumption	338	395	436	439
消费量分组二	Consumption Group 2.	2021	2166	2323	2184
1.终端消费	Terminal Consumption	1907	2040	2194	2077
#工业	Industry	1206	1223	1291	1203
2.输配电损失量	Distribution Loss	114	126	129	107
三、平衡差额	**Balance**				

注:根据第四次全国经济普查结果对2018及之前年度数据进行了修订。
Note: Based on the results of the fourth national economic census, the data of 2018 and previous years are revised.

6-8 分市州单位GDP能耗降低率

Reduction Rate of Energy Consumption per Unit GDP by Cities and Prefectures

地 区	Region	2017年单位GDP能耗比2016年降低(±%) 2017year Unit GDP Energy Consumption lower than in 2016	2018年单位GDP能耗比2017年降低(±%) 2018year Unit GDP Energy Consumption lower than in 2017	2019年单位GDP能耗比2018年降低(±%) 2019year Unit GDP Energy Consumption lower than in 2018	2020年单位GDP能耗比2019年降低(±%) 2020year Unit GDP Energy Consumption lower than in 2019
全省	**Total**	**-5.6**	**-4.4**	**-3.2**	**-1.2**
武汉市	Wuhan	-4.9	-4.9	-3.3	-5.2
黄石市	Huangshi	-5.0	-3.8	-2.5	5.9
十堰市	Shiyan	-7.1	-6.5	-4.3	-5.1
宜昌市	Yichang	-4.8	-4.5	-4.3	-1.6
襄阳市	Xiangyang	-5.2	-4.7	-4.8	-3.9
鄂州市	Ezhou	-8.1	-4.9	-4.5	5.1
荆门市	Jingmen	-4.3	-5.2	-3.2	6.1
孝感市	Xiaogan	-5.1	-5.7	-1.2	-0.9
荆州市	Jingzhou	-4.7	-3.1	-6.9	2.2
黄冈市	Huanggang	-5.6	-4.1	-0.8	3.8
咸宁市	Xianning	1.0	-3.5	-3.7	-1.6
随州市	Suizhou	-4.3	6.4	-3.1	-2.9
恩施自治州	Enshi	-4.1	-2.6	-3.2	0.5
仙桃市	Xiantao	-4.1	-4.6	-4.1	2.0
潜江市	Qianjiang	-9.2	-5.0	-4.5	6.0
天门市	Tianmen	-4.9	-4.9	-4.1	1.9
神农架林区	Shennongjia	-2.5	-2.0	-0.3	-0.2

注:表中数据根据第四次全国经济普查结果修订核算。
Note: The data in the table are revised according to the results of the fourth national economic census.

主要统计指标解释

能源生产总量 指一定时期内，一次能源生产量的总和。该指标是观察能源生产水平、规模、构成和发展速度的总量指标。一次能源生产量包括原煤、原油、天然气、水电、核能及其他动力能(如风能、地热能等)发电量，不包括低热值燃料生产量、生物质能、太阳能等的利用和由一次能源加工转换而成的二次能源产量。

能源消费总量 指一定区域内(国家或地区)国民经济各行业和居民家庭在一定时期消费的各种能源的总和。能源消费总量分为三部分，即终端能源消费量、能源加工转换损失量和能源损失量。

(1)终端能源消费量：指一定时期内地区各行业和居民生活消费的各种能源在扣除了用于加工转换二次能源消费量和损失量以后的数量。

(2)能源加工转换损失量：指一定时期内地区投入加工转换的各种能源数量之和与产出各种能源产品之和的差额。该指标是观察能源在加工转换过程中损失量变化的指标。

(3)能源损失量：指一定时期内，能源在输送、分配、储存过程中发生的损失和由客观原因造成的各种损失量，不包括各种气体能源放空、放散量。

单位国内生产总值能耗 指一定时期内，一个国家或地区每生产一个单位的国内生产总值所消耗的能源。计算公式为：

$$单位国内生产总值能耗=\frac{能源消费总量}{国内生产总值}$$

Explanatory Notes on Main Statistical Indicators

Total Energy Production refers to the total production of primary energy by all energy producing enterprises in a given period of time. It is a comprehensive indicator to show the capacity, scale, composition and development of energy production. The production of primary energy includes that of coal, crude oil, natural gas, hydro-power and electricity generated by nuclear energy and other means such as wind power and geothermal power. However, it excludes the production of fuels of low calorific value, bio-energy, solar energy and the secondary energy converted from the primary energy.

Total Domestic Energy Consumption refers to the total consumption of energy of various kinds by material production sectors, non material production sectors and households in a given period of time. It is a comprehensive indicator to show the scale, composition and development of energy consumption. The total energy consumption includes that of coal, crude oil and their products, natural gas and electricity, However, it excludes the consumption of fuel of low calorific value, bio-energy and solar energy. Total domestic energy consumption can be divided into three parts: final energy consumption, loss during the process of energy conversion, and energy loss.

(1)Final Energy Consumption: It refers to the total energy consumption by material production sectors, non material production sectors and households in a given period of time, but excludes the consumption in conversion of the primary energy into the secondary energy and the loss in the process of energy conversion.

(2)Loss During the Process of Energy Conversion: It refers to the total input of various kinds of energy for conversion, minus the total output of various kinds of energy in a given period of time. It is an indicator to show the loss that occurs during the process of energy conversion.

(3)Energy Loss: It refers to the total of the loss of energy during the course of energy transport, distribution and storage and the loss caused by any objective reason in a given period of time. The loss of various kinds of gas due to gas discharges and stocktaking is excluded.

Energy Consumption per Unit of GDP refers to the energy consumption per unit of gross domestic production in a country or the gross region production in a region in the same reference period. The formula is:

Energy Consumption per Unit of GDP = Total Energy Consumption / Gross Domestic Production

7

财政和金融

Government Finance and Banking

资料整理人员:金　花

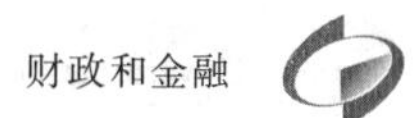

财政和金融
Government Finance and Banking
2020

地方一般公共预算收入	(亿元)	Local Public Financial Revenue	(100 million yuan)	2511.52
地方一般公共预算支出	(亿元)	Local Public Financial Expenditure	(100 million yuan)	8439.04
金融机构(含外资)本外币存款年末余额	(亿元)	Balance of Deposits in Financial Organizations (including Foreign Investment) at Year-end	(100 million yuan)	67159.32
#住户存款	(亿元)	People′s Savings Deposit	(100 million yuan)	34144.37
金融机构(含外资)本外币贷款年末余额	(亿元)	Balance of Loans in Financial Organizations (including Foreign Investment) at Year-end	(100 million yuan)	59872.13

一般公共预算收入与一般公共预算支出(亿元)
Local Budgetary Revenue and Expenditure(100 million yuan)

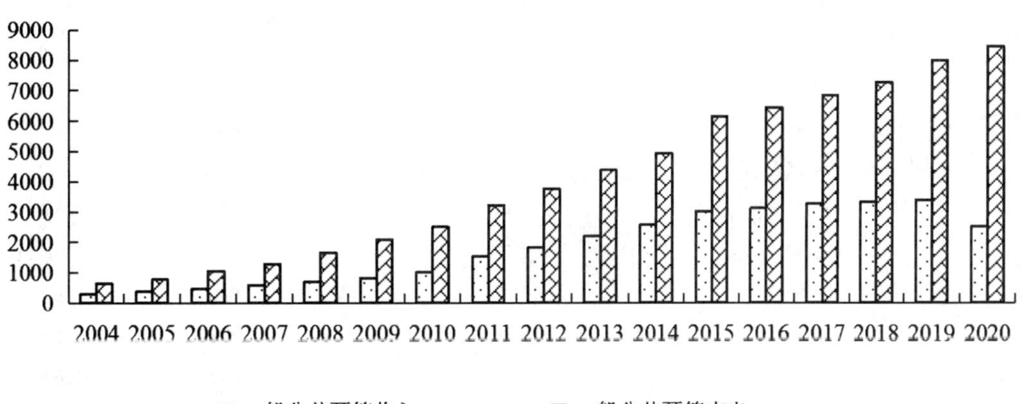

一般公共预算收入与一般公共预算支出(亿元)
Local Budgetary Revenue and Expenditure (100 million yuan)

年份(Year)	2004	2005	2006	2007	2008	2009	2010	2011	2012	2013	2014	2015	2016	2017	2018	2019	2020
一般公共预算收入 (Local Public Financial Revenue)	311	376	476	590	711	815	1011	1527	1823	2191	2567	3006	3102	3248	3307	3389	2512
一般公共预算支出 (Local Public Financial Expenditure)	646	779	1047	1274	1650	2091	2501	3215	3760	4372	4934	6133	6423	6832	7258	7970	8439

7-1 历年地方财政收支额及指数

Amount and Indices of Local Financial Revenue and Expenditure over the Years

单位:亿元 (100 million yuan)

年 份 Year	财政总收入 Total Fiscal Revenue	地方一般公共预算收入 Local Public Financial Revenue	地方一般公共预算支出 Local Public Financial Expenditure	指数(上年=100) Index (previous year=100) 收入 Revenue	 支出 Expenditure
1952	3.81	3.81	1.96	100.0	100.0
1957	6.27	6.27	3.55	109.8	96.7
1965	11.26	11.26	6.85	97.4	105.2
1970	15.20	15.20	15.73	170.6	158.1
1975	24.05	24.05	17.52	139.5	103.9
1978	31.38	31.38	29.98	149.0	148.6
1980	34.01	34.01	26.53	107.6	94.5
1985	50.26	50.26	43.60	119.3	137.5
1990	77.85	77.85	84.82	100.8	106.1
1995	180.57	99.69	162.43	128.7	118.4
1996	216.68	124.51	197.44	124.9	121.6
1997	246.35	139.89	223.70	112.4	113.3
1998	284.44	168.95	280.12	120.8	125.2
1999	314.91	194.44	336.46	115.1	120.1
2000	343.98	214.35	368.77	110.2	109.6
2001	374.15	231.94	484.40	108.2	131.4
2002	435.50	243.44	511.39	105.0	105.6
2003	483.90	259.76	540.44	106.7	105.7
2004	589.65	310.45	646.29	119.5	119.6
2005	727.61	375.52	778.72	121.0	120.5
2006	901.17	476.08	1047.00	126.8	134.5
2007	1115.47	590.36	1274.27	124.0	121.7
2008	1338.75	710.85	1650.28	120.4	129.5
2009	1541.55	814.87	2090.92	114.6	126.7
2010	1918.94	1011.23	2501.40	124.1	119.7
2011	2639.81	1526.91	3214.74	151.0	128.5
2012	3115.63	1823.05	3759.79	119.4	117.0
2013	3566.89	2191.22	4371.65	120.2	116.3
2014	4096.00	2566.90	4934.15	117.1	112.9
2015	4705.00	3005.53	6132.84	117.1	124.3
2016	4974.00	3102.06	6422.98	107.3	104.7
2017	5441.42	3248.44	6831.74	108.4	105.9
2018	5684.85	3307.08	7258.27	101.8	106.2
2019	5787.04	3388.57	7970.21	102.5	109.8
2020	4580.89	2511.52	8439.04	74.1	105.9

注:2020 年数据为财政收支月报数。

Note: The data for 2020 are monthly data on fiscal revenue and expenditure.

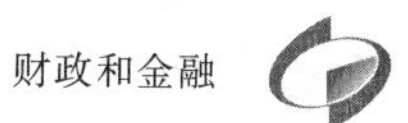

7–2 财政收支
Financial Revenue and Expenditure

单位:亿元 (100 million yuan)

指 标	Item	2017	2018	2019	2020
地方一般公共预算收入	**Local Public Financial Revenue**	**3248.44**	**3307.08**	**3388.57**	**2511.52**
#税收收入	Revenue	2247.60	2463.52	2530.82	1923.40
#增值税	Taxes on Value Added	493.75	937.57	975.87	753.37
营业税	Run Taxes	366.92			
企业所得税	Enterprise Income Taxes	349.40	394.37	407.05	349.79
个人所得税	Individual Income Taxes	121.94	135.87	98.23	90.04
城市维护建设税	Taxes on City Maintenance and Construction	162.73	181.87	179.97	146.28
房产税	Real Estate Taxews	82.67	89.31	100.67	68.65
耕地占用税	Taxes on Use of Cultivated Land	106.37	105.47	98.71	29.51
地方一般公共预算支出	**Local Public Financial Expenditure**	**6831.74**	**7258.27**	**7970.21**	**8439.04**
1.一般公共服务	General Public Service	726.84	739.21	795.05	776.06
2.外交	Foreign Affairs				
3.国防	National Defence		4.61	5.83	
4.公共安全	Public Security	402.14	428.99	452.92	437.39
5.教育	Education	1114.57	1065.64	1147.1	1191.53
6.科学技术	Science and Technology	236.37	268.49	319.28	284.90
7.文化体育与传媒	Culture, Sports and Media	92.32	113.15	148.53	145.33
8.社会保障和就业	Social Security and Employment	1109.41	1172.00	1267.01	1416.94
9.卫生健康	Medical Care and Family Planning	633.91	575.74	601.82	1022.15
10.节能环保	Environmental Protecction	151.27	211.30	282.13	218.90
11.城乡社区	Community Service in Urban and Rural Community	745.62	848.56	924.62	742.97
12.农林水	Water Affairs of Agriculture and Forestry	650.95	785.55	828.21	867.73
13.交通运输	Transportation	272.05	370.64	429.39	501.10
14.其他支出	Others	696.29	674.39	768.32	834.03

注:2020 年数据为财政收支月报数。
Note: The data for 2020 are monthly data on fiscal revenue and expenditure.

7-3 财政收入占地区生产总值的比重
Percentage of Local Financial Revenue to GDP

年 份 Year	地方一般公共预算收入(亿元) Local Public Financial Revenue (100 million yuan)	地区生产总值(亿元) Gross Domestic Product (100 million yuan)	一般公共预算收入占地区生产总值的比重(%) Percentage of Local Financial Revenue to GDP (%)
1980	26.53	199.38	13.31
1985	43.50	396.26	10.98
1986	58.04	442.04	13.13
1987	60.98	517.77	11.78
1988	68.66	626.52	10.96
1989	79.07	717.08	11.03
1990	84.82	824.38	10.29
1991	95.09	913.38	10.41
1992	94.14	1088.39	8.65
1993	115.07	1325.83	8.68
1994	77.46	1700.92	4.55
1995	99.69	2109.38	4.73
1996	124.51	2499.77	4.98
1997	139.89	2856.47	4.90
1998	168.95	3114.02	5.43
1999	194.44	3229.29	6.02
2000	214.35	3545.39	6.05
2001	231.94	3880.53	5.98
2002	243.44	4212.82	5.78
2003	259.76	4757.45	5.46
2004	310.45	5664.15	5.48
2005	375.52	6631.65	5.66
2006	476.08	7670.83	6.21
2007	590.36	9396.62	6.28
2008	710.85	11413.87	6.23
2009	814.87	13082.03	6.23
2010	1011.23	16114.59	6.28
2011	1526.91	19815.57	7.71
2012	1823.05	22479.66	8.11
2013	2191.22	25064.92	8.74
2014	2566.90	27693.04	9.27
2015	3005.53	29882.83	10.06
2016	3102.06	32665.38	9.50
2017	3248.44	35478.09	9.16
2018	3307.08	39366.55	8.40
2019	3388.57	45828.31	7.40
2020	2511.52	43443.46	5.78

注:2020 年数据为财政收支月报数。
Note: The data for 2020 are monthly data on fiscal revenue and expenditure.

7-4 市州一般公共预算收入
Local Public Financial Revenue of Cities and Prefecture

单位:亿元 (100 million yuan)

市 州	Municipalities	2005	2010	2012	2013	2014	2015	2016	2017	2018	2019	2020
全省	**Total**	**375.52**	**1011.23**	**1823.05**	**2191.22**	**2566.90**	**3005.53**	**3102.06**	**3248.44**	**3307.08**	**3388.57**	**2511.52**
省级	Provinial	94.59	206.78	130.07	126.27	133.16	155.96	169.23	231.33	144.27	143.95	129.99
武汉市	Wuhan	138.82	390.19	828.58	978.52	1101.02	1245.63	1322.10	1402.93	1528.70	1564.12	1230.29
黄石市	Huangshi	11.96	34.10	65.64	78.36	89.38	100.53	105.47	111.09	117.02	119.55	88.23
十堰市	Shiyan	11.37	43.77	76.93	73.53	85.77	93.38	100.27	107.66	113.30	119.96	89.36
荆州市	Jingzhou	12.05	27.60	56.76	71.95	88.17	103.95	115.45	122.50	134.31	139.42	105.41
宜昌市	Yichang	22.53	70.24	153.25	206.31	271.51	339.10	300.04	242.08	237.24	240.79	139.97
襄阳市	Xiangyang	18.40	51.01	139.85	191.53	249.24	339.10	320.70	314.91	295.52	300.24	160.00
鄂州市	Ezhou	4.93	15.66	33.02	38.43	42.74	47.17	52.91	58.33	57.93	60.05	48.47
荆门市	Jingmen	9.34	23.25	50.69	59.84	69.82	80.43	91.73	101.25	105.76	110.48	79.84
孝感市	Xiaogan	10.78	34.20	69.50	89.05	107.22	122.77	129.23	131.95	130.19	135.53	100.17
黄冈市	Huanggang	13.14	38.98	62.92	79.98	96.04	112.82	119.52	133.33	139.24	141.40	104.00
咸宁市	Xianning	7.43	23.34	45.82	58.71	70.76	80.12	83.34	87.70	91.32	94.62	70.90
恩施自治州	Enshi	8.35	22.16	40.43	50.05	57.82	67.23	71.91	74.93	80.21	80.65	57.65
随州市	Suizhou	4.25	9.53	22.99	29.67	36.68	43.34	45.55	48.60	47.38	49.10	35.88
仙桃市	Xiantao	2.81	7.35	17.14	21.00	24.16	27.69	29.08	30.90	33.35	34.63	31.98
天门市	Tianmen	1.37	4.71	11.00	15.02	17.35	19.59	17.97	19.25	20.40	21.36	14.23
潜江市	Qianjiang	3.02	7.25	16.02	20.00	22.69	22.85	23.32	25.09	25.84	27.50	21.32
神农架林区	Shennongjia	0.42	1.10	2.44	3.00	3.37	3.86	4.25	4.63	5.10	5.22	3.82

7-5 市州一般公共预算支出
Local Public Financial Expenditure of Cities and Prefecture

单位:亿元 (100 million yuan)

市 州	Municipalities	2005	2010	2012	2013	2014	2015	2016	2017	2018	2019	2020
全省	**Total**	**778.70**	**2501.40**	**3759.79**	**4371.65**	**4934.15**	**6132.84**	**6422.98**	**6831.74**	**7258.27**	**7970.21**	**8439.04**
省级	Provinial	205.75	273.40	449.69	484.45	661.60	893.13	758.76	822.87	789.90	713.80	757.96
武汉市	Wuhan	176.88	583.55	885.55	1122.88	1175.10	1338.05	1524.68	1728.28	1929.54	2238.16	2407.19
黄石市	Huangshi	23.47	102.56	140.43	150.79	152.97	225.94	224.10	224.27	246.50	265.37	286.34
十堰市	Shiyan	33.42	146.98	207.75	231.42	258.87	307.65	323.70	341.35	374.02	406.95	458.62
荆州市	Jingzhou	39.51	163.15	226.83	255.92	276.29	346.48	384.71	406.23	433.18	489.57	533.11
宜昌市	Yichang	47.63	196.51	297.45	364.44	439.92	537.53	531.97	493.77	503.58	596.99	588.80
襄阳市	Xiangyang	49.19	184.92	313.97	364.87	437.93	584.50	624.12	666.99	670.97	729.68	670.10
鄂州市	Ezhou	10.38	43.01	62.69	70.87	75.65	86.80	100.24	116.37	121.67	124.95	127.61
荆门市	Jingmen	24.58	95.46	142.20	158.79	178.96	225.90	246.09	267.52	269.31	293.68	313.68
孝感市	Xiaogan	32.50	133.58	201.79	227.90	253.18	290.38	356.87	360.06	382.52	408.84	425.26
黄冈市	Huanggang	44.40	188.13	278.92	305.16	344.66	401.03	439.87	454.48	482.59	535.34	594.84
咸宁市	Xianning	21.41	100.02	143.03	158.14	176.97	190.85	216.15	226.10	248.34	280.27	312.29
恩施自治州	Enshi	32.12	129.79	179.69	216.69	216.32	332.59	320.24	339.25	391.76	446.04	469.71
随州市	Suizhou	14.11	57.23	85.55	100.04	103.70	153.10	148.32	149.70	154.14	157.98	191.09
仙桃市	Xiantao	8.29	32.91	47.71	50.08	59.56	69.30	74.58	78.93	90.67	92.82	106.49
天门市	Tianmen	6.22	28.27	41.84	46.53	54.36	64.73	67.96	74.02	78.38	88.65	93.06
潜江市	Qianjiang	6.99	28.60	42.01	46.80	51.27	64.11	63.54	61.76	70.10	77.21	81.98
神农架林区	Shennongjia	1.86	13.33	12.69	15.88	16.84	20.78	17.08	19.76	21.10	23.92	20.90

7-6 金融机构(含外资)本外币存款年末余额
Balance of Deposits in Financial Organizations (Including Foreign Investment) at Year-end

单位:亿元 (100 million yuan)

指标	Item	2020
各项存款	**Deposits**	**67159.32**
一、境内存款	**Domestic Deposits**	**66939.82**
1.住户存款	Household Deposits	34144.37
(1)活期存款	Demand Deposits	11855.38
(2)定期及其他存款	Regular and Other Deposits	22288.99
2.非金融企业存款	Non Financial Enterprise Deposits	19513.01
(1)活期存款	Demand Deposits	9818.79
(2)定期及其他存款	Regular and Other Deposits	9694.22
3.广义政府存款	General Government Deposits	11664.16
(1)财政性存款	Public Financial Deposits	2126.98
(2)机关团体存款	Bank Deposits	9537.17
4.非银行业金融机构存款	Non Banking Financial Institutions Deposits	1618.29
二、境外存款	**Offshore Deposits**	**219.51**

7-7 金融机构(含外资)本外币贷款年末余额
Balance of Loans in Financial Organizations (Including Foreign Investment) at Year-end

单位:亿元 (100 million yuan)

指标	Item	2020
各项贷款	**Loans**	**59872.13**
一、境内贷款	**Domestil Loans**	**58889.63**
1.住户贷款	Household Loans	18706.43
(1)短期贷款	Short-term Loans	2399.40
消费贷款	Consumer Loans	971.00
经营贷款	Operating Loans	1428.41
(2)中长期贷款	Medium-term and Long-term Loans	16307.03
消费贷款	Consumer Loans	14235.33
经营贷款	Operating Loans	2071.70
2.非金融企业及机关团体贷款	Non Financial Enterprise and Institution Loans	40165.08
(1)短期贷款	Short-term Loans	8406.91
(2)中长期贷款	Medium and Long Term Loans	26941.71
(3)票据融资	Bill Financing	3019.30
(4)融资租赁	Loans for Accomodation and Rent	1786.19
(5)各项垫款	Money Advanced Payment for Others	10.97
3.非银行业金融机构贷款	Non Banking Financial Institution Loans	18.12
二、境外贷款	**Foreign Loans**	**982.50**

7-8 保险业务主要指标
Major Indicators of Insurance Business

项目	Item	2017	2018	2019	2020
一、保险密度 (元/人)	**Density of Insurance (yuan/person)**	**2281.89**	**2485.93**	**2916.43**	**3210.91**
二、保险深度 (%)	**Depth of Insurance (%)**	**3.69**	**3.74**	**3.77**	**4.27**
三、保费收入 (亿元)	**Premium (100 million yuan)**	**1346.77**	**1470.92**	**1728.57**	**1854.38**
(一)财产保险	Property Insurnce	308.53	351.97	397.85	370.25
1.财产险	Property Insurnce	14.37	16.41	17.83	15.65
2.机动车辆保险	Machine Driving Cars Insurnce	249.85	272.56	299.16	275.56
3.责任险	Responsibility Insurance	12.95	17.74	23.65	27.56
4.信用保证险	Credit Guarantee Insurance	12.59	22.97	29.44	15.87
5.其它	Others	18.77	22.29	27.77	35.62
(二)人身保险	Life Insurance	1038.24	1118.95	1330.72	1484.14
1.人身意外伤害保险	Accident Insurance	35.45	39.90	43.73	42.16
团体保险	Group Insurance	12.59	13.33	14.95	15.05
个人保险	Individual Insurance	22.86	26.58	28.78	27.10
2.健康险	Healthy Insurance	172.72	238.28	312.03	346.70
团体保险	Group Insurance	39.47	55.02	74.64	84.22
个人保险	Individual Insurance	133.25	183.26	237.39	262.48
3.寿险	Personal Insurance	830.07	840.76	974.95	1095.28
团体保险	Group Insurance	0.79	0.72	1.14	1.29
个人保险	Individual Insurance	829.28	840.04	973.81	1093.98
四、各项赔款和给付 (亿元)	**Claim and Payment (100 million yuan)**	**406.47**	**466.67**	**512.26**	**518.15**
(一)财产保险	Property Insurnce	153.30	182.35	210.43	218.15
1.财产险	Property Insurnce	6.24	6.64	7.97	9.39
2.机动车辆保险	Machine Driving Cars Insurnce	127.06	145.36	156.22	147.95
3.责任险	Responsibility Insurance	6.56	8.46	12.47	13.65
4.信用保证险	Credit Guarantee Insurance	2.42	6.03	14.07	24.67
5.其它	Others	11.02	15.86	19.71	22.49
(二)人身保险	Life Insurance	253.18	284.32	301.82	300.01
1.人身意外伤害保险	Accident Insurance	8.84	10.51	12.53	12.59
团体保险	Group Insurance	4.37	4.76	5.56	6.62
个人保险	Individual Insurance	4.46	5.76	6.97	5.96
2.健康险	Healthy Insurance	52.70	79.01	110.84	125.46
团体保险	Group Insurance	31.79	48.49	66.49	66.52
个人保险	Individual Insurance	20.91	30.52	44.35	58.94
3.寿险	Personal Insurance	191.64	194.80	178.45	161.96
团体保险	Group Insurance	8.77	7.90	5.40	5.10
个人保险	Individual Insurance	182.87	186.90	173.05	156.86

注:2020 年采用数据为保险业新口径数据。
Note: The data adopted for 2020 are insurance data based on new standards.

主要统计指标解释

财政总收入　指地方一般预算收入与上划中央税收收入之和。

公共财政收入　是指各级政府为履行职能，按照国家法律、法规规定收取的纳入一般预算管理的各项税收及非税收入总和。主要包括：

(1)各项税收：包括国内增值税、国内消费税、进口货物增值税和消费税、出口货物退增值税和消费税、营业税、企业所得税、个人所得税、资源税、城市维护建设税、房产税、印花税、城镇土地使用税、土地增值税、车船税、船舶吨税、车辆购置税、关税、耕地占用税、契税、烟叶税等。

(2)非税收入：包括专项收入、行政事业性收费、罚没收入和其他收入。

公共财政支出　国家财政将筹集起来的资金进行分配使用，以满足经济建设和各项事业的需要。主要包括：

(1)一般公共服务：指政府提供基本公共管理与服务的支出，包括人大事务、政协事务、政府办公厅(室)及相关机构事务、发展与改革事务、统计信息事务、财政事务、税收事务、审计事务、海关事务、人力资源事务、纪检监察事务、人口与计划生育事务、商贸事务、知识产权事务、工商行政管理事务、国土资源事务、海洋管理事务、测绘事务、地震事务、气象事务、民族事务、宗教事务、港澳台侨事务、档案事务、共产党事务、民主党派事务及工商联事务、群众团体事务、彩票事务等。

(2)外交：指政府外交事务支出，包括外交行政管理、驻外机构、对外援助、国际组织、对外合作与交流、边界勘界联检等方面的支出。

(3)国防：指政府用于国防方面的支出，包括用于现役部队、预备役部队、民兵、国防科研事业、专项工程、国防动员等方面的支出。

(4)公共安全：指政府维护社会公共安全方面的支出，包括武装警察、公安、国家安全、检察、法院、司法行政、监狱、劳教、国家保密、缉私警察等。

(5)教育：指政府教育事务支出，包括教育行政管理、学前教育、小学教育、初中教育、普通高中教育、普通高等教育、初等职业教育、中专教育、技校教育、职业高中教育、高等职业教育、广播电视教育、留学生教育、特殊教育、干部继续教育、教育机关服务等。

(6)科学技术：指用于科学技术方面的支出，包括科学技术管理事务、基础研究、应用研究、技术研究与开发、科技条件与服务、社会科学、科学技术普及、科技交流与合作等。

(7)文化教育与传媒：指政府在文化、文物、体育、广播影视、新闻出版等方面的支出。

(8)社会保障和就业：指政府在社会保障与就业方面的支出，包括社会保障和就业管理事务、民政管理事务、财政对社会保险基金的补助、补充全国社会保障基金、行政事业单位离退休、企业改革补助、就业补助、抚恤、退役安置、社会福利、残疾人事业、城市居民最低生活保障、其他城镇社会救济、农村社会救济、自然灾害生活救助、红十字事务等。

(9)医疗卫生：指政府医疗卫生方面的支出，包括医疗卫生管理事务支出、医疗服务支出、医疗保障支出、疾病预防控制支出、卫生监督支出、妇幼保健支出、农村卫生支出等。

(10)节能环保：指政府环境保护支出，包括环境保护管理事务支出、环境监测与监察支出、污染治理支出、自然生态保护支出、天然林保护工程支出、退耕还林支出、风沙荒漠治理支出、退牧还草支出、已垦草原退耕还草、能源节约利用、污染减排、可再生能源和资源综合利用等支出。

(11)城乡社区事务：指政府城乡社区事务支出，包括城乡社区管理事务支出、城乡社区规划与管理支出、城乡社区公共设施支出、城乡社区住宅支出、城乡社区环境卫生支出、建设市场管理与监督支出等。

(12)农林水事务：指政府农林水事务支出，包括农业支出、林业支出、水利支出、扶贫支出、农业综合开发支出等。

(13)交通运输：指政府交通运输和邮政业方面的支出，包括公路运输支出、水路运输支出、铁路运输支出、民用航空运输支出、邮政业支出等。

信贷资金　指金融机构以信用方式积聚和分配的货币资金。金融机构信贷资金的来源有各项存款、金融债券发行、应付及暂收款、对国际金融机构负债、流通中货币、各项准备、所有者权益和其他项目等；信贷资金的运用有各项贷款、有价证券及投资、应收及预付款、委托投资、金银占款、外汇占款、库存现金、财政借款及在国际金融机构中的资产等。

存款　指企业、机关、团体或居民根据资金必须收回的原则，把货币资金存入银行或其他信贷机构保管并取得一定利息的一种信用活动形式。根据存款对象或性质的不同可划分为企业存款、财政存款、机关团体存款、基本建设存款、储蓄存款、农村存款、委托存款、其他存款等科目。它是银行信贷资金的主要来源。

贷款 指银行或其他信贷机构根据资金必须归还的原则,按一定利率,为企业、个人等提供资金的一种信用活动形式。我国银行贷款分为短期贷款、中期流动资金贷款、中长期贷款、信托贷款、融资租赁、委托贷款、票据融资、各项垫款等。

保险公司 在中国境内的、经过保险监督管理部门批准设立,并依法登记注册的各类商业保险公司。

保险金额 指保险人承担赔偿或者给付保险金责任的最高限额。

保费 指投保人为取得保险人在约定范围内所承担赔偿责任而支付给保险人的费用。

赔款 指保险人根据保险合同的规定,向被保险人支付的赔偿保险责任损失的金额。

给付 包括死伤医疗给付和满期给付。死伤医疗给付是指保险人根据人寿保险及长期健康保险合同的规定,因被保险人在保险期内发生保险责任范围内的保险事故支付给被保险人(或受益人)的金额。满期给付是指被保险人生存期满,保险人按人寿保险合同规定支付给被保险人的满期保险金额。

Explanatory Notes on Main Statistical Indicators

Total income refers to the local fiscal revenue and the general budget tax revenue and central planning.

Public Financial revenue is to perform its functions in accordance with national laws and regulations collected into the general budget of the revenue management and non-tax revenues combined.

Public Financial Expenditure refers to the distribution and use of the funds the government finances has risen, so as to meet the needs of economic construction and various causes. It includes the following main items:

(1) Expenditure for general public services: It refers to the spending on the basic public management and services which provided by governments, including the expense on affairs of People's Congress, affairs of People's Political Consultative Conference, affairs of government general office and relative institutions, affairs of development and reform, affairs of statistics, affairs of finance, affairs of taxation, affairs of audit, affairs of customs, affairs of human resources and social security, affairs of discipline inspection and supervision, affairs of population and family planning, affairs of commerce and trade, affairs of intellectual property, affairs of administration for industry and commerce, affairs of land and resources, affairs of oceanic administration, affairs of surveying and mapping, affairs of earthquake, ethnic affairs, religious affairs, affairs of Hong Kong, Macao, Taiwan, and Overseas Chinese, affairs of archives administration, affairs of Chinese Communist Party, affairs of democratic parties and federation of industry and commerce, affairs of mass organization, and affairs of lottery, etc.

(2) Expenditure for foreign affairs: It refers to the spending of government on foreign affairs, including the expense on administration of foreign affairs, missions overseas, external assistance, international organizations, foreign cooperation and communication, surveying and joint inspection on borderline, etc.

(3) Expenditure for national defence: It refers to the spending of government on national defence, including the expense on active force, reserve force, militia, scientific research on national defence, special projects, mobilization of national defence, etc.

(4) Expenditure for public security: It refers to the spending of government on maintaining social and public security, including the expense on armed police force, public security, state security, prosecution, courts, justice, prison, labour education and rehabilitation, protection of state secrecy, anti-smuggling police, etc.

(5) Expenditure for education: It refers to the spending of government on education, including the expense on the administration of education, pre-primary education, primary education, secondary education, high school education, regular higher education, primary vocational education, secondary vocational education, technical school education, vocational high school education and higher vocational education, radio and television education, student abroad education, special education, on the job training of cadres, education authorities services, etc.

(6) Expenditure for science and technology: It refers to the spending of government on science and technology (S&T), including the expense on the administration of S&T, basic research, applied research, research and development, conditions and services of S&T, popularization of social science, science and technology, exchanges and cooperation of S&T, etc.

(7) Expenditure for culture, sport and media: It refers to the spending of government on culture, cultural heritage, sports, radio, film, television, press and publication, etc.

(8) Expenditure for social safety net and employment effort: It refers to the spending of government on social safety net and employment, including the expense on administration of social safety net and employment, civil affairs, budgetary subsidy on the social insurance funds, subsidy on National Social Security Fund, retirees of administrative units and institutions, subsidy on enterprise reform, subsidy on employment effort, pension, placement of ex-serviceman, social welfare, the handicapped undertakings, the system of cost of living allowances for urban residents, other urban social relief, rural social relief, living relief of natural disasters, affairs of Red Cross Society, etc.

(9) Expenditure for medical and health care: It refers to the spending of government on medical and health care, includ-

ing the expense on administration of medical and health care, medical services, health care, disease prevention and control, health inspection and supervision, women and children's health, rural health care, etc.

(10) Expenditure for environment protection: It refers to the spending of government on environment protection, including the expense on administration of environment protection, environment monitoring and supervision, pollution control, natural ecology protection, project of virgin forests protection, reforesting farmland, controlling the sources of dust storms, returning pastureland to grassland, returning pastureland to grassland, returning cultivated land to grassland, energy conservation, emissions reduction, comprehensive utilization of renewable energy and resources, etc.

(11) Expenditure for urban and rural community affairs: It refers to the spending of government on urban and rural community affairs, including the expense on administration of urban and rural community, planning and management of urban and rural community, public facilities of urban and rural community, housing of urban and rural community, sanitation of urban and rural community, management and supervision on the construction market, etc.

(12) Expenditure for agriculture, forestry and water conservancy: It refers to the spending of government on agriculture, forestry and water conservancy, including the expense on agriculture, forestry, water conservancy, poverty alleviation, comprehensive agricultural development, etc.

(13) Expenditure for transportation: It refers to the spending of government on transportation and postal services, including the expense on road transportation, waterway transportation, railway transportation, civil aviation transportation, and postal services.

Credit Funds refer to the funds issued as loans by banking institutions. The sources of credit funds of the banking institutions included deposits, issue of financial bonds, account-payable and temporary gathering, liabilities to international financial institutions, currency in circulation, various reserves, owners' rights and interests and other items. The credit funds can be used in forms of loans, securities and investment, account receivable and advance payment, entrusted investment, gold, foreign exchange, cash on hand, government debt and assets in the international financial institutions.

Deposit is a form of credit by which enterprises, institutions, organizations or households can put money into banks and other credit institutions for safekeeping and interest earning under the principle of free withdrawal. According to different depositors, deposits are divided into enterprise deposits, treasury deposits, deposits of government agencies and organizations, capital construction deposits, savings deposits, rural saving deposits, entrusted deposits and other deposits. Deposits are major sources of the credit funds of banks.

Loan is a form of credit by which banks and other credit institutions provide funds at certain interest rate to enterprises and individuals in the light of the principle of unconditional repayment. Loans from Chinese banks include circulating capital loans, fixed assets loans, loans to urban and rural individuals engaged in industrial and commercial business and agricultural loans.

Insurance Companies refer to commercial insurance companies of various forms registered by law and established in China with the approval of insurance regulatory agencies.

Amount Insured refers to the maximum that the insurant will get for the claim of the case insured.

Premium is the fee paid by the insurant to the insurer to obtain the obligation of compensation from the insurance within the agreed terms.

Settled Claim is the compensation paid by the insurer to the insurant in accordance with the insurance contract.

Payment includes payment for death, injury or medical treatment and mature payment. Payment for death, injury or medical treatment refers to the money paid to the insurant (or the beneficiary) in accordance with the life or health insurance contract when the insurant encounters accidents within the insured period covered in the contract. Mature payment refers to the mature payment to the insurant in accordance with the life insurance contract at the end of the insured period.

8 价格 Prices

资料整理人员:阳　夏　　潘　路

8-1 物价总指数(2020)
General Price Indices (2020)

基 期	Base Period	商品零售价格总指数 General Rtail Price Index	居民消费价格总指数 General Consumption Price Index
以 1950 年价格为 100	The Price of 1950 Equals 100	707.3	1153.8
以 1952 年价格为 100	The Price of 1952 Equals 100	627.3	1015.1
以 1957 年价格为 100	The Price of 1957 Equals 100	567.9	899.8
以 1965 年价格为 100	The Price of 1965 Equals 100	508.9	791.7
以 1970 年价格为 100	The Price of 1970 Equals 100	512.8	794.7
以 1975 年价格为 100	The Price of 1975 Equals 100	513.6	786.9
以 1978 年价格为 100	The Price of 1978 Equals 100	509.5	784.0
以 1980 年价格为 100	The Price of 1980 Equals 100	480.3	715.8
以 1985 年价格为 100	The Price of 1985 Equals 100	418.8	601.8
以 1990 年价格为 100	The Price of 1990 Equals 100	259.8	379.5
以 1995 年价格为 100	The Price of 1995 Equals 100	139.2	178.5
以 2000 年价格为 100	The Price of 2000 Equals 100	141.8	166.2
以 2005 年价格为 100	The Price of 2005 Equals 100	136.6	150.6
以 2010 年价格为 100	The Price of 2010 Equals 100	120.1	129.8
以 2015 年价格为 100	The Price of 2015 Equals 100	107.4	112.0
以上年价格为 100	The Price of Last Year Equals 100	102.2	102.7

8-2 各市、县物价指数(2020)
General Price Indices of Cities and Counties (2020)

(上年=100) (preceding year = 100)

地 区	Region	居民消费价格指数 Consumer Price Index	商品零售价格指数 Retail Price Index	农业生产资料价格指数 Agricultural Production Material Price Index
湖北省	**Total**	**102.7**	**102.2**	**106.4**
武汉市	Wuhan	102.4	102.2	
黄石市	Huangshi	102.3	101.8	
十堰市	Shiyan	102.3	101.8	
竹山县	Zhushan	103.8	103.9	103.9
宜昌市	Yichang	102.7	102.3	
宜都市	Yidu	103.7	103.3	114.4
襄阳市	Xiangyang	102.9	103.1	
老河口市	Laohekou	104.0	103.2	109.2
鄂州市	Ezhou	102.5	102.2	
荆门市	Jingmen	102.5	101.6	
孝感市	Xiaogan	102.4	101.1	
大悟县	Dawu	103.6	103.6	107.6
荆州市	Jingzhou	102.6	100.8	
洪湖市	Honghu	103.6	102.9	106.4
黄冈市	Huanggang	102.6	102.6	
浠水县	Xishui	103.8	102.8	105.1
麻城市	Macheng	103.0	102.8	104.0
咸宁市	Xianning	102.5	101.6	
崇阳县	Chongyang	103.8	103.4	105.1
随州市	Suizhou	101.9	100.9	
恩施州	Enshi	102.2	101.2	
天门市	Tianmen	102.1	102.7	103.4

8-3 全省居民消费、商品零售价格分类指数(2020)
Provincial Consumer Price Indices and Retail Price Indices by Category (2020)

(上年=100) (preceding year=100)

类 别	Item	全 省 Provincial Indices	城 市 Urban Indices	农 村 Rural Indices
居民消费价格总指数	**General Consumer Price Index**	**102.7**	**102.5**	**103.5**
*服务价格指数	Service Price Index	100.3	100.2	100.6
一、食品烟酒	Food Tobacco and Alcohol	109.3	108.6	110.8
二、衣着	Clothing	99.7	99.6	100.1
三、居住	Residence	99.2	99.0	99.6
四、生活用品及服务	Daily Necessities and Services	100.1	100.0	100.2
五、交通通信	Transportation and Communication	96.5	96.4	96.7
六、教育文化娱乐	Education, Culture and Recreation	100.9	100.8	101.2
七、医疗保健	Medicine	102.2	101.9	102.9
八、其他用品及服务	Other Supplies and Services	104.8	105.5	103.1
商品零售价格总指数	**General Price Index**	**102.2**	**102.1**	**103.0**
一、食品	Foods	111.0	110.5	113.4
二、饮料、烟酒	Beverage, Tobacco and Liquor	100.4	100.4	100.8
三、服装、鞋帽	Garments, Shoes and Hats	99.2	99.1	99.6
四、纺织品	Texiles	100.4	100.6	99.7
五、家用电器及音像器材	Household Electric Appliance and Stereo	96.9	96.8	97.4
六、文化办公用品	Stationery and Business Articles	101.4	101.5	100.5
七、日用品	Daily Use Articles	100.6	100.6	100.6
八、体育娱乐用品	Sports and Receation Articles	100.2	100.2	100.2
九、交通、通信用品	Transportation and Communication Articles	97.4	97.6	96.2
十、家具	Furniture	100.5	100.4	101.0
十一、化妆品	Cosmetics	102.8	102.9	102.4
十二、金银饰品	Gold and Silver Jewelery	116.1	116.4	113.9
十三、中西药品及医疗保健用品	Chinese Traditional Medicine, Western Medicines and Health Care Appliances	102.3	102.0	103.7
十四、书报杂志及电子出版物	Books, Newspaper, Magzines and Electronic Publications	100.2	100.2	100.2
十五、燃料	Fuels	92.7	92.5	93.6
十六、建筑材料及五金电料	Building and Decoration Materials	100.4	100.3	100.6
农业生产资料价格指数	**General Price Index of Means of Agricultural**	**106.4**		

8-4 工业生产者出厂价格指数
Producer Price Indices for Industrial Products

分 类	Group Name	上年=100 preceding year=100	2015 年=100 2015=100	
		2020	2019	2020
总指数	**General Indices**	**99.1**	**109.4**	**108.9**
一、按轻重工业分	**Grouped by Light Industry and Heavy Industry**			
1.轻工业	Light Industry	101.0	105.8	106.7
以农产品为原料	Using Farm Products as Raw Material	101.3	105.4	106.8
以非农产品为原料	Using Non-Farm Products as Raw Material	99.8	107.7	106.4
2.重工业	Heavy Industry	98.1	111.1	109.9
采掘	Mining and Quarrying	101.3	130.2	134.3
原料	Raw Material	95.3	115.9	111.8
加工	Processing	98.7	108.7	108.0
二、按两大部类分	**Grouped by Two Sectors**			
1.生产资料	Means of Production	98.1	111.3	110.3
采掘	Mining and Quarrying	101.3	130.2	134.3
原料	Raw Material	95.1	115.0	110.5
加工	Processing	98.6	109.3	108.9
2.生活资料	Consumer Goods	101.2	105.0	105.6
食品	Foods	102.2	105.0	106.6
衣着	Clothing	100.7	104.3	105.0
一般日用品	Daily Use Articles	100.2	111.6	111.0
耐用消费品	Durable Consumer Goods	99.1	99.8	98.2

8-5 原材料、燃料、动力购进价格指数
Purchasing Price Indices for Raw Materials, Fuels and Power

分 类	Group Name	上年=100 preceding year=100	2015 年=100 2015=100	
		2020	2019	2020
总指数	**General Index**	**98.4**	**111.2**	**110.6**
燃料、动力类	Fuel Powers	89.6	115.7	100.8
黑色金属材料类	Ferrous Metal	100.6	131.5	139.8
有色金属材料类	Non-ferrous Metal	100.3	117.9	127.2
化工原材料类	Chemical Materials	94.1	103.0	100.4
木材及纸浆类	Timber and Pulp	95.9	106.2	104.4
建筑材料及非金属矿类	Construction Materials and Non-Metal Mining Industry	98.5	119.9	117.8
其它工业原材料及半成品类	Other Industrial Raw Materials and Semi-Finished Products	100.5	101.4	102.6
农副产品类	Farm and Sideline Products	108.6	113.4	118.5
纺织原料类	Textile Raw Materials	99.0	106.6	112.6

8-6 固定资产投资价格指数(2019)
Price Indices for Investment in Fixed Assets(2019)

分 类	Name of Group	上年=100 preceding year=100	1990 年=100 1990=100
		2019	2019
总指数	**Total Indices**	**104.0**	**354.02**
建筑安装工程	Construction and Installation	104.4	422.09
设备、工器具	Equipment and Devices	100.5	181.10
其他费用	Others	105.7	415.93

主要统计指标解释

居民消费价格指数 是反映一定时期内城乡居民所购买的生活消费品价格和服务项目价格变动趋势和程度的相对数，是对城市居民消费价格指数和农村居民消费价格指数进行综合汇总计算的结果。该指数可以观察和分析消费品的零售价格和服务价格变动对城乡居民实际生活费支出的影响程度。

城市居民消费价格指数 是反映一定时期内城市居民家庭所购买的生活消费品价格和服务项目价格变动趋势和程度的相对数。该指数可以观察和分析消费品的零售价格和服务项目价格变动对城镇职工货币工资的影响，作为研究职工生活和确定工资政策的依据。

农村居民消费价格指数 是反映一定时期内农村居民家庭所购买的生活消费品价格和服务项目价格变动趋势和程度的相对数。该指数可以观察农村消费品的零售价格和服务项目价格变动对农村居民生活消费支出的影响，直接反映农民生活水平的实际变化情况，为分析和研究农村居民生活问题提供依据。

商品零售价格指数 是反映一定时期内城乡商品零售价格变动趋势和程度的相对数。商品零售价格的变动直接影响到城乡居民的生活支出和国家的财政收入，影响居民购买力和市场供需的平衡，影响到消费与积累的比例关系。因此，该指数可以从一个侧面对上述经济活动进行观察和分析。

农业生产资料价格指数 指反映一定时期内农业生产资料价格变动趋势和程度的相对数。农业生产资料价格指数分为小农具、饲料、产品畜、役畜、半机械化农具、机械化农具、化学肥料、农药及农药械、农机用油、其他农业生产资料十大类。其编制目的是了解农业生产中物质资料投入价格的变动状况，服务于国民经济核算。1994 年以前，农业生产资料价格指数仅仅是商品零售价格指数的一个类别，此后，从商品零售价格指数中分离出来，单独编制。

农产品生产者价格指数 是反映一定时期内，农产品生产者出售农产品价格水平变动趋势及幅度的相对数。该指数可以客观反映全国农产品生产价格水平和结构变动情况，满足农业与国民经济核算需要。其中某代表品生产价格指数是通过对全部有出售该产品行为的调查单位的个体指数进行几何平均求得的，类价格指数是通过对其所属的类(或代表品)的价格指数进行加权平均求得的。季度累计价格指数的计算方法与分季指数的计算方法相同。

工业生产者出厂价格指数 是反映一定时期内全部工业产品出厂价格总水平的变动趋势和程度的相对数，包括工业企业售给本企业以外所有单位的各种产品和直接售给居民用于生活消费的产品。该指数可以观察出厂价格变动对工业总产值及增加值的影响。

工业生产者购进价格指数 是反映工业企业作为生产投入，而从物资交易市场和能源、原材料生产企业购买原材料、燃料和动力产品时，所支付的价格水平变动趋势和程度的统计指标，是扣除工业企业物质消耗成本中的价格变动影响的重要依据。

目前，我国编制的原材料、燃料和动力购进价格指数所调查的产品包括燃料动力、黑色金属、有色金属、化工、建材等九大类的近 1800 种产品。

固定资产投资价格指数 是反映一定时期内固定资产投资品及项目的价格变动趋势和程度的相对数。固定资产投资额是由建筑安装工程投资完成额、设备工器具购置投资完成额和其他费用投资完成额三部分组成的。编制固定资产投资价格指数应首先分别编制上述三部分投资的价格指数，然后采用加权算术平均法求出固定资产投资价格总指数。

该指数可以准确地反映固定资产投资中涉及的各类投资品和取费项目价格变动趋势和变动幅度，消除按现价计算的固定资产投资指标中的价格变动因素，真实地反映固定资产投资的规模、速度、结构和效益，为国家科学地制定、检查固定资产投资计划并提高宏观调控水平，为完善国民经济核算体系提供科学的、可靠的依据。

Explanatory Notes on Main Statistical Indicators

Consumer Price Indices reflect the trend and degree of changes in prices of consumer goods and services purchased by urban and rural households during a given period. It can be used to observe and analyze the impact of price changes in consumer goods and services on wages (in monetary terms) of urban and rural staff and workers, and provide basis for policy-making concerning the living cost and wages of staff and workers.

Urban Consumer Price Indices reflect the trend and degree of changes in prices of consumer goods and services purchased by urban households during a given period. It can be used to observe the impact of change in retail prices of consumer goods and service prices in urban areas on the wage of urban workers′ money. It provides basis for analysis and research on condition of life in urban areas.

Rural Consumer Price Indices reflect the trend and degree of changes in prices of consumer goods and services purchased by rural households during a given period. It can be used to observe the impact of change in retail prices of consumer goods and service prices in rural areas on living expenditure of rural households, and to show the changes in the living standard of peasants. It provides basis for analysis and research on condition of life in rural areas.

Retail Price Indices reflect the trend and degree of change in retail prices of commodities during a given period. The change in retail prices of commodities directly affect the living expenditure of urban and rural residents, government revenue, purchasing power of residents and the equilibrium of market supply and demand, and the ratio of consumption to accumulation. Therefore, the retail price indices are useful to analyze the changes of the above economic activities.

Price Indices of Means of Agricultural Production reflect the trend and degree of changes in prices of means of agricultural production during a given period. Price indices of means of agricultural production are composed of 10 categories including small farm tools, feeds, domestic animals for meat, draught domestic animals, semi-mechanized farm machinery, mechanized farm machinery, chemical fertilizers, pesticides and spraying machinery, fuels for farm machinery and other means of agricultural production. Compilation of these indices helps to understand the changes in prices of input into agricultural production and facilitate the compilation of national account statistics. Before 1994, price indices of means of agricultural production was a sub-category in the in the retail price indices of commodities, and it has been compiled separately since 1994.

Indices of Producers' Prices for Farm Products reflect the trend and degree of changes in producers' prices received by farmers when they sell farm products during a given period. These indices depict the change in the level and structure of producers' prices of farm products of the country and meet the needs of agriculture statistics and national account statistics. The producers' price index of a given product is calculated through geometrical mean of individual indices of all surveyed units who sell such product, and the indices of a product category is obtained through weighted mean of price indices of all products in the category. Method for calculating accumulative quarterly indices is the same as for calculating the distinctive quarterly indices.

Producer Price Indices for Industrial Producers reflect the trend and degree of changes in general ex-factory prices of all industrial products during a given period, including sales of industrial products by an industrial enterprise to all units outside the enterprise, as well as sales of consumer goods to residents. It can be used to analyze the impact of ex-factory prices on gross output value and value-added of the industrial sector.

Purchasing Price Indices for Industrial Producers reflect changes in the level and degree of prices paid by industrial enterprises when they purchase production input such as raw materials, fuels and power from the market or from other energy or raw materials producing enterprises. These indices provide important basis for measuring the material consumption of industrial enterprises after removing influence of price changes.

At present, close to 1,800 products in 9 categories, including fuels and power, ferrous metals, non-ferrous metals, chemicals, building materials, are covered in China for the survey to produce indices of purchasing prices of raw materials, fuels and power.

Price Indices of Investment in Fixed Assets reflect the trend and degree of changes in prices of investment goods and projects in fixed assets during a given period. The investment in fixed assets consists of three components, namely the investment in construction and installation, the investment in purchases of equipment and instrument, and the investment in other items. Price indices of investment in fixed assets are calculated as the weighted arithmetic mean of the price indices of the three components of investment in fixed assets.

Removing the factor of price change in the aggregates of investment at current prices, this indicator shows the changes in the prices of commodities and fees involved in the investment of fixed assets, and can be used to observe the actual size, growth, structure, and efficiency of investment in fixed assets and provides reliable and scientific data for government planning, management, decision-making, and further improving the current national accounting system.

9

人民生活

People's Livelihoods

资料整理人员:盛 坤 孙胜男 程文懿

9-1 居民生活水平情况
People′s Living Standard

项 目		Item		2005	2010	2015	2019	2020
一、城乡就业		**Employment**						
每一农村劳动力负担人数	(人)	Average Person Supported by a Rural Laborer	(person)	1.34	1.27	1.41	1.46	1.45
每一城镇就业者负担人数	(人)	Average Person Supported by a Urban Laborer	(person)	1.96	2.01	1.86	1.88	1.36
城镇登记失业率	(%)	The Rate of Registered Unemployment	(percentage)	4.33	4.18	2.64	2.44	3.35
二、城乡居民收入		**Revenue**						
农村居民人均可支配收入	(元)	Net Income of Rural Residents Per Capita	(yuan)	3099.00	5832.00	11843.89	16390.86	16305.91
农村居民人均可支配收入指数(1990=100)	(%)	Indices of Net Income of Rural Residents Per Capita (1990=100)	(percentage)	461.80	869.24	1765.63	2443.00	2430.34
城镇居民人均可支配收入	(元)	Annual Disposable Income of Urban Residents	(yuan)	8786.00	16058.00	27051.47	37601.36	36705.74
城镇居民人均可支配收入指数(1990=100)	(%)	Indices of Net Annual Disposable Income of Urban Residents (1990=100)	(percentage)	615.80	1125.45	1895.42	2635.35	2572.58
国有职工平均工资	(元)	Average Wages of Staff and Workers in State-Owned Units	(yuan)	14774	35981	60615	91665	101253
三、城乡居民人平消费水平		**Consumption Level**						
农村居民	(元)	Rural Residents	(yuan)	2503	4758	9542		
城镇居民	(元)	Urban Residents	(yuan)	8051	13576	23561		
四、储蓄		**Savings**						
城乡居民人平储蓄存款余额	(元)	Balance of Saving Deposits of Rural and Urban Residents Per Capita	(yuan)	7929	17216	33539	50329	58206
五、平均每人居住面积								
城市(大、中)	(平方米)	Floor Area of Housing Per Capita Municipalities (Large and Medium-sized)	(sq.m)	29.90	33.20	43.18	46.31	43.08
农村	(平方米)	Rural Areas	(sq.m)	36.05	40.99	55.61	58.68	57.79
六、交通		**Transportations**						
城镇每百户拥有汽车	(辆)	Cars Ouned Per 100	(set)		5.53	17.68	37.33	49.33
七、文化		**Culture**						
每百人每天有报纸	(份)	Newspaper Owned Per 100 Persons Every Day	(unit)	8.89	8.70	7.23	3.41	2.68
每人每年有图书、杂志	(册)	Books and Magazines Owned Per Capita Annually	(unit)	8.99	9.90	8.82	6.53	6.27
八、教育		**Education**						
学龄儿童入学率	(%)	Emrollment Ratio of School-Age Children	(percentsge)	99.65	99.96	99.99	100.00	100.00
每万人口有大学生数	(人)	Number of University Students Per 10 000 Persons	(person)	167.91	226.58	240.75	252.75	276.51
九、卫生		**Health Care**						
每千人口卫生机构床位数	(张)	Number of Hospital-Beds Owned By Per 1 000 Person	(unit)	2.31	3.26	5.87	6.86	7.05
每千人有医生	(人)	Number of Doctors Owned By Per 1 000 Persons	(person)	1.49	1.62	2.32	2.62	2.74

注:1.平均每人居住面积中,城市(大、中)从 2002 年起为建筑面积,以前年份为居住面积。

2.2014 年起使用城乡一体化住户收支与生活状况调查数据,与之前的分城镇和农村住户调查的范围、方法、指标口径有所不同(此后相关表同)。

Note: a)Of Average Housing Areas, it refers to Construction Area of Municipalities (large and medium-sized) areas.since 2002, before2002, it refers to living areas.

b)The integrated household income and expenditure survey has been used since 2014, including both urban and rural households. The coverage, methodology and definitions used in the survey are different from those used for the separate urban and rural household survey prior to 2014.

9-2 居民消费水平
People's Consumption Level

年 份 Year	居民消费（亿元） People's Consumption (100 million yuan)	农村居民 Rural Residents	城镇居民 Urban Residents	居民消费水平（元） Level of Consumption (yuan)	农村居民 Rural Residents	城镇居民 Urban Residents
1982	126.75	90.67	36.08	266	227	462
1983	141.49	101.17	40.32	293	251	502
1984	172.19	120.41	51.78	352	300	592
1985	203.23	129.78	73.45	411	328	738
1986	247.13	158.31	88.82	493	402	825
1987	271.22	172.47	98.75	533	434	891
1988	328.82	204.21	124.61	638	509	1092
1989	398.09	255.09	143.00	762	630	1218
1990	434.62	273.27	161.35	813	659	1341
1991	475.85	286.08	189.77	869	674	1541
1992	546.61	301.60	245.01	986	706	1926
1993	694.49	357.14	337.35	1236	831	2554
1994	845.15	413.40	431.75	1486	964	3086
1995	1095.97	504.12	591.85	1908	1183	3989
1996	1346.74	594.80	751.94	2323	1396	4892
1997	1438.12	614.90	823.22	2459	1441	5208
1998	1518.87	610.20	908.67	2579	1427	5632
1999	1507.12	558.43	948.69	2545	1302	5802
2000	1594.07	559.11	1034.96	2680	1302	6250
2001	1767.37	585.41	1181.96	2962	1365	7042
2002	1951.54	606.80	1344.74	3263	1418	7899
2003	2188.04	637.70	1550.34	3853	1926	6547
2004	2452.62	700.77	1751.85	4309	2134	7277
2005	2785.42	815.32	1970.10	4883	2503	8051
2006	3154.40	912.15	2242.25	5533	2832	9041
2007	3709.69	1051.82	2657.87	6513	3300	10593
2008	4225.38	1217.95	3007.43	7406	3864	11780
2009	4456.31	1277.72	3178.59	7791	4137	12080
2010	5136.78	1419.65	3717.13	8977	4758	13576
2011	6241.95	1597.69	4644.26	10873	5653	15935
2012	7085.46	1830.83	5254.63	12283	6705	17296
2013	8053.82	2064.74	5989.08	13912	7755	19156
2014	9124.48	2292.06	6832.42	15712	8788	21355
2015	10167.87	2434.73	7733.14	17429	9542	23561
2016	11379.23	2709.89	8669.34	19391	10860	25703
2017	12914.48	3185.97	9728.51	21913	13090	28121
2018	14832.97	3871.33	10961.64	25100	16296	31018

9-3 居民消费水平指数
Indices of People's Consumption Level

(1978 年=100)

年 份 Year	居民消费 (%) People's Consumption (%)	农村居民 Rural Residents	城镇居民 Urban Residents	居民消费水平 (%) Level of Consumption (%)	农村居民 Rural Residents	城镇居民 Urban Residents
1982	156.2	169.2	132.3	149.0	164.2	111.5
1983	172.2	186.6	145.4	162.1	179.7	119.0
1984	196.6	205.4	181.4	183.3	198.7	136.6
1985	218.4	212.2	233.3	201.1	208.2	154.2
1986	253.2	247.7	267.4	229.7	244.3	163.5
1987	263.0	255.1	282.4	235.4	249.4	167.4
1988	268.8	257.1	295.6	237.8	248.6	170.4
1989	278.8	273.6	292.7	243.0	262.6	163.9
1990	290.5	281.2	312.9	247.6	263.3	170.8
1991	275.4	257.6	314.1	229.3	235.7	167.6
1992	281.7	254.0	339.6	231.8	230.5	175.3
1993	338.3	276.9	460.8	274.7	250.1	229.1
1994	380.3	292.4	553.4	304.9	264.6	259.6
1995	421.7	303.5	653.0	334.8	276.3	288.9
1996	474.9	340.2	737.9	373.6	310.0	315.2
1997	499.1	342.9	802.9	389.3	311.8	333.1
1998	549.5	354.6	927.3	425.5	321.8	377.1
1999	571.5	356.0	989.4	440.0	322.1	397.1
2000	599.5	361.0	1062.6	459.8	326.0	420.9
2001	661.3	377.2	1206.1	505.8	341.3	471.0
2002	738.6	391.9	1394.3	564.0	355.3	537.0
2003	807.3	393.9	1578.3	614.7	359.2	595.0
2004	868.7	405.3	1726.7	659.6	372.5	640.2
2005	963.4	458.4	1899.3	729.5	425.0	692.7
2006	1074.5	502.7	2133.2	814.1	471.3	767.5
2007	1191.6	556.8	2366.7	903.7	527.9	841.9
2008	1280.1	599.2	2540.8	969.7	574.4	888.2
2009	1353.2	630.8	2690.5	1022.0	616.9	913.1
2010	1508.6	675.9	3046.2	1138.5	684.1	993.5
2011	1723.1	710.1	3586.1	1295.7	758.7	1098.8
2012	1898.9	785.5	3946.9	1421.3	868.7	1160.3
2013	2107.4	862.9	4395.3	1572.0	979.0	1255.4
2014	2343.1	940.2	4920.1	1741.8	1088.6	1373.4
2015	2577.9	984.0	5499.9	1907.2	1164.9	1497.1
2016	2844.6	1075.3	6087.3	2092.2	1301.1	1612.3
2017	3166.0	1248.4	6683.9	2318.2	1549.7	1725.2
2018	3511.1	1418.2	7357.7	2563.9	1803.8	1859.8

9-4 城镇居民家庭基本情况

年 份 Year	调查户数 （户） Number of Households Surveyed (household)	平均每户家庭人口 （人） Average Number of People Per Household (person)	平均每户就业人口 （人） Number of Employees Per Household (person)	每一就业者负担人数 （人） Average Persons Supported by a Labor (person)
1963	240	5.30	1.63	3.25
1964	299	5.36	1.61	3.33
1965	370	5.22	1.60	3.26
1980	571	4.20	2.32	1.81
1985	1658	3.84	2.15	1.79
1987	1900	3.73	2.12	1.76
1988	1950	3.61	2.07	1.74
1989	1990	3.52	2.05	1.72
1990	1990	3.47	2.04	1.70
1991	1990	3.45	2.04	1.69
1992	1940	3.36	2.02	1.66
1993	1890	3.29	1.98	1.66
1994	1330	3.23	1.95	1.66
1995	1330	3.22	1.92	1.68
1996	1390	3.24	1.95	1.66
1997	1790	3.23	1.89	1.71
1998	1640	3.19	1.90	1.68
1999	1540	3.15	1.86	1.69
2000	1540	3.14	1.81	1.73
2001	1540	3.10	1.77	1.75
2002	1600	3.07	1.64	1.87
2003	1600	3.06	1.68	1.82
2004	1700	3.03	1.65	1.83
2005	1800	2.98	1.52	1.96
2006	1800	2.96	1.55	1.91
2007	1850	2.95	1.59	1.86
2008	1900	2.96	1.50	1.97
2009	1900	2.94	1.48	1.99
2010	1900	2.93	1.46	2.01
2011	1900	2.90	1.47	1.97
2012	1900	2.89	1.48	1.95
2013	1718	2.77	1.53	1.81
2014	3060	2.85	1.59	1.79
2015	3073	2.85	1.53	1.86
2016	3053	2.86	1.52	1.88
2017	3031	2.84	1.51	1.89
2018	3489	3.00	1.60	1.87
2019	3409	3.01	1.60	1.88
2020	3210	3.03	1.46	1.36

注：1.2002 年方法制度重新修订，部分指标有所变化：原“平均每人居住面积”改为“平均每人建筑总面积”；原“平均每人实际收入”改为“平均每人总收入”；原“平均每人实际支出”改为“平均每人总支出”。

2.2014 年起使用城乡一体化住户收支与生活状况调查数据，与之前的分城镇和农村住户调查的范围、方法、指标口径有所不同（此后相关表同）。

3.2014 年起为城镇常住居民人均可支配收入，与 2014 年以前不同。

Basic Conditions of Urban Households

平均每户就业面 (%) Percentage of Employed Persons Per Household (%)	平均每人 Per Capita 总收入(元) Actual Income (yuan)	# 可支配收入(元) Disposable Income (yuan)	平均每人 Per Capita 总支出(元) Actual Expenditures (yuan)	消费性支出 Living Expenditures	# 食品 Food	平均每人建筑面积(平方米) Average Living Floor Space Per Cappita (sq.m)
30.75	238.1	238.1	237.2	218.4	133.9	
30.04	232.9	232.9	228.3	211.7	122.7	
30.65	224.3	224.3	218.8	204.4	118.0	3.3
55.24	413.7	413.7	394.2	369.3	210.6	5.1
55.99	713.3	704.2	693.1	644.2	324.5	7.9
56.84	960.6	951.8	919.1	836.1	443.2	8.4
57.34	1136.4	1128.1	1153.1	1058.8	538.9	8.9
58.24	1271.6	1262.6	1250.0	1130.7	607.0	9.1
58.79	1437.1	1427.2	1349.4	1220.3	652.4	9.8
59.13	1603.7	1592.9	1538.2	1380.2	717.4	9.6
60.12	1886.4	1874.2	1799.9	1577.7	799.0	9.9
60.18	2453.5	2438.7	2358.1	2097.6	941.5	10.5
60.37	3360.0	3346.0	3588.6	2733.1	1307.1	11.1
59.63	4031.9	4016.7	3977.3	3433.8	1680.6	11.9
60.19	4367.0	4350.2	4290.6	3713.5	1731.4	11.8
58.51	4693.8	4673.2	4549.7	3855.6	1773.6	12.8
59.56	4849.4	4826.4	4903.1	4074.4	1787.7	12.7
59.04	5234.5	5212.8	5333.8	4340.6	1783.4	13.2
57.64	5542.6	5524.5	5643.6	4644.5	1779.4	13.9
57.10	5888.7	5856.0	5774.8	4804.8	1799.4	15.2
53.42	7142.2	6789.0	7159.7	5608.9	2087.8	26.2
54.90	7745.8	7322.0	7551.1	5963.3	2279.6	26.3
54.46	8522.1	8022.8	8076.1	6398.5	2516.2	27.3
51.01	9395.1	8786.0	8582.8	6737.0	2625.4	29.9
52.36	10533.3	9803.0	9839.7	7397.0	2868.4	31.0
53.90	12421.8	11485.0	11476.7	8701.0	3456.0	32.3
50.68	14174.3	13153.0	12471.0	9478.0	3996.0	32.0
50.34	15698.0	14367.0	13868.0	10294.0	4160.5	32.8
49.83	17572.8	16058.4	15612.3	11451.0	4429.3	33.2
50.69	20193.3	18373.9	18123.4	13163.8	5363.7	35.5
51.21	22903.9	20839.6	20107.1	14496.0	5837.9	35.8
55.23	25180.5	22906.4	20419.5	15749.5	6259.2	38.8
55.73	27538.9	24852.3	23175.1	16681.4	3688.3	41.9
53.69	30057.4	27051.5	24798.4	18192.3	3897.6	43.2
53.23	32239.8	29385.8	27376.3	20040.0	4262.6	44.5
52.97	34972.3	31889.4	28784.6	21275.6	4244.0	45.1
52.32	38860.2	34454.6	35600.7	23995.9	3883.4	45.0
53.10	42207.9	37601.4	40544.4	26421.8	4154.2	46.3
48.17	40196.3	36705.7	31006.2	22885.5	7112.4	43.1

Note: a)"Per Capita Living Space (sq.m)" in the above table was changed into "Per Capita Living Floor Space (sq.m)"; "Per Capita Actual Income (yuan)" into; "Per Capita Actual Expenditures(yuan)" into "Per Capita Total Expenditures(yuan)"; owing to the changes of items in the reversion of 2002 mearurement system.

b)The integrated household income and expenditure survey has been used since 2014, including both urban and rural households. The coverage, methodology and definitions used in the survey are different from those used for the separate urban and rural household survey prior to 2014.

c)The concept is Per Capita Disposable Income of Rural Permanent Pesident since 2014, different from that before 2014.

9-5 城镇居民家庭收支情况(2020)

单位：元

项 目		Item		总 计 Total	低收入户 Low Income Households
调查户数	(户)	Households Surveyed	(household)	3210	642
比重	(%)	Ratio	(%)	100.00	20.00
平均每户家庭人口	(人)	Average Number of Residents Per Household	(person)	3.03	3.45
平均每户离退休人口	(人)	Average Number of Retirees Per Household	(person)	0.52	0.16
平均每一就业者负担人数	(人)	Average Persons Supported by a Urban Labor	(person)	2.08	2.23
平均每户就业面	(%)	Average Employment Rate Per Household	(%)	48.17	44.81
平均每人总收入		Per Capita Total Income		40196.30	15469.51
#可支配收入		Disposable Income		36705.74	12459.53
平均每人借贷收入		Income of Loans Per Capita		514.65	541.87
#提取储蓄存款		Savings Withdrawn		277.56	285.78
平均每人借贷支出		Expenditures of Loans Per Capita		1753.93	801.91
#存入储蓄款		Money Saved		39.80	1.37
平均每人总支出		Total Expenditure Per Capita		31006.17	19332.73
#消费性支出		Consumption Expenditure		22885.47	13847.89
一、食品烟酒		**Food Cigarettes and Wine**		**7112.39**	**4878.37**
食品		Food		4824.93	3580.24
谷物		Grain		723.41	523.54
薯类		Patato		51.51	51.00
豆类		Bean		71.30	60.82
食用油		Edible Oil		173.61	164.01
蔬菜和食用菌		Vegetable and Edible Fungi		699.05	537.07
肉类		Meat		1287.57	995.42
禽类		Poultry		227.34	168.99
水产品		Aquatic Products		359.59	237.72
蛋类		Egg		122.33	100.52
奶类		Milk		265.59	188.15
干鲜瓜果类		Fruits and Processed Products		449.60	284.00
糖果糕点类		Sweet		135.79	80.09
其他食品		Others		258.23	188.94
烟酒		Cigarettes and Wine		680.35	472.16
饮料		Drink		119.73	76.50
饮食服务		Food Service		1487.38	749.47
二、衣着		**Clothing**		**1472.31**	**836.98**
衣类		Clothing		1230.81	683.48
鞋类		Shoes		241.50	153.50
三、居住		**Residence**		**5774.27**	**3035.78**
租赁房房租		Rent		171.44	140.13
住房维修及管理		Management		700.87	397.85
水电燃料及其他		Water and Power		850.24	582.66
自有住房折算租金		Converted Rent of Zts Own		4051.72	1915.13
四、生活用品及服务		**Household Facilities Articles and Services**		**1316.02**	**728.07**
家具及室内装饰品		Furniture		183.81	123.40
家用器具		Appliances		324.14	149.81
家用纺织品		Drygoods		95.87	37.95
家庭日用杂品		Commodity		330.40	211.88
个人用品		Personal Helongings		319.19	186.33
家庭服务		Households Service		62.61	18.70
五、交通通信		**Transport and Communication**		**2852.48**	**1849.79**
交通		Transport		2113.66	1387.87
通信		Communication		738.82	461.92
六、教育文化娱乐		**Education Culture and Recreation**		**2040.84**	**1317.69**
教育		Education		1491.34	1092.74
文化娱乐用品		Cultural Recreation Articals		311.31	160.14
文化娱乐服务		Cultural Recreation Services		238.19	64.80
七、医疗保健		**Medicine and Medical Service**		**1922.34**	**1004.39**
医疗器具及药品		Medical Apparatus and Instruments		546.83	307.25
医疗服务		Medical Service		1375.51	697.14
八、其他用品和服务		**Miscellaneous Goods and Services**		**394.82**	**196.83**
其他用品		Goods		167.06	80.93
其他服务		Services		227.75	115.90

注:2014年起城镇居民消费居住支出中自有住房折算租金指现住房为自有住房的住户为自身消费提供住房服务的折算价值，属于实物消费，不包括在现金消费支出中。

Income and Consumption Expenditure of Urban Households (2020)

(yuan)

中低收入户 Lower Middle Income Households	中等收入户 Middle Income Households	中高收入户 Upper Middle Income Households	高收入户 High Income Households
642	642	642	642
20.00	20.00	20.00	20.00
3.39	3.02	2.74	2.56
0.35	0.58	0.79	0.70
2.12	2.03	2.08	1.89
47.12	49.24	48.01	53.00
25168.71	35956.38	50422.63	87401.65
23031.60	33194.54	46806.98	80748.63
454.36	302.93	546.15	773.55
354.34	181.49	225.15	333.77
1160.50	1280.77	2012.42	4099.97
140.44		24.83	20.89
21673.67	28529.16	38395.52	54085.29
16579.45	22451.36	28339.96	38073.56
5873.10	**7241.60**	**8688.35**	**9922.55**
4130.71	4880.97	5812.50	6297.62
577.01	719.06	816.47	1091.68
46.89	48.95	58.65	53.72
60.84	73.59	84.57	82.40
165.44	173.34	197.28	172.43
601.30	700.55	867.05	865.26
1123.40	1326.03	1519.83	1604.61
209.06	235.68	267.42	277.35
298.37	371.75	451.79	491.82
108.27	124.00	141.31	148.08
241.12	260.30	332.09	337.33
365.96	443.91	580.38	650.12
99.94	148.55	177.07	199.08
233.13	255.25	318.58	323.73
519.28	716.95	863.87	934.65
91.83	115.81	155.87	180.85
1131.28	1527.88	1856.11	2509.43
1101.29	**1474.67**	**1819.52**	**2444.23**
914.76	1232.89	1518.65	2075.30
186.52	241.78	300.87	368.93
3748.32	**5822.12**	**7394.63**	**10352.37**
121.34	200.26	223.50	190.44
322.51	933.13	804.51	1225.17
633.18	813.63	928.44	1456.84
2671.28	3875.10	5438.18	7479.92
823.31	**1136.98**	**1778.13**	**2476.51**
91.05	127.31	243.45	390.76
163.80	278.36	468.20	670.98
67.79	92.65	145.06	162.22
250.44	316.44	405.40	531.97
226.89	296.63	452.56	504.30
23.34	25.59	63.47	216.27
1870.69	**2964.67**	**3075.14**	**5130.16**
1289.28	2159.14	2191.87	4043.45
581.41	805.53	883.26	1086.71
1695.60	**1883.81**	**2369.31**	**3304.11**
1357.54	1356.60	1688.05	2152.82
191.84	298.07	412.99	579.80
146.22	229.14	268.26	571.48
1258.42	**1585.99**	**2716.36**	**3584.22**
338.97	548.74	823.57	846.73
919.45	1037.26	1892.79	2737.49
208.72	**341.52**	**498.52**	**859.42**
79.00	151.93	194.87	387.56
129.71	189.59	303.66	471.85

Note: Home ownership conversion in urban household residence consumption expenditure in 2014, refers to a resident who lives on a self-owned house now, provides housing service the conversion value for their own consumption. It belongs to material consumption, not included in cash consumption expenditure.

9-6 城镇居民家庭平均每百户年末耐用品拥有量(2020)

品 名		Item		总平均 Total Average	低收入户 Low Income Households
摩托车	(辆)	Motorcycles	(unit)	32.11	47.21
助力车	(辆)	Auxiliary Drving Bikes	(unit)	44.21	50.12
家用汽车	(辆)	Cars for Household Use	(unit)	37.85	29.34
洗衣机	(台)	Washing Machins	(unit)	99.32	95.00
电冰箱	(台)	Refrigerators	(unit)	104.90	101.84
彩色电视机	(台)	Color TV Sets	(unit)	120.85	116.21
家用电脑	(台)	Computers	(unit)	74.59	55.33
照相机	(架)	Cameras	(unit)	14.94	4.20
中高档乐器	(件)	Medium and High-Grade Musical Instruments	(unit)	7.77	3.28
微波炉	(台)	Microwave Stove	(unit)	47.05	26.89
空调器	(台)	Air Conditioners	(unit)	169.89	128.42
热水器	(台)	Showers	(unit)	104.72	99.22
洗碗机	(台)	Dishwasher	(unit)	1.71	0.91
健身器材	(件)	Health Care Instruments	(unit)	7.05	4.21
固定电话	(部)	Fixed Telephone	(set)	9.25	7.31
移动电话	(部)	Mobile Phones	(set)	263.87	269.50
空气净化器(含新风系统)	(台)		(unit)	5.71	1.35

Main Durable Goods Owned per 100 Urban Households (2020)

中低收入户 Lower Middle Income Households	中等收入户 Middle Income Households	中高收入户 Upper Middle Income Households	高收入户 High Income Households
40.44	29.73	21.24	21.94
52.60	45.88	42.75	29.72
35.14	39.22	36.21	49.33
99.47	101.21	101.00	99.91
106.19	106.04	104.28	106.16
118.94	119.60	120.79	128.71
66.66	75.51	79.57	95.82
8.75	12.50	19.93	29.29
4.32	9.25	8.99	12.99
41.81	48.45	54.67	63.38
148.66	170.87	186.78	214.65
104.40	106.10	105.78	108.06
0.53	1.43	1.00	4.67
4.60	6.88	8.55	11.00
5.86	6.98	11.49	14.63
277.40	271.27	253.07	248.12
2.32	6.40	7.08	11.42

9-7 城镇居民家庭房屋居住分布情况
Housing Distribution of Urban Households

分组	Group	各组户数占总户数比重(%) Percentage of Household in Each Group of the Total Households				
		2016	2017	2018	2019	2020
总计	**Total**	**3053.0**	**3031.0**	**3488.7**	**3409.4**	**3210.0**
一、房屋产权	**Building Property Right**					
租赁公房	Leased Pubilc Houses	3.4	3.4	2.8	2.1	2.4
租赁私房	Leased Private Houses	5.4	5.0	3.9	3.0	3.9
原有私房	Original Private Houses	30.7	30.4	41.1	43.3	40.0
房改私房	Private Houses	22.3	22.4	11.5	11.0	11.9
商品房	Commercial Houses	29.6	30.6	39.3	39.1	40.3
借用房	Borrowed	1.0	1.3	0.8	0.7	0.7
其他	Others	7.6	6.8	0.6	0.7	0.9
二、住宅样式	**Housing Pattens**					
单栋住宅	Sole-Unit Houses	36.0	36.3	35.5	37.0	59.9
四居室	Four-Room Houses	3.7	3.8	3.5	3.6	2.1
三居室	Three-Room Houses	24.7	24.4	29.4	30.0	18.9
二居室	Two-Room Houses	27.9	28.0	26.1	24.7	15.7
一居室	One-Room Houses	5.6	5.6	4.6	4.0	2.8
普通楼房	Ordinary Houses					
平房及其他	Bungalow and Others	2.1	1.9	0.8	0.7	0.6
三、用水情况	**Waters**					
独用自来水	Private Tap Water	95.8	95.6	92.3	92.6	94.7
公用自来水	Public Tap Water					
井、河水	Water from Rivers and Wells	3.7	3.7	5.1	5.1	3.0
其他	Others	0.6	0.6	2.6	2.3	2.4
四、卫生设备	**Sanitary Faciities**					
无卫生设备	Have not	1.6	1.3	1.7		
独立卫生设备	Independent Health Facilities	94.1	94.4	97.8	98.5	98.6
公用卫生设备	Public Health Facilities	4.3	4.2	0.5	1.5	1.4
五、取暖设备	**Warming Facilities**					
无取暖设备	Have not	37.5	36.8	36.3	34.4	32.5
空调设备	Air Conditioner					
暖气	Heater					
其他	Others	62.5	63.2	63.7	65.6	67.5
六、燃料使用情况	**Fuel Material Usage Conditions**					
煤	Coal	0.9	0.8	0.2	0.0	0.1
罐装液化石油气	LPG Cylinders	46.5	44.4	31.7	33.6	32.8
管道液化石油气	LPG Pipeline	2.0	2.1	2.3	1.4	0.8
管道煤气	Piped Coal Gas	1.1	0.9	1.3	0.9	0.1
管道天然气	Gas Pipeline	38.1	39.9	50.5	52.6	58.2
其他	Others	11.4	11.9	14.0	11.4	8.0
七、通信设备使用情况	**Telecommunication Facilities Usage Conditions**					
1.每百户固定电话	Per 100 Fixed Telephone	28.7	27.1	13.2	10.1	9.3
2.每百户移动电话	Mobile Phones Per 100 Households	233.5	234.6	261.3	261.3	263.9

注:2014 年起住宅样式为四居室的数据包含四居室及以上单元房的占比。
Note: The data refers to four bedroom and above for four bedroom units since 2014.

9-8 市、州城镇(常住)居民年人均可支配收入
Annual Per Capita Disposable Income of Urban Household (Permanent Residents) of Cities and Prefectures

单位：元 (yuan)

地区	Item	城镇居民人均可支配收入 Per Capita Disposable Income of Urban Households					
		2008	2009	2010	2011	2012	2013
全省	**Province**	**13153**	**14367**	**16058**	**18374**	**20840**	**22906**
武汉市	Wuhan	16712	18385	20806	23738	27061	29821
黄石市	Huangshi	11734	13119	14666	17003	19417	21330
十堰市	Shiyan	10535	11376	12653	14172	16011	17694
宜昌市	Yichang	11001	12005	14282	16451	18775	20934
襄阳市	Xiangyang	11733	12843	13333	15352	17532	19329
鄂州市	Ezhou	10946	11951	14788	17008	19307	20878
荆门市	Jingmen	12244	13408	13601	15526	17678	19820
孝感市	Xiaogan	11110	12214	13796	15888	18091	19819
荆州市	Jingzhou	11461	12507	13285	14947	17010	18706
黄冈市	Huanggang	9952	11336	12832	14731	16765	18432
咸宁市	Xianning	10597	11626	12968	14875	16913	18581
随州市	Suizhou	11298	12333	13824	15870	18171	19806
恩施自治州	Enshi	9446	10307	11406	13174	15058	16639
仙桃市	Xiantao	10761	11783	13021	15052	17280	19065
潜江市	Qianjiang	10448	11243	13879	15561	17451	19187
天门市	Tianmen	11426	12571	12210	13886	15685	17112
神农架林区	Shennongjia	9164	10116	11146	12312	13567	14937

9-8 续表 1 continued

单位：元 (yuan)

地区	Item	城镇常住居民人均可支配收入 Per Capita Disposable Income of Urban Permanent Residents							
		2013	2014	2015	2016	2017	2018	2019	2020
全省	**Province**	**22668**	**24852**	**27051**	**29386**	**31889**	**34455**	**37601**	**36706**
武汉市	Wuhan	30286	33270	36436	39737	43405	47359	51706	50362
黄石市	Huangshi	22968	25208	27536	29906	32535	35327	38725	37912
十堰市	Shiyan	20185	22143	24057	26030	28518	30771	33577	32771
宜昌市	Yichang	22826	25025	27275	29735	32316	35011	38463	37232
襄阳市	Xiangyang	21957	24113	26282	28794	31316	33947	37297	37707
鄂州市	Ezhou	20813	22763	24774	26986	29399	31742	34541	35025
荆门市	Jingmen	22470	24627	26731	28920	31317	33779	36805	35958
孝感市	Xiaogan	21439	23491	25753	27939	30264	32685	35695	35374
荆州市	Jingzhou	21063	23128	25382	27666	29973	32590	35910	34474
黄冈市	Huanggang	18851	20729	22620	24796	26884	28978	31812	30826
咸宁市	Xianning	19671	21591	23505	25839	28053	30337	33191	32394
随州市	Suizhou	19131	20959	22791	24799	26959	29237	31961	30587
恩施自治州	Enshi	18329	20245	22198	24410	26766	28918	31561	30930
仙桃市	Xiantao	20429	22503	24641	26845	29266	31672	34541	35750
潜江市	Qianjiang	20541	22609	24721	26985	29284	31574	34627	33623
天门市	Tianmen	18703	20622	22618	24475	26528	28825	31753	31308
神农架林区	Shennongjia	18133	19810	21404	23452	25767	28176	30728	32203

注：2013 年前分城镇和农村开展住户调查，指标为城镇居民人均可支配收入。2014 年起使用城乡一体化住户收支与生活状况调查数据，指标改为城镇常住居民人均可支配收入。

Note: Urban and rural household surveys are separate prior to 2013, the concept is Per Capita Disposable Income of Urban Households, The data from an integrated household income and expenditure survey has been used since 2014, the concept was changed into Per Capita Disposable Income of Urban Permanent Residents.

9-9 农民家庭基本情况
Basic Conditions of Rural Households

年份 Year	调查户数 Number of Households Surveyed	常住人口（人） Permanent Residents (person)	平均每户常住人口（人） Average Permanent Residents Per Households (person)	平均每户整半劳动力（人） Average Full-Time and Part-Time Labors Per Household (person)	平均每个劳动力负担人口（人） Average Person Supported by Each Labor (person)
1982	948	5364	5.66	2.73	2.08
1983	1470	8267	5.62	2.99	1.88
1984	1510	8317	5.51	3.02	1.83
1985	3300	16473	5.07	2.98	1.71
1986	3300	16432	4.98	2.96	1.68
1987	3300	16195	4.91	2.94	1.67
1988	3300	15966	4.84	2.93	1.65
1989	3300	15567	4.72	2.86	1.65
1990	3300	15411	4.67	2.84	1.65
1991	3300	15094	4.57	2.66	1.72
1992	3300	14900	4.52	2.63	1.71
1993	3300	14651	4.44	2.65	1.67
1994	3300	14466	4.38	2.72	1.61
1995	3300	14447	4.38	2.77	1.58
1996	3300	14053	4.26	2.75	1.55
1997	3200	13453	4.20	2.64	1.60
1998	3200	13239	4.14	2.62	1.58
1999	3200	13082	4.09	2.63	1.55
2000	3300	13557	4.11	2.76	1.49
2001	3300	13490	4.09	2.75	1.49
2002	3300	13420	4.07	2.78	1.46
2003	3300	13385	4.06	2.86	1.42
2004	3300	13356	4.05	2.92	1.39
2005	3300	13228	4.01	2.99	1.34
2006	3300	13259	4.02	3.03	1.34
2007	3300	13186	4.00	3.06	1.30
2008	3300	13163	3.99	3.08	1.29
2009	3300	13151	3.99	3.12	1.28
2010	3300	13123	3.98	3.14	1.27
2011	3300	13120	3.98	3.12	1.27
2012	3300	13140	3.98	3.12	1.28
2013	2096	7921	3.78	2.88	1.31
2014	2522	7233	2.87	2.03	1.41
2015	2540	7309	2.88	2.04	1.41
2016	2549	7360	2.89	2.05	1.41
2017	2538	7287	2.87	2.06	1.40
2018	2140	6594	3.08	2.10	1.46
2019	2220	6838	3.08	2.12	1.46
2020	2420	7500	3.10	2.14	1.45

注：1.2014 年起使用城乡一体化住户收支与生活状况调查数据，与之前的分城镇和农村住户调查的范围、方法、指标口径有所不同（此后相关表同）。
2.2014 年起农民人均纯收入改为农村常住居民人均可支配收入。

Note: a)The integrated household income and expenditure survey has been used since 2014, including both urban and rural households. The coverage, methodology and definitions used in the survey are different from those used for the separate urban and rural household survey prior to 2014. (Related tables the same ever since).
b)Per Capita Income of Rural Households has been changed into Per Capita Disposable Income of Rural Permanent Residents since 2014.

9-9 续表 1 continued

年 份 year	平均每户经营耕地面积（亩）Space of Cultivation Land Per Household (mu)	平均每户年末拥有生产性固定资产原值(元) Value of Production Fixed Assets Per Household (yuan)	平均每户年内新建购房屋面积（平方米）Floor Space of Rooms Newly Built Per Household (sq.m)	平均每人年末使用房屋面积（平方米）Lving Space Per Capita (sq.m)
1982	0.57	159.2	5.36	16.45
1983	8.95	389.97	5.65	18.04
1984	8.66	530.20	6.70	19.03
1985	7.60	557.86	8.24	21.18
1986	7.48	610.47	8.45	22.63
1987	7.31	672.87	7.79	23.50
1988	7.04	759.61	4.90	24.15
1989	6.95	819.53	5.50	25.10
1990	6.79	861.91	6.20	25.73
1991	6.58	1068.45	4.56	27.33
1992	6.47	1146.94	4.07	27.94
1993	6.36	1281.66	3.75	25.80
1994	6.69	1542.58	3.91	25.22
1995	6.73	1775.57	4.66	25.92
1996	6.82	2291.6	4.25	26.58
1997	6.56	2688.67	4.98	27.99
1998	6.08	2604.21	4.74	28.38
1999	6.08	2543.61	4.19	29.87
2000	5.93	2482.02	3.48	30.11
2001	5.94	2773.52	2.98	31.19
2002	6.01	2953.37	4.65	31.55
2003	6.03	2989.82	4.01	32.44
2004	6.15	3046.47	2.82	33.68
2005	6.15	4121.2	3.88	36.05
2006	6.12	4297.19	4.22	36.77
2007	6.41	4996.00	3.36	37.96
2008	6.36	5434.99	5.90	39.04
2009	6.51	6368.83	4.40	40.11
2010	6.73	7078.46	5.05	40.99
2011	6.44	9636.11	7.88	44.24
2012	6.80	10813.13	5.46	44.98
2013	7.08	13839.73	6.06	41.84
2014	6.97	12048.41	5.81	54.78
2015	7.90	12226.49	4.08	55.61
2016	8.24	12709.63	2.51	57.67
2017	8.10	13287.33	2.85	58.71
2018	7.30	17213.25	3.19	57.76
2019	7.30	16299.52		58.68
2020	7.38	16409.08		57.79

9-9 续表 2 continued

年 份 year	平均每户年末使用房屋价值（元） Value of Per Households Living Space(yuan)	平均每人总收入（元） Total Income Per Capita (yuan)	平均每人纯收入（元） Net Income Per Capita (yuan)	平均每人生活消费支出（元） Living Expenditures Per Capita (yuan)
1982	1261.51	311.51	286.07	226.96
1983	1688.93	405.14	299.24	252.47
1984	1786.54	525.86	392.29	305.03
1985	2068.78	569.74	421.24	334.63
1986	2319.44	605.67	445.13	373.53
1987	2514.22	638.64	460.66	408.69
1988	2751.40	710.47	497.84	450.62
1989	3095.15	820.70	571.84	540.13
1990	3545.50	957.01	670.80	607.58
1991	4661.58	936.57	626.92	615.40
1992	4885.77	1015.62	677.82	611.84
1993	5004.02	1135.77	783.18	722.09
1994	5887.81	1690.49	1170.06	1012.95
1995	6729.46	2184.20	1511.22	1245.10
1996	10050.26	2642.45	1863.62	1630.41
1997	11432.61	2913.16	2102.20	1660.13
1998	12966.45	2917.66	2172.24	1699.43
1999	13654.80	2871.62	2217.08	1572.90
2000	13717.28	3008.13	2268.50	1555.61
2001	16007.50	3124.10	2352.16	1649.18
2002	16581.94	3239.81	2444.06	1745.63
2003	19010.48	3378.80	2566.76	1801.63
2004	20254.50	3826.27	2890.01	2088.98
2005	24815.99	4221.81	3099.20	2430.19
2006	27772.00	4580.79	3419.35	2732.46
2007	31696.83	5365.78	3997.48	3090.00
2008	36250.27	6266.27	4656.38	3652.57
2009	41493.01	6663.13	5035.26	3725.40
2010	47606.56	7699.27	5832.27	4090.78
2011	61870.37	9387.20	6897.92	5010.74
2012	77338.15	10525.66	7851.71	5726.73
2013	101314.51	11896.06	8866.95	6279.52
2014	110492.00	14836.14	10849.06	8680.93
2015	125534.00	15819.16	11843.89	9803.15
2016	145244.08	16807.81	12724.97	10938.30
2017	148155.46	17927.34	13812.09	11632.51
2018	181945.74	20158.66	14977.82	13946.26
2019	191268.89	22524.84	16390.86	15328.02
2020	198840.25	21908.75	16305.91	14472.50

9-10 农民家庭年人均纯收入(可支配收入)及构成
Annual Per Capita Net Income (Disposable Income) and Composition of Rural Households

单位：元 (yuan)

指 标	Item	2005	2010	2011	2012	2013	2014	2015	2016	2017	2018	2019	2020
全年总收入	**Total Revenue**	**4221.81**	**7699.27**	**9387.20**	**10525.66**	**11896.06**	**14836.14**	**15819.16**	**16807.81**	**17927.34**	**20158.66**	**22524.84**	**21908.75**
全年纯收入	**Annual Net Income**	**3099.20**	**5832.27**	**6897.92**	**7851.71**	**8866.95**	**10849.06**	**11843.89**	**12724.97**	**13812.09**	**14977.82**	**16390.86**	**16305.91**
工资性收入	Money Wage	941.64	2186.11	2703.05	3189.84	3648.20	3298.61	3682.91	4023.04	4389.58	4886.79	5352.90	5271.63
家庭经营纯收入	House Business Revenue	2049.04	3234.94	3731.34	4123.49	4616.55	5009.34	5281.41	5534.01	5963.95	6270.85	6807.69	6745.37
转移性收入	Transfer Income	91.71	304.30	379.08	472.51	518.07	2415.66	2718.79	3009.32	3292.77	3634.24	4019.61	214.39
财产性收入	Property Income	16.81	106.92	84.45	65.87	84.13	125.44	160.78	158.60	165.79	185.94	210.66	4074.51
比重(纯收入=100)	**Ratio(net income = 100)**												
工资性收入	Money Wage	30.38	37.48	39.19	40.63	41.14	30.40	31.10	31.62	31.78	32.63	32.66	32.33
家庭经营纯收入	House Business Revenue	66.12	55.47	54.09	52.52	52.06	46.17	44.59	43.49	43.18	41.87	41.53	41.37
转移性收入	Transfer Income	2.96	5.22	5.50	6.02	5.84	22.27	22.96	23.65	23.84	24.26	24.52	24.99
财产性收入	Property Income	0.54	1.83	1.22	0.84	0.95	1.16	1.35	1.25	1.20	1.24	1.29	1.31

注:2014 年起为农村常住居民人均可支配收入、工资性收入、家庭经营净收入、财产净收入、转移净收入。

Note: It has been Per Capita Disposable Income of Rural Permanent Residents, Money Wage, House Business Revenue. Property Income, Transfer Income since 2014.

9-11 农民家庭年人均纯收入(可支配收入)分组
Annual Grouping of Per Capita Net Income (Disposable Income)of Rural Households

单位：户 (household)

指 标	Item	2007	2008	2009	2010	2011	2012	2013	2014	2015	2016	2017	2018	2019	2020
调查户总计	**Total Households Surveyed**	**3300**	**3300**	**3300**	**3300**	**3300**	**3300**	**2096**	**2522**	**2540**	**2549**	**2538**	**2140**	**2220**	**2420**
2000 元以下	Below 2000 yuan	508	414	411	257	233	155	48	70	69	70	59	80	68	62
2000-3000 元	2000-3000 yuan	659	519	478	365	295	197	83	57	51	35	58	29	15	25
3000-4000 元	3000-4000 yuan	660	559	492	419	313	289	127	118	85	71	61	67	46	42
4000-5000 元	4000-5000 yuan	510	510	460	469	373	286	170	139	147	117	79	71	61	65
5000 元以上	5000 yuan and Over	969	1298	1459	1790	2086	2373	1668							
5000-10000 元	5000-10000 yuan								814	796	689	648	546	462	526
10000-15000 元	10000-15000 yuan								661	612	621	589	518	499	553
15000-20000 元	15000-20000 yuan								353	349	386	400	331	383	392
20000 元以上	20000 yuan and Over								311	431	561	644	498	686	755

注:2014 年起为农村常住居民人均可支配收入分组。

Note: It has been Rural Permanent Grouped by Per Capita Disposable Income since 2014.

9-12 农民家庭年人均经营总收入
Annual Per Capita Total Business Income of Rural Households

单位：元 (yuan)

指 标	Item	2013	2014	2015	2016	2017	2018	2019	2020
家庭经营总收入	**Total Income of Family Business**	**7022.00**	**8699.22**	**8928.74**	**9242.06**	**9625.59**	**10927.48**	**12299.81**	**11769.81**
农业收入	Farming	4049.41	4663.10	4927.80	4875.69	4887.51	4011.98	4346.83	4498.19
林业收入	Forestry	140.80	272.35	292.41	345.81	271.17	99.46	105.77	96.75
牧业收入	Animal Husbandry	1077.50	1610.39	1235.80	1199.91	1242.35	1694.16	1951.14	2491.50
渔业收入	Fishery	403.93	476.41	696.02	654.65	846.48	1381.42	1642.34	1558.50
工业收入	Industry	60.66	204.82	160.40	167.05	167.68	354.24	288.86	215.84
建筑业收入	Construction	307.83	188.27	110.67	261.24	359.50	546.40	900.20	601.47
交通运输邮电业收入	Transportation, Post Services	328.76	353.50	461.56	472.43	551.38	490.88	530.99	422.49
批零贸易餐饮业收入	Wholesales, Retail Sales and Catering	401.46	572.30	646.44	886.04	887.31	1864.94	2011.22	1259.23
社会服务和文教卫生业收入	Social Services and Public Health Services	177.96	211.73	189.00	141.72	137.63	167.96	205.32	189.71
农林牧渔服务业收入	Agriculture and Forestry Services		133.44	171.08	189.94	222.58	254.81	262.25	244.52
其他家庭经营收入	Other Family Revenue	10.54	12.93	37.56	47.59	51.99	61.23	54.89	191.60

9-13 农民家庭年人均生产支出
Annual Per Capita Production Expenditures of Rural Households

单位：元 (yuan)

指 标	Item	2012	2013	2014	2015	2016	2017	2018	2019	2020
一、家庭经营费用支出	**Expenditures of Family Business**	**2402.73**	**2408.72**	**3413.49**	**3366.25**	**3412.31**	**3349.56**	**4277.95**	**5134.74**	**4670.94**
农业生产支出	Agricultural Expenditures	1076.28	1049.49	1329.35	1566.04	1535.20	1387.20	1105.56	1288.39	1226.57
林业生产支出	Forestry Expenditures	16.33	19.52	27.68	23.91	126.05	25.67	13.86	31.88	18.55
牧业生产支出	Animal Husbandary Expenditures	693.65	753.88	1279.08	923.32	765.09	795.14	1222.16	1459.20	1917.75
渔业生产支出	Fishery Expenditures	230.50	174.04	217.63	366.77	276.83	420.32	663.93	833.36	688.23
工业生产支出	Industrial Expenditures	84.17	28.31	78.83	57.14	81.29	54.87	150.34	171.19	117.54
建筑业支出	Construction Expenditures	54.28	120.30	158.47	43.86	143.14	218.87	110.29	313.12	106.92
交通运输邮电业支出	Expenditures of Transportation and Post Services	120.00	81.99	74.77	136.61	114.81	132.11	79.25	87.42	39.99
批零贸易餐饮业支出	Expenditures of Wholesales, Retail Sales and Catering	100.13	82.03	166.42	175.88	276.11	215.23	832.21	802.40	347.32
社会服务和文教卫生业支出	Expenditures of Social Services and Public Health Services	20.52	69.33	39.98	18.10	25.19	16.19	18.19	46.11	30.62
农林牧渔服务业支出	Agriculture and Forestry Services			36.77	44.08	60.89	74.14	67.38	85.44	67.86
其他家庭经营支出	Other Family Expenditures	6.85	2.19	4.51	10.54	7.70	9.82	14.78	16.24	109.58
二、购置住房、生产性固定资产支出	**Purchase of Housing, the Productive Expenditure of Fixed Assets**	**240.00**	**315.23**	**876.97**	**1244.33**	**862.13**	**762.17**	**1098.59**	**1293.24**	**1380.44**
三、税费支出	**Expenditures of Taxation**	**11.09**								

9-14 农民家庭年人均生活消费支出
Annual Per Capita Living Consumption Expenditure of Rural Households

单位：元 (yuan)

指 标	Item	2012	2013	2014	2015	2016	2017	2018	2019	2020
全年总支出	**Total Annual Expenditures**	**8923.73**	**9477.33**	**16775.27**	**18257.83**	**19372.81**	**19739.32**	**23946.03**	**26484.28**	**24232.53**
生活消费支出	**Living Expenditures**	**5726.73**	**6279.52**	**8680.93**	**9803.15**	**10938.30**	**11632.51**	**13946.26**	**15328.02**	**14472.50**
一、食品消费	**Food Consumption**	**2154.01**	**2308.45**	**2724.10**	**2952.69**	**3295.30**	**3332.38**	**3928.22**	**4163.70**	**4304.48**
主食	Grain	350.86	334.10	440.21	446.36	466.19	486.50	478.65	501.05	534.12
副食	Non-Staple Food	969.20	1037.53	1401.57	1539.65	1734.74	1663.16	1885.15	2004.27	2306.80
其他食品	Others	542.32	514.98	691.15	744.25	828.79	862.39	947.36	1003.67	938.88
在外饮食	Travelling Catering Service	282.94	393.63	191.17	222.44	265.57	320.34	617.06	654.71	465.16
二、衣着消费	**Clothing Consumption**	**316.41**	**347.67**	**495.73**	**549.14**	**568.71**	**626.40**	**783.07**	**825.71**	**780.44**
三、居住消费	**Residence Consumption**	**1206.16**	**1415.73**	**1944.56**	**2150.27**	**2407.90**	**2512.27**	**2954.25**	**3277.95**	**3197.57**
住房	Housing	973.60	1013.20	1523.05	1693.72	1931.67	2047.55	2516.83	2750.42	2638.05
电费	Electricity Fees	112.57	138.37	209.40	230.15	248.22	254.18	256.19	310.50	322.98
燃料	Fuel	91.16	197.33	115.15	116.80	107.37	113.77	104.71	122.61	137.50
四、家庭设备用品及服务	**Familty facilities and Services**	**397.86**	**425.00**	**574.31**	**599.92**	**669.01**	**706.20**	**852.22**	**839.58**	**790.90**
耐用消费品	Durable Consumer Goods	238.55	249.85	298.95	298.90	328.12	343.23	414.88	385.84	347.68
日用杂品	Daily Necessities	142.41	164.10	260.06	286.12	320.73	338.53	410.01	430.71	422.86
五、交通通讯消费	**Transportation and Telecommunication Fees**	**496.10**	**605.95**	**816.43**	**1218.42**	**1381.37**	**1384.68**	**1933.05**	**2228.83**	**2175.32**
交通工具	Transportation	235.85	324.51	378.07	743.70	835.55	826.12	1310.21	1592.14	847.85
通讯工具	Telecommunication	39.84	45.85	76.43	89.87	94.07	116.12	136.61	118.35	146.52
交通、邮电服务费	Transport, Postal Services	220.41	235.48	361.94	384.85	451.76	442.44	486.24	518.35	1180.95
六、教育文化娱乐	**Culture, Education and Receation**	**394.63**	**407.42**	**1010.19**	**1118.15**	**1156.60**	**1330.67**	**1551.43**	**1807.64**	**1382.30**
文教娱乐用品	Cultural, Educational and Receational Articles	107.87	104.20	122.61	156.33	145.88	164.33	205.32	222.93	202.64
学杂费	School Fees	136.21	159.18	98.51	90.58	93.95	85.73	147.41	183.61	192.63
技术培训费	Technical Training	12.85	28.88	20.89	36.57	51.56	74.32	116.35	128.92	82.26
一揽子教育服务费	Education Service Charge			661.05	712.83	693.66	761.58	823.98	989.45	739.77
文体休闲娱乐费	Sports Recreation Fee	23.05	35.58	62.47	78.67	76.99	102.87	111.71	110.78	53.76
七、医疗保健消费	**Medicine and Medical Services Fees**	**591.87**	**624.40**	**907.33**	**985.09**	**1213.47**	**1438.32**	**1588.03**	**1921.78**	**1558.47**
医疗保健用品	Health Care Supplies	117.28	127.71	200.10	225.14	269.73	303.46	382.47	375.22	351.42
医疗保健服务费	Health Care Service Fees	474.59	496.69	707.22	759.94	943.74	1134.86	1205.57	1546.56	1207.05
八、其他商品和服务	**Other Commdities and Services**	**169.68**	**144.90**	**208.28**	**229.48**	**245.94**	**301.59**	**355.99**	**262.83**	**283.01**

9-15 农民家庭年人均现金收支
Annual Per Capita Cash Revenue and Expenditure of Rural Households

单位：元 (yuan)

指 标	Item	2013	2014	2015	2016	2017	2018	2019	2020
期内现金收入合计	**Total Cash Income at Year-End**	**10819.88**	**13243.58**	**13958.40**	**15145.85**	**16228.97**	**18888.95**	**21154.30**	**20517.47**
一、工资性现金收入	**Cash Income By Wages**	**3858.97**	**3282.57**	**3663.96**	**4000.55**	**4370.51**	**4866.90**	**5328.80**	**5233.28**
二、家庭经营现金收入	**Cash Income By Family Business**	**5959.60**	**7328.03**	**7336.22**	**7921.93**	**8318.33**	**10084.50**	**11390.05**	**10866.41**
农业	Farm Products	3179.27	3614.71	3658.73	3873.47	3751.74	3304.21	3690.44	3871.21
林业	Forestry Products	142.91	163.40	172.04	241.80	224.36	77.18	78.48	66.21
牧业	Animal Husbandary Products	891.19	1404.35	1039.15	995.89	1128.45	1596.84	1738.25	2267.03
渔业	Fishery Products	395.83	468.59	689.58	644.76	835.71	1365.82	1629.16	1537.09
工业	Industry Products	60.66	204.82	160.40	167.05	167.68	354.24	288.86	215.84
建筑业	Building Industry	307.83	188.27	110.67	261.24	359.50	546.40	900.20	601.47
交通运输邮电业	Transportation and Post Service	328.76	353.50	461.56	472.43	551.38	490.88	530.99	422.49
批零贸易餐饮业	Retail Sales and Catering	401.46	572.30	646.44	886.04	887.31	1864.94	2011.22	1259.23
社会服务和文教卫生业	Social Services and Educational Sector	177.96	211.73	189.00	141.72	137.63	167.96	205.32	189.71
农林牧渔服务业	Agriculture and Forestry Services		133.44	171.08	189.94	222.58	254.81	262.25	244.52
其他家庭经营收入	Cash Income of Other	10.54	12.93	37.56	47.59	51.99	61.23	54.89	191.60
三、转移性现金收入	**Transfer Cash Income**	**902.05**	**2497.66**	**2791.31**	**3053.31**	**3361.28**	**3738.76**	**226.18**	**233.74**
四、财产性现金收入	**Property Cash Income**	**99.26**	**135.33**	**166.91**	**170.07**	**178.85**	**198.80**	**4209.27**	**4184.04**
期内现金支出合计	**Total Cash Expenditures at Year-End**	**8563.81**	**14688.88**	**15923.32**	**16677.01**	**17014.59**	**21165.56**	**23472.02**	**21057.67**
一、家庭经营费用现金支出	**Cash Expenditures By Family Business**	**2243.66**	**3249.87**	**3222.08**	**3290.04**	**3230.71**	**4143.15**	**5019.04**	**4561.61**
购买化肥	Fertilizers Purchases	396.06	456.72	515.12	482.81	411.64	319.30	422.11	
购买农药	Purchases of Farm Chemical	112.80	140.48	142.26	154.19	149.47	137.07	144.28	
购买农用薄膜	Purchase of Agricultural Film	4.80	7.94	8.01	8.65	7.26	4.01	3.90	
二、购买住房、生产性固定资产支出	**Purchase of Housing, the Productive Expenditure**	**315.23**	**876.97**	**1244.33**	**862.13**	**762.17**	**1098.59**	**1293.24**	**1380.44**
三、税费现金支出	**Cash Expenditures of Taxations**								
四、生活消费现金支出	**Cash Expenditures of Living Consumption**	**5531.07**	**6738.17**	**7612.82**	**8364.76**	**9026.62**	**11300.60**	**12431.46**	**11406.97**
五、转移性现金支出	**Transfer Cash Expenditures**	**471.72**	**287.31**	**321.74**	**363.36**	**440.55**	**511.35**	**626.33**	**19.35**
六、财产性现金支出	**Property Cash Expenditures**	**2.13**	**8.67**	**6.12**	**11.47**	**13.06**	**12.86**	**15.52**	**559.05**

9-16 农民家庭年人均出售主要农副产品情况
Annual Per Capita Selling of Farm and Sideline Products of Rural Households

单位：千克 (kg)

品 名	Item	2005	2010	2011	2012	2013	2014	2015	2016	2017	2018	2019	2020
粮食	Grain	383.48	447.78	451.98	489.22	591.56	770.96	888.88	982.69	960.01	924.51	938.02	893.65
小麦	Wheat	54.25	75.44	86.70	91.93	79.55	111.05	129.72	151.98	138.05	128.72	112.16	128.58
稻谷	Paddy	302.70	331.71	302.69	329.15	432.85	528.86	588.64	656.03	684.99	674.81	671.05	662.32
棉花	Cotton	55.95	55.03	88.30	93.94	72.29	48.98	30.33	19.31	23.01	18.98	15.24	8.34
油料	Oil Producer	77.73	72.15	60.91	58.57	73.99	77.34	52.15	45.97	40.04	38.21	53.04	51.52
糖料	Sugar	5.47	6.43	0.16	0.17	2.16	2.08	2.21	3.43	1.80	0.13		
烟草	Tobacco	2.34	2.77	2.97	3.82	7.89	7.07	14.35	13.67	7.37	2.76	5.20	3.46
蔬菜	Vegetable	135.09	139.41	137.62	143.53	99.54	134.68	163.39	125.98	181.69	152.25	155.06	134.38
瓜类	Melon	14.21	19.69	17.40	17.60	40.74	33.63	10.12	15.49	20.49	7.60	31.69	5.22
水果	Fruits	69.54	78.09	66.13	109.87	62.86	111.30	97.70	93.46	109.78	104.67	137.01	156.65
茶叶	Tea	1.24	1.95	4.17	8.08	5.02	5.01	7.55	8.39	8.00	7.61	8.07	6.67
猪肉	Pork	29.70	30.92	22.91	25.68	28.51	58.86	41.76	32.19	40.52	30.98	27.82	23.79
家禽	Poultry	4.47	8.38	2.28	2.80	1.65	8.63	4.26	3.61	1.99	13.26	9.84	13.51
蛋类	Eggs	11.98	11.19	10.33	13.01	16.54	29.12	14.59	13.58	19.47	78.07	85.04	72.70
水产品	Aquatic Products	28.59	38.70	43.09	43.25	39.61	40.65	68.30	62.48	72.54	77.75	116.76	113.22

9-17 农民家庭主要生活用品购买量
Purchases of Articles for Main Daily Necessities of Rural Households

品名	Item	2010	2012	2013	2014	2015	2016	2017	2018	2019	2020
粮食 (千克/人)	Grain (kg/person)	29.46	44.45	38.34	44.06	47.43	49.61	50.47	61.25	68.59	61.32
植物油 (千克/人)	Edible Vegetable Oil (kg/person)	3.61	5.70	5.11	7.41	8.07	7.88	7.50	7.38	9.22	9.57
动物油 (千克/人)	Edible Animal Oil (kg/person)	0.33	0.39	0.27	0.47	0.49	0.42	0.44	0.40	0.39	0.37
蔬菜 (千克/人)	Vegetables (kg/person)	17.73	18.27	16.51	25.95	27.28	31.31	33.07	44.99	41.61	48.44
猪肉 (千克/人)	Pork (kg/person)	7.43	8.71	8.76	13.13	14.32	13.80	14.74	18.35	15.61	11.83
牛羊肉 (千克/人)	Beef and Mutton (kg/person)	0.51	0.47	0.54	0.85	1.04	1.14	1.22	1.38	1.54	2.08
家禽 (千克/人)	Poultry (kg/person)	1.17	1.24	0.97	2.40	2.46	2.95	2.58	3.60	4.60	4.88
鲜蛋 (千克/人)	Fresh Eggs (kg/person)	1.30	2.20		2.83	4.32	4.16	3.77	3.81	4.39	5.64
鲜活鱼类 (千克/人)	Fresh Fish (kg/person)	6.99	7.06		9.58	10.13	10.31	9.30	11.14	12.72	13.55
卷烟 (盒/人)	Tobacco (pack/person)	27.50	31.42	26.93	41.00	40.03	40.62	38.60	36.79	38.82	35.89
酒 (千克/人)	Wine (kg/person)	10.72	11.06	10.06	14.24	12.76	11.78	10.72	8.88	7.70	7.13
水果 (千克/人)	Fruits (kg/person)	6.22	8.27		17.63	19.69	23.07	25.35	30.07	27.97	29.49
服装 (件/人)	Clothing (piece/person)	1.95	2.52								
鞋类 (双/人)	Footwear (two/person)	1.36	1.80		2.10	2.37	2.35	2.23	2.11	2.09	2.01
水泥 (千克/人)	Cement (kg/person)	150.72	149.81								
钢材 (千克/人)	Steel (kg/person)	10.21	9.72								
生活用煤 (千克/人)	Coal (kg/person)	19.70	13.18		14.84	15.18	18.06	18.18	10.85	14.81	15.37
电视机 (台/百户)	TV Sets (set/100 households)	3.70	6.48	5.76	5.31	7.17	6.39	5.66	6.38	5.69	4.34
洗衣机 (台/百户)	Washing Machine (set/100 households)	3.21	5.09	4.44	4.93	4.35	4.48	4.29	4.92	4.20	4.84
电风扇 (台/百户)	Electric Fans (set/100 households)	10.52	13.67								
电冰箱 (台/百户)	Refrigerators (set/100 households)	7.00	7.12	6.16	6.03	6.61	6.62	5.62	7.26	6.57	6.34
自行车（含电动）(辆/百户)	Bycicle (set/100 households)	4.67	7.30	6.54	6.99	6.27	5.63	5.37	6.90	6.39	2.49
摩托车 (辆/百户)	Motocycle (set/100 households)	3.88	5.30	3.91	3.65	3.51	3.18	2.99	4.13	3.05	2.47
热水器 (台/百户)	Shower (set/100 households)	4.36	5.70	3.58	2.75	3.20	3.19	2.66	4.05	4.58	4.61
电话机 (部/百户)	Telephone Sets (set/100 households)	3.36	2.76	1.86	1.03	1.37	0.83	0.99	0.88	0.49	0.08
手机 (部/百户)	Mobile Phones (set/100 households)	18.92	28.00	33.40	39.75	39.44	34.97	31.79	30.82	26.95	41.76

9-18 农民家庭年人均主要食品消费量
Annual Per Capita Major Foods' Consumption of Rural Households

单位：千克 (kg)

品 名	Item	2010	2012	2013	2014	2015	2016	2017	2018	2019	2020
一、粮食	**Grain**	**178.37**	**151.06**	**125.59**	**153.08**	**152.05**	**137.15**	**136.85**	**136.07**	**147.01**	**136.26**
#小麦	Wheat	17.60	15.55	10.17	16.74	17.90	14.74	15.70	16.60	18.11	26.04
稻谷	Paddy	146.13	126.67	104.27	121.21	118.83	107.22	106.54	103.38	112.62	105.11
豆类	Bean	3.22	1.97	3.85	7.25	7.86	8.72	7.70	9.20	9.85	11.98
二、蔬菜及菜制品	**Fresh Vegetables and Vegetable Products**	**137.51**	**119.33**	**88.16**	**118.03**	**123.06**	**123.22**	**113.01**	**113.78**	**118.58**	**134.52**
鲜菜	Fresh Vegetables	136.22	118.25	86.56	116.30	121.40	121.10	111.36	111.49	116.26	132.35
三、油脂类	**Oil and Fats**	**5.49**	**10.39**	**11.05**	**29.71**	**16.04**	**15.52**	**14.10**	**12.27**	**14.08**	**14.57**
植物油	Edible Vegetable Oil	5.13	9.93	10.61	29.02	15.24	14.89	13.51	11.86	13.61	14.18
动物油	Edible Animal Oil	0.36	0.47	0.43	0.70	0.79	0.62	0.58	0.41	0.46	0.40
四、肉禽及其制品	**Meat and Processed Products**	**22.79**	**22.80**	**22.91**	**29.82**	**31.20**	**29.15**	**27.52**	**31.54**	**24.31**	**26.78**
猪肉	Pork	17.98	17.63	18.11	23.12	24.12	21.43	20.29	23.44	20.90	16.14
牛羊肉	Beef and Mutton	0.57	0.53	0.63	0.93	1.14	1.26	1.28	1.41	1.55	2.11
家禽	Poultry	2.91	2.94	2.87	4.19	4.27	4.60	4.00	4.70	5.97	6.85
五、蛋类及蛋制品	**Eggs and Processed Products**	**4.47**	**5.02**	**4.68**	**6.65**	**8.31**	**8.08**	**7.26**	**6.61**	**7.43**	**9.52**
六、奶及奶制品	**Milk and Dariy Products**	**1.22**	**1.67**	**2.11**	**3.53**	**3.58**	**4.12**	**3.70**	**4.17**	**4.32**	**4.75**
七、水产品	**Aquatic Products**	**8.33**	**8.54**	**7.93**	**11.10**	**11.75**	**12.15**	**11.09**	**13.12**	**14.90**	**16.52**
鱼类	Fish	7.93	8.09	7.58	10.55	10.97	11.20	10.06	11.98	13.48	14.83
八、干鲜瓜果	**Fresh and Dry**	**15.70**	**16.83**	**13.33**	**20.74**	**22.42**	**26.28**	**28.68**	**34.02**	**32.93**	**33.65**
九、酒类	**Liquor and Drinks**	**10.77**	**11.12**	**10.08**	**14.25**	**12.78**	**11.85**	**10.81**	**8.92**	**7.80**	**7.20**
白酒	Wine Spirit	3.70	3.52	3.65	5.82	5.51	5.22	5.27	4.43	3.40	3.21
啤酒	Beer	7.01	7.53	6.41	8.41	7.24	6.58	5.52	4.48	4.37	3.96

9-19 农民家庭每百户主要耐用消费品拥有量
Main Durable Goods Owned per 100 Rural Households

品 名		Item		2010	2012	2013	2014	2015	2016	2017	2018	2019	2020
彩电	(台)	Color TV Set	(unit)	109.18	116.24	114.35	116.50	118.46	120.09	121.73	121.00	121.26	121.93
照相机	(架)	Camera	(unit)	2.64	3.64	5.24	4.89	3.84	2.97	3.72	2.57	2.65	2.59
洗衣机	(台)	Washing Machine	(unit)	47.97	62.42	53.79	57.94	65.02	73.13	75.52	84.52	86.52	86.91
电冰箱	(台)	Refrigerator	(unit)	51.48	80.18	75.82	79.53	84.75	93.01	95.81	102.11	104.93	106.74
摩托车	(辆)	Motocycle	(unit)	64.12	74.76	68.84	76.52	77.87	78.47	80.16	82.24	83.19	82.74
摄像机	(台)	Videorecorder	(unit)	0.70	1.52	0.62	0.50	0.44	0.37				
抽油烟机	(台)	Ventilator	(unit)	10.03	15.82	10.94	13.59	14.89	14.86	17.35	30.39	32.24	34.37
空调机	(台)	Air Conditioner	(unit)	18.36	33.15	33.05	37.79	43.49	56.47	62.65	86.25	88.14	93.75
热水器	(台)	Shower	(unit)	32.00	55.91	52.16	58.01	61.71	68.63	71.21	84.74	87.17	91.39
电话机	(部)	Telephone Set	(set)	55.70	40.06	31.44	37.15	27.43	20.71	19.49	9.79	7.62	5.79
移动电话	(部)	Moblile Phone	(set)	152.27	215.06	211.52	223.46	232.18	236.26	238.70	268.13	270.85	274.90
家用计算机	(台)	PC	(unit)	7.39	19.73	22.14	25.72	26.23	27.04	27.94	31.92	33.61	34.32

9-20 市、州农民年人均纯收入(可支配收入)
Annual Per Capita Net Income of Rural Household of Cities and Prefectures

单位：元 (yuan)

地 区	Item	农村居民人均纯收入 Per Capita Net Income of Rural Households						农村常住居民人均可支配收入 Per Capita Disposable Income of Rural Permanent Residents							
		2008	2009	2010	2011	2012	2013	2013	2014	2015	2016	2017	2018	2019	2020
全省	**Province**	**4656**	**5035**	**5832**	**6898**	**7852**	**8867**	**9692**	**10849**	**11844**	**12725**	**13812**	**14978**	**16391**	**16306**
武汉市	Wuhan	6349	7161	8295	9814	11190	12713	14390	16160	17722	19152	20887	22652	24776	24057
黄石市	Huangshi	4374	4811	5524	6487	7477	8492	9781	10957	12004	12925	13972	15125	16516	16549
十堰市	Shiyan	2841	3110	3499	4044	4566	5226	6212	7046	7779	8514	9373	10295	11378	11731
宜昌市	Yichang	4686	5186	5980	7055	8046	9121	10458	11837	12990	14057	15253	16514	18134	18515
襄阳市	Xiangyang	4880	5440	6365	7549	8684	9785	11176	12534	13650	14762	16005	17305	18933	18422
鄂州市	Ezhou	5096	5718	6645	7909	9072	10210	11309	12692	13812	14813	16168	17609	19313	18792
荆门市	Jingmen	5332	5956	6951	8248	9387	10615	12082	13481	14716	15811	17167	18776	20556	19980
孝感市	Xiaogan	4636	5131	5943	7029	7988	9023	10360	11597	12655	13554	14744	15988	17510	17090
荆州市	Jingzhou	4889	5464	6453	7664	8710	9909	11280	12625	13728	14707	15962	17300	18893	18817
黄冈市	Huanggang	3744	4130	4634	5438	6142	6966	8385	9388	10252	11076	12116	13238	14490	14693
咸宁市	Xianning	4411	4873	5606	6588	7505	8480	9709	10891	11940	12812	13925	15116	16591	16359
随州市	Suizhou	4967	5457	6279	7427	8419	9490	10702	11984	13022	14077	15268	16538	18094	17624
恩施自治州	Enshi	2519	2810	3255	3939	4571	5235	6364	7194	7969	8728	9588	10524	11620	11887
仙桃市	Xiantao	5248	5856	6807	8006	9076	10365	11809	13193	14422	15462	16736	18177	19891	20647
潜江市	Qianjiang	4929	5531	6486	7684	8785	10017	11448	12862	14076	15113	16397	17797	19494	18948
天门市	Tianmen	4761	5326	6207	7407	8507	9608	10809	12086	13178	14107	15367	16598	18138	18356
神农架林区	Shennongjia	3330	3707	4083	4640	5110	5677	6305	6920	7578	8342	9205	10091	11171	11417

注：2013 年前分城镇和农村开展住户调查，指标为农民人均纯收入。2014 年起使用城乡一体化住户收支与生活状况调查数据，指标改为农村常住居民人均可支配收入。

Note：Urban and rural household surveys are separate prior to 2013,the concept is Per Capita Net Income of Rural Households, The data from an integrated household income and expenditure survey has been used since 2014 , the concept was changed into Per Capita Disposable Income of Rural Permanent Residents.

主要统计指标解释

一、城镇住户调查(到 2012 年)

城镇家庭人口 指居住在一起，经济上合在一起共同生活的家庭成员。凡计算为家庭人口的成员其全部收支都包括在本家庭中。

城镇就业面 指就业人口占家庭人口的百分比。

城镇就业者负担人数 指家庭人口与就业人口之比。

城镇家庭总收入 指家庭成员得到的工资性收入、经营净收入、财产性收入、转移性收入之和,不包括出售财物收入和借贷收入。

城镇居民家庭可支配收入 指家庭成员得到可用于最终消费支出和其它非义务性支出以及储蓄的总和，即居民家庭可以用来自由支配的收入。它是家庭总收入扣除交纳的个人所得税、个人交纳的社会保障支出以及记账补贴后的收入。计算公式为：

城镇居民家庭可支配收入=家庭总收入-交纳所得税-个人交纳的社会保障支出-记帐补贴

城镇家庭总支出 指家庭除借贷支出以外的全部实际支出。包括现金消费支出、财产性支出、转移性支出、社会保障支出、购房与建房支出。

城镇家庭现金消费支出 指家庭用于日常生活的全部现金支出,包括食品、衣着、家庭设备及用品、交通通信、文教娱乐、医疗保健、其他等八大类支出。

城镇家庭服务性消费支出 指家庭用于支付社会提供的各种文化和生活方面的非商品性服务费用。

城镇家庭收入分组方法 是将所有调查户依户人均可支配收入由低到高排队，按 10%,10%,20%,20%,20%,10%,10%的比例依次分成:最低收入户、较低收入户、中等偏下收入户、中等收入户、中等偏上收入户、高收入户、最高收入户等七组。总体中最低 5%的户为困难户。

恩格尔系数 指食品支出在现金消费支出中所占的比例。计算公式为：

$$恩格尔系数=\frac{食品支出}{现金消费支出}\times100\%$$

二、农村住户调查(到 2012 年)

农村住户 指农村常住户。农村常住户指长期(一年以上)居住在乡镇(不包括城关镇)行政管理区域内的住户,以及长期居住在城关镇所辖行政村范围内的农村住户。户口不在本地而在本地居住一年及以上的住户也包括在本地农村常住户范围内;有本地户口,但举家外出谋生一年以上的住户，无论是否保留承包耕地都不包括在本地农村住户范围内。

常住人口 指全年经常在家或在家居住 6 个月以上，而且经济和生活与本户连成一体的人口。外出从业人员在外居住时间虽然在 6 个月以上,但收入主要带回家中,经济与本户连为一体,仍视为家庭常住人口;在家居住,生活和本户连成一体的国家职工、退休人员也为家庭常住人口。但是现役军人、中专及以上(走读生除外)的在校学生、以及常年在外(不包括探亲、看病等)且已有稳定的职业与居住场所的外出从业人员,不算家庭常住人口。家庭常住人口主要作为计算农村住户平均每人收入、消费和积累水平及分析家庭人口状况的依据。

整、半劳动力 整劳动力指男子 18 周岁到 50 周岁,女子 18 周岁到 45 周岁;半劳动力指男子 16 周岁到 17 周岁,51 周岁到 60 周岁；女子 16 周岁到 17 周岁,46 周岁到 55 周岁,同时具有劳动能力的人。虽然在劳动年龄之内,但已丧失劳动能力的人,不应算为劳动力;超过劳动年龄,但能经常参加劳动,计入半劳动力数内。常住人口中的职工,若这些职工为劳动力,就包括在本户的整半劳动力中。

总收入 指调查期内农村住户和住户成员从各种来源渠道得到的收入总和。按收入的性质划分为工资性收入、家庭经营收入、财产性收入和转移性收入。

工资性收入 指农村住户成员受雇于单位或个人,靠出卖劳动而获得的收入。

家庭经营收入 指农村住户以家庭为生产经营单位进行生产筹划和管理而获得的收入。农村住户家庭经营活动按行业划分为农业、林业、牧业、渔业、工业、建筑业、交通运输业邮电业、批发和零售贸易餐饮业、社会服务业、文教卫生业和其他家庭经营。

财产性收入 指金融资产或有形非生产性资产的所有者向其他机构单位提供资金或将有形非生产性资产供其支配,作为回报而从中获得的收入。

转移性收入 指农村住户和住户成员无须付出任何对应物而获得的货物、服务、资金或资产所有权等,不包括无偿提供的用于固定资本形成的资金。一般情况下,是指农村住户在二次分配中的所有收入。

现金收入 指农村住户和住户成员在调查期内得到以

现金形态表现的收入。按来源分成工资性收入、家庭经营现金收入、财产性收入、转移性收入。

农村居民家庭纯收入 指农村住户当年从各个来源得到的总收入相应地扣除所发生的费用后的收入总和。计算方法：

农村居民家庭纯收入=总收入-家庭经营费用支出-税费支出-生产性固定资产折旧-赠送农村内部亲支

纯收入主要用于再生产投入和当年生活消费支出，也可用于储蓄和各种非义务性支出。“农民人均纯收入”按人口平均的纯收入水平，反映的是一个地区农村居民的平均收入水平。

总支出 指农村住户用于生产、生活和再分配的全部支出。包括家庭经营费用支出、购置生产性固定资产支出、税费支出、消费支出、财产性支出和转移性支出。

三、一体化住户调查

从2012年四季度起，国家统计局对分别进行的城乡住户调查实施了一体化改革，统一了城乡居民收入指标名称、分类和统计标准，建立了城乡统一的一体化住户调查《住户收支与生活状况调查》，并据此获得全国居民有关数据。

居民可支配收入 居民可支配收入指居民可用于最终消费支出和储蓄的总和，即居民可用于自由支配的收入。既包括现金收入、也包括实物收入。按照收入的来源，可支配收入包含四项，分别为：工资性收入、经营性净收入、转移性净收入和财产性净收入。

居民消费支出 居民消费支出是指居民用于满足家庭日常生活消费需要的全部支出，既包括现金消费支出，也包括实物消费支出。消费支出可划分为食品烟酒、衣着、居住、生活用品及服务、交通和通信、教育文化和娱乐、医疗保健以及其他用品及服务八大类。

Explanatory Notes on Main Statistical Indicators

Ⅰ.Urban Households(to the year of 2012)

Population of Urban Households refer to members of the household living and sharing economically together. All income and expenditure of the population of the household are included in the income and expenditure of the household.

Proportion of Urban Employment refer to the proportion of employed population to the population of urban households.

Number of Dependents per Urban Employee refers to the ratio between number of persons in urban households and the number of dependents.

Total Income of Urban Households refers to the sum of wage and salary, net business income, income from properties, and income from transfers of members of the households, excluding income from selling of properties and income from borrowings.

Disposable Income of Urban Households refers to the actual income at the disposal of members of the households which can be used for final consumption, other non-compulsory expenditure and savings. This equals to total income minus income tax, personal contribution to social security and sample household subsidy for keeping diaries. Following formula is used:

Disposable income = total household income – income tax – personal contribution to social security – sample household subsidy for keeping diaries

Total Expenditure of Urban Households refer to all expenditure of the households except expenditure on leading. It includes expenditure on consumption, on purchasing or building houses, on transfers, on properties and on social security.

Consumption Expenditure of Urban Households refers to total expenditure of the sample households for consumption in daily life, including expenditure on eight categories such as food, clothing, household appliances and services, health care and medical services, transport and communications, recreation, education and cultural services, housing, miscellaneous goods and services.

Expenditure of Urban Households on Consumption of Services refers to expenditure of households on services of various kinds provided by the society.

Urban Households by Income Group All households in the sample are grouped, by per capita disposable income of the household, into groups of lowest income, low income, lower middle income, middle income, upper middle income, high income and highest income, each group consisting of 10%, 10%, 20%, 20%, 20%, 10% and 10% of all households respectively. The lowest 5% of households are also referred to as poor households.

Engel Coefficient refers to the percentage of expenditure on food in the total consumption expenditure, using the following formula:

Engel Coefficient = (expenditure on food / total living consumption expenditure) x 100%

Ⅱ.Rural Households(to the year of 2012)

Rural Households refer to resident households in rural areas. Resident households in rural areas are the households residing for more than one year in the areas under the jurisdiction of administration of township governments (excluding county towns), and in the areas under the jurisdiction of administration of villages in county towns. Migrated households residing in the current addresses for over one year with their household registration in other places are included in the resident households of their current addresses. For households with their household registration in one place but all members of the households moving away for living in another place for over one year, they will not be included in the rural households of the area where they are registered, irrespective of whether they still keep their contracted land.

Resident Population refers to population staying at home permanently or for over 6 months during a year and sharing life economically with the household. Members of the household staying away from the household for over 6 months but keeping a close economic relation with the household by sending the majority of income to the household are regarded as resident population of the household. Government staff and workers or retirees living as close members of the household are also considered as resident population. However, servicemen, students of secondary technical schools or schools of higher education and persons with stable jobs and residence outside the household (excluding those visiting relatives or seeking medical service) are not included as resident population of the household. Resident population is used in calculating income, consumption, accumulation on per capita basis of rural households and in analyzing composition of rural households.

Full/Semi Labor Force Full labor force refers to persons capable of work, aged 18–50 for males and 18–45 for females. Semi labor force refers to persons capable of work, aged 16–17 and 51–60 for males and 16–17 and 46–55 for females. Persons at their working ages but not capable of work are not to be included as labor force. Persons not at working ages but participating regularly in work are included in semi labor force. For staff and workers as resident population of the household, they are included as full or semi labor force of the household if they are in the labor force.

Total Income refers to the sum of income earned from various sources by the rural households and their members during the reference period, and is classified as income from wages and salaries, income from household operations, income from properties and income from transfers.

Income from Wages and Salaries refers to income from labor earned by the members of rural households employed by other units or individuals.

Income from Household Operations refers to income by the rural households as units of production and operations. Operations by rural households are classified by economic activities as agriculture, forestry, animal husbandry, fishery, manufacturing, construction, transportation, post and telecommunications, wholesale, retail and catering, social service, culture, education, health, and other household operations.

Income from Properties refers to the income received as returns by owners of financial assets or tangible non–productive assets by providing capitals or tangible non–productive assets to other institutional units.

Income from Transfers refers to the receipt by rural households and their members of goods, services, capitals or rights of assets without giving or repaying accordingly, excluding capitals provided to them for the formation of fixed assets. In general, it refers to all income received by rural households through redistribution.

Cash Income refers to income received by rural households and their members in the form of cash during the reference period. It is classified, by source of income, into income from wages and salaries, cash income from household operations, income from properties and income from transfers.

Net Income refers to the total income of rural households from all sources minus all corresponding expenses. The formula for calculation is as follows:

Net income = total income – taxes and fees paid – household operation expenses – taxes and fees depreciation of fixed assets for production – subsidy for participating in household survey – gifts to non–rural relatives

Net income is mainly used as input for reproduction and as consumption expenditure of the year, and also used for savings and non–compulsory expenses of various forms. "Per capital net income of farmers" is the level of net income averaged by population which reflects the average income level of rural households in a given area.

Total Expenditure refers to total expenses of rural households on production, consumption and redistribution, including expenditure on household operations, on purchase of productive fixed assets, depreciation of productive fixed assets, taxes and fees, expenses on household consumption, expenses on properties and expenses on transfers.

Ⅲ.Integrated Household Survey

In the fourth quarter of 2012, the NBS launched its reform on the household survey program in order to produce aggregates with the same concepts and definitions for urban and rural population. This new survey program is an integrated one whereas there had existed two separate household surveys for the urban and rural households. The reform took a number of measures, including the integration of concepts, classifications and standards, which provided a basis for producing data covering all households.The new survey includes the following indicators:

Disposable Income of Households has a national coverage comparable between urban and rural households, and refers to the kind of income that households call have at them disposal. It includes income both in cash and in kind from four categories: income from wages and salaries, cash income from household operations, income from properties and income from transfers.

Consumption Expenditure of Households has a national coverage comparable between urban and rural households, and refers to the all the expenditures of households for consumption in daily life. It includes expenditure in cash and in kind on eight categories: food; clothing; housing; household appliances and services; transport and communications; education, cultural and recreational activities; and medical care. The expenditure on housing also includes rents, water, electricity, fuels and imputed rents of owner–occupied dwellings.

10 城市概况

City Overview

资料整理人员:程文懿

10-1 主要城市土地面积、人口情况(2020)
Land Area and Populations of Major Cities (2020)

城市	Cities	土地面积(平方公里) Land Area (sq.km)	常住人口(万人) Resident Population (10 000 persons)	人口密度(人/平方公里) Population Desity (person/sq.km)
武汉	Wuhan	8569	1244.77	1452.64
黄石	Huangshi	4583	246.91	538.75
十堰	Shiyan	23666	320.90	135.60
宜昌	Yichang	21230	389.64	183.53
襄阳	Xiangyang	19728	526.10	266.68
鄂州	Ezhou	1596	107.94	676.32
荆门	Jingmen	12404	259.69	209.36
孝感	Xiaogan	8904	427.04	479.60
荆州	Jingzhou	14099	523.12	371.03
黄冈	Huanggang	17457	588.27	336.98
咸宁	Xianning	9751	265.83	272.62
随州	Suizhou	9614	204.79	213.01

10-2 主要城市就业情况(2020)
Employment of Major Cities (2020)

单位：人 (person)

城市	Cities	从业人员期末人数(城镇) Employment (year-end)	从业人员按三次产业分 Employment Grouped by Type of Industry			城镇登记失业率(%) Unemployment Registered Rate (%)
			第一产业 Primary Industry	第二产业 Secondary Industry	第三产业 Tertiary Industry	
武汉	Wuhan	1763564	954	682479	1080131	3.04
黄石	Huangshi	288474	799	152316	135359	3.85
十堰	Shiyan	701761	8023	319087	374651	3.78
宜昌	Yichang	822900	10911	386719	365165	3.47
襄阳	Xiangyang	1083382	41340	503577	538465	3.59
鄂州	Ezhou	232895	302	149205	83388	2.90
荆门	Jingmen	410196	1102	211745	197349	3.63
孝感	Xiaogan	844002	7069	437592	399341	4.14
荆州	Jingzhou	374472	5277	226726	142469	3.26
黄冈	Huanggang	530631	2896	375217	152518	2.91
咸宁	Xianning	202552	406	57381	144765	3.34
随州	Suizhou	135624	423	54111	81090	4.86

10-3 主要城市地区生产总值(2020)
Gross Domestic Products of Major Cities (2020)

城市	Cities	地区生产总值(亿元) Gross Domestic Product (100 million yuan)	(当年价格) 第一产业 Primary Industry	第二产业 Secondary Industry	第三产业 Tertiary Industry	人均地区生产总值(元) Per Capita GDP (yuan)
武汉	Wuhan	15616	402	5558	9656	131441
黄石	Huangshi	1641	116	798	727	66439
十堰	Shiyan	1915	190	793	932	57971
宜昌	Yichang	4261	460	1828	1973	104807
襄阳	Xiangyang	4602	513	2104	1985	84773
鄂州	Ezhou	1005	99	435	471	93986
荆门	Jingmen	1906	251	849	806	70162
孝感	Xiaogan	2194	343	861	990	51367
荆州	Jingzhou	2369	453	806	1110	44143
黄冈	Huanggang	2170	438	750	982	36888
咸宁	Xianning	1524	217	629	678	58319
随州	Suizhou	1097	173	477	446	54474

10-4 主要城市固定资产投资(2020)
Investment in Fixed Assets of Major Cities (2020)

城市	Cities	固定资产投资增速(%) Growth Rate of Fixed Assert Investment(%)	商品房屋销售额(亿元) Commercial Housing Sales (100 million yuan)	#住宅 Residential Buildings	待售面积(万平方米) Area of Sale (10 000 sq.m)
武汉	Wuhan	-11.8	3769.49	3304.62	183.85
黄石	Huangshi	-18.4	174.22	163.49	36.11
十堰	Shiyan	-21.1	155.38	135.61	115.95
宜昌	Yichang	-20.5	283.12	264.30	44.19
襄阳	Xiangyang	-20.6	361.95	329.77	43.69
鄂州	Ezhou	-17.2	113.87	112.29	15.95
荆门	Jingmen	-21.3	136.56	122.71	169.33
孝感	Xiaogan	-20.8	145.23	136.45	55.00
荆州	Jingzhou	-22.4	242.77	231.44	91.27
黄冈	Huanggang	-21.9	174.37	160.58	206.59
咸宁	Xianning	-21.7	191.13	170.48	102.12
随州	Suizhou	-23.3	59.71	56.30	12.65

10-5 主要城市规模以上工业基本情况(2020)
Basic Statistics on Industry above Designated Size of Major Cities (2020)

单位:亿元 (100 million yuan)

城 市	Cities	工业企业单位数(个) Number of Industrial Enterprises (unit)	资产总计 Total Assets	利润总额 Total Profits
武 汉	Wuhan	2958	17223.44	656.56
黄 石	Huangshi	704	2027.90	106.83
十 堰	Shiyan	950	2348.17	95.79
宜 昌	Yichang	1293	4951.79	419.62
襄 阳	Xiangyang	1697	3661.49	323.40
鄂 州	Ezhou	492	745.03	72.77
荆 门	Jingmen	982	2004.18	172.96
孝 感	Xiaogan	1174	1602.66	110.62
荆 州	Jingzhou	1239	2173.72	129.01
黄 冈	Huanggang	1264	1424.13	82.80
咸 宁	Xianning	945	1114.60	144.55
随 州	Suizhou	700	940.75	80.34

10-6 主要城市规上工业经济效益状况(2020)
Economic Efficiency of Industry above Designated Size of Major Cities (2020)

单位:% (%)

城 市	Cities	企业亏损面 Loss Making Rate of Enterprises	资产负债率 Assets Liability Ratio	成本费用利润率 Ratio of Profits to Industrial Cost	产品销售率 Proportion of Products Sold
武 汉	Wuhan	20.4	53.74	5.87	98.44
黄 石	Huangshi	22.8	54.57	6.72	98.02
十 堰	Shiyan	17.6	66.89	5.32	95.55
宜 昌	Yichang	8.1	49.88	14.94	95.70
襄 阳	Xiangyang	9.2	48.52	6.50	97.31
鄂 州	Ezhou	10.6	53.85	6.22	96.83
荆 门	Jingmen	9.2	48.37	6.36	96.10
孝 感	Xiaogan	10.9	51.22	4.81	96.98
荆 州	Jingzhou	14.2	46.37	7.03	96.28
黄 冈	Huanggang	14.6	55.02	5.05	96.59
咸 宁	Xianning	6.6	45.57	8.93	97.34
随 州	Suizhou	6.6	48.20	9.62	96.76

10-7 主要城市财政收支(2020)
Government Revenue and Expenditures of Major Cities (2020)

单位：亿元 (100 million yuan)

城市	Cities	公共财政收入 The Public Finance Income	#各项税收 Taxes	公共财政支出 The Public Finance Expenditures	#社会保障和就业支出 Subsides Expenditures for Social Security	#城乡社区事务支出 Expenditures for City Maintenance
武汉	Wuhan	1230.29	1041.06	2407.81	384.64	409.01
黄石	Huangshi	88.23	62.84	286.34	50.67	20.72
十堰	Shiyan	89.36	67.12	459.23	67.95	18.77
宜昌	Yichang	139.97	114.06	589.59	89.24	47.20
襄阳	Xiangyang	160.00	124.25	670.28	109.02	85.51
鄂州	Ezhou	48.47	38.93	127.41	22.01	8.31
荆门	Jingmen	79.84	61.05	312.94	51.60	27.28
孝感	Xiaogan	100.17	77.90	425.26	74.91	19.64
荆州	Jingzhou	105.41	77.36	532.82	119.37	24.16
黄冈	Huanggang	104.00	76.47	594.84	101.05	29.26
咸宁	Xianning	70.90	53.03	312.26	47.88	13.40
随州	Suizhou	35.88	27.31	190.94	34.87	8.16

10-8 主要城市金融机构存贷款余额(2020)
Deposits and Loans Balance of Banking Institutions of Major Cities (2020)

单位：亿元 (100 million yuan)

城市	Cities	年末金融机构人民币各项存款余额 Deposit Balance	#住户存款余额 Balance of Deposits of Households	年末金融机构人民币各项贷款余额 Loans Balance
武汉	Wuhan	30329.15	10213.24	35491.87
黄石	Huangshi	2006.36	1210.17	1568.72
十堰	Shiyan	2810.02	1864.31	1719.91
宜昌	Yichang	4361.32	2571.30	3987.54
襄阳	Xiangyang	4278.11	2977.90	2817.87
鄂州	Ezhou	897.78	505.89	708.79
荆门	Jingmen	2449.43	1665.01	1427.41
孝感	Xiaogan	2860.24	2082.63	1601.70
荆州	Jingzhou	3701.55	2663.36	2191.70
黄冈	Huanggang	3995.03	2900.92	2168.25
咸宁	Xianning	1797.12	1090.63	1288.80
随州	Suizhou	1634.80	1194.77	885.44

10-9 主要城市贸易、外经情况(2020)
Domestic Trade and Foreign Economy of Major Cities (2020)

城 市	Cities	社会消费品零售总额(亿元) Total Retail Sales of Consumer Goods (100 million yuan)	进出口总额(亿元) Total Import and Export (100 million yuan)	进口 Imports	出口 Exports	当年实际使用外资金额(万美元) Actual Foreign Direct Investment (USD 10 000)
武 汉	Wuhan	6149.84	2704.30	1282.60	1421.70	833073
黄 石	Huangshi	758.81	238.45	118.36	120.09	19875
十 堰	Shiyan	974.01	53.31	4.78	48.54	7212
宜 昌	Yichang	1391.12	206.20	21.99	184.21	14144
襄 阳	Xiangyang	1567.26	218.13	20.26	197.87	83122
鄂 州	Ezhou	326.57	29.31	18.22	11.09	4742
荆 门	Jingmen	779.31	86.42	28.25	58.17	12507
孝 感	Xiaogan	981.24	110.22	18.53	91.69	29245
荆 州	Jingzhou	1284.49	119.70	16.53	103.17	8684
黄 冈	Huanggang	1150.13	65.50	5.80	59.70	5967
咸 宁	Xianning	604.04	73.92	8.14	65.78	3749
随 州	Suizhou	519.53	80.00	4.60	75.40	4759

10-10 主要城市邮电、电力情况(2020)
Postal and Telecommunication Services and Electricity in Major Cities (2020)

城 市	Cities	邮电业务收入(亿元) Revenue from Posts and Telecommunication Services(100 million yuan)	固定电话用户(万户) Telephones (10 000 subscribers)	移动电话用户(万户) Mobile Telephones (10 000 subscribers)	国际互联网用户(万户) Internet Service (10 000 subscribers)	全年用电量(亿千瓦小时) Electricity Consumption (100 million kwh)	#城乡居民生活用电 Urban and Rural Residents Electricity Consumption
武 汉	Wuhan	283.97	156.45	1557.37	479.53	568.79	115.46
黄 石	Huangshi	74.57	18.98	256.62	82.71	144.80	19.29
十 堰	Shiyan	26.59	20.00	321.00	153.56	104.12	22.59
宜 昌	Yichang	36.37	33.03	431.96	157.44	225.00	28.82
襄 阳	Xiangyang	45.34	35.83	545.62	160.36	160.34	35.13
鄂 州	Ezhou	15.73	8.59	98.20	42.75	70.57	8.85
荆 门	Jingmen	25.54	19.40	243.75	86.48	105.91	17.49
孝 感	Xiaogan	42.70	26.09	359.85	96.98	139.01	31.26
荆 州	Jingzhou	51.07	35.13	469.20	163.12	147.86	39.37
黄 冈	Huanggang	51.06	42.54	461.07	203.51	141.60	39.50
咸 宁	Xianning	23.27	29.76	245.12	89.86	93.41	21.28
随 州	Suizhou	18.50	10.04	197.16	62.97	46.51	13.50

10–11 主要城市居民收支情况(2020)
Income and Expenditure of Major Urban Households (2020)

单位:元 (yuan)

城市	Cities	城镇常住居民人均可支配收入 Per Capita Disposable Income of Urban Residents	城镇常住居民人均消费性支出 Per Capita Living Expenditure of Urban Residents	城镇人均住房建筑面积(平方米) Per Capita Housing Construction Area of Urban(sq.m)
武汉	Wuhan	50362	31115	
黄石	Huangshi	37912	23718	38.90
十堰	Shiyan	32771	20538	37.36
宜昌	Yichang	37232	21866	46.80
襄阳	Xiangyang	37707	20337	
鄂州	Ezhou	35025	19281	46.00
荆门	Jingmen	35958	21459	35.40
孝感	Xiaogan	35374	22775	45.00
荆州	Jingzhou	34474	21294	49.46
黄冈	Huanggang	30826	20236	40.00
咸宁	Xianning	32394	19493	45.12
随州	Suizhou	30587	18691	48.00

10–12 主要城市居民消费支出、价格(2020)
Consumption Expenditures and Price of Major Urban Households (2020)

单位:元 (yuan)

城市	Cities	城镇常住居民人均消费性支出 Per Capita Living Expenditures for Consumption of Urban Residents				居民消费价格指数(上年=100) Consumer Price Index (preceding year=100)
		#医疗保健 Medicine and Medicine and Medical Service	#交通和通讯 Transport and Telecommunication	#娱乐、教育、文化服务 Recreation, Education and Cultural Services	#居 住 Residence	
武汉	Wuhan	2314	3614	3053	8591	102.4
黄石	Huangshi	2112	2511	3267	3717	102.3
十堰	Shiyan	1506	2802	2629	3676	102.3
宜昌	Yichang	1735	2565	2843	5262	102.7
襄阳	Xiangyang	1515	2524	2278	4098	102.9
鄂州	Ezhou	1776	1573	1995	3299	102.5
荆门	Jingmen	2168	2366	2404	3558	102.5
孝感	Xiaogan	1476	2136	2441	2555	102.4
荆州	Jingzhou	1694	2743	1979	4542	102.6
黄冈	Huanggang	1305	1783	2201	2486	102.6
咸宁	Xianning	1408	2129	2198	4475	102.5
随州	Suizhou	1773	2074	2012	3362	101.9

10-13 主要城市文教、科技、卫生情况(2020)

Culture and Education, Science and Technology, Public Health of Major Cities (2020)

城 市	Cities	普通本专科在校学生数(万人) Number of Students Enrolled in Institutions of Higher Education (10 000 persons)	公共图书馆图书总藏量(万册) Total Volume of Collection of Public Libraries (10 000 volumes)	医疗卫生机构数(个) Number of Health Care Institutions (unit)	医疗卫生机构床位数(万张) Number of Beds In Health Care Intitutions (10 000 units)	执业(助理)医师(万人) PractionerDoctors (Assitant) (10 000 persons)
武 汉	Wuhan	106.72	933.05	6446	9.38	4.19
黄 石	Huangshi	5.43	191.00	1427	1.78	0.67
十 堰	Shiyan	5.63	161.20	2785	3.23	1.08
宜 昌	Yichang	6.11	377.09	2634	2.93	1.19
襄 阳	Xiangyang	7.24	288.37	3693	3.90	1.43
鄂 州	Ezhou	1.66	135.00	476	0.58	0.22
荆 门	Jingmen	2.28	93.68	1960	1.88	0.75
孝 感	Xiaogan	3.68	192.00	2430	2.65	1.00
荆 州	Jingzhou	9.83	136.00	3012	3.42	1.25
黄 冈	Huanggang	4.54	419.61	4248	3.95	1.58
咸 宁	Xianning	4.05	139.19	1358	1.61	0.74
随 州	Suizhou	0.78	53.03	1312	1.34	0.56

主要统计指标解释

商品房销售额 指房地产开发企业本年出售商品房屋的合同总价款（即双方签署的正式买卖合同中所确定的合同总价）。该指标与商品房销售面积同口径。

城镇私营和个体就业人员 城镇私营就业人员指在工商管理部门注册登记，其经营地址设在县城关镇（含县城关镇）以上的私营企业就业人员，包括私营企业投资者和雇工。城镇个体就业人员指在工商管理部门注册登记，并持有城镇户口或在城镇长期居住，经批准从事个体工商经营的就业人员，包括个体经营者和在个体工商户劳动的家庭帮工和雇工。

医疗卫生机构 指从卫生（卫生计生）行政部门取得《医疗机构执业许可证》《中医诊所备案证》《计划生育技术服务许可证》，或从民政、工商行政、机构编制管理部门取得法人单位登记证书，为社会提供医疗服务、公共卫生服务或从事医学科研和医学在职培训等工作的单位。医疗卫生机构包括医院、基层医疗卫生机构、专业公共卫生机构、其他医疗卫生机构。

Explanatory Notes on Main Statistical Indicators

Value of Commercialized Housing Sold refers to the total contracted value (i.e. value of sales/purchase for selling/purchase of commercialized housing as designated in the contract signed by both sides) received from the sales of the buildings by real estate development companies during the reference time. This indicator has the same coverage as the area of commercialized housing sold.

Persons Employed in Private Enterprises and Self-Employed Individuals in Urban Areas Persons employed in private enterprises refer to the persons employed in the private enterprises which have been registered at the departments of industrial and commercial administration for which the business operation are situated at a county town (i.e. a town where the county government is located), or at urban areas with administrative hierarchy higher than a county town. The self-employed individuals in urban areas refer to persons who hold the certificates of residence in urban areas or have resided in the urban areas for a long time and have been registered at the departments of industrial and commercial administration and approved to be engaged in individual industrial or commercial business, including self-employed persons as well as helpers and hired laborers who work in individual households.

Medical and Health Care Institutions refer to the units which have been qualified the *Certification of Health Care Institution, Filing Certificate of Traditional Chinese Medicine Clinic, Certification of Family Planning Technical Service* by the administration of public health (family planning), or qualified the Certification of Corporate Unit by the civil affairs, administration for industry and commerce, commission office for public sector reform, and engaging in medical health care services, public health services, or medicine research and on-job training, etc., including: hospitals, health care institutions at grass-root level, specialized public health institutions, and other medical and health care institutions.

11

资源和环境

Resources and Environment

资料整理人员:康世华　　高　媛

11-1 “三废”排放和处理综合利用情况

Comprehensive Utilization Situation of “Three Wastes” Discharge and Treatment

分 类	Item	2015	2016	2017	2018	2019
一、废水排放总量 (万吨)	**Total Volume of Waste Water Discharged (10 000 tons)**	**313785**	**274787**	**272694**	**269605**	**332993**
工业废水排放总量	Total Volume of Industrial Waste Water Discharged	80817	49090	44158	45849	57088
二、工业废气排放量 (亿标立方米)	**Total Volume of Waste Gas Discharged (100 million cu.m)**	**23643**	**29519**	**20176**	**24241**	**24240**
三、废气中污染物排放量 (万吨)	**Pollutants Discharged in Waste Gas (10 000 tons)**					
二氧化硫	Sulfur Dioxide	55.14	28.56	22.01	17.70	11.68
#工业二氧化硫	Industrial Sulfur Dioxide	47.07	18.55	11.61	9.13	9.63
烟粉尘	Soot and Dust	44.69	27.58	18.80	15.85	31.87
四、工业固体废物产生量 (万吨)	**Volume of Industrial Solid Wastes Producced (10 000 tons)**	**7750**	**7109**	**8112**	**8472**	**13368**
已处置的	Teated	2078	1494	1021	636	2467
已综合利用的	Utilized In a Comprehensive Way	5253	4332	4812	5599	10060
已贮存的	Stored	488	1505	2624	2582	1943
工业固体废物排放量	Volume of Industrial Solid Wastes Emission	0.50	0.22	0.58	0.25	0.23
五、工业锅炉数 (台)	**Total Number of Boiler (unit)**	**3107**	**2694**	**2407**	**2293**	**2606**
工业锅炉蒸吨数 (蒸吨)	Steam Tons of Boiler (steam ton)	83972	81870	100748	93046	111741
六、工业炉窑 (座)	**Number of Industrial Kiln Stove (unit)**	**2157**	**1589**	**1667**	**2078**	**4626**

11-2 工业污染治理情况
Statistics on Treatment of Industrial Pollution

项目	Item	2013	2014	2015	2016	2017	2018	2019
一、汇总工业企业单位数（个）	**Total Number of Industrial Enterprises (unit)**	**147**	**152**	**161**	**305**	**302**	**201**	**241**
二、污染治理项目本年投资来源合计（万元）	**Total Resource of Investment in Pollutant Treatment Projects (10 000 yuan)**	**251745**	**262884**	**157944**	**169061**	**188536**	**137427**	**133861**
国家预算内资金	State Budgetary Funds	3667	1890	1035	631	38	265	244
其他	Others	247868	258817	155917	167800	188472	137162	133617
三、污染治理项目本年完成投资合计（万元）	**Total Investment in Pollutant Treatment Projects (10 000 yuan)**	**251745**	**262884**	**157944**	**169061**	**174632**	**137434**	**133861**
治理废水	Waste Water	15873	18409	26067	39707	31296	22807	31287
治理废气	Waste Gas	216673	230712	120301	98518	124206	88293	77832
治理固体废物	Solid Waste	1720	2762	1375	8475	5542	828	273
治理噪声	Noise Abatement	52	104	275	367	637	1172	217
其他	Others	17427	10896	9927	21994	1219	24335	24252
四、本年施工项目数（个）	**Projects Carried Out in This Year (unit)**	**113**	**127**	**199**	**302**	**233**	**187**	**179**
治理废水	Waste Water	28	38	63	99	52	34	27
治理废气	Waste Gas	59	78	96	151	141	112	114
治理固体废物	Solid Waste	3	2	7	21	2	3	4
治理噪声	Noise Abatement	1	4	5	4	2	6	2
其他	Others	22	5	28	27	36	32	32
五、本年竣工项目（个）	**Projects Completed in This Year (unit)**	**148**	**134**	**146**	**238**	**164**	**128**	**134**
治理废水	Waste Water	42	37	41	80	30	20	20
治理废气	Waste Gas	83	88	73	116	108	81	88
治理固体废物	Solid Waste	3	1	4	17	2	2	3
治理噪声	Noise Abatement		3	5	4	2	5	1
其他	Others	20	5	23	21	22	20	22

11-3 工业企业废水处理设施情况
Statistics on Industrial Waste Water Treatment Facilities

项 目	Item	2014	2015	2016	2017	2018	2019
汇总企业单位数 （个）	Total Number of Enterprises (unit)	3911	4555	4198	3834	3775	5242
治理设施数量 （套）	Number of Treatment Facilities (set)	2238	2562	1942	2109	2139	2562
处理能力 （万吨/日）	Treatment Capacity (10 000 tons/day)	1043	1052	566	625	629	721
运行费用 （万元）	Operation Fees (10 000 yuan)	232869	224053	195593	249534	273845	303646

主要统计指标解释

工业废水排放量 指经过企业厂区所有排放口排到企业外部的工业废水量。包括生产废水、外排的直接冷却水、超标排放的矿井地下水和与工业废水混排的厂区生活污水,不包括外排的间接冷却水(清污不分流的间接冷却水应计算在内)。

工业废气排放量 指报告期内企业厂区内燃料燃烧和生产工艺过程中产生的各种排入大气的含有污染物的气体的总量,以标准状态(273K,101325Pa)计算。测算公式为:

工业废气排放量 = 燃料燃烧过程中废气排放量

+ 生产工艺过程中废气排放量

工业烟尘排放量 指企业厂区内燃料燃烧过程中产生的烟气中夹带的颗粒物排放量。

工业粉尘排放量 指企业在生产工艺过程中排放的能在空气中悬浮一定时间的固体颗粒物排放量。如钢铁企业的耐火材料粉尘、焦化企业的筛焦系统粉尘、烧结机的粉尘、石灰窑的粉尘、建材企业的水泥粉尘等。不包括电厂排入大气的烟尘。

工业固体废物产生量 指报告期内企业在生产过程中产生的固体状、半固体状和高浓度液体状废弃物的总量,包括危险废物、冶炼废渣、粉煤灰、炉渣、煤矸石、尾矿、放射性废物和其他废物等;不包括矿山开采的剥离废石和掘进废石(煤矸石和呈酸性或碱性的废石除外)。酸性或碱性废石指采掘的废石其流经水、雨淋水的 pH 值小于 4 或 pH 值大于 10.5 者。

Explanatory Notes on Main Statistical Indicators

Waste Water Discharged by Industry refers to the volume of waste water discharged by industrial enterprises through all their outlets, including waste water from production process, directly cooled water, groundwater from mining wells which does not meet discharge standards and sewage from households mixed with waste water produced by industrial activities, but excluding indirectly cooled water discharged (It should be included if the discharge is not separated with waste water).

Industrial Waste Air Emission refers to discharge into atmosphere of waste air containing pollutants generated from fuel burning and production process in enterprises within a given period of time. It is calculated at standard status (273K, 101325Pa) as:

Industrial waste air emission = emission through fuel burning + emission through production process

Industrial Soot Emission refers to volume of soot in smoke emitted in process of fuel burning in premises of enterprises.

Industrial Dust Emission refers to volume of dust emitted by production process of enterprises and suspended in the air for a given period of time, including dust from refractory material of iron and steel works, dust from coke-screening systems and sintering machines of coke plants, dust from lime kilns and dust from cement production in building material enterprises, but excluding soot and dust emitted from power plants.

Industrial Solid Wastes Produced refers to total volume of solid, semi-solid and high concentration liquid residues produced by industrial enterprises from production process in a given period of time, including hazardous wastes, slag, coal ash, gangue, tailings, radioactive residues and other wastes, but excluding stones stripped or dug out in mining (gangue and acid or alkaline stones not included). A stone is acid or alkaline depending on the pH value of the water below 4 or above 10.5 when the stone is in, or soaked by, the water.

12 农业 Agriculture

资料整理人员:周　真

12-1 农村基层组织和农业基本情况
Basic Conditions of Rural Grassroots Units and Agriculture

指 标	Item	2000	2005	2010	2015	2018	2019	2020
农村组织情况 (个)	**Rural Units (unit)**							
乡个数	Township	476	217	201	168	163	162	161
镇个数	Town Governments	853	737	742	761	762	760	761
村委会个数	Village Committees	32400	26678	26018	25343	23571	23202	22532
村民小组个数	Villager Group	259250	212587	209598	208546	205059	203005	208002
农业生产条件	**Agricultural Production Conditions**							
年末实有耕地面积 (千公顷)	Cultivated Areas (Year-End) (1 000 hectares)			5312.28	5255.00	5235.40		
农业机械总动力 (万千瓦)	Total Agricultural Machinery Power (10 000 kw)	1414.00	2057.37	2796.99	4465.51	4424.59	4515.73	4626.07
化肥施用量 (万吨)	Consumption of Chemical Fertilizers (10 000 tons)	247.08	285.83	350.77	333.87	295.82	273.89	267.23
农村用电量 (亿千瓦小时)	Electricity Consumed in Rural Areas (100 million kwh)	60.86	70.09	109.78	149.10	165.21	178.55	186.87
农作物播种面积 (千公顷)	**Total Sown Area of Farm Crops (1 000 hectares)**							
总播种面积	Total Sown Area	7584.07	7391.30	7383.59	7986.30	7952.90	7815.89	7974.44
其中:粮食	Grain Crops	4156.20	4068.15	4139.12	4784.38	4847.01	4608.60	4645.27
棉花	Cotton Crops	318.07	360.95	482.37	267.62	159.26	162.83	129.73
油料	Oil-Bearing Crops	1503.44	1460.20	1390.30	1389.39	1255.82	1278.60	1377.93
# 油菜籽	Rapeseed	1158.94	1178.65	1089.43	1070.11	932.97	938.31	1034.36
花生	Peanuts	193.42	171.71	198.50	221.65	232.60	243.62	248.72
甘蔗	Sugarcane	22.17	9.95	7.04	6.30	6.45	6.48	6.63
烤烟	Flue-Cured Tobacco	48.10	43.68	39.36	39.60	33.63	30.38	31.58
主要农产品产量 (万吨)	**Volume of Major Agricultural Products (10 000 tons)**							
其中:粮食	Grain Crops	2218.49	2177.38	2304.26	2914.75	2839.47	2724.98	2727.43
棉花	Cotton Crops	30.43	37.50	47.41	30.08	14.93	14.36	10.79
油料	Oil-Bearing Crops	269.98	293.90	302.28	316.71	302.48	313.95	344.45
# 油菜籽	Rapeseed	192.40	219.15	220.35	226.02	205.31	211.35	241.06
花生	Peanuts	53.46	60.19	66.64	73.21	80.67	85.71	87.10
肉类产量	Output of Meat	271.19	342.63	383.48	443.66	430.95	349.20	307.44
水产品产量	Output of Aquatic Products	234.34	318.21	353.09	455.80	458.40	469.54	467.93

注:主要农产品播种面积、产量2007-2017年数据依据第三次全国农业普查结果进行了修订。
Note: Statistics of major farm products output of 2007-2017 is adjusted according to the Third Agricultural Census.

12-2 农林牧渔业总产值
Gross Output Value of Farming, Forestry, Animal Husbandry and Fishery

单位:亿元 当年价格 (At current price, 100 million yuan)

年 份 Year	农林牧渔业总产值 Gross Output Value of Farming, Forestry, Animal Husbandry and Fishery	农业 Farming	林业 Foresty	畜牧业 Animal Husbandry	渔业 Fishery	农林牧渔专业及辅助性活动 Professional and Ancillary Service for Farming, Forestry, Animal Husbandry and Fishery
1949	10.72	7.22	0.69	0.97	0.10	
1952	16.59	12.08	0.79	1.48	0.18	
1957	28.59	20.55	1.46	3.81	0.46	
1962	33.66	26.52	1.71	3.61	0.46	
1965	47.48	37.44	1.98	6.02	0.51	
1970	51.27	40.62	2.07	6.41	0.92	
1975	74.68					
1978	84.46					
1979	109.85					
1980	94.95	64.70	7.28	17.29	1.46	
1985	192.32	129.61	8.15	39.08	8.18	
1986	219.10	146.79	8.75	43.86	10.77	
1987	249.68	160.13	9.97	54.86	14.19	
1988	297.51	175.12	10.98	80.80	18.83	
1989	335.04	198.56	11.75	91.47	20.66	
1990	402.23	252.92	14.15	98.04	23.88	
1991	405.04	247.01	16.81	102.19	25.06	
1992	435.42	265.53	17.36	110.37	27.59	
1993	501.17	301.99	22.39	134.02	42.77	
1994	786.84	481.82	26.47	219.53	59.01	
1995	988.53	612.12	28.33	268.09	79.98	
1996	1140.76	670.27	33.62	337.02	99.86	
1997	1243.68	711.91	37.33	381.40	113.04	
1998	1222.58	688.06	41.29	371.37	121.86	
1999	1126.10	645.98	40.86	311.43	127.83	
2000	1125.64	615.74	40.24	338.77	130.89	
2001	1172.82	658.26	27.11	352.63	134.82	
2002	1203.30	671.20	28.33	354.84	148.93	
2003	1342.09	733.36	34.78	383.71	170.43	
2004	1695.44	921.59	31.78	514.52	205.68	21.87
2005	1775.58	932.15	37.30	545.40	236.49	24.24
2006	1842.20	995.46	40.50	487.09	221.42	97.73
2007	2281.21	1147.31	41.86	678.27	310.83	102.90
2008	2900.59	1385.21	49.69	985.51	372.98	107.20
2009	2924.66	1490.91	57.67	851.62	413.14	111.30
2010	3407.64	1883.22	65.37	883.09	458.58	117.40
2011	4110.16	2244.55	86.10	1137.84	508.80	132.90
2012	4542.16	2416.35	100.10	1244.29	626.20	155.22
2013	4920.13	2585.15	122.00	1286.55	748.40	178.03
2014	5162.94	2651.16	157.00	1301.06	844.20	209.53
2015	5387.13	2674.07	180.60	1354.28	922.77	255.42
2016	5863.98	2794.79	203.43	1527.29	1030.01	308.46
2017	6129.72	2962.49	213.26	1478.10	1089.08	386.79
2018	6207.83	3033.76	235.23	1386.53	1105.95	446.36
2019	6681.85	3257.85	258.47	1521.49	1152.68	491.36
2020	7303.64	3492.54	245.37	1864.78	1156.78	544.16

注:农林牧渔业总产值2007-2017年数据依据第三次全国农业普查结果进行了修订。
Note: Gross output value of farm, forestry, animal husbandry and fishery of 2007-2017 is adjusted according to the Third Agricultural Census.

12-3 农、林、牧、渔业总产值指数(上年=100)
Indices of Gross Output Value of Farming, Forestry, Animal Husbandry and Fishery (preceding year=100)

单位:% 上年=100 (preceding year=100)

年份 Year	合计 Total	农业 Farming	林业 Forestry	畜牧业 Animal Husbandry	渔业 Fishery	农林牧渔专业及辅助性活动 Professional and Ancillary Service for Farming, Forestry, Animal Husbandry and Fishery
1978	104.00	103.10	104.90	107.60	94.20	
1980	88.80	83.70	102.80	108.10	111.30	
1985	106.30	101.70	103.00	127.80	133.30	
1986	103.40	100.60	98.50	107.30	129.80	
1987	102.70	101.20	104.50	101.00	120.10	
1988	97.20	93.90	90.60	105.40	105.60	
1989	105.00	104.50	101.60	105.20	108.30	
1990	107.10	108.40	106.00	104.90	106.70	
1991	100.70	97.66	118.80	104.23	104.94	
1992	107.50	107.50	103.27	108.00	110.10	
1993	115.10	113.73	128.97	121.43	155.02	
1994	157.00	159.55	118.27	163.80	137.93	
1995	125.63	127.04	106.99	122.12	135.54	
1996	115.40	109.50	118.67	125.71	124.87	
1997	109.02	106.21	111.04	113.17	113.20	
1998	98.30	96.65	110.61	97.37	107.80	
1999	92.11	93.88	98.95	83.86	104.90	
2000	99.96	95.32	98.48	108.78	102.39	
2001	104.19	106.91	67.37	104.09	103.00	
2002	102.60	101.97	104.50	100.63	110.47	
2003	111.53	109.26	122.77	108.14	114.44	
2004	126.33	125.67	91.37	134.09	120.68	
2005	104.73	101.15	117.37	106.00	114.98	110.84
2006	105.37	109.29	108.58	96.04	109.87	116.05
2007	103.90	104.15	99.50	102.90	105.10	105.40
2008	106.20	102.80	105.00	110.00	112.00	102.00
2009	105.40	104.05	107.60	106.90	107.20	101.80
2010	104.50	103.40	117.50	105.30	105.80	101.50
2011	104.40	106.11	109.90	101.20	102.10	106.90
2012	105.60	103.65	108.10	107.70	108.80	106.60
2013	105.60	104.70	110.70	104.50	108.70	112.60
2014	105.60	103.22	123.30	105.90	107.20	119.20
2015	105.40	104.69	121.50	101.65	106.07	122.87
2016	104.90	104.90	112.00	99.00	108.34	118.70
2017	105.00	104.60	110.10	102.60	102.70	123.50
2018	103.40	103.80	109.10	102.50	99.80	111.20
2019	103.47	103.92	109.73	97.13	106.65	108.37
2020	100.74	103.94	97.08	92.52	101.16	105.95

注:农林牧渔业总产值2007-2017年数据依据第三次全国农业普查结果进行了修订。
Note: Gross output value of farm, forestry, animal husbandry and fishery of 2007-2017 is adjusted according to the Third Agricultural Census.

12-4 农、林、牧、渔业总产值指数(1978 年=100)

Indices of Gross Output Value of Farming, Forestry, Animal Husbandry and Fishery (year of 1978 =100)

单位:% 1978 年=100 (year 1978 =100)

年份 Year	合计 Total	农业 Farming	林业 Forestry	牧业 Animal Husbandry	渔业 Fishery
1980	97.3	91.4	104.7	127.9	121.5
1985	157.7	142.4	114.0	206.2	338.6
1987	167.5	145.0	117.3	282.7	527.8
1988	162.9	136.1	106.3	285.5	557.3
1989	171.0	142.3	108.0	301.0	603.6
1990	183.1	154.2	114.5	315.7	644.0
1991	181.7	147.7	125.9	334.0	631.8
1992	194.4	158.7	120.1	360.7	689.3
1993	207.4	168.0	129.5	410.9	936.1
1994	227.8	175.0	152.0	461.7	1203.0
1995	259.9	195.3	156.0	535.1	1530.2
1996	277.6	198.0	168.5	611.1	1732.0
1997	304.0	213.4	179.3	671.6	2007.4
1998	307.3	209.1	204.6	682.3	2164.0
1999	309.5	220.2	196.7	627.9	2270.0
2000	318.1	226.3	194.2	650.4	2324.5
2001	327.6	238.7	141.6	669.6	2382.4
2002	334.2	233.1	145.9	700.2	2677.3
2003	351.8	237.2	167.2	730.8	2824.4
2004	374.7	257.9	153.9	760.8	2979.6
2005	392.4	260.9	180.6	806.4	3425.9
2006	171.8	137.9	58.7	502.2	2214.2
2007	178.5	143.6	58.4	516.8	2327.1
2008	189.6	147.7	61.3	568.4	2606.4
2009	199.8	153.6	66.0	607.7	2794.0
2010	208.8	158.9	77.5	639.9	2956.1
2011	218.0	168.6	85.2	647.5	3018.2
2012	230.2	174.7	92.1	697.4	3283.8
2013	243.1	183.0	102.0	728.8	3569.5
2014	256.7	188.8	125.7	771.8	3826.5
2015	270.6	197.7	152.8	784.5	4058.9
2016	283.8	207.4	171.1	776.7	4397.5
2017	298.0	216.9	188.4	796.9	4516.3
2018	308.2	225.2	205.6	816.7	4507.0
2019	318.9	234.0	225.6	793.2	4806.9
2020	321.2	243.2	219.0	733.8	4862.7

注:农林牧渔业总产值、增加值 2007-2017 年数据依据第三次全国农业普查结果进行了修订。
Note: Grass output value of farm, forestry, animal husbandry and fishery of 2007-2017 is adjusted according to the Third Agricultural Census.

12-5 农作物播种面积
Sown Areas of Farm Crops

单位：千公顷 (1 000 hectares)

年 份 Year	总播种面积 Total Sown Areas	粮食作物 Grain Crops	小麦 Wheat	稻谷 Rice	薯类 Tubers	玉米 Corn	大豆 Soybean	经济作物 Economic Crops
1978	7931.05	5544.78	1122.28	2894.63	427.23	403.14	173.43	2386.27
1980	7477.06	5352.04	1292.29	2708.22	387.46	406.91	138.94	2125.02
1985	7331.71	5108.25	1331.42	2538.57	354.01	374.17	134.64	2223.46
1990	7361.14	5200.01	1352.10	2636.47	391.90	386.11	164.65	2161.13
1991	7423.92	5194.50	1347.53	2622.79	402.38	395.19	150.61	2229.42
1992	7183.83	4955.35	1287.91	2537.49	392.59	376.18	140.23	2228.48
1993	7125.47	4812.05	1271.23	2377.82	384.33	365.96	181.69	2313.42
1994	7181.43	4797.95	1225.60	2373.26	203.39	373.02	201.52	2383.48
1995	7431.71	4776.65	1179.93	2408.66	397.65	393.77	188.01	2655.06
1996	7579.01	4880.28	1230.14	2448.58	419.53	405.07	174.71	2698.73
1997	7739.21	4944.66	1276.52	2467.51	415.74	400.30	182.51	2794.55
1998	7695.98	4737.15	1212.08	2244.74	431.02	442.84	201.32	2958.83
1999	7788.66	4673.11	1074.43	2284.98	448.72	460.82	207.01	3115.55
2000	7584.07	4156.20	845.10	1995.29	467.61	424.10	224.75	3427.87
2001	7488.99	4015.73	735.85	1953.77	237.75	401.11	218.01	3473.26
2002	7281.61	3816.08	679.02	1888.75	430.61	384.04	217.82	3465.53
2003	7153.24	3572.74	603.43	1808.75	208.56	349.81	196.47	3580.50
2004	7225.13	3817.89	605.08	2084.02	403.79	357.49	186.05	3407.24
2005	7391.30	4068.05	730.61	2162.39	397.75	428.79	179.79	3323.25
2006	7100.59	3902.27	1016.93	1975.07	218.67	431.93	118.40	3198.32
2007	6993.69	4032.18	1099.41	2027.17	217.51	444.55	117.20	2961.51
2008	7132.86	3891.72	1006.35	1956.92	212.20	488.24	115.60	3241.14
2009	7330.17	4072.96	1001.98	2093.62	230.05	536.46	111.36	3257.20
2010	7380.25	4135.78	1011.70	2087.84	260.83	572.53	109.94	3244.47
2011	7457.92	4191.52	1028.32	2081.07	283.93	603.37	108.12	3266.40
2012	7687.83	4294.51	1084.08	2086.42	275.94	663.58	105.67	3393.32
2013	7734.78	4416.60	1117.11	2202.55	272.53	653.43	103.27	3318.17
2014	7794.75	4522.12	1099.38	2201.79	274.15	745.72	136.79	3272.64
2015	7986.31	4784.38	1122.15	2383.35	276.80	813.53	144.40	3201.92
2016	7908.50	4816.14	1140.67	2358.67	276.35	797.33	202.25	3092.36
2017	7956.13	4852.99	1153.21	2368.07	282.72	794.78	212.34	3103.14
2018	7952.90	4847.01	1104.96	2390.99	308.13	781.20	219.77	3105.89
2019	7815.89	4608.60	1017.74	2286.75	322.47	727.53	211.72	3207.29
2020	7974.44	4645.27	1031.38	2280.73	319.23	751.99	219.72	3329.17

注：2007-2017 年数据依据第三次全国农业普查结果进行了修订。
Note: Statistics of 2007-2017 is adjusted according to the Third Agricultural Census.

12-5 续表 continued

年 份 Year	棉花 Cotton	油菜籽 Rape-Seed	花生 Peanuts	芝麻 Sesame	黄红麻 Jute and Ambary	甘蔗 Sugar-cane	甜菜 Beet-Roots	烤烟 Flue-Cured Tobacco
1978	593.19	165.27	34.14	102.71	8.39	2.31	0.13	24.75
1980	591.67	175.75	40.76	113.51	12.17	1.49	0.12	9.69
1985	464.97	361.42	65.94	173.31	94.17	7.85	0.08	37.67
1990	455.92	744.31	63.75	126.85	27.33	8.07	0.01	46.35
1991	461.55	610.10	61.59	128.17	20.42	8.47	0.02	56.83
1992	507.19	534.41	64.73	126.32	18.15	10.64	0.02	72.76
1993	486.06	522.14	79.70	127.24	22.41	15.00	0.03	64.32
1994	497.58	615.87	86.97	114.77	11.70	15.73		38.69
1995	502.03	838.82	91.91	110.04	10.83	15.97	0.03	41.16
1996	474.38	855.26	90.82	107.72	8.59	16.59		51.92
1997	480.56	829.80	95.20	107.35	10.10	18.00		70.99
1998	431.58	887.01	121.48	113.62	7.94	19.97		48.47
1999	310.70	1003.64	143.87	127.14	4.30	23.34		48.32
2000	318.07	1158.94	193.42	143.82	3.14	22.17		48.10
2001	346.65	1118.06	210.06	129.93	2.65	18.88		40.43
2002	286.37	1155.25	206.04	138.88	5.13	19.18		42.90
2003	355.02	1174.63	201.11	124.00	2.97	17.24		39.45
2004	408.30	1186.10	173.03	111.20	1.36	10.01		39.94
2005	360.95	1178.65	171.71	102.52	0.98	9.95		43.68
2006	496.40	1001.20	140.10	97.24	0.69	3.70		32.13
2007	514.84	912.69	139.45	88.14	0.53	3.48		32.42
2008	544.31	1056.00	180.24	87.79	0.41	6.19		45.97
2009	461.74	1112.36	190.41	91.45	0.26	9.36		54.42
2010	482.37	1089.43	198.50	82.46	0.07	7.04		39.36
2011	491.61	1055.39	203.96	77.28	0.06	6.60		45.61
2012	476.29	1062.61	257.57	74.28	0.05	6.37		49.40
2013	419.11	1098.94	217.77	69.06	0.04	5.95		46.69
2014	348.13	1101.62	218.37	71.50	0.02	5.83		36.53
2015	267.62	1070.11	221.65	66.75	0.02	6.30		39.60
2016	204.96	983.62	232.14	64.31	0.04	6.42	0.02	40.89
2017	204.80	971.17	230.53	62.69	0.03	6.57	0.02	36.62
2018	159.26	932.97	232.60	67.87	0.01	6.45	0.02	33.63
2019	162.83	938.31	243.62	77.22	0.01	6.48		30.38
2020	129.73	1034.36	248.72	80.10	0.01	6.63		31.58

12-6 主要农作物播种面积和产量(2020)
Sown Areas and Output of Major Farm Crops (2020)

指 标	Item	播种面积(千公顷) Sown Areas (1 000 hectares)	总产量(万吨) Total Output (10 000 tons)
农作物总播种面积	**Total Sown Areas of Farm Crops**	**7974.44**	–
粮食作物总计	**Total Grain**	**4645.27**	**2727.43**
夏粮	Summer Grain	1276.06	471.96
小麦	Wheat	1031.38	400.66
大麦	Barley	7.05	2.35
秋粮	Autumn Grain	3369.21	2255.47
稻谷	Rice	2280.73	1864.34
# 中稻	Semilate Rice	1998.97	1687.34
双季晚稻	Late Double-crop Rice	159.33	108.70
薯类	Tubers	99.13	40.30
玉米	Corn	751.99	311.54
高粱	Sorghum	5.07	1.83
大豆	Soybeans	219.72	35.54
绿豆	Green Beans	7.25	0.95
经济作物	**Economic Crops**	**3329.17**	–
棉花	Cotton	129.73	10.79
油料	Oil-Bearing Crops	1377.93	344.45
# 花生	Peanuts	248.72	87.10
油菜籽	Rapeseed	1034.36	241.06
芝麻	Sesame	80.10	13.06
麻类	Hemp Crops	3.33	0.83
# 黄红麻	Jute	0.01	0.003
苎麻	Ramie	3.32	0.83
糖料	Sugar Crops	6.63	28.15
# 甘蔗	Sugarcane	6.63	28.15
烟叶	Tobacco Crops	36.37	6.30
中草药材	Crude Drugs	269.85	–
蔬菜及食用菌	Vegetable	1279.90	4119.36
瓜果类	Melon and Fruits	99.07	350.45
其他农作物	Others	126.36	–

注:2007-2017 年数据依据第三次全国农业普查结果进行了修订。
Note: Statistics of 2007-2017 is adjusted according to the Third Agricultural Census.

12-7 主要农产品产量
Output of Major Farm Products

单位:万吨 (10 000 tons)

年份 Year	粮食 Grain	夏粮 Summer Grain	秋粮 Autumn Grain	棉花 Cotton	油料 Oil Bearing Crops	花生 Peanuts	油菜籽 Rapeseed
1949	578.13	101.85	476.28	5.74	13.37	3.17	4.12
1952	747.54	148.81	598.73	12.17	22.34	4.56	7.09
1957	986.08	180.87	805.21	21.02	25.26	11.23	4.86
1962	960.41	246.34	714.07	14.22	18.30	3.81	4.29
1965	1241.34	255.01	986.33	38.29	22.32	5.15	6.76
1970	1268.67	187.06	1081.62	29.64	14.93	4.82	3.94
1975	1561.51	230.10	1331.41	40.61	21.44	5.12	10.65
1978	1725.60	315.04	1410.56	36.67	23.71	4.90	10.72
1980	1536.43	341.32	1195.11	31.63	20.58	5.85	11.59
1985	2216.13	429.58	1786.56	49.22	72.98	13.52	41.14
1990	2475.03	474.96	2000.07	51.73	95.75	12.79	70.90
1991	2244.10	476.20	1767.90	49.11	106.29	11.44	83.75
1992	2426.60	450.90	2022.83	60.99	99.74	15.72	70.86
1993	2325.70	471.87	1853.85	42.50	111.74	20.68	78.35
1994	2422.10	472.70	1949.40	45.00	137.77	24.81	98.07
1995	2463.84	447.20	2016.64	58.60	189.44	27.28	146.24
1996	2484.40	465.24	2019.16	43.01	181.82	30.77	134.88
1997	2634.40	542.60	2091.80	58.09	195.47	31.24	147.53
1998	2475.79	501.69	1974.10	32.50	216.69	42.87	154.76
1999	2451.88	392.71	2059.17	28.15	228.27	48.15	159.97
2000	2218.49	322.39	1896.10	30.43	269.98	53.46	192.40
2001	2138.49	319.14	1819.35	37.35	279.45	63.99	194.79
2002	2047.00	232.27	1841.73	32.26	245.29	72.25	151.40
2003	1921.02	255.65	1665.37	32.50	272.72	68.37	187.10
2004	2100.12	271.24	1828.96	39.54	314.38	63.19	235.12
2005	2177.38	302.49	1874.89	37.50	293.90	60.19	219.15
2006	2099.10	369.08	1730.02	55.20	254.45	48.40	191.83
2007	2139.07	409.86	1729.21	55.80	252.78	49.01	190.71
2008	2145.47	382.28	1763.19	49.98	279.20	50.24	209.17
2009	2291.05	392.08	1898.97	48.22	306.83	64.21	227.13
2010	2304.26	411.90	1892.36	47.41	302.28	66.64	220.35
2011	2407.45	415.67	1991.78	52.90	293.13	71.67	206.02
2012	2485.14	437.75	2047.39	53.53	305.13	78.16	212.15
2013	2586.21	490.08	2096.13	46.36	315.57	72.21	227.90
2014	2658.26	493.82	2164.44	36.30	321.18	73.83	230.86
2015	2914.75	493.09	2421.66	30.08	316.71	73.21	226.02
2016	2796.35	497.59	2298.76	19.00	305.15	77.98	211.14
2017	2846.12	488.25	2357.87	18.40	307.69	78.37	213.17
2018	2839.47	467.60	2371.87	14.93	302.48	80.67	205.31
2019	2724.98	457.00	2267.98	14.36	313.95	85.71	211.35
2020	2727.43	471.96	2255.47	10.79	344.45	87.10	241.06

注:2007-2017 年数据依据第三次全国农业普查结果进行了修订。
Note: Statistics of 2007-2017 is adjusted according to the Third Agricultural Census.

12-8 人均占有主要农产品产量
Per Capita Output of Major Farm Products

单位:千克/人 (kg/person)

年 份 Year	粮 食 Grain	棉 花 Cotton	油 料 Oil Bearing Crops	猪、牛、羊肉 Output of Pork, Beef and Mutton	水产品 Output of Aquatic Products
1952	275	4.5	8.2		2.9
1957	327	7.0	8.4		4.0
1962	302	4.4	5.8		2.3
1965	359	11.1	6.4		3.3
1970	319	7.5	3.8		2.8
1975	357	9.3	4.9		2.6
1978	379	8.1	5.2		2.4
1980	330	6.8	4.4	11.9	2.9
1985	452	10.0	14.9	20.7	7.6
1990	467	9.8	18.1	27.7	13.4
1991	415	8.9	19.6	29.0	12.9
1992	443	11.1	18.2	31.9	14.9
1993	416	7.6	20.0	35.3	18.1
1994	431	8.0	24.5	41.8	23.0
1995	429	10.2	33.0	48.6	26.3
1996	428	7.4	31.4	40.4	30.1
1997	450	9.9	33.4	44.4	34.6
1998	419	5.5	36.7	44.2	37.0
1999	413	5.0	38.4	44.8	38.6
2000	372	5.1	45.3	45.5	39.3
2001	358	6.3	46.8	48.3	40.5
2002	342	5.4	41.0	49.4	45.4
2003	316	6.5	45.5	51.4	47.8
2004	349	6.6	52.3	54.1	50.2
2005	361	6.2	48.7	56.8	52.8
2006	365	7.4	46.2	42.0	46.7
2007	376	9.8	44.4	45.2	49.1
2008	376	8.8	48.9	50.4	54.9
2009	401	8.4	53.7	53.8	59.1
2010	403	8.3	52.8	55.3	61.7
2011	419	9.2	51.1	55.9	62.1
2012	431	9.3	52.9	60.8	67.4
2013	447	8.0	54.5	63.3	70.9
2014	458	6.3	55.3	65.2	74.6
2015	500	5.2	54.3	63.8	78.1
2016	477	3.2	52.0	62.0	80.2
2017	483	3.1	52.2	61.9	79.0
2018	481	2.5	51.2	60.7	77.6
2019	460	2.4	53.0	45.4	79.3
2020	467	1.8	59.0	39.1	80.2

注:按全省常住人口计算的人均占有量。
Note: The data is caculated by resident population.

12-9 蚕、茶、果生产情况
Statistics on Production of Silkworm Cocoons, Tea and Fruits

指 标	Item	1995	2000	2005	2010	2015	2018	2019	2020
蚕茧产量 （万吨）	**Silkworm Cocoons (10 000 tons)**	**2.24**	**1.22**	**1.07**	**0.68**	**0.62**	**0.40**	**0.38**	**0.11**
茶叶产量 （万吨）	**Tea (10 000 tons)**	**3.90**	**6.37**	**8.50**	**16.36**	**26.13**	**32.98**	**35.25**	**36.08**
# 红茶	Red Tea	0.12		0.65	1.51	2.97	3.34	3.70	4.23
绿茶	Green Tea	3.05	5.15	6.72	13.59	19.06	23.54	24.12	25.57
其他茶	Others			0.18	0.30	0.28	0.64	0.83	0.52
园林水果产量（万吨）	**Garden Fruit Production (10 000 tons)**	**114.70**	**215.68**	**260.79**	**446.81**	**646.94**	**655.46**	**661.04**	**716.38**
# 苹果	Apples	3.21	3.02	1.24	0.99	1.39	0.97	0.79	0.67
柑桔	Citrus	58.14	94.62	146.26	320.41	490.92	488.05	478.22	509.96
梨	Pears	26.02		46.80	44.35	42.52	37.31	40.37	41.53
葡萄	Grapes			4.97	11.82	21.40	27.88	29.81	31.29
桃子	Peaches	14.59	30.87	46.88	52.87	68.16	77.27	86.54	108.63
猕猴桃	Kiwi Fruit			0.85	1.42	5.04	7.42	8.42	7.39
红枣	Dates			2.02	2.79	3.63	3.26	3.07	2.66
柿子	Persimmons			4.77	4.51	5.14	5.16	5.01	4.97
茶园面积 （千公顷）	**Area of Tea Plantations (1 000 hectares)**	**113.39**	**121.02**	**138.43**	**195.08**	**261.50**	**321.50**	**347.71**	**358.39**
# 当年采摘面积	Pick Area	7.42		101.62	142.21	188.02	232.68	264.79	273.95
果园 （千公顷）	**Area of Orchards (1 000 hectares)**	**199.80**	**233.93**	**265.05**	**343.72**	**338.28**	**366.17**	**380.86**	**400.83**
# 苹果园	Apples	13.66	8.98	3.30	1.51	0.97	1.03	0.96	0.80
柑桔园	Citrus	98.39	99.13	143.15	220.04	218.95	227.23	232.76	237.40
梨园	Pears	35.42	33.49	35.90	29.59	24.06	23.88	24.53	24.78
葡萄园	Grapes			4.77	5.22	10.27	15.47	15.70	16.19

注：2007–2017 年数据依据第三次全国农业普查结果进行了修订。
Note: Statistics of 2007–2017 is adjusted according to the Third Agricultural Census.

12-10 林业生产情况
Statistics on Production of Forestry

单位:公顷 (hectare)

指标名称	Item	2018	2019	2020
造林面积	Build Forestry Areas	181597	199645	159438
用材林	Material Forests	65479	57976	64581
经济林	Economic Forests	39446	42924	38560
防护林	Windbreak Forests	74612	97026	53586
薪炭林	Firewood Forests	1609	1107	1365
特种用途林	Forests for Soecial Puppse	451	612	1346
更新造林	Updateing Areas	4098	5913	8592
四旁(零星)植树 (万株)	Planting	11404		
育苗面积	Raise Seedlings Areas	42105		
主要林产品产量 (吨)	Output of Forestry Products (ton)			
生漆	Lacquer	2664		
油桐籽	Tung-oil Seeds	21400		
乌柏籽	Tea-oil Seeds	10234		
油茶籽	Tallow Seeds	194836	209419	221790
五倍子	Gallnut	2767		
棕片	Palm Pieces	3014		
松脂	Turpentine	13280		
竹笋干	Bamboo Shoots	16547	19891	19896
核桃	Walnut	123487	122401	104242
板栗	Chestnut	405495	390281	380797
花椒	Pepper	1940		
八角	Star Anise	124		
食用菌	Edible Fungi	193714		
木材采伐量 (万立方米)	Output of Timber Cut (10 000 cu.m)	368	534	406
竹材采伐量 (万根)	Output of Bamboo Cut (10 000 cu.m)	3744	3724.5	3269

注:1.林业数据来源于林业部门。2.主要林产品产量包括人工种植和林下采集产量。

Note: a)Statistics of forestry sources from the Department of Forestry of Hubei Province.

b)The output of main forest products includes the output of artificial planting and non-timber forest-based products gathering.

12-11 畜牧业生产情况
Statistics on Production of Livestock

指 标	Item	2000	2005	2010	2015	2018	2019	2020
牲畜年末存栏头数 （万头）	**(10 000 heads)**							
大牲畜	Large Animals	431.50	384.32	266.08	226.93	241.53	243.55	242.28
牛	Cattles and Buffalloes	428.38	382.14	264.78	226.31	241.09	243.15	242.08
马	Horses	1.83	1.58	0.83	0.43	0.35	0.33	0.11
驴	Donkeys	0.98	0.44	0.34	0.15	0.07	0.06	0.06
骡	Mules	0.30	0.16	0.12	0.03	0.02	0.02	0.02
猪	Hogs	2132.79	2289.05	2526.60	2613.15	2521.80	1617.86	2161.46
羊 （万只）	Sheep (10 000 heads)	224.80	337.66	414.96	501.14	546.79	553.35	533.26
畜产品产量 （万头）	**Livestock Products (10 000 heads)**							
猪牛羊出栏头数	Hogs, Sheep and Goats	3023.96	3841.82	4536.52	5269.97	5081.06	3914.69	3265.77
当年肉猪出栏头数	Hogs	2714.44	3345.18	3905.44	4566.00	4363.50	3189.24	2631.12
当年出售和自宰的肉用牛	Ox by Sold and Killed	104.26	115.49	104.86	111.49	108.33	109.52	101.96
当年出售和自宰的肉用羊 （万只）	Sheep by Slod and Killed (10 000 heads)	205.26	381.15	526.22	592.48	609.23	615.93	532.68
肉类总产量 （万吨）	Output of Meat (10 000 tons)	271.19	342.63	383.48	443.66	430.95	349.20	307.44
猪肉	Pork	215.84	271.23	292.91	346.83	333.18	242.95	203.84
牛肉	Beef	13.80	16.91	15.07	16.03	15.82	15.99	15.40
羊肉	Mutton	3.04	6.00	8.36	9.48	9.75	9.85	8.86
禽肉	Poultry	38.51	48.49	66.34	69.92	71.35	79.48	79.00
其他畜禽产品产量 （吨）	Others (ton)							
牛奶产量	Milk Cow	56400	122223	111324	134071	128100	133800	133893
绵羊毛产量	Sheep´s Wool	34.57	4.00	3.13	7.16	9.00	9.00	7.37
山羊毛产量	Goats´ Wool	52.17	16.00	8.21	32.67	48.00	48.00	43.24
蜂蜜	Cashmere	9187	7890	10832	31532	23434	22914	20240
禽蛋 （万吨）	Poultry Eggs (10 000 tons)	102.56	121.25	133.68	168.37	171.53	178.75	193.23

注：畜牧业 2007-2017 年数据依据第三次全国农业普查结果进行了修订。
Note: Statistics of Livestock is adjusted according to the Third Agricultural Census.

12-12 水产品产量
Output of Aquatic Products

指 标	Item	2000	2005	2010	2015	2018	2019	2020
水产品产量 （万吨）	**Output of Aquatic Products (10 000 tons)**	**234.34**	**318.03**	**353.00**	**455.89**	**458.40**	**469.54**	**467.93**
#鱼类产量	Fish	219.88	277.82	308.42	379.60	348.86	349.08	343.54
虾蟹产量	Shrimp, Prawn and Crab	7.51	7.71	35.93	67.38	101.69	112.60	116.24
贝类产量	Shell Fish	5.38	1.13	4.32	2.74	0.92	0.80	0.62
其它类产量	Others	1.58		3.66	5.37	6.93	7.06	7.53
养殖产量	Artificially Cultivated	194.84	274.45	321.56	435.99	440.30	432.54	438.62
#精养鱼池	Intensive Fish Culture Pond					303.16	308.29	306.18
稻田养虾	Shrimp Farming in Rice Paddies					67.30	78.89	83.55
捕捞产量	Captured	39.50	43.58	31.44	19.10	18.11	16.18	7.53
鱼苗产量 （亿尾）	Young Fry (100 million tons)	444.01	521.39	750.00	1020.00	1184.00	1192.18	1218.20
鱼种产量 （万吨）	Advanced Fry (10 000 tons)	38.79	54.04	82.03	128.16	105.14	103.82	103.71
投放鱼种量 （万吨）	Volume of Advanced Fry (10 000 tons)	40.16	57.08	80.74	115.64	99.64	95.26	101.14
水产养殖面积 （千公顷）	**Aquatic Raised Areas (1 000 hectares)**							
池塘	Ponds	291.10	339.57	340.40	484.17	535.15	532.56	525.89
#精养鱼池	Intensive Fish Culture Pond					390.91	397.91	391.97
稻田	Paddy				257.84	393.50	460.51	490.27
#稻田养虾	Shrimp Farming in Rice Paddies					381.46	448.59	477.75

注：数据来源于省水产局，2012-2017年数据依据第三次全国农业普查结果进行了修订。
Note: Data sources from the Fisheries Bureau of Hubei Province. Statistics of 2012-2017 is adjusted according to the Third Agricultural Census.

12-13 农业现代化情况
Statistics on Agricultural Modernization

单位:千公顷 (1 000 hectares)

指 标	Item	2000	2005	2010	2015	2018	2019	2020
农业机械化情况	**Statistics on Agricultural Machinery**							
机耕面积	Areas Ploughed by Tractors	1969.55	2015.93	4517.14	6036.19	6099.78	5983.54	6127.64
机播面积	Seeded Areas by Tractors	255.69	233.66	815.61	2335.23	3049.25	3099.30	3362.60
机械植保面积	Plant Protection Area by Tractors	2426.95	2848.66	4074.38	4850.88	5002.67	5071.48	5058.40
机械收获面积	Harvest Area by Tractors	643.65	1407.62	2780.52	4233.67	4589.12	4539.20	4633.18
农村电气化情况	**Electrification of Rural Area**							
农村用电量(亿千瓦小时)	Electricity Consumed in Rural Area (100 million kwh)	60.86	70.09	109.78	149.10	165.21	178.55	186.87
农用物资使用情况	**Used Agricultural Product Material**							
化肥施用量(折纯量)(万吨)	Consumption of Chemical Fertilizers (10 000 tons)	247.08	285.83	350.77	333.87	295.82	273.89	267.32
每亩耕地施用化肥(折纯量)(千克)	Per Mu Consumption of Chemical Fertilizers (kg)			44.02	42.36	37.64		
农用塑料薄膜使用量(万吨)	Used Plastic Film (10 000 tons)		5.46	6.38	7.13	6.36	5.88	5.80
农用柴油使用量 (万吨)	Used Diesel Oil (10 000 tons)	107.81	41.31	58.29	65.61	65.10	63.54	62.78
农药使用量(万吨)	Used Agricultural Chemical Insecticides (10 000 tons)	11.54	11.02	14.00	12.07	10.33	9.70	9.31
农田水利情况	**Irrigation and Water Conservancy**							
耕地灌溉面积	Irrigation Area of Cultivated Land			2522.47	2899.15	2931.90	2968.99	3086.04
占耕地面积的比重 (%)	Share of Caltivated Area (%)			47.5	55.2	56.0		

注:1.农业机械化情况数据由省农业农村厅提供。
2.农田水利情况由省水利厅提供。

Note: a)The data on agricultural mechanization are provided by the Provincial Department of Agriculture and Rural Affairs.
b)The data on farmland water conservancy are provided by the Provincial Department of Water Resources.

12-14 主要农业机械
Major Agricultural Machinery

年 份 Year	农业机械总动力 (万千瓦) Total Power of Agricultural Machinery (10 000 kw)	农用大中型拖拉机 (万台) Large and Medium Agricultural Tractors (10 000 units)	农用小型及手扶拖拉机 (万台) Mini and Walking Agricultural Tractors (10 000 units)	农用水泵 (万台) Agricultual Water Pump (10 000 units)	联合收割机 (台) Combine Hearvesters (unit)
1978	616.07	2.80	7.75	21.22	425
1980	772.53	3.60	10.90	23.70	602
1985	910.94	5.72	14.62	21.06	479
1990	1099.62	8.60	17.70	24.30	2335
1991	1120.92	8.60	18.30	24.10	455
1992	1120.90	8.45	17.92	23.98	390
1993	1108.99	7.89	16.99	23.95	345
1994	1136.13	7.38	15.72	24.37	346
1995	1174.34	7.12	15.47	26.56	312
1996	1222.20	7.03	16.47	27.62	553
1997	1276.04	7.11	18.50	28.76	1521
1998	1325.90	7.13	20.60	29.59	2338
1999	1363.70	7.03	22.67	32.57	2559
2000	1414.00	6.82	23.63	35.47	2704
2001	1469.24	6.58	24.88	40.46	3363
2002	1557.40	6.64	26.68	43.89	5722
2003	1661.70	6.59	28.23	45.63	6708
2004	1768.60	6.83	32.09	50.82	10585
2005	2057.37	7.66	48.39	55.92	16085
2006	2263.15	8.50	55.69	71.42	22407
2007	2551.08	9.30	74.12	82.70	29803
2008	2796.99	10.42	85.23	87.73	34983
2009	3057.24	11.85	90.84	87.70	41904
2010	3371.00	12.71	99.10	85.40	50509
2011	3571.23	13.08	106.48	89.48	58398
2012	3842.16	13.84	111.56	103.30	66860
2013	4081.05	14.94	114.12	105.63	73808
2014	4292.90	15.85	112.98	110.60	81410
2015	4468.12	16.84	113.81	110.13	88704
2016	4187.75	18.18	114.67	110.97	95747
2017	4335.47	18.97	115.12	111.38	99432
2018	4424.59	16.15	115.87	108.96	102197
2019	4515.73	17.22	114.94	116.91	106069
2020	4626.07	18.17	112.58	118.33	109080

注:1.2018 年调整了农用拖拉机大中小型划分方法。2.本表数据由湖北省农业农村厅提供。

Note: a)The classification method of large, medium and small agricultural tractors was adjusted in 2018.

b)The data in this table are provided by the Department of Agriculture and Rural Affairs of Hubei Province.

12-15 市、州农、林、牧、渔业总产值及指数
Gross Output Value and Its Indices of Farming, Forestry, Animal Husbandry and Fishery of Cities and Prefectures

市、州	Municipalities and Prefectures	绝对数(亿元) Absolute Number (100 million yuan)		指数(%) Indices (%)	
		2019	2020	2019	2020
全 省	**Province**	**6681.85**	**7303.64**	**103.5**	**100.7**
武汉市	Wuhan	653.17	695.53	103.3	95.4
黄石市	Huangshi	177.91	198.95	103.7	100.6
十堰市	Shiyan	299.73	335.30	103.6	100.9
宜昌市	Yichang	719.19	799.67	103.6	102.8
襄阳市	Xiangyang	789.95	909.29	103.6	103.0
鄂州市	Ezhou	173.15	171.76	103.6	96.9
荆门市	Jingmen	431.87	451.63	103.5	101.8
孝感市	Xiaogan	545.99	611.16	103.5	102.2
荆州市	Jingzhou	766.45	808.07	103.6	100.8
黄冈市	Huanggang	710.61	773.14	103.5	100.3
咸宁市	Xianning	352.74	388.61	103.6	100.7
随州市	Suizhou	280.84	314.47	103.6	103.9
恩施自治州	Enshi	329.14	370.59	103.7	100.9
仙桃市	Xiaotao	155.67	164.21	103.4	98.3
潜江市	Qianjiang	141.73	147.30	103.6	100.5
天门市	Tianmen	149.64	159.78	103.5	98.3
神农架林区	Shennongjia	4.08	4.18	103.8	99.5

注:本表数据依据第三次全国农业普查结果进行了修订。
Note: Statistics of this table is adjusted according to the Third Agricultural Census.

12-16 市、州农、林、牧、渔业产值（现价）（2020）
Gross Output Value of Farming, Forestry, Animal Husbandry and Fishery of Cities and Prefectures (At Current Prices)(2020)

单位：亿元 (100 million yuan)

市、州	Municipalities and Prefectures	合 计 Total	农 业 Farming	林 业 Forestry	牧 业 Animal Husbandry	渔 业 Fishery	农林牧渔专业及辅助性活动 Professional and Ancillary Service for Farming, Forestry, Animal Husbandry and Fishery
全 省	**Province**	**7303.64**	**3492.54**	**245.37**	**1864.78**	**1156.78**	**544.16**
武汉市	Wuhan	695.53	417.47	13.43	98.21	112.80	53.62
黄石市	Huangshi	198.95	78.47	8.81	45.84	56.90	8.92
十堰市	Shiyan	335.30	174.96	30.80	104.80	15.51	9.23
宜昌市	Yichang	799.67	465.35	25.33	206.87	46.57	55.56
襄阳市	Xiangyang	909.29	431.00	20.73	345.11	48.45	64.00
鄂州市	Ezhou	171.76	43.38	3.30	34.00	80.92	10.15
荆门市	Jingmen	451.63	209.05	9.58	106.07	83.40	43.53
孝感市	Xiaogan	611.16	264.60	18.66	180.83	99.88	47.19
荆州市	Jingzhou	808.07	343.18	13.33	132.51	241.25	77.80
黄冈市	Huanggang	773.14	342.22	36.34	220.60	119.25	54.74
咸宁市	Xianning	388.61	190.69	23.98	84.99	57.08	31.87
随州市	Suizhou	314.47	142.24	12.08	101.56	32.73	25.87
恩施自治州	Enshi	370.59	197.75	22.26	125.40	1.28	23.90
仙桃市	Xiaotao	164.21	56.75	1.48	25.98	70.86	9.14
潜江市	Qianjiang	147.30	59.06	2.28	24.78	48.18	12.99
天门市	Tianmen	159.78	73.84	2.35	26.34	41.69	15.55
神农架林区	Shennongjia	4.18	2.51	0.64	0.90	0.03	0.10

12-17 市、州耕地面积(2018)
Cultivated Area of Cities and Prefectures(2018)

单位:公顷 (hectare)

市、州	Municipalities and Prefectures	耕 地 Cultivated Land	水 田 Paddy Field	水浇地 Irrigated Land	旱 地 Dry Land
全 省	**Province**	**5235395**	**2647870**	**479411**	**2108114**
武汉市	Wuhan	293857	139783	84117	69957
黄石市	Huangshi	117297	63743	1196	52358
十堰市	Shiyan	239317	45055	2905	191357
宜昌市	Yichang	347355	122680	18040	206635
襄阳市	Xiangyang	703432	259801	11147	432484
鄂州市	Ezhou	55289	25743	16367	13180
荆门市	Jingmen	501773	324148	8588	169037
孝感市	Xiaogan	439275	277101	57870	104303
荆州市	Jingzhou	682706	435123	225768	21816
黄冈市	Huanggang	532728	349428	16124	167176
咸宁市	Xianning	200830	130628	17075	53127
随州市	Suizhou	253609	178309	5242	70058
恩施自治州	Enshi	451653	107301	312	344039
仙桃市	Xiantao	119424	61193	4750	53481
潜江市	Qianjiang	122230	62168	5261	54801
天门市	Tianmen	167344	65626	4379	97339
神农架林区	Shennongjia	7277	40	272	6965

注:本表数据来源于湖北省自然资源厅。
Note: The data in this table come from the Department of Natural Resources of Hubei Province.

12-18 市、州农作物总播种面积
Total Sown Areas of Farm Crops of Cities and Prefectures

单位：千公顷 (1 000 hectares)

市、州	Municipalities and Prefectures	2019	粮食作物 Total Grain	2020	粮食作物 Total Grain
全 省	**Province**	**7815.89**	**4608.60**	**7974.44**	**4645.27**
武汉市	Wuhan	406.84	143.05	414.33	144.00
黄石市	Huangshi	174.40	87.84	173.64	82.95
十堰市	Shiyan	408.92	209.80	413.48	210.75
宜昌市	Yichang	596.11	314.58	626.71	317.81
襄阳市	Xiangyang	1022.92	781.67	1040.07	786.69
鄂州市	Ezhou	91.64	41.19	86.91	38.34
荆门市	Jingmen	654.55	459.02	677.00	462.43
孝感市	Xiaogan	570.93	344.95	590.67	348.10
荆州市	Jingzhou	1061.24	702.28	1081.07	707.08
黄冈市	Huanggang	810.16	391.09	828.47	394.39
咸宁市	Xianning	420.79	194.45	430.51	196.53
随州市	Suizhou	287.20	192.44	302.31	206.92
恩施自治州	Enshi	711.33	367.20	704.22	369.02
仙桃市	Xiantao	216.75	115.93	217.22	115.31
潜江市	Qianjiang	141.70	99.81	142.06	100.81
天门市	Tianmen	230.18	157.40	235.55	158.98
神农架林区	Shennongjia	10.24	5.90	10.23	5.16

12-19 市、州主要农作物产量(2020)

单位:万吨 (10 000 tons)

市、州	Municipalities and Prefectures	粮食 Grain	稻谷 Rice	小麦 Wheat	玉米 Corn	薯类 Tubers	大豆 Soybean	棉花 Cotton
全　省	**Province**	**2727.43**	**1864.34**	**400.66**	**311.54**	**106.33**	**35.54**	**10.79**
武汉市	Wuhan	89.60	76.85	2.73	7.27	1.08	1.45	0.82
黄石市	Huangshi	51.29	43.64	2.19	3.02	1.91	0.40	0.28
十堰市	Shiyan	82.38	19.18	16.46	29.98	12.53	2.54	0.01
宜昌市	Yichang	151.08	65.02	13.32	51.23	18.59	1.76	0.52
襄阳市	Xiangyang	472.43	186.25	186.11	89.38	8.68	0.94	0.69
鄂州市	Ezhou	24.55	20.91	1.47	0.46	0.59	0.45	0.33
荆门市	Jingmen	286.80	218.73	39.42	22.57	1.29	4.68	0.33
孝感市	Xiaogan	232.71	201.82	23.21	5.44	1.19	0.84	0.73
荆州市	Jingzhou	449.82	374.67	50.44	15.02	0.72	7.82	2.82
黄冈市	Huanggang	269.11	243.46	11.25	4.30	7.10	2.60	2.02
咸宁市	Xianning	116.83	99.47	1.71	7.31	6.64	1.32	0.30
随州市	Suizhou	146.17	116.81	19.15	6.76	3.00	0.26	0.35
恩施自治州	Enshi	144.12	38.32	0.49	59.82	40.67	3.67	
仙桃市	Xiaotao	69.74	54.26	7.41	5.83	0.44	1.49	0.81
潜江市	Qianjiang	59.00	47.58	8.41	1.02	0.42	1.53	0.13
天门市	Tianmen	80.06	57.36	16.83	1.35	0.76	3.73	0.65
神农架林区	Shennongjia	1.74	0.01	0.07	0.79	0.71	0.05	

Output of Major Farm Crops of Cities and Prefectures (2020)

单位:万吨 (10 000 tons)

油料 Oil Bearing Crops	花生 Peanuts	油菜籽 Rapeseed	芝麻 Sesame	麻类 Hemp Crops	苎麻 Ramie	糖类 Sugar Crops	甘蔗 Crane	烟叶 Tobacoo Crops	烤烟 Tobacco
344.45	**87.10**	**241.06**	**13.06**	**0.83**	**0.83**	**28.15**	**28.15**	**6.30**	**5.34**
13.92	4.42	8.26	1.24			1.95	1.95		
11.66	1.63	8.29	1.69	0.35	0.35	0.56	0.56		
16.42	5.54	8.92	1.83	0.01	0.00	2.11	2.11	1.15	1.15
22.11	3.40	18.35	0.35			0.07	0.07	0.70	0.58
37.62	24.90	9.56	2.55			0.83	0.83	0.59	0.59
4.34	0.79	2.79	0.05			0.56	0.56		
37.21	6.36	30.16	0.69			1.15	1.15	0.002	
26.74	8.18	18.06	0.50	0.004	0.004	1.83	1.83		
50.49	0.64	48.67	1.17	0.048	0.048	3.65	3.65		
53.01	17.11	34.44	1.23	0.29	0.29	3.35	3.35		
18.82	3.36	14.57	0.59	0.13	0.13	7.59	7.59		
10.29	3.88	5.21	0.19			0.20	0.20		
11.90	2.05	9.60	0.04					3.85	3.01
13.21	0.40	12.23	0.57			3.40	3.40		
4.19	0.59	3.40	0.20			0.35	0.35		
12.49	3.82	8.52	0.16			0.56	0.56		
0.03	0.01	0.02	0.00					0.004	0.004

12-20 市、州大牲畜、羊、猪年末存栏、出栏、肉产量(2020)

市、州	Municipalities and Prefectures	牛存栏（万只）Cattles and Bufflaoes (10 000 heads)	羊存栏（万只）Sheep in Stock (10 000 heads)	家禽存笼（万只）Poultry Stockpile (10 000 heads)	年末生猪存栏（万头）Hogs in Stock at Year-end (10 000 heads)	年内出栏肉猪（万头）Hogs out of Stock at Year-end (10 000 heads)
全省	**Province**	**242.08**	**533.26**	**38289.98**	**2161.46**	**2631.12**
武汉市	Wuhan	4.44	3.01	1976.02	105.24	113.94
黄石市	Huangshi	2.25	2.94	825.12	50.89	65.39
十堰市	Shiyan	15.54	81.12	1625.87	81.70	114.02
宜昌市	Yichang	9.72	99.08	1432.06	271.77	355.95
襄阳市	Xiangyang	60.86	88.62	7586.81	285.76	383.62
鄂州市	Ezhou	1.77	0.38	427.20	35.68	44.60
荆门市	Jingmen	17.31	30.19	3516.95	199.76	223.31
孝感市	Xiaogan	17.91	20.32	4233.49	130.87	188.90
荆州市	Jingzhou	5.19	4.27	3389.86	198.47	209.42
黄冈市	Huanggang	63.44	78.96	5871.90	249.68	258.42
咸宁市	Xianning	3.67	19.15	1354.59	117.07	141.91
随州市	Suizhou	15.27	50.28	3280.75	95.12	136.91
恩施自治州	Enshi	16.71	50.70	889.38	234.09	282.89
仙桃市	Xiaotao	1.28	0.23	496.17	28.45	36.99
潜江市	Qianjiang	3.19	1.03	509.69	33.72	36.70
天门市	Tianmen	3.20	1.30	848.00	40.99	35.29
神农架林区	Shennongjia	0.32	1.67	26.12	2.21	2.88

Statistics on Live Animals, Sheep, Hogs in Stock/out of Stock at Year-end and Output of Meat of Cities and Prefectures(2020)

年内出栏羊 (万只) Sheep out of Stock at Year-end (10 000 heads)	出笼禽 (万只) Poultry out of Stock at Year-end (10 000 heads)	猪肉产量 (万吨) Output of Pork Meat (10 000 tons)	牛肉产量 (万吨) Beef (10 000 tons)	羊肉 (万吨) Muttom (10 000 tons)	禽蛋产量 (万吨) Output of Eggs (10 000 tons)
532.68	**59325.84**	**203.84**	**15.40**	**8.86**	**193.23**
2.01	3446.30	8.63	0.30	0.03	10.47
2.84	1995.59	5.07	0.12	0.05	4.95
76.52	3051.49	9.03	0.89	1.27	6.71
113.23	2855.95	27.90	0.64	1.88	6.80
103.44	7729.49	29.72	4.56	1.72	36.88
1.10	1095.20	3.45	0.13	0.02	4.27
40.14	4405.99	17.00	1.28	0.67	13.49
18.69	9886.79	14.63	1.08	0.31	26.32
8.62	6241.47	16.02	0.36	0.14	18.91
57.66	4834.86	20.02	3.48	0.96	31.46
13.69	3381.26	10.99	0.20	0.23	5.25
36.88	6698.84	10.61	0.92	0.61	14.58
53.63	1148.52	22.12	0.92	0.89	4.42
0.29	593.09	2.82	0.09	0.00	1.96
1.71	953.33	2.87	0.22	0.03	2.53
0.88	974.00	2.73	0.20	0.01	4.20
1.38	33.66	0.22	0.02	0.02	0.03

12-21 市、州主要土特产品产量(2020)
Output of Main Native Products of Cities and Prefectures (2020)

市、州	Municipalities and Prefectures	茶叶（万吨）Tea (10 000 tons)	蚕茧（吨）Silkworm Coccons (ton)	桑蚕茧 Mulbeery Silkworm Coccons	园林水果（万吨）Fruits (10 000 tons)	桃子 Peaches	柑橘 Citrus	苹果 Apples	黑木耳（吨）Black Fungus (ton)
全　省	**Province**	**36.08**	**1090**	**991**	**716.38**	**108.63**	**509.96**	**0.67**	**24379**
武汉市	Wuhan	0.26			14.88	5.45	3.65	0.03	535
黄石市	Huangshi	0.11	133	133	11.07	1.74	7.62		196
十堰市	Shiyan	1.69	121	121	36.51	2.81	29.80	0.04	4836
宜昌市	Yichang	9.50	318	318	397.83	4.31	386.39	0.07	488
襄阳市	Xiangyang	1.06	359	359	64.05	53.76	2.44	0.20	3186
鄂州市	Ezhou	0.02			4.56	0.40	2.65		11
荆门市	Jingmen	0.03			40.47	6.93	13.04		1767
孝感市	Xiaogan	0.85			15.38	8.47	1.97	0.10	681
荆州市	Jingzhou	0.03			49.11	2.73	30.45		
黄冈市	Huanggang	3.93	12	12	8.59	3.60	2.58	0.06	392
咸宁市	Xianning	5.99			9.72	1.33	4.49		439
随州市	Suizhou	0.38	99		17.74	12.97	0.34	0.04	11801
恩施自治州	Enshi	12.24	48	48	36.92	1.52	23.32	0.13	1
仙桃市	Xiaotao				1.68	0.43	0.54		
潜江市	Qianjiang				5.96	1.80	0.30		24
天门市	Tianmen				1.89	0.38	0.39		
神农架林区	Shennongjia	0.01			0.02	0.001		0.0002	22

12-22 市、州人平粮、棉、油、肉、水产品生产水平(2020)
Per Capita Production Level of Grain, Cotton, Oil, Meat and Aquatic Products of Cities and Prefectures(2020)

单位:千克 (kg)

市、州	Municipalities and Prefectures	粮食 Grain	棉花 Cotton	油料 Oil Bearing Crops	猪肉 Pork	水产品 Aquatic Products	禽蛋 Eggs
按常住人口平均	**Average of Total Population**						
全省	**Province**	**467.35**	**1.85**	**59.02**	**34.93**	**80.18**	**33.11**
武汉市	Wuhan	75.41	0.69	11.72	7.26	35.92	8.82
黄石市	Huangshi	207.64	1.13	47.21	20.51	90.88	20.04
十堰市	Shiyan	250.82	0.02	49.98	27.50	15.65	20.43
宜昌市	Xiangyang	371.60	1.27	54.39	68.61	44.55	16.72
襄阳市	Ezhou	870.27	1.28	69.30	54.75	36.20	67.94
鄂州市	Jingmen	229.13	3.09	40.53	32.16	262.59	39.87
荆门市	Xiaogan	1055.50	1.23	136.93	62.57	170.72	49.64
孝感市	Jingzhou	513.65	1.62	59.03	32.30	92.69	58.08
荆州市	Yichang	838.17	5.25	94.08	29.86	210.90	35.24
黄冈市	Huanggang	443.86	3.33	87.44	33.02	72.81	51.88
咸宁市	Xianning	446.88	1.15	71.97	42.05	85.55	20.06
随州市	Suizhou	690.39	1.66	48.61	50.10	39.88	68.86
恩施自治州	Enshi	420.21		34.70	64.48	0.80	12.89
仙桃市	Xiaotao	613.44	7.16	116.17	24.83	249.64	17.22
潜江市	Tianmen	642.48	1.36	45.66	31.29	163.20	27.59
天门市	Qianjiang	670.44	5.44	104.60	22.87	97.13	35.14
神农架林区	Shennongjia	247.62		4.40	31.66		4.43

12-23 市、州农业机械、用电、化肥、水利情况(2020)
Agricultural Machinery, Electricity Consumption, Chemical Fertilizers and Irrigationof Cities and Prefectures (2020)

市、州	Municipalities and Prefectures	农业机械总动力(万千瓦特) Total Power of Agricultural Machinery (10 000 kw)	当年实际机耕面积(千公顷) Actual Sown Areas (1 000 hectares)	农村用电量(万千瓦小时) Rural Electricity Consumption (10 000 kw/h)	化肥施用量(折纯量)(万吨) Consumption of Chemical Fertilizers (pure)(10 000 tons)	耕地灌溉面积(千公顷) Irrigation Area of Cultivated Land (1 000 hectares)
全 省	**Province**	**4626.07**	**6127.64**	**1868739.62**	**267.32**	**3086.04**
武汉市	Wuhan	241.00	259.84	142793.00	10.75	169.88
黄石市	Huangshi	125.32	112.21	118312.00	4.57	73.24
十堰市	Shiyan	183.12	264.24	77385.00	8.86	61.69
宜昌市	Yichang	320.68	441.98	121560.00	29.51	172.94
襄阳市	Xiangyang	707.78	933.55	180576.00	35.20	367.53
鄂州市	Ezhou	57.34	542.50	57669.00	6.71	55.84
荆门市	Jingmen	504.43	592.72	130109.12	27.68	283.15
孝感市	Xiaogan	280.00	431.23	179136.00	17.72	358.23
荆州市	Jingzhou	661.68	931.16	301217.00	30.11	574.02
黄冈市	Huanggang	388.38	670.67	230980.60	30.25	323.42
咸宁市	Xianning	194.74	297.38	52777.57	10.20	127.35
随州市	Suizhou	227.10	232.26	54384.44	14.98	115.25
恩施自治州	Enshi	249.94	350.80	71366.12	23.06	105.70
仙桃市	Xiaotao	148.50	176.26	63290.80	5.23	113.53
潜江市	Qianjiang	151.04	135.00	51755.81	5.10	73.28
天门市	Tianmen	173.01	246.26	35343.00	7.02	110.26
神农架林区	Shennongjia	11.96	5.00	84.16	0.38	0.73

注:本表数据由湖北省农业农村厅和湖北省水利厅提供。

Note: The data in this table are provided by the Department of Agriculture and Rural Affairs of Hubei Province and the Department of Water Resources of Hubei Province.

主要统计指标解释

农林牧渔业总产值 指以货币表现的农、林、牧、渔业全部产品和对农林牧渔业生产活动进行的各种支持性服务活动的价值总量，它反映一定时期内农林牧渔业生产总规模和总成果。1957年以前的农林牧渔业总产值中包括了厩肥和农民自给性手工业(如农民自制衣服、鞋、袜，自己从事粮食初步加工等)。1958年及以后，林业中增加了村及村以下竹木采伐产值；牧业中取消了厩肥产值；副业中取消了农民自给性手工业产值，增加了村及村以下办的工业产值；渔业中增加了海洋捕捞水产品产值。1980年及以后，在副业中增加了农民家庭兼营工业商品部分的产值。从1984年起村及村以下工业产值划归工业。从1993年起取消副业，将野生动物的捕猎划入牧业，野生植物采集和农民家庭兼营商品性工业划归农业。从2003年起，执行新的国民经济行业分类标准，农林牧渔业总产值中包括了农林牧渔服务业产值。林业中增加了森林采运业产值。农业中取消了家庭兼营商品性工业产值，将野生林产品的采集划归林业。第一次农业普查以后，由于畜牧业产品年报数据与普查数据之间存在一定的差距，国家统计局农调总队对畜牧业年报数据与普查数据进行衔接，对畜牧业产值进行相应调整。

农林牧渔业总产值的计算方法通常是按农、林、牧、渔业产品及其副产品的产量分别乘以各自单位产品价格求得；少数生产周期较长，当年没有产品或产品产量不易统计的，则采用间接方法匡算其产值；然后将四业产品产值相加即为农林牧渔业总产值。

粮食产量 指全社会的产量。包括国有经济经营的、集体统一经营的和农民家庭经营的粮食产量，还包括工矿企业办的农场和其他生产单位的产量。粮食除包括稻谷、小麦、玉米、高粱、谷子及其他杂粮外，还包括薯类和豆类。其产量计算方法，豆类按去豆荚后的干豆计算；薯类(包括甘薯和马铃薯，不包括芋头和木薯)1963年以前按每4公斤鲜薯折1公斤粮食计算，从1964年开始改为按5公斤鲜薯折1公斤粮食计算。城市郊区作为蔬菜的薯类(如马铃薯等)按鲜品计算，并且不作粮食统计。其他粮食一律按脱粒后的原粮计算。1989年以前全国粮食产量数据主要靠全面报表取得，1989年开始使用抽样调查数据。

棉花产量 指全社会的产量。包括春播棉和夏播棉。产量按皮棉计算。不包括木棉。

油料产量 指全部油料作物的生产量。包括花生、油菜籽、芝麻、向日葵籽、胡麻籽(亚麻籽)和其他油料。不包括大豆、木本油料和野生油料。花生以带壳干花生计算。

水产品产量 指人工养殖的水产品和天然生长的水产品的捕捞量。包括海水的鱼类、虾蟹类、贝类和藻类以及内陆水域的鱼类、虾蟹类和贝类，不包括淡水生植物。水产品产量是通过各级水产和统计部门逐级上报取得数据。1995年及以前，贝类中牡蛎按鲜肉计算；蚶、蛤、蛙按5斤鲜品折1斤计算。1996年以后则统一按鲜品计算。

猪、牛、羊肉产量 指当年出栏并已屠宰、除去头蹄下水后带骨肉(即胴体重)的重量。包括全社会范围内的产量。1996年前为各级逐级上报数据。1996年第一次农业普查以后，由于畜牧业产品年报数据与普查数据之间存在一定的差距，国家统计局农调总队对畜牧业年报数据与普查数据进行衔接。1999年以后，国家统计局开展了猪、牛、羊、禽等主要畜禽品种的抽样调查，并用抽样数据作为国家定案数据使用。未开展抽样调查的品种，仍使用各级统计部门逐级上报数据。

期初(末)畜禽存栏头(只)数 指报告期初(末)农村各种合作经济组织和国营农场、农民个人、机关、团体、学校、工矿企业、部队等单位以及城镇居民饲养的大牲畜、猪、羊、家禽等畜禽的存栏数。数据上报方式及数据调整情况同猪、牛、羊肉产量。

常用耕地 是指耕地总资源中专门种植农作物并经常进行耕种、能够正常收获的土地。包括当年实际耕种的熟地；弃耕、休闲不满三年，随时可以复耕的地；开荒利用三年以上的土地。在统计口径上包括南方小于1米、北方小于2米宽的沟、渠、路和田埂。不包括临时种植农作物的坡度在25度以上的陡坡地；在河套、湖畔、库区临时开发的成片或零星土地；也不包括已列为国家和省(区、市)退耕计划但临时耕种的土地。常用耕地是国家需要重点保护的耕地，是反映我国农业综合生产能力的一个重要指标。

农作物播种面积 指实际播种或移植有农作物的面积。凡是实际种植有农作物的面积，不论种植在耕地上还是种植在非耕地上，均包括在农作物播种面积中。在播种季节基本结束后，因遭灾而重新改种和补种的农作物面积，也包括在内。它是反映我国耕地面积利用情况的一个重要指标。目前，农作物播种面积主要包括粮食、棉花、油料、糖料、麻类、烟叶、蔬菜和瓜类、药材和其他农作物九大类。

有效灌溉面积 指具有一定的水源，地块比较平整，灌溉工程或设备已经配套，在一般年景下，当年能够进行正常灌溉的耕地面积。在一般情况下，有效灌溉面积应等于灌溉工程或设备已经配备，能够进行正常灌溉的水田和水浇地面积之和。它是反映我国耕地抗旱能力的一个重要指标。

农用化肥施用量 指本年内实际用于农业生产的化肥数量，包括氮肥、磷肥、钾肥和复合肥。化肥施用量要求按折纯量计算数量。折纯量是指把氮肥、磷肥、钾肥分别按含氮、含五氧化二磷、含氧化钾的百分之百成份进行折算后的数量。复合肥按其所含主要成分折算。公式为：

折纯量=实物量×某种化肥有效成份含量的百分比

农业机械总动力 指主要用于农、林、牧、渔业的各种动力机械的动力总和。包括耕作机械、排灌机械、收获机械、农用运输机械、植物保护机械、牧业机械、林业机械、渔业机械和其他农业机械〔内燃机按引擎马力折成瓦(特)计算、电动机按功率折成瓦(特)计算〕。不包括专门用于乡、镇、村、组办工业、基本建设、非农业运输、科学试验和教学等非农业生产方面用的动力机械与作业机械。这个指标的统计数据主要来源于农机部门。

乡村从业人员 指乡村人口中劳动年龄在16周岁以上实际参加生产经营活动并取得实物或货币收入的人员，包括劳动年龄内经常参加劳动的人员，也包括超过劳动年龄但经常参加劳动的人员，但不包括户口在家的在外学生、现役军人和丧失劳动能力的人，也不包括待业人员和家务劳动者。从业人员按从事主业时间最长(时间相同按收入)分为农林牧渔业从业人员、工业从业人员、建筑业从业人员、交通运输业、仓储及邮电通信业从业人员、批零贸易业、餐饮业从业人员、其他非农行业从业人员。

Explanatory Notes on Main Statistical Indicators

Gross Output Value of Farming, Forestry, Animal Husbandry and Fishery refers to the total value of products of farming, forestry, animal husbandry and fishery, and total value of services rendered to support farming, forestry, animal husbandry and fishery activities. It reflects the total scale and results of agricultural production during a given period. Prior to 1957, Chinese gross agricultural output value included barnyard manure and handicraft products for self-consumption (clothes, shoes, stockings, and initial grain processing undertaken by peasants). Since 1958, cutting and felling of bamboo and trees by villages and other cooperative organizations under villages have been included in forestry; value of barnyard manure has been excluded from animal husbandry; self consumed handicrafts has been excluded from sideline occupations, while the output value of industries run by villages and cooperative organizations under village had been included in sideline occupations and the output value of fish catches by motor fishing boats has been added to fishery. Since 1980, the value of handicraft products made for sale by individuals in households had been added to sideline occupations. Since 1984, industries run by villages and under villages have been included in the sector of industry. Since 1993, the subdivision of sideline occupations has been canceled, and the hunting of wild animals has been classified into animal husbandry, and the gathering of wild plants and commodity industry run by rural household have been included in farming. A new industrial classification of economic activities was introduced in 2003. Under the new classification, value of services to farming, forestry, animal husbandry and fishery is included in the gross output value of agriculture, value of wood felling and transport is included in forestry, value of industrial output by rural households is not included in agriculture, and the collection of wild forest products is taken from agriculture and included in the forestry. The first agriculture census of China revealed some discrepancy between the production of animal products from the annual reports and that from the census. Efforts were made by the Rural Socio-economic Survey Organization of NBS to adjust the output value of animal husbandry to make the figures from the annual reports consistent with the census data.

Gross output value of agriculture is obtained by first multiplying the output of each product or by product by its price, resulting in the output value of each single item. For a small number of products, annual output of which is not available or difficult to get due to the long production (growing) process involved, the output value is estimated through an indirect approach. The sum of output value of all products of farming, forestry, animal husbandry and fishery is then equal to the gross output value of agriculture.

Grain Output refers to the total output in the whole country including grains produced by state farms, collective units, rural households, as well as by farms affiliated to industrial and mining enterprises and other production units. Grain includes rice, wheat, corn, sorghum, millet and other miscellaneous grains as well as tubers and bean. Output of beans refers to dry beans without pods. The output of tubers (sweet potatoes and potatoes, not including taros and cassava) was converted into that of grain at the ratio 4:1, i.e. 4 kilograms of fresh tubers was equivalent to 1 kilogram of grain up to 1963. Since 1964 the ratio for conversion has been 5:1. Tubers supplied as vegetables (such as potatoes) in cities and suburbs are calculated as fresh vegetables and their output is not included in the output of grain. Output of all other grains refers to husked grain. Data on grain production before 1989 were obtained through Comprehensive Statistical Reporting System. Since 1989, data from sample surveys are used.

Cotton Output refers to the cotton production in the whole country including cotton sown in spring and in autumn. Output is measured as the weight of ginned cotton. Ceiba is not included.

Output of Oil-bearing Crops refers to the total production of oil-bearing crops of various kinds, including peanuts, (dry, in shell) rapeseeds, sesame, sunflower seeds, flax seeds, and other oil-bearing crops. Soybeans, oil-bearing woody plants, and wild oil-bearing crops are not included.

Output of Aquatic Products refers to catches of both artificially cultured and naturally grown aquatic products, including fish, shrimps, crabs and shellfish in sea and inland water as well as seaweed. Freshwater plants are not included. Data on output of aquatic products are reported by aquatic product and statistical agencies level by level. Before 1995, among the shellfish, the oyster was counted as fresh meat; 5 kilograms of ark shell, clams and frogs are equivalent to 1 kilogram of fresh aquatic products; they are all counted as fresh aquatic products since 1996.

Output of Pork, Beef, and Mutton refers to the meat of slaughtered hogs, cattle, sheep and goats with head, feet, and offal taken away. Data refers to the production of the whole country. The first agriculture census of China in 1996 revealed some discrepancy between the production of animal products from the annual reports and that from the census. Efforts were made by the Rural Socio-economic Survey Organization of NBS to adjust the output value of animal husbandry to make the figures from the annual reports consistent with the census data. Since 1999, NBS conducted sample survey for the major animal husbandry products, such as hogs, cattle, sheep and goats and fowls, and the data from sample surveys are used as national finalized data. Those products, which are not covered by the sample survey, are still reported by statistical agencies level by level.

Number of Livestock or Poultry in Stock at Beginning (or End) refers to the total number of large animals, pigs, sheep, fowls, etc. raised by rural cooperative organizations, state farms, rural individuals, government agencies, schools, industrial and mining enterprises, army, and urban residents at the beginning (or end) of the reference period. Data reporting system and data adjustment are the same as that in the output of pork, beef and mutton.

Regularly Cultivated Land refers to farmland among the total land resources, which is exclusively used for farming and is under regular cultivation with harvest in normal years. Included are currently cultivated land, land that has been abandoned or put in idle for less than 3 years and could be re-used for cultivation at any time, and new-claimed land that has been put into cultivation for more than 3 years. According to statistical coverage, it includes the gouges, dykes, roads and ridges of field with 1 meter wide in Southern areas and 2 meters wide in Northern areas. Excluded under this category are steep slope land over 25 degrees under temporary cultivation, land (large or small plots) that is claimed along river bends, lake sides or banks of reservoirs, as well as land that has been designated under the "Green for Grain" programme of the state and provincial governments but is still temporarily under cultivation. The regularly cultivated land is the key protection land of the nation, an important indicator reflecting the comprehensive productivity of agriculture of China.

Sown Area of Crops refers to area of land sown or transplanted with crops regardless of being in cultivated area or non-cultivated area. Area of land re-sown due to natural disasters is also included. This is an important indicator that can reflect the utilization condition of the cultivated land in China. At present, the sown area of crops mainly include the following 9 categories of crops: grain, cotton, oil-bearing crops, sugar crops, fiber crops, Tobacco, Vegetables and melons, medicinal materials and other farm crops.

Irrigated Area refers to areas that are effectively irrigated, i.e. level land, which has water source and complete sets of irrigation facilities to lift and move adequate water for irrigation purpose under normal conditions. Under normal conditions, irrigated area is the sum of watered fields and irrigated fields where irrigation systems or equipment have been installed for regular irrigation purpose. This important indicator reflects drought resistance capacity of the cultivated land in China.

Consumption of Chemical Fertilizers in Agriculture refers to the quantity of chemical fertilizers applied in agriculture in the year, including nitrogenous fertilizer, phosphate fertilizer, potash fertilizer, and compound fertilizer. The consumption of chemical fertilizers is required in calculation to convert the gross weight into weight containing 100% effective component (e.g. 100% nitrogen content in nitrogenous fertilizer, 100% phosphorous pent oxide contents in phosphate fertilizer, 100% potassium oxide contents in potash fertilizer). Compound fertilizer is converted with its major component. The formula is :

Volume of effective component= physical quantity x effective component of certain chemical fertilizer (%)

Total Power of Farm Machinery refers to total mechanical power of machinery used in farming, forestry, animal husbandry, and fishery, including ploughing, irrigation and drainage, harvesting, transport, plant protection, stock breeding, forestry and fishery. The power of internal combustion engines is required to convert horsepower into watts and the power of electric motors is required to be converted into watts. Machinery employed for non-agricultural purposes, such as the machines used in township run and village-run industry, construction, non-agricultural transport, scientific experiments and teaching, is excluded. Data are mainly from agricultural machinery agencies.

Rural Employed Persons refer to rural labor forces aged over 16 years old who are engaged in real production and management activities and receive payment in kind or wages, including those covered within the age frame and regularly participating in production activities, and those who are out of the range of age frame and also participating in production activities regularly. Excluding students studying in other places with their permanent residence registered in local areas, servicemen and persons incapable of working; also excluding those who are waiting for jobs and those engaged in household work. Persons employed are classified as persons engaged in agriculture, forestry, animal husbandry or fishery activities; persons engaged in industrial activities; persons engaged in construction activities; persons engaged in transport, storage and telecommunications activities; persons engaged in whole sales and retail sales trade and catering activities; and persons engaged in other non-agriculture activities, depending upon the longest period of employment in major activities (or using income indicator when period of employment is the same).

13 工业 Industry

资料整理人员：魏燕子　刘洪韬　高　媛

工 业
Industry
2020

规模以上工业企业		Industrial Enterprises Above Designated Size		
工业总产值(现价)	(亿元)	Total Output Value (at current price)	(100 million yuan)	42767.04
#轻工业	(亿元)	Light Industry	(100 million yuan)	14356.84
重工业	(亿元)	Heavy Industry	(100 million yuan)	28410.2
#大型企业	(亿元)	Large Scale Enterprises	(100 million yuan)	13760.58
中型企业	(亿元)	Medium Scale Enterprises	(100 million yuan)	8767.11
资产总计	(亿元)	Total Assets	(100 million yuan)	44195.49
负债合计	(亿元)	Total Liability	(100 million yuan)	23100.74
营业收入	(亿元)	Business Revenue	(100 million yuan)	40925.19
利税总额	(亿元)	Total Profits and Taxes	(100 million yuan)	4439.79
从业人员年平均人数	(万人)	Annually Average Number of Employment	(10 000 persons)	274.51

规模以上工业总产值构成(%)
Composition of Industry above Desginated Size

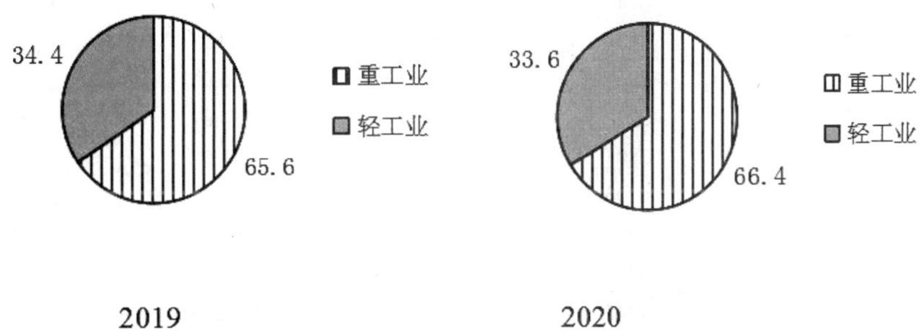

2019 2020

规模以上工业增长指数(上年=100)
Added Value Index of Industries above the Scale (previous year=100)

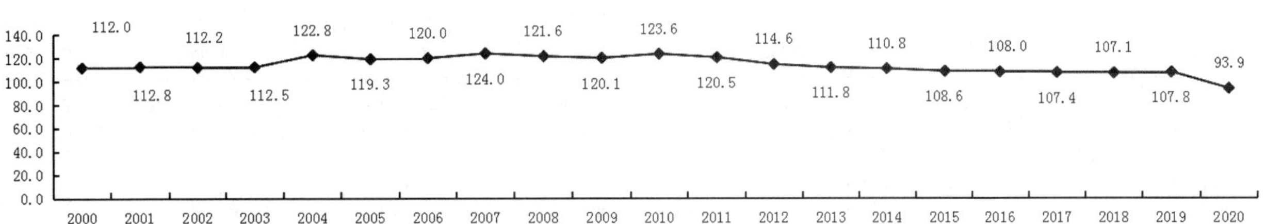

13-1 工业发展基本情况
Basic Situation of Industrial Development

年份 Year	工业企业单位数(个) Number of Industrial Enterprises (unit)	轻工业 Light Industry	重工业 Heavy Industry	工业总产值(当年价)(亿元) Total Output Value (currentprice) (100 million yuan)	轻工业 Light Industry	重工业 Heavy Industry
1979	16073	10100	5973	220.82	93.45	107.37
1985	25011	15309	9702	467.22	216.47	250.75
1986	27697	16890	10807	538.28	256.06	282.22
1987	26294	15528	10766	659.19	315.49	343.70
1988	26016	15279	10737	834.84	405.13	429.71
1989	25999	15035	10964	976.93	463.35	513.58
1990	25913	14885	11028	1008.20	476.76	531.44
1991	25204	14317	10887	1136.02	531.26	604.76
1992	23985	13428	10557	1373.66	605.11	768.55
1993	22600	11958	10642	1992.31	770.20	1222.11
1994	23275	12096	11179	3024.72	1360.78	1663.94
1995	27815	14827	12988	3697.91	1870.12	1827.79
1996	25986	13618	12368	4836.33	2470.90	2365.43
1997	24498	12723	11775	5977.00	3158.47	2818.53
1998	7399	3581	3818	6731.31	3534.67	3196.64
1999	6874	3308	3566	2831.70	1109.92	1721.78
2000	6282	3026	3256	3064.43	1177.24	1887.18
2001	6197	2981	3216	3239.51	1194.90	2044.61
2002	6183	2947	3236	3589.26	1184.78	2404.48
2003	6271	2789	3482	3631.29	1192.46	2438.82
2004	6232	2632	3600	4960.25	1180.07	3780.17
2005	6813	2953	3860	6066.96	1503.00	4563.95
2006	7546	3272	4274	7454.07	1898.34	5555.73
2007	8996	3808	5188	9601.52	2492.88	7108.64
2008	12067	4806	7261	13454.94	3344.80	10110.14
2009	14027	5515	8512	15567.02	4234.52	11332.50
2010	16106	6326	9780	21623.12	5935.78	15687.33
2011	10633	4347	6286	28072.73	8370.27	19702.45
2012	12441	5012	7429	33450.66	10941.70	22508.95
2013	14650	5855	8795	39208.98	13405.24	25803.74
2014	15957	6453	9504	43393.87	15378.14	28015.73
2015	16413	6646	9767	45809.57	16810.65	28998.91
2016	16296	6680	9616	48766.71	18027.68	30739.04
2017	15097	6100	8997	45642.59	15630.86	30011.74
2018	15222	6272	8950	45765.33	15817.24	29948.09
2019	15520	6230	9290	47572.06	16352.06	31220.00
2020	15708	6240	9468	42767.04	14356.84	28410.20

注:1.本表规模以上工业1997年及以前统计范围为乡及乡以上工业。1998-2006年为全部国有工业及年销售收入500万元以上非国有工业企业;2007年-2010年为主营业务收入500万元以上工业企业。2011年起为主营业务收入2000万元及以上的工业法人企业。(下表同)

2."国有及国有控股经济"一栏,1998年以前统计范围为国有工业。

3.2017年行业小类码按照《国民经济行业分类》(GB/T4754-2017)填写。(下表同)

Note: a)The scopes of industrial statistics are all township and above town industrial enterprises before 1998. The scopes are all state-owned industrial enterprises and non-state-owned industrial enterprise with revenue from principal business over 5 million yuan from 1998 to 2006. For 2007 to 2010, the scopes are all industrial enterprices with revenue from principal business over 5 million yuan. From 2011, the scopes are all industrial enterprises with revenue from principal business over 20 millon yuan.The same applies to the talbe following.

b)"State-owned and state-controlled economy" a column, prior to 1998 statistics the range of state-owned industries.

c)Accordring to GB/T4754-2017, the small classes code of industries are filled in the table from 2017. The same applies to the talbe following.

13-1 续表 continued

年 份 Year	主营业务收入(亿元) Main Business Income (100 million yuan)	利润总额(亿元) Total Profits (100 million yuan)	利税总额(亿元) Total Profits and Taxes (100 million yuan)	职工人数(万人) Number of Employees (10 000 persons)
1979	163.52	20.70	34.19	161.98
1985	381.43	43.64	80.82	306.83
1986	438.95	40.22	82.14	333.63
1987	526.95	48.54	96.16	343.43
1988	654.72	58.85	117.28	356.43
1989	706.99	50.99	112.12	360.88
1990	705.97	26.73	88.40	358.65
1991	800.01	31.79	103.46	367.41
1992	1041.66	43.19	127.15	357.74
1993	1500.71	67.00	167.92	357.97
1994	1690.94	74.06	190.29	381.45
1995	2066.38	52.26	181.57	379.84
1996	2305.57	43.93	181.41	369.80
1997	2681.36	57.71	221.53	362.50
1998	2433.92	44.71	195.96	274.43
1999	2602.26	68.82	232.24	250.07
2000	2870.36	106.47	293.58	230.36
2001	3043.82	134.49	335.36	212.48
2002	3378.31	175.60	404.23	205.82
2003	3993.99	194.40	444.96	198.60
2004	4832.43	270.98	559.28	176.70
2005	5962.54	371.84	727.48	188.30
2006	7314.81	454.00	897.19	190.85
2007	9390.43	647.85	1229.16	200.35
2008	13081.90	909.03	1761.47	235.90
2009	15331.62	1092.47	1987.88	272.39
2010	21151.56	1668.55	2950.08	294.97
2011	27072.02	1864.46	3093.57	279.59
2012	32325.95	2046.28	3528.80	311.13
2013	38183.39	2475.07	4451.87	346.29
2014	41401.49	2402.63	4465.72	359.45
2015	43179.21	2456.00	4599.15	352.64
2016	45850.64	2713.46	4754.74	339.51
2017	43210.52	2608.03	4603.47	309.78
2018	43515.86	3752.76	6542.53	315.55
2019	44492.00	3049.57	5274.52	335.87
2020	39809.10	2646.93	4439.79	274.51

13-2 规模以上工业企业单位数和产销总值(2020)

单位:亿元

项 目	Item	企业单位数(个) Number of Enterprises (unit)
总计	**Total**	**15708**
一、按登记注册类型分组:	**Grouped by Type of Registration**	
内资企业	Inner Funded Enterprises	14928
国有企业	State Owned Enterprises	151
中央企业	Central Enterprises	48
地方企业	Local Enterprises	103
集体企业	Collective - Owned Enterprise	32
股份合作企业	Share Holding Cooperative Enterprises	8
联营企业	Joint Owned Enterprise	7
国有联营企业	State Joint Ownership	3
集体联营企业	Collective Joint Ownership	1
国有与集体联营企业	Joint State - Collective Ownership	1
其他联营企业	Other Joint Owned Enterprise	2
有限责任公司	Responsibility Co. Ltd	2865
国有独资公司	State Solely Funded Co.	131
其他有限责任公司	Others	2734
股份有限公司	Share Holding Co. Ltd.	619
私营企业	Private - Owned Enterprises	11238
私营独资企业	Solely Private - Owned Enterprises	199
私营合伙企业	Private Joint Venture	40
私营有限责任公司	Private Responsibility Co. Ltd	10091
私营股份有限公司	Private Share Holding Co. Ltd.	908
其他企业	Others	8
港、澳、台商投资企业	Hongkong, Macao and Taiwan Funded Enterprises	292
合资经营企业(港或澳、台资)	Joint Venture with Hongkong, Macao and Taiwan	107
合作经营企业(港或澳、台资)	Cooperate with Hongkong, Macao and Taiwan Funded	1
港澳台商独资经营企业	Enterprises Solely Funded by Hongkong, Macao and Taiwan Businessmen	164
港澳台商投资股份有限公司	Share Holding Co. Ltd. With Hongkong, Macao and Taiwan Investment	9
其他港澳台商投资企业	Other Hongkong, Macao and Taiwan Funded Enterprises	11
外商投资企业	Foreign Funded Enterprises	488
中外合资经营企业	Sino - Foreign Joint Funded Enterprises	224
中外合作经营企业	Sino - Foreign Cooperative Funded Enterprises	5
外资企业	Foreign Solely Funded Enterprises	239
外商投资股份有限公司	Foreign Funded Share Holding Co. Ltd.	10
其他外商投资企业	Other Foreign Funded Enterprises	10
二、在总计中:亏损企业	**Of the Total: Enterprises Running under Deficit**	**2060**
在总计中:国有控股企业	Of the Total: State-Owned Share Holding Enterprises	798
在总计中:轻工业	Of the Total: Light Industry	6240
重工业	Heavy Industry	9468
在总计中:大型企业	Of the Total: Large Scale Enterprises	280
中型企业	Medium Scale Enterprises	1372
小型企业	Small Enterprises	14056

Number of Industrial Enterprises above Designated Size and Gross Production and Sales(2020)

(100 million yuan)

工业总产值(当年价格) Total Output Value (current price)	资产总计 Total Assets	流动资产合计 Circulating Funds	应收帐款 Accounts Received	固定资产原价 Original Price of Fixed Assets
42767.04	**44195.49**	**21434.85**	**5282.60**	**25418.10**
35599.14	37437.83	17484.44	4238.38	21986.36
1650.83	3039.17	1004.67	279.98	3245.89
1449.71	2581.19	817.46	219.42	2964.40
201.12	457.98	187.20	60.56	281.49
44.03	30.60	17.52	7.07	16.07
7.79	7.49	4.47	1.07	5.04
13.94	16.62	9.92	2.63	9.58
6.88	11.29	7.99	1.59	3.80
0.04	0.12	0.10	0.08	0.04
0.41	3.53	0.88	0.82	3.17
6.60	1.68	0.95	0.14	2.58
10351.46	14114.39	6878.35	1578.25	7894.89
2200.54	2525.49	1339.11	223.87	2096.37
8150.93	11588.90	5539.23	1354.38	5798.53
4011.27	9509.03	4045.35	760.54	4292.01
19513.71	10711.85	5517.59	1606.10	6520.03
330.73	140.87	83.84	14.69	92.17
43.72	20.14	7.98	1.86	13.86
17285.02	9240.44	4765.52	1434.82	5750.35
1854.26	1310.40	660.25	154.73	663.65
6.10	8.68	6.58	2.74	2.84
1696.39	1969.97	1032.77	244.50	1041.41
778.80	888.44	548.18	100.28	413.52
0.98	1.54	0.48	0.04	1.62
788.58	813.21	353.65	129.61	528.46
79.33	194.57	88.69	5.43	62.54
48.69	72.20	41.76	9.13	35.27
5471.52	4787.68	2917.64	799.71	2390.33
3971.30	3265.90	1898.11	301.20	1729.54
31.02	50.91	27.25	2.89	40.72
1378.18	1374.39	936.07	478.12	567.78
52.68	48.91	26.99	7.55	30.28
38.34	47.58	29.23	9.95	22.01
4452.81	**9188.14**	**3110.55**	**719.14**	**6744.19**
10998.17	19598.26	8282.20	1519.84	12425.86
14356.84	9964.78	5554.70	1102.11	5375.25
28410.20	34230.71	15880.14	4180.48	20042.85
13760.58	21200.14	9475.71	1736.10	12653.13
8767.11	8530.15	4584.76	1328.79	4766.75
20239.35	14465.20	7374.37	2217.70	7998.22

13-2 续表 1 continued

单位：亿元

项 目	Item	累计折旧 Accumulated Depreciation
总计	**Total**	**11901.60**
一、按登记注册类型分组:	**Grouped by Type of Registration**	
内资企业	Inner Funded Enterprises	10283.58
国有企业	State Owned Enterprises	1623.66
中央企业	Central Enterprises	1547.34
地方企业	Local Enterprises	76.32
集体企业	Collective - Owned Enterprise	6.39
股份合作企业	Share Holding Cooperative Enterprises	2.67
联营企业	Joint Owned Enterprise	4.31
国有联营企业	State Joint Ownership	1.24
集体联营企业	Collective Joint Ownership	0.04
国有与集体联营企业	Joint State - Collective Ownership	0.53
其他联营企业	Other Joint Owned Enterprise	2.50
有限责任公司	Responsibility Co. Ltd	3385.52
国有独资公司	State Solely Funded Co.	1299.84
其他有限责任公司	Others	2085.68
股份有限公司	Share Holding Co. Ltd.	2195.09
私营企业	Private - Owned Enterprises	3064.01
私营独资企业	Solely Private - Owned Enterprises	52.00
私营合伙企业	Private Joint Venture	4.11
私营有限责任公司	Private Responsibility Co. Ltd	2704.69
私营股份有限公司	Private Share Holding Co. Ltd.	303.21
其他企业	Others	1.94
港、澳、台商投资企业	Hongkong, Macao and Taiwan Funded Enterprises	424.16
合资经营企业(港或澳、台资)	Joint Venture with Hongkong, Macao and Taiwan	170.96
合作经营企业(港或澳、台资)	Cooperate with Hongkong, Macao and Taiwan Funded	0.66
港澳台商独资经营企业	Enterprises Solely Funded by Hongkong, Macao and Taiwan Businessmen	217.78
港澳台商投资股份有限公司	Share Holding Co. Ltd. With Hongkong, Macao and Taiwan Investment	22.13
其他港澳台商投资企业	Other Hongkong, Macao and Taiwan Funded Enterprises	13.00
外商投资企业	Foreign Funded Enterprises	1193.86
中外合资经营企业	Sino - Foreign Joint Funded Enterprises	901.93
中外合作经营企业	Sino - Foreign Cooperative Funded Enterprises	27.19
外资企业	Foreign Solely Funded Enterprises	244.16
外商投资股份有限公司	Foreign Funded Share Holding Co. Ltd.	11.64
其他外商投资企业	Other Foreign Funded Enterprises	9.00
二、在总计中:亏损企业	**Of the Total: Enterprises Running under Deficit**	**2942.04**
在总计中:国有控股企业	Of the Total: State - Owned Share Holding Enterprises	6219.46
在总计中:轻工业	Of the Total: Light Industry	2559.48
重工业	Heavy Industry	9342.12
在总计中:大型企业	Of the Total: Large Scale Enterprises	6253.54
中型企业	Medium Scale Enterprises	2324.78
小型企业	Small Enterprises	3323.29

(100 million yuan)

固定资产净额 NBV of Fixed Assets	负债合计 Total Liability	流动负债合计 Total Circulating Liability	应付账款 Account Payable
12533.09	**23100.74**	**17514.61**	**5738.98**
10799.88	18972.77	13868.61	4293.97
1582.70	1967.98	1477.26	547.19
1406.99	1650.43	1291.33	503.68
175.71	317.56	185.93	43.51
8.58	14.88	6.95	0.71
2.33	3.24	3.11	1.08
5.27	11.11	8.21	3.04
2.55	7.38	7.33	2.86
	0.06		
2.64	2.21	0.40	
0.08	1.47	0.49	0.18
4289.62	7787.41	5583.40	1878.25
774.63	1289.98	1081.78	421.90
3515.00	6497.43	4501.62	1456.36
2010.07	4037.16	2747.19	610.93
2900.59	5144.86	4037.79	1251.43
32.56	67.42	56.63	8.28
8.33	8.56	6.82	1.46
2551.04	4476.66	3520.45	1122.50
308.66	592.22	453.88	119.19
0.70	6.12	4.69	1.34
585.38	988.38	846.06	236.86
234.29	533.95	485.18	124.74
	0.18	0.11	0.03
288.27	356.36	288.38	99.12
40.41	67.03	47.59	4.85
22.41	30.86	24.80	8.13
1147.84	3139.59	2799.94	1208.15
796.88	2165.23	1931.33	726.75
12.74	32.62	24.47	3.15
307.13	891.75	803.00	459.98
18.13	25.77	23.22	10.50
12.96	24.21	17.92	7.76
3659.28	**5736.42**	**3775.57**	**1132.91**
6036.09	10480.32	7570.79	2330.45
2472.60	4584.89	3650.18	974.66
10060.50	18515.85	13864.42	4764.31
6299.44	11295.51	8409.75	2818.19
2311.27	4447.20	3640.17	1261.02
3922.38	7358.02	5464.69	1659.76

13-2 续表 2 continued

单位:亿元

项 目	Item	所有者权益合计 Total Rights of Owners	实收资本 Assets Recevied
总计	**Total**	**21007.97**	**8850.97**
一、按登记注册类型分组:	**Grouped by Type of Registration**		
内资企业	Inner Funded Enterprises	18378.07	7603.08
国有企业	State Owned Enterprises	1068.17	761.54
中央企业	Central Enterprises	930.76	657.24
地方企业	Local Enterprises	137.40	104.30
集体企业	Collective - Owned Enterprise	15.53	5.23
股份合作企业	Share Holding Cooperative Enterprises	4.24	1.86
联营企业	Joint Owned Enterprise	5.51	2.90
国有联营企业	State Joint Ownership	3.91	1.51
集体联营企业	Collective Joint Ownership	0.06	0.01
国有与集体联营企业	Joint State - Collective Ownership	1.32	1.28
其他联营企业	Other Joint Owned Enterprise	0.21	0.11
有限责任公司	Responsibility Co. Ltd	6314.91	3612.13
国有独资公司	State Solely Funded Co.	1234.80	400.10
其他有限责任公司	Others	5080.11	3212.02
股份有限公司	Share Holding Co. Ltd.	5458.94	1041.23
私营企业	Private - Owned Enterprises	5508.21	2176.95
私营独资企业	Solely Private - Owned Enterprises	73.01	20.45
私营合伙企业	Private Joint Venture	11.32	4.78
私营有限责任公司	Private Responsibility Co. Ltd	4709.66	1896.21
私营股份有限公司	Private Share Holding Co. Ltd.	714.22	255.52
其他企业	Others	2.56	1.26
港、澳、台商投资企业	Hongkong, Macao and Taiwan Funded Enterprises	980.43	409.25
合资经营企业(港或澳、台资)	Joint Venture with Hongkong, Macao and Taiwan	354.49	127.87
合作经营企业(港或澳、台资)	Cooperate with Hongkong, Macao and Taiwan Funded	1.36	1.17
港澳台商独资经营企业	Enterprises Solely Funded by Hongkong, Macao and Taiwan Businessmen	455.69	240.76
港澳台商投资股份有限公司	Share Holding Co. Ltd. With Hongkong, Macao and Taiwan Investment	127.54	21.20
其他港澳台商投资企业	Other Hongkong, Macao and Taiwan Funded Enterprises	41.34	18.25
外商投资企业	Foreign Funded Enterprises	1649.48	838.64
中外合资经营企业	Sino - Foreign Joint Funded Enterprises	1100.51	571.36
中外合作经营企业	Sino - Foreign Cooperative Funded Enterprises	18.28	12.66
外资企业	Foreign Solely Funded Enterprises	481.75	223.86
外商投资股份有限公司	Foreign Funded Share Holding Co. Ltd.	23.00	15.49
其他外商投资企业	Other Foreign Funded Enterprises	25.93	15.27
二、在总计中:亏损企业	**Of the Total: Enterprises Running under Deficit**	**3446.99**	**2991.31**
在总计中:国有控股企业	Of the Total: State - Owned Share Holding Enterprises	9113.00	3669.61
在总计中:轻工业	Of the Total: Light Industry	5331.19	1860.32
重工业	Heavy Industry	15676.79	6990.65
在总计中:大型企业	Of the Total: Large Scale Enterprises	9904.63	3848.16
中型企业	Medium Scale Enterprises	4082.95	1604.39
小型企业	Small Enterprises	7020.39	3398.42

(100 million yuan)

国家资本 National Assets	集体资本 Collective Assets	法人资本 Corperative Assets	个人资本 Individual Assets	港澳台资本 Assets from Hongkong, Macao and Taiwan Funded Enterprises	外商资本 Total Rights of the Owners Foreign Assets
1998.86	**193.36**	**4235.82**	**1716.89**	**226.51**	**474.44**
1750.15	172.44	3920.27	1689.46	13.73	51.92
587.82	0.80	165.58	3.64	0.07	0.77
516.31	0.29	140.31	0.32		
71.51	0.51	25.27	3.32	0.07	0.77
	3.81	0.37	0.94	0.11	
	0.83	0.70	0.33		
0.73	0.01	1.84	0.33		
0.73		0.50	0.28		
	0.01				
		1.28			
		0.06	0.05		
872.17	63.17	2315.74	330.36	0.41	28.12
268.15		128.72	3.21		0.03
604.02	63.17	2187.02	327.15	0.41	28.10
257.20	52.63	488.85	207.45	12.44	22.66
32.23	51.21	946.81	1145.53	0.71	0.37
	0.33	7.66	12.46		
	0.03	2.26	2.49		
27.03	28.93	858.61	980.55	0.71	0.30
5.21	21.92	78.28	150.04		0.07
		0.38	0.88		
64.62	3.62	101.72	8.30	190.93	40.06
4.25	2.54	42.57	4.07	59.32	15.13
				1.17	
58.79	0.20	40.52	4.11	121.50	15.64
		15.81	0.12	2.12	3.15
1.57	0.88	2.83		6.82	6.14
184.09	17.30	213.83	19.13	21.85	382.46
165.22	16.30	176.70	13.13	11.16	188.85
4.82		2.49			5.35
7.78	0.96	27.67	5.60	6.12	175.71
0.03	0.03	5.29	0.03	4.56	5.55
6.24		1.68	0.36		6.99
916.69	**31.28**	**1653.58**	**223.81**	**52.72**	**113.22**
1803.73	63.42	1542.52	81.55	16.89	158.64
131.79	43.82	827.95	635.24	113.41	108.08
1867.07	149.54	3407.87	1081.64	113.09	366.35
1301.68	45.74	1987.53	227.10	84.76	201.35
334.48	52.08	729.41	291.40	55.02	141.96
362.70	95.54	1518.87	1198.39	86.72	131.12

13-2 续表 3 continued

单位:亿元

项 目	Item	营业收入 Business Revenue
总计	**Total**	**40925.19**
一、按登记注册类型分组:	**Grouped by Type of Registration**	
内资企业	Inner Funded Enterprises	33765.52
国有企业	State Owned Enterprises	1661.28
中央企业	Central Enterprises	1451.01
地方企业	Local Enterprises	210.27
集体企业	Collective - Owned Enterprise	39.49
股份合作企业	Share Holding Cooperative Enterprises	6.67
联营企业	Joint Owned Enterprise	12.05
国有联营企业	State Joint Ownership	6.49
集体联营企业	Collective Joint Ownership	0.04
国有与集体联营企业	Joint State - Collective Ownership	0.41
其他联营企业	Other Joint Owned Enterprise	5.11
有限责任公司	Responsibility Co. Ltd	10066.21
国有独资公司	State Solely Funded Co.	2096.82
其他有限责任公司	Others	7969.39
股份有限公司	Share Holding Co. Ltd.	3966.41
私营企业	Private - Owned Enterprises	18006.60
私营独资企业	Solely Private - Owned Enterprises	322.40
私营合伙企业	Private Joint Venture	42.06
私营有限责任公司	Private Responsibility Co. Ltd	16010.56
私营股份有限公司	Private Share Holding Co. Ltd.	1631.59
其他企业	Others	6.81
港、澳、台商投资企业	Hongkong, Macao and Taiwan Funded Enterprises	1723.52
合资经营企业(港或澳、台资)	Joint Venture with Hongkong, Macao and Taiwan	716.81
合作经营企业(港或澳、台资)	Cooperate with Hongkong, Macao and Taiwan Funded	0.98
港澳台商独资经营企业	Enterprises Solely Funded by Hongkong, Macao and Taiwan Businessmen	889.74
港澳台商投资股份有限公司	Share Holding Co.Ltd. With Hongkong, Macao and Taiwan Investment	64.29
其他港澳台商投资企业	Other Hongkong, Macao and Taiwan Funded Enterprises	51.70
外商投资企业	Foreign Funded Enterprises	5436.15
中外合资经营企业	Sino - Foreign Joint Funded Enterprises	3731.19
中外合作经营企业	Sino - Foreign Cooperative Funded Enterprises	31.25
外资企业	Foreign Solely Funded Enterprises	1596.20
外商投资股份有限公司	Foreign Funded Share Holding Co. Ltd.	41.81
其他外商投资企业	Other Foreign Funded Enterprises	35.71
二、在总计中:亏损企业	**Of the Total: Enterprises Running under Deficit**	**4452.51**
在总计中:国有控股企业	Of the Total: State - Owned Share Holding Enterprises	10682.36
在总计中:轻工业	Of the Total: Light Industry	13465.35
重工业	Heavy Industry	27459.84
在总计中:大型企业	Of the Total: Large Scale Enterprises	13713.88
中型企业	Medium Scale Enterprises	8401.23
小型企业	Small Enterprises	18810.08

(100 million yuan)

主营业务收入 Revenue of Major Business	营业成本 Operating Costs	税金及附加 Tax	销售费用 Selling Expenses
39809.10	**33842.09**	**916.31**	**1190.29**
32879.27	27899.62	761.34	962.26
1642.82	1569.48	8.52	12.54
1440.23	1386.35	5.41	6.55
202.59	183.13	3.11	5.99
39.19	32.61	0.69	0.56
5.68	4.84	0.04	0.58
11.97	9.82	0.03	0.68
6.41	5.35	0.03	0.17
0.04	0.04		
0.41	0.19		
5.11	4.25		0.51
9578.13	7980.12	522.12	282.41
2021.47	1376.04	452.68	25.02
7556.66	6604.07	69.44	257.40
3830.44	3034.74	96.10	148.53
17764.31	15261.58	133.83	516.85
317.27	262.29	3.49	16.51
40.41	35.00	0.64	1.10
15792.46	13620.19	118.80	450.24
1614.17	1344.10	10.90	48.99
6.73	6.43	0.01	0.11
1583.55	1398.53	9.74	79.70
706.24	562.82	4.89	43.25
0.98	0.67	0.01	
762.13	762.02	3.87	21.02
63.93	34.49	0.68	11.51
50.28	38.53	0.28	3.92
5346.28	4543.94	145.22	148.33
3675.86	3070.55	137.47	106.04
30.98	27.72	0.18	0.54
1562.93	1386.05	7.12	39.51
41.41	30.19	0.32	1.42
35.10	29.43	0.13	0.82
4141.95	**4097.03**	**171.19**	**98.91**
10382.83	8404.57	676.09	250.59
13203.49	10627.57	550.82	534.90
26605.61	23214.52	365.48	655.40
13100.51	11019.65	723.01	377.71
8225.65	6897.76	58.03	269.59
18482.93	15924.68	135.27	542.99

13-2 续表 4 continued

单位:亿元

项 目	Item	管理费用 Management Expenses
总计	**Total**	**1417.05**
一、按登记注册类型分组:	**Grouped by Type of Registration**	
内资企业	Inner Funded Enterprises	1167.32
国有企业	State Owned Enterprises	49.69
中央企业	Central Enterprises	38.00
地方企业	Local Enterprises	11.68
集体企业	Collective - Owned Enterprise	2.29
股份合作企业	Share Holding Cooperative Enterprises	0.40
联营企业	Joint Owned Enterprise	0.57
国有联营企业	State Joint Ownership	0.43
集体联营企业	Collective Joint Ownership	
国有与集体联营企业	Joint State - Collective Ownership	
其他联营企业	Other Joint Owned Enterprise	0.13
有限责任公司	Responsibility Co. Ltd	351.68
国有独资公司	State Solely Funded Co.	73.93
其他有限责任公司	Others	277.76
股份有限公司	Share Holding Co. Ltd.	150.63
私营企业	Private - Owned Enterprises	611.77
私营独资企业	Solely Private - Owned Enterprises	13.38
私营合伙企业	Private Joint Venture	1.71
私营有限责任公司	Private Responsibility Co. Ltd	536.70
私营股份有限公司	Private Share Holding Co. Ltd.	59.97
其他企业	Others	0.29
港、澳、台商投资企业	Hongkong, Macao and Taiwan Funded Enterprises	59.38
合资经营企业(港或澳、台资)	Joint Venture with Hongkong, Macao and Taiwan	27.15
合作经营企业(港或澳、台资)	Cooperate with Hongkong, Macao and Taiwan Funded	0.09
港澳台商独资经营企业	Enterprises Solely Funded by Hongkong, Macao and Taiwan Businessmen	27.22
港澳台商投资股份有限公司	Share Holding Co. Ltd. With Hongkong, Macao and Taiwan Investment	2.80
其他港澳台商投资企业	Other Hongkong, Macao and Taiwan Funded Enterprises	2.00
外商投资企业	Foreign Funded Enterprises	190.36
中外合资经营企业	Sino - Foreign Joint Funded Enterprises	137.15
中外合作经营企业	Sino - Foreign Cooperative Funded Enterprises	0.67
外资企业	Foreign Solely Funded Enterprises	50.01
外商投资股份有限公司	Foreign Funded Share Holding Co. Ltd.	1.03
其他外商投资企业	Other Foreign Funded Enterprises	1.00
二、在总计中:亏损企业	**Of the Total: Enterprises Running under Deficit**	**216.83**
在总计中:国有控股企业	Of the Total: State - Owned Share Holding Enterprises	376.58
在总计中:轻工业	Of the Total: Light Industry	478.26
重工业	Heavy Industry	938.79
在总计中:大型企业	Of the Total: Large Scale Enterprises	415.54
中型企业	Medium Scale Enterprises	319.85
小型企业	Small Enterprises	681.67

(100 million yuan)

财务费用 Financial Expenses	利息费用 Interest Expenses	利息收入 Interest Income	其他收益 Other Income
336.03	**306.96**	**71.01**	**140.79**
315.52	268.84	52.83	121.32
17.02	19.48	3.15	8.91
13.33	15.63	3.13	6.27
3.69	3.86	0.01	2.64
0.14	0.04		−0.40
0.03	0.03	−0.01	
0.37	0.16		0.03
0.11	0.11		0.03
0.22			
0.05	0.05		
77.78	90.12	20.35	71.91
4.80	10.72	6.34	5.10
72.98	79.40	14.01	66.81
56.76	76.23	24.89	18.51
163.32	82.77	4.52	22.36
3.78	1.69	0.08	0.15
0.26	0.05	0.01	0.02
141.04	69.27	3.39	17.81
18.23	11.76	1.03	4.38
0.10		−0.07	
11.70	20.28	7.88	4.85
5.41	10.01	5.76	1.49
			0.01
5.04	4.94	1.31	2.89
0.93	4.75	0.54	0.18
0.32	0.58	0.28	0.29
8.82	17.84	10.30	14.62
5.33	13.55	10.45	10.66
0.30	0.37	−0.07	0.15
2.84	3.69	−0.22	3.39
0.16	0.15	0.06	0.25
0.18	0.07	0.08	0.17
65.13	**66.93**	**8.47**	**51.08**
94.44	140.05	49.32	66.91
107.36	71.85	11.58	25.89
228.67	235.10	59.43	114.89
75.19	144.08	58.98	85.14
78.26	61.26	6.96	24.60
182.59	101.62	5.07	31.05

13-2 续表 5 continued

单位:亿元

项 目	Item	投资收益 Investment Income
总计	**Total**	**250.94**
一、按登记注册类型分组:	**Grouped by Type of Registration**	
内资企业	Inner Funded Enterprises	230.04
国有企业	State Owned Enterprises	21.05
中央企业	Central Enterprises	1.46
地方企业	Local Enterprises	19.59
集体企业	Collective – Owned Enterprise	
股份合作企业	Share Holding Cooperative Enterprises	
联营企业	Joint Owned Enterprise	
国有联营企业	State Joint Ownership	
集体联营企业	Collective Joint Ownership	
国有与集体联营企业	Joint State – Collective Ownership	
其他联营企业	Other Joint Owned Enterprise	
有限责任公司	Responsibility Co. Ltd	25.83
国有独资公司	State Solely Funded Co.	16.69
其他有限责任公司	Others	9.14
股份有限公司	Share Holding Co.Ltd.	172.75
私营企业	Private – Owned Enterprises	10.41
私营独资企业	Solely Private – Owned Enterprises	0.04
私营合伙企业	Private Joint Venture	
私营有限责任公司	Private Responsibility Co. Ltd	7.03
私营股份有限公司	Private Share Holding Co. Ltd.	3.35
其他企业	Others	
港、澳、台商投资企业	Hongkong, Macao and Taiwan Funded Enterprises	7.54
合资经营企业(港或澳、台资)	Joint Venture with Hongkong, Macao and Taiwan	1.74
合作经营企业(港或澳、台资)	Cooperate with Hongkong, Macao and Taiwan Funded	
港澳台商独资经营企业	Enterprises Solely Funded by Hongkong, Macao and Taiwan Businessmen	5.80
港澳台商投资股份有限公司	Share Holding Co.Ltd. With Hongkong, Macao and Taiwan Investment	
其他港澳台商投资企业	Other Hongkong, Macao and Taiwan Funded Enterprises	-0.01
外商投资企业	Foreign Funded Enterprises	13.36
中外合资经营企业	Sino – Foreign Joint Funded Enterprises	10.35
中外合作经营企业	Sino – Foreign Cooperative Funded Enterprises	-0.01
外资企业	Foreign Solely Funded Enterprises	3.50
外商投资股份有限公司	Foreign Funded Share Holding Co.Ltd.	
其他外商投资企业	Other Foreign Funded Enterprises	-0.47
二、在总计中:亏损企业	**Of the Total: Enterprises Running under Deficit**	**17.50**
在总计中:国有控股企业	Of the Total: State-Owned Share Holding Enterprises	196.80
在总计中:轻工业	Of the Total: Light Industry	33.35
重工业	Heavy Industry	217.59
在总计中:大型企业	Of the Total: Large Scale Enterprises	176.36
中型企业	Medium Scale Enterprises	28.89
小型企业	Small Enterprises	45.70

(100 million yuan)

营业利润 Operating Profits	营业外收入 Non-operating Income	营业外支出 Non-operating Expenses	利润总额 Total Profits	所得税费用 Income Tax
2630.29	**122.43**	**105.57**	**2646.93**	**379.80**
2139.27	102.43	78.20	2163.27	275.20
-8.43	5.98	21.32	-23.78	8.35
-2.82	3.96	3.31	-2.17	5.31
-5.62	2.02	18.01	-21.61	3.04
2.52	0.09	0.03	2.58	0.04
0.70	0.07	0.06	0.71	0.18
0.28	0.01	0.02	0.28	0.04
0.22	0.01	0.01	0.22	0.03
-0.01	0.01			
0.01		0.01		
0.07			0.07	0.01
571.67	28.18	24.27	575.58	107.05
148.64	3.64	3.79	148.49	33.85
423.03	24.54	20.48	427.09	73.20
512.91	17.32	15.33	514.68	74.04
1059.76	48.88	17.18	1091.46	85.51
18.23	0.28	0.21	18.30	2.02
3.32	0.03	0.10	3.25	0.46
920.46	43.21	14.45	949.22	72.63
117.75	5.35	2.42	120.68	10.39
-0.14	1.91		1.76	
146.33	7.15	2.77	150.71	27.83
56.85	4.38	1.07	60.16	10.56
0.22			0.22	0.07
71.76	2.49	1.44	72.82	14.64
12.09	0.10	0.14	12.05	1.44
5.40	0.18	0.12	5.46	1.11
344.70	12.85	24.60	332.96	76.77
240.50	3.60	18.29	225.80	53.56
1.95	0.01	0.49	1.47	0.63
93.54	8.93	4.65	97.83	21.15
6.32	0.05	0.15	6.23	1.37
2.38	0.25	1.02	1.62	0.06
-351.38	**23.84**	**35.49**	**-363.03**	**7.37**
755.18	29.37	53.85	730.71	162.23
994.65	46.85	22.47	1018.81	123.44
1635.65	75.58	83.09	1628.13	256.37
921.78	26.27	49.63	898.43	174.99
637.00	39.25	15.81	660.45	104.42
1071.51	56.90	40.13	1088.06	100.39

13-2 续表 6 continued

单位:亿元

项 目	Item	亏损企业亏损总额 Total Loss of Enterprises Running under Deficit
总计	**Total**	**363.03**
一、按登记注册类型分组:	**Grouped by Type of Registration**	
内资企业	Inner Funded Enterprises	285.41
国有企业	State Owned Enterprises	64.06
中央企业	Central Enterprises	30.14
地方企业	Local Enterprises	33.92
集体企业	Collective - Owned Enterprise	0.26
股份合作企业	Share Holding Cooperative Enterprises	0.11
联营企业	Joint Owned Enterprise	0.08
国有联营企业	State Joint Ownership	0.08
集体联营企业	Collective Joint Ownership	
国有与集体联营企业	Joint State- Collective Ownership	
其他联营企业	Other Joint Owned Enterprise	
有限责任公司	Responsibility Co. Ltd	140.27
国有独资公司	State Solely Funded Co.	3.83
其他有限责任公司	Others	136.45
股份有限公司	Share Holding Co.Ltd.	38.62
私营企业	Private - owned enterprises	42.01
私营独资企业	Solely Private - owned enterprises	0.35
私营合伙企业	Private Joint Venture	0.04
私营有限责任公司	Private Responsibility Co. Ltd	37.60
私营股份有限公司	Private Share Holding Co.Ltd.	4.03
其他企业	Others	
港、澳、台商投资企业	Hongkong, Macao and Taiwan Funded Enterprises	11.11
合资经营企业(港或澳、台资)	Joint Venture with Hongkong, Macao and Taiwan	4.94
合作经营企业(港或澳、台资)	Cooperate with Hongkong, Macao and Taiwan Funded	
港澳台商独资经营企业	Enterprises Solely Funded by Hongkong, Macao and Taiwan Businessmen	5.94
港澳台商投资股份有限公司	Share Holding Co.Ltd. With Hongkong, Macao and Taiwan Investment	0.01
其他港澳台商投资企业	Other Hongkong, Macao and Taiwan Funded Enterprises	0.00
外商投资企业	Foreign Funded Enterprises	66.51
中外合资经营企业	Sino - Foreign Joint Funded Enterprises	53.30
中外合作经营企业	Sino - Foreign Cooperative Funded Enterprises	1.30
外资企业	Foreign Solely Funded Enterprises	10.74
外商投资股份有限公司	Foreign Funded Share Holding Co.Ltd.	0.59
其他外商投资企业	Other Foreign Funded Enterprises	0.58
二、在总计中:亏损企业	**Of the Total: Enterprises Running under Deficit**	**363.03**
在总计中:国有控股企业	Of the Total: State-Owned Share Holding Enterprises	197.57
在总计中:轻工业	Of the Total: Light Industry	48.93
重工业	Heavy Industry	314.10
在总计中:大型企业	Of the Total: Large Scale Enterprises	170.52
中型企业	Medium Scale Enterprises	70.57
小型企业	Small Enterprises	121.94

(100 million yuan)

应交税金及附加 Tax and Extra Charges	本年应付职工薪酬 Wages Welfarism Payable This Year	本年应交增值税 Value Added Payable of the Current Year	全部从业人员年平均人数(万人) Average Number of Empolyment of the Current Year (10 000 persons)
2172.65	**2671.87**	**876.55**	**274.51**
1750.97	2287.43	714.43	238.66
51.82	189.75	34.95	10.50
40.55	170.36	29.83	8.57
11.28	19.39	5.13	1.93
1.73	1.99	0.99	0.39
0.51	0.53	0.29	0.08
0.10	1.30	0.04	0.15
0.09	1.01	0.03	0.11
	0.01		
0.01	0.28		0.03
895.46	752.41	266.29	68.09
590.49	146.93	103.96	8.17
304.97	605.48	162.33	59.92
273.80	362.59	103.66	27.68
527.47	978.40	308.14	131.67
11.78	11.81	6.27	1.72
1.96	2.81	0.86	0.30
468.05	865.96	276.62	116.64
45.68	97.82	24.39	13.01
0.07	0.47	0.06	0.11
73.66	115.31	36.09	14.24
31.04	57.74	15.58	7.56
0.15	0.07	0.07	0.01
34.50	47.22	16.00	5.66
5.47	5.13	3.34	0.56
2.50	5.15	1.10	0.46
348.02	269.13	126.03	21.62
293.78	167.56	102.75	11.37
1.55	2.35	0.74	0.14
49.00	91.56	20.72	9.35
2.87	3.49	1.18	0.35
0.82	4.17	0.64	0.41
271.35	**435.69**	**92.79**	**42.18**
1189.45	883.61	351.14	53.98
968.22	826.83	293.96	106.73
1204.43	1845.04	582.59	167.78
1271.26	1054.23	373.26	74.69
321.84	673.52	159.40	72.75
579.56	944.12	343.90	127.07

13-2　续表 7　continued

单位:亿元

项　目	Item	企业单位数(个) Number of Enterprises (unit)
按行业分	**Grouped by sector**	
采矿业	**Mining and Qarrying**	**367**
煤炭开采和洗选业	Coal Mining and Processing	4
石油和天然气开采业	Petroleum and Natural Gas Extraction	1
黑色金属矿采选业	Ferrous Metals Mining and Processing	27
有色金属矿采选业	Non-ferrous Metals Mining and Processing	20
非金属矿采选业	Non-metal Minerals Mining and Processing	312
开采辅助活动	Mining Auxiliary Activities	1
其他采矿业	Other Minerals Mining and Processing	2
制造业	**Manufacturing**	**14878**
农副食品加工业	Food Processing	1459
食品制造业	Food Production	356
酒、饮料和精制茶制造业	Wine, Beverage and Refined Tea Production	401
烟草制品业	Tobacco Processing	7
纺织业	Textile Industry	894
纺织服装、服饰业	Textile, Garments, and Fashion Industry	451
皮革、毛皮、羽毛及其制品和制鞋业	Leather, Furs, Down and Related Products	149
木材加工和木、竹、藤、棕、草制品业	Timber Processing, Wood, Bamboo, Cane, Palm and Sraw Products	288
家具制造业	Furniture Manufacturing	130
造纸和纸制品业	Papermaking and Paper Products	199
印刷和记录媒介复制业	Printing and Record Processing	334
文教、工美、体育和娱乐用品制造业	Stationery, Education and Sports Goods	304
石油加工、炼焦和核燃料加工业	Petroleum Processing, Coking Products and Nuclear Fuel Processing	53
化学原料和化学制品制造业	Raw Chemical Material and Chemical Products	954
医药制造业	Medical and Pharmaceutical Products	447
化学纤维制造业	Chemical Fibers	18
橡胶和塑料制品业	Rubber and Plastic Products	575
非金属矿物制品业	Nonmetal Material Products	2028
黑色金属冶炼和压延加工业	Smelting and Pressing of Ferrous Metals	104
有色金属冶炼和压延加工业	Smelting and Pressing of Nonferrous Metals	153
金属制品业	Metal Products	856
通用设备制造业	Ordinary Machinery Manufacturing	726
专用设备制造业	Special Purpose Equipment Manufacturing	769
汽车制造业	Motor Manufacturing	1547
铁路、船舶、航空航天和其他运输设备制造业	Railway, Watercraft, Aviation and other Transporlation Equipment Manufacturing	151
电气机械和器材制造业	Electric Machinery and Equipment	691
计算机、通信和其他电子设备制造业	Telecommunication Computer, Equipment and Other Electronic Equipment Manufacturing	497
仪器仪表制造业	Instruments and Meters, Manufacturing	164
其他制造业	Other Manufacturing	43
废弃资源综合利用业	Waste Comprehensive Vtilization of Resources Industry	108
金属制品、机械和设备修理业	Metal Products, Machinery and Equipment Repairing	22
电力、燃气及水的生产和供应业	**Electric Power, Gas and Water Production and Supply**	**463**
电力、热力生产和供应业	Electric Power, Steam and Hot Water Production and Supply	246
燃气生产和供应业	Gas Production and Supply	91
水的生产和供应业	Tap Water Production and Supply	126

(100 million yuan)

工业总产值（当年价格） Total Output Value (current price)	资产总计 Total Assets	流动资产合计 Circulating Funds	应收帐款 Accounts Received	固定资产原价 Original Price of Fixed Assets
627.93	**816.98**	**326.34**	**60.83**	**598.73**
1.07	3.33	1.27	0.24	2.08
25.30	259.03	61.90	2.03	332.27
104.67	98.74	43.82	18.54	82.20
32.24	44.21	23.74	2.60	25.06
456.72	403.30	191.12	34.92	147.93
0.29	0.49	0.43	0.07	0.16
7.65	7.87	4.07	2.42	9.03
39886.07	**36849.97**	**20186.71**	**4918.58**	**17749.75**
3499.46	1552.48	805.41	162.85	1028.15
863.65	620.68	331.38	69.48	331.40
889.50	1084.90	711.80	72.51	424.65
716.24	634.77	499.46	38.27	135.62
2139.39	996.03	491.17	92.03	825.26
673.85	314.05	153.64	27.87	205.11
213.76	79.40	45.02	8.73	68.33
371.95	317.11	154.84	18.69	159.43
178.01	167.27	76.97	17.41	94.22
486.12	531.54	206.12	40.69	348.77
553.34	426.99	235.00	66.02	228.75
523.66	360.15	217.26	28.96	186.91
443.23	222.04	84.52	12.63	194.96
3345.73	3261.34	1182.26	213.68	2045.77
1252.41	1471.24	767.45	151.94	619.67
39.32	36.97	15.55	3.37	37.78
945.37	596.77	317.55	93.98	355.63
3115.55	2375.58	1185.71	432.38	1334.98
1826.01	1457.73	576.89	53.38	1727.89
869.50	349.37	176.53	30.29	231.14
1550.80	1215.62	784.28	229.74	514.39
1287.72	1073.72	620.01	184.28	499.74
1275.87	1230.05	813.06	256.71	532.03
6860.37	7642.70	4836.93	1026.61	2448.08
571.99	1115.70	721.09	131.31	360.98
1842.07	1656.65	1088.61	432.47	617.15
2588.08	5250.79	2599.95	902.21	1912.15
271.95	256.68	178.26	60.27	85.83
88.20	76.65	53.99	8.08	28.88
497.08	392.97	201.33	32.14	130.81
105.90	82.01	54.67	19.60	35.26
2253.04	**6528.54**	**921.80**	**303.18**	**7069.62**
1986.87	5654.43	596.00	243.19	6600.11
169.42	289.30	119.47	15.18	180.65
96.76	584.80	206.32	44.81	288.87

13-2 续表 8 continued

单位:亿元

项 目	Item	固定资产净额 NBV of Fixed Assets
按行业分	**Grouped by Sector**	
采矿业	**Mining and Qarrying**	**223.37**
煤炭开采和洗选业	Coal Mining and Processing	1.27
石油和天然气开采业	Petroleum and Natural Gas Extraction	103.55
黑色金属矿采选业	Ferrous Metals Mining and Processing	34.71
有色金属矿采选业	Non-ferrous Metals Mining and Processing	9.43
非金属矿采选业	Non-metal Minerals Mining and Processing	72.10
开采辅助活动	Mining Auxiliary Activities	0.02
其他采矿业	Other Minerals Mining and Processing	2.28
制造业	**Manufacturing**	**8601.63**
农副食品加工业	Food Processing	415.89
食品制造业	Food Production	156.82
酒、饮料和精制茶制造业	Wine, Beverage and Refined Tea Production	210.05
烟草制品业	Tobacco Processing	56.53
纺织业	Textile Industry	305.36
纺织服装、服饰业	Textile, Garments, and Fashion Industry	79.90
皮革、毛皮、羽毛及其制品和制鞋业	Leather, Furs, Down and Related Products	20.57
木材加工和木、竹、藤、棕、草制品业	Timber Processing, Wood, Bamboo, Cane, Palm and Sraw Products	72.59
家具制造业	Furniture Manufacturing	57.06
造纸和纸制品业	Papermaking and Paper Products	240.35
印刷和记录媒介复制业	Printing and Record Processing	111.91
文教、工美、体育和娱乐用品制造业	Stationery, Education and Sports Goods	68.71
石油加工、炼焦和核燃料加工业	Petroleum Processing, Coking Products and Nuclear Fuel Processing	90.00
化学原料和化学制品制造业	Raw Chemical Material and Chemical Products	864.68
医药制造业	Medical and Pharmaceutical Products	341.26
化学纤维制造业	Chemical Fibers	11.16
橡胶和塑料制品业	Rubber and Plastic Products	164.15
非金属矿物制品业	Nonmetal Material Products	656.91
黑色金属冶炼和压延加工业	Smelting and Pressing of Ferrous Metals	638.68
有色金属冶炼和压延加工业	Smelting and Pressing of Nonferrous Metals	122.28
金属制品业	Metal Products	242.78
通用设备制造业	Ordinary Machinery Manufacturing	218.83
专用设备制造业	Special Purpose Equipment Manufacturing	231.14
汽车制造业	Motor Manufacturing	1102.06
铁路、船舶、航空航天和其他运输设备制造业	Railway,Watercraft, Aviation and other Transporlation Equipment Manufacturing	201.45
电气机械和器材制造业	Electric Machinery and Equipment	332.88
计算机、通信和其他电子设备制造业	Telecommunication Computer, Equipment and Other Electronic Equipment Manufacturing	1438.43
仪器仪表制造业	Instruments and Meters, Manufacturing	36.76
其他制造业	Other Manufacturing	14.48
废弃资源综合利用业	Waste Comprehensive Vtilization of Resources Industry	87.37
金属制品、机械和设备修理业	Metal Products, Machinery and Equipment Repairing	10.60
电力、燃气及水的生产和供应业	**Electric Power, Gas and Water Production and Supply**	**3708.10**
电力、热力生产和供应业	Electric Power, Steam and Hot Water Production and Supply	3410.52
燃气生产和供应业	Gas Production and Supply	123.88
水的生产和供应业	Tap Water Production and Supply	173.70

(100 million yuan)

累计折旧 Accumulated Depreciation	负债合计 Total Liability	流动负债合计 Total Circulating Liability	应付账款 Account Payable
351.14	**436.16**	**268.69**	**49.25**
0.81	4.07	4.06	2.32
228.72	129.14	76.41	9.85
44.88	58.50	36.99	10.25
13.95	14.06	11.06	1.37
56.40	226.07	137.49	24.15
0.14	0.22	0.22	0.10
6.23	4.09	2.46	1.21
8291.37	**19161.87**	**15180.39**	**5243.86**
520.10	706.87	549.29	141.35
159.24	270.71	222.93	56.27
196.52	555.38	499.16	56.18
78.80	199.14	197.52	61.85
473.10	441.69	338.46	73.69
95.87	145.51	120.32	26.13
38.01	36.33	26.36	10.13
72.89	150.54	88.86	18.74
28.51	76.84	43.03	14.90
91.46	302.54	210.88	53.98
101.47	201.57	157.58	48.26
100.05	199.61	75.75	19.13
98.11	134.69	109.44	19.05
1092.35	1695.10	1140.57	281.00
249.44	616.03	501.84	105.17
25.66	18.96	15.22	4.21
171.92	263.46	216.34	64.78
583.96	1070.27	882.22	349.75
1071.15	792.30	722.27	265.79
99.68	217.46	167.46	45.57
242.00	684.26	582.94	172.68
246.81	569.67	442.65	143.58
252.57	688.76	606.95	200.93
1220.92	4124.51	3552.53	1386.08
147.42	705.58	625.14	223.55
263.72	913.38	798.62	355.44
452.90	2957.07	1924.95	964.36
44.23	132.02	103.90	37.32
13.48	42.82	40.10	9.67
36.39	204.92	182.67	17.93
22.63	43.89	34.44	16.36
3259.10	**3502.70**	**2065.53**	**445.87**
3101.69	2955.60	1735.61	385.77
53.17	191.06	171.97	27.61
104.23	356.04	157.95	32.50

13-2 续表 9 continued

单位:亿元

项 目	Item	所有者权益合计 Total Rights of Owners	实收资本 Assets Recevied
按行业分	**Grouped by sector**		
采矿业	**Mining and Qarrying**	**378.76**	**118.80**
煤炭开采和洗选业	Coal Mining and Processing	-0.74	1.06
石油和天然气开采业	Petroleum and Natural Gas Extraction	129.89	
黑色金属矿采选业	Ferrous Metals Mining and Processing	40.10	37.12
有色金属矿采选业	Non-ferrous Metals Mining and Processing	30.15	6.74
非金属矿采选业	Non-metal Minerals Mining and Processing	175.32	70.16
开采辅助活动	Mining Auxiliary Activities	0.26	0.20
其他采矿业	Other Minerals Mining and Processing	3.78	3.50
制造业	**Manufacturing**	**17606.26**	**7356.98**
农副食品加工业	Food Processing	830.97	309.59
食品制造业	Food Production	346.07	131.27
酒、饮料和精制茶制造业	Wine, Beverage and Refined Tea Production	528.43	144.74
烟草制品业	Tobacco Processing	435.63	31.62
纺织业	Textile Industry	543.06	183.90
纺织服装、服饰业	Textile, Garments, and Fashion Industry	166.38	77.64
皮革、毛皮、羽毛及其制品和制鞋业	Leather, Furs, Down and Related Products	42.62	16.36
木材加工和木、竹、藤、棕、草制品业	Timber Processing, Wood, Bamboo, Cane, Palm and Sraw Products	165.03	69.50
家具制造业	Furniture Manufacturing	89.74	36.67
造纸和纸制品业	Papermaking and Paper Products	228.84	156.18
印刷和记录媒介复制业	Printing and Record Processing	225.05	100.65
文教、工美、体育和娱乐用品制造业	Stationery, Education and Sports Goods	158.81	70.02
石油加工、炼焦和核燃料加工业	Petroleum Processing, Coking Products and Nuclear Fuel Processing	86.58	88.25
化学原料和化学制品制造业	Raw Chemical Material and Chemical Products	1546.69	589.75
医药制造业	Medical and Pharmaceutical Products	855.18	255.20
化学纤维制造业	Chemical Fibers	18.01	13.17
橡胶和塑料制品业	Rubber and Plastic Products	331.64	128.67
非金属矿物制品业	Nonmetal Material Products	1298.30	515.82
黑色金属冶炼和压延加工业	Smelting and Pressing of Ferrous Metals	665.42	232.21
有色金属冶炼和压延加工业	Smelting and Pressing of Nonferrous Metals	131.82	72.68
金属制品业	Metal Products	527.77	235.44
通用设备制造业	Ordinary Machinery Manufacturing	504.87	242.33
专用设备制造业	Special Purpose Equipment Manufacturing	540.32	227.80
汽车制造业	Motor Manufacturing	3512.36	966.85
铁路、船舶、航空航天和其他运输设备制造业	Railway, Watercraft, Aviation and other Transporlation Equipment Manufacturing	410.00	220.52
电气机械和器材制造业	Electric Machinery and Equipment	742.07	341.70
计算机、通信和其他电子设备制造业	Telecommunication Computer, Equipment and Other Electronic Equipment Manufacturing	2290.81	1686.76
仪器仪表制造业	Instruments and Meters, Manufacturing	124.12	48.26
其他制造业	Other Manufacturing	33.49	13.00
废弃资源综合利用业	Waste Comprehensive Vtilization of Resources Industry	187.78	139.49
金属制品、机械和设备修理业	Metal Products, Machinery and Equipment Repairing	38.39	10.93
电力、燃气及水的生产和供应业	**Electric Power, Gas and Water Production and Supply**	**3022.95**	**1375.19**
电力、热力生产和供应业	Electric Power, Steam and Hot Water Production and Supply	2699.00	1250.41
燃气生产和供应业	Gas Production and Supply	98.24	52.86
水的生产和供应业	Tap Water Production and Supply	225.71	71.93

(100 million yuan)

国家资本 National Assets	集体资本 Collective Assets	法人资本 Corperative Assets	个人资本 Individual Assets	港澳台资本 Assets from Hongkong, Macao and Taiwan Funded Enterprises	外商资本 Total Rights of the Owners Foreign Assets
43.06	**4.46**	**38.53**	**31.97**	**0.11**	**0.66**
		0.96	0.10		
32.08	0.48	0.80	3.76		
2.00	0.10	2.45	1.53		0.66
5.68	3.68	34.14	26.56	0.11	
		0.18	0.02		
3.30	0.20				
1188.84	**173.15**	**3697.35**	**1655.25**	**191.24**	**448.91**
4.31	5.62	110.07	151.81	18.84	18.93
16.95	3.04	51.27	44.56	2.96	12.49
16.36	2.90	50.38	33.17	19.20	22.73
30.20	1.05	0.37			
10.88	6.33	75.23	83.80	2.52	5.14
4.09	3.11	28.67	38.93	2.37	0.43
1.27		3.39	7.35	0.09	4.26
0.69	0.31	47.17	21.32		
1.25	0.02	26.51	8.72	0.16	
0.06	1.51	107.37	29.50	11.26	6.49
7.24	0.92	55.81	34.83	1.60	0.24
0.66	3.89	20.16	32.72	11.25	1.33
62.51	0.18	19.56	3.82	1.00	1.19
103.29	20.06	272.47	128.02	15.97	49.95
22.04	9.73	120.98	66.30	31.99	4.17
		4.38	2.23		6.55
1.79	0.88	67.23	53.31	4.07	1.39
33.93	12.61	234.14	199.42	7.05	26.54
120.58	1.62	78.19	30.40	1.22	0.20
12.90	0.81	28.48	15.55		14.94
33.94	2.30	103.05	88.52	6.49	1.13
52.45	21.99	85.47	71.83	3.39	7.18
35.42	6.20	108.45	68.77	0.33	8.64
283.36	56.25	310.60	124.47	12.03	180.09
73.56	0.06	131.09	11.58	3.00	1.23
28.82	7.87	170.52	99.30	2.40	32.79
223.27	3.15	1300.48	88.16	31.39	40.32
2.29	0.33	30.16	14.93	0.02	0.54
0.03	0.01	11.06	1.89		0.01
1.90	0.40	37.59	98.98	0.62	
2.81		7.06	1.06		
766.95	**15.75**	**499.94**	**29.67**	**35.16**	**24.87**
725.50	6.35	449.57	15.92	31.32	18.89
6.73	5.13	32.16	4.11	3.84	0.89
34.72	4.27	18.21	9.64		5.09

13-2 续表 10 continued

单位:亿元

项 目	Item	营业收入 Business Revenue
按行业分	**Grouped by sector**	
采矿业	**Mining and Qarrying**	**568.61**
煤炭开采和洗选业	Coal Mining and Processing	0.98
石油和天然气开采业	Petroleum and Natural Gas Extraction	61.18
黑色金属矿采选业	Ferrous Metals Mining and Processing	95.06
有色金属矿采选业	Non-ferrous Metals Mining and Processing	27.70
非金属矿采选业	Non-metal Minerals Mining and Processing	375.77
开采辅助活动	Mining Auxiliary Activities	0.28
其他采矿业	Other Minerals Mining and Processing	7.65
制造业	**Manufacturing**	**38059.10**
农副食品加工业	Food Processing	3235.91
食品制造业	Food Production	846.78
酒、饮料和精制茶制造业	Wine, Beverage and Refined Tea Production	765.31
烟草制品业	Tobacco Processing	791.98
纺织业	Textile Industry	2017.85
纺织服装、服饰业	Textile, Garments, and Fashion Industry	628.34
皮革、毛皮、羽毛及其制品和制鞋业	Leather, Furs, Down and Related Products	197.49
木材加工和木、竹、藤、棕、草制品业	Timber Processing, Wood, Bamboo, Cane, Palm and Sraw Products	329.46
家具制造业	Furniture Manufacturing	162.10
造纸和纸制品业	Papermaking and Paper Products	453.30
印刷和记录媒介复制业	Printing and Record Processing	511.64
文教、工美、体育和娱乐用品制造业	Stationery, Education and Sports Goods	482.98
石油加工、炼焦和核燃料加工业	Petroleum Processing, Coking Products and Nuclear Fuel Processing	564.16
化学原料和化学制品制造业	Raw Chemical Material and Chemical Products	3156.85
医药制造业	Medical and Pharmaceutical Products	1141.10
化学纤维制造业	Chemical Fibers	39.60
橡胶和塑料制品业	Rubber and Plastic Products	878.30
非金属矿物制品业	Nonmetal Material Products	2926.72
黑色金属冶炼和压延加工业	Smelting and Pressing of Ferrous Metals	1860.17
有色金属冶炼和压延加工业	Smelting and Pressing of Nonferrous Metals	801.42
金属制品业	Metal Products	1503.10
通用设备制造业	Ordinary Machinery Manufacturing	1232.60
专用设备制造业	Special Purpose Equipment Manufacturing	1223.52
汽车制造业	Motor Manufacturing	6535.27
铁路、船舶、航空航天和其他运输设备制造业	Railway, Watercraft, Aviation and other Transporlation Equipment Manufacturing	508.33
电气机械和器材制造业	Electric Machinery and Equipment	1813.74
计算机、通信和其他电子设备制造业	Telecommunication Computer, Equipment and Other Electronic Equipment Manufacturing	2568.96
仪器仪表制造业	Instruments and Meters, Manufacturing	242.00
其他制造业	Other Manufacturing	85.11
废弃资源综合利用业	Waste Comprehensive Vtilization of Resources Industry	452.45
金属制品、机械和设备修理业	Metal Products, Machinery and Equipment Repairing	102.56
电力、燃气及水的生产和供应业	**Electric Power, Gas and Water Production and Supply**	**2297.48**
电力、热力生产和供应业	Electric Power, Steam and Hot Water Production and Supply	2012.30
燃气生产和供应业	Gas Production and Supply	176.89
水的生产和供应业	Tap Water Production and Supply	108.29

(100 million yuan)

主营业务收入 Revenue of Major Business	营业成本 Business Cost	税金及附加 Tax	销售费用 Selling Expenses
525.44	**451.09**	**14.20**	**23.98**
0.98	0.76	0.02	0.01
25.15	59.76	1.73	0.64
93.54	76.88	1.52	1.85
27.10	14.64	0.81	0.14
371.91	293.10	9.92	20.91
0.28	0.23		0.01
6.48	5.73	0.20	0.42
37043.08	**31545.05**	**886.23**	**1151.65**
3205.67	2853.39	17.67	79.26
831.26	698.85	5.04	40.29
742.51	531.35	21.37	57.34
743.30	210.65	445.22	11.62
1989.05	1663.77	18.97	59.03
623.96	538.44	5.34	17.65
196.38	171.90	0.86	3.43
323.61	285.99	2.58	8.84
161.29	135.05	1.73	4.67
448.97	382.88	2.62	19.23
507.31	421.52	3.12	16.28
478.98	411.51	4.83	11.75
364.06	460.37	80.38	2.85
3095.93	2611.68	79.82	90.54
1110.40	749.60	8.50	134.70
36.80	36.06	0.38	1.07
867.59	732.77	5.54	26.86
2891.14	2385.36	26.61	100.14
1701.26	1720.34	7.62	12.01
774.30	689.87	3.97	5.46
1478.78	1297.84	8.16	40.95
1221.73	1035.77	7.79	40.44
1209.61	1015.02	6.17	40.57
6420.19	5503.22	92.19	188.86
499.75	446.10	2.21	6.75
1751.86	1548.29	10.88	53.92
2497.90	2241.51	8.12	56.59
238.70	178.89	1.43	12.49
84.43	73.85	0.34	1.29
444.13	428.96	3.86	4.43
102.25	84.25	2.89	2.36
2240.58	**1845.95**	**15.87**	**14.65**
1973.00	1610.91	14.42	1.19
168.98	149.31	0.53	6.64
98.60	85.73	0.92	6.82

13-2 续表 11 continued

单位:亿元

项　目	Item	管理费用 Management Expenses
按行业分	Grouped by sector	
采矿业	**Mining and Qarrying**	**34.08**
煤炭开采和洗选业	Coal Mining and Processing	0.15
石油和天然气开采业	Petroleum and Natural Gas Extraction	8.84
黑色金属矿采选业	Ferrous Metals Mining and Processing	6.29
有色金属矿采选业	Non-ferrous Metals Mining and Processing	2.22
非金属矿采选业	Non-metal Minerals Mining and Processing	16.10
开采辅助活动	Mining Auxiliary Activities	0.02
其他采矿业	Other Minerals Mining and Processing	0.45
制造业	**Manufacturing**	**1325.31**
农副食品加工业	Food Processing	73.86
食品制造业	Food Production	29.48
酒、饮料和精制茶制造业	Wine, Beverage and Refined Tea Production	35.88
烟草制品业	Tobacco Processing	21.46
纺织业	Textile Industry	78.52
纺织服装、服饰业	Textile, Garments, and Fashion Industry	23.09
皮革、毛皮、羽毛及其制品和制鞋业	Leather, Furs, Down and Related Products	7.50
木材加工和木、竹、藤、棕、草制品业	Timber Processing, Wood, Bamboo, Cane, Palm and Sraw Products	10.01
家具制造业	Furniture Manufacturing	5.26
造纸和纸制品业	Papermaking and Paper Products	15.99
印刷和记录媒介复制业	Printing and Record Processing	22.21
文教、工美、体育和娱乐用品制造业	Stationery, Education and Sports Goods	18.38
石油加工、炼焦和核燃料加工业	Petroleum Processing, Coking Products and Nuclear Fuel Processing	6.10
化学原料和化学制品制造业	Raw Chemical Material and Chemical Products	115.53
医药制造业	Medical and Pharmaceutical Products	67.73
化学纤维制造业	Chemical Fibers	1.33
橡胶和塑料制品业	Rubber and Plastic Products	34.00
非金属矿物制品业	Nonmetal Material Products	104.57
黑色金属冶炼和压延加工业	Smelting and Pressing of Ferrous Metals	32.33
有色金属冶炼和压延加工业	Smelting and Pressing of Nonferrous Metals	9.35
金属制品业	Metal Products	50.39
通用设备制造业	Ordinary Machinery Manufacturing	56.75
专用设备制造业	Special Purpose Equipment Manufacturing	52.27
汽车制造业	Motor Manufacturing	260.69
铁路、船舶、航空航天和其他运输设备制造业	Railway, Watercraft, Aviation and other Transporlation Equipment Manufacturing	24.78
电气机械和器材制造业	Electric Machinery and Equipment	63.91
计算机、通信和其他电子设备制造业	Telecommunication Computer, Equipment and Other Electronic Equipment Manufacturing	70.53
仪器仪表制造业	Instruments and Meters, Manufacturing	15.30
其他制造业	Other Manufacturing	4.11
废弃资源综合利用业	Waste Comprehensive Vtilization of Resources Industry	8.93
金属制品、机械和设备修理业	Metal products, Machinery and Equipment Repairing	5.09
电力、燃气及水的生产和供应业	**Electric Power, Gas and Water Production and Supply**	**57.67**
电力、热力生产和供应业	Electric Power, Steam and Hot Water Production and Supply	42.50
燃气生产和供应业	Gas Production and Supply	5.47
水的生产和供应业	Tap Water Production and Supply	9.70

(100 million yuan)

财务费用 Financial Expenses	利息费用 Interest Expenses	利息收入 Interest Income	其他收益 Other Income
10.26	**7.43**	**0.72**	**1.82**
1.95	2.33	0.39	1.31
1.64	1.41	0.17	0.37
0.03	0.11	0.12	0.01
6.54	3.48	0.04	0.12
0.11	0.11		0.01
243.76	**221.59**	**68.32**	**133.80**
25.53	14.86	0.78	2.22
3.50	3.39	1.44	1.59
7.10	6.49	2.03	2.17
–4.14	0.01	3.61	0.47
25.97	10.44	0.82	1.24
4.70	2.51	0.11	0.13
0.83	0.17	0.01	0.01
3.63	2.29	0.03	0.26
1.44	0.93	0.11	0.23
6.99	5.70	0.38	1.80
3.83	2.53	–0.23	0.66
3.64	1.38	0.01	0.92
1.68	2.37	0.93	0.05
36.91	32.17	3.40	5.79
10.35	12.32	2.84	7.66
0.58	0.44	0.01	0.08
7.93	5.53	0.13	1.93
27.37	10.96	1.05	4.86
6.53	7.28	1.87	0.80
4.67	4.63	0.67	2.97
12.34	7.70	0.94	4.44
11.80	7.95	0.95	3.34
11.14	8.87	0.95	3.59
7.01	27.80	30.42	19.40
–0.03	3.47	3.13	4.43
10.37	6.95	0.35	8.32
2.27	24.29	11.25	43.19
2.82	1.84	0.12	2.35
0.05	0.11	0.14	0.31
5.84	5.05	0.06	8.58
1.09	1.16	0.02	0.02
82.01	**77.93**	**1.97**	**5.17**
75.60	71.87	1.78	4.20
2.12	2.02	0.09	0.22
4.30	4.04	0.09	0.74

13-2 续表 12 continued

单位:亿元

项 目	Item	投资收益 Investment Income
按行业分	Grouped by sector	
采矿业	Mining and Qarrying	**0.30**
煤炭开采和洗选业	Coal Mining and Processing	
石油和天然气开采业	Petroleum and Natural Gas Extraction	
黑色金属矿采选业	Ferrous Metals Mining and Processing	
有色金属矿采选业	Non-ferrous Metals Mining and Processing	
非金属矿采选业	Non-metal Minerals Mining and Processing	0.30
开采辅助活动	Mining Auxiliary Activities	
其他采矿业	Other Minerals Mining and Processing	
制造业	Manufacturing	**207.41**
农副食品加工业	Food Processing	8.24
食品制造业	Food Production	3.23
酒、饮料和精制茶制造业	Wine, Beverage and Refined Tea Production	5.26
烟草制品业	Tobacco Processing	6.56
纺织业	Textile Industry	2.88
纺织服装、服饰业	Textile, Garments, and Fashion Industry	0.49
皮革、毛皮、羽毛及其制品和制鞋业	Leather, Furs, Down and Related Products	
木材加工和木、竹、藤、棕、草制品业	Timber Processing, Wood, Bamboo, Cane, Palm and Sraw Products	0.01
家具制造业	Furniture Manufacturing	0.13
造纸和纸制品业	Papermaking and Paper Products	0.08
印刷和记录媒介复制业	Printing and Record Processing	0.44
文教、工美、体育和娱乐用品制造业	Stationery, Education and Sports Goods	0.20
石油加工、炼焦和核燃料加工业	Petroleum Processing, Coking Products and Nuclear Fuel Processing	-0.18
化学原料和化学制品制造业	Raw Chemical Material and Chemical Products	15.99
医药制造业	Medical and Pharmaceutical Products	4.01
化学纤维制造业	Chemical Fibers	
橡胶和塑料制品业	Rubber and Plastic Products	1.61
非金属矿物制品业	Nonmetal Material Products	7.59
黑色金属冶炼和压延加工业	Smelting and Pressing of Ferrous Metals	3.40
有色金属冶炼和压延加工业	Smelting and Pressing of Nonferrous Metals	-20.68
金属制品业	Metal Products	0.13
通用设备制造业	Ordinary Machinery Manufacturing	1.50
专用设备制造业	Special Purpose Equipment Manufacturing	1.08
汽车制造业	Motor Manufacturing	150.89
铁路、船舶、航空航天和其他运输设备制造业	Railway, Watercraft, Aviation and other Transporlation Equipment Manufacturing	4.28
电气机械和器材制造业	Electric Machinery and Equipment	3.38
计算机、通信和其他电子设备制造业	Telecommunication Computer, Equipment and Other Electronic Equipment Manufacturing	6.28
仪器仪表制造业	Instruments and Meters, Manufacturing	0.72
其他制造业	Other Manufacturing	-0.01
废弃资源综合利用业	Waste Comprehensive Vtilization of Resources Industry	-0.08
金属制品、机械和设备修理业	Metal Products, Machinery and Equipment Repairing	0.01
电力、燃气及水的生产和供应业	Electric Power, Gas and Water Production and Supply	**43.24**
电力、热力生产和供应业	Electric Power, Steam and Hot Water Production and Supply	40.37
燃气生产和供应业	Gas Production and Supply	1.12
水的生产和供应业	Tap Water Production and Supply	1.75

(100 million yuan)

营业利润 Operating Profits	营业外收入 Non-operating Income	营业外支出 Non-operating Expense	利润总额 Total Profits	所得税费用 Income Tax
30.92	**1.88**	**3.68**	**29.11**	**6.73**
0.04		0.03	0.01	
-12.43	0.88	0.59	-12.14	1.78
6.92	0.09	1.54	5.46	0.75
9.22	0.15	0.21	9.16	1.81
26.65	0.75	1.16	26.25	2.32
0.51	0.01	0.15	0.37	0.06
2276.34	**112.81**	**94.05**	**2294.88**	**301.67**
163.69	8.07	3.76	167.78	8.21
61.78	2.78	1.84	62.72	6.84
101.96	5.15	6.46	100.65	19.33
109.04	0.19	1.20	108.02	24.78
148.62	4.54	1.31	151.85	17.53
34.90	0.88	0.51	35.27	1.57
10.76	0.25	0.06	10.95	0.61
12.59	0.54	0.98	12.15	0.74
11.40	0.72	0.04	12.08	1.26
19.45	10.61	0.53	29.53	5.12
36.49	2.04	0.78	37.75	3.83
26.75	0.64	0.23	27.17	1.71
2.30	0.32	0.51	2.11	0.70
182.37	7.83	9.69	180.52	17.95
140.26	4.81	3.58	141.49	17.87
-0.34	0.14	0.02	-0.23	0.10
57.73	2.36	0.46	59.64	4.51
257.88	6.74	5.32	259.30	33.87
47.04	3.52	1.64	48.91	10.77
8.65	6.10	0.78	13.98	0.73
66.82	4.07	2.89	68.00	7.25
57.30	4.31	1.27	60.34	4.01
65.04	3.65	1.51	67.18	6.74
466.98	15.31	42.34	439.95	76.72
30.29	0.92	0.45	30.76	1.92
85.49	4.33	2.34	87.48	10.35
41.03	8.13	2.48	46.67	11.00
17.52	0.95	0.42	18.05	2.43
3.83	0.35	0.06	4.12	0.32
4.77	2.14	0.59	6.32	2.77
3.96	0.41	0.01	4.36	0.14
323.04	**7.75**	**7.84**	**322.95**	**71.41**
306.84	4.75	7.11	304.47	67.18
13.88	0.60	0.32	14.16	3.04
2.32	2.40	0.40	4.31	1.19

13-2 续表 13 continued

单位:亿元

项 目	Item	亏损企业亏损总额 Total Loss of Enterprises Running
按行业分	**Grouped by sector**	
采矿业	**Mining and Qarrying**	**15.49**
煤炭开采和洗选业	Coal Mining and Processing	0.03
石油和天然气开采业	Petroleum and Natural Gas Extraction	12.14
黑色金属矿采选业	Ferrous Metals Mining and Processing	0.06
有色金属矿采选业	Non-ferrous Metals Mining and Processing	0.13
非金属矿采选业	Non-metal Minerals Mining and Processing	3.11
开采辅助活动	Mining Auxiliary Activities	
其他采矿业	Other Minerals Mining and Processing	0.02
制造业	**Manufacturing**	**321.42**
农副食品加工业	Food Processing	8.05
食品制造业	Food Production	1.83
酒、饮料和精制茶制造业	Wine, Beverage and Refined Tea Production	3.06
烟草制品业	Tobacco Processing	0.06
纺织业	Textile Industry	4.69
纺织服装、服饰业	Textile, Garments, and Fashion Industry	2.10
皮革、毛皮、羽毛及其制品和制鞋业	Leather, Furs, Down and Related Products	0.33
木材加工和木、竹、藤、棕、草制品业	Timber Processing, Wood, Bamboo, Cane, Palm and Sraw Products	3.09
家具制造业	Furniture Manufacturing	0.45
造纸和纸制品业	Papermaking and Paper Products	2.47
印刷和记录媒介复制业	Printing and Record Processing	3.17
文教、工美、体育和娱乐用品制造业	Stationery, Education and Sports Goods	0.54
石油加工、炼焦和核燃料加工业	Petroleum Processing, Coking Products and Nuclear Fuel Processing	7.58
化学原料和化学制品制造业	Raw Chemical Material and Chemical Products	28.67
医药制造业	Medical and Pharmaceutical Products	10.71
化学纤维制造业	Chemical Fibers	1.53
橡胶和塑料制品业	Rubber and Plastic Products	1.97
非金属矿物制品业	Nonmetal Material Products	8.94
黑色金属冶炼和压延加工业	Smelting and Pressing of Ferrous Metals	2.02
有色金属冶炼和压延加工业	Smelting and Pressing of Nonferrous Metals	3.94
金属制品业	Metal Products	12.58
通用设备制造业	Ordinary Machinery Manufacturing	7.82
专用设备制造业	Special Purpose Equipment Manufacturing	10.83
汽车制造业	Motor Manufacturing	98.94
铁路、船舶、航空航天和其他运输设备制造业	Railway, Watercraft, Aviation and other Transporlation Equipment Manufacturing	0.41
电气机械和器材制造业	Electric Machinery and Equipment	13.06
计算机、通信和其他电子设备制造业	Telecommunication Computer, Equipment and Other Electronic Equipment Manufacturing	69.03
仪器仪表制造业	Instruments and Meters, Manufacturing	6.78
其他制造业	Other Manufacturing	0.08
废弃资源综合利用业	Waste Comprehensive Vtilization of Resources Industry	6.39
金属制品、机械和设备修理业	Metal Products, Machinery and Equipment Repairing	0.28
电力、燃气及水的生产和供应业	**Electric Power, Gas and Water Production and Supply**	**26.12**
电力、热力生产和供应业	Electric Power, Steam and Hot Water Production and Supply	19.01
燃气生产和供应业	Gas Production and Supply	1.47
水的生产和供应业	Tap Water Production and Supply	5.65

(100 million yuan)

应交税金及附加 Tax and Extra Charges	本年应付职工薪酬 Wages Welfarism Payable this year	本年应交增值税 Value Added Payable of the	全部从业人员年平均人数(万人) Average Number of Empolyment of the Current Year (10 000 persons)
35.34	**53.63**	**14.41**	**4.89**
0.08	0.15	0.06	0.03
4.92	19.14	1.40	1.02
5.49	10.53	3.22	1.00
3.98	3.93	1.36	0.40
20.35	18.35	8.11	2.36
	0.02		
0.52	1.50	0.26	0.08
1957.72	**2397.12**	**769.82**	**258.60**
50.92	115.37	25.04	14.98
27.17	49.17	15.28	6.78
63.75	53.46	23.05	6.16
548.48	25.87	78.49	0.73
71.84	144.13	35.33	19.59
16.62	66.42	9.71	9.64
4.41	11.87	2.94	2.28
8.15	18.46	4.83	2.92
5.08	13.40	2.08	1.87
18.67	24.53	10.93	3.13
17.61	45.39	10.66	6.29
14.53	28.63	7.99	4.14
91.96	9.47	10.88	0.70
144.02	160.61	46.25	17.27
63.89	108.29	37.51	12.69
1.35	3.34	0.87	0.51
21.89	50.01	11.84	7.23
127.74	168.45	67.26	20.43
48.91	86.22	30.52	5.32
22.99	37.66	18.29	3.24
45.74	95.20	30.33	12.29
31.92	89.63	20.12	10.37
34.10	101.88	21.19	10.25
330.48	410.72	161.57	35.28
9.55	63.50	5.42	5.25
48.96	119.60	27.73	12.56
46.10	233.09	26.98	20.06
10.51	27.84	6.65	2.68
1.42	7.85	0.76	0.75
24.40	9.82	17.77	1.24
4.58	17.24	1.55	2.01
179.60	**221.12**	**92.32**	**11.02**
168.05	189.02	86.45	7.88
6.26	9.92	2.69	0.95
5.28	22.18	3.18	2.19

13-3 国有控股工业企业单位数和主要经济指标(2020)

单位:亿元

项 目	Item	企业单位数(个) Number of Enterprises (unit)	工业总产值(当年价格) Total Output Value (current price)
总计	**Total**	**798**	**10998.17**
在总计中:	**Of the Total**		
亏损企业	Enterprises Running Under Deficit	159	2101.39
在总计中:	**Of the Total:**		
中央企业	Central Enterprises	279	8401.96
地方企业	Local Enterprises	519	2596.21
在总计中:	**Of the Total:**		
轻工业	Light Industry	152	1379.92
重工业	Heavy Industry	646	9618.25
在总计中:	**Of the Total:**		
大型企业	Large Scale Enterprises	94	8345.08
中型企业	Medium Scale Enterprises	183	1534.28
小型企业	Small Enterprises	521	1118.82
按行业分	**Grouped by Sector**		
采矿业	**Mining and Qarrying**	**28**	**122.62**
煤炭开采和洗选业	Coal Mining and Processing		
石油和天然气开采业	Petroleum and Natural Gas Extraction	1	25.30
黑色金属矿采选业	Ferrous Metals Mining and Processing	3	56.24
有色金属矿采选业	Non-ferrous Metals Mining and Processing	2	11.37
非金属矿采选业	Non-metal Minerals Mining and Processing	21	22.30
开采辅助活动	Mining Auxiliary Activities		
其他采矿业	Other Minerals Mining and Processing	1	7.41
制造业	**Manufacturing**	**557**	**8959.98**
农副食品加工业	Food Processing	33	130.34
食品制造业	Food Production	12	79.41
酒、饮料和精制茶制造业	Wine, Beverage and Refined Tea Production	13	26.16
烟草制品业	Tobacco Processing	6	716.03
纺织业	Textile Industry	10	50.30
纺织服装、服饰业	Textile, Garments, and Fashion Industry	8	9.83
皮革、毛皮、羽毛及其制品和制鞋业	Leather, Furs, Down and Related Products		
木材加工和木、竹、藤、棕、草制品业	Timber Processing, Wood, Bamboo, Cane, Palm and Sraw Products	4	4.68
家具制造业	Furniture Manufacturing		
造纸和纸制品业	Papermaking and Paper Products	3	13.59
印刷和记录媒介复制业	Printing and Record Processing	15	49.32
文教、工美、体育和娱乐用品制造业	Stationery, Education and Sports Goods	3	1.29
石油加工、炼焦和核燃料加工业	Petroleum Processing, Coking Products and Nuclear Fuel Processing	7	262.02
化学原料和化学制品制造业	Raw Chemical Material and Chemical Products	49	853.97
医药制造业	Medical and Pharmaceutical Products	20	94.49
化学纤维制造业	Chemical Fibers		
橡胶和塑料制品业	Rubber and Plastic Products	10	53.54
非金属矿物制品业	Nonmetal Material Products	60	233.51
黑色金属冶炼和压延加工业	Smelting and Pressing of Ferrous Metals	11	1013.02
有色金属冶炼和压延加工业	Smelting and Pressing of Nonferrous Metals	5	449.27
金属制品业	Metal Products	24	224.45
通用设备制造业	Ordinary Machinery Manufacturing	27	114.18
专用设备制造业	Special Purpose Equipment Manufacturing	32	171.32
汽车制造业	Motor Manufacturing	79	2882.58
铁路、船舶、航空航天和其他运输设备制造业	Railway, Watercraft, Aviation and other Transporlation Equipment Manufacturing	33	373.21
电气机械和器材制造业	Electric Machinery and Equipment	36	299.68
计算机、通信和其他电子设备制造业	Telecommunication Computer, Equipment and Other Electronic Equipment Manufacturing	33	726.32
仪器仪表制造业	Instruments and Meters, Manufacturing	14	39.40
其他制造业	Other Manufacturing	3	44.79
废弃资源综合利用业	Waste Comprehensive Vtilization of Resources Industry	3	17.69
金属制品、机械和设备修理业	Metal Products, Machinery and Equipment Repairing	4	25.59
电力、燃气及水的生产和供应业	**Electric Power, Gas and Water Production and Supply**	**213**	**1915.56**
电力、热力生产和供应业	Electric Power, Steam and Hot Water Production and Supply	126	1789.34
燃气生产和供应业	Gas Production and Supply	15	69.02
水的生产和供应业	Tap Water Production and Supply	72	57.20

Number and Main Economic Indicators of State-Holding Industrial Enterprises(2020)

(100 million yuan)

资产总计 Total Assets	流动资产合计 Circulating Funds	固定资产原价 Original Value of Fixed Assets	固定资产净额 NBV of Fixed Assets	营业收入 Revenue	全部从业人员年平均人数(万人) Average Number of Empolyment of the Curreat Year (10 000 Persons)
19598.26	**8282.20**	**12425.86**	**6036.09**	**10682.36**	**53.98**
4798.45	1147.08	4725.07	2347.09	2184.21	13.75
13299.89	5637.28	9428.95	4263.09	7979.00	31.18
6298.37	2644.92	2996.91	1773.01	2703.36	22.80
1462.16	982.04	455.89	228.05	1492.09	5.94
18136.09	7300.16	11969.97	5808.04	9190.27	48.04
14950.08	6101.17	9720.74	4585.59	7997.41	37.32
2447.93	1249.01	1309.25	620.44	1578.15	10.43
2200.24	932.02	1395.87	830.06	1106.81	6.23
394.03	**130.58**	**414.72**	**134.93**	**152.46**	**1.84**
259.03	61.90	332.27	103.55	61.18	1.02
54.66	27.97	48.05	17.48	51.96	0.44
22.32	10.16	15.75	4.67	11.57	0.19
50.56	26.71	9.84	7.06	20.34	0.12
7.46	3.84	8.81	2.17	7.41	0.07
13650.84	**7520.34**	**5704.38**	**2688.09**	**8561.90**	**43.02**
39.85	24.72	17.51	8.61	124.59	0.37
114.24	58.14	36.39	21.70	100.40	0.76
43.01	21.98	22.64	8.45	21.30	0.42
632.66	499.20	133.80	55.21	791.78	0.72
72.55	48.66	29.55	15.19	52.06	0.54
33.37	22.39	9.48	3.11	8.70	0.52
6.62	1.93	1.68	0.09	2.75	0.04
27.18	13.80	15.68	8.24	13.16	0.08
83.70	49.90	44.88	20.02	56.46	0.31
1.98	1.49	0.24	0.15	1.39	0.03
112.63	25.23	132.54	61.82	247.60	0.32
1443.74	353.99	853.95	380.00	882.01	3.82
205.01	98.37	79.31	48.37	96.91	0.87
56.55	29.09	21.49	17.26	53.17	0.37
331.11	154.63	148.98	92.47	221.81	1.26
883.45	325.83	1404.90	438.16	858.90	2.33
192.78	89.99	151.44	77.68	411.83	1.21
377.15	272.19	115.56	57.83	233.30	1.66
256.36	169.99	89.85	44.75	110.59	1.82
266.83	185.16	109.01	47.97	180.68	1.42
4530.06	3003.28	905.77	342.51	2625.75	10.19
970.46	625.21	306.94	179.51	345.95	3.59
450.39	295.24	144.48	84.22	313.85	2.12
2372.22	1042.75	876.56	648.72	674.39	5.90
64.23	44.44	23.87	12.71	38.43	0.56
48.41	35.28	17.63	8.64	44.08	0.34
7.37	5.01	2.03	1.67	17.75	0.02
26.93	22.45	8.22	3.03	32.31	1.43
5553.33	**631.29**	**6306.78**	**3213.09**	**1967.98**	**9.15**
4997.04	443.22	5987.74	3013.73	1824.37	7.21
109.49	26.80	92.14	66.36	72.23	0.35
446.80	161.27	226.90	133.00	71.38	1.59

13-4 集体工业企业单位数和主要经济指标（2020）

单位：亿元

项 目	Item	企业单位数（个）Number of Enterprises (unit)	工业总产值（当年价格）Total Output Value (current price)
总计	**Total**	**32**	**44.03**
在总计中：	**Of the Total:**		
亏损企业	Enterprises Running Under Deficit	3	4.58
在总计中：	**Of the Total:**		
轻工业	Light Industry	9	10.13
重工业	Heavy Industry	23	33.90
在总计中：	**Of the Total:**		
大型企业	Large Scale Enterprises		
中型企业	Medium Scale Enterprises	3	7.72
小型企业	Small Enterprises	29	36.31
按行业分	**Grouped by sector**		
采矿业	**Mining and Qarrying**	**9**	**17.49**
煤炭开采和洗选业	Coal Mining and Processing		
石油和天然气开采业	Petroleum and Natural Gas Extraction		
黑色金属矿采选业	Ferrous Metals Mining and Processing	3	7.51
有色金属矿采选业	Non-ferrous Metals Mining and Processing	1	0.42
非金属矿采选业	Non-metal Minerals Mining and Processing	5	9.56
开采辅助活动	Mining Auxiliary Activities		
其他采矿业	Other Minerals Mining and Processing		
制造业	**Manufacturing**	**20**	**21.01**
农副食品加工业	Food Processing		
食品制造业	Food Production		
酒、饮料和精制茶制造业	Wine, Beverage and Refined Tea Production		
烟草制品业	Tobacco Processing		
纺织业	Textile Industry	1	1.19
纺织服装、服饰业	Textile, Garments, and Fashion Industry	2	0.48
皮革、毛皮、羽毛及其制品和制鞋业	Leather, Furs, Down and Related Products		
木材加工和木、竹、藤、棕、草制品业	Timber Processing, Wood, Bamboo, Cane, and Nuclear Fuel Processing		
家具制造业	Furniture Manufacturing		
造纸和纸制品业	Papermaking and Paper Products		
印刷和记录媒介复制业	Printing and Record Processing	2	4.07
文教、工美、体育和娱乐用品制造业	Stationery, Education and Sports Goods		
石油加工、炼焦和核燃料加工业	Petroleum Processing, Coking Products and Nuclear Fuel Processing		
化学原料和化学制品制造业	Raw Chemical Material and Chemical Products		
医药制造业	Medical and Pharmaceutical Products	1	0.31
化学纤维制造业	Chemical Fibers		
橡胶和塑料制品业	Rubber and Plastic Products	3	4.07
非金属矿物制品业	Nonmetal Material Products	3	5.46
黑色金属冶炼和压延加工业	Smelting and Pressing of Ferrous Metals	1	3.33
有色金属冶炼和压延加工业	Smelting and Pressing of Nonferrous Metals		
金属制品业	Metal Products		
通用设备制造业	Ordinary Machinery Manufacturing	1	
专用设备制造业	Special Purpose Equipment Manufacturing		
汽车制造业	Motor Manufacturing	3	1.65
铁路、船舶、航空航天和其他运输设备制造业	Railway, Watercraft, Aviation and other Transporlation Equipment Manufacturing	2	0.45
电气机械和器材制造业	Electric Machinery and Equipment		
计算机、通信和其他电子设备制造业	Telecommunication Computer, Equipment and Other Electronic Equipment Manufacturing		
仪器仪表制造业	Instruments and Meters, Manufacturing		
其他制造业	Other Manufacturing		
废弃资源综合利用业	Waste Comprehensive Vtilization of Resources Industry	1	
金属制品、机械和设备修理业	Metal Products, Machinery and Equipment Repairing		
电力、燃气及水的生产和供应业	**Electric Power, Gas and Water Production and Supply**	**3**	**5.53**
电力、热力生产和供应业	Electric Power, Steam and Hot Water Production and Supply		
燃气生产和供应业	Gas Production and Supply		
水的生产和供应业	Tap Water Production and Supply	3	5.53

Number and Main Economic Indicators of Collective-Owned Industrial Enterprises(2020)

(100 million yuan)

资产总计 Total Assets	流动资产合计 Circulating Funds	固定资产原价 Original Value of Fixed Assets	固定资产净额 NBV of Fixed Assets	营业收入 Revenue	全部从业人员年平均人数(万人) Average Number of Empolyment of the Curreat Year (10 000 Persons)
30.60	**17.52**	**16.07**	**8.58**	**39.49**	**0.39**
12.55	5.70	7.55	5.53	3.94	0.07
4.07	2.61	1.41	0.70	9.92	0.13
26.54	14.91	14.66	7.88	29.56	0.26
13.33	6.07	7.70	5.55	6.35	0.11
17.27	11.46	8.37	3.04	33.14	0.27
5.77	**2.58**	**2.36**	**1.43**	**16.2**	**0.12**
2.14	0.81	0.94	0.85	7.43	0.05
0.08	0.04	0.05	0.03	0.42	
3.55	1.73	1.37	0.55	8.35	0.07
13.57	**9.83**	**6.62**	**1.74**	**20.47**	**0.21**
0.24	0.11	0.08	0.07	1.19	0.01
0.52	0.41	0.11	0.02	0.58	0.02
0.66	0.25	0.28	0.05	4.06	0.02
0.38	0.05	0.31	0.25	0.29	
2.27	1.79	0.63	0.32	3.80	0.07
6.27	5.49	3.26	0.61	5.20	0.03
2.04	0.66	1.03	0.32	3.30	0.03
0.57	0.51	0.74	0.09	1.6	0.02
0.62	0.56	0.18	0.01	0.45	0.01
11.25	**5.12**	**7.09**	**5.40**	**2.82**	**0.05**
11.25	5.12	7.09	5.40	2.82	0.05

13-5 外商投资和港澳台商投资工业企业单位数和主要经济指标(2020)

单位:亿元

项 目	Item	企业单位数(个) Number of Enterprises(unit)	工业总产值(当年价格) Total Output Value (current price)
总计	**Total**	**780**	**7167.91**
在总计中:	**Of the Total:**		
亏损企业	Enterprises Running Under Deficit	177	692.56
在总计中:	**Of the Total:**		
港、澳、台商投资企业	Hongkong, Macao and Taiwan Funded Enterprises	292	1696.39
合资经营企业(港或澳、台资)	Joint Venture with Hongkong, Macao and Taiwan	107	778.80
合作经营企业(港或澳、台资)	Cooperate with Hongkong, Macao and Taiwan Funded	1	0.98
港澳台商独资经营企业	Enterprises Solely Funded by Hongkong, Macao and Taiwan Businessmen	164	788.58
港澳台商投资股份有限公司	Share Holding Co.Ltd. With Hongkong, Macao and Taiwan Businessmen	9	79.33
其他港澳台投资	Othes	11	48.69
外商投资企业	Foreign Funded Enterprises	488	5471.52
中外合资经营企业	Sino - Foreign Joint Funded Enterprises	224	3971.30
中外合作经营企业	Sino - Foreign Cooperative Funded Enterprises	5	31.02
外资企业	Foreign Solely Funded Enterprises	239	1378.18
外商投资股份有限公司	Foreign Funded Share Holding Co.Ltd.	10	52.68
其他外商投资	Othes	10	38.34
在总计中:	**Of the Total:**		
国有控股企业	State-Owned Share Holding Enterprises	33	2454.48
在总计中:	**Of the Total:**		
轻工业	Light Industry	287	1676.00
重工业	Heavy Industry	493	5491.90
在总计中:	**Of the Total:**		
大型企业	Large Scale Enterprises	62	4447.16
中型企业	Medium Scale Enterprises	193	1556.82
小型企业	Small Enterprises	525	1163.93
按行业分	**Grouped by Sector**		
采矿业	**Mining and Qarrying**	**2**	**0.89**
煤炭开采和洗选业	Coal Mining and Processing		
石油和天然气开采业	Petroleum and Natural Gas Extraction		
黑色金属矿采选业	Ferrous Metals Mining and Processing		
有色金属矿采选业	Non-ferrous Metals Mining and Processing	2	0.89
非金属矿采选业	Non-metal Minerals Mining and Processing		
开采辅助活动	Mining Auxiliary Activities		
其他采矿业	Other Minerals Mining and Processing		

Number and Main Economic Indicators of Industrial Enterprises with Hong Kong, Macao, Taiwan and Foreign Funds(2020)

(100 million yuan)

资产总计 Total Assets	流动资产合计 Circulating Funds	固定资产原价 Original Value of Fixed Assets	固定资产净额 Total Fixed Assets	营业收入 Revenue	全部从业人员年平均人数(万人) Average Number of Empolyment of the Curreat Year (10 000 Persons)
6757.65	**3950.41**	**3431.74**	**1733.22**	**7159.67**	**35.86**
1212.49	396.86	960.15	448.08	722.89	6.82
1969.97	1032.77	1041.41	585.38	1723.52	14.24
888.44	548.18	413.52	234.29	716.81	7.56
1.54	0.48	1.62		0.98	0.01
813.21	353.65	528.46	288.27	889.74	5.66
194.57	88.69	62.54	40.41	64.29	0.56
72.20	41.76	35.27	22.41	51.70	0.46
4787.68	2917.64	2390.33	1147.84	5436.15	21.62
3265.90	1898.11	1729.54	796.88	3731.19	11.37
50.91	27.25	40.72	12.74	31.25	0.14
1374.39	936.07	567.78	307.13	1596.20	9.35
48.91	26.99	30.28	18.13	41.81	0.35
47.58	29.23	22.01	12.96	35.71	0.41
2015.64	1294.59	901.45	373.80	2221.04	4.41
1481.33	815.52	764.27	405.40	1641.02	13.27
5276.32	3134.89	2667.47	1327.82	5518.65	22.59
3758.19	2336.39	1691.05	780.67	4464.83	16.80
1622.62	917.49	907.10	510.39	1534.34	10.83
1376.85	696.53	833.60	442.15	1160.50	8.23
1.78	**1.00**	**1.01**	**0.63**	**0.76**	**0.05**
1.78	1.00	1.01	0.63	0.76	0.05

13-5 续表 continued

单位:亿元

项目	Item	企业单位数(个) Number of Enterprises (unit)	工业总产值(当年价格) Total Output Value (current price)
制造业	**Manufacturing**	**719**	**6925.61**
农副食品加工业	Food Processing	41	329.94
食品制造业	Food Production	21	148.09
酒、饮料和精制茶制造业	Wine, Beverage and Refined Tea Production	28	210.48
烟草制品业	Tobacco Processing		
纺织业	Textile Industry	36	125.05
纺织服装、服饰业	Textile, Garments, and Fashion Industry	27	38.82
皮革、毛皮、羽毛及其制品和制鞋业	Leather, Furs, Down and Related Products	9	14.64
木材加工和木、竹、藤、棕、草制品业	Timber Processing, Wood, Bamboo, Cane, Palm and Sraw Products	3	4.27
家具制造业	Furniture Manufacturing	3	0.71
造纸和纸制品业	Papermaking and Paper Products	10	89.54
印刷和记录媒介复制业	Printing and Record Processing	12	27.65
文教、工美、体育和娱乐用品制造业	Stationery, Education and Sports Goods	15	70.25
石油加工、炼焦和核燃料加工业	Petroleum Processing, Coking Products and Nuclear Fuel Processing	2	10.47
化学原料和化学制品制造业	Raw Chemical Material and Chemical Products	44	447.58
医药制造业	Medical and Pharmaceutical Products	37	311.20
化学纤维制造业	Chemical Fibers	1	5.97
橡胶和塑料制品业	Rubber and Plastic Products	13	29.26
非金属矿物制品业	Nonmetal Material Products	37	166.19
黑色金属冶炼和压延加工业	Smelting and Pressing of Ferrous Metals	6	123.64
有色金属冶炼和压延加工业	Smelting and Pressing of Nonferrous Metals	2	0.50
金属制品业	Metal Products	15	26.88
通用设备制造业	Ordinary Machinery Manufacturing	36	78.82
专用设备制造业	Special Purpose Equipment Manufacturing	24	102.61
汽车制造业	Motor Manufacturing	203	3505.41
铁路、船舶、航空航天和其他运输设备制造业	Railway, Watercraft, Aviation and other Transporlation Equipment Manufacturing	7	12.33
电气机械和器材制造业	Electric Machinery and Equipment	36	311.74
计算机、通信和其他电子设备制造业	Telecommunication Computer, Equipment and Other Electronic Equipment Manufacturing	42	715.68
仪器仪表制造业	Instruments and Meters, Manufacturing	6	9.10
其他制造业	Other Manufacturing		
废弃资源综合利用业	Waste Comprehensive Vtilization of Resources Industry	3	8.79
金属制品、机械和设备修理业	Metal Products, Machinery and Equipment Repairing		
电力、燃气及水的生产和供应业	**Electric Power, Gas and Water Production and Supply**	**59**	**241.39**
电力、热力生产和供应业	Electric Power, Steam and Hot Water Production and Supply	25	141.25
燃气生产和供应业	Gas Production and Supply	28	90.72
水的生产和供应业	Tap Water Production and Supply	6	9.42

(100 million yuan)

资产总计 Total Assets	流动资产合计 Circulating Funds	固定资产原价 Original Value of Fixed Assets	固定资产净额 Total Fixed Assets	营业收入 Revenue	全部从业人员年平均人数(万人) Average Number of Empolyment of the Curreat Year (10 000 Persons)
6236.44	**3796.07**	**2941.06**	**1437.66**	**6911.14**	**34.91**
203.97	111.75	100.36	60.59	327.67	1.37
122.99	80.87	76.03	29.64	164.69	1.08
188.62	99.23	146.36	59.44	196.55	1.25
64.07	39.72	40.34	18.1	125.41	1.41
40.37	26.25	19.09	6.45	33.07	1.03
10.90	4.93	7.11	5.12	12.80	0.42
2.14	0.98	0.65	0.14	4.17	0.09
2.54	1.24	1.40	0.95	0.71	0.02
154.81	61.56	88.52	66.21	88.93	0.58
26.09	17.36	12.91	6.03	26.48	0.26
41.44	23.08	22.03	13.89	71.10	0.61
14.14	10.23	4.99	2.66	11.38	0.02
415.43	88.26	361.84	185.4	437.39	1.36
401.92	199.71	144.16	88.64	277.86	2.87
7.00	3.76	8.34	2.61	7.54	0.06
31.68	20.76	15.30	7.86	31.81	0.23
184.29	82.63	156.91	69.39	140.33	1.38
191.22	72.69	73.99	49.91	232.2	0.31
3.36	0.86	2.12	2.04	0.79	0.01
38.65	15.28	25.60	14.78	25.52	1.51
92.62	65.32	31.16	16.47	79.41	0.79
117.30	82.55	24.15	13.30	103.76	1.20
2785.02	1869.54	1245.00	529.02	3315.08	10.47
14.46	12.76	3.36	1.13	13.36	0.18
223.34	154.9	124.73	55.55	356.85	2.23
848.53	643.57	200.16	129.48	807.83	3.83
8.25	5.18	4.37	2.85	9.04	0.32
1.29	1.10	0.08	0.01	9.41	0.02
519.43	**153.36**	**489.7**	**294.92**	**247.78**	**0.92**
343.62	89.22	384.20	220.48	145.01	0.22
134.46	54.18	89.29	62.84	93.29	0.50
41.35	9.96	16.21	11.60	9.48	0.20

13-6 私营工业企业单位数和主要经济指标(2020)

单位:亿元

项目	Item	企业单位数(个) Number of Enterprises (unit)	工业总产值(当年价格) Total Output Value (current price)
总计	**Total**	**11238**	**19513.71**
在总计中:	**Of the Total:**		
亏损企业	Enterprises Running Under Deficit	1205	1074.76
在总计中:	**Of the Total:**		
轻工业	Light Industry	4802	8852.10
重工业	Heavy Industry	6436	10661.61
在总计中:	**Of the Total:**		
大型企业	Large Scale Enterprises	64	1214.65
中型企业	Medium Scale Enterprises	681	3637.61
小型企业	Small Enterprises	10493	14661.46
按行业分	**Grouped by sector**		
采矿业	**Mining and Qarrying**	**251**	**357.11**
煤炭开采和洗选业	Coal Mining and Processing	4	1.07
石油和天然气开采业	Petroleum and Natural Gas Extraction		
黑色金属矿采选业	Ferrous Metals Mining and Processing	15	30.62
有色金属矿采选业	Non-ferrous Metals Mining and Processing	10	12.36
非金属矿采选业	Non-metal Minerals Mining and Processing	222	313.06
开采辅助活动	Mining Auxiliary Activities		
其他采矿业	Other Minerals Mining and Processing		
制造业	**Manufacturing**	**10877**	**19078.03**
农副食品加工业	Food Processing	1158	2610.88
食品制造业	Food Production	254	465.49
酒、饮料和精制茶制造业	Wine, Beverage and Refined Tea Production	297	400.46
烟草制品业	Tobacco Processing		
纺织业	Textile Industry	761	1764.19
纺织服装、服饰业	Textile, Garments, and Fashion Industry	372	558.78
皮革、毛皮、羽毛及其制品和制鞋业	Leather, Furs, Down and Related Products	125	177.96
木材加工和木、竹、藤、棕、草制品业	Timber Processing, Wood, Bamboo, Cane, Palm and Sraw Products	236	263.04
家具制造业	Furniture Manufacturing	108	152.01
造纸和纸制品业	Papermaking and Paper Products	155	303.87
印刷和记录媒介复制业	Printing and Record Processing	247	351.75
文教、工美、体育和娱乐用品制造业	Stationery, Education and Sports Goods	248	374.93
石油加工、炼焦和核燃料加工业	Petroleum Processing, Coking Products and Nuclear Fuel Processing	29	20.19
化学原料和化学制品制造业	Raw Chemical Material and Chemical Products	658	1530.82
医药制造业	Medical and Pharmaceutical Products	270	449.46
化学纤维制造业	Chemical Fibers	12	25.52
橡胶和塑料制品业	Rubber and Plastic Products	450	718.69
非金属矿物制品业	Nonmetal Material Products	1628	2172.68
黑色金属冶炼和压延加工业	Smelting and Pressing of Ferrous Metals	71	470.31
有色金属冶炼和压延加工业	Smelting and Pressing of Nonferrous Metals	124	336.91
金属制品业	Metal Products	656	942.21
通用设备制造业	Ordinary Machinery Manufacturing	514	844.33
专用设备制造业	Special Purpose Equipment Manufacturing	533	653.92
汽车制造业	Motor Manufacturing	952	1690.32
铁路、船舶、航空航天和其他运输设备制造业	Railway, Watercraft, Aviation and other Transporlation Equipment Manufacturing	86	126.77
电气机械和器材制造业	Electric Machinery and Equipment	433	642.90
计算机、通信和其他电子设备制造业	Telecommunication Computer, Equipment and Other Electronic Equipment Manufacturing	289	540.44
仪器仪表制造业	Instruments and Meters, Manufacturing	95	134.36
其他制造业	Other Manufacturing	32	28.05
废弃资源综合利用业	Waste Comprehensive Vtilization of Resources Industry	71	273.61
金属制品、机械和设备修理业	Metal Products, Machinery and Equipment Repairing	13	53.18
电力、燃气及水的生产和供应业	**Electric Power, Gas and Water Production and Supply**	**110**	**78.55**
电力、热力生产和供应业	Electric Power, Steam and Hot Water Production and Supply	62	51.21
燃气生产和供应业	Gas Production and Supply	25	15.39
水的生产和供应业	Tap Water Production and Supply	23	11.95

Number and Main Economic Indicators of Private Industrial Enterprises(2020)

(100 million yuan)

资产总计 Total Assets	流动资产合计 Circulating Funds	固定资产原价 Original Value of Fixed Assets	固定资产净额 NBV of Fixed Assets	营业收入 Revenue	全部从业人员年平均人数(万人) Average Number of Empolyment of the Curreat Year (10 000 Persons)
10711.85	**5517.59**	**6520.03**	**2900.59**	**18006.60**	**131.67**
1329.65	683.57	529.84	318.58	907.64	12.85
4365.59	2172.43	3083.57	1265.14	8117.64	64.70
6346.27	3345.16	3436.47	1635.44	9888.97	66.97
897.64	475.39	490.58	255.92	1182.39	9.50
2223.95	1141.66	1566.07	678.19	3335.66	34.69
7590.26	3900.54	4463.39	1966.48	13488.55	87.47
209.73	**94.91**	**96.61**	**44.8**	**286.57**	**1.77**
3.33	1.27	2.08	1.27	0.98	0.03
25.53	9.71	14.10	7.80	25.34	0.15
15.57	10.39	6.14	3.25	9.17	0.11
165.3	73.54	74.29	32.48	251.08	1.48
10249.01	**5348.4**	**6243.17**	**2734.01**	**17643.97**	**129.28**
1069.72	537.15	772.14	298.26	2374.4	10.99
267.30	133.00	158.70	79.46	433.85	3.47
264.17	129.84	154.01	84.90	361.87	2.69
728.62	346.00	653.90	233.10	1640.26	15.21
216.93	92.15	160.62	63.10	520.42	6.93
61.71	36.02	56.85	13.34	166.44	1.63
139.61	61.11	92.27	42.27	227.16	1.97
124.81	59.53	68.53	38.04	137.19	1.44
164.63	77.87	119.07	60.07	276.92	1.99
217.52	121.16	120.19	50.83	308.67	2.95
182.07	79.26	139.75	49.42	341.29	3.01
34.05	24.13	4.93	3.72	16.86	0.11
781.43	363.35	618.01	211.11	1362.40	7.30
364.99	194.44	201.01	97.15	411.16	4.60
14.88	5.78	16.90	5.21	25.17	0.14
376.56	194.57	260.44	109.70	659.05	5.15
1297.19	670.12	742.32	355.21	2056.11	14.20
250.81	113.29	152.44	100.19	490.16	1.91
114.17	60.72	63.02	35.38	314.88	1.64
460.13	266.84	246.51	109.81	888.50	6.02
494.50	244.96	295.38	118.84	788.38	5.57
462.89	278.67	235.98	105.72	606.54	5.05
1041.76	597.49	468.84	230.25	1592.46	11.46
73.76	41.26	35.46	15.61	108.52	1.05
477.47	289.29	180.95	98.52	600.73	4.85
337.38	201.92	127.80	80.01	509.77	5.89
78.28	53.38	28.07	11.33	108.12	0.89
19.07	11.37	7.97	4.26	26.41	0.27
110.82	55.02	45.32	27.54	240.85	0.60
21.78	8.71	15.79	1.66	49.43	0.30
253.1	**74.3**	**180.23**	**121.78**	**76.05**	**0.64**
193.48	48.36	146.32	99.94	48.55	0.33
31.50	17.11	14.53	10.10	16.13	0.12
28.12	8.83	19.38	11.74	11.37	0.19

13-7 大中型工业企业单位数和产销总值(2020)

单位:亿元

项 目	Item	企业单位数(个) Number of Enterprises (unit)	工业总产值(当年价格) Total Output Value (current price)
总计	**Total**	**1652**	**22527.69**
一、按登记注册类型分组:	**Grouped by Type of Registration**		
内资企业	Inner Funded Enterprises	1397	16523.72
国有企业	State Owned Enterprises	46	1498.79
中央企业	Central Enterprises	27	1394.33
地方企业	Local Enterprises	19	104.46
集体企业	Collective-owned Enterprise	3	7.72
股份合作企业	Share Holding Cooperative Enterprises		
联营企业	Joint Owned Enterprise	1	4.65
国有联营企业	State Joint Ownership	1	4.65
集体联营企业	Collective Joint Ownership		
国有与集体联营企业	Joint State- Collective Ownership		
其他联营企业	Other Joint Owned Enterprise		
有限责任公司	Responsibility Co. Ltd	438	6815.90
国有独资公司	State Solely Funded Co.	39	2062.86
其他有限责任公司	Others	399	4753.04
股份有限公司	Share Holding Co.Ltd.	163	3342.15
私营企业	Private - owned Enterprises	745	4852.26
私营独资企业	Solely Private - owned Enterprises	7	76.24
私营合作企业	Private Joint Venture	1	1.92
私营有限责任公司	Private Responsibility Co. Ltd	644	4030.13
私营股份有限公司	Private Share Holding Co.Ltd.	93	743.96
其他企业	Others	1	2.26
港、澳、台商投资企业	Hongkong, Macao and Taiwan Funded Enterprises	103	1320.23
合资经营企业(港或澳、台资)	Joint Venture with Hongkong, Macao and Taiwan	46	644.68
合作经营企业(港或澳、台资)	Cooperate with Hongkong, Macao and Taiwan Funded		
港澳台商独资经营企业	Enterprises Solely Funded by Hongkong, Macao and Taiwan Businessmen	47	556.98
港澳台商投资股份有限公司	Share Holding Co.Ltd. With Hongkong, Macao and Taiwan Investment	4	75.61
其他港澳台投资	Others	6	42.97
外商投资企业	Foreign Funded Enterprises	152	4683.74
中外合资经营企业	Sino - Foreign Joint Funded Enterprises	68	3592.84
中外合作经营企业	Sino - Foreign Cooperative Funded Enterprises	3	19.36
外资企业	Foreign Solely Funded Enterprises	74	994.79
外商投资股份有限公司	Foreign Funded Share Holding Co.Ltd.	4	42.66
其他外商投资	Others	3	34.09
二、在总计中:亏损企业	**Of the Total: enterprises running under deficit**	**230**	**3035.40**
在总计中:国有控股企业	Of the Total: State-Owned Share Holding Enterprises	277	9879.35
在总计中:轻工业	Of the Total: Light Industry	754	6296.66
重工业	Heavy Industry	898	16231.03
在总计中:大型企业	Of the Total: Large Scale Enterprises	280	13760.58
中型企业	Medium Scale Enterprises	1372	8767.11

Number and Gross Production and Sales of Large and Medium-sized Industrial Enterprises (2020)

(100 million yuan)

资产总计 Total Assets	流动资产合计 Circulating Funds	固定资产原价 Original Value of Fixed Assets	固定资产净额 NBV of Fixed Assets	营业收入 Revenue	全部从业人员年平均人数(万人) Average Number of Empolyment of the Curreat Year (10 000 Persons)
29730.29	**14060.48**	**17420**	**8610.71**	**22115.11**	**147.45**
24349.49	10806.60	14822	7319.65	16115.94	119.82
2620.67	859.40	2944	1394.15	1497.82	9.30
2426.78	763.18	2846	1331.22	1385.39	8.37
193.89	96.22	98	62.93	112.43	0.94
13.33	6.07	8	5.55	6.35	0.11
7.29	5.25	3	1.69	4.65	0.08
7.29	5.25	3	1.69	4.65	0.08
10024.87	4834.20	5857	3119.42	6729.88	43.53
2203.35	1198.59	1928	671.84	1958.56	7.19
7821.52	3635.61	3928	2447.58	4771.32	36.34
8555.87	3479.57	3951	1864.32	3355.62	22.56
3121.59	1617.06	2057	934.11	4518.05	44.20
52.30	39.77	24	9.64	75.35	0.28
1.15	0.34	1	0.56	1.69	0.03
2444.83	1277.31	1733	769.01	3801.94	38.11
623.31	299.63	299	154.91	639.07	5.78
5.86	5.06	2	0.40	3.58	0.03
1424.66	805.25	650	364.62	1366.07	10.65
722.04	464.59	327	181.91	601.10	5.29
447.25	217.21	230	122.73	658.26	4.42
192.06	86.70	62	39.96	60.63	0.54
63.32	36.75	32	20.02	46.09	0.39
3956.14	2448.62	1948	926.45	4633.10	16.98
2856.04	1688.65	1500	684.00	3361.44	9.05
35.43	21.85	10	3.95	19.57	0.11
990.64	694.21	396	214.90	1188.63	7.21
39.28	23.68	23	12.69	32.21	0.28
34.74	20.24	19	10.90	31.24	0.33
6662.58	**1861.53**	**5646**	**3011.64**	**3179.31**	**24.67**
17398.02	7350.18	11030	5206.04	9575.55	47.75
5395.19	3196.22	2666	1322.30	6015.53	53.27
24335.10	10864.26	14754	7288.41	16099.58	94.18
21200.14	9475.71	12653.13	6299.44	13713.88	74.69
8530.15	4584.76	4766.75	2311.27	8401.23	72.75

13-7 续表 continued

单位:亿元

项 目	Item	企业单位数(个) Number of Enterprises (unit)	工业总产值(当年价格) Total Output Value (current price)
按行业分	**Grouped by Sector**		
采矿业	**Mining and Qarrying**	**20**	**140.71**
煤炭开采和洗选业	Coal Mining and Processing		
石油和天然气开采业	Petroleum and Natural Gas Extraction	1	25.30
黑色金属矿采选业	Ferrous Metals Mining and Processing	6	65.62
有色金属矿采选业	Non-ferrous Metals Mining and Processing	5	16.47
非金属矿采选业	Non-metal Minerals Mining and Processing	7	25.91
开采辅助活动	Mining Auxiliary Activities		
其他采矿业	Other Minerals Mining and Processing	1	7.41
制造业	**Manufacturing**	**1584**	**20664.16**
农副食品加工业	Food Processing	79	872.05
食品制造业	Food Production	50	357.66
酒、饮料和精制茶制造业	Wine, Beverage and Refined Tea Production	43	502.13
烟草制品业	Tobacco Processing	2	699.96
纺织业	Textile Industry	175	987.60
纺织服装、服饰业	Textile, Garments, and Fashion Industry	87	298.31
皮革、毛皮、羽毛及其制品和制鞋业	Leather, Furs, Down and Related Products	12	29.88
木材加工和木、竹、藤、棕、草制品业	Timber Processing, Wood, Bamboo, Cane, Palm and Sraw Products	13	61.16
家具制造业	Furniture Manufacturing	18	75.31
造纸和纸制品业	Papermaking and Paper Products	30	295.10
印刷和记录媒介复制业	Printing and Record Processing	33	171.90
文教、工美、体育和娱乐用品制造业	Stationery, Education and Sports Goods	23	144.10
石油加工、炼焦和核燃料加工业	Petroleum Processing, Coking Products and Nuclear Fuel Processing	4	389.02
化学原料和化学制品制造业	Raw Chemical Material and Chemical Products	105	1789.86
医药制造业	Medical and Pharmaceutical Products	78	732.80
化学纤维制造业	Chemical Fibers	3	15.27
橡胶和塑料制品业	Rubber and Plastic Products	47	269.72
非金属矿物制品业	Nonmetal Material Products	95	688.59
黑色金属冶炼和压延加工业	Smelting and Pressing of Ferrous Metals	26	1663.91
有色金属冶炼和压延加工业	Smelting and Pressing of Nonferrous Metals	24	483.78
金属制品业	Metal Products	53	459.30
通用设备制造业	Ordinary Machinery Manufacturing	67	393.66
专用设备制造业	Special Purpose Equipment Manufacturing	56	485.05
汽车制造业	Motor Manufacturing	210	4955.03
铁路、船舶、航空航天和其他运输设备制造业	Railway, Watercraft, Aviation and other Transporlation Equipment Manufacturing	29	406.15
电气机械和器材制造业	Electric Machinery and Equipment	80	1019.14
计算机、通信和其他电子设备制造业	Telecommunication Computer, Equipment and Other Electronic Equipment Manufacturing	108	1999.95
仪器仪表制造业	Instruments and Meters, Manufacturing	18	106.33
其他制造业	Other Manufacturing	4	49.28
废弃资源综合利用业	Waste Comprehensive Vtilization of Resources Industry	5	198.26
金属制品、机械和设备修理业	Metal Products, Machinery and Equipment Repairing	7	63.90
电力、燃气及水的生产和供应业	**Electric Power, Gas and Water Production and Supply**	**48**	**1722.84**
电力、热力生产和供应业	Electric Power, Steam and Hot Water Production and Supply	26	1634.21
燃气生产和供应业	Gas Production and Supply	4	55.90
水的生产和供应业	Tap Water Production and Supply	18	32.73

(100 million yuan)

资产总计 Total Assets	流动资产合计 Circulating Funds	固定资产原价 Original Value of Fixed Assets	固定资产净额 NBV of Fixed Assets	营业收入 Revenue	全部从业人员年平均人数(万人) Average Number of Empolyment of the Curreat Year (10 000 Persons)
397.49	**132.17**	**435.51**	**139.38**	**162.28**	**2.38**
259.03	61.90	332.27	103.55	61.18	1.02
69.43	32.57	65.85	25.42	61.26	0.78
27.27	14.37	16.91	5.31	13.60	0.26
34.30	19.49	11.67	2.93	18.83	0.25
7.46	3.84	8.81	2.17	7.41	0.07
24688.67	**13470.33**	**11569.33**	**5809.04**	**20192.58**	**137.09**
367.54	193.21	309.60	111.05	756.51	4.81
305.78	152.22	185.28	83.45	363.99	3.70
780.94	577.50	257.51	116.56	445.23	3.43
597.86	470.05	124.42	51.30	768.69	0.66
548.23	289.55	440.48	163.92	963.76	11.10
165.54	86.10	115.56	50.89	281.01	5.27
25.26	14.20	14.98	9.17	27.01	1.22
99.47	54.22	46.88	15.80	57.57	0.76
101.46	45.71	54.72	41.87	68.98	0.97
409.80	149.18	259.60	199.22	272.31	1.74
156.88	107.75	56.94	30.63	162.30	2.08
76.94	39.26	45.74	26.19	133.05	1.28
157.47	41.84	172.83	79.12	508.19	0.48
2284.66	734.91	1423.23	638.54	1729.68	9.78
943.33	486.80	387.59	227.48	669.41	7.61
19.08	9.93	19.38	5.20	16.20	0.38
271.51	143.85	127.14	72.21	265.97	2.67
752.15	341.96	447.23	225.34	656.83	5.68
1368.06	517.77	1686.88	619.42	1701.54	4.67
236.62	111.43	184.03	94.97	439.49	2.28
553.85	380.99	237.59	105.74	468.97	4.21
574.03	330.02	224.43	105.24	391.95	4.43
563.40	382.97	286.03	97.28	492.43	4.48
6188.93	3962.38	1833.06	807.00	4729.46	22.32
940.76	606.66	316.38	181.38	376.40	4.16
971.25	658.28	350.32	192.60	1033.84	7.11
4735.46	2275.25	1785.80	1366.39	2014.19	15.77
146.19	99.17	51.30	22.38	101.83	1.39
52.05	37.44	19.55	9.20	48.37	0.44
231.32	124.95	72.83	50.41	183.32	0.44
62.85	44.78	32.02	9.09	64.10	1.77
4644.14	**457.99**	**5415.02**	**2662.30**	**1760.24**	**7.99**
4240.81	314.47	5205.62	2534.07	1661.33	6.60
81.06	30.55	56.22	39.68	56.31	0.31
322.27	112.97	153.18	88.55	42.60	1.08

13-8 规模以上工业企业生产能力(2020)
Production Capacity of Industrial Enterprises above Designated Size(2020)

产品名称	计量单位	Item	Measurement	年初生产能力 Capacity at the Beginning of the Year	年末生产能力 Capacity at the End of the Year
原煤	(万吨)	Coal	(10 000 tons)	40.0	40.0
天然原油	(万吨)	Crude Petroleum Oil	(10 000 tons)	54.0	54.2
卷烟	(万支)	Cigarettes	(10 000 pieces)	20905290	14484804
棉纺锭/纺纱量	(万锭/万吨)	Knitting Spindle/Capacity	(10 000 spindle/10 000 tons)	700.2	698.2
气流纺锭/纺纱量	(万头/万吨)	Air Spindle/Capacity	(10 000 spindle/10 000 tons)	22.3	23.9
棉布织机/布	(万台/亿米)	Cotton Loom/Cloth	(10 000 piece/hundred million meters)	19.9	20.7
原油加工能力/原油加工量	(万吨/万吨)	Crude Oil Processing pacity	(10 000 ton/10 000 tons)	1745.5	1750.5
焦炭	(万吨)	Coke	(10 000 tons)	903.0	848.0
烧碱(折 100%)	(万吨)	Caustic Soda (100%)	(10 000 tons)	101.3	101.3
碳化钙(电石,折 300 升/千克)	(万吨)	Calcium Carbide (300 L/kg)	(10 000 tons)	22.0	22.0
农用氮、磷、钾化学肥料总计(折纯)	(万吨)	Chemical Fertilizers	(10 000 tons)	930.7	908.5
初级形态塑料	(万吨)	Primary Plastic	(10 000 tons)	210.6	213.4
化学纤维	(万吨)	Chemical Fiber	(10 000 tons)	39.6	39.9
硅酸盐水泥熟料	(万吨)	Portland Cement Clinker	(10 000 tons)	7236.8	7579.0
水泥	(万吨)	Cement	(10 000 tons)	14284.3	14357.8
平板玻璃	(万重量箱)	Plain Glass	(10 000 weight case)	10902.3	11177.8
生铁	(万吨)	Pig Ion	(10 000 tons)	2606.2	2646.6
粗钢	(万吨)	Crude Steel	(10 000 tons)	3850.5	3893.6
钢材	(万吨)	Rolled Steel	(10 000 tons)	4407.5	4249.9
铁合金	(万吨)	Ferroalloy	(10 000 tons)	36.2	38.4
原铝(电解铝)	(万吨)	Electrolyzed Aluminum	(10 000 tons)	11.8	12.1
金属切削机床	(万台)	Metal-cutting Machine Tools	(10 000 pieces)	1.6	1.4
汽车	(万辆)	Automobile	(10 000 units)	323.2	308.3
其中:基本型乘用车(轿车)		Cars		256.2	237.9
家用电冰箱	(万台)	Home Refrigerators	(10 000 pieces)	600.0	650.0
房间空气调节器	(万台)	Air Conditioners	(10 000 pieces)	2031.7	2032.3
微型计算机设备	(万台)	computers	(10 000 pieces)	1865.2	2519.6
移动通信手持机(手机)	(万台)	Mobile Phones	(10 000 pieces)	9004.2	9140.0
发电设备容量总计/发电量	(万千瓦/万千瓦小时)	Generating Capacity	(10 000 kwh)	6880.3	7108.6
其中:火电设备容量/发电量		Thermal Power		2897.3	3029.3
水电设备容量/发电量		Hydropower		3431.3	3476.9
风电设备容量/发电量		Wind Power		330.3	373.0

13-9 规模以上工业主要产品产量(2020)
Main Products' Output of Industry above Designated Size(2020)

名 称	计量单位	Name	Measurement	产品产量
原煤	(吨)	Original Coal	(ton)	402674.75
天然原油	(吨)	Natural Oil	(ton)	535024.00
天然气	(万立方米)	Natural Gas	(10 000 cu.m)	10111.00
铁矿石原矿	(吨)	Iron Ore	(ton)	5914853.67
铜金属含量	(吨)	Copper	(ton)	67599.53
锌金属含量	(吨)	Zinc	(ton)	14579.50
钨精矿折合量(折三氧化钨 65%)	(吨)	Tungsten Concentrate Equivalent Amount	(ton)	302.55
钼精矿折合量(折纯钼 45%)	(吨)	Molybdenum Concentrate Equivalent Amount	(ton)	113.00
磷矿石(折含五氧化二磷 30%)	(吨)	Phosphate Rock (30% of Phosphorus Pentoxide)	(ton)	38281366.13
原盐	(吨)	Crude Salt	(ton)	4265829.00
小麦粉	(吨)	Wheat Flour	(ton)	2660841.01
大米	(吨)	Rice	(ton)	26039140.03
饲料	(吨)	Feed	(ton)	14354378.93
# 配合饲料	(吨)	Compoud Feed	(ton)	7263559.34
混合饲料	(吨)	Mixed feed	(ton)	2316995.70
精制食用植物油	(吨)	Refined Edible Vegetable oil	(ton)	3079442.82
鲜、冷藏肉	(吨)	Fresh and Chilled Meat	(ton)	864568.04
冷冻水产品	(吨)	Frozen Seafood	(ton)	575780.09
糖果	(吨)	Candy	(ton)	299861.17
速冻米面食品	(吨)	Frozen Rice\Flour Food	(ton)	59525.30
方便面	(吨)	Instant Noodles	(ton)	171841.47
乳制品	(吨)	Dairy Products	(ton)	1200703.16
# 液体乳	(吨)	Liquid Dairies	(ton)	1098965.41
乳粉	(吨)	Milk Powder	(ton)	7660.44
罐头	(吨)	Can	(ton)	589731.30
酱油	(吨)	Soy Sauce	(ton)	68743.00
冷冻饮品	(吨)	Frozen Drinks	(ton)	172234.87
食品添加剂	(吨)	Food Additives	(ton)	1229589.83
饮料酒	(千升)	Alcoholic Beverage	(kl)	2166195.66
# 白酒(折 65 度,商品量)	(千升)	Liquor (of 65 degrees, the amount of goods)	(kl)	358680.07

13-9 续表 1 continued

名 称	计量单位	Name	Measurement	产品产量
啤酒	(千升)	Beer	(kl)	975435.53
葡萄酒	(千升)	Wine	(kl)	671.90
饮料	(吨)	Drinks	(ton)	9962696.09
#碳酸饮料类(汽水)	(吨)	Carbonated Beverages (soft drinks)	(ton)	780478.39
包装饮用水类	(吨)	Packaging of Drinking Water	(ton)	3533351.07
果汁和蔬菜汁饮料类	(吨)	Fruit Juice and Vegetable Juice	(ton)	774291.05
精制茶	(吨)	Refined Tea	(ton)	398385.32
卷烟	(万支)	Cigarette	(10 000 pieces)	13304649.50
纱	(吨)	Yarn	(ton)	2698423.19
#棉纱	(吨)	Cotton Yarn	(ton)	1742091.03
棉混纺纱	(吨)	Cotton Blended Yarn	(ton)	373990.97
化学纤维纱	(吨)	Chemical Fiber Yarn	(ton)	583865.19
布	(万米)	Fabric	(10 000 meters)	419217.20
#棉布	(万米)	Cotton	(10 000 meters)	318414.14
棉混纺布	(万米)	Cotton Blended Cloth	(10 000 meters)	76369.42
化学纤维短纤布	(万米)	Chemical-Fiber Cloth	(10 000 meters)	24433.64
印染布	(万米)	Dyed Cloth	(10 000 meters)	18640.17
亚麻布(含亚麻≥55%)	(万米)	Linen Fabric (containing linen≥55%)	(10 000 meters)	12.28
苎麻布(含苎麻≥55%)	(万米)	Ramie fabric (containing linen≥55%)	(10 000 meters)	535.01
蚕丝	(吨)	Silk	(ton)	275.20
蚕丝被	(万条)	Silk Quilt	(10 000 pieces)	30.09
无纺布(无纺织物)	(吨)	Non-woven Fabric	(ton)	457908.08
服装	(万件)	Clothing	(10 000 pieces)	98030.66
#梭织服装	(万件)	Tated Garments	(10 000 pieces)	80704.09
#羽绒服	(万件)	Down Jacket	(10 000 pieces)	863.11
西服套装	(万件)	Western-style	(10 000 pieces)	1631.62
衬衫	(万件)	Shirt	(10 000 pieces)	780.87
针织服装	(万件)	Knitted Garments	(10 000 pieces)	17326.57
天然毛皮服装	(万件)	Leather Clothes	(piece)	103.41
皮革鞋靴	(万双)	Leather Footwear	(10 000 pairs)	3363.08
人造板	(立方米)	Artificial Board	(cu.m)	8965725.05
#胶合板	(立方米)	Plywood	(cu.m)	2867204.04
纤维板	(立方米)	Fibre Board	(cu.m)	3220687.05
刨花板	(立方米)	Shaving Board	(cu.m)	363356.00
人造板表面装饰板	(平方米)	Artificial Board for Surface Decoration	(sq.m)	35527986.44
复合木地板	(平方米)	Composite Wood Flooring	(sq.m)	50720933.33
家具	(件)	Furniture	(piece)	9131728.00

13-9 续表 2 continued

名 称	计量单位	Name	Measurement	产品产量
#木质家具	(件)	Wood Furniture	(piece)	5500603.00
金属家具	(件)	Metal Furniture	(piece)	1105061.00
软体家具	(件)	Upholstered Furniture	(piece)	897176.00
纸浆(原生浆及废纸浆)	(吨)	Pulp (original pulp and waste paper pulp)	(ton)	1763036.51
机制纸及纸板（外购原纸加工除外）	(吨)	Machine Made Paper and PaperBoard (excludingprocessing outsourcing base paper)	(ton)	4675351.42
#未涂布印刷书写用纸	(吨)	Uncoating Writing Paper	(ton)	366007.00
卫生用纸原纸	(吨)	Toilet Paper	(ton)	86414.00
箱纸板	(吨)	Case Board	(ton)	839830.94
纸制品	(吨)	Paper Products	(ton)	4992455.28
#瓦楞纸箱	(吨)	Corrugated Case	(ton)	1955349.37
单色印刷品	(令)	Monochrome Print	(ream)	4947141.76
多色印刷品	(对开色令)	Multi-color Print	(folio color ream)	28856472.53
原油加工量	(吨)	Crude Oil Processing Capacity	(ton)	12684628.33
汽油	(吨)	Gasoline	(ton)	3443992.18
煤油	(吨)	Kerosene	(ton)	832286.83
柴油	(吨)	Diesel Fuel	(ton)	3950269.62
润滑油	(吨)	Lubricating Oil	(ton)	76676.73
燃料油	(吨)	Fuel Oil	(ton)	138719.16
石脑油	(吨)	Naphtha	(ton)	1212745.92
溶剂油	(吨)	Megilp	(ton)	0.00
液化石油气	(吨)	LPG	(ton)	511002.71
石油焦	(吨)	Petroleum Coke	(ton)	787694.68
石油沥青	(吨)	Petroleum Pitch	(ton)	190864.68
焦炭	(吨)	Coke	(ton)	8011773.00
硫酸(折 100%)	(吨)	Sulfuric Acid (100% discount)	(ton)	8376267.21
盐酸(氯化氢,含量 31%)	(吨)	Hydrochloric Acid (hydrogen chloride, 31%)	(ton)	474635.56
浓硝酸(折 100%)	(吨)	Concentrated Nitric Acid (100% discount)	(ton)	5199.82
烧碱(折 100%)	(吨)	Caustic Soda (100% discount)	(ton)	804271.00
#离子膜法烧碱(折 100%)	(吨)	Ionic Membrane Method(100% discount)	(ton)	599166.00
纯碱(碳酸钠)	(吨)	Soda Ash (sodium carbonate)	(ton)	1732943.77
乙烯	(吨)	Ethylene	(ton)	697828.93
丙烯	(吨)	Propylene	(ton)	354567.00
纯苯	(吨)	Pure benzene	(ton)	153040.32
精甲醇	(吨)	Refined Methanol	(ton)	736255.00
合成氨(无水氨)	(吨)	Anhydrous Amonia	(ton)	3938985.14
农用氮、磷、钾化学肥料总计(折纯)	(吨)	Agricultural Nitrogen, Phosphorus and Potassium Fertilizer	(ton)	4820954.63

13-9 续表 3 continued

名 称	计量单位	Name	Measurement	产品产量
#氮肥(折含 N100%)	(吨)	N (of N 100%)	(ton)	2381630.24
#尿素(折含 N100%)	(吨)	Urea (of N 100%)	(ton)	673680.12
磷肥(折五氧化二磷 100 %)	(吨)	P (of 100% phosphorus pentoxide)	(ton)	2321059.85
磷酸一铵(实物量)	(吨)	MAP (physical quantity)	(ton)	10316723.99
磷酸二铵(实物量)	(吨)	DAP (physical quantity)	(ton)	5091545.91
化学农药原药(折有效成分 100%)	(吨)	Chemical Pesticide Active Compound	(ton)	149140.57
#杀虫剂原药	(吨)	Pesticide Active Compound	(ton)	5641.00
除草剂原药	(吨)	Herbicide Active Compound	(ton)	121347.44
涂料	(吨)	Paint	(ton)	1366322.44
初级形态的塑料	(吨)	Primary Form Plastic	(ton)	1740385.24
#聚丙烯树脂	(吨)	Polypropylene Resin	(ton)	606054.33
聚氯乙烯树脂	(吨)	PVC Resin	(ton)	208366.05
聚苯乙烯树脂	(吨)	Polystyrene Resin	(ton)	46238.00
ABS 树脂	(吨)	ABS Resin	(ton)	25986.00
合成橡胶	(吨)	Synthetic Rubber	(ton)	4969.24
化学试剂	(吨)	Chemical Reagent	(ton)	1034828.89
合成洗涤剂	(吨)	Synthetic Detergent	(ton)	388057.90
化学药品原药	(吨)	Original Drug Chemicals	(ton)	183300.05
中成药	(吨)	Chinese Patent Medicine	(ton)	231302.94
化学纤维用浆粕	(吨)	Chemical Fiber Pulp	(ton)	29097.33
化学纤维	(吨)	Chemical Fiber	(ton)	325396.84
#人造纤维(纤维素纤维)	(吨)	Artificid Fiber	(ton)	63490.00
#粘胶短纤维	(吨)	Fibranne	(ton)	52487.00
粘胶纤维长丝	(吨)	Viscose Filament	(ton)	11003.00
合成纤维	(吨)	Synthetic Fiber	(ton)	257159.84
#涤纶纤维	(吨)	Polyester Fiber	(ton)	26851.48
丙纶纤维	(吨)	Polypropylene Fiber	(ton)	61934.00
橡胶轮胎外胎	(条)	Rubber Cover Tyre	(piece)	6704139.00
#子午线轮胎外胎	(条)	Radial Tire	(piece)	4370784.00
塑料制品	(吨)	Plastic Products	(ton)	4310125.25
#塑料薄膜	(吨)	Plastic Film	(ton)	425570.74
#农用薄膜	(吨)	Agricultural Film	(ton)	16648.90
泡沫塑料	(吨)	Foam	(ton)	64357.81
塑料人造革、合成革	(吨)	Plastic Leather and Synthetic Leather	(ton)	5592.00
日用塑料制品	(吨)	Household Plastic Products	(ton)	549315.69
硅酸盐水泥熟料	(吨)	Cement Clinker	(ton)	59836898.76

13-9 续表 4 continued

名 称	计量单位	Name	Measurement	产品产量
#窑外分解窑水泥熟料	(吨)	Cement Kiln Clinker	(ton)	44307546.74
水泥	(吨)	Cement	(ton)	98867740.19
#强度等级 42.5 水泥(含 R 型)	(吨)	Strength Grade 42.5 Cement (including R-type)	(ton)	35299842.22
强度等级 52.5 水泥(含 R 型)	(吨)	Strength Grade 52.5 Cement (including R-type)	(ton)	1137868.99
商品混凝土	(立方米)	Concrete	(cu.m)	106194606.64
水泥混凝土排水管	(千米)	Concrete Drainage Pipe	(km)	12349.89
水泥混凝土压力管	(千米)	Concrete Pressure Pipe	(km)	201.60
水泥混凝土电杆	(根)	Cement Concrete Pole	(piece)	1087401.00
预应力混凝土桩	(米)	Prestressed Concrete Pile	(meter)	18238387.00
石膏板	(万平方米)	Gypsum Board	(10 000 sq.m)	45810.00
砖	(万块)	Brick	(10 000 pieces)	4024100.95
瓦	(万片)	Tile	(10 000 pieces)	103168.89
瓷质砖	(平方米)	Porcelain Tile	(sq.m)	117346120.23
陶质砖	(平方米)	Ceramic Tile	(sq.m)	54745244.11
天然大理石建筑板材	(平方米)	Natural Marble Building Boards	(sq.m)	26510549.57
天然花岗石建筑板材	(平方米)	Natural Granite Building Boards	(sq.m)	216441056.75
沥青和改性沥青防水卷材	(平方米)	Asphalt and Modified Bitumen Sheet	(sq.m)	213302213.76
平板玻璃	(重量箱)	Plate Glass	(weight case)	95654975.20
钢化玻璃	(平方米)	Tempered Glass	(sq.m)	25130672.20
夹层玻璃	(平方米)	Laminated Glass	(sq.m)	4968543.21
中空玻璃	(平方米)	Insulating Glass	(sq.m)	5076359.43
日用玻璃制品	(吨)	Daily Glass Products	(ton)	669741.06
玻璃包装容器	(吨)	Glass Containers	(ton)	663059.70
玻璃纤维纱	(吨)	Glass Fiber Yarn	(ton)	7688.00
纤维增强塑料制品	(吨)	Fiber Reinforced Plastic Products	(ton)	14586.72
卫生陶瓷制品	(吨)	Sanitary Ceramic Products	(piece)	11455206.00
耐火材料制品	(吨)	Refractory Products	(ton)	1781251.03
石墨及炭素制品	(吨)	Graphite and Carbon Products	(ton)	324610.17
生铁	(吨)	Pig Iron	(ton)	27274393.00
粗钢	(吨)	Crude Steel	(ton)	36218302.26
铸铁件	(吨)	Iron Casting	(ton)	4032997.01
铸钢件	(吨)	Steel Casting	(ton)	475535.89
钢材	(吨)	Steel	(ton)	36491090.11
#铁道用钢材	(吨)	Railway Steel	(ton)	530640.00
#重轨	(吨)	Heavy Rail	(ton)	514901.00
大型型钢	(吨)	Large-scale Steel	(ton)	163739.40
中小型型钢	(吨)	Small and Medium Scale Steel	(ton)	1198111.00

13-9 续表 5 continued

名 称	计量单位	Name	Measurement	产品产量
棒材	(吨)	Bar	(ton)	2613922.50
钢筋	(吨)	Steel Bar	(ton)	9979742.95
线材(盘条)	(吨)	Wire (coil)	(ton)	3165887.77
特厚板	(吨)	Special Plate	(ton)	414626.00
厚钢板	(吨)	Thick Steel Plate	(ton)	656397.00
中板	(吨)	Middle Plate	(ton)	1275470.00
热轧薄板	(吨)	Hot-rolled Sheet	(ton)	13689.00
冷轧薄板	(吨)	Cold-rolled Sheet	(ton)	794283.10
中厚宽钢带	(吨)	Thick Wide Strip	(ton)	2769963.00
热轧薄宽钢带	(吨)	Hot-rolled Thin Wide Strip	(ton)	2377271.72
冷轧薄宽钢带	(吨)	Cold-rolled Wide Strip	(ton)	2261053.66
热轧窄钢带	(吨)	Hot-rolled Narrow Strip	(ton)	626488.62
冷轧窄钢带	(吨)	Cold-rolled Narrow Strip	(ton)	29701.00
镀层板(带)	(吨)	Coated Plate	(ton)	2931510.17
涂层板(带)	(吨)	Coated Plate	(ton)	888316.47
铁合金	(吨)	Ferroalloy	(ton)	300964.64
十种有色金属	(吨)	10 Kinds of Nonferrous Metals	(ton)	805662.98
#精炼铜(电解铜)	(吨)	Refined Copper (electrolytic copper)	(ton)	512025.00
铅	(吨)	Lead	(ton)	204604.04
原铝(电解铝)	(吨)	Electrolytic Aluminum	(ton)	73157.18
黄金	(千克)	Gold	(kg)	6728.51
白银(银锭)	(千克)	Silver (silver bullion)	(kg)	869570.55
铝合金	(吨)	Aluminum Alloy	(ton)	154381.35
铜材	(吨)	Copper	(ton)	417226.68
铝材	(吨)	Aluminum	(ton)	1223167.30
金属切削工具	(万件)	Metal Cutting Tools	(10 000 pieces)	7005.86
钢丝	(吨)	Wire	(ton)	80998.69
钢丝绳	(吨)	Wire Rope	(ton)	54075.00
钢绞线	(吨)	Strand	(ton)	151431.96
锻件	(吨)	Forge Piece	(ton)	310474.63
粉末冶金零件	(吨)	Powder Metallurgy	(ton)	6916.10
工业锅炉	(蒸发量吨)	Industrial Boiler	(ton)	1331.25
发动机	(千瓦)	Engine	(kw)	167711651.00
#汽车用发动机	(千瓦)	Automotive Engine	(kw)	167711651.00
电站用汽轮机	(千瓦)	Power Plant Steam Turbine	(kw)	1247400.00
电站水轮机	(千瓦)	Turbine	(kw)	3020.00
金属切削机床	(台)	Metal Cutting Machine	(piece)	8275.00

13-9 续表 6 continued

名 称	计量单位	Name	Measurement	产品产量
#数控金属切削机床	(台)	CNC Metal Cutting Machine	(piece)	3753.00
金属成形机床	(台)	Metal Forming Machine	(piece)	2147.00
#数控金属成形机床(数控锻压设备)	(台)	CNC Metal Forming Machine	(piece)	1559.00
铸造机械	(台)	Foundry Machinery	(piece)	14380.00
电焊机	(台)	Electric Welding Machine	(piece)	392.97
机床数控装置	(套)	Machine Digital Control Device	(piece)	1573.00
起重机	(吨)	Crane	(piece)	37173.71
电动车辆(电动叉车)	(台)	Electric Vehicles (electric forklift)	(piece)	32604.00
输送机械(输送机和提升机)	(吨)	Transportation Machinery (conveyors and elevators)	(ton)	105481.50
泵	(台)	Pump	(piece)	693282.00
#真空泵	(台)	Vacuum Pump	(piece)	15145.00
气体压缩机	(台)	Gas Compressor	(piece)	29830117.00
#制冷设备用压缩机	(台)	Refrigeration Equipment with Compressor	(piece)	29823861.00
阀门	(吨)	Valve	(ton)	63395.98
液压元件	(件)	Hydraulic Components	(piece)	847696.00
滚动轴承	(万套)	Roller	(10 000 pieces)	12150.51
齿轮	(吨)	Gear	(ton)	176657.50
风机	(台)	Fans	(piece)	97036.00
包装专用设备	(台)	Special Equipment Package	(piece)	6906.00
金属密封件	(万件)	Metal Sealing Element	(10 000 pieces)	7005.65
金属紧固件	(吨)	Metal Fastenings	(ton)	282811.35
弹簧	(吨)	Spring	(ton)	72715.68
减速机	(台)	Reducer	(piece)	265616.00
矿山专用设备	(吨)	Mining Special Equipment	(ton)	245683.95
混凝土机械	(台)	Concrete Machinery	(piece)	1241.00
金属冶炼设备	(吨)	Metal Smelting Equipment	(ton)	21747.00
金属轧制设备	(吨)	Metal Rolling Equipment	(ton)	6220.30
炼油、化工生产专用设备	(吨)	Oil Refining and Chemical Production Special Equipment	(ton)	32415.49
塑料加工专用设备	(台)	Plastics Processing Special Equipment	(piece)	672.00
模具	(套)	Mold	(piece)	540333.00
农产品初加工机械	(台)	Equipment for Agricultural Products Pretreating	(piece)	74842.00
饲料生产专用设备	(台)	Equipment for Feed Production	(piece)	1984.00
小型拖拉机	(台)	Small Tractor	(piece)	1341.00
收获机械	(台)	Harvesting Machinery	(piece)	28.00
收获后处理机械	(台)	Post-harvesting Processing Machinery	(piece)	38715.00
环境污染防治专用设备	台(套)	Equipment for Environmental Pollution Control	(piece)	12945.00

13-9 续表 7 continued

名 称	计量单位	Name	Measurement	产品产量
#大气污染防治设备	台(套)	Air Pollution Control Equipment	(piece)	6850.00
水质污染防治设备	台(套)	Water Pollution Control Equipment	(piece)	4997.00
固体废弃物处理设备	台(套)	Solid Waste Handling Equipment	(piece)	1098.00
工业机器人	(套)	Industrial Robot	(piece)	9857.00
汽车	(辆)	Car	(piece)	2105348.00
#基本型乘用车(轿车)	(辆)	Passenger Vehicles	(piece)	849546.00
#1 升<排量≤1.6 升	(辆)	1.0 Liter < Displacement ≤ 1.6 Liter	(piece)	463897.00
1.6 升<排量≤2.0 升	(辆)	1.6 Liter < Displacement ≤ 2.0 Liter	(piece)	353851.00
多功能乘用车(MPV)	(辆)	MPV	(piece)	67724.00
运动型多用途乘用车(SUV)	(辆)	SUV	(piece)	623944.00
客车	(辆)	Bus	(piece)	22794.00
#中型客车(7 米<车长≤10 米)	(辆)	Medium Passenger Bus(7 m<car length≤10 m)	(piece)	522.00
轻型客车(车长≤7 米)	(辆)	Light buses (car length≤ 7 m)	(piece)	22197.00
载货汽车	(辆)	Lorry	(piece)	485398.00
#新能源汽车	(辆)	New Energy Vehicles	(piece)	32019.00
改装汽车	(辆)	Modified Cars	(piece)	260221.00
低速载货汽车	(辆)	Low Speed Truck	(piece)	11701.00
铁路货车	(辆)	Railway Wagon	(piece)	3081.00
城市轨道车辆	(辆)	Railway Wagon	(piece)	502.00
民用钢质船舶	(载重吨)	Civil Steel Ships	(ton)	569271.00
电动自行车	(辆)	Electric Bicycle	(piece)	529754.00
发电机组(发电设备)	(千瓦)	Generating Units (power equipment)	(kw)	1139118.00
#水轮发电机组	(千瓦)	Generator Group	(kw)	30900.00
汽轮发电机	(千瓦)	Turbonator	(kw)	1104000.00
交流电动机	(千瓦)	AC Motors	(kw)	2500380.90
变压器	(千伏安)	Transformer	(kva)	20428826.67
互感器	(台)	Mutual Inductor	(kva)	188129.00
高压开关板	(面)	High-voltage Switch Board	(piece)	50383.00
低压开关板	(面)	Low-voltage Switch Board	(piece)	293895.00
高压开关设备(11 万伏以上)	(台)	High Voltage Switchgear (11 KV and above)	(piece)	155270.00
通信及电子网络用电缆	(对千米)	Communication and Electronic Networks Cables	(km)	850591.28
电力电缆	(千米)	Power Cable	(km)	1353093.40
光纤	(千米)	Optical Fiber	(km)	45443956.66
光缆	(芯千米)	Optical Cable	(km)	50285463.15
绝缘制品	(吨)	Insulation Products	(ton)	106582.76
锂离子电池	只(自然只)	Li-ion Battery	(piece)	1117789354.00
铅酸蓄电池	(千伏安时)	Lead-acid Battery	(kvah)	22467717.37

13-9 续表 8 continued

名 称	计量单位	Name	Measurement	产品产量
碱性蓄电池	只(自然只)	Alkaline Battery	(piece)	5994641.00
原电池及原电池组(非扣式)	(万只)	Primary Cells and Primary Batteries	(10 000 pieces)	2490.16
太阳能电池	(千瓦)	Solar Battery	(kw)	375625.12
家用电冰箱	(台)	Household Refrigerator	(piece)	5700645.00
家用冷柜(家用冷冻箱)	(台)	Household Refrigerator (household freezers)	(piece)	1957044.00
房间空气调节器	(台)	Room Air Conditioners	(piece)	17603075.00
家用吸排油烟机	(台)	Home Ventilator	(piece)	10383.00
家用电热水器	(台)	Water Heater	(piece)	2554147.00
家用燃气灶具	(台)	Kitchen Range	(piece)	1051961.00
太阳能热水器	(平方米)	Solar Water Heater	(sq.m)	9922.84
电光源	(万只)	Light Sources	(10 000 pieces)	45732.78
# 白炽灯泡	(万只)	Incandescent Bulb	(10 000 pieces)	2017.46
荧光灯	(万只)	Fluorescent Lamp	(10 000 pieces)	1644.27
灯具及照明装置	套(台、个)	Lamps and Lighting Fittings	(pieces)	29950168.00
电子计算机整机	(台)	Computers	(pieces)	17686318.00
# 微型计算机设备	(台)	Micro-computer Equipment	(pieces)	17200129.00
# 平板电脑	(台)	Tablet PC	(pieces)	14485960.00
显示器	(台)	Monitor	(pieces)	14558485.00
移动通信手持机(手机)	(台)	Mobile Handset (cell phone)	(pieces)	26670089.00
# 智能手机	(台)	Intelligent Mobile Phone	(pieces)	25051975.00
半导体分立器件	(万只)	Semiconductor Discrete Devices	(10 000 pieces)	898691.30
集成电路圆片	(万片)	IC Wafer	(10 000 pieces)	52.83
光电子器件	万只(片、套)	Optoelectronic Devices	(10 000 pieces)	768801.34
# 发光二极管(LED)	(万只)	Light-emitting Diode (LED)	(10 000 pieces)	438276.00
电子元件	(万只)	Electronic Component	(10 000 pieces)	1084183.53
印制电路板	(平方米)	Printed Board	(sq.m)	11486361.17
工业自动调节仪表与控制系统	台(套)	Automatic Adjustment and Control System	(piece)	346544.00
电工仪器仪表	(台)	Electric Instrument	(piece)	2635998.00
分析仪器及装置	台(套)	Analytical Instrument	(piece)	2656.00
汽车仪器仪表	(台)	Car Instrument	(piece)	499741.00
光学仪器	台(个)	Optical Instrument	(piece)	1213538.00
发电量	(万千瓦小时)	Power Generation	(10 000 kwh)	29113503.00
# 火力发电量	(万千瓦小时)	Thermal Capacity	(10 000 kwh)	12206143.11
水力发电量	(万千瓦小时)	Hydroelectricity	(10 000 kwh)	15745319.21
风力发电量	(万千瓦小时)	Wind Power Capacity	(10 000 kwh)	727891.00
煤气生产量	(万立方米)	Coal Gas	(10 000 cu.m)	4134265.00
自来水生产量	(万立方米)	Water Production	(10 000 cu.m)	391126.12

13-10 规模以上工业企业主要经济效益指标(2020)

项 目	Item	企业亏损面(%) Enterprises deficit (%)
总计	**Total**	**13.1**
一、按登记注册类型分组:	**Grouped by Type of Registration**	
内资企业	Inner Funded Enterprises	12.6
国有企业	State Owned Enterprises	19.9
中央企业	Central Enterprises	20.8
地方企业	Local Enterprises	19.4
集体企业	Collective-owned Enterprise	9.4
股份合作企业	Share Holding Cooperative Enterprises	25.0
联营企业	Joint Owned Enterprise	42.9
国有联营企业	State Joint Ownership	33.3
集体联营企业	Collective Joint Ownership	100.0
国有与集体联营企业	Joint State-Collective Ownership	100.0
其他联营企业	Other Joint Owned Enterprise	
有限责任公司	Responsibility Co. Ltd	18.8
国有独资公司	State Solely Funded Co.	22.9
其他有限责任公司	Others	18.7
股份有限公司	Share Holding Co.Ltd.	16.2
私营企业	Private - owned Enterprises	10.7
私营独资企业	Solely Private - owned Enterprises	7.5
私营合伙企业	Private Joint Venture	10.0
私营有限责任公司	Private Responsibility Co. Ltd	10.9
私营股份有限公司	Private Share Holding Co.Ltd.	9.5
其他企业	Others	
港、澳、台商投资企业	Hongkong, Macao and Taiwan Funded Enterprises	21.6
合资经营企业(港或澳、台资)	Joint Venture with Hongkong, Macao and Taiwan	18.7
合作经营企业(港或澳、台资)	Cooperate with Hongkong, Macao and Taiwan Funded	
港澳台商独资经营企业	Enterprises Solely Funded by Hongkong, Macao and Taiwan Businessmen	22.0
港澳台商投资股份有限公司	Share Holding Co.Ltd. With Hongkong, Macao and Taiwan Investment	22.2
其他港澳台商投资企业	Others	45.5
外商投资企业	Foreign Funded Enterprises	23.4
中外合资经营企业	Sino - Foreign Joint Funded Enterprises	23.7
中外合作经营企业	Sino - Foreign Cooperative Funded Enterprises	20.0
外资企业	Foreign Solely Funded Enterprises	23.0
外商投资股份有限公司	Foreign Funded Share Holding Co.Ltd.	20.0
其他外商投资企业	Others	30.0
二、在总计中:亏损企业	**Of the Total: Enterprises Running Under Deficit**	**100.0**
在总计中:国有控股企业	Of the Total: State-Owned Share Holding Enterprises	19.9
在总计中:轻工业	Of the Total: Light Industry	11.9
重工业	Heavy Industry	13.9
在总计中:大型企业	Of the Total: Large Scale Enterprises	15.4
中型企业	Medium Scale Enterprises	13.6
小型企业	Small Enterprises	13.0

Main Economic Efficiency Indicators of Industrial Enterprises above Designated Size(2020)

资产负债率(%) Assets Liability Ratio(%)	总资产贡献率(%) Contributing Ratie of Tatal Assets(%)	流动资产周转率(次/年) Current Asset Tuinover (Times/year)	成本费用利润率(%) Ratio of Riofits to Industrial Cost(%)
52.27	**10.58**	**1.91**	**7.04**
50.68	10.30	1.93	6.97
64.75	1.19	1.65	-1.43
63.94	1.77	1.78	-0.15
69.34	-2.08	1.12	-10.36
48.62	14.06	2.25	7.20
43.35	14.37	1.49	11.86
66.87	2.99	1.21	2.38
65.34	3.40	0.81	3.49
47.57	2.41	0.38	-1.00
62.64	-0.09	0.47	-0.82
87.34	6.76	5.40	1.29
55.17	10.16	1.46	6.42
51.08	28.09	1.57	9.76
56.07	6.25	1.44	5.74
42.46	8.05	0.98	14.59
48.03	15.05	3.26	6.49
47.86	21.06	3.85	6.08
42.50	23.81	5.27	8.52
48.45	15.26	3.36	6.33
45.19	12.72	2.47	8.02
70.48	21.98	1.04	25.37
50.17	10.61	1.67	9.56
60.10	9.55	1.31	9.18
11.91	19.55	2.02	29.35
43.82	11.84	2.52	8.86
34.45	10.43	0.72	23.33
42.74	9.91	1.24	11.84
65.58	12.78	1.86	6.71
66.30	14.36	1.97	6.72
64.09	5.54	1.15	5.04
64.88	9.43	1.71	6.52
52.70	16.00	1.55	17.68
50.88	5.00	1.22	4.94
62.43	**-0.44**	**1.43**	**-7.90**
53.48	9.43	1.29	7.79
46.01	19.31	2.42	8.52
54.09	8.04	1.73	6.35
53.28	9.81	1.45	7.35
52.14	10.93	1.83	8.54
50.87	11.50	2.55	6.18

13-10 续表 continued

项 目	Item	企业亏损面(%) Enterprises Deficit(%)
按行业分	**Grouped by Sector**	
采矿业	**Mining and Qarrying**	**12.3**
煤炭开采和洗选业	Coal Mining and Processing	50.0
石油和天然气开采业	Petroleum and Natural Gas Extraction	100.0
黑色金属矿采选业	Ferrous Metals Mining and Processing	11.1
有色金属矿采选业	Non-ferrous Metals Mining and Processing	25.0
非金属矿采选业	Non-metal Minerals Mining and Processing	10.6
开采辅助活动	Mining Auxiliary Activities	
其他采矿业	Other Minerals Mining and Processing	50.0
制造业	**Manufacturing**	**13.1**
农副食品加工业	Food Processing	11.0
食品制造业	Food Production	12.4
酒、饮料和精制茶制造业	Wine, Beverage and Refined Tea Production	10.5
烟草制品业	Tobacco Processing	14.3
纺织业	Textile Industry	11.0
纺织服装、服饰业	Textile, Garments, and Fashion Industry	13.1
皮革、毛皮、羽毛及其制品和制鞋业	Leather, Furs, Down and Related Products	9.4
木材加工和木、竹、藤、棕、草制品业	Timber Processing, Wood, Bamboo, Cane, Palm and Sraw Products	10.1
家具制造业	Furniture Manufacturing	13.8
造纸和纸制品业	Papermaking and Paper Products	12.1
印刷和记录媒介复制业	Printing and Record Processing	15.3
文教、工美、体育和娱乐用品制造业	Stationery, Education and Sports Goods	7.9
石油加工、炼焦和核燃料加工业	Petroleum Processing, Coking Products and Nuclear Fuel Processing	22.6
化学原料和化学制品制造业	Raw Chemical Material and Chemical Products	11.5
医药制造业	Medical and Pharmaceutical Products	17.0
化学纤维制造业	Chemical Fibers	16.7
橡胶和塑料制品业	Rubber and Plastic Products	10.1
非金属矿物制品业	Nonmetal Material Products	9.2
黑色金属冶炼和压延加工业	Smelting and Pressing of Ferrous Metals	23.1
有色金属冶炼和压延加工业	Smelting and Pressing of Nonferrous Metals	27.5
金属制品业	Metal Products	13.7
通用设备制造业	Ordinary Machinery Manufacturing	11.6
专用设备制造业	Special Purpose Equipment Manufacturing	11.4
汽车制造业	Motor Manufacturing	19.1
铁路、船舶、航空航天和其他运输设备制造业	Railway, Watercraft, Aviation and other Transporlation Equipment Manufacturing	13.9
电气机械和器材制造业	Electric Machinery and Equipment	16.9
计算机、通信和其他电子设备制造业	Telecommunication Computer, Equipment and Other Electronic Equipment Manufacturing	19.7
仪器仪表制造业	Instruments and Meters, Manufacturing	14.6
其他制造业	Other Manufacturing	14.0
废弃资源综合利用业	Waste Comprehensive Vtilization of Resources Industry	23.1
金属制品、机械和设备修理业	Metal products, Machinery and Equipment Repairing	13.6
电力、燃气及水的生产和供应业	**Electric Power, Gas and Water Production and Supply**	**13.0**
电力、热力生产和供应业	Electric Power, Steam and Hot Water Production and Supply	13.4
燃气生产和供应业	Gas Production and Supply	6.6
水的生产和供应业	Tap Water Production and Supply	16.7

资产负债率(%) Assets Liability Ratio(%)	总资产贡献率(%) Contributing Ratie of Tatal Assets(%)	流动资产周转率(次/年) Current Asset Tuinover (Times/year)	成本费用利润率(%) Ratio of Riofits to Industrial Cost(%)
53.39	**7.89**	**1.74**	**5.54**
122.34	2.71	0.77	1.02
49.86	-2.73	0.99	-16.57
59.25	11.59	2.17	6.28
31.80	25.61	1.17	52.44
56.05	11.83	1.97	7.73
45.92	1.62	0.64	1.40
51.99	11.85	1.88	5.28
52.00	**11.14**	**1.89**	**6.55**
45.53	14.47	4.02	5.49
43.61	13.69	2.56	8.00
51.19	13.78	1.08	15.59
31.37	98.95	1.59	44.66
44.34	21.66	4.11	8.19
46.33	16.79	4.09	5.99
45.76	18.79	4.39	5.89
47.47	6.88	2.13	3.89
45.94	9.99	2.11	8.11
56.92	9.10	2.20	6.80
47.21	12.72	2.18	7.99
55.42	11.48	2.22	6.01
60.66	42.70	6.67	0.44
51.98	10.28	2.67	6.19
41.87	13.39	1.49	14.12
51.28	3.92	2.55	-0.57
44.15	13.81	2.77	7.29
45.05	15.28	2.47	9.78
54.35	6.34	3.22	2.69
62.24	11.51	4.54	1.95
56.29	9.32	1.92	4.75
53.06	8.87	1.99	5.15
55.99	8.33	1.50	5.82
53.97	9.04	1.35	7.22
63.24	3.47	0.70	6.25
55.13	8.01	1.67	5.07
56.32	1.81	0.99	1.85
51.43	10.85	1.36	8.14
55.87	6.77	1.58	5.06
52.15	8.38	2.25	1.40
53.52	12.12	1.88	4.56
53.65	**7.77**	**2.49**	**16.09**
52.27	8.41	3.38	17.53
66.04	6.68	1.48	8.65
60.88	2.11	0.52	4.02

13-11 规模以上工业企业产销总值及主要经济指标(分地区)(2020)

单位:亿元

地 区	Region	企业单位数(个) Number of Enterprises(unit)	亏损企业 Enterprises Running under Deficit
全 省	**Province**	**15708**	**2060**
武汉市	Wuhan	2971	607
黄石市	Huangshi	705	161
十堰市	Shiyan	950	167
宜昌市	Yichang	1299	105
襄阳市	Xiangyang	1704	157
鄂州市	Ezhou	472	50
荆门市	Jingmen	982	90
孝感市	Xiaogan	1183	129
荆州市	Jingzhou	1241	176
黄冈市	Huanggang	1243	181
咸宁市	Xianning	945	62
随州市	Suizhou	679	45
恩施自治州	Enshi	329	51
仙桃市	Xiantao	452	36
潜江市	Qianjiang	227	14
天门市	Tianmen	316	26
神农架林区	Shennongjia	10	3

Gross Production and Sales and Main Economic Indicators of Industrial Enterprises above Designated Size (By Region) (2020)

(100 million yuan)

资产总计 Total Assets	流动资产合计 Circulating Funds	应收帐款 Accounts Receivable
44195.49	**21434.85**	**5282.60**
18041.00	9599.75	2452.69
2045.20	1156.32	181.62
2348.17	1441.68	313.19
5416.64	1485.35	279.36
3829.17	2082.69	662.11
745.03	317.88	104.44
2004.18	875.09	180.28
1718.34	800.66	201.82
2196.15	1127.34	284.36
1459.13	665.92	173.71
1114.60	518.56	143.39
933.02	397.87	114.12
447.48	146.23	39.92
665.39	328.89	72.16
739.83	265.31	39.36
451.28	204.92	39.69
40.85	20.39	0.37

13-11 续表 1 continued

单位:亿元

地 区	Region	固定资产原价 Original Price of Fixed Assets	累计折旧 Accumulated
全 省	**Province**	**25418.10**	**11901.60**
武汉市	Wuhan	9431.11	4536.39
黄石市	Huangshi	918.13	363.81
十堰市	Shiyan	811.26	330.34
宜昌市	Yichang	3557.04	1599.37
襄阳市	Xiangyang	1908.48	853.28
鄂州市	Ezhou	544.59	250.28
荆门市	Jingmen	1297.51	541.14
孝感市	Xiaogan	1881.38	1307.44
荆州市	Jingzhou	1163.22	550.50
黄冈市	Huanggang	810.87	240.77
咸宁市	Xianning	609.75	209.49
随州市	Suizhou	481.59	137.00
恩施自治州	Enshi	401.13	145.98
仙桃市	Xiantao	422.86	183.46
潜江市	Qianjiang	699.24	378.52
天门市	Tianmen	459.81	266.88
神农架林区	Shennongjia	20.12	6.95

(100 million yuan)

固定资产净额 Total Fixed Assets	负债合计 Total Liability	流动负债合计 Total Circulating Liability	应付账款 Aaounts Payable	所有者权益合计 Total Rights of Owners
12533.09	**23100.74**	**17514.61**	**5738.98**	**21007.97**
4744.67	9694.62	7499.67	3194.21	8336.87
521.92	1116.04	945.07	197.62	928.64
458.11	1570.68	1312.11	410.63	777.19
1909.88	2701.66	1779.77	306.25	2714.26
914.37	1858.03	1435.61	425.40	1929.58
269.45	401.17	325.33	103.52	341.61
683.38	969.46	750.81	152.28	1031.18
484.49	880.11	541.79	144.44	836.32
497.41	1018.25	820.10	239.00	1173.60
514.97	802.81	608.26	157.10	644.65
318.16	507.91	390.86	111.12	599.90
289.38	449.74	302.86	86.66	482.10
237.49	241.96	168.87	29.42	203.28
204.20	302.78	254.29	70.45	362.62
302.40	362.89	237.18	59.71	376.94
169.65	192.99	125.66	47.98	257.99
13.17	29.61	16.38	3.18	11.24

13-11 续表 2 continued

单位:亿元

地区	Region	所有者权益合计 Total Rights of Owners	
		实收资本 Assets Recevied	国家资本 National Assets
全 省	**Province**	**8850.97**	**1998.86**
武汉市	Wuhan	3790.61	1173.51
黄石市	Huangshi	355.53	84.00
十堰市	Shiyan	409.49	121.13
宜昌市	Yichang	778.21	68.73
襄阳市	Xiangyang	657.77	125.56
鄂州市	Ezhou	221.71	129.46
荆门市	Jingmen	433.85	63.74
孝感市	Xiaogan	419.30	52.20
荆州市	Jingzhou	458.87	37.78
黄冈市	Huanggang	367.85	25.75
咸宁市	Xianning	247.27	10.78
随州市	Suizhou	230.27	30.91
恩施自治州	Enshi	118.63	46.18
仙桃市	Xiantao	103.81	6.72
潜江市	Qianjiang	117.34	16.45
天门市	Tianmen	136.10	5.77
神农架林区	Shennongjia	4.35	0.20

(100 million yuan)

集体资本 Collective Assets	法人资本 Corperative Assets	个人资本 Individual Assets	港澳台资本 Assets from Hongkong, Macao and Taiwan	外商资本 Foreign Assets	营业成本 Cost
193.36	**4235.82**	**1716.89**	**226.51**	**474.44**	**33842.09**
40.52	1899.10	329.22	98.97	247.11	10186.44
23.00	154.23	52.43	5.23	36.63	1467.83
14.52	157.70	66.17	1.82	48.16	1610.60
19.64	491.61	145.17	38.66	14.40	2492.92
40.32	279.94	158.14	14.70	39.09	4597.76
6.10	41.44	42.67	0.78	1.23	1057.46
4.56	168.74	182.79	5.37	8.65	2476.54
3.68	184.86	150.85	17.34	10.38	2142.25
6.23	201.50	174.43	4.34	34.61	1708.81
11.69	187.31	119.10	15.39	8.63	1058.64
7.42	121.91	93.09	11.15	2.92	1489.11
5.69	97.41	91.93	3.64	0.70	1107.41
1.45	42.17	25.08	0.89		131.95
2.89	41.44	25.54	6.52	20.71	870.83
4.69	66.07	29.06	0.70	0.38	708.00
0.99	97.45	30.04	1.01	0.85	731.15
	2.96	1.19			4.37

13-11 续表 3 continued

单位:亿元

地 区	Region	税金及附加 Tax of Business	销售费用 Selling Expenses
全 省	**Province**	**916.31**	**1190.29**
武汉市	Wuhan	622.26	380.57
黄石市	Huangshi	13.98	37.78
十堰市	Shiyan	12.58	60.34
宜昌市	Yichang	28.89	118.80
襄阳市	Xiangyang	34.31	122.60
鄂州市	Ezhou	7.90	38.65
荆门市	Jingmen	86.14	86.02
孝感市	Xiaogan	29.42	77.95
荆州市	Jingzhou	11.60	60.79
黄冈市	Huanggang	10.33	34.88
咸宁市	Xianning	10.34	39.43
随州市	Suizhou	8.91	39.58
恩施自治州	Enshi	1.31	5.71
仙桃市	Xiantao	8.45	45.19
潜江市	Qianjiang	26.00	12.23
天门市	Tianmen	2.95	29.67
神农架林区	Shennongjia	0.94	0.08

(100 million yuan)

管理费用 Management Expense	财务费用 Financial Expenses	利息费用 Interest Expenses	其他收益 Other Income	投资收益 Investment Income	营业利润 Operating Profits
1417.05	**336.03**	**306.96**	**140.79**	**250.94**	**2630.29**
462.78	27.66	79.32	74.33	165.57	671.31
43.39	13.53	13.34	1.27	−19.39	108.25
66.55	14.09	13.39	7.37	8.37	101.53
115.87	69.22	72.54	14.10	57.94	430.96
178.19	35.22	21.14	10.93	12.60	317.65
51.36	9.16	6.54	0.44	3.67	71.80
89.33	26.02	16.04	7.12	3.76	170.88
91.30	33.06	9.65	4.95	2.30	106.83
60.60	19.75	13.95	3.72	13.67	130.75
48.57	16.92	12.68	6.69	0.85	58.41
41.85	14.28	8.27	5.73	0.79	142.38
40.47	17.90	8.89	1.22	0.43	116.47
8.33	6.01	4.36	0.29	0.48	21.96
54.84	9.89	6.90	0.32	−0.57	116.26
24.46	5.95	5.44	2.08	0.26	19.76
38.73	16.13	13.58	0.21		43.60
0.43	1.23	0.92	0.01	0.22	1.49

13-11 续表 4 continued

单位:亿元

地 区	Region	营业外收入 Non-operating Income	营业外支出 Non-operating Expense	利润总额 Total Profits	所得税费用 Income Tax
全 省	**Province**	**122.43**	**105.57**	**2646.93**	**379.80**
武汉市	Wuhan	40.01	44.72	666.60	135.51
黄石市	Huangshi	6.19	7.44	107.00	18.96
十堰市	Shiyan	5.75	11.49	95.79	7.91
宜昌市	Yichang	11.98	12.91	430.04	67.81
襄阳市	Xiangyang	16.67	7.94	326.37	35.78
鄂州市	Ezhou	2.49	1.53	72.77	11.48
荆门市	Jingmen	5.24	3.17	172.96	13.60
孝感市	Xiaogan	10.59	2.53	114.89	8.49
荆州市	Jingzhou	6.46	4.52	132.48	16.91
黄冈市	Huanggang	4.65	3.21	59.85	11.54
咸宁市	Xianning	3.83	1.66	144.55	15.84
随州市	Suizhou	2.12	1.45	117.14	4.16
恩施自治州	Enshi	1.69	0.83	22.82	3.71
仙桃市	Xiantao	2.16	0.87	117.55	16.54
潜江市	Qianjiang	1.83	1.01	20.57	5.19
天门市	Tianmen	0.63	0.12	44.12	6.02
神农架林区	Shennongjia	0.14	0.18	1.45	0.33

(100 million yuan)

亏损企业亏损总额 Total Loss of Enterprises Running under Deficit	应交税金及附加 Tax alafor Business	本年应付工资薪酬 Wases Welfarism Payable This Year	本年应交增值税 Value Added Payable of the Current Year	全部从业人员年平均人数(万人) Average Number of Empolyment of the Current Year (10 000 persons)
363.03	**2172.65**	**2671.87**	**876.55**	**274.51**
205.73	1087.08	888.36	329.31	70.09
10.59	61.65	110.80	28.72	12.89
16.13	69.89	134.21	49.40	13.76
25.73	207.02	187.97	110.33	23.02
16.34	174.02	334.18	103.93	30.00
1.35	42.48	120.31	23.09	11.79
11.30	139.53	116.33	39.79	14.88
10.72	75.85	150.34	37.95	18.41
11.96	60.71	145.59	32.20	17.10
24.50	48.44	89.79	26.57	14.70
5.73	54.01	84.66	27.83	11.38
3.35	22.99	64.82	9.91	8.37
1.14	11.79	16.48	6.78	2.20
4.48	58.33	89.82	33.34	11.70
12.72	42.22	70.00	11.04	5.54
0.92	14.75	67.52	5.78	8.61
0.35	1.88	0.67	0.60	0.08

13-12 分市州规模以上工业企业主要经济效益指标(2020)

单位:%

地 区	Item	企业亏损面 Loss Making Rate of Enterprises	资产负债率 Assets Liability Ratio
全 省	**Province**	**13.1**	**52.27**
武汉市	Wuhan	20.4	53.74
黄石市	Huangshi	22.8	54.57
十堰市	Shiyan	17.6	66.89
宜昌市	Yichang	8.1	49.88
襄阳市	Xiangyang	9.2	48.52
鄂州市	Ezhou	10.6	53.85
荆门市	Jingmen	9.2	48.37
孝感市	Xiaogan	10.9	51.22
荆州市	Jingzhou	14.2	46.37
黄冈市	Huanggang	14.6	55.02
咸宁市	Xianning	6.6	45.57
随州市	Suizhou	6.6	48.20
恩施自治州	Enshi	15.5	54.07
仙桃市	Xiantao	8.0	45.50
潜江市	Qianjiang	6.2	49.05
天门市	Tianmen	8.2	42.77
神农架林区	Shennongjia	30.0	72.48

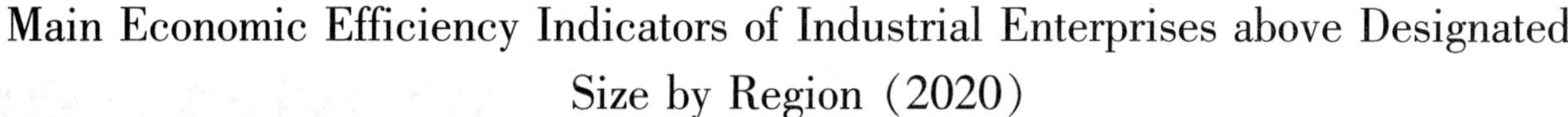

Main Economic Efficiency Indicators of Industrial Enterprises above Designated Size by Region (2020)

总资产贡献率 Contributing Rate of Total Assets	流动资产周转率(次/年) Current Asset Turnover(Times/Year)	成本费用利润率 Ratio of Profits to Industrial Cost
10.58	**1.91**	**7.04**
9.15	1.30	5.87
7.78	1.55	6.72
7.07	1.32	5.32
11.75	2.20	14.94
12.60	2.57	6.50
14.77	3.91	6.22
15.64	3.40	6.36
11.09	3.15	4.81
8.68	1.78	7.03
7.47	1.87	5.05
17.07	3.41	8.93
15.51	3.37	9.62
7.92	1.21	14.79
24.88	3.42	11.78
8.33	3.04	2.70
14.72	4.24	5.37
9.58	0.41	23.59

主要统计指标解释

工业　指从事自然资源的开采，对采掘品和农产品进行加工和再加工的物质生产部门。具体包括：(1)对自然资源的开采，如采矿、晒盐等（但不包括禽兽捕猎和水产捕捞）；(2)对农副产品的加工、再加工，如粮油加工、食品加工、缫丝、纺织、制革等；(3)对采掘品的加工、再加工，如炼铁、炼钢、化工生产、石油加工、机器制造、木材加工等，以及电力、自来水、煤气的生产和供应等；(4)对工业品的修理、翻新，如机器设备的修理、交通运输工具（如汽车）的修理等。

工业统计调查单位为独立核算法人工业企业。

独立核算法人工业企业指从事工业生产经营活动的单位。独立核算法人工业企业应同时具备以下条件：①依法成立，有自己的名称、组织机构和场所，能够承担民事责任；②独立拥有和使用资产，承担负债，有权与其他单位签订合同；③独立核算盈亏，并能够编制资产负债表。

本年鉴中涉及的企业登记注册类型：

国有及国有控股企业　指国有企业加上国有控股企业。国有企业（即原全民所有制工业或国营工业）指企业全部资产归国家所有，并按《中华人民共和国企业法人登记管理条例》规定登记注册的非公司制的经济组织。包括国有企业、国有独资公司和国有联营企业。1957年以前的公私合营和私营工业，后均改造为国营工业，1992年改为国有工业，这部分工业的资料不单独分列时，均包括在国有企业内。国有控股企业是对混合所有制经济的企业进行的“国有控股”分类。它是指这些企业的全部资产中国有资产（股份）相对其他所有者中的任何一个所有者占资（股）最多的企业。该分组反映了国有经济控股情况。

集体企业　指企业资产归集体所有，并按《中华人民共和国企业法人登记管理条例》规定登记注册的经济组织。是社会主义公有制经济的组成部分。包括城乡所有使用集体投资举办的企业，以及部分个人通过集资自愿放弃所有权并依法经工商行政管理机关认定为集体所有制的企业。

股份合作企业　指以合作制为基础，由企业职工共同出资入股，吸收一定比例的社会资产投资组建，实行自主经营，自负盈亏，共同劳动，民主管理，按劳分配与按股分红相结合的一种集体经济组织。

联营企业　指两个及两个以上相同或不同所有制性质的企业法人或事业单位法人，按自愿、平等、互利的原则，共同投资组成的经济组织。联营企业包括：

国有联营企业指国有企业与国有企业间的联营；

集体联营企业指集体企业与集体企业间的联营；

国有与集体联营企业指国有企业与集体企业间的联营。

有限责任公司　指根据《中华人民共和国公司登记管理条例》规定登记注册，由两个以上，五十个以下的股东共同出资，每个股东以其所认缴的出资额对公司承担有限责任，公司以其全部资产对其债务承担责任的经济组织。

有限责任公司包括国有独资公司以及其他有限责任公司。

股份有限公司　指根据《中华人民共和国企业法人登记管理条例》规定登记注册，其全部注册资本由等额股份构成并通过发行股票筹集资本，股东以其认购的股份对公司承担有限责任，公司以其全部资产对其债务承担责任的经济组织。

私营企业　指由自然人投资设立或由自然人控股，以雇佣劳动为基础的营利性经济组织。包括按照《公司法》、《合伙企业法》、《私营企业暂行条例》规定登记注册的私营有限责任公司、私营股份有限公司、私营合伙企业和私营独资企业。

港、澳、台商投资企业　指企业注册登记类型中的港、澳、台资合资、合作、独资经营企业和股份有限公司之和。

外商投资企业　指企业注册登记类型中的中外合资、合作经营企业、外资企业和外商投资股份有限公司之和。

“三资”企业系指港、澳、台商投资企业和外资企业的简称。

轻工业　指主要提供生活消费品和制作手工工具的工业。按其所使用的原料不同，可分为两大类：(1)以农产品为原料的轻工业，是指直接或间接以农产品为基本原料的轻工业。主要包括食品制造、饮料制造、烟草加工、纺织、缝纫、皮革和毛皮制作、造纸以及印刷等工业；(2)以非农产品为原料的轻工业，是指以工业品为原料的轻工业。主要包括文教体育用品、化学药品制造、合成纤维制造、日用化学制品、日用玻璃制品、日用金属制品、手工工具制造、医疗器械制造、文化和办公用机械制造等工业。

重工业　指为国民经济各部门提供物质技术基础的主要生产资料的工业。按其生产性质和产品用途，可以分为下

列三类:(1)采掘(伐)工业,是指对自然资源的开采,包括石油开采、煤炭开采、金属矿开采、非金属矿开采等工业;(2)原材料工业,指向国民经济各部门提供基本材料、动力和燃料的工业。包括金属冶炼及加工、炼焦及焦炭、化学、化工原料、水泥、人造板以及电力、石油和煤炭加工等工业;(3)加工工业,是指对工业原材料进行再加工制造的工业。包括装备国民经济各部门的机械设备制造工业、金属结构、水泥制品等工业,以及为农业提供的生产资料如化肥、农药等工业。

根据上述划分原则,修理业中以重工业产品为修理作业对象的划为重工业,反之划为轻工业。

工业总产值

(1)定义:

工业总产值是以货币形式表现的,工业企业在一定时期内生产的工业最终产品或提供工业性劳务活动的总价值量。它反映一定时间内工业生产的总规模和总水平。

(2)计算原则:

工业生产的原则,即凡是企业在报告期生产的经检验合格的产品,不管是否在报告期销售,均包括在内。

最终产品的原则,即凡是计入工业总产值的产品,必须是本企业生产的经检验合格的,不需要再进行任何加工的最终产品。如果企业有中间产品(半成品)对外销售,则对外销售的中间产品应视为企业的最终产品。

工厂法原则,即工业总产值是以工业企业作为基本计算(核算)单位,即按企业的最终产品计算工业总产值。按这种方法计算的工业总产值,不允许同一产品价值在企业内部重复计算,不能把企业内部各个车间(分厂)生产的成果相加,但允许企业间的重复计算。

(3)内容及计算方法:

1995 年全国工业普查对工业总产值(原规定)的内容及计算原则和方法做了某些修订,修订后的工业总产值(新规定)包括三项内容:即本期生产成品价值、对外加工费收入、在制品半成品期末期初差额价值三部分。

本期生产成品价值:指企业本期生产,并在报告期内不再进行加工,经检验、包装入库的全部工业成品(半成品)价值合计,包括企业生产的自制设备及提供给本企业在建工程、其他非工业部门和福利部门等单位使用的成品价值。本期生产成品价值为按自备原材料生产的产品的数量乘以本期不含增值税(销项税额)的产品实际销售平均单价计算;会计核算中按成本价格转帐的自制设备和自产自用的成品,按成本价格计算生产成品价值。生产成品价值中不包括用定货者来料加工的成品(半成品)价值。

对外加工费收入:指企业在报告期内完成的对外承接的工业品加工(包括用定货者来料加工产品)的加工费收入和对外工业修理作业所取得的加工费收入。对外加工费收入按不含增值税(销项税额)的价格计算,可根据会计“产品销售收入”科目的有关资料取得。

对于本企业对内非工业部门提供的加工修理、设备安装的劳务收入,如果企业会计核算基础较好,能取得这部分资料,而且这部分价值所占比重较大,应包括在对外加工费收入中。

自制半成品在制品期末期初差额价值:指企业报告期在制品期末减期初的差额价值,本指标一般可以从会计核算资料中取得。如果会计产品成本核算中不计算半成品、在制品的成本,则总产值中也不包括这部分价值,反之则包括。

(4)工业总产值统计范围变化和计算方法修订情况:

1984 年以前工业总产值不包括村办工业,村办工业总产值划归农业。1984 年以后工业总产值包括村办工业。

1995 年工业普查对工业总产值计算方法做了修订,即从 1995 年始按新修订(新规定)方法计算工业总产值。新规定与原规定的区别如下:

全价与加工费的计算原则不同:新规定为凡自备原材料,不论其生产繁简程度如何,一律按全价计算工业总产值;凡来料加工,允许按加工费计算工业总产值。原规定则视生产加工的繁简程度不同,规定哪些行业按全价,哪些行业按加工费计算工业总产值。

自制半成品、在产品期末期初差额价值的计算原则不同;新规定要求,凡会计产品成本核算时计算了成本的差额价值,总产值中就应包括,否则可不包括;原规定则按生产周期六个月的界限区分,凡生产周期六个月以上的企业,总产值计算中应包括这部分差额价值,否则可不包括。

计算价格不同:新规定按不含增值税(销项税额)的价格计算;原规定则按含增值税(销项税额)的价格计算。

工业增加值 指工业企业在报告期内以货币表现的工业生产活动的最终成果。

工业增加值有两种计算方法:一是生产法,即工业总产出减去工业中间投入加上应交增值税;二是收入法,即从收入的角度出发,根据生产要素在生产过程中应得到的收入份额计算,具体构成项目有固定资产折旧、劳动者报酬、生产税净额、营业盈余,这种方法也称要素分配法。本年鉴中的工业增加值是以生产法计算的。

生产法工业增加值的计算方法为:

工业增加值=工业总产出-工业中间投入+应交增值税

(1)工业总产出:指工业企业在一定时期内工业生产活动的总成果。工业总产出包括:成品生产价值,对外加工费收入,自制半成品、在产品期末期初差额价值。1995 年后用新规定计算的工业总产值代替。

(2)工业中间投入：指工业企业在工业生产活动中消耗的外购物质产品和对外支付的服务费用。服务费用包括支付给物质生产部门(工业、农业、批发零售贸易业、建筑业、运输邮电业）的服务费用和支付给非物质生产部门（如保险、金融、文化教育、科学研究、医疗卫生、行政管理等)的服务费用。工业中间投入的确定须遵循以下原则：必须从外部购入的，并已计入工业总产出的产品和服务价值；必须是本期投入生产，并一次性消耗掉(包括本期摊销的低值易耗品等)的产品和服务价值。

工业中间投入包括直接材料费用、制造费用中的工业中间投入、管理费用中的工业中间投入、销售费用中的工业中间投入和利息支出五部分。

资产总计 指企业拥有或控制的能以货币计量的经济资源，包括各种财产、债权和其他权利。资产按流动性分为流动资产、长期投资、固定资产、无形资产、递延资产和其他资产。该指标根据企业会计“资产负债表”中“资产总计”项目的期末数增列。

流动资产 指企业可以在一年内或者超过一年的一个生产周期内变现或者耗用的资产，包括现金及各种存款、短期投资，应收及预付款项、存货等。

流动资产平均余额 指企业在报告期内全部流动资产的平均余额。

固定资产原价 指企业在建造、购置、安装、改建、扩建、技术改造某项固定资产时所支出的全部货币总额。它一般包括买价、包装费、运杂费和安装费等。

固定资产净值年平均余额 指固定资产净值在报告期内余额的平均数。计算公式为：

$$\text{固定资产净值年平均余额}=\frac{\text{1至12月各月月初、月末固定资产净值之和}}{24}$$

该指标根据“资产负债表”中“固定资产原价”、“累计折旧”指标的期初、期末数计算填列。

固定资产净值指固定资产原价减去历年已提折旧额后的净额。计算公式为：

固定资产净值=固定资产原价-累计折旧

负债合计 指企业所承担的能以货币计量，将以资产或劳务偿付的债务，偿还形式包括货币、资产或提供劳务。负债一般按偿还期长短分为流动负债和长期负债。根据会计“资产负债表”中“负债合计”的年末数填列。

所有者权益 指企业投资人对企业净资产的所有权。企业净资产等于企业全部资产减去全部负债后的余额，包括企业投资人对企业的最初投入的实际到位的资产及资本公积金、盈余公积金和未分配利润。所有者权益合计数小于零，表示企业资不抵债。

主营业务收入 指会计“利润表”中对应指标的本年累计数。未执行2001年《企业会计制度》的企业，用“产品销售收入”的本期累计数代替。

主营业务成本 指会计“利润表”中对应指标的本年累计数。未执行2001年《企业会计制度》的企业，用“产品销售成本”的本期累计数代替。

主营业务税金及附加 指会计“利润表”中对应指标的本年累计数。未执行2001年《企业会计制度》的企业，用“产品销售税金及附加”的本期累计数代替。

利润总额 指企业生产经营活动的最终成果，是企业在一定时期内实现的盈亏相抵后的利润总额(亏损以“-”号表示)，它等于营业利润加上补贴收入加上投资收益加上营业外净收入再加上以前年度损益调整。

本年应交增值税 指企业在报告期内应交纳的增值税额。它等于本年销项税额加上出口退税加上进项税额转出数减去本年进项税额。小规模纳税企业直接按全年计税销售额乘以征收率计算取得。

从业人员平均人数 是指报告期内每天拥有的从业人员人数。其计算公式为：

$$\text{季平均人数}=\frac{\text{季内各月平均人数之和}}{3}$$

$$\text{月平均人数}=\frac{\text{报告月内每天实有人数之和}}{\text{报告月日历日数}}$$

$$\text{年平均人数}=\frac{\text{年内各月平均人数之和}}{12}$$

总资产贡献率 反映企业全部资产的获利能力，是企业经营业绩和管理水平的集中体现，是评价和考核企业盈利能力的核心指标。计算公式为：

$$\text{总资产贡献率(\%)}=\frac{\text{利润总额+税金总额+利息支出}}{\text{平均资金总额}}\times100\%$$

公式中：税金总额为产品销售税金及附加与应交增值税之和；平均资产总额为期初期末资产之和的算术平均值。

资产负债率 该指标既反映企业经营风险的大小，也反映企业利用债权人提供的资金从事经营活动的能力。计算公式为：

$$\text{资产负债率(\%)}=\frac{\text{负债总额}}{\text{资产总额}}\times100\%$$

资产与负债均为报告期期末数。

流动资产周转次数 指一定时期内流动资产完成的周转次数，反映投入工业企业流动资金的周转速度。计算公式为：

$$\text{流动资产周转资转次数}=\frac{\text{营业收入}}{\text{流动资产合计}}$$

公式中：全部流动资产平均余额为期初和期末的流动资产之和的算术平均值。

成本费用利润率 反映企业投入的生产成本及费用的经济效益，同时也反映企业降低成本所取得的经济效益。计算公式为：

$$\text{成本费用利润率(\%)}=\frac{\text{利润总额}}{\text{成本费用总额}}\times 100\%$$

公式中：成本费用总额为产品销售成本、销售费用、管理费用、财务费用之和。

全员劳动生产率 该指标反映企业的生产效率和劳动投入的经济效益。计算公式为：

$$\text{全员劳动生产率(元/人)}=\frac{\text{工业增加值}}{\text{全部从业人员平均人数}}$$

产品销售率 该指标反映工业产品已实现销售的程度，是分析工业产销衔接情况，研究工业产品满足社会需求的指标。计算公式为：

$$\text{产品销售率(\%)}=\frac{\text{工业销售产值}}{\text{工业总产值(现价)}}\times 100\%$$

Explanatory Notes on Main Statistical Indicators

Industry refers to the material production sector which is engaged in extraction of natural resources and processing and re-processing of minerals and agricultural products, including (1) extraction of natural resources, such as mining, salt production (but not including hunting and fishing); (2) processing and reprocessing of farm and sideline produces, such as rice husking, flour milling, wine making, oil pressing, silk reeling, spinning and weaving, and leather making; (3) manufacture of industrial products, such as steel making, iron smelting, chemicals manufacturing, petroleum processing, machine building, timber processing; water and gas production and electricity generation and supply; (4)repairing of industrial products such as the repairing of machinery and means of transport (including cars).

Units of industrial statistics survey corporate industrial enterprises with independent accounting system.

Corporate industrial enterprises with independent accounting system refer to enterprises engaging in industrial production activities, which meet the following requirements: (1)They are established legally, having their own names, organizations, location, able to take civil liability; (2)They possess and use their assets independently, assume liabilities, and are entitled to sign contracts with other units; (3)They are financially independent and compile their own balance sheets.

Enterprises covered in the industrial statistics in the Yearbook include following categories by their registration:

State-owned and State-holding Enterprises refer to state-owned enterprises plus state-holding enterprises. State-owned enterprises (originally known as state-run enterprises with ownership by the whole society) are non-corporate economic entities registered in accordance with the Regulation of the People's Republic of China on the Management of Registration of Legal Enterprises, where all assets are owned by the state. Included in this category are state-owned enterprises, state-funded corporations and state-owned joint-operation enterprises. Joint state-private industries and private industries, which existed before 1957, were transformed into state-run industries since 1957, and into state-owned industries after 1992. Statistics on those enterprises are included in the state-owned industries instead of grouping them separately. State-holding enterprises is a sub-classification of enterprises with mixed ownership, referring to enterprises where the percentage of state assets (or shares by the state) is larger than any other single share holder of the same enterprise. This sub-classification illustrates the control of the state over a particular industry.

Collective-owned Enterprises refer to economic entities registered in accordance with the Regulation of the People's Republic of China on the Management of Registration of Legal Enterprises, where assets are owned by collectively. Collective enterprises constitute an integral part of the socialist economy with public ownership. They include urban and rural enterprises invested by collectives, and some enterprises registered in industrial and commercial administration agency as collective units where funds are pulled together by individuals who voluntarily give up their right of ownership.

Share-holding Cooperative Enterprises refer to economic units set up on cooperative basis, with funding partly from members of the enterprise and partly from outside investment, where the operation and management is decided by the members who also participate in the production, and the distribution of income is based both on work (labour input) and on shares (capital input).

Joint-operation enterprises refer to economic units that are established by joint investment by two or more corporate enterprises or institutions of the same or different types of ownership on voluntary, equal and mutual-beneficial basis. They include:

a) state-owned joint-operation enterprises (joint operation between state-owned enterprises);

b) collective joint-operation enterprises (joint operation between collective enterprises; and

c) state-collective joint-operation enterprises (joint operation between state and collective enterprises).

Limited Liability Corporations refer to economic units registered in accordance with the Regulation of the People's Republic of China on the Management of Registration of Corporations, with capitals from 2 to 49 investors, each investor bears limited liability to the corporation depending on his/her holding of shares, and the corporation bears liability to its debt to the maximum of its total assets.

Share-holding Corporations Ltd. refer to economic units registered in accordance with the Regulation of the People's Republic of China on the Management of Registration of Corporate Enterprises, with total registered capitals divided into equal shares and raised through issuing stocks. Each investor bears limited liability to the corporation depending on the holding of shares, and the corporation bears liability to its debt to the maximum of its total assets.

Private Enterprises refer to economic units invested or controlled (by holding the majority of the shares) by natural persons who hire labours for profit-making activities. Included in this category are private limited liability corporations, private share-holding corporations Ltd., private partnership enterprises and private sole investment enterprises registered in accordance with the Corporation Law, Partnership Enterprise Law and Tentative Regulation on Private Enterprises.

Enterprises with Funds from Hong Kong, Macao and Taiwan refers to all industrial enterprises registered as the joint-venture, cooperative, sole (exclusive) investment industrial enterprises and limited liability corporations with funds from Hong Kong, Macao and Taiwan.

Foreign Funded Enterprises refers to all industrial enterprises registered as the joint-venture, cooperative, sole (exclusive) investment industrial enterprises and limited liability corporations with foreign funds.

Enterprise with Hong Kong, Macao, Taiwan and foreign fund refer to all the enterpries with funds from Hong Kong Macao and Taiwan and foreign funded enterprises.

Light Industry refers to the industry that produces consumer goods and hand tools. It consists of two categories, depending on the materials used:

(1) Industries using farm products as raw materials. These are branches of light industry which directly or indirectly use farm products as basic raw materials, including the manufacture of food and beverages, tobacco processing, textile, clothing, fur and leather manufacturing, paper making, printing, etc.

(2) Industries using non farm products as raw materials. These are branches of light industry which use manufactured goods as raw materials, including the manufacture of cultural, educational articles and sports goods, chemicals, synthetic fiber, chemical products for daily use, glass products for daily use, metal products for daily use, hand tools, medical apparatus and instruments, and the manufacture of cultural and clerical machinery.

Heavy Industry refers to the industry which produces capital goods, and provides various sectors of the national economy with necessary material and technical basis. It consists of the following three branches according to the purpose of production or the use of products:

(1) Mining, quarrying and logging industry refers to the industry that extracts natural resources, including extraction of petroleum, coal, metal and non-metal ores.

(2) Raw materials industry refers to the industry that provides various sectors of the national economy with raw materials, fuels and power. It includes smelting and processing of metals, coking and coke chemistry, chemical materials and building materials such as cement, plywood, and power, petroleum refining and coal dressing.

(3) Manufacturing industry refers to the industry that processes raw materials. It includes machine-building industry which equips sectors of the national economy, industries of metal structure and cement products, industries producing means of agricultural production, such as chemical fertilizers and pesticides.

According to the above principle of classification, the repairing trades, which are engaged primarily in repairing products of heavy industry are classified into heavy industry while these engaged in repairing products of light industry are classified into light industry.

Gross Industrial Output Value

(1) Definition: Gross industrial output value is the total volume of final industrial products produced and industrial services provided during a given period. It reflects the total achievements and overall scale of industrial production during a given period.

(2) Principles for calculation:

Statistics on industrial production follow the principle that all products produced by the enterprises and accepted during the reference period are to be included no matter whether they are sold or not during the reference period.

Determination of final products follow the principle that all products that are included in the calculation of grow industrial output value are the final products of the enterprise which have been accepted through quality check and require no further processing. If an enterprise has intermediate (semi-finished) products to sell, these intermediate products are considered as the final products of the enterprise.

Gross industrial output value is calculated following the principle of factory approach, i.e. industrial enterprise is used as the basic accounting unit in calculating the gross industrial output value. By this approach, value of the same product is not to be double counted, and the output value of different workshops (branch factories) should not be added. However, this approach does not exclude the possibility of double counting between enterprises.

(3) Content and calculation method: The old definition of gross industrial output value was modified during the national industrial census in 1995. The revised (new) definition of gross industrial output value consists of 3 components: value of the finished products during the reference period, income from external processing, and value of change in semi-finished products at the end and at the beginning of the reference period.

Value of the finished products during the reference period: refers to the value of all finished (semi-finished) industrial products that are produced during the reference period without the need for further processing, checked for acceptance, packed and put into the warehouse of the enterprise, including the value of own-produced equipment and the value of products provided to the projects under construction of the enterprise, and to other non-industrial or welfare units. Value of finished products during the reference period is calculated by the quantity of products produced using own materials multiplied by the average unit prices at which products are sold (excluding value-added tax). Own-produced equipment and products produced for own use are value at cost prices as in the case of enterprise accounting. Value of finished products does not include the value of finished products (semi-finished products) that are produced using the materials from the clients who make the orders.

Income from external processing: refers to income from contracted external processing of industrial products (including processing of industrial products using materials from the clients), and the income from industrial repairing work provided to other units. Income from external processing is calculated using information from the item "products sales income" in the enterprise accounting at the prices excluding value-added tax.

For income from services such as processing, repairing and installation of equipment provided to non-industrial units within the enterprise, if the accounting work of the enterprise is good enough to separate it from other records, and the share of such services is significant, it should also be included in the income from external processing.

Value of change in semi-finished products at the end and at the beginning of the reference period: refers to the value of change in semi-finished products at the end and at the beginning of the reference period, which generally can be obtained from accounting records of enterprises. If the enterprise accounting excludes the cost of semi-finished products, then it should not be included in the gross industrial output value, and vice versa.

(4) Changes in the coverage and method of calculation of gross industrial output value

Prior to 1984, the value of rural industry run by villages was classified into agriculture instead of industry. Since 1984, it has been included in the gross industrial output value. Method of calculation for the gross industrial output value was modified in the industrial census in 1995. The difference in the new method as compared with the old one is outlined below:

Principle in using full value vs. processing fee: The new method stipulates that all products produced using own materials are to be calculated with full value in reporting the gross industrial output value irrespective of sophistication of production, and for external processing, it allows calculation using processing fee. In the old method, however, the use of full value or processing fee was determined by the degree of sophistication of production in different branches of industries.

Principle in determining the value of change in semi-finished products: The new method requires that value of the change in semi-finished products should be included in the gross industrial output value if it is included in the accounting record of the enterprise, otherwise it should not be included. By the old method, it is determined by the type of enterprises in terms of production cycle. If the production cycle is over 6 months, the value of change in semi-finished products is included in the gross industrial output value, otherwise it is excluded.

Difference in prices: The new method uses prices excluding value-added tax in the calculation of gross industrial output value, while the old method used prices including value-added tax.

Value-added of Industry refers to the final results of industrial production of industrial enterprises in money terms during the reference period.

Industrial value-added can be calculated by two approaches: the production approach, i.e. gross industrial output value minus intermediate input plus value-added tax, and the income approach, i.e. income for various factors used in the course of production, including depreciation of fixed assets, remuneration of labourers, net of production tax, and operating surplus. Value-added of industry in the Yearbook is calculated by production approach as following:

Value-added of industry = gross industrial output industrial intermediate input + value-added tax

(1) Gross industrial output: refers to the total achievements of industrial production during a given period. Gross industrial output includes value of finished products, income from external processing, and value of change in semi-finished products at the end and at the beginning of the reference period. Since 1995, it was substituted by the gross industrial output value by new method.

(2) Industrial intermediate input: refers to purchased goods and paid services consumed during the industrial production of enterprises. Fees paid for services include fees paid for the services provided by material production sectors (industry, agriculture, wholesale and retail trade, construction, transport, post and telecommunications) and by non-material production sectors (insurance, banking, culture, education, scientific research, health and medical care, public administration, etc.). The determination of industrial intermediate input follows the principle that the goods and services must be purchased from outside and included in the gross industrial output, and that the goods and services are inputted into production and consumed (include low-value consumables) during the reference period.

Industrial intermediate input includes 5 components, namely direct consumption of materials, industrial intermediate input in manufacturing cost, industrial intermediate input in management cost, industrial intermediate input in marketing cost and expenditure on interest.

Total Assets refer to all economic resources, in monetary terms, that is owned or controlled by enterprises, including properties, creditors equity and other economic rights of all forms. Classified by the degree of equitability, total assets include circulating assets, long-term investment, fixed assets, intangible assets and deferred assets, and other assets. Data on this indicator can be obtained by the year-end figures of total assets in the Assets and Liability Table of accounting records of enterprises.

Working Capitals refer to capitals that an enterprise can cash or use during one year or one production cycle that may exceeds one year, including cash and savings deposits of various forms, short-term investment, money receivable and prepaid money, inventories, etc.

Annual Average Value of Working Capitals refers to the average value of all working capitals of the enterprise during the reference period.

Original Value of Fixed Assets refers to the total value, in monetary terms, that an enterprise spent on fixed assets, through construction, purchase, installation, transformation, expansion or technical upgrading. Generally, it covers cost of purchase, packing, transportation and installation, etc.

Annual Average of Net Value of Fixed Assets refer to average of the net value of fixed assets during the reference period, calculated with the following formula:

Annual Average of Net Value of Fixed Assets = sum of net value of fixed assets at the beginning and at the end of each month from January to December / 24.

Information on this indicator can be obtained from the beginning and ending figures of the original value of fixed assets and cumulative depreciation from the Assets and Liability Table of enterprises.

Net value of fixed assets refers to the original value of fixed assets minus depreciation over the years, i.e.:

Net value of fixed assets = original value of fixed assets cumulative depreciation

Total Liabilities refer to payable liabilities of enterprises that have to repay in terms of money, assets or labour services. In terms of payment, it can be divided into liquid liabilities and long-term liabilities. Data on this item is obtained from the ending figures on total liabilities from theAssets and Liability Table from the enterprises.

Owner's Equity refers to the ownership of net assets of enterprise by its investors. The net assets equal the total assets minus total liabilities of the enterprise, including the actual assets invested into the enterprise by investors, accumulation of capitals and operating surplus and non-distributed profits. The enterprise's assets is less than its liabilities if the sum of owner's equity is smaller than zero.Revenue from Principal Business refers to the annual accumulation of corresponding item in the "profit table" of the accountant. For enterprises that do not follow the 2001 Enterprise Accounting Standards, the year-end accumulation of revenue from the sales of products is used as a substitute.

Cost of Principal Business refers to the annual accumulation of corresponding item in the "profit table" of the accountant. For enterprises that do not follow the 2001 Enterprise Accounting Standards, the year-end accumulation of cost for the sales of products is used as a substitute.

Tax and Extra Charges from Principal Business refer to the annual accumulation of corresponding item in the "profit table" of the accountant. For enterprises that do not follow the 2001 Enterprise Accounting Standards, the year-end accumulation of tax and extra charges from the sales of products is used as a substitute.

Total Profits refer to the final achievements of production and operation of the enterprises, represented by the total profits after deducting losses (loss is expressed by the negative figure). It is the sum of profits from operation, income from subsidies, investment earnings, net income from activities other than operation, and adjustment of profits and losses of previous years.

Value-added Tax Payable refers to the amount of the value-added tax which should be paid by the enterprises during the reference period. It is the sum of tax on sales, export rebate, and transferred tax on purchases of the current year, minus the tax on purchases of the current year. Value-added tax payable of small-size enterprises is determined by the taxable sales of the year multiplied by the tax rate.

Average Annual Number of Employed Persons Employed persons refer to all those who are employed in enterprises and receive remunerations therefrom, including currently working employees, retirees who are re-employed, teachers of local-run schools, as well as foreigners, staff from Hong Kong, Macao and Taiwan, part-time employees and persons with second job who are employed by the enterprise, and employees of other units temporarily working in the enterprises, but excluding former employees who left the enterprise with their employment records still kept by the enterprises.

Average number of employed persons refers to the number of employees everyday during the reference period, calculated with the following formula:

Monthly average number = sum of actual employees everyday in reference month/number of calendar dates in reference month

Quarterly average number = sum of monthly average number in reference quarter/3

Annual average number = sum of monthly average number in reference year/12

Ratio of Profits, Taxes and Interests to Average Assets reflects the profit-making capability of all assets of the enterprise and is a key indicator manifesting the performance and management and evaluating the profit-making potential of the enterprise. It is calculated as follows:

Ratio of Profits, Taxes and Interests to Average Assets (%) = [(total profits + total taxes + interest payment) / average assets]× 100%

In the above formula, total taxes is the sum of tax and extra charges on the sales of products and value-added tax payable; and average assets is the arithmetic mean of the sum of beginning assets and ending assets.

Ratio of Debts to Assets reflect both the operation risk and the capability of the enterprise in making use of the capital from the creditors. It is calculated as follows:

Ratio of Debts to Assets (%) = (total debts / total assets)× 100%

Both assets and debts are figures at the end of the reference period.

Turnover of Working Capitals refers to the number of times of turnover of working capital in a given period of time, which reflects the speed of the turnover of working capital of industrial enterprises, and is calculated as follows:

Turnover of Working Capital=(sales revenue of products) / (average balance of total working capital)

In the above formula, average balance of total working capital refers to the arithmetic mean of the sum of working capital at the beginning and at the end of the reference period.

Ratio of Profits to Total Industrial Costs refers to the ratio of profits realized in a given period to the total costs in the same period, which reflects the economic efficiency of input cost and is calculated as follows:

Ratio of Profits to Total Industrial Cost (%)=(total profits/ total costs)×100%

Total costs in the above formula is the sum of cost of products sold, marketing cost, management cost and financial cost.

Overall Labour Productivity is an indicator reflecting the production efficiency of an enterprise and the economic efficiency of its labour input, calculated by the formula:

Overall Labour Productivity (yuan/person) = industrial value-added / average of all persons engaged

Sales Ratio of Products is an indicator reflecting the actual sale of industrial products, analyzing the production-selling and supply-demand relations. It is calculated as:

Sales Ratio of Products (%) = value of industrial sales / gross industrial output value (current prices) * 100%

资料整理人员:王　曦

14-1 建筑业企业概况
Basic Statistics on Construction Enterprises

项 目 Item	总 计 Total	国有及控股 State - Owned	地 方 Local - Owned	中 央 Central- Owned	其他经济 Others
企业单位个数(个) Number of Enterprises (unit)					
1995	912	323	277	46	50
1996	1696	403	250	53	95
1997	1761	429	378	51	125
1998	1838	433	379	54	199
1999	2120	491	432	59	332
2000	2070	488	440	48	409
2001	1661	393	350	43	459
2002	1625	363	327	36	782
2003	1808	558	488	70	906
2004	2357	433	378	55	2566
2005	2114	524	448	76	1322
2006	2238	320	279	41	1695
2007	2516	449	383	66	1876
2008	2975	440	374	66	2374
2009	2878	396	331	65	2330
2010	2845	388	334	54	2315
2011	2640	376	330	46	2134
2012	2952	390	335	55	2440
2013	3376	399	334	66	2879
2014	3217	386	324	62	2741
2015	3346	384	323	61	2875
2016	3534	389	325	64	3145
2017	3873	391	329	62	3482
2018	4196	375	316	59	3821
2019	4566	367	304	63	4199
2020	4632	368	306	62	4264
职工平均人数(万人) Average Staff and Workers (10 000 persons)					
1995	57.28	38.05	18.86	19.19	2.61
1996	76.31	36.83	18.58	18.25	3.48
1997	76.09	36.36	18.60	17.76	3.77
1998	82.63	38.22	19.22	19.00	5.59
1999	85.72	39.57	22.57	17.00	9.46
2000	82.76	36.58	21.73	14.83	10.82
2001	83.11	36.16	19.99	16.44	17.65
2002	93.50	34.20	21.25	12.95	35.80
2003	108.82	50.20	30.72	19.48	41.64
2004	105.30	44.40	28.10	16.30	48.70
2005	110.09	41.70	22.85	18.85	56.79
2006	114.25	27.26	15.18	12.08	76.71
2007	136.14	39.73	19.52	20.21	86.97
2008	137.61	38.51	18.40	20.11	92.49
2009	146.02	41.68	18.76	22.92	97.12
2010	170.71	54.40	22.31	32.09	110.74
2011	141.88	42.61	15.06	27.55	94.49
2012	169.33	50.83	15.10	35.73	114.29
2013	174.18	40.50	14.83	25.67	130.64
2014	206.37	49.04	19.48	29.56	153.98
2015	232.85	55.21	19.07	36.14	174.45
2016	269.17	61.15	17.25	43.91	208.02
2017	254.74	60.35	18.57	41.78	194.39
2018	254.34	55.78	14.55	41.23	198.56
2019	251.26	57.36	18.02	39.34	193.90
2020	214.55	57.10	15.96	41.14	157.45

14-1 续表 1 continued

项 目 Item	总 计 Total	国有及国有控股 State - Owned	地 方 Local - Owned	中 央 Central - Owned	其他经济 Others
建筑业总产值(亿元) Gross Output Value of Construction Enterprises (100 million yuan)					
1995	227.41	178.51	58.96	119.55	15.19
1996	284.43	187.00	60.83	126.17	18.29
1997	305.97	199.53	63.59	135.94	21.75
1998	343.65	223.80	73.98	149.82	26.70
1999	399.02	246.58	88.07	158.51	45.13
2000	454.35	266.03	106.76	159.27	64.86
2001	529.02	279.39	112.32	167.07	131.93
2002	639.11	301.93	143.90	158.03	238.29
2003	876.26	535.71	227.72	307.99	257.56
2004	1114.33	676.45	285.29	391.16	370.63
2005	1349.32	776.70	268.77	507.92	502.71
2006	1667.00	545.64	184.87	360.77	1048.92
2007	2110.80	1065.26	234.03	831.23	976.85
2008	2710.80	1333.87	241.63	1092.24	1319.41
2009	3421.89	1621.66	191.86	1429.80	1722.37
2010	4344.39	2287.08	414.78	1872.30	1996.10
2011	5586.45	2934.99	501.47	2433.52	2566.42
2012	7040.65	3428.40	627.89	2800.51	3478.70
2013	8465.50	3933.36	757.54	3175.82	4465.39
2014	10059.59	4755.30	921.65	3833.65	5232.75
2015	10591.71	4695.04	1072.67	3622.37	5825.87
2016	11862.40.	5549.57	1071.13	4478.43	6312.83
2017	13391.23	6350.70	1325.65	5025.05	7040.53
2018	15133.87	6737.91	1205.66	5532.25	8395.96
2019	16979.67	8058.87	1713.24	6345.63	8920.80
2020	16136.10	8766.77	1702.00	7064.77	7369.33
施工房屋面积(万平方米) Floor Space of Buildings Under Construction (10 000 sq.m)					
1995	3284.30	2122.80	1185.20	937.60	293.90
1996	4548.80	2224.60	1203.30	1021.30	315.80
1997	4604.20	2330.60	1226.90	1103.70	388.30
1998	5310.00	2488.80	1288.80	1200.00	573.70
1999	5797.00	2703.40	1578.40	1125.00	764.20
2000	6256.50	2889.10	1564.50	1324.60	919.20
2001	6662.59	2792.50	1480.20	1312.30	1817.10
2002	7215.88	2836.00	1452.00	1384.00	2637.90
2003	8933.44	3817.50	2102.60	1714.90	3541.10
2004	11772.31	5089.10	2522.60	2566.50	5334.30
2005	12091.16	4568.90	1993.30	2575.60	6257.50
2006	14478.24	3811.18	1016.18	2795.00	9545.40
2007	16679.70	5503.80	1666.40	3837.40	10139.80
2008	18376.50	5703.90	1060.40	4643.50	11920.60
2009	20499.30	5672.40	522.50	5149.90	14027.50
2010	25046.70	6752.80	968.80	5784.00	17660.30
2011	31023.80	9209.70	1549.00	7660.70	21031.70
2012	39112.20	10747.20	1661.70	9085.50	27459.10
2013	48937.96	14424.51	1734.33	12690.18	33914.19
2014	62227.88	22903.06	2137.75	20765.31	38763.33
2015	62195.32	21339.76	2258.52	19081.24	40349.12
2016	72759.57	32325.74	3165.63	29160.12	40433.82
2017	79257.69	35888.37	3085.28	32803.09	43369.32
2018	88238.10	39202.58	3151.11	36051.47	49035.52
2019	92042.23	43717.24	3845.39	39871.85	48324.99
2020	85268.18	45173.86	4173.33	41000.53	40094.32

14-1 续表 2 continued

项 目 Item	总 计 Total	国有控股 State - Owned	地 方 Local - Owned	中 央 Central - Owned	其他经济 Others
竣工房屋面积(万平方米) Floor Space of Buildings Completed (10 000 sq.m)					
1995	1175.90	622.20	466.90	155.30	69.40
1996	1880.70	653.30	501.30	152.00	103.90
1997	1982.30	765.30	522.10	243.20	92.50
1998	2374.00	836.00	624.00	212.00	239.40
1999	2873.00	1023.10	776.10	247.00	365.60
2000	3150.10	1096.30	836.10	260.20	481.80
2001	3673.40	1237.00	828.30	408.70	1102.30
2002	4146.60	1261.80	889.30	372.50	1738.80
2003	4840.80	1578.80	1143.40	435.40	2268.30
2004	6647.10	2561.30	1563.20	998.10	3265.30
2005	6896.90	2125.60	923.70	1201.90	3979.80
2006	7376.20	1137.10	450.40	686.70	5560.30
2007	8425.00	1620.90	858.60	762.30	5895.30
2008	9256.10	1386.00	537.90	848.10	7394.00
2009	10280.70	1587.10	255.90	1331.20	8198.90
2010	12813.40	2185.70	364.50	1821.20	10174.90
2011	16468.10	2593.00	600.00	1993.00	13274.20
2012	20395.20	1938.00	649.80	1288.30	17751.90
2013	22773.70	2278.00	571.70	1706.30	20077.10
2014	24867.30	2393.00	1105.00	1288.00	22165.10
2015	26825.20	3717.00	908.50	2808.50	22719.00
2016	28599.93	4714.59	772.76	3941.82	23885.34
2017	30836.86	5596.78	854.54	4742.24	25240.08
2018	32691.00	5336.02	508.38	4827.64	27354.98
2019	33907.92	8228.57	842.09	7386.48	25679.35
2020	26559.53	7094.84	828.65	6266.19	19464.69
房屋建筑面积竣工率(%) Rate of Floor Space of Buildings Completed (%)					
1995	35.80	41.20	39.40	16.60	23.60
1996	41.30	29.40	41.70	14.90	32.90
1997	43.10	32.70	42.60	22.00	23.80
1998	44.70	33.60	48.40	17.70	41.70
1999	49.60	37.80	49.20	22.00	47.80
2000	50.30	37.90	53.40	19.60	52.40
2001	55.10	44.30	56.00	31.10	60.70
2002	57.50	44.50	61.20	26.90	65.90
2003	54.20	41.30	51.10	25.40	64.10
2004	56.50	50.30	62.00	38.90	61.20
2005	57.00	46.50	46.30	46.70	63.60
2006	50.90	29.80	44.30	24.60	58.30
2007	50.50	29.50	51.50	19.90	58.10
2008	50.40	24.30	50.70	18.30	62.00
2009	50.20	28.00	49.00	25.80	58.40
2010	51.20	32.40	37.60	31.50	57.60
2011	53.10	28.20	38.70	26.00	63.10
2012	52.10	18.00	39.10	14.20	64.60
2013	46.50	15.80	33.00	13.40	59.20
2014	40.00	10.40	51.70	6.20	57.20
2015	43.10	17.40	40.20	14.70	56.30
2016	39.31	14.58	24.41	13.52	59.07
2017	38.91	15.59	27.70	14.46	58.20
2018	37.05	13.61	16.13	13.39	55.79
2019	36.84	18.82	21.90	18.53	53.14
2020	31.15	15.71	19.86	15.28	48.55

注:本表资料包括施工总承包和专业承包企业,不含劳务分包企业(下同)。

Note: In this table, the data including general contract and specilized contract enterprises under construction, excluding labor divided contract (the same as the following tables)

14-2 按登记注册类型分的企业数及合同情况(2020)

单位:亿元

指标名称	Item	有工作量的建筑业企业个数(个) Number of Construction Enterprises with Work (unit)
总计	**Total**	**4632**
其中:国有及国有控股企业	State-owned and State-holding Enterprises	368
按登记注册类型分组	**Grouped by Status of Registration**	
内资企业	Domestic Funded Enterprises	4621
国有企业	State-owned Enterprises	126
集体企业	Collective-owned Enterprises	51
股份合作企业	Cooperative Enterprises	3
联营企业	Joint Ownership Enterprises	1
国有联营企业	State Joint Ownership Enterprises	
集体联营企业	Collective Joint Ownership Enterprises	1
国有与集体联营企业	Joint State-collective Enterprises	
其他联营企业	Other Joint Ownership Enterprises	
有限责任公司	Limited Liability Corporations	1230
国有独资公司	State Sole Funded Corporations	70
其他有限责任公司	Other Limited Liability Corporations	1160
股份有限公司	Share-holding Corporations Ltd.	97
私营企业	Private Enterprises	3111
私营独资企业	Private-funded Enterprises	19
私营合伙企业	Private Partnership Enterprises	
私营有限责任公司	Private Limited Liability Corporations	3026
私营股份有限公司	Private Share-holding Corporations Ltd.	66
其他企业	Other Enterprises	2
港、澳、台商投资企业	Enterprises with Funds from Hong Kong,Macao and Taiwan	4
合资经营企业(港或澳、台资)	Joint-venture Enterprises	4
合作经营企业(港或澳、台资)	Cooperative Enterprises	
港、澳、台商独资经营企业	Enterprises with Sole Fund	
港、澳、台商投资股份有限公司	Share-holding Corporations Ltd.	
其他港澳台投资	Other Enterprises with Funds from Hong Kong, Macao and Taiwan	
外商投资企业	Foreign Funded Enterprises	7
中外合资经营企业	Joint-venture Enterprises	4
中外合作经营企业	Cooperative Enterprises	
外资企业	Enterprises with Sole Fund	1
外商投资股份有限公司	Share-holding Corporations Ltd.	2
其他外商投资	Other Foreign Funded Enterprises	

Number of Enterprises and Contract Status by Registration Status(2020)

(100 million yuan)

合同情况(亿元) Condition on Contracts (100 million yuan)		
签订的合同额 Total Value of Contracts	1.上年结转合同额 Value from Contracts Signed in Last Year	2.本年新签合同额 Value from New Contracts Signed in This Year
43596.88	**21536.47**	**22060.41**
32060.63	17235.84	14824.79
43498.89	21492.31	22006.58
379.67	139.99	239.69
60.16	10.78	49.39
9.32	5.47	3.85
3.67	1.30	2.36
3.67	1.30	2.36
33904.60	18126.14	15778.47
14889.84	8995.58	5894.26
19014.76	9130.56	9884.20
1339.65	544.41	795.23
7803.88	2664.96	5138.92
15.55	1.26	14.29
7333.82	2532.94	4800.88
454.51	130.76	323.75
1.24	0.44	0.79
2.23	0.61	1.63
2.23	0.61	1.63
95.76	43.55	52.21
91.70	43.12	48.58
0.75	0.00	0.75
3.31	0.43	2.88

14-3 按登记注册类型分的建筑业总产值(2020)

单位:亿元

指标名称	Item	建筑业总产值 Total Output Value
总计	**Total**	**16136.10**
其中:国有及国有控股企业	State-owned and State-holding Enterprises	8766.77
按登记注册类型分组	**Grouped by Status of Registration**	
内资企业	Domestic Funded Enterprises	16076.22
国有企业	State-owned Enterprises	191.64
集体企业	Collective-owned Enterprises	53.27
股份合作企业	Cooperative Enterprises	8.94
联营企业	Joint Ownership Enterprises	0.31
国有联营企业	State Joint Ownership Enterprises	
集体联营企业	Collective Joint Ownership Enterprises	0.31
国有与集体联营企业	Joint State-collective Enterprises	
其他联营企业	Other Joint Ownership Enterprises	
有限责任公司	Limited Liability Corporations	9996.78
国有独资公司	State Sole Funded Corporations	3471.41
其他有限责任公司	Other Limited Liability Corporations	6525.37
股份有限公司	Share-holding Corporations Ltd.	684.17
私营企业	Private Enterprises	5140.22
私营独资企业	Private-funded Enterprises	13.09
私营合伙企业	Private Partnership Enterprises	
私营有限责任公司	Private Limited Liability Corporations	4797.80
私营股份有限公司	Private Share-holding Corporations Ltd.	329.33
其他企业	Other Enterprises	0.87
港、澳、台商投资企业	Enterprises with Funds from Hong Kong, Macao and Taiwan	1.07
合资经营企业(港或澳、台资)	Joint-venture Enterprises	1.07
合作经营企业(港或澳、台资)	Cooperative Enterprises	
港、澳、台商独资经营企业	Enterprises with Sole Fund	
港、澳、台商投资股份有限公司	Share-holding Corporations Ltd.	
外商投资企业	Foreign Funded Enterprises	58.81
中外合资经营企业	Joint-venture Enterprises	55.54
外资企业	Enterprises with Sole Fund	0.73
外商投资股份有限公司	Share-holding Corporations Ltd.	2.54
其他外商投资	Other Foreign Funded Enterprises	

Total Output Value of Construction by Status of Registration(2020)

(100 million yuan)

其中:装饰装修产值 Output Value of Decoration	其中:在外省完成的产值 Output Value Completed in Other Provinces	建筑工程产值 Output Value of Construction	安装工程产值 Output Vaule of Installation	其他产值 Others
511.67	**6871.19**	**14294.92**	**1264.35**	**576.83**
76.17	5822.34	7852.44	632.34	281.99
510.26	6862.85	14236.22	1263.32	576.67
0.38	10.32	172.89	5.19	13.57
0.16	0.41	48.07	5.20	0.06
0.00	0.00	8.94	0.00	0.00
0.00	0.00	0.31	0.00	0.00
0.00	0.00	0.31	0.00	0.00
152.81	5887.18	8990.75	766.08	239.95
7.74	2476.91	3242.91	185.85	42.66
145.08	3410.27	5747.83	580.24	197.30
4.06	88.86	442.77	77.19	164.21
352.80	875.71	4571.68	409.62	158.94
1.03	0.77	11.40	1.38	0.31
338.34	826.24	4270.46	395.20	132.14
13.42	48.70	289.82	13.04	26.48
0.05	0.36	0.82	0.05	0.00
0.14	0.00	1.05	0.03	0.00
0.14	0.00	1.05	0.03	0.00
1.27	8.34	57.65	1.01	0.16
1.27	8.34	55.54	0.00	0.00
0.00	0.00	0.00	0.73	0.00
0.00	0.00	2.10	0.28	0.16

14-4 按隶属关系和资质等级分的建筑业总产值的构成(2020)

单位:亿元

指标名称	Item	建筑业总产值 Total Output Value
总计	**Total**	**16136.10**
一、按隶属关系分组	**Grouped by Jurisdiction of Management**	
中央	Centre	7064.77
地方	Province (Autonomous Region、Municipality)	3399.20
其他	Others	5672.13
二、按企业资质等级分组	**Grouped by Qualification Criteria**	
企业资质等级(施工总承包)	General Contracting	15385.96
特级	Special Grade	6884.45
一级	First Grade	5927.65
二级	Second Grade	1580.03
三级及以下	Third Grade and Below	993.83
企业资质等级(专业总承包)	Professional Contraction Construction	750.14
一级	First Grade	499.20
二级	Second Grade	149.84
三级及以下	Third Grade and Below	101.10

Composition of Total Output Value of Construction Enterprises by Affiliation and Qualification Criteria(2020)

(100 million yuan)

其中:装饰装修产值 Output Value of Decoration	其中:在外省完成的产值 Output Value Completed in Other Provinces	建筑工程产值 Output Value of Construction	安装工程产值 Output Vaule of Installation	其他产值 Others
511.67	**6871.19**	**14294.92**	**1264.35**	**576.83**
39.55	5505.24	6424.40	494.01	146.36
80.87	358.26	2924.36	267.37	207.46
391.25	1007.69	4946.16	502.97	223.00
377.45	6693.66	13801.67	1080.47	503.81
55.33	4527.13	6375.86	375.92	132.67
253.75	2006.65	5138.06	527.94	261.65
32.56	111.71	1419.90	105.08	55.05
35.81	48.17	867.85	71.53	54.44
141.60	177.54	490.52	184.94	74.68
126.84	149.94	343.34	109.60	46.26
12.74	13.24	76.60	54.54	18.70
2.02	14.36	70.58	20.80	9.72

14-5 按登记注册类型分的建筑业企业完成房屋建筑竣工面积(2020)

单位:万平方米

指标名称	Item	合计 Total	住宅房屋 Residential Buildings
总计	**Total**	**26559.53**	**17899.38**
其中:国有及国有控股企业	State-owned and State-holding Enterprises	7094.84	4379.83
按登记注册类型分组	**Grouped by Status of Registration**		
内资企业	Domestic Funded Enterprises	26460.79	17805.08
国有企业	State-owned Enterprises	62.59	48.63
集体企业	Collective-owned Enterprises	265.79	172.23
股份合作企业	Cooperative Enterprises	27.38	25.03
联营企业	Joint Ownership Enterprises	0.83	0.83
国有联营企业	State Joint Ownership Enterprises		
集体联营企业	Collective Joint Ownership Enterprises	0.83	0.83
国有与集体联营企业	Joint State-collective Enterprises		
其他联营企业	Other Joint Ownership Enterprises		
有限责任公司	Limited Liability Corporations	10904.92	7235.69
国有独资公司	State Sole Funded Corporations	3156.44	1432.27
其他有限责任公司	Other Limited Liability Corporations	7748.48	5803.42
股份有限公司	Share-holding Corporations Ltd.	589.23	402.79
私营企业	Private Enterprises	14610.06	9919.88
私营独资企业	Private-funded Enterprises	69.12	55.77
私营合伙企业	Private Partnership Enterprises		
私营有限责任公司	Private Limited Liability Corporations	14092.02	9620.98
私营股份有限公司	Private Share-holding Corporations Ltd.	448.93	243.14
其他企业	Other Enterprises		
港、澳、台商投资企业	Enterprises with Funds from Hong Kong, Macao and Taiwan	0.84	0.00
合资经营企业(港或澳、台资)	Joint-venture Enterprises	0.84	0.00
合作经营企业(港或澳、台资)	Cooperative Enterprises		
港、澳、台商独资经营企业	Enterprises with Sole Fund		
港、澳、台商投资股份有限公司	Share-holding Corporations Ltd.		
外商投资企业	Foreign Funded Enterprises	97.90	94.30
中外合资经营企业	Joint-venture Enterprises	94.30	94.30
中外合作经营企业	Cooperative Enterprises		
外资企业	Enterprises with Sole Fund		
外商投资股份有限公司	Share-holding Corporations Ltd.	3.60	
其他外商投资	Other Foreign Funded Enterprises		

Completed Floor Space of Buildings Constructed by Construction Enterprises by Registration Status(2020)

(10 000 sq.m)

商业及服务用房屋 Houses for Business and Service	办公用房屋 Office Buildings	科研、教育、医疗用房屋 Houses for Scientific Research、Education and Medical Treatment	文化、体育、娱乐用房屋 Houses for Culture、Sports and Entertainment	厂房及建筑物 Workshop and Buildings	仓 库 Storage	其他未列明的房屋建筑物 Others
2352.24	**1113.89**	**1605.06**	**299.74**	**2424.90**	**98.27**	**766.05**
727.32	299.10	483.70	114.05	608.84	41.68	440.32
2352.17	1113.89	1605.06	299.74	2420.57	98.27	766.02
6.21	1.56	2.13	0.11	3.16	0.64	0.15
27.35	19.14	7.29	0.00	35.68	3.72	0.38
0.00	1.50	0.00	0.00	0.85	0.00	0.00
0.00	0.00	0.00	0.00	0.00	0.00	0.00
0.00	0.00	0.00	0.00	0.00	0.00	0.00
944.72	439.71	567.49	118.63	1008.58	59.92	530.17
525.85	75.30	257.99	83.59	407.01	12.86	361.57
418.88	364.42	309.50	35.03	601.57	47.06	168.60
51.78	14.66	16.20	14.24	61.41	0.40	27.73
1322.11	637.31	1011.94	166.75	1310.89	33.59	207.59
0.00	0.42	0.04	0.00	7.12	0.00	5.78
1275.67	585.24	979.80	157.37	1250.26	25.03	197.67
46.44	51.65	32.10	9.38	53.51	8.56	4.14
0.07	0.01	0.00	0.00	0.73	0.00	0.03
0.07	0.01	0.00	0.00	0.73	0.00	0.03
0.00	0.00	0.00	0.00	3.60	0.00	0.00
				3.60		

14-6 按隶属关系和资质等级分的建筑业企业工程完成情况(2020)

单位:万平方米

指标名称	Item	房屋建筑施工面积 Floor Space of Buildings under Construcion
一、按隶属关系分组	Grouped by Jurisdiction of Management	
中央	Centre	41000.53
地方	Province (Autonomous Region、Municipality)	15181.01
其他	Others	29086.63
二、按企业资质等级分组	Grouped by Qualification Criteria	
企业资质等级(施工总承包)	Enterprises Qualification Criteria (General Contracting)	84259.98
特级	Special Grade	51180.30
一级	First Grade	21789.19
二级	Second Grade	7495.53
三级及以下	Third Grade and Below	3794.96
企业资质等级(专业总承包)	Enterprises Qualification Criteria (Professional Contraction Construction)	1008.19
一级	First Grade	435.13
二级	Second Grade	126.38
三级及以下	Third Grade and Below	446.68

Project Completion Situation of Construction Enterprises by Affiliation and Qualification Criteria(2020)

(10 000 sq.m)

本年新开工面积 Floor Space of New Construction This Year	房屋建筑竣工面积 Floor Space of Buildings Completed	住宅房屋 Residential Buildings	商业及服务用房屋 Houses for Business Use
10344.30	6266.19	4021.69	694.40
7829.99	7633.27	4665.08	820.48
14312.70	12660.08	9212.61	837.36
31961.71	26184.01	17755.81	2258.10
16443.90	10614.62	6441.84	1271.93
9523.52	9271.41	7076.20	670.49
3789.05	3881.77	2617.01	207.56
2205.24	2416.21	1620.76	108.12
525.29	375.52	143.57	94.14
105.08	214.90	63.21	74.39
79.37	41.97	20.22	6.28
340.84	118.65	60.14	13.47

14-7 分市州建筑业企业生产情况(2020)
Statistics on Production of Construction Enterprises by Cities and Prefectures(2020)

单位:亿元 (100 million yuan)

项　目	Item	建筑业总产值 Total Output Value of Construction Industry	建筑工程产值 Output Value of Construction Projects	安装工程产值 Output Value of Installation Projects	其他产值 Output Value of Other Projects	竣工产值 Output Value of Projects Completed
湖北省	**Hubei**	**16136.10**	**14292.19**	**1265.41**	**578.50**	**6997.82**
武汉市	Wuhan	10590.83	9383.46	872.97	334.40	4319.07
黄石市	Huangshi	405.89	366.72	20.68	18.49	225.80
十堰市	Shiyan	495.15	463.27	18.46	13.42	173.72
宜昌市	Yichang	1149.65	1037.01	89.27	23.36	352.01
襄阳市	Xiangyang	1003.05	904.79	79.92	18.35	471.63
鄂州市	Ezhou	103.57	88.47	11.85	3.25	56.15
荆门市	Jingmen	151.06	136.10	10.73	4.23	97.50
孝感市	Xiaogan	349.23	291.88	48.78	8.57	248.98
荆州市	Jingzhou	245.35	226.64	12.12	6.59	134.38
黄冈市	Huanggang	824.66	769.03	42.80	12.83	403.71
咸宁市	Xianning	202.34	181.32	15.04	5.98	120.07
随州市	Suizhou	107.98	98.17	3.39	6.42	67.89
恩施自治州	Enshi	95.81	89.00	4.60	2.21	56.77
仙桃市	Xiantao	112.93	101.60	6.80	4.53	77.71
潜江市	Qianjiang	151.01	36.80	11.44	102.76	99.81
天门市	Tianmen	141.48	112.44	16.53	12.51	87.61
神农架林区	Shennongjia	6.11	5.49	0.03	0.60	5.01

14-8 分市州建筑业企业工程完成情况(2020)
Project Completion Situation of Construction Enterprises by Cities and Prefectures(2020)

单位:万平方米 (10 000 sq.m)

项 目	Item	房屋建筑施工面积 Floor Space of Housing Construction	本年新开工面积 Beginning Projects in This Year	房屋建筑竣工面积 Floor Space of Housing Projects Completed	#住 宅 Residential Buildings	#办公用房 Office Buildings
湖北省	**Hubei**	**85268.18**	**32486.99**	**26559.53**	**17899.38**	**1113.89**
武汉市	Wuhan	59722.97	19767.98	15217.23	10082.65	587.89
黄石市	Huangshi	2292.99	929.48	1135.33	738.24	44.18
十堰市	Shiyan	1363.21	700.71	667.54	501.74	9.56
宜昌市	Yichang	3917.77	1564.98	1156.34	771.26	48.82
襄阳市	Xiangyang	2999.49	1552.80	1527.18	1087.22	82.81
鄂州市	Ezhou	472.43	269.69	267.09	191.28	1.80
荆门市	Jingmen	689.01	411.08	367.78	247.23	13.93
孝感市	Xiaogan	2008.37	1297.64	1363.06	861.47	70.37
荆州市	Jingzhou	1156.10	540.75	553.66	382.19	15.02
黄冈市	Huanggang	6852.01	3625.48	2257.02	1523.79	150.37
咸宁市	Xianning	1092.94	631.82	596.32	478.98	20.67
随州市	Suizhou	741.17	213.80	428.48	322.17	18.21
恩施自治州	Enshi	477.35	156.65	167.73	106.53	10.74
仙桃市	Xiantao	518.81	321.86	365.49	277.58	14.66
潜江市	Qianjiang	298.35	76.35	51.48	15.58	3.08
天门市	Tianmen	641.05	409.42	431.08	308.87	20.19
神农架林区	Shennongjia	24.15	16.51	6.71	2.60	1.57

主要统计指标解释

建筑业统计单位 指从事房屋、构筑物建造和设备安装活动的法人企业。建筑业法人企业应具有建筑业资质并能够独立核算，同时其应具备以下条件：①依法成立，有自己的名称、组织机构和场所，能够承担民事责任；②独立拥有和使用资产，承担负债，有权与其他单位签订合同；③独立核算盈亏，能够编制资产负债表。

建筑业总产值 是以货币形式表现的建筑业企业在一定时期内生产的建筑业产品和提供的服务的总和。建筑业总产值包括：

(1)建筑工程产值：指列入建筑工程预算内的各种工程价值。

(2)安装工程产值：指设备安装工程价值，不包括被安装设备本身的价值。

(3)其他产值：建筑业总产值中除建筑工程、安装工程以外的产值。包括房屋构筑物修理产值、非标准设备制造产值、总包企业向分包企业收取的管理费以及不能明确划分的施工活动所完成的产值。

a.房屋构筑物修理产值：指房屋和构筑物修理所完成的产值，但不包括被修理房屋、构筑物本身价值和生产设备的修理产值。

b.非标准设备制造产值：指加工制造没有定型的非标准生产设备的加工费和原材料价值(如化工厂、炼油厂用的各种罐、槽，矿井生产统一使用的各种漏斗、三角槽、阀门等)以及附属加工厂为本企业承建工程制作的非标准设备的价值。

房屋建筑施工面积 指在报告期内施过工的全部房屋建筑面积，包括本期新开工的房屋面积、上期施工跨入本期继续施工的房屋面积、上期停缓建在本期恢复施工的房屋面积、本期竣工的房屋面积及本期施工后又停缓建的房屋面积。

房屋建筑竣工面积 指在报告期内房屋建筑按照设计要求全部完工，达到了使用条件，经验收鉴定合格，正式移交使用单位的房屋建筑面积。

Explanatory Notes on Main Statistical Indicators

Statistical Unit in Construction refers to corporate enterprise engaged in the construction of buildings and structures and in the installation of equipment. A corporate construction enterprise should have qualification certificates with independent accounting system, and should meet the following 3 requirements: a) being set up in line with relevant legal basis, having its full name, organization and location, and capable of taking civil liabilities; b) independently possessing and using its assets and assuming its liabilities, and entitled to sign contracts with other institutions; and c) making independent accounts of its profits and losses, and capable of compiling its own balance sheet.

Gross Output Value of Construction refers to total of construction products and services, expressed in money terms, produced or rendered by construction and installation enterprises during a given period of time. It includes:

(1) Output value of construction projects, that is the value of projects covered by the project budgets;

(2) Output value of installation projects, that is the value of the installation of equipment, (excluding the value of the equipment to be installed);

(3) Output value of others, that is the output value of construction industry excluding that of construction projects and installation projects. It includes: output value of repair of buildings and structures; output value of non-standard equipment manufacturing; overhead expenses received by contracted enterprises to the sub-contracted enterprises and the completed output value of construction activities that have no clear definition.

a. Output value of repair of buildings and structures, that is the value created through the repairs of buildings or structures, but does not include the value of buildings or structures being repaired and the value of the repair of production equipment;

b. Output value of manufactured non-standard equipment, that is the value of non-standard production equipment including raw materials and manufacturing cost made for the construction project (i.e., chemical plant; kettles or tanks used by refineries; various fillers, triangle tanks, valves used by mines), and the output value of equipment manufactured by subsidiary workshops.

Floor Space of Buildings Under Construction refers to floor space of buildings under construction during the reference period, including newly started buildings, buildings started earlier and continued during the reference period, and buildings suspended earlier but restarted during the reference period, buildings completed during the reference period, and buildings under construction and then suspended during the reference period.

Floor Space of Buildings Completed refers to the floor space of buildings that are completed in the reference period in accordance with the requirements of the design, up to the standard for putting them into use, and have been checked and accepted by concerned departments as qualified ones.

资料整理人员:朱　昳

15-1 主要年份规模以上服务业企业财务状况主要指标
Main Indicators of Financial Status of Service Enterprises above Designated Size in Major Years

单位:亿元 (100 million yuan)

年 份 Year	企业单位数(个) Number of Enterprises (unit)	营业收入 Bussiness Revenue	营业成本 Business Cost	利润总额 Total Profits	税金总额 Total Taxes	资产总计 Total Assets
2013	4037	3514.8	2501.4	367.9	134.3	15547.3
2014	4072	3736.2	2771.8	446.8	125.9	18374.1
2015	3999	3718.8	2800.9	390.7	133.8	20189.8
2016	4495	4119.8	3192.1	390.0	133.1	22092.0
2017	4627	4493.0	3420.9	454.7	140.5	28032.3
2018	6132	6352.7	4705.5	754.2	261.8	35733.6
2019	6156	6869.0	5304.5	721.3	193.8	36756.8
2020	6307	6578.8	5290.6	458.2	157.9	39636.9

15-2 分类型规模以上服务业企业财务状况主要指标(2020)
Main Indicators of Financial Status of Service Enterprises above Designated Size by Type (2020)

单位:亿元 (100 million yuan)

指 标	Indicators	企业单位数(个) Number of Enterprises (unit)	营业收入 Bussiness Revenue	营业成本 Business Cost	利润总额 Total Profits	税金总额 Total Taxes	资产总计 Total Assets
按登记注册类型分	**By Status of Registration**	**6307**	**6578.82**	**5290.60**	**458.21**	**157.91**	**39636.91**
内资企业	**Domestic Funded Enterprises**	**6129**	**6140.11**	**4987.14**	**409.65**	**145.08**	**38621.06**
国有企业	State-owned Enterprises	298	365.10	291.33	45.98	7.10	2093.91
集体企业	Collective-owned Enterprises	36	13.76	7.79	-4.81	0.57	106.59
股份合作企业	Cooperative Enterprises	9	13.67	3.62	9.69	0.47	52.34
联营企业	Joint Ownership Enterprises	7	2.14	1.56	0.26	0.08	5.89
有限责任公司	Limited Liability Corporations	2055	3310.91	2774.91	220.72	82.87	32021.76
股份有限公司	Share-holding Corporations Ltd.	161	396.02	282.84	53.28	8.33	1906.06
私营企业	Private Enterprises	3339	1949.23	1558.04	80.49	44.92	2260.58
其他企业	Other Enterprises	224	89.28	67.05	4.04	0.74	173.93
港、澳、台商投资企业	**Enterprises with Investment from Hong Kong, Macao and Taiwan**	**73**	**234.81**	**143.18**	**39.86**	**7.56**	**464.13**
外商投资企业	**Foreign Funded Enterprises**	**105**	**203.90**	**160.28**	**8.70**	**5.27**	**551.72**
按企业划型标准分	**By Size of Enterprises**						
大型企业	Large Enterprises	216	2111.15	1742.78	107.01	42.14	7361.54
中型企业	Medium-sized Enterprises	863	1496.36	1120.85	221.34	37.34	7484.90
小型企业	Small Enterprises	3848	1900.07	1451.71	150.59	58.22	16590.19
微型企业	Micro-sized Enterprises	797	244.31	207.13	9.96	6.92	895.57

注:部分行业无大中小微型企业划分标准。
Note: In some sectors, there is no defferentiation of large, medium-sized and small enterprises.

15-3 分行业规模以上服务业企业财务状况主要指标(2020)

单位:亿元

行 业	Item	企业单位数(个) Number of Enterprises (unit)	营业成本 Business Cost
总计	**Total**	**6307**	**5290.60**
交通运输、仓储和邮政业	**Transport, Storage and Post**	**1326**	**1761.55**
铁路运输业	Railway Transport	8	595.94
道路运输业	Road Transport	903	580.65
水上运输业	Water Transport	85	94.89
航空运输业	Air Transport	12	45.26
管道运输业	Transport Via Pipelines	7	58.99
多式联运和运输代理业	Intermodality and Forwarding Agency	72	46.80
装卸搬运和仓储业	Loading, Unloading and Storage	182	173.75
邮政业	Post	57	165.26
信息传输、软件和信息技术服务业	**Information Transmission, Software and Information Technology**	**666**	**974.34**
电信、广播电视和卫星传输服务	Telecommunication, Radio and television and Satellite Transmission Service	85	361.46
互联网和相关服务	Internet and Related Service	73	172.62
软件和信息技术服务业	Software and Information Technology	508	440.26
房地产业(不含房地产开发经营业)	**Real Estate (Excluding Real Estate Development and Operation)**	**596**	**192.53**
租赁和商务服务业	**Leasing and Business Services**	**1261**	**948.29**
租赁业	Leasing	74	43.45
商务服务业	Business Services	1187	904.85
科学研究和技术服务业	**Scientific Research and Technical Services**	**879**	**928.60**
研究和试验发展	Research and Experimental Development	62	29.88
专业技术服务业	Professional Technical Services	674	855.46
科技推广和应用服务业	Science and Technology Popularization and Application Services	143	43.26
水利、环境和公共设施管理业	**Management of Water Conservancy, Environment and Public Facilities**	**208**	**202.79**
水利管理业	Management of Water Conservancy	8	13.04
生态保护和环境治理业	Ecological protection and Environmental Treatment	29	28.89
公共设施管理业	Management of Public Facilities	148	69.51
土地管理业	Management of Land	23	91.34
居民服务、修理和其他服务业	**Service to Households, Repair and Other Services**	**267**	**33.62**
居民服务业	Services to Households	109	9.85
机动车、电子产品和日用产品修理业	Repair of Motor Vehicles, Electronics and Household Products	70	10.80
其他服务业	Other Services	88	12.97
教育	**Education**	**238**	**43.57**
教育	Education	238	43.57
卫生和社会工作	**Health and Social Security**	**270**	**106.32**
卫生	Health	241	104.93
社会工作	Social Service	29	1.39
文化、体育和娱乐业	**Culture, Sports and Entertainment**	**596**	**98.99**
新闻和出版业	Journalism and Publishing Activities	72	31.68
广播、电视、电影和录音制作业	Radio, Television, Motion Picture and Audio-visual Programme Production Services	156	27.84
文化艺术业	Culture and Art Activities	62	6.22
体育	Sports Activities	34	2.32
娱乐业	Entertainment	272	30.92

Main Indicators of Financial Status of Service Enterprises above Designated Size by Sector (2020)

(100 million yuan)

营业收入 Bussiness Revenue	利润总额 Total Profits	税金总额 Total Taxes	资产总计 Total Assets	平均用工人数(万人) Annual Average Employees (10 000 persons)
6578.82	**458.21**	**157.91**	**39636.90**	**114.76**
1918.01	**7.82**	**35.62**	**15732.06**	**30.97**
580.20	-60.64	7.91	4652.35	8.33
689.29	24.12	16.18	9299.98	14.78
104.33	7.88	1.41	206.12	1.04
30.26	-16.23	0.87	357.78	0.68
97.11	37.47	4.67	427.00	0.10
51.96	0.96	0.53	44.09	0.40
175.97	9.76	2.30	645.62	1.34
188.89	4.50	1.75	99.13	4.29
1416.26	**160.43**	**38.41**	**2359.59**	**15.90**
547.03	95.25	14.99	1077.64	4.68
210.46	5.03	2.87	181.71	1.00
658.77	60.15	20.55	1100.24	10.23
260.13	**34.51**	**12.59**	**2670.47**	**13.78**
1162.10	**65.61**	**30.38**	**7848.78**	**25.46**
48.27	-2.84	0.95	73.53	0.57
1113.84	68.45	29.43	7775.24	24.89
1167.86	**106.10**	**28.88**	**2134.44**	**11.17**
43.52	1.79	0.76	276.98	0.43
1062.75	97.80	26.78	1749.95	9.73
61.60	6.52	1.34	107.51	1.00
272.29	**68.63**	**6.11**	**7683.46**	**2.85**
9.54	-7.03	0.53	457.93	0.07
35.31	-4.98	0.89	457.99	0.43
88.12	7.53	1.74	1348.75	2.25
139.33	73.12	2.97	5418.78	0.10
46.99	**3.65**	**1.04**	**56.65**	**2.52**
17.60	2.25	0.25	31.34	0.88
13.01	0.29	0.40	10.69	0.31
16.37	1.11	0.38	14.63	1.33
65.29	**4.21**	**0.58**	**149.23**	**3.55**
65.29	4.21	0.58	149.23	3.55
141.51	**1.05**	**0.50**	**223.28**	**4.63**
139.51	0.87	0.49	213.66	4.48
2.00	0.17	0.01	9.62	0.15
128.38	**6.20**	**3.80**	**778.94**	**3.94**
48.71	11.18	1.62	353.46	0.94
28.27	-4.33	0.63	102.06	0.85
6.92	-0.25	0.25	47.50	0.40
3.15	-0.77	0.14	51.34	0.18
41.33	0.36	1.16	224.58	1.57

15-4 分地区规模以上服务业企业财务状况主要指标(2020)
Main Indicators of Financial Status of Service Enterprises Above Designated Size by Territory (2020)

单位:亿元 (100 million yuan)

地 区	Territory	营业收入 Bussiness Revenue	营业成本 Business Cost	利润总额 Total Profits	税金总额 Total Taxes	资产总计 Total Assets
湖北省	**Hubei Province**	**6578.82**	**5290.60**	**458.21**	**157.91**	**39636.91**
武汉市	Wuhan	4838.54	3942.00	236.40	114.70	29481.02
黄石市	Huangshi	125.49	97.95	10.39	2.78	1498.00
十堰市	Shiyan	116.76	97.46	0.96	2.33	720.54
宜昌市	Yichang	372.85	294.47	28.14	12.27	2491.33
襄阳市	Xiangyang	360.18	268.41	100.21	7.63	2150.65
鄂州市	Ezhou	38.80	29.56	0.81	1.17	147.79
荆门市	Jingmen	84.47	57.62	16.28	2.60	889.41
孝感市	Xiaogan	140.90	118.84	10.19	3.79	160.62
荆州市	Jingzhou	135.84	106.90	14.47	2.78	799.48
黄冈市	Huanggang	81.92	56.69	15.04	2.15	337.3
咸宁市	Xianning	74.26	53.20	5.39	2.27	354.73
随州市	Suizhou	46.59	42.74	3.70	0.75	136.15
恩施自治州	Enshi	65.01	49.41	5.04	0.93	142.35
仙桃市	Xiantao	29.95	21.54	4.14	0.70	49.52
潜江市	Qianjiang	23.53	18.67	2.38	0.62	27.03
天门市	Tianmen	42.30	33.69	6.24	0.42	224.97
神农架林区	Shennongjia	1.41	1.46	-1.55	0.03	26.02

主要统计指标解释

营业收入 指企业从事销售商品、提供劳务和让渡资产使用权等生产经营活动形成的经济利益流入。营业收入包括“主营业务收入”和“其他业务收入”。

营业成本 指企业从事销售商品、提供劳务和让渡资产使用权等生产经营活动发生的实际成本。包括“主营业务成本”和“其他业务成本”。

利润总额 指企业在一定会计期间的经营成果，是生产经营过程中各种收入扣除各种耗费后的盈余，反映企业在报告期内实现的盈亏总额。

税金合计 指企业发生的除企业所得税和允许抵扣的增值税以外的各项税金及其附加。税金合计=税金及附加+应交增值税。

税金及附加 指企业因从事生产经营活动按税法规定应缴纳的消费税、城市维护建设税、资源税、环境保护税、教育费附加、房产税、城镇土地使用税、车船税、印花税等相关税费。

应交增值税 指按照税法规定，以销售货物、服务、无形资产、不动产或提供加工、修理修配劳务的增值额和货物进口金额为计税依据而课征的一种流转税。按权责发生制核算本期应负担的增值税。

资产总计 指企业过去的交易或者事项形成的、由企业拥有或者控制的、预期会给企业带来经济利益的资源。包括企业拥有的土地、办公楼、厂房、机器、运输工具、存货等实物资产和现金、存款、应收账款和预付账款等金融资产。资产一般按流动性(资产的变现或耗用时间长短)分为流动资产和非流动资产。其中流动资产可分为货币资金、交易性金融资产、应收票据、应收账款、预付款项、其他应收款、存货等;非流动资产可分为长期股权投资、固定资产、无形资产及其他非流动资产等。

平均用工人数 指报告期企业平均实际拥有的，参与本企业生产经营活动的人员数。

Explanatory Notes on Main Statistical Indicators

Business Revenue refers to the inflow of economic benefits generated by an enterprise from production and operation activities such as selling goods, providing labor services and transferring the right to use assets. Operating Income includes "main business income" and "other business income".

Business Cost refers to the actual cost incurred by an enterprise in production and operation activities such as selling goods, providing services and transferring the right to use assets. Operating Cost includes "main business cost" and "other business cost".

Total Profit refers to the operating result of an enterprise in a certain accounting period. It is the surplus after various costs are deducted from various incomes from production and operation, and reflects the total profit and loss realized by an enterprise during the reporting period.

Total Taxes refer to all taxes and surcharges incurred by an enterprise in addition to the corporate income tax and the VAT that is allowed to be deducted. Total taxes = Taxes and surcharges + VAT payable.

Taxes and Surcharges refer to the relevant taxes and dues that an enterprise shall pay according to the provisions of the tax law for its production and business activities, such as goods and services tax, urban maintenance and construction tax, resource tax, environmental protection tax, education surcharge, housing property tax, urban land use tax, vehicle and vessel tax, stamp tax and so on.

VAT Payable refers to a kind of turnover tax levied based on the added value of selling goods, services, intangible assets, immovable properties, or providing services of processing, repairing and replacement, and the import amount of goods in accordance with the tax law. The VAT to be borne in the current period is calculated on the accrual basis.

Total Assets refer to the resources owned or controlled by an enterprise and expected to bring economic benefits to the enterprise, formed by past transactions or events of the enterprise, including the land, office buildings, factory buildings, machinery, transportation tools, inventory and other physical assets and financial assets such as cash, deposits, accounts receivable and prepayments owned by an enterprise. The assets are generally divided into current assets and non–current assets according to the liquidity (the length of time it takes to realize or consume the assets). Among them, current assets can be divided into monetary funds, transactional financial assets, notes receivable, accounts receivable, prepayments, other receivables, inventories, etc.; non–current assets can be divided into long–term equity investments, fixed assets, intangible assets and other non–current assets, etc.

Annual Average Employees refer to the number of persons engaged in the production and operation activities of enterprises in the reporting period, which are actually employed by the enterprises.

16

交通运输和邮电

Transport, Postal and Telecommunication Services

资料整理人员：杨　旸

交通运输和邮电

Transport, Postal and Telecommunication Services

2020

客运量	(万人) Passenger Capacity of The Whole Society	(10 000 persons)	30900.20
#公路	(万人) Public Road	(10 000 persons)	21730.86
货运量	(万吨) Volume of Freight Traffic	(10 000 tons)	160427.50
#公路	(万吨) Public Road	(10 000 tons)	114345.95
邮电业务总量	(亿元) Business Volume of Post and Telecommunications	(100 million yuan)	4676.68
#函件	(万件) Letters	(10 000 pcs)	3096.17
年末固定电话用户	(万户) Fixed Telephone Subscribers at Year-end	(10 000 units)	481.61
年末移动电话用户	(万户) Mobile Telephone Subscribers at Year-end	(10 000 units)	5681.07

全社会客货运量

Passenger Capactity of The Whole Society

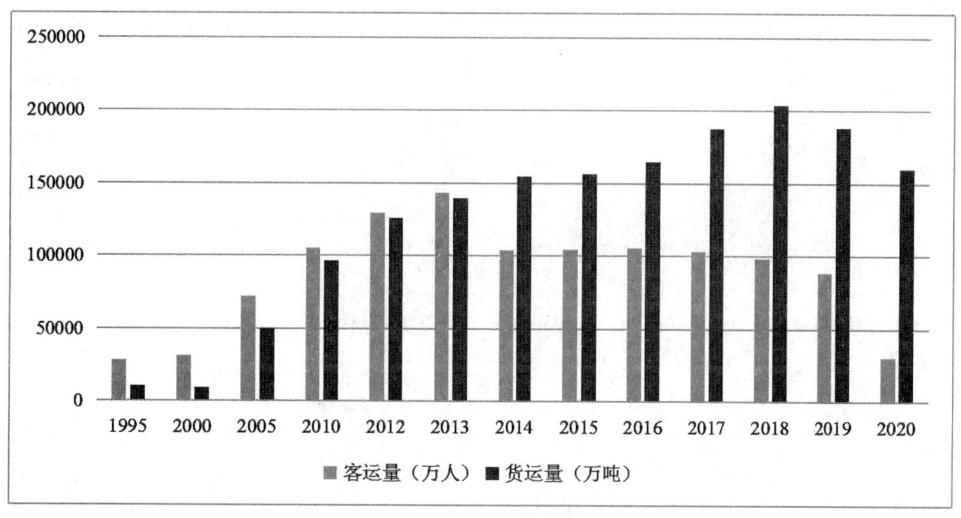

附:客货运量

Passenger Capacity of The Whole Society

年份 Year	客运量(万人) Passenger Capacity (10 000 persons)	货运量(万吨) Volume of Freight Traffic (10 000 tons)
1995	28508	10174
2000	31593	9345
2005	71892	49924
2010	105132	96938
2012	129511	126195
2013	143100	139740
2014	103672	154736
2015	104694	156357
2016	105813	165125
2017	103549	187638
2018	98720	203704
2019	88926	188143
2020	30900	160428

注:1.2014 年因公路运输统计方法调整,数据与前期不可比(下同)。
2.2017 年因运输调整统计方法,数据与前期不可比(下同)。
3.2019 年因公路运输统计方法调整,数据与前期不可比(下同)。

Note: a)From 2014, due to the statistics method of road transport has been adjusted, the data can not be compared with the previous period(the same below).
b)From 2017, due to the statistics method of transportation has been adjusted, the data can not be compared with the previous(the same below).
c)From 2019, due to the statistics method of road transport has been adjusted, the data can not be compared with the previous period(the same below).

16-1 交通运输业基本情况

指 标	Item	1995	2000	2005
运输线路长度 （公里）	Length of Transportation Routes (km)			
铁路营业里程	Total Railway's Length in Operation	1940	2025	2758
公路总里程	Total Highway in Operation	48728	57850	91131
#等级公路里程	Length of Expressway and Class I to IV Highway	30910	48062	76075
#高速公路	Expressway		569	1649
一级公路	Class I Highway	641	611	1092
二级公路	Class II Highway	4967	7911	15225
内河航道里程	Navigable Inland Waterways	8969	8309	8988
客运量总计 （万人）	Total Passenger Traffic (10 000 persons)	28508.20	31593.00	71892.00
铁路	Railway	2300.00	3469.00	4615.00
公路	Highway	24315.00	27184.00	66183.00
水运	Waterway	1745.00	679.00	601.00
民用航空	Civil Aviation	150.00	261.00	494.00
旅客周转量 （亿人公里）	Turnover Volume of Passenger Traffic (100 million persons-km)	285.29	398.32	803.90
货运量总计 （万吨）	Total Freight Traffic (10 000 tons)	10173.62	9345.19	49923.52
铁路	Railway	3986.00	3857.00	8491.00
公路	Highway	2600.00	2228.00	33481.00
水运	Waterway	3585.00	3255.00	7944.00
货物周转量 （亿吨公里）	Turnover Volume of Freight Traffic (100 million tons-km)	776.44	831.64	1682.48
民用车辆拥有量 （万辆）	Civil Moto Vehicles			393.90
民用汽车拥有量	Civil Vehicles	34.89	47.55	103.04
载客汽车	Passenger Vehicles	14.96	24.69	53.40
载货汽车	Trucks	18.61	21.72	30.96
营运汽车	Moto Vehicles in Operation			20.33
私人汽车	Private Vehicles		41.72	59.66
民用运输船舶拥有量 （艘）	Civil Transpot Vessels (units)		5905	5362
机动船	Moto Vessels		4188	4158
驳船	Barges		1717	1204
港口货物吞吐量 （万吨）	Cargo Handled at Ports (10 000 tons)		4113.46	13992.51

注：1.2014 年因公路运输统计方法调整，数据与前期不可比（下同）。
2.2017 年因运输调整统计方法，数据与前期不可比（下同）。
3.2019 年因公路运输统计方法调整，数据与前期不可比（下同）。
4.2019 年因港口货物吞吐量统计方法调整，数据与前期不可比（下同）

Basic Conditions of Transport

2010	2015	2016	2017	2018	2019	2020
3032	4062	4140	4216	4341	5165	5185
206212	252980	260179	269484	275039	289029	289960
187812	240936	249819	259591	265912	281422	283053
3674	6204	6204	6252	6367	6860	7230
2210	5231	5460	5874	6093	6465	7064
16159	21555	22005	22712	23179	23936	24628
8988	9066	9066	9066	9067	9067	9067
105415.50	104693.75	105813.14	103549.03	98719.70	88926.43	30900.20
7281.30	15083.90	15855.30	14876.60	15700.40	17216.06	8148.04
96873.00	87953.26	88220.89	86772.19	80989.51	69584.36	21730.86
375.80	574.46	572.22	624.63	647.79	631.63	232.90
885.40	1082.13	1164.73	1275.61	1382.00	1494.37	788.40
1262.26	1490.81	1521.05	1365.87	1348.98	1386.79	612.42
97006.94	156356.93	165124.84	187637.83	203703.74	188143.15	160427.51
10145.60	6579.00	6744.20	3773.40	4116.40	5479.90	5362.70
71020.00	115800.30	122654.50	147710.51	163145.18	143548.61	114345.95
15832.00	33968.00	35715.80	36143.90	36431.99	39104.66	40713.70
3370.37	5908.40	6159.90	6276.67	6605.49	6133.74	5295.68
761.11	959.35	902.95	1008.15	1081.82	1174.57	1277.48
224.60	504.36	593.33	683.42	775.70	864.10	934.80
151.51	424.70	515.17	601.48	683.57	762.34	824.93
53.29	70.16	69.71	74.32	84.35	93.48	101.19
36.60	55.25	51.92	52.50	57.32	61.93	74.83
165.39	433.90	524.16	609.12	693.95	775.25	842.77
5502	4357	4010	3595	3278	3366	3321
4634	4155	3857	3466	3172	3270	3227
868	202	153	129	106	96	94
18782.67	32949.52	35191.90	36903.31	34620.55	30661.00	37976.00

Note: a) From 2014, due to the statistics method of road transport has been adjusted, the data can not be compared with the previous period(the same below).
b) From 2017, due to the statistics method of transportation has been adjusted, the data can not be compared with the previous(the same below).
c) From 2019, due to the statistics method of road transport has been adjusted, the data can not be compared with the previous period(the same below).
d) From 2019, due to the statistics method of port handling capacity has been adjusted, the data can not be compared with the previous period(the same below).

16-2 客运量
Passenger Traffic

单位:万人　　(10 000 persons)

年 份 Year	总 计 Total	铁 路 Railway	公 路 Highway	水 运 Waterway	民用航空 Civil Aviation
1978	12009.20	2854.00	7429.00	1722.00	4.20
1980	16629.26	3217.00	11282.00	2123.00	7.26
1985	28178.22	3353.00	22378.00	2433.00	14.22
1990	32145.93	2107.00	27333.00	2693.00	12.93
1991	33982.62	2016.00	29279.00	2654.00	33.62
1992	34726.00	2077.00	29635.00	2894.00	120.00
1993	30152.00	2265.00	25116.00	2665.00	106.00
1994	29607.00	2358.00	24819.00	2210.00	120.00
1995	28508.20	2300.00	24315.00	1743.00	150.00
1996	29045.40	2248.00	25180.00	1449.00	168.00
1997	29503.08	2127.00	25684.00	1538.00	154.08
1998	28208.00	2218.00	24540.00	1306.00	144.00
1999	29360.14	2545.00	25596.00	1080.00	139.14
2000	63306.00	3469.00	58897.00	679.00	261.00
2001	62696.00	3632.00	58018.00	767.00	279.00
2002	63382.00	3813.00	58623.00	638.00	308.00
2003	62880.00	3602.00	58371.00	573.00	334.42
2004	68167.00	4072.00	63127.00	522.00	446.11
2005	71892.00	4615.00	66183.00	601.00	494.00
2006	75440.00	4850.00	69335.00	706.00	549.00
2007	84088.00	5125.00	77514.00	736.00	712.70
2008	89720.00	6027.00	82532.00	388.00	774.00
2009	96219.00	6440.00	88703.00	371.00	705.00
2010	105415.50	7281.30	96873.00	375.80	885.40
2011	114736.92	8503.80	104971.00	347.60	914.52
2012	129510.90	9764.90	118369.00	443.50	933.50
2013	143100.28	12101.80	129533.75	528.00	936.73
2014	103671.40	14302.70	87804.00	533.80	1031.30
2015	104693.73	15083.90	87953.26	574.46	1082.13
2016	105813.14	15855.30	88220.89	572.22	1164.73
2017	103549.03	14876.60	86772.19	624.63	1275.61
2018	98719.70	15700.40	80989.51	647.79	1382.00
2019	88926.43	17216.06	69584.36	631.63	1494.37
2020	30900.20	8148.04	21730.86	232.90	788.40

注:1.2014 年因公路运输统计方法调整,数据与前期不可比(下同)。
2.2017 年因铁路运输调整统计方法,数据与前期不可比(下同)。
3.2019 年因公路运输统计方法调整,数据与前期不可比(下同)。

Note: a)From 2014, due to the statistics method of has been adjusted, the data can not be compared with the previous period(the same below).
b)From 2017, due to the statistics method of railway transportation has been adjusted, the data can not be compared with the previous(the same below).
c)From 2019, due to the statistics method of road transport has been adjusted, the data can not be compared with the previous period(the same below).

16-3 旅客周转量
Passenger-Kilometers

单位:亿人公里 (100 million passenger-km)

年 份 Year	总 计 Total	铁 路 Railway	公 路 Highway	水 运 Waterway	民用航空 Civil Aviation
1978	69.38	30.72	24.85	13.54	0.17
1980	95.88	41.79	36.20	17.52	0.37
1985	185.25	84.00	81.33	19.40	0.52
1990	225.85	82.83	112.83	29.28	0.91
1991	257.68	98.09	126.70	30.19	2.70
1992	286.35	104.89	135.61	34.72	11.13
1993	281.28	113.60	123.64	33.50	10.54
1994	283.98	121.91	121.40	28.71	11.96
1995	285.29	129.47	117.76	22.71	15.35
1996	285.04	121.17	124.97	21.09	17.81
1997	282.53	118.62	123.39	24.14	16.38
1998	278.66	126.68	118.51	18.79	14.68
1999	300.38	146.54	124.46	14.09	15.29
2000	563.78	232.00	297.46	8.84	25.48
2001	574.24	248.00	293.35	5.87	27.02
2002	633.69	283.00	317.02	3.60	30.07
2003	617.68	271.00	309.00	4.00	33.68
2004	703.95	322.80	334.00	3.20	43.95
2005	803.90	389.40	358.00	4.20	52.30
2006	847.42	408.10	374.80	5.10	59.42
2007	947.71	440.80	423.80	5.30	77.81
2008	1077.68	474.01	522.57	2.30	78.80
2009	1096.31	466.70	562.34	2.49	64.78
2010	1262.26	528.90	631.39	2.92	99.05
2011	1444.66	639.15	700.06	2.49	102.97
2012	1576.00	663.60	804.07	2.94	106.36
2013	1761.10	756.40	892.25	3.14	109.31
2014	1458.24	854.40	483.89	2.85	120.10
2015	1490.81	869.30	489.29	3.32	128.90
2016	1521.05	895.80	487.33	3.35	134.57
2017	1365.87	734.70	482.27	4.06	144.84
2018	1348.98	731.80	453.44	4.74	159.00
2019	1386.79	803.51	392.09	4.76	186.43
2020	612.42	390.31	131.60	1.01	89.50

16-4 货运量
Freight Traffic

单位:万吨 (10 000 tons)

年份 Year	总计 Total	铁路 Railway	公路 Highway	水运 Waterway	#内河 Inland Waterway	#海运 Seashipping
1978	10199	3513	3556	3130		
1980	8420	3211	2199	3110		
1985	11059	2659	3852	3463		
1990	10916	3901	2941	3784		
1991	11217	3957	2999	3996		
1992	11565	4018	2828	4364		
1993	11184	4029	2734	4248		
1994	10663	3964	2666	3641		
1995	10174	3986	2600	3585		
1996	9928	3779	2537	3268		
1997	9389	3882	2280	3119		
1998	10154	3999	2009	4040		
1999	10517	3964	2141	4313		
2000	40949	6558	27863	6270	6202	68
2001	41476	7094	29851	4275	4198	77
2002	42064	7400	28777	5630	5390	240
2003	44661	7825	30348	6195	5830	365
2004	47073	7872	31584	7259	6823	436
2005	50317	8491	33481	7944	7466	478
2006	52885	8990	35361	8242	7679	536
2007	58523	9728	39568	9027	7765	1262
2008	75778	10202	52759	12681	8182	4499
2009	82714	9839	59563	13305	8108	5197
2010	97007	10145	71020	15832	9916	6082
2011	110168	10059	82741	17358	10817	6536
2012	125392	9177	97136	19070	11836	7275
2013	139740	9010	108824	21897	13575	8042
2014	154736	7681	116280	30765	21152	8476
2015	156357	6579	115800	33968	27564	6226
2016	165125	6744	122655	35716	29898	5728
2017	187638	3773	147711	36144	30482	5537
2018	203704	4116	163145	36432	31110	5322
2019	188143	5480	143549	39105	31526	7579
2020	160428	5363	114346	40714	32624	8089

16-5 货物周转量
Freight Ton-Kilometers

单位:亿吨公里 (100 million ton-km)

年 份 Year	总 计 Total	铁 路 Railway	公 路 Highway	水 运 Waterway	#内 河 Inland Waterway	#海 运 Seashipping
1978	281.09	191.72	9.22	80.15		
1980	326.85	206.14	9.85	110.85		
1985	507.57	320.37	16.59	169.94		
1990	670.53	415.17	14.72	235.04		
1991	720.23	455.00	14.67	245.41		
1992	757.00	461.81	13.89	272.70		
1993	753.52	477.64	11.99	259.90		
1994	743.21	505.57	10.23	222.32		
1995	776.44	544.40	9.62	222.20		
1996	775.79	552.32	9.93	208.05		
1997	725.34	501.77	8.72	212.21		
1998	696.62	465.81	7.59	220.63		
1999	696.27	457.70	8.25	227.76		
2000	1156.57	618.37	227.16	305.29	295.07	10.22
2001	1097.60	634.90	218.97	237.31	226.15	11.16
2002	1212.82	680.00	211.49	313.60	271.30	42.29
2003	1313.13	703.80	224.00	377.00	315.38	61.61
2004	1485.76	781.83	235.60	461.08	395.75	65.33
2005	1689.86	987.60	251.00	443.20	391.05	105.00
2006	1730.93	1021.40	266.10	437.90	379.81	58.10
2007	1902.17	1138.20	302.09	458.00	361.93	95.83
2008	2699.97	1096.90	789.37	810.46	416.17	394.29
2009	2808.46	1032.40	930.10	845.18	402.82	442.36
2010	3370.37	1144.60	1079.13	1145.52	547.77	470.00
2011	4044.45	1226.80	1277.71	1538.83	625.26	609.61
2012	4693.61	1194.10	1565.45	1590.65	740.76	683.36
2013	4883.01	1195.70	1818.18	1868.08	946.02	756.69
2014	5798.12	1109.10	2340.56	2347.32	1347.07	891.82
2015	5908.40	995.70	2380.62	2530.91	1851.27	618.02
2016	6159.90	971.50	2506.85	2680.34	2040.82	600.69
2017	6276.67	744.80	2741.91	2788.80	2143.64	585.12
2018	6605.49	798.80	2955.53	2850.00	2222.91	627.08
2019	6133.74	938.73	2268.11	2925.55	2158.62	766.93
2020	5295.68	915.10	1639.91	2739.94	2001.75	738.19

16-6 全省民用车辆拥有量(2020)
Number of Civil Vehicles Owned in the Province(2020)

单位:辆 (unit)

指标	Item	总计 Total	营运 Working	非营运 Non-Working
合计	**Total**	**12774781**	**748293**	**11979616**
汽车	Civil Vehicles	9347989	602978	8698139
载客汽车	Passenger Vehicles	8249347	130675	8071803
#大型	Lage Scale	59674	40496	12575
中型	Medium Scale	26129	9248	9501
小型	Small Scale	8147501	80931	8033684
#轿车	Cars	4861079	76054	4753103
载货汽车	Trucks	1011945	455947	555998
#重型	Heavy Scale	264947	246877	18070
中型	Medium Scale	54628	45355	9273
轻型	Light Scale	692134	163693	528441
其他汽车	Other Vehicles	86697	16356	70341
#三轮汽车	Tricycle Motocars	5333	470	4863
低速货车	Low Speed Vehicles	22882	8644	14238
摩托车	Motorear	3337831	57525	3280306
#普通	Ordinary Motor	3161934	57513	3104421
轻便	Light Motor	175897	12	175885
挂车	Freight Trailers	88893	87747	1146
其他类型车	Other Motor Vehicles	28	3	25

注:本表"其他汽车"中,包括三轮和四轮农用运输车。
Note: Tricycles and four-wheel farming vehicles are inclued in"Other Vehicles".

16-7 私人车辆拥有量
Possession of Private Vehicles

单位:辆 (unit)

指 标	Item	2000	2005	2010	2015	2017	2018	2019	2020
私人汽车	Private Vehicles	475500	596601	1653948	4338967	6091207	6939463	7752483	8427672
载客汽车	Passenger Vehicles	245500	297095	1153728	3796713	5543501	6333079	7082548	7706067
#大型	Lage Scale	29200	3312	2939	770	432	385	360	332
#轿车	Cars		177650	773727	2414210	3387453	3827327	4249714	4591579
载货汽车	Ordinary Trucks	211400	135352	327509	473513	498195	558088	620493	672171
#重型	Heavy Scale		8766	33281	59388	65158	76314	87219	95976
其它汽车	Others		164154	172711	68741	49511	48296	49442	49434
摩托车	Motors	1241000	2853113	4971619	4501871	3188833	2989016	3012446	3311622
挂车	Freight Trailers	4400	1714	6467	11405	15037	17863	24246	28126

16-8 水路运输工具拥有量(2020)
Possession of Waterway Transport Vehicles(2020)

指 标	Item	机动船 Power Boat	客 船 Passenger Ship	货 船 Cargo Ship	拖 船 Tugboat
数量 (艘)	Quantity (ship)	3227	308	2868	51
总载重量 (吨)	Total Carrying Capacity (tonage)	7425352	866	7424486	
净载重量 (吨)	Net Load (tonage)	7216988	524	7216464	
载客量 (客位)	Passenger Carrying Capacity (person)	36219	36219		
标准箱位	TEU	3272		3272	
功率 (千瓦)	Power (kw)	1855264	92722	1724003	38539

16-9 分市、州公路旅客运输完成情况(2020)
Completion of Highway Passenger Transportation by Cities and Prefectures(2020)

地 区	Region	客运量（万人）Passenger Traffic (10 000 persons)	旅客周转量（万人公里）Turnover Volume of Passenger Traffic (100 million passenger-km)
武汉市	Wuhan	803	97437
黄石市	Huangshi	1227	88349
十堰市	Shiyan	781	68961
宜昌市	Yichang	3149	161956
襄阳市	Xiangyang	2093	154733
鄂州市	Ezhou	518	28809
荆门市	Jingmen	706	49255
孝感市	Xiaogan	2139	102069
荆州市	Jingzhou	2312	151465
黄冈市	Huanggang	2241	115899
咸宁市	Xianning	1017	64645
随州市	Suizhou	1219	66018
恩施自治州	Enshi	2344	118937
仙桃市	Xiantao	369	13596
潜江市	Qianjiang	153	7221
天门市	Tianmen	547	23340
神农架林区	Shennongjia	112	3322

16-10 邮电业务基本情况
Basic Conditions of Postal and Telecommunication Services

指标	Item	2005	2010	2015	2019	2020
邮电业务总量 (亿元)	Business Volume of Postal and Telecommunicaion (100 million yuan)	373.63	1028.09	962.66	3824.44	4676.68
邮政业务总量	Business Volume of Postal Services	23.40	55.71	137.41	458.51	471.77
电信业务总量	Business Volume of Telecommunication Services	350.20	972.38	825.25	3365.93	4204.91
函件 (亿件)	Letters (100 million pcs)	1.30	1.00	0.68	0.65	0.31
包裹 (万件)	Package (10 000 pcs)	320.00	210.10	105.80	54.91	30.82
快递业务量 (万件)	Pieces of Express Mail Services (10 000 pcs)	685.30	5476.60	50847.30	168499.77	178505.52
报刊期发数 (万份)	Issue of Newspapers and Magzines (10 000 pcs)	643.00	557.00	587.00	371.90	372.49
年末固定电话用户 (万户)	Number of Fixed Telephone Subscribers at Year-end (10 000 subscribers)	1236.00	1026.40	872.50	518.93	481.61
年末移动电话用户 (万户)	Number of Mobile Telephone Subscribers at Year-end (10 000 subscribers)	1401.00	3454.70	4650.60	5688.02	5681.07
互联网宽带接入用户 (万户)	Broadband Users (10 000 subscribers)	128.00	459.40	983.50	1708.32	1870.16
年末城市宽带用户 (万户)	Urban Broadband Users at Year-end (10 000 subscribers)			703.70	1208.57	1299.90
年末农村宽带用户 (万户)	Rural Broadband Users at Year-end (10 000 subscribers)			154.90	499.75	570.30
邮路总长度(单程) (公里)	Length of Postal Routes(One Way) (km)		57483	163136	265400	308739
邮路线路总条数 (条)	Postal Routes (unit)		411	767	1683	1262
农村投递线路条数 (条)	Rural Delivery Routes (unit)		4198	3562	3634	3536
农村投递线路长度(单程) (公里)	Rural Delivery Routes(One Way) (km)		194656	205502	187419	175879
移动电话交换机容量 (万户)	Capacity of Mobile Telephone Swicthboard (10 000 units)		5862.70	8748.70	9043.50	9084.24
互联网宽带接入端口 (万个)	Broadband Subscribers Port of Internet (10 000 ports)			1600.30	3062.28	3221.40
长途光缆线路长度 (万公里)	Length of Long-Distance Optical Cable Lines (10 000 km)		2.70	3.14	3.08	3.21

注:1.邮电业务总量统计口径2011年发生变化,与以前各年份不可比。
2.2017年2月,工信部调整了统计口径,2017年电信行业数据与2016年及以往年度电信行业数据不可比。
3.2019年邮路线路总条数统计口径有调整,与以往各年份不可比。

Note: a)The statistic on total volume of post and telecommunication have been reconfigured from 2011. Datas of other year can not compare with the data of 2011.
b)In February 2017, the Ministry of Industry and Information Technology adjusted its statistical calibre. The 2017 telecommunications industry data is not comparable with the 2016 and previous years ′ telecommunications industry data.
c)Form 2019, due to the statistics method of Postal Routes has been adjusted, the data can not be compared with the previous period.

16-11 邮电通信水平
Postal and Telecommunication Services Available

指 标	Item	2005	2010	2015	2017	2018	2019	2020
每百人平均函件量 (件/百人)	Annual Average Number of Letters Mailed per 100 persons (unit/100 persons)	228.0	174.7	115.5	114.9	125.7	110.3	53.9
每百人平均订阅报刊量 (份/百人)	Annual Average Number of Newspaper and Magazine Subscribed per 100 persons (unit/100 persons)	977.9	962.7	1211.8	1145.0	1129.5	1095.7	1113.8
每百人平均包裹 (件/百人)	Annual Average Number of Package per 100 persons (unit/100 persons)	5.6	3.4	1.8	1.2	1.0	0.9	0.5
电话普及率 (部/百人)	Popularization Rate of Telephone per 100 persons (unit/100 persons)	43.9	78.3	94.4	95.8	103.7	104.9	104.0
移动电话普及率 (部/百人)	Popularization Rate of Mobile Telephone per 100 persons (unit/100 persons)	23.3	60.4	79.5	84.6	94.1	96.1	98.9

主要统计指标解释

铁路营业里程 又称营业长度（包括正式营业和临时营业里程），指办理客货运输业务的铁路正线总长度。凡是全线或部分建成双线及以上的线路，以第一线的实际长度计算；复线、站线、段管线、岔线和特殊用途线以及不计算运费的联络线都不计算营业里程。该指标可以反映铁路运输业基础设施的发展水平，也是计算客货周转量、运输密度和机车车辆运用效率等指标的基础资料。

公路总里程 指在一定时期内实际达到《公路工程[WTBZ]技术标准JTJ01-88》规定的等级公路，并经公路主管部门正式验收交付使用的公路里程数。包括大中城市的郊区公路以及通过小城镇街道部分的公路里程和桥梁、渡口的长度，不包括大中城市的街道、厂矿、林区生产用道和农业生产用道的里程。两条或多条公路共同经由同一路段，只计算一次，不得重复计算里程长度。该指标可以反映公路建设的发展规模，也是计算运输网密度等指标的基础资料。

内河航道里程 也称内河通航里程，指在一定时期内，能通航运输船舶及排筏的天然河流、湖泊水库、运河及通航渠道的长度。包括全年季节性通航累计三个月以上的航道，不包括仅供零散流放竹、木排的河道。该指标可以反映内河水运网的规模、水平和发展情况。

货（客）运量 指在一定时期内，各种运输工具实际运送的货物（旅客）数量。该指标是反映运输业为国民经济和人民生活服务的数量指标，也是制定和检查运输生产计划、研究运输发展规模和速度的重要指标。货运按吨计算，客运按人计算。货物不论运输距离长短、货物类别，均按实际重量统计。旅客不论行程远近或票价多少，均按一人一次客运量统计；半价票、小孩票也按一人统计。

货物（旅客）周转量 指在一定时期内，由各种运输工具运送的货物（旅客）数量与其相应运输距离的乘积之总和。该指标可以反映运输业生产的总成果，也是编制和检查运输生产计划，计算运输效率、劳动生产率以及核算运输单位成本的主要基础资料。计算货物周转量通常按发出站与到达站之间的最短距离，也就是计费距离计算。计算公式为：

货物（旅客）周转量=∑（货物（旅客）运输量×运输距离）

民用汽车拥有量 指报告期末，在公安交通管理部门按照《机动车注册登记工作规范》，已注册登记领有民用车辆牌照的全部汽车数量。汽车拥有量统计的主要分类：根据汽车结构分为载客汽车、载货汽车及其他汽车；根据汽车所有者不同分为个人（私人）汽车、单位汽车；根据汽车的使用性质分为营运汽车、非营运汽车；根据汽车大小规格不同载客汽车分为大型、中型、小型和微型，载货汽车分为重型、中型、轻型和微型。

邮电业务总量 指以货币形式表示的邮政、电信通信企业为社会提供各类邮政、电信通信服务的总数量。计算方法为各类业务的实物量分别乘以相应的不变单价，求出各类业务的货币量加总求得。没有不变单价的业务按其业务收入直接相加。

年末固定电话用户 指接入本地电信运营商固定电话网上的电话用户。包括：住宅用户、单位用户、公用电话用户等。

年末移动电话用户 指通过移动电话交换机进入移动电话网、占用移动电话号码的各类电话用户。包括签约用户和智能网预付费用户。一个移动电话号码统计为一户。

Explanatory Notes on Main Statistical Indicators

Length of Railways in Operation refers to the total length of the trunk line under passenger and freight transportation (including both full operation and temporary operation). The calculation is based on the actual length of the first line even if this line has a full or partial double track or more tracks, excluding double tracks, station sidings, tracks under the charge of stations, branch lines, special-purpose lines and the non-payable connecting lines. The length of railways in operation is an important indicator to show the development of the infrastructure for the railway transport, and also the essential data to calculate volume of passenger freight transport, traffic density and utilization efficiency of the locomotives and carriages.

Length of Highways refers to the length of highways which are built in conformity with the grades specified by the highway engineering standard formulated by the Ministry of Communications, and have been formally checked and accepted by the departments of highways and put into use. The length of highways includes that of the suburb highways at large and medium-sized cities, highways passing through streets at small cities and towns, and also the length of bridges and ferries. It does not include the length of streets in big and medium-sized cities and highways built for the production purpose at factories, mines, forest areas and agricultural areas. If two or more highways go the same section of the way, the length of the section is only calculated for once and no duplication is allowed. The length of highways is an important indicator to show the development of the highway construction and to provide essential information to calculate the transport network density.

Length of Navigable Inland Waterways it is an indicator reflecting the size and development of inland water network, it refers to the length of the natural rivers, lakes, reservoirs, canals, and ditches open to navigation during a given period, which enables the transport by ships and rafts. It includes the channels open to navigation for over an accumulative 3 months in a year, yet this does not include the river courses, which are only used to float odd logs and bamboo rafts. This indicator can reflect the scale, level and development situation of the inland waterway network.

Freight (Passenger) Traffic refers to the volume of freight (passenger) transported with various means. Freight transport is calculated in tons and passenger traffic is calculated in the number of persons. Despite the type of freight and traveling distance, the freight transport is calculated in the actual weight of the goods: and despite the traveling distance and ticket price, the passenger traffic is calculated by the principle that one person can be counted only once in one travel. The passengers who travel with a half price ticket or a child ticket is also calculated as one person. The freight (passenger) traffic provides a quantitative measure to show how the transport industry serves the national economy and people, and is also an important indicator for planning the transport industry and for studying the development scale and speed of the transport industry.

Freight Ton-kilometers (Passenger-kilometers) refer to the sum of the products of the volume of transported cargo (passengers) multiplying by the transport distance. It is an important indicator to reflect the achievement of transportation industry. Normally, the shortest distance between the departure station and the destination station (i.e., the payable distance) is the basis to calculate the freight ton-kilometers. This is an important indicator to show the total results of the transport industry, to prepare and examine the transport plan and to measure the efficiency, the labour productivity and the unit cost of transport.

The formula is as follows:

Freight ton-kilometers (passenger-kilometers) = Σ {freight (passenger) traffic × distance of transportation}

Possession of Civil Motor Vehicles refer to the total numbers of vehicles that are registered and received vehicles license tags according to the Work Standard for Motor Vehicles Registration formulated by transport management office under department of public security at the end of reference period. They are divided into following categories according to the structure of motor vehicles: passenger vehicles, trucks and others; and private vehicles and vehicles for units use according to ownerships; working vehicles and non-working vehicles according to kind of usage; large passenger vehicles, medium passenger vehicles, small passenger vehicles and mini passenger vehicle, heavy

trucks, light-heavy trucks, light trucks and mini trucks according to sizes of vehicles.

Business Volume of Postal and Telecommunications refers to the total amount of postal and telecommunication services, expressed in value terms, provided by the post and telecommunications departments for society. Business volume of post and telecommunications is the sum of each service in kind multiplying with its correspondent unit price (constant price). Business without constant price add their business revenue directly.

Number of Fixed Telephone Subscribers at Year-end refers to the persons who own mobile telephone numbers and are connected with the mobile telephone communication network through the mobile telephone switchboards, including contracted subscribers and pre-paid subscribers for intelligent network. One mobile telephone is taken as a subscriber.

Number of Mobile Telephone Subscribers at Year-end refers to subscribers that are connected to the local telecommunication service provider through fix line network, including household subscribers, institutional subscribers and public telephones.

17

国内贸易

Domestics Trade

资料整理人员:朱　莉　　王　芳

国内贸易

Domestic Trade

2020

社会消费品零售总额	(亿元)	Total Retail Sales of Consumer Goods	(100 million yuan)	17984.87
商品零售额	(亿元)	Retail Sales	(100 million yuan)	15796.68
餐饮收入额	(亿元)	Food and Beverage Revenue	(100 million yuan)	2188.19

社会消费品零售总额(亿元)
Total Retail Sales of Consumer Goods(100 million yuan)

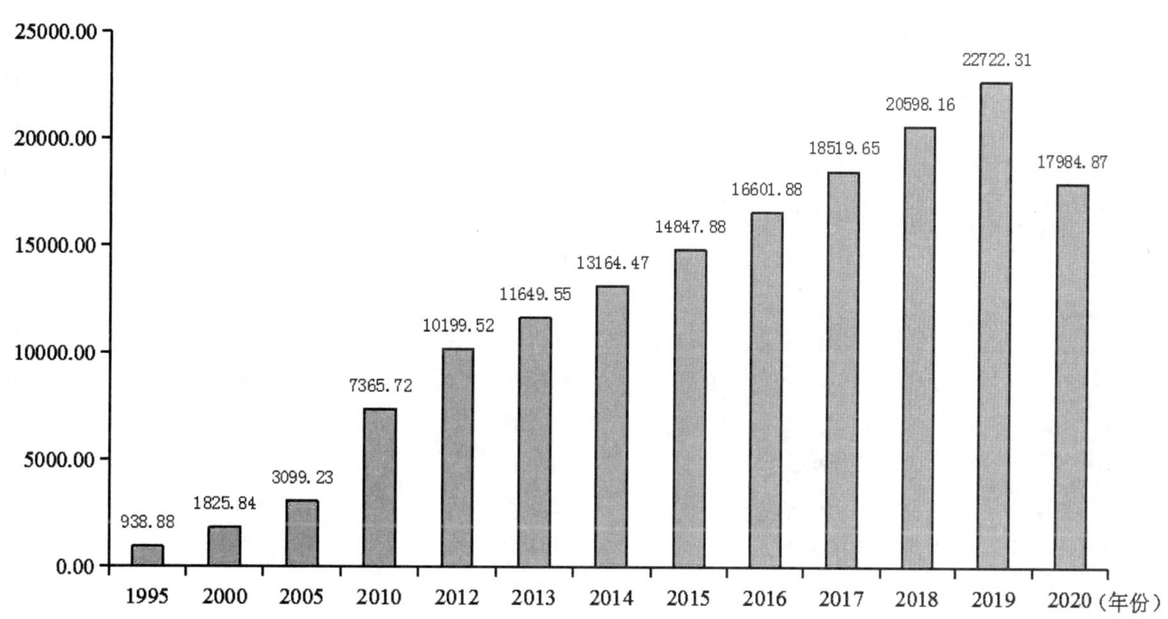

社会消费品零售总额(亿元)
Total Retail Sales of Consumer Goods(100 million yuan)

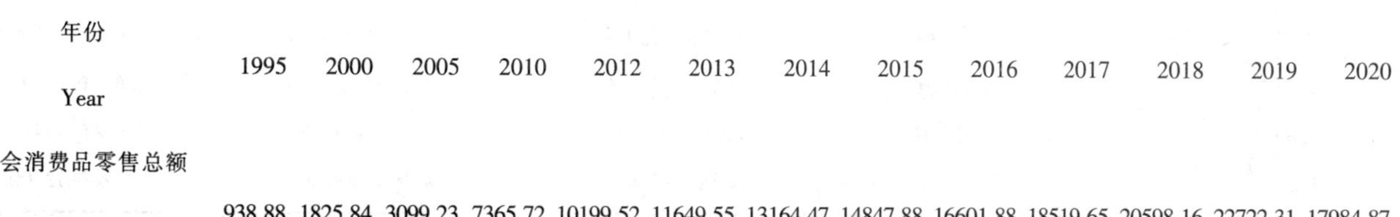

年份 Year	1995	2000	2005	2010	2012	2013	2014	2015	2016	2017	2018	2019	2020
社会消费品零售总额 Total Retail Sales of Consumer Goods	938.88	1825.84	3099.23	7365.72	10199.52	11649.55	13164.47	14847.88	16601.88	18519.65	20598.16	22722.31	17984.87

17-1 按地区分社会消费品零售总额
Total Retail Sales of Consumer Goods by Region

单位:亿元 (100 million yuan)

年 份 Year	零售额 Total Retail Sales of Consumer Goods	市 City	县 County	县以下 Below County Level
1978	59.84	19.24	16.56	24.04
1980	81.91	28.98	17.01	35.92
1985	181.17	75.26	31.64	74.17
1990	326.36	166.44	45.62	114.30
1991	362.26	190.65	50.04	121.57
1992	411.52	221.59	55.04	134.89
1993	522.67	294.56	69.05	159.05
1994	727.41	413.71	102.25	211.44
1995	938.88	543.89	128.73	266.26
1996	1157.35	695.38	131.60	330.37
1997	1362.42	812.56	148.47	401.39
1998	1503.98	909.75	158.45	435.78
1999	1645.96	1037.75	153.64	454.57
2000	1825.84	1151.48	181.27	493.08
2001	2020.53	1296.20	198.67	525.66
2002	2183.80	1466.37	205.82	511.61
2003	2425.08	1610.79	223.90	590.39
2004	2711.28	2105.44	284.86	320.99
2005	3099.23	2160.36	290.04	648.83
2006	3601.89	2528.90	338.91	734.07
2007	4294.36	3014.43	410.45	869.48
2008	5346.00	3753.37	514.16	1078.46
2009	6216.20	4328.55	615.30	1272.35
2010	7365.72	(城镇)6235.18	(城区)5282.73	(乡村)1130.53
2011	8792.13	(城镇)7453.26	(城区)6216.18	(乡村)1338.87
2012	10199.52	(城镇)8680.56	(城区)7139.30	(乡村)1518.96
2013	11649.55	(城镇)9855.37	(城区)7624.26	(乡村)1794.18
2014	13164.47	(城镇)11170.41	(城区)8632.97	(乡村)1994.06
2015	14847.88	(城镇)12588.85	(城区)9636.71	(乡村)2259.03
2016	16601.88	(城镇)14088.49	(城区)10685.95	(乡村)2513.39
2017	18519.65	(城镇)15729.03	(城区)11825.29	(乡村)2790.62
2018	20598.16	(城镇)17501.70	(城区)13035.36	(乡村)3096.45
2019	22722.31	(城镇)19311.04	(城区)14245.87	(乡村)3411.27
2020	17984.87	(城镇)15284.69	(城区)10668.04	(乡村)2700.18

注:1.1996 年及以后社会消费品零售总额及各分组指标中不含售给城乡居民生活用住房的零售额。
2.2010 年起采用国家新制定的城乡划分标准:城镇(其中:城区)、乡村

Note: a)Since 1996, the residential house was exclued in the total retail sales of consumer goods and all the targets by groups.
b)Since 2010, a new towm and country division national standard is applied:town(including urban area), country.

17-2 分市、州社会消费品零售总额
Total Retail Sales of Consumer Goods by Cities and Prefectures

单位：亿元 (100 million yuan)

地 区	Region	2013	2014	2015	2016	2017	2018	2019	2020
全 省	**Province**	**11649.55**	**13164.47**	**14847.88**	**16601.88**	**18519.65**	**20598.16**	**22722.31**	**17984.87**
武汉市	Wuhan	4205.74	4788.39	5301.82	5843.66	6493.24	7169.70	7774.49	6149.84
黄石市	Huangshi	532.70	587.52	655.70	735.40	827.02	921.34	1026.38	758.81
十堰市	Shiyan	566.76	628.05	729.39	832.28	948.85	1064.33	1193.01	974.01
宜昌市	Yichang	911.85	996.47	1116.42	1273.20	1373.13	1530.34	1710.43	1391.12
襄阳市	Xiangyang	999.11	1085.03	1217.73	1388.75	1562.75	1747.86	1955.18	1567.26
鄂州市	Ezhou	226.55	248.34	280.74	321.05	365.01	411.03	455.72	326.57
荆门市	Jingmen	430.14	479.37	570.52	649.14	732.09	822.03	917.06	779.31
孝感市	Xiaogan	659.22	728.20	836.10	929.39	1030.35	1148.46	1278.66	981.24
荆州市	Jingzhou	860.84	957.74	1075.99	1208.61	1350.77	1505.48	1671.47	1284.49
黄冈市	Huanggang	703.67	785.51	961.70	1068.03	1197.65	1334.86	1470.72	1150.13
咸宁市	Xianning	369.10	407.38	449.69	499.03	566.02	634.74	708.40	604.04
随州市	Suizhou	344.47	384.21	430.64	482.68	535.80	595.24	654.64	519.53
恩施自治州	Enshi	247.11	440.80	491.03	553.63	620.94	689.59	763.78	562.59
仙桃市	Xiantao	221.05	248.80	281.60	315.40	355.37	398.74	445.25	381.93
潜江市	Qianjiang	161.90	166.42	185.92	208.38	233.20	260.54	291.35	248.90
天门市	Tianmen	202.27	224.31	248.66	277.47	309.82	344.33	384.96	289.76
神农架林区	Shennongjia	7.07	7.96	14.23	15.77	17.64	19.56	20.83	15.34

注：本表各市、州数据包含了“其他”部分的全口径数据；
Note: “Others” was included in the total retail sales of consumer goods in the form.

17-3 批发和零售业连锁经营情况
Basic Conditions of Wholesale and Retail Sale Chain Stores Industries

指标名称	Item	合计 Total		直营店 Direct Sales Store		加盟店 League Store	
		2019	2020	2019	2020	2019	2020
一、门店总数 （个）	**Number of Stores (unit)**	**12177**	**10894**	**8581**	**8568**	**3596**	**2326**
其中：批发业 （个）	Number of Stores (unit)	858	1269	495	906	363	363
零售业 （个）	Number of Stores (unit)	11319	9625	8086	7662	3233	1963
二、零售营业面积 （百平方米）	**Floor Space of Retail Business (100 sq.m)**	**69419**	**49112**	**66752**	**46632**	**2666**	**2480**
其中：批发业 （百平方米）	Floor Space of Retail Business (100 sq.m)	4175	4441	3491	3757	684	684
零售业 （百平方米）	Floor Space of Retail Business (100 sq.m)	65244	44671	63261	42875	1982	1796
三、从业人员 （人）	**Person Engaged (person)**	**126744**	**105629**	**119268**	**101908**	**7476**	**3721**
其中：批发业 （人）	Person Engaged (person)	7904	7314	7058	6467	846	847
零售业 （人）	Person Engaged (person)	118840	98315	112210	95441	6630	2874
四、商品购进总额 （亿元）	**Total Value of Commodities Purchased (100 million yuan)**	**1978.23**	**1086.15**	**1942.82**	**1067.09**	**35.40**	**19.06**
#统一配送商品购进额	Total Purchasing Value	1200.32	795.36	1191.04	784.58	9.29	10.78
#自有配送中心配送商品购进额	Commodities Purchased From Dispatching Center	797.62	464.99	788.69	455.97	8.94	9.01
#非自有配送中心配送商品购进额	Commodities Purchased From Nondispatching Center	103.07	54.63	102.91	53.04	0.16	1.59
五、商品销售额 （亿元）	**Sales Amount (100 million yuan)**	**2195.76**	**1326.95**	**2149.96**	**1304.88**	**45.80**	**22.08**
#零售额	Retail Sales	1816.22	1063.64	1801.29	1046.66	14.93	16.99

17-4 住宿和餐饮业连锁经营情况

Basic Conditions of Hotels and Catering Services Chain Stores Industries

指标名称	Item	合计 Total		直营店 Direct Sales Store		加盟店 League Store	
		2019	2020	2019	2020	2019	2020
一、门店总数 (个)	**Number of Stores (unit)**	**1666**	**1898**	**1646**	**1872**	**20**	**26**
二、餐饮营业面积 (百平方米)	**Floor Space of Restaurant Business (100 sq.m)**	**5405**	**5780**	**5353**	**5727**	**52**	**53**
三、从业人员 (人)	**Person Engaged (person)**	**34726**	**42415**	**34027**	**41818**	**699**	**597**
四、客房数 (间)	**Number of Hotel Rooms (unit)**	**6733**	**7038**	**6671**	**6325**	**62**	**713**
五、床位数 (个)	**Number of Beds (unit)**	**9155**	**10274**	**9057**	**9280**	**98**	**994**
六、餐位数 (位)	**Restaurant Seating Capacity (unit)**	**136987**	**159212**	**135657**	**157882**	**1330**	**1330**
七、商品购进总额 (万元)	**Total Value of Commodities Purchased (10 000 yuan)**	**274764**	**331308**	**271296**	**327810**	**3468**	**3498**
#统一配送商品购进额	Total Purchasing Value	220334	120815	216866	117316	3468	3498
#自有配送中心配送商品购进额	Commodities Purchased From Dispatching Center	106302	5578	106300	5578	2	
非自有配送中心配送商品购进额	Commodities Purchased From Nondispatching Center	55565	59132	55565	58898		234
八、营业额 (万元)	**Turnover (10 000 yuan)**	**930715**	**742499**	**920843**	**732663**	**9872**	**9836**
#餐费收入	Meals Revenue	877763	698573	868145	692080	9618	6493
#商品销售额	Merchandise Sales	15240	16816	15238	16816	2	

17-5 按登记注册类型分限额以上批发零售业基本情况(2020)
Basic Conditions of Enterprises above Designated Size of Wholesale and Retail Trade by Registration Type(2020)

登记注册类型	Type of Registration	法人企业数（个）Number of Corperations (unit)	年末从业人数（人）Person Engaged at Year-end (person)	零售营业面积（万平方米）Floor Space of Retail Business (10 000 sq.m)
总计	**Total**	**8719**	**453195**	**2147.0**
一、批发业	**Wholesales**	**3542**	**165586**	**526.5**
按登记注册类型分组	**Grouped by Registration Type**			
内资	Domestic Funded Enterprises	3478	147766	496.2
国有	State-owned Enterprises	57	17511	24.0
集体	Collective-owned Enterprises	8	202	0.4
股份合作	Cooperative Enterprises	4	182	0.4
联营企业	Joint Ownership Enterprises			
国有联营	State Joint Ownership Enterprises			
集体联营	Collective Joint Ownership Enterprises			
国有与集体联营	Joint State-collective Enterprises			
其他联营	Other Joint Ownership Enterprises			
有限责任公司	Limited Liability Corporations	854	45971	177.7
国有独资公司	State Sole Funded Corporations	28	2223	35.6
其他有限责任公司	Other Limited Liability Corporations	826	43748	142.2
股份有限公司	Share-holding Corporations Ltd.	55	14036	26.3
私营企业	Private Enterprises	2462	68172	264.1
私营独资	Private-funded Enterprises	59	1099	4.3
私营合伙	Private Partnership Enterprises	1	11	0.4
私营有限责任公司	Private Limited Liability Corporations	2361	65163	253.7
私营股份有限公司	Private Share-holding Corporations Ltd.	41	1899	5.6
其他	Other Enterprises	38	1692	3.3
港澳台商投资企业	Enterprises with Funds from Hongkong, Macao and Taiwan	32	10883	6.6
合资经营	Joint-venture Enterprises	5	521	0.0
合作经营	Cooperative Enterprises			
独资经营	Enterprises with Sole Investment	25	9928	6.2
投资股份有限公司	Share-holding Corporations Ltd.	2	434	0.336
外商投资企业	Foreign Funded Enterprises	32	6937	23.8
中外合资经营	Sino-foreign Joint-venture Enterprises	17	2716	11.2
外资企业	Enterprises with Sole Foreign Investment	12	3691	8.5
外商投资股份有限公司	Share-holding Co. Ltd. with Foreign Investment	2	391	4.1
其他外资企业	Other Enterprises with Sole Foreign Investment	1	139	

17-5 续表 continued

登记注册类型	Type of Registration	法人企业数（个） Number of Corperations (unit)	年末从业人数（人） Person Engaged at Year-end (person)	零售营业面积（万平方米） Floor Space of Retail Business (10 000 sq.m)
二、零售业	**Retail Trade**	**5177**	**287609**	**1620.5**
按登记注册类型分组	**Grouped by Registration Type**			
内资	Domestic Funded Enterprises	5119	260930	1476.7
国有	State-owned Enterprises	52	2656	7.8
集体	Collective-owned Enterprises	26	6271	30.4
股份合作	Cooperative Enterprises	5	187	0.3
联营企业	Joint Ownership Enterprises	1	60	0.8
国有联营	State Joint Ownership Enterprises	1	60	0.8
集体联营	Collective Joint Ownership Enterprises			
国有与集体联营	Joint State-collective Enterprises			
其他联营	Other Joint Ownership Enterprises			
有限责任公司	Limited Liability Corporations	975	106483	627.3
国有独资公司	State Sole Funded Corporations	11	1379	10.9
其他有限责任公司	Other Limited Liability Corporations	964	105104	616.5
股份有限公司	Share-holding Corporations Ltd.	63	19815	143.6
私营企业	Private Enterprises	3978	124764	665.6
私营独资	Private-funded Enterprises	372	5777	33.3
私营合伙	Private Partnership Enterprises	30	534	2.9
私营有限责任公司	Private Limited Liability Corporations	3530	114764	613.6
私营股份有限公司	Private Share-holding Corporations Ltd.	46	3689	15.8
其他	Other Enterprises	19	694	0.8
港澳台商投资企业	Enterprises with Funds from Hongkong, Macao and Taiwan	30	12622	42.9
合资经营	Joint-venture Enterprises	8	2006	13.8
合作经营	Cooperative Enterprises			
独资经营	Enterprises with Sole Investment	22	10616	29.1
其他港澳台投资企业	Other Enterprises with Funds from Hongkong, Macao and Taiwan			
外商投资企业	Foreign Funded Enterprises	28	14057	100.9
中外合资经营	Sino-foreign Joint-venture Enterprises	4	1792	25.2
中外合作经营	Sino-foreign Cooperative Enterprises			
外资企业	Enterprises with Sole Foreign Investment	22	12076	73.0
外商投资股份有限公司	Share-holding Co. Ltd. with Foreign Investment	2	189	2.7

17-6 按国民经济行业分限额以上批发零售业基本情况(2020)
Basic Conditions of Enterprises above Designated Size of Wholesale and Retail Trade by Sector(2020)

项 目	Item	法人企业数(个) Number of Corperations (unit)	年末从业人数(人) Person Engaged at Year-end (person)	零售营业面积(万平方米) Floor Space of Retail Business (10 000 sq.m)
总计	**Total**	**8719**	**453195**	**2147.0**
一、批发业	**Wholesales**	**3542**	**165586**	**526.5**
农、林、牧、渔产品批发业	Wholesales of Agriculture, Forestry, Animal Husbandry and Fishery Products	260	7009	141.8
食品、饮料及烟草制品批发业	Wholesales of Foods, Beverage and Tobacco	568	49076	88.0
米、面制品及食用油批发业	Wholesales of Rice, Noodles and Edible Oil	105	5434	13.2
烟草制品批发业	Wholesales of Tobacco	20	11458	0.6
纺织、服装及家庭用品批发业	Wholesales of Textile Products, Garments and Household Articles	168	9858	9.6
服装批发业	Wholesales of Garments	44	2909	4.5
家用视听设备批发业	Wholesales of Household Audio-visual Equipment	14	930	1.1
文化、体育用品及器材批发业	Wholesales of Cultural and Sports Goods and Equipments	73	6591	20.1
医药及医疗器材批发业	Wholesales of Medicnes and Medical Appliances	601	40597	52.4
矿产品、建材及化工产品批发业	Wholesales of Mineral Products, Building Materials and Chemical Products	1223	32242	169.6
煤炭及制品批发业	Wholesales of Coal and Coal-made Products	117	2048	2.2
石油及制品批发业	Wholesales of Petroleum Products	132	11546	108.7
非金属矿及制品批发	Wholesales of Non-metal and Non-metal Mines	53	1201	0.6
金属及金属矿批发业	Wholesales of Metal and Metal Mines	353	5792	14.5
建材批发业	Wholesales of Construction Materials	268	4050	25.7
化肥批发业	Wholesales of Chemical Fertilizers	82	3674	14.5
机械设备、五金产品及电子产品批发	Wholesales of Machinery Equipment, Hardware, and Electronic Products	558	17454	38.2
汽车及零配件批发业	Wholesales of Cars and Spare Parts	193	4983	9.2
计算机、软件及辅助设备批发业	Wholesales of Computers, Softwares and Assisted Equipments	32	1539	0.6
贸易经纪与代理	Trade Agent	6	92	0.1
其他批发业	Other Wholesales	85	2667	6.8
二、零售业	**Retail Sales**	**5177**	**287609**	**1620.5**
综合零售业	Retail Sales of Department	757	122674	762.3
百货零售业	Department Stores	406	37354	360.7
超级市场零售业	Supermarkets	261	80619	358.2
食品、饮料及烟草制品专门零售业	Monopoly Retail of Foods, Beverage and Tobacco	636	21762	81.9
纺织、服装及日用品专门零售业	Monopoly Retail of Textile, Garments, and Daily Used Articles	238	13180	65.1
服装零售业	Retail Sales of Garments	110	7575	50.4
文化、体育用品及器材专门零售业	Monopoly Retail of Cultural, Sports Products and Equipments	229	7028	28.5
体育用品及器材零售业	Retail Sales of Sports Goods and Equipment	5	54	0.1
图书报刊零售业	Retail Sales of Books, Newspapers and Periodicals	19	1314	4.0
医药及医疗器材专门零售业	Monopoly Retail of Medicine and Medical Appliances	247	28629	71.1
汽车、摩托车、零配件和燃料及其他动力销售	Monopoly Retail of Cars, Motorcycle, Spare Parts, Fuel and Other Power	1508	53529	383.5
汽车新车零售业	Retail Sales of New Cars	1102	41166	271.8
机动车燃油零售业	Retail Sales of Motor Vehicles Fuels	256	9687	82.2
家用电器及电子产品专门零售业	Monopoly Retail of Home Appliances and Electronic Products	743	23089	126.2
家用视听设备零售业	Retail Sales of Home Audio-visual Equipment	319	8852	59.0
计算机、软件及辅助设备零售业	Retail Sales of Computers, Softwares and Assisted Equipments	121	2987	3.4
通信设备零售业	Retail Sales of Communication Equipments	63	4987	11.1
五金、家具及室内装修材料专门零售业	Monopoly Retail of Hardware, Furnitures and Decorative Materials	396	7448	53.0
货摊、无店铺及其他零售业	Retail Sales of Stalls ,Storeless and Others	423	10270	48.8
互联网零售	Retail on the Internet	294	7107	19.9

17-7 按登记注册类型分限额以上住宿和餐饮业基本情况(2020)
Basic Conditions of Enterprises above Designated Size in Hotels and Catering Services by Registration Type(2020)

项目	Item	法人企业数(个) Number of Corporations (unit)	年末从业人数(人) Person Engaged at Year-end (person)	餐饮营业面积(万平方米) Floor Space of Catering Business (10 000 sq.m)
总计	**Total**	**2354**	**147686**	**725.36**
一、住宿业	**Hotel Trade**	**934**	**47565**	**365.59**
按登记注册类型分组	**Grouped by Registration Type**			
内资	Domestic Funded Enterprises	913	44299	350.13
国有	State-owned Enterprises	23	1828	12.95
集体	Collective-owned Enterprises	10	713	4.51
股份合作	Cooperative Enterprises			
联营企业	Joint Ownership Enterprises	1	143	0.07
国有联营	State Joint Ownership Enterprises	1	143	0.07
集体联营	Collective Joint Ownership Enterprises			
国有与集体联营	Joint State-collective Enterprises			
其他联营	Other Joint Ownership Enterprises			
有限责任公司	Limited Liability Corporations	185	13403	94.58
国有独资公司	State Sole Funded Corporations	9	935	7.02
其他有限责任公司	Other Limited Liability Corporations	176	12468	87.56
股份有限公司	Share-holding Corporations Ltd.	13	1208	5.75
私营企业	Private Enterprises	679	26949	232.22
私营独资	Private-funded Enterprises	38	782	4.80
私营合伙	Private Partnership Enterprises	7	254	0.95
私营有限责任公司	Private Limited Liability Corporations	633	25853	226.32
私营股份有限公司	Private Share-holding Corporations Ltd.	1	60	0.15
其他	Other Enterprises	2	55	0.04
港澳台商投资企业	Enterprises with Funds from Hongkong, Macao and Taiwan	13	2000	9.41
合资经营	Joint-venture Enterprises	2	349	2.99
合作经营	Cooperative Enterprises	1	262	0.14
独资经营	Enterprises with Sole Investment	8	953	5.80
投资股份有限公司	Share-holding Co. Ltd. With Investment	2	436	0.48
外商投资企业	Foreign Funded Enterprises	8	1266	6.05
中外合资经营	Sino-foreign Joint-venture Enterprises	2	469	2.32
中外合作经营	Sino-foreign Cooperative Enterprises			
外资企业	Enterprises with Sole Foreign Investment	4	543	2.01
外商投资股份有限公司	Share-holding Co. Ltd. with Foreign Investment	2	254	1.72
二、餐饮业	**Catering Trade**	**1420**	**100121**	**359.77**
按登记注册类型分组	**Grouped by Registration Type**			
内资	Domestic Funded Enterprises	1396	63545	320.04
国有	State-owned Enterprises	7	406	2.01
集体	Collective-owned Enterprises	3	207	0.85
股份合作	Cooperative Enterprises			
联营企业	Joint Ownership Enterprises			
国有联营	State Joint Ownership Enterprises			
集体联营	Collective Joint Ownership Enterprises			
国有与集体联营	Joint State-collective Enterprises			
其他联营	Other Joint Ownership Enterprises			
有限责任公司	Limited Liability Corporations	192	11126	57.71
国有独资公司	State Sole Funded Corporations	1	294	0.60
其他有限责任公司	Other Limited Liability Corporations	191	10832	57.11
股份有限公司	Share-holding Corporations Ltd.	6	1595	1.33
私营企业	Private Enterprises	1187	50181	258.12
私营独资	Private-funded Enterprises	198	3544	22.46
私营合伙	Private Partnership Enterprises	11	266	1.57
私营有限责任公司	Private Limited Liability Corporations	963	43663	224.33
私营股份有限公司	Private Share-holding Corporations Ltd.	15	2708	9.75
其他	Other Enterprises	1	30	0.03
港澳台商投资企业	Enterprises with Funds from Hongkong, Macao and Taiwan	13	29317	31.02
合资经营	Joint-venture Enterprises	1	138	0.25
合作经营	Cooperative Enterprises			
独资经营	Enterprises with Sole Investment	11	29068	30.63
投资股份有限公司	Share-holding Co. Ltd. With Investment	1	111	0.14
外商投资企业	Foreign Funded Enterprises	11	7259	8.71
中外合资经营	Sino-foreign Joint-venture Enterprises	2	255	0.42
外资企业	Enterprises with Sole Foreign Investment	9	7004	8.28

17-8 按国民经济行业分限额以上住宿和餐饮业基本情况(2020)
Basic Conditions of Enterprises above Designated Size of Hotels and Catering Services by Sector(2020)

行 业	Item	法人企业数（个）Number of Corperations (unit)	年末从业人数（人）Person Engaged at Year-end (person)	餐饮营业面积（万平方米）Floor Space of Catering Business (10 000 sq.m)
总计	**Total**	**2354**	**147686**	**725.36**
一、住宿业	**Hotel**	**934**	**47565**	**365.59**
按国民经济行业分组	**Grouped by Sector**			
旅游饭店	Tourist Hotel	394	29976	204.16
一般旅馆	Regular Hotel	499	15587	136.89
民宿服务	B&B Service	2	23	0.15
其他住宿服务	Other Accomodation Service	39	1979	24.39
二、餐饮业	**Catering**	**1420**	**100121**	**359.77**
按国民经济行业分组	**Grouped by Sector**			
正餐服务	Dinner	1354	62874	316.85
快餐服务	Fast Food	29	28681	33.34
饮料及冷饮服务	Beverage and Cold Drink Services	13	4780	5.11
餐饮配送及外卖送餐服务	Catering Distribution and Takeaway Service	16	3624	4.27
其他餐饮业	Others	8	162	0.20

17-9 按国民经济行业分限额以上住宿和餐饮业经营情况(2020)
Business Conditions of Enterprises above Designated Size of Hotels and Catering Services by Sector(2020)

行 业	Item	营业额(亿元) Turn over (100 million yuan)	客房收入 Revnue from Guest Rooms	餐费收入 Revenue from Catering Bills	商品销售收入 Revenue from Commo dity Sales	其他收入 Revenue from Others	年末住宿和餐饮企业拥有床位数(万个) Number of Beds owned by Hotels and Catering Enterprises at Year-end (10 000 units)	年末住宿和餐饮企业拥有餐位数(万位) Number of Seats owned by Hotels and Catering Enterprises at Year-end (10 000 units)
总计	**Total**	**326.39**	**73.51**	**232.61**	**10.74**	**9.54**	**29.47**	**107.28**
一、住宿业	**Hotel**	**96.56**	**57.22**	**30.78**	**2.25**	**6.30**	**21.90**	**23.68**
按国民经济行业分组	**Grouped by Sector**							
旅游饭店	Tourist Hotel	57.41	31.10	19.85	1.13	5.34	13.43	15.81
一般旅馆	Regular Hotel	35.44	23.98	9.61	1.05	0.80	7.71	6.88
民宿服务	B&B Service	0.18	0.12	0.06	0.00		0.02	0.00
其他住宿业	Other Accomodation Service	3.53	2.03	1.26	0.07	0.17	0.74	0.99
二、餐饮业	**Catering**	**229.83**	**16.29**	**201.82**	**8.48**	**3.24**	**7.57**	**83.60**
按国民经济行业分组	**Grouped by Sector**							
正餐服务	Dinner	157.09	16.29	131.35	6.80	2.66	7.57	67.83
快餐服务	Fast Food	45.78		45.44	0.00	0.33		9.28
饮料及冷饮服务	Beverage and Cold Drink Services	18.65		16.86	1.66	0.13		3.36
餐饮配送及外卖送餐服务	Catering Distribution and Takeaway Service	7.82		7.68	0.02	0.12		3.07
其他餐饮业	Others	0.49		0.49	0.00	0.00		0.05

17-10 按登记注册类型分限额以上住宿和餐饮业经营情况(2020)

单位:亿元

项 目	Item	营业额 Turnover	客房收入 Revnue from Guest Rooms
总计	**Total**	**326.39**	**73.51**
一、住宿业	**Hotels**	**96.56**	**57.22**
按登记注册类型分组	**Grouped by Registration Type**		
内资	Domestic Funded Enterprises	90.37	53.54
国有	State-Owned Enterprises	2.58	1.20
集体	Collective-owned Enterprises	1.35	0.71
股份合作	Cooperative Enterprises		
联营企业	Joint Ownership Enterprises	0.14	0.07
国有联营	State Joint Ownership Enterprises	0.14	0.07
集体联营	Collective Joint Ownership Enterprises		
国有与集体联营	Joint State-collective Enterprises		
其他联营	Other Joint Ownership Enterprises		
有限责任公司	Limited Liability Corporations	24.84	13.37
国有独资公司	State Sole Funded Corporations	1.58	0.71
其他有限责任公司	Other Limited Liability Corporations	23.26	12.66
股份有限公司	Share-holding Corporations Ltd.	1.86	1.07
私营企业	Private Enterprises	59.44	36.99
私营独资	Private-funded Enterprises	2.48	1.71
私营合伙	Private Partnership Enterprises	0.58	0.25
私营有限责任公司	Private Limited Liability Corporations	56.17	34.90
私营股份有限公司	Private Share-holding Corporations Ltd.	0.20	0.13
其他	Other Enterprises	0.16	0.14
港澳台商投资企业	Enterprises with Funds from Hongkong, Macao and Taiwan	3.66	2.18
合资经营	Joint-venture Enterprises	0.72	0.37
合作经营	Cooperative Enterprises	0.41	0.24
独资经营	Enterprises with Sole Investment	1.73	1.02
投资股份有限公司	Share-holding Co. Ltd. With Investment	0.80	0.54
外商投资企业	Foreign Funded Enterprises	2.54	1.50
中外合资经营	Sino-foreign Joint-venture Enterprises	0.81	0.35
中外合作经营	Sino-foreign Cooperative Enterprises		
外资企业	Enterprises with Sole Foreign Investment	1.08	0.64
外商投资股份有限公司	Share-holding Co. Ltd. with Foreign Investment	0.65	0.52
二、餐饮业	**Catering**	**229.83**	**16.29**
按登记注册类型分组	**Grouped by Registration Type**		
内资	Domestic Funded Enterprises	168.59	16.11
国有	State-Owned Enterprises	0.41	0.11
集体	Collective-owned Enterprises	0.35	0.00
股份合作	Cooperative Enterprises		
联营企业	Joint Ownership Enterprises		
国有联营	State Joint Ownership Enterprises		
集体联营	Collective Joint Ownership Enterprises		
国有与集体联营	Joint State-collective Enterprises		
其他联营	Other Joint Ownership Enterprises		
有限责任公司	Limited Liability Corporations	25.93	2.42
国有独资公司	State Sole Funded Corporations	2.36	
其他有限责任公司	Other Limited Liability Corporations	23.57	2.42
股份有限公司	Share-holding Corporations Ltd.	1.63	0.07
私营企业	Private Enterprises	140.25	13.51
私营独资	Private-funded Enterprises	19.67	1.70
私营合伙	Private Partnership Enterprises	0.50	0.05
私营有限责任公司	Private Limited Liability Corporations	113.89	11.45
私营股份有限公司	Private Share-holding Corporations Ltd.	6.19	0.31
其他	Other Enterprises	0.03	
港澳台商投资企业	Enterprises with Funds from Hongkong, Macao and Taiwan	51.07	0.13
合资经营	Joint-venture Enterprises	0.22	0.08
合作经营	Cooperative Enterprises		
独资经营	Enterprises with Sole Investment	50.70	0.05
投资股份有限公司	Share-holding Co. Ltd. With Investment	0.15	
外商投资企业	Foreign Funded Enterprises	10.17	0.04
中外合资经营	Sino-Foreign Joint-venture Enterprises	0.61	
外资企业	Enterprises with Sole Foreign Investment	9.56	0.04

Business Conditions of Enterprises above Designated Size of Hotels and Catering Services by Registration Type(2020)

(100 million yuan)

餐费收入 Revenue from Catering Bills	商品销售收入 Revenue from Commodity Sales	其他收入 Revenue from Others	年末床位数 (万个) Number of Beds at Year-end (10 000 units)	年末餐位数 (万位) Number of Seats at Year-end (10 000 units)
232.61	**10.74**	**9.54**	**29.47**	**107.28**
30.78	**2.25**	**6.30**	**21.90**	**23.68**
28.76	2.09	5.98	21.03	22.52
1.18	0.01	0.19	0.47	0.93
0.58	0.00	0.06	0.23	0.52
0.07		0.01	0.03	0.04
0.07		0.01	0.03	0.04
7.93	0.73	2.82	4.73	6.13
0.53	0.01	0.34	0.28	0.50
7.40	0.72	2.48	4.45	5.63
0.61	0.09	0.09	0.42	0.47
18.38	1.26	2.82	15.11	14.43
0.64	0.13	0.01	1.34	0.55
0.32	0.00	0.00	0.10	0.10
17.34	1.13	2.81	13.64	13.77
0.07		0.00	0.04	0.01
0.01	0.00	0.01	0.04	0.01
1.20	0.13	0.16	0.48	0.60
0.33	0.01	0.01	0.07	0.04
0.15	0.02		0.05	0.14
0.50	0.08	0.12	0.28	0.30
0.21	0.02	0.03	0.08	0.13
0.82	0.04	0.17	0.39	0.56
0.35	0.01	0.10	0.10	0.12
0.38	0.02	0.05	0.19	0.36
0.09	0.01	0.03	0.10	0.09
201.82	**8.48**	**3.24**	**7.57**	**83.60**
142.98	6.87	2.64	7.48	71.18
0.26	0.01	0.02	0.08	0.23
0.35	0.00		0.03	0.37
21.40	1.49	0.63	1.60	10.33
1.21	1.15			0.17
20.18	0.34	0.63	1.60	10.16
1.51	0.05		0.05	0.83
119.45	5.32	1.98	5.72	59.39
16.82	1.00	0.15	0.37	4.72
0.45		0.00	0.03	1.74
96.30	4.32	1.82	5.20	49.18
5.88	0.00	0.00	0.12	3.76
0.02		0.01		0.03
48.80	1.61	0.52	0.08	10.14
0.02		0.12	0.04	0.03
48.64	1.61	0.39	0.04	10.04
0.14		0.01		0.07
10.04	0.00	0.08	0.02	2.27
0.60	0.00			0.27
9.44	0.00	0.08	0.02	2.00

17-11 按登记注册类型分限额以上批发和零售业商品购、销、存总额(2020)

Total Purchases, Sales and Stock of Enterprises above Designated Size of Wholesale and Retail Trades by Registration Type(2020)

单位:亿元 (100 million yuan)

项目	Item	购进总额 Total Purchasing Value	销售总额 Total Sales Value	批发 Whole Sales	零售 Retail Sales	年末库存总额 Total Value of Inventory at Year-end
总计	**Total**	**14385.35**	**15934.33**	**10696.63**	**5192.78**	**1472.29**
一、批发业	**Wholesales**	**10387.06**	**11222.01**	**10370.08**	**807.34**	**775.85**
按登记注册类型分组	**Grouped by Registration Type**					
内资	Domestic Funded Enterprises	8185.02	8795.70	8100.99	650.56	714.03
国有	State-owned Enterprises	738.87	983.50	943.65	39.85	64.53
集体	Collective-owned Enterprises	10.63	11.14	10.51	0.63	0.37
股份合作	Cooperative Enterprises	2.27	2.36	1.98	0.38	0.07
联营企业	Joint Ownership Enterprises					
国有联营	State Joint Ownership Enterprises					
集体联营	Collective Joint Ownership Enterprises					
国有与集体联营	Joint State-collective Enterprises					
其他联营	Other Joint Ownership Enterprises					
有限责任公司	Limited Liability Corporations	3635.50	4002.80	3650.28	324.25	213.41
国有独资公司	State Sole Funded Corporations	514.32	551.12	521.04	30.08	13.00
其他有限责任公司	Other Limited Liability Corporations	3121.18	3451.68	3129.23	294.17	200.41
股份有限公司	Share-holding Corporations Ltd.	910.16	587.72	549.96	37.69	233.50
私营企业	Private Enterprises	2859.69	3175.42	2920.46	239.34	200.44
私营独资	Private-funded Enterprises	32.35	36.60	28.99	7.23	1.63
私营合伙	Private Partnership Enterprises	0.22	0.26	0.24	0.02	0.00
私营有限责任公司	Private Limited Liability Corporations	2794.06	3100.10	2861.35	223.52	195.91
私营股份有限公司	Private Share-holding Corporations Ltd.	33.05	38.46	29.88	8.57	2.90
其他	Other Enterprises	27.91	32.76	24.15	8.43	1.71
港澳台商投资企业	Enterprises with Funds from Hongkong, Macao and Taiwan	343.57	493.59	471.48	21.67	17.66
合资经营	Joint-venture Enterprises	14.55	15.08	15.03	0.05	1.64
合作经营	Cooperative Enterprises					
独资经营	Enterprises with Sole Investment	320.82	468.63	446.57	21.62	13.96
投资股份有限公司	Share-holding Corporations Ltd.	8.20	9.88	9.88		2.06
外商投资企业	Foreign Funded Enterprises	1858.46	1932.72	1797.61	135.11	44.17
中外合资经营	Sino-foreign Joint-venture Enterprises	1667.91	1699.52	1660.62	38.90	37.59
外资企业	Enterprises with Sole Foreign Investment	177.89	217.82	126.50	91.32	6.21
外商投资股份有限公司	Share-holding Co. Ltd. with Foreign Investment	9.92	12.00	7.12	4.89	0.23
其他外资企业	Other Enterprises with Sole Foreign Investment	2.74	3.37	3.37		0.13
二、零售业	**Retail Trade**	**3998.29**	**4712.33**	**326.55**	**4385.44**	**696.44**
按登记注册类型分组	**Grouped by Registration Type**					
内资	Domestic Funded Enterprises	3432.70	4062.88	235.62	3826.92	671.74
国有	State-owned Enterprises	20.69	22.77	0.88	21.89	1.83
集体	Collective-owned Enterprises	48.54	54.57	0.26	54.31	5.32
股份合作	Cooperative Enterprises	1.15	1.18	0.11	1.07	0.05
联营企业	Joint Ownership Enterprises	0.21	0.22		0.22	0.03
国有联营	State Joint Ownership Enterprises	0.21	0.22		0.22	0.03
集体联营	Collective Joint Ownership Enterprises					
国有与集体联营	Joint State-collective Enterprises					
其他联营	Other Joint Ownership Enterprises					
有限责任公司	Limited Liability Corporations	1683.18	1981.43	108.86	1872.57	144.82
国有独资公司	State Sole Funded Corporations	43.19	69.45	25.91	43.55	1.36
其他有限责任公司	Other Limited Liability Corporations	1639.98	1911.98	82.95	1829.03	143.46
股份有限公司	Share-holding Corporations Ltd.	194.79	295.54	30.38	265.15	18.12
私营企业	Private Enterprises	1479.33	1701.41	94.58	1606.49	501.43
私营独资	Private-funded Enterprises	71.34	82.17	4.96	77.21	4.32
私营合伙	Private Partnership Enterprises	5.97	6.20	0.02	6.18	0.44
私营有限责任公司	Private Limited Liability Corporations	1380.90	1587.70	88.95	1498.41	493.99
私营股份有限公司	Private Share-holding Corporations Ltd.	21.12	25.35	0.65	24.70	2.69
其他	Other Enterprises	4.82	5.75	0.56	5.19	0.15
港澳台商投资企业	Enterprises with Funds from Hongkong, Macao and Taiwan	210.36	249.88	6.73	243.15	15.02
合资经营	Joint-venture Enterprises	8.91	19.61	1.66	17.95	4.12
合作经营	Cooperative Enterprises					
独资经营	Enterprises with Sole Investment	201.45	230.27	5.07	225.20	10.89
其他港澳台投资企业	Other Enterprises with Funds from Hongkong, Macao and Taiwan					
外商投资企业	Foreign Funded Enterprises	355.23	399.57	84.20	315.37	9.69
中外合资经营	Sino-foreign Joint-venture Enterprises	95.55	115.67	9.46	106.20	0.48
中外合作经营	Sino-foreign Cooperative Enterprises					
外资企业	Enterprises with Sole Foreign Investment	258.18	282.67	74.69	207.98	9.19
外商投资股份有限公司	Share-holding Co. Ltd. with Foreign Investment	1.50	1.23	0.04	1.19	0.01

17-12 按国民经济行业分限额以上批发和零售业商品购、销、存总额(2020)
Total Purchases, Sales and Stock of Enterprises above Designated Size of Wholesale and Retail Trade by Sector(2020)

单位:亿元 (100 million yuan)

项 目	Item	购进总额 Total Purchasing Value	销售总额 Total Sales Value	批发 Whole Sales	零售 Retail Sales	年末库存总额 Total Value of Inventory at Year-end
总计	**Total**	**14385.35**	**15934.33**	**10696.63**	**5192.78**	**1472.29**
一、批发业	**Wholesales**	**10387.06**	**11222.01**	**10370.08**	**807.34**	**775.85**
农、林、牧、渔产品批发业	Wholesales of Agriculture, Forestry, Animal Husbandry and Fishery Products	307.93	337.59	285.93	48.02	48.35
食品、饮料及烟草制品批发业	Wholesales of Foods, Beverage and Tobacco	1514.25	1950.24	1787.82	158.04	146.58
米、面制品及食用油批发业	Wholesales of Rice, Noodles and Edible Oil	240.22	239.45	221.01	17.74	30.54
烟草制品批发业	Wholesales of Tobacco	495.29	723.41	716.97	6.44	42.78
纺织、服装及家庭用品批发业	Wholesales of Textile Products, Garments and Household Articles	281.31	321.98	240.16	81.19	38.25
服装批发业	Wholesales of Garments	88.45	112.25	43.92	68.32	6.56
家用视听设备批发业	Wholesales of Household Audio-visual Equipment	45.46	47.08	44.70	1.84	10.19
文化、体育用品及器材批发业	Wholesales of Cultural and Sports Goods and Equipments	187.35	225.58	174.84	50.73	19.41
医药及医疗器材批发业	Wholesales of Medicnes and Medical Appliances	1235.24	1401.51	1357.95	41.51	277.97
矿产品、建材及化工产品批发业	Wholesales of Mineral Products, Building Materials and Chemical Products	5396.11	5411.34	5050.27	330.45	148.66
煤炭及制品批发业	Wholesales of Coal and Coal-made Products	297.58	317.89	308.09	7.92	3.78
石油及制品批发业	Wholesales of Petroleum Products	2360.30	2075.12	1817.48	257.58	52.71
非金属矿及制品批发	Wholesales of Non-metal and Non-metal Mines	38.49	44.35	42.79	1.56	3.04
金属及金属矿批发业	Wholesales of Metal and Metal Mines	1764.45	1935.65	1909.47	26.18	56.94
建材批发业	Wholesales of Construction Materials	266.01	286.74	263.07	22.80	9.03
化肥批发业	Wholesales of Chemical Fertilizers	197.85	248.14	214.32	7.12	3.90
机械设备、五金产品及电子产品批发	Wholesales of Machinery Equipment, Hardware, and Electronic Products	1314.46	1410.07	1325.66	82.10	92.19
汽车及零配件批发业	Wholesales of Cars and Spare Parts	618.79	654.99	605.73	47.31	60.84
计算机、软件及辅助设备	Wholesales of Computers, Softwares and Assisted Equipments	280.17	283.93	281.33	2.52	10.40
贸易经纪与代理	Trade Agent	8.06	8.31	8.31	0.00	0.32
其他批发业	Other Wholesales	142.35	155.40	139.13	15.29	4.12
二、零售业	**Retail Sales**	**3998.29**	**4712.33**	**326.55**	**4385.44**	**696.44**
综合零售业	Retail Sales of Department	809.39	1062.54	36.65	1025.89	89.74
百货零售业	Department Stores	348.83	452.08	7.17	444.91	26.71
超级市场零售业	Supermarkets	416.01	551.86	27.89	523.97	58.22
食品、饮料及烟草制品专门零售业	Monopoly Retail of Foods, Beverage and Tobacco	185.31	225.08	27.98	197.03	15.55
纺织、服装及日用品专门零售业	Monopoly Retail of Textile, Garments, and Daily Used Articles	87.71	110.68	11.60	99.07	22.01
服装零售业	Retail Sales of Garments	50.86	68.24	6.00	62.24	12.51
文化、体育用品及器材专门零售业	Monopoly Retail of Cultural, Sports Products and Equipments	56.17	68.52	5.89	62.60	11.59
体育用品及器材零售业	Retail Sales of Sports Goods and Equipment	1.73	1.90	0.14	1.76	0.07
图书报刊零售业	Retail Sales of Books, Newspapers and Periodicals	7.87	9.48	0.91	8.57	2.61
医药及医疗器材专门零售业	Monopoly Retail of Medicine and Medical Appliances	170.89	203.01	19.59	183.42	367.80
汽车、摩托车、零配件和燃料及其他动力销售	Monopoly Retail of Cars, Motorcycle, Spare Parts, Fuel and Other Power	1504.07	1698.37	80.11	1618.26	152.15
汽车新车零售业	Retail Sales of New Cars	1223.18	1312.82	24.99	1287.83	135.64
机动车燃油零售业	Retail Sales of Motor Vehicles Fuels	234.94	331.62	51.26	280.36	11.80
家用电器及电子产品专门零售业	Monopoly Retail of Home Appliances and Electronic Products	363.99	409.07	91.53	317.44	21.18
家用视听设备零售业	Retail Sales of Home Audio-visual Equipment	93.22	113.64	5.83	107.71	9.30
计算机、软件及辅助设备零售业	Retail Sales of Computers, Softwares and Assisted Equipments	32.69	37.41	3.59	33.83	2.35
通信设备零售业	Retail Sales of Communication Equipments	132.60	146.49	77.88	68.61	2.73
五金、家具及室内装修材料专门零售业	Monopoly Retail of Hardware, Furnitures and Decorative Materials	76.94	98.81	11.57	87.23	7.01
货摊、无店铺及其他零售业	Retail Sales of Stalls、Storeless and Others	743.83	836.24	41.62	794.49	9.41
互联网零售	Retail on the Internet	716.11	800.44	37.21	763.10	7.84

17-13 限额以上批发和零售业企业资产及负债(2020)
Assets and Liabilities of Enterprises above Designated Size of Wholesale and Retail Trade(2020)

单位:亿元 (100 million yuan)

项 目	Item	流动资产合计 Total Circulating Funds	固定资产原价 Original Price of Fixed Assets	资产总计 Total Assets	负债合计 Total Liabilities	所有者权益合计 Total Creditor's Equity
总计	**Total**	**5818.96**	**1069.94**	**7853.41**	**5652.84**	**2180.92**
一、批发业	**Wholesales**	**4343.66**	**527.03**	**5516.07**	**4033.90**	**1476.66**
按登记注册类型分组	**Grouped by Registration Type**					
内资	Domestic Funded Enterprises	3656.82	459.27	4700.18	3338.98	1355.69
国有	State-owned Enterprises	387.44	102.20	518.59	258.02	260.57
集体	Collective-owned Enterprises	4.69	0.42	5.23	4.70	0.53
股份合作	Cooperative Enterprises	1.33	0.11	1.50	1.09	0.40
联营企业	Joint Ownership Enterprises					
国有联营	State Joint Ownership Enterprises					
集体联营	Collective Joint Ownership Enterprises					
国有与集体联营	Joint State-collective Enterprises					
其他联营	Other Joint Ownership Enterprises					
有限责任公司	Limited Liability Corporations	1869.13	156.16	2296.41	1829.83	465.84
国有独资公司	State Sole Funded Corporations	218.55	15.40	336.03	258.12	77.91
其他有限责任公司	Other Limited Liability Corporations	1650.58	140.76	1960.38	1571.71	387.93
股份有限公司	Share-holding Corporations Ltd.	409.50	36.03	652.87	380.82	271.64
私营企业	Private Enterprises	980.71	159.10	1215.70	861.79	349.70
私营独资	Private-funded Enterprises	8.33	2.83	11.23	5.55	5.57
私营合伙	Private Partnership Enterprises	0.02	0.00	0.02	0.04	-0.01
私营有限责任公司	Private Limited Liability Corporations	958.33	147.98	1180.89	847.54	329.24
私营股份有限公司	Private Share-holding Corporations Ltd.	14.02	8.29	23.57	8.67	14.90
其他	Other Enterprises	4.02	5.25	9.88	2.72	7.01
港澳台商投资企业	Enterprises with Funds from Hongkong, Macao and Taiwan	447.43	18.48	501.48	370.47	131.01
合资经营	Joint-venture Enterprises	88.91	0.25	106.45	74.22	32.24
合作经营	Cooperative Enterprises					
独资经营	Enterprises with Sole Investment	336.04	15.04	362.69	278.51	84.17
投资股份有限公司	Share-holding Co. Ltd. With Investment	22.48	3.18	32.34	17.75	14.60
外商投资企业	Foreign Funded Enterprises	239.41	49.29	314.41	324.44	-10.03
中外合资经营	Sino-foreign Joint-venture Enterprises	178.96	37.40	243.28	213.19	30.09
外资企业	Enterprises with Sole Foreign Investment	55.45	7.71	64.11	106.83	-42.72
外商投资股份有限公司	Share-holding Co. Ltd. with Foreign Investment	4.64	4.07	6.40	4.03	2.37
其他外资企业	Other Enterprises with Sole Foreign Investment	0.36	0.11	0.61	0.39	0.22
按国民经济行业分组	**Grouped by Sector**					
农、林、牧、渔产品批发业	Wholesales of Agriculture, Forestry, Animal Husbandry and Fishery Products	160.43	38.05	216.81	163.24	53.21
食品、饮料及烟草制品批发业	Wholesales of Foods, Beverage and Tobacco	879.69	160.22	1083.08	674.43	407.49
米、面制品及食用油批发业	Wholesales of Rice, Noodles and Edible Oil	146.67	22.65	193.70	132.26	61.39
烟草制品批发业	Wholesales of Tobacco	175.98	64.67	222.40	55.52	166.88
纺织、服装及家庭用品批发业	Wholesales of Textile Products, Garments and Household Articles	110.02	10.34	123.41	97.74	25.20
服装批发业	Wholesales of Garments	32.25	3.93	35.84	26.95	9.07
家用视听设备批发业	Wholesales of Household Audio-visual Equipment	24.51	0.41	24.80	22.93	1.63
文化、体育用品及器材批发业	Wholesales of Cultural and Sports Goods and Equipments	222.59	19.31	247.27	187.57	59.70
医药及医疗器材批发业	Wholesales of Medicnes and Medical Appliances	1164.19	45.45	1502.92	1090.81	410.09
矿产品、建材及化工产品批发业	Wholesales of Mineral Products, Building Materials and Chemical Products	1175.87	206.14	1578.05	1105.63	471.38
煤炭及制品批发业	Wholesales of Coal and Coal-made Products	85.61	14.00	116.74	69.14	47.96
石油及制品批发业	Wholesales of Petroleum Products	248.43	137.26	419.46	252.13	166.73
非金属及金属矿批发业	Wholesales of Non-metellic Mineral and Metal Industry	41.74	4.12	73.97	67.92	6.05
金属及金属矿批发业	Wholesales of Metal and Metal Mines	564.78	23.64	656.10	486.12	169.97
建材批发业	Wholesales of Construction Materials	89.71	10.90	105.37	70.26	34.61
化肥批发业	Wholesales of Chemical Fertilizers	50.70	5.35	60.67	44.48	16.07
机械设备、五金产品及电子产品批发业	Wholesales of Machinery Equipment, Hardware and Electronic Products	582.01	40.75	708.34	670.39	37.61
汽车及零配件批发业	Wholesales of Cars and Spare Parts	318.80	15.88	401.45	381.86	19.41
计算机、软件及辅助设备批发业	Wholesales of Computers, Softwares and Assisted Equipments	120.26	0.63	121.56	106.04	15.27
贸易经纪与代理	Trade Agent	3.44	0.50	3.84	2.96	0.88
其他批发业	Other Wholesales	45.42	6.27	52.34	41.12	11.11

17-13 续表 continued

单位:亿元 (100 million yuan)

项 目	Item	流动资产合计 Total Circulating Funds	固定资产原价 Original Price of Fixed Assets	资产总计 Total Assets	负债合计 Total Liabilities	所有者权益合计 Total Creditor's Equity
二、零售业	**Retail Trade**	**1475.30**	**542.90**	**2337.35**	**1618.94**	**704.25**
按登记注册类型分组	**Grouped by Registration Type**					
内资	Domestic Funded Enterprises	1310.99	475.16	2057.06	1403.50	639.99
国有	State-owned Enterprises	8.28	5.37	12.65	6.68	5.97
集体	Collective-owned Enterprises	7.18	4.20	11.23	7.28	3.95
股份合作	Cooperative Enterprises	0.26	1.04	1.02	0.50	0.52
联营企业	Joint Ownership Enterprises	0.05	0.04	0.13	0.50	-0.36
国有联营	State Joint Ownership Enterprises	0.05	0.04	0.13	0.50	-0.36
集体联营	Collective Joint Ownership Enterprises					
国有与集体联营	Joint State-collective Enterprises					
其他联营	Other Joint Ownership Enterprises					
有限责任公司	Limited Liability Corporations	634.10	184.13	888.94	647.82	238.97
国有独资公司	State Sole Funded Corporations	4.30	18.49	32.80	16.81	16.07
其他有限责任公司	Other Limited Liability Corporations	629.79	165.64	856.14	631.01	222.91
股份有限公司	Share-holding Corporations Ltd.	101.84	104.41	366.57	224.89	139.36
私营企业	Private Enterprises	557.45	173.43	772.44	513.75	249.58
私营独资	Private-funded Enterprises	14.03	13.54	27.45	7.92	18.80
私营合伙	Private Partnership Enterprises	1.41	0.85	2.18	1.17	1.01
私营有限责任公司	Private Limited Liability Corporations	522.23	153.82	708.96	482.21	218.37
私营股份有限公司	Private Share-holding Corporations Ltd.	19.79	5.22	33.84	22.45	11.39
其他	Other Enterprises	1.84	2.52	4.08	2.08	2.00
港澳台商投资企业	Enterprises with Funds from Hongkong, Macao and Taiwan	65.47	24.26	95.38	80.26	14.56
合资经营	Joint-venture Enterprises	6.66	9.43	16.62	12.00	4.62
合作经营	Cooperative Enterprises					
独资经营	Enterprises with Sole Investment	58.81	14.82	78.76	68.26	9.94
其他港澳台投资企业	Other Enterprises with Funds from Hongkong, Macao and Taiwan					
外商投资企业	Foreign Funded Enterprises	98.83	43.49	184.91	135.18	49.70
中外合资经营	Sino-foreign Joint-venture Enterprises	12.24	15.38	44.37	37.05	7.32
中外合作经营	Sino-foreign Cooperative Enterprises					
外资企业	Enterprises with Sole Foreign Investment	85.63	28.01	139.54	97.54	41.97
外商投资股份有限公司	Share-holding Co. Ltd. with Foreign Investment	0.96	0.10	0.99	0.59	0.41
按国民经济行业分组	**Grouped by Sector**					
综合零售业	Retail Sales of Department	367.35	227.95	806.18	531.24	272.93
百货零售业	Department Stores	201.79	126.61	514.07	331.69	181.38
超级市场零售业	Supermarkets	145.43	95.95	262.14	178.80	83.18
食品、饮料及烟草制品专门零售业	Monopoly Retail of Foods, Beverage and Tobacco	148.17	34.30	197.91	123.41	72.75
纺织、服装及日用品专门零售业	Monopoly Retail of Textile, Garments,and Daily Used Articles	51.56	21.76	75.55	56.55	18.82
服装零售业	Retail Sales of Garments	37.33	16.66	57.39	45.96	11.23
文化、体育用品及器材专门零售业	Monopoly Retail of Cultural, Sports Products and Equipments	30.81	10.81	43.49	27.40	13.59
体育用品及器材零售业	Retail Sales of Sports Goods and Equipment	0.33	0.01	2.51	1.62	-1.46
图书报刊零售业	Retail Sales of Books, Newspapers and Periodicals	9.03	4.11	12.79	7.39	5.41
医药及医疗器材专门零售业	Monopoly Retail of Medicine and Medical Appliances	92.54	12.95	117.15	94.08	22.86
汽车、摩托车、零配件和燃料及其他动力销售	Monopoly Retail of Cars, Motorcycle, Spare Parts, Fuel and Other Power	411.21	172.09	650.73	456.38	188.20
汽车新车零售业	Retail Sales of New Cars	360.94	85.47	464.56	341.63	117.09
机动车燃油零售业	Retail Sales of Motor Vehicles Fuels	26.32	79.58	153.58	96.19	57.39
家用电器及电子产品专门零售业	Monopoly Retail of Home Appliances and Electronic Products	140.43	19.55	168.50	108.49	58.99
家用视听设备零售业	Retail Sales of Home Audio-visual Equipment	33.12	12.54	48.83	26.49	22.20
计算机、软件及辅助设备零售业	Retail Sales of Computers, Softwares and Assisted Equipments	16.13	1.37	17.63	9.11	8.51
通信设备零售业	Retail Sales of Communication Equipments	32.10	1.10	34.46	28.62	5.21
五金、家具及室内装修材料专门零售业	Monopoly Retail of Hardware, Furnitures and Decorative Materials	38.33	18.69	60.32	36.34	23.69
货摊、无店铺及其他零售业	Retail Sales of Stalls ,Storeless and Others	194.88	24.80	217.52	185.04	32.42
互联网零售	Retail on the Internet	178.51	11.12	189.43	169.68	19.72

17-14 限额以上批发和零售业企业主要财务指标(2020)
Main Financial Indicators of Enterprises above Designated Size of Wholesale and Retail Trade(2020)

单位:亿元 (100 million yuan)

项目	Item	营业收入 Revenue of Business	营业成本 Cost of Business	其他业务利润 Profits of Other Business	利润总额 Total Profits
总计	**Total**	**14462.86**	**12993.54**	**62.62**	**387.12**
一、批发业	**Wholesales**	**10112.32**	**9233.15**	**17.40**	**278.64**
按登记注册类型分组	**Grouped by Registration Type**				
内资	Domestic Funded Enterprises	7928.95	7218.93	16.40	232.62
国有	State-owned Enterprises	893.84	676.73	0.82	80.68
集体	Collective-owned Enterprises	10.17	9.56	0.03	0.19
股份合作	Cooperative Enterprises	2.25	1.77		0.17
联营企业	Joint Ownership Enterprises				
国有联营	State Joint Ownership Enterprises				
集体联营	Collective Joint Ownership Enterprises				
国有与集体联营	Joint State-collective Enterprises				
其他联营	Other Joint Ownership Enterprises				
有限责任公司	Limited Liability Corporations	3615.39	3392.18	9.12	69.21
国有独资公司	State Sole Funded Corporations	488.82	475.46	0.03	7.35
其他有限责任公司	Other Limited Liability Corporations	3126.58	2916.72	9.09	61.86
股份有限公司	Share-holding Corporations Ltd.	533.15	509.34	3.86	15.50
私营企业	Private Enterprises	2844.34	2604.50	2.57	64.34
私营独资	Private-funded Enterprises	34.19	28.01		2.13
私营合伙	Private Partnership Enterprises	0.24	0.22		0.02
私营有限责任公司	Private Limited Liability Corporations	2775.16	2545.90	2.47	60.74
私营股份有限公司	Private Share-holding Corporations Ltd.	34.75	30.36	0.10	1.44
其他	Other Enterprises	29.81	24.86		2.53
港澳台商投资企业	Enterprises with Funds from Hongkong, Macao and Taiwan	441.55	313.50	0.99	44.04
合资经营	Joint-venture Enterprises	14.49	12.73	0.00	-1.68
合作经营	Cooperative Enterprises				
独资经营	Enterprises with Sole Investment	418.21	293.47	0.99	45.31
投资股份有限公司	Share-holding Co. Ltd. With Investment	8.85	7.31	0.00	0.41
外商投资企业	Foreign Funded Enterprises	1741.82	1700.71	0.01	1.98
中外合资经营	Sino-foreign Joint-venture Enterprises	1519.61	1507.30	-0.05	2.71
外资企业	Enterprises with Sole Foreign Investment	208.06	180.51	0.06	-0.61
外商投资股份有限公司	Share-holding Co. Ltd. with Foreign Investment	11.08	10.34		-0.15
其他外资企业	Other Enterprises with Sole Foreign Investment	3.07	2.57		0.03
按国民经济行业分组	**Grouped by Sector**				
农、林、牧、渔产品批发业	Wholesales of Agriculture, Forestry, Animal Husbandry and Fishery Products	309.25	284.77	0.20	8.81
食品、饮料及烟草制品批发业	Wholesales of Foods, Beverage and Tobacco	1770.26	1350.87	2.69	161.90
米、面制品及食用油批发业	Wholesales of Rice, Noodles and Edible Oil	219.31	205.89	1.07	4.04
烟草制品批发业	Wholesales of Tobacco	649.07	451.64	0.24	76.75
纺织、服装及家庭用品批发业	Wholesales of Textile Products, Garments and Household Articles	299.05	262.86	0.77	1.80
服装批发业	Wholesales of Garments	107.26	87.92	0.14	1.13
家用视听设备批发业	Wholesales of Household Audio-visual Equipment	42.06	39.29	0.00	0.14
文化、体育用品及器材批发业	Wholesales of Cultural and Sports Goods and Equipments	201.08	170.55	0.40	9.82
医药及医疗器材批发业	Wholesales of Medicnes and Medical Appliances	1264.36	1095.82	10.57	65.04
矿产品、建材及化工产品批发业	Wholesales of Mineral Products, Building Materials and Chemical Products	4835.69	4709.43	2.03	29.57
煤炭及制品批发业	Wholesales of Coal and Coal-made Products	286.04	273.97	0.17	4.29
石油及制品批发业	Wholesales of Petroleum Products	1868.39	1846.30	0.43	1.56
非金属及金属矿批发业	Wholesales of Non-metellic Mineral and Metal Industry	41.39	36.64	0.64	0.17
金属及金属矿批发业	Wholesales of Metal and Metal Mines	1724.57	1687.74	0.77	9.53
建材批发业	Wholesales of Construction Materials	228.79	212.68	0.00	4.17
化肥批发业	Wholesales of Chemical Fertilizers	232.89	218.86	0.02	3.87
机械设备、五金产品及电子产品批发业	Wholesales of Machinery Equipment, Hardware and Electronic Products	1282.55	1216.11	0.67	-1.88
汽车及零配件批发业	Wholesales of Cars and Spare Parts	579.33	557.21	0.11	-7.86
计算机、软件及辅助设备批发业	Wholesales of Computers, Softwares and Assisted Equipments	274.30	265.88	0.03	-1.69
贸易经纪与代理	Trade Agent	7.74	7.28	0.00	0.19
其他批发业	Other Wholesales	142.34	135.45	0.08	3.39

17-14 续表 continued

单位:亿元 (100 million yuan)

项 目	Item	营业收入 Revenue of Business	营业成本 Cost of Business	其他业务 Profits of Other Business	利润总额 Total Profits
二、零售业	**Retail Trade**	**4350.54**	**3760.40**	**45.22**	**108.48**
按登记注册类型分组	**Grouped by Registration Type**				
内资	Domestic Funded Enterprises	3747.11	3238.96	24.78	95.59
国有	State-owned Enterprises	21.45	17.66	0.10	1.53
集体	Collective-owned Enterprises	39.49	36.97	0.57	0.61
股份合作	Cooperative Enterprises	1.06	0.83	0.06	0.06
联营企业	Joint Ownership Enterprises	0.20	0.17	0.00	-0.09
国有联营	State Joint Ownership Enterprises	0.20	0.17	0.00	-0.09
集体联营	Collective Joint Ownership Enterprises				
国有与集体联营	Joint State-collective Enterprises				
其他联营	Other Joint Ownership Enterprises				
有限责任公司	Limited Liability Corporations	1831.67	1605.86	18.10	30.97
国有独资公司	State Sole Funded Corporations	63.95	61.20	0.01	-0.98
其他有限责任公司	Other Limited Liability Corporations	1767.71	1544.66	18.08	31.95
股份有限公司	Share-holding Corporations Ltd.	292.75	242.49	1.83	8.35
私营企业	Private Enterprises	1555.27	1330.74	4.13	53.68
私营独资	Private-funded Enterprises	73.92	57.19	0.04	6.79
私营合伙	Private Partnership Enterprises	5.57	4.69		0.16
私营有限责任公司	Private Limited Liability Corporations	1450.54	1247.99	3.77	46.29
私营股份有限公司	Private Share-holding Corporations Ltd.	25.23	20.87	0.31	0.45
其他	Other Enterprises	5.22	4.23		0.49
港澳台商投资企业	Enterprises with Funds from Hongkong, Macao and Taiwan	243.09	204.44	18.09	9.20
合资经营	Joint-venture Enterprises	18.21	15.75	0.09	0.95
合作经营	Cooperative Enterprises				
独资经营	Enterprises with Sole Investment	224.87	188.69	18.00	8.25
其他港澳台投资企业	Other Enterprises with Funds from Hongkong, Macao and Taiwan				
外商投资企业	Foreign Funded Enterprises	360.34	316.99	2.34	3.69
中外合资经营	Sino-foreign Joint-venture Enterprises	100.25	84.38	0.38	1.75
中外合作经营	Sino-foreign Cooperative Enterprises				
外资企业	Enterprises with Sole Foreign Investment	258.97	231.78	1.97	1.94
外商投资股份有限公司	Share-holding Co. Ltd. with Foreign Investment	1.12	0.84		0.00
按国民经济行业分组	**Grouped by Sector**				
综合零售业	Retail Sales of Department	1020.87	808.72	35.74	32.80
百货零售业	Department Stores	434.39	332.50	23.09	22.51
超级市场零售业	Supermarkets	529.51	429.21	11.61	8.89
食品、饮料及烟草制品专门零售业	Monopoly Retail of Foods, Beverage and Tobacco	212.67	163.20	1.32	14.87
纺织、服装及日用品专门零售业	Monopoly Retail of Textile, Garments,and Daily Used Articles	100.35	78.40	1.30	2.27
服装零售业	Retail Sales of Garments	61.78	47.70	1.17	-0.17
文化、体育用品及器材专门零售业	Monopoly Retail of Cultural, Sports Products and Equipments	64.75	52.30	0.30	4.92
体育用品及器材零售业	Retail Sales of Sports Goods and Equipment	3.01	2.81		0.12
图书报刊零售业	Retail Sales of Books, Newspapers and Periodicals	9.33	7.29	0.19	1.20
医药及医疗器材专门零售业	Monopoly Retail of Medicine and Medical Appliances	184.64	149.62	0.60	4.98
汽车、摩托车、零配件和燃料及其他动力销售	Monopoly Retail of Cars, Motorcycle, Spare Parts, Fuel and Other Power	1551.51	1428.20	4.58	25.05
汽车新车零售业	Retail Sales of New Cars	1194.33	1105.43	4.03	18.55
机动车燃油零售业	Retail Sales of Motor Vehicles Fuels	306.17	277.65	0.39	4.89
家用电器及电子产品专门零售业	Monopoly Retail of Home Appliances and Electronic Products	375.62	326.43	0.92	11.43
家用视听设备零售业	Retail Sales of Home Audio-visual Equipment	107.88	90.13	0.22	5.46
计算机、软件及辅助设备零售业	Retail Sales of Computers, Softwares and Assisted Equipments	35.97	28.75	0.11	3.44
通信设备零售业	Retail Sales of Communication Equipments	130.56	120.60	0.36	0.95
五金、家具及室内装修材料专门零售业	Monopoly Retail of Hardware, Furnitures and Decorative Materials	89.97	72.13	0.21	5.06
货摊、无店铺及其他零售业	Retail Sales of Stalls、Storeless and Others	750.16	681.41	0.24	7.12
互联网零售	Retail on the Internet	716.15	654.65	0.04	4.37

17-15 限额以上餐饮业企业资产及负债(2020)
Assets and Liabilities of Enterprises above Designated Size of Catering Services(2020)

单位:亿元 (100 million yuan)

项 目	Item	流动资产合计 Total Circulating Funds	固定资产原价 Original Price of Fixed Assets	资产总计 Total Assets	负债合计 Total Liabilities	所有者权益合计 Total Creditor's Equity
总计	**Total**	**119.26**	**119.89**	**265.78**	**190.71**	**78.45**
按国民经济行业分组	**Grouped by Sector**					
正餐服务	Dinner	99.34	105.43	221.52	163.78	61.10
快餐服务	Fast Food	5.48	10.86	22.53	18.41	4.11
饮料及冷饮服务	Beverage and Cold Drink Services	10.00	2.82	15.39	5.46	9.99
餐饮配送及外卖送餐服务	Catering Distribution and Takeaway Service	4.32	0.46	5.90	2.79	3.10
其他餐饮业	Others	0.11	0.32	0.45	0.27	0.15
按登记注册类型分组	**Grouped by Registration Type**					
内资	Domestic Funded Enterprises	103.14	103.21	224.43	162.99	64.83
国有	State-Owned Enterprises	0.54	0.59	0.94	0.30	0.64
集体	Collective-owned Enterprises	6.60	1.75	9.67	6.47	3.20
股份合作	Cooperative Enterprises					
联营企业	Joint Ownership Enterprises					
国有联营	State Joint Ownership Enterprises					
集体联营	Collective Joint Ownership Enterprises					
国有与集体联营	Joint State-collective Enterprises					
其他联营	Other Joint Ownership Enterprises					
有限责任公司	Limited Liability Corporations	16.09	16.49	32.57	25.71	6.76
国有独资公司	State Sole Funded Corporations	1.68	0.79	2.29	1.71	0.58
其他有限责任公司	Other Limited Liability Corporations	14.41	15.70	30.28	24.00	6.19
股份有限公司	Share-holding Corporations Ltd.	1.90	1.79	4.10	1.43	2.67
私营企业	Private Enterprises	78.00	82.51	177.05	129.07	51.46
私营独资	Private-funded Enterprises	4.09	8.22	11.69	4.00	7.44
私营合伙	Private Partnership Enterprises	0.17	0.14	0.32	0.08	0.24
私营有限责任公司	Private Limited Liability Corporations	70.55	71.64	158.12	121.19	40.66
私营股份有限公司	Private Share-holding Corporations Ltd.	3.19	2.51	6.92	3.80	3.11
其他	Other Enterprises	0.01	0.09	0.10		0.10
港澳台商投资企业	Enterprises with Funds from Hongkong, Macao and Taiwan	12.68	15.16	34.02	22.00	12.02
合资经营	Joint-venture Enterprises	0.18	1.50	1.12	2.24	-1.12
合作经营	Cooperative Enterprises					
独资经营	Enterprises with Sole Investment	12.33	13.64	32.67	19.50	13.17
投资股份有限公司	Share-holding Co. Ltd. With Investment	0.17	0.02	0.23	0.26	-0.03
外商投资企业	Foreign Funded Enterprises	3.45	1.52	7.33	5.73	1.60
中外合资经营	Sino-Foreign Joint-venture Enterprises	0.52	0.04	0.75	0.36	0.39
外资企业	Enterprises with Sole Foreign Investment	2.93	1.48	6.58	5.36	1.21
外商投资股份有限公司	Share-holding Co. Ltd. with Foreign Investment					
其他外商投资企业	Other Enterprises with Sole Foreign Investment					

17-16 限额以上餐饮业企业主要财务指标(2020)

Main Financial Indicators of Enterprises above Designated Size of Catering Services(2020)

单位:亿元 (100 million yuan)

项目	Item	营业收入 Revenue of Business	营业成本 Cost of Business	其他业务利润 Profits of Other Business	利润总额 Total Profits
总计	**Total**	**220.54**	**130.76**	**0.40**	**10.09**
按国民经济行业分组	**Grouped by Sector**				
正餐服务	Dinner	151.06	92.40	0.40	7.93
快餐服务	Fast Food	43.65	25.75	0.00	-0.77
饮料及冷饮服务	Beverage and Cold Drink Services	17.80	6.28		2.50
餐饮配送及外卖送餐服务	Catering Distribution and Takeaway Service	7.55	6.06	0.00	0.43
其他餐饮业	Others	0.49	0.27	0.00	0.00
按登记注册类型分组	**Grouped by Registration Type**				
内资	Domestic Funded Enterprises	162.42	104.44	0.40	8.17
国有	State-Owned Enterprises	0.40	0.19	0.00	0.01
集体	Collective-owned Enterprises	0.34	0.38		-0.20
股份合作	Cooperative Enterprises				
联营企业	Joint Ownership Enterprises				
国有联营	State Joint Ownership Enterprises				
集体联营	Collective Joint Ownership Enterprises				
国有与集体联营	Joint State-collective Enterprises				
其他联营	Other Joint Ownership Enterprises				
有限责任公司	Limited Liability Corporations	25.23	16.32	0.20	-0.27
国有独资公司	State Sole Funded Corporations	2.28	1.94		0.05
其他有限责任公司	Other Limited Liability Corporations	22.94	14.39	0.20	-0.32
股份有限公司	Share-holding Corporations Ltd.	1.52	1.15		0.19
私营企业	Private Enterprises	134.90	86.36	0.19	8.81
私营独资	Private-funded Enterprises	18.63	13.76	0.01	2.50
私营合伙	Private Partnership Enterprises	0.48	0.27		0.08
私营有限责任公司	Private Limited Liability Corporations	109.67	68.03	0.18	5.55
私营股份有限公司	Private Share-holding Corporations Ltd.	6.12	4.29	0.00	0.68
其他	Other Enterprises	0.03	0.03		0.00
港澳台商投资企业	Enterprises with Funds from Hongkong, Macao and Taiwan	48.40	21.94	0.01	1.97
合资经营	Joint-venture Enterprises	0.20	0.02		-0.05
合作经营	Cooperative Enterprises				
独资经营	Enterprises with Sole Investment	48.05	21.85	0.01	2.04
投资股份有限公司	Sole Investment Co. Ltd. With Investment	0.14	0.07		-0.02
外商投资企业	Foreign Funded Enterprises	9.72	4.38		-0.05
中外合资经营	Sino-Foreign Joint-venture Enterprises	0.60	0.55		-0.09
外资企业	Enterprises with Sole Foreign Investment	9.12	3.84		0.04
外商投资股份有限公司	Share-holding Co. Ltd. with Foreign Investment				
其他外商投资企业	Other Enterprises with Sole Foreign Investment				

17-17 限额以上住宿业企业资产及负债(2020)
Assets and Liabilities of Enterprises above Designated Size of Hotels Services(2020)

单位:亿元 (100 million yuan)

项 目	Item	流动资产合计 Total Circulating Funds	固定资产原价 Original Price of Fixed Assets	资产总计 Total Assets	负债合计 Total Liabilities	所有者权益合计 Total Creditor's Equity
总计	**Total**	**100.05**	**226.34**	**320.57**	**239.75**	**79.92**
按国民经济行业分组	**Grouped by Sector**					
旅游饭店	Tourist Hotel	66.62	176.61	234.15	180.26	53.70
一般旅馆	Regular Hotel	26.59	42.54	71.11	47.73	22.69
民宿服务	B&B Service	0.02	0.07	0.12	0.04	0.08
其他住宿业	Other Accomodation Service	6.82	7.12	15.19	11.73	3.46
按登记注册类型分组	**Grouped by Registration Type**					
内资	Domestic Funded Enterprises	93.95	197.78	294.94	216.07	77.97
国有	State-Owned Enterprises	2.85	9.18	9.47	9.15	0.32
集体	Collective-owned Enterprises	2.49	6.74	5.72	3.24	2.48
股份合作	Cooperative Enterprises					
联营企业	Joint Ownership Enterprises	0.13	0.11	0.61	0.87	-0.27
国有联营	State Joint Ownership Enterprises	0.13	0.11	0.61	0.87	-0.27
集体联营	Collective Joint Ownership Enterprises					
国有与集体联营	Joint State-collective Enterprises					
其他联营	Other Joint Ownership Enterprises					
有限责任公司	Limited Liability Corporations	32.45	73.93	108.03	76.18	31.72
国有独资公司	State Sole Funded Corporations	3.75	9.61	19.61	9.04	10.56
其他有限责任公司	Other Limited Liability Corporations	28.70	64.32	88.42	67.14	21.16
股份有限公司	Share-holding Corporations Ltd.	2.10	6.01	12.65	5.50	7.15
私营企业	Private Enterprises	53.90	101.78	158.22	121.03	36.42
私营独资	Private-funded Enterprises	0.69	1.73	3.37	1.29	2.02
私营合伙	Private Partnership Enterprises	0.57	0.59	1.07	0.79	0.28
私营有限责任公司	Private Limited Liability Corporations	52.59	99.08	152.87	118.71	33.46
私营股份有限公司	Private Share-holding Corporations Ltd.	0.06	0.38	0.91	0.24	0.66
其他	Other Enterprises	0.03	0.04	0.25	0.10	0.15
港澳台商投资企业	Enterprises with Funds from Hongkong, Macao and Taiwan	3.22	8.11	10.24	10.96	-0.73
合资经营	Joint-venture Enterprises	1.60	0.84	2.98	2.23	0.75
合作经营	Cooperative Enterprises	0.27	0.41	0.37	0.50	-0.13
独资经营	Enterprises with Sole Investment	0.60	3.98	4.72	5.73	-1.00
投资股份有限公司	Share-holding Co. Ltd. With Investment	0.75	2.89	2.16	2.51	-0.34
外商投资企业	Foreign Funded Enterprises	2.88	20.44	15.39	12.71	2.68
中外合资经营	Sino-foreign Joint-venture Enterprises	1.89	11.90	9.16	5.33	3.83
外资企业	Enterprises with Sole Foreign Investment	0.74	2.80	2.84	2.75	0.10
外商投资股份有限公司	Share-holding Co. Ltd. with Foreign Investment	0.25	5.74	3.39	4.63	-1.24
其他外商投资企业	Other Enterprises with Sole Foreign Investment					

17-18 限额以上住宿业企业主要财务指标(2020)

Main Financial Indicators of Enterprises above Designated Size of Hotels Services(2020)

单位:亿元 (100 million yuan)

项 目	Item	营业收入 Revenue of Business	营业成本 Cost of Business	其他业务利润 Profits of Other Business	利润总额 Total Profits
总计	**Total**	**93.22**	**44.95**	**0.65**	**-4.91**
按国民经济行业分组	**Grouped by Sector**				
旅游饭店	Tourist Hotel	55.61	25.14	0.47	-4.81
一般旅馆	Regular Hotel	33.98	18.00	0.15	0.12
民宿服务	B&B Service	0.18	0.14		0.01
其他住宿业	Other Accomodation Service	3.46	1.68	0.03	-0.23
按登记注册类型分组	**Grouped by Registration Type**				
内资	Domestic Funded Enterprises	87.34	43.14	0.64	-3.74
国有	State-Owned Enterprises	2.56	1.25	0.00	-0.25
集体	Collective-owned Enterprises	1.40	0.48		-0.08
股份合作	Cooperative Enterprises				
联营企业	Joint Ownership Enterprises	0.13	0.12		-0.04
国有联营	State Joint Ownership Enterprises	0.13	0.12		-0.04
集体联营	Collective Joint Ownership Enterprises				
国有与集体联营	Joint State-collective Enterprises				
其他联营	Other Joint Ownership Enterprises				
有限责任公司	Limited Liability Corporations	24.24	10.87	0.41	-2.76
国有独资公司	State Sole Funded Corporations	1.55	0.70	0.00	-0.11
其他有限责任公司	Other Limited Liability Corporations	22.69	10.16	0.41	-2.65
股份有限公司	Share holding Corporations Ltd.	1.72	0.50	0.10	-0.26
私营企业	Private Enterprises	57.13	29.86	0.12	-0.35
私营独资	Private-funded Enterprises	2.33	1.51	0.01	0.25
私营合伙	Private Partnership Enterprises	0.54	0.33		0.01
私营有限责任公司	Private Limited Liability Corporations	54.00	27.75	0.11	-0.61
私营股份有限公司	Private Share holding Corporations Ltd.	0.26	0.26		0.00
其他	Other Enterprises	0.16	0.06		0.01
港澳台商投资企业	Enterprises with Funds from Hongkong, Macao and Taiwan	3.47	1.26	0.01	-0.89
合资经营	Joint-venture Enterprises	0.62	0.17	0.01	0.00
合作经营	Cooperative Enterprises	0.40	0.22		-0.17
独资经营	Enterprises with Sole Investment	1.68	0.53		-0.73
投资股份有限公司	Sole Investment Co. Ltd. With Investment	0.77	0.33		0.03
外商投资企业	Foreign Funded Enterprises	2.41	0.56		-0.29
中外合资经营	Sino-Foreign Joint-venture Enterprises	0.77	0.11		-0.30
外资企业	Enterprises with Sole Foreign Investment	1.03	0.38		-0.07
外商投资股份有限公司	Share-holding Co. Ltd. with Foreign Investment	0.61	0.07		0.08
其他外商投资企业	Other Enterprises with Sole Foreign Investment				

17-19 亿元以上商品交易市场基本情况(2020)
Basic Statistics on Commodity Exchange Markets of Transaction Value over 100 Million Yuan(2020)

市 场	Market	市场数量(个) Number of Markets (unit)	摊位数(个) Number of Booths (unit)	营业面积(万平方米) Operating Area (10 000 sq.m)	成交额(亿元) Turnover (100 million yuan)
总计	**Total**	**108**	**85302**	**723.33**	**2090.01**
综合市场	**Integrated Markets**	**38**	**30804**	**262.96**	**779.29**
综合贸易市场	Integrated Trade Markets	38	30804	262.96	779.29
生产资料综合市场	Production Comprehensive Market	2	6473	107.00	292.94
工业消费品综合市场	Industrial Consumable Comprehensive Markets	5	4526	36.54	50.42
农产品综合市场	Farm Produce Comprehensive Markets	20	13161	82.95	277.19
其他综合市场	Other Comprehensive Markets	11	6644	36.47	158.74
专业市场	**Special Markets**	**70**	**54498**	**460.37**	**1310.72**
生产资料市场	Production Markets	12	5428	79.25	383.11
农业生产用具市场	Agricultural Production Equipment Markets				
农用生产资料市场	Agricultural Production Markets				
煤炭市场	Coal and Charcoal Markets				
木材市场	Wood Markets				
建材市场	Building Material Markets	8	3433	53.91	100.16
化工材料及制品市场	Chemical Materials and Products Markets				
金属材料市场	Metal Materials Markets	4	1995	25.34	282.94
机械设备市场	Mechanical Equipments Markets				
其他生产资料市场	Others				
农产品市场	Farm Produce Markets	8	7504	65.34	371.29
粮油市场	Grain and Oil Markets				
肉禽蛋市场	Meat, Poultry and Eggs Markets				
水产品市场	Aquatic Products Markets	3	3105	35.39	255.25
蔬菜市场	Vegetables Markets	2	320	4.70	5.03
干鲜果品市场	Dried and Fresh Melons and Fruits Markets	2	3549	20.75	106.11
棉麻土畜、烟叶市场	Cotton, Local & Livestock Products, and Tobacco Markets				
其他农产品市场	Others	1	530	4.50	4.89
食品、饮料及烟酒市场	Food, Beverages, Tobacco and Liquor Markets	7	4189	19.12	69.77
食品饮料市场	Food and Beverages Markets	1	351	1.05	4.10
茶叶市场	Tea Markets	3	1420	2.74	31.55
烟酒市场	Tobacco and Liquor Markets	1	258	8.00	1.11
其他食品饮料及烟酒市场	Others	2	2160	7.32	33.01
纺织、服装、鞋帽市场	Textiles, Clothing, Shoes and Hats Markets	18	24970	123.62	107.88
布料及纺织品市场	Cloth and Textiles Markets	2	235	1.07	1.75
服装市场	Clothing Markets	12	11741	65.25	64.90
鞋帽市场	Shoes and Hats Markets	2	720	5.00	2.80
其他纺织服装鞋帽市场	Others	2	12274	52.30	38.43
日用品及文化用品市场	Daily Use Articles and Cultural Goods Markets	2	935	8.17	17.55

17-19 续表 continued

市 场	Market	市场数量（个）Number of Markets (unit)	摊位数（个）Number of Booths (unit)	营业面积（万平方米）Operating Area (10 000 sq.m)	成交额（亿元）Turnover (100 million yuan)
小商品市场	Merchandise Markets	1	315	0.40	2.35
箱包市场	Luggage Markets				
玩具市场	Toys Markets				
文具市场	Stationary Markets				
图书、报刊杂志市场	Books, Newspapers and Magazines Markets				
音像制品及电子出版物市场	Video Products and E-journal Markets				
体育用品市场	Sports Markets				
其他日用品及文化用品市场	Others	1	620	7.77	15.20
黄金、珠宝、玉器等首饰市场	Gold, Jewelry, Jade Markets				
电器、通讯器材、电子设备市场	Electrical Appliances, Communication Appliances and	1	435	2.50	15.07
家电市场	Electronical Appliances Markets				
通讯器材市场	Household Appliances Markets	1	435	2.50	15.07
照相、摄像器材市场	Communication Appliances Markets				
计算机及辅助设备市场	Cameras and Video Equipments Markets				
其他电器、通讯器材、电子设备市场	Others				
医药、医疗用品及器材市场	Medicine, Medical Materials and Medical Instruments Markets				
中药材市场	Chinese Medicine Markets				
其他医药、医疗用品及器材市场	Others				
家具、五金及装饰材料市场	Furniture, Hardware and Decoration Materials Markets	16	8777	111.22	161.12
家具市场	Furniture Markets	3	525	10.89	5.23
装饰材料市场	Decoration Materials Markets	11	4709	86.14	139.07
灯具市场	Lamps Markets				
厨具、盥洗设备市场	Kitchen Utensils, Washing Equipments Markets				
五金材料市场	Hardware Materials Markets	2	3543	14.18	16.81
其他装修市场	Others				
汽车、摩托车及零配件市场	Cars, Motorcycles and Spare Parts Markets	6	2260	51.15	184.94
汽车市场	Cars Markets	5	560	21.15	72.74
摩托车市场	Motorcycles Markets				
机动车零配件市场	Vehicle Spare Parts Markets	1	1700	30.00	112.20
花、鸟、鱼、虫市场	Flower, Bird, Fish and Insects Markets				
花卉市场	Flower Markets				
鸟市场	Bird Markets				
观赏鱼市场	Fish Markets				
其他花鸟鱼虫市场	Others				
旧货市场	Second Hand Markets				
古玩、古董、字画市场	Antiques, Calligraphy and Painting Markets				
邮票、硬币市场	Stamps and Coins Markets				
其他旧货市场	Others				
其他专业市场	Others				

主要统计指标解释

社会消费品零售总额 指企业(单位、个体户)通过交易直接售给个人、社会集团非生产、非经营用的实物商品金额,以及提供餐饮服务所取得的收入金额。个人包括城乡居民和入境人员,社会集团包括机关、社会团体、部队、学校、企事业单位、居委会或村委会等。

批发业 指向其他批发或零售单位(含个体经营者)及其他企事业单位、机关团体等批量销售生活用品、生产资料的活动,以及从事进出口贸易和贸易经纪与代理的活动,包括拥有货物所有权,并以本单位(公司)的名义进行交易活动,也包括不拥有货物的所有权,收取佣金的商品代理、商品代售活动;还包括各类商品批发市场中固定摊位的批发活动,以及以销售为目的的收购活动。

零售业 指百货商店、超级市场、专门零售商店、品牌专卖店、售货摊等主要面向最终消费者(如居民等)的销售活动,以互联网、邮政、电话、售货机等方式的销售活动,还包括在同一地点,后面加工生产,前面销售的店铺(如面包房);谷物、种子、饲料、牲畜、矿产品、生产用原料、化工原料、农用化工产品、机械设备(乘用车、计算机及通信设备除外)等生产资料的销售不作为零售活动;多数零售商对其销售的货物拥有所有权,但有些则是充当委托人的代理人,进行委托销售或以收取佣金的方式进行销售。

批发和零售业商品购进、销售、库存额 指各种登记注册类型的批发和零售业企业(单位)以本企业(单位)为总体的,从国内、国外市场购进的商品总价,销售和出口的商品总价,库存的商品总价等情况。该指标可以反映商品流转过程中商品的购进、销售、库存之间的比例关系和存在的问题。

商品购进额 指从本企业以外的单位和个人购进(包括从国外直接进口)作为转卖或加工后转卖的商品金额(含增值税)。商品购进包括:(1)从工农业生产者、批发和零售业企业、住宿和餐饮业企业、出版社或报社的出版发行部门和其他服务业企业购进的商品;(2)从机关团体、社会团体购进的商品;(3)从海关、市场管理部门购进的缉私和没收的商品;(4)从居民收购的废旧商品等。不包括:(1)企业为本单位自身经营用,不是作为转卖而购进的商品,如材料物资、包装物、低值易耗品、办公用品等;(2)未通过买卖行为而收入的商品,如接受其他部门移交的商品、借入的商品、收入代其他单位保管的商品、其他单位赠送的样品、加工回收的成品等;(3)经本单位介绍,由买卖双方直接结算,本单位只收取手续费的业务;(4)销售退回和买方拒付货款的商品;(5)商品溢余;(6)期货交易商品。

商品销售额 指对本单位以外的单位和个人出售的商品金额(包括售给本单位消费用的商品,含增值税)。商品销售包括:(1)售给个人和社会集团消费用的商品;(2)售给农业、工业、建筑业、服务业等国民经济各行业用于生产、经营用的商品,包括售予批发和零售业作为转卖或加工后转卖的商品;(3)对国(境)外直接出口的商品。商品销售不包括:(1)未通过买卖行为付出的商品,如因机构变动移交给其他企业单位的商品、借出的商品、归还受其他单位委托代保管的商品、付出的加工原料和赠送给其他单位的样品等;(2)促销返券所销售的、不计入营业收入的商品;(3)经本单位介绍,由买卖双方直接结算,本单位只收取手续费的业务;(4)未发生所有权转移的商品预付卡销售,如加油卡;(5)汽车维修、电话卡销售等服务性经济活动;(6)购货退回的商品;(7)商品损耗和损失;(8)出售本单位自用的废旧物资;(9)期货交易商品;(10)自来水供应企业、电力企业、天然气供应企业提供的水、电、气。

商品库存额 对于批发和零售业法人单位和个体经营户,是指报告期末取得所有权的全部商品金额(含增值税);对于批发和零售业产业活动单位,是指报告期末实际在库且归属法人具有所有权的全部商品金额(含增值税)。库存商品包括:(1)存放在本单位(如门市部、批发站、采购站、经营处)的仓库、货场、货柜和货架中的商品;(2)挑选、整理、包装中的商品;(3)已记入购进而尚未运到本单位的商品,即发货单或银行承兑凭证已到而货未到的商品;(4)寄放他处的商品,如因购货方拒绝付款而暂时存在购货方的商品;(5)委托其他单位代销(未作销售或调出)尚未售出的商品;(6)代其他单位购进尚未交付的商品。不包括:所有权不属于本单位的商品;委托外单位加工的商品;外贸企业代理其他单位从国外进口,尚未付给订货单位的商品;代国家储备部门保管的商品。

住宿业 指为旅行者提供短期留宿场所的活动,有些单位只提供住宿,也有些单位提供住宿、饮食、商务、娱乐一体的服务,不包括主要按月或按年长期出租房屋住所的活动。

餐饮业 指通过即时制作加工、商业销售和服务性劳动等,向消费者提供食品和消费场所及设施的服务。

营业额 指住宿和餐饮业单位在经营活动中，因提供服务或销售商品等取得的全部收入(含增值税),收入主要来源于提供客房、餐费服务、商品销售和其他服务,如商务服务。不包括多产业法人企业附营的其他行业产业活动单位的餐费收入、商品销售收入等各项收入。其中,客房收入指住宿和餐饮业单位在经营活动中因提供住宿服务取得的收入(含增值税)。不包括多产业法人企业附营的其他行业产业活动单位的客房收入。餐费收入指本单位为顾客提供就餐服务取得的收入(含增值税)。包括:经烹饪、调制加工后出售的各种食品,如主食、炒菜、凉拌菜等的收入。不包括多产业法人企业附营的其他行业产业活动单位的餐费收入。

连锁总店(总部) 指负责连锁企业资源(商号、商誉、经营模式、服务标准、管理模式等等)的开发、配置、控制或使用等功能的企业核心管理机构。连锁经营是指经营同类商品或服务,使用统一商号的若干店铺,在同一总店(总部)的管理下,采取统一采购或特许经营等方式,实现规模效益的组织形式，包括直营连锁、特许连锁和自愿连锁三种形式。其中,直营连锁是指连锁店铺由连锁公司全资或控股开设,在总部的直接控制下,开展统一经营的连锁经营形式;特许连锁是指拥有注册商标、企业标志、专利、专有技术等经营资源的企业(特许人),以合同形式将其拥有的经营资源许可其他经营者(被特许人)使用,被特许人按合同约定在统一的经营模式下开展经营，并向特许人支付特许经营费用的连锁经营形式；自愿连锁是指若干个店铺或企业自愿组合起来,在不改变各自资产所有权关系的情况下,以同一个品牌形象面对消费者，以共同进货为纽带开展的连锁经营形式。

亿元以上商品交易市场 指年成交额在亿元及以上的商品交易市场。商品交易市场是指经有关部门和组织批准设立,有固定场所、设施,有经营管理部门和监管人员,若干市场经营者入内,常年或实际开业三个月以上,集中、公开、独立地进行生活消费品、生产资料等现货商品交易以及提供相关服务的交易场所,包括各类消费品市场、生产资料市场等。

Explanatory Notes on Main Statistical Indicators

Total Retail Sales of Consumer Goods refer to the amount obtained by enterprises (units, self-employed individuals) through direct sales of non-production and non-business physical commodity to individuals, social institutions, and revenue from providing catering services. Individuals include rural and urban households, population from abroad, social institutions include government agencies, social organizations, military units, schools, institutions, neighborhood (village) committees.

Wholesale Trade refers to the activities of selling wholesale commodities for daily use and capital goods to enterprises of wholesale and retail trades (including self-employed individuals) and other enterprises, institutions and government organs and organizations, and the activities of engaging in import and export and acting as a trade agent. The wholesaler may have the ownership of the commodities for wholesale and trade in the name of its own (a company), and the wholesaler can act as commission agent or commodity broker without the ownership of commodities. Also included are the wholesale activities at the fixed stalls in wholesale market and the acquisition for sales purpose.

Retail Trade refers to the activities of department store, supermarket, franchised store, brand store, retail stall and on-the-spot-making-selling store selling commodities to the final consumers (residents) by any means including internet, post, telephone, sales machine. It also includes shops with sales and production located in the same places (such as bakeries). Retail trade excludes the activities of sales of capital goods such as grain, seed, feed, livestock, mineral products, raw material for production, industrial chemicals, chemical products for agricultural use, machine and equipment (excluding vehicles, computers and communication equipment). Most retailers have the ownership of commodities to sell, but some are acting as agents or brokers to make transactions for a commission.

Purchase, Sales and Stock of Commodities by Wholesale and Retail Trades refer to the total volume of commodities purchased, total volume of sales and exports, and the stock of commodities by wholesale and retail enterprises (establishments) of different status of registration from domestic and overseas markets. This indicator reflects the relationship among purchase, sales and stock of commodities in the circulation of goods and reveals the existing problems.

Total Purchases of Commodities refer to the total value of purchases of commodities by enterprises (establishments) from other establishments or individuals (including direct import from abroad) for the purpose of re-selling, either with or without further processing of the commodities purchased. The commodities include: (1) commodities purchased from agricultural and industrial producer, wholesaler, retailer, publishing house and other enterprises,institutions and individual operators of service business; (2) commodities purchased from institutions and government departments; (3) confiscated goods purchased from the customs authorities or market management agencies; (4) second-hand goods and wastes purchased from residents; The commodities exclude (1) commodities purchased by enterprises (establishments) for use in their own business operation, commodities obtained without buying or selling procedures such as materials, consumable goods of low value, office appliance, etc. (2) received goods without trading, such as goods handed over from others, borrowed goods, preserved goods for others, donated goods from others, processed and retrieved goods, etc. (3) goods of direct settlement between buyer and seller with handling fees introduced by others, (4) goods returned or refused to pay by the buyer, (5) excessive goods,(6)futures trading commodities.

Total Sales of Commodities refer to value of commodities sold by the establishments to other establishments and individuals (including goods sold for self-consumption, including the value-added tax). The commodities include: (1) commodities sold to individuals and social groups for their consumption; (2) commodities sold to establishments in all industries for their production and operation, including agriculture, industry, construction, and catering services including commodities sold to wholesale and retail establishments for re-selling, with or without further processing; and (3) commodities for direct export to abroad. Excluded are (1) extended commodities without trading, such as goods handed over to other enterprises and institutions because of the change of organizations, lent goods, returned goods preserved for others, extended processing materials and samples donated to others; (2) commodities sold in shopping coupon promotion and not included in sales revenue; (3) goods of direct settlement between buyer and seller with handling fees introduced by others; (4) sales of prepaid cards without transfer of ownership, such as fuel cards ; (5) service economic activities such as vehicle maintenance and telephone card sales; (6) goods returned after purchase; (7) damaged and spoiled goods; (8) waste and used goods of self-use;(9) commodities traded in futures; (10) water, electricity and gas provided by water supply enterprises, power enterprises and natural gas supply enterprises.

Total Stock of Commodities For the legal entities and self-employed individuals engaged in wholesale and retail trade, it refers to total value (including VAT) of commodities possessed at the end of the reference period; and for wholesale and retail establishments, it refers to the value (including VAT) of all commodities actually in stock and owned by their legal persons at the end of reference period. The commodities in stock includes: (1) commodities located in storage, garages, counters, and shelves of operating places of wholesale and retail trades (such as sale stores, wholesale centres, procurement stations and operating offices); (2) commodities in the process of being selected, sorted, and packed; (3) commodities not arrived but recorded as purchase in the account, i.e. commodities not arrived but payment receipts for the commodities from the sellers or the banks arrived; (4) commodities deposited in other places rather than places mentioned above, for instance: commodities in the hold of purchasers temporarily due to the refusal of payment; (5) commodities entrusted to other units to sell but not sold yet; (6) commodities purchased for other units but not delivered yet. Commodities not included as stock are those not owned by the enterprises (units), commodities on commission for processing, imported commodities of agency of foreign trade enterprise but not yet delivered to ordering units and finally those put in stock on behalf of the state reserves units.

Hotel Services refer to the accommodation services provided to visitors. Some units may provide only accommodation while others provide a combination of accommodation, meals, business services and/or recreational facilities. It excludes activities related to the provision of long-term primary residences in facilities such as apartments typically leased on a monthly or annual basis.

Catering Services refer to the activities of providing foods, serving locations and facilities to customers through instant processing, commercial sales and service-type labor.

Business Revenue refers to total revenue (including VAT) of hotels and catering services received from providing services or selling commodities through business activities, income comes mainly from providing hotels, catering services, selling of commodities and other services, such as commodity services. It does not include revenue such as meal fees, selling of commodities of other industrial units affiliated with multi industrial legal entities. Income from hotels refers to income(including VAT) of hotels and catering services by providing lodging services through business activities. Income from catering services refers to income (including VAT) from providing catering services, including selling of cooked or prepared foods, such as staple food, cooked dishes, or cold dishes. It does not include meal fees of other industrial units affiliated with multi industrial legal entities.

Chain Head Stores (headquarter) refer to the core leading stores responsible for development, allocation, administration and utilization of resources (name of stores, brand of stores, operation model, service standard, management way, etc.) of chain stores. Chain stores refers to the stores engaged in providing homogeneous commodities or services, with the central leadership of head store (headquarters) and guided by common policies, conduct centralized purchase and distributed selling of commodities, in order to gain better efficiency through standardized operation. The chain stores include regular chain stores, franchise chain stores and voluntary chain stores.

Regular Chain store refers to chain stores that are invested or controlled by the headquarters. They operate under direct and unified management from the headquarters.

Franchise chain store refers to the chain stores (franchisees) which are franchised with operation resources such as trade marks, names, patent and operation know-how by the franchisors in form of contract and pay the operation fees to the franchisors.

Voluntary chain store refers to the stores operate jointly on the voluntary bases while maintaining their status of independent legal entities with full ownership of their assets. They sell goods of same brand from same channel of resource to the consumers.

Large Commodity Markets with Transaction Value over 100 Million Yuan refer to the commodity markets with an annual transaction at and above 100 million. The commodity market refers to the markets approved and managed by related departments, where there are fixed sites, facilities, managers and administration offices, where there are a certain number of traders to operate for three month and above or all the year, where the commodities including the articles for daily consumption and capital goods and services are traded in a centralized, independent and open way. Such market includes markets of daily goods and market of capital goods, etc.

18

科技和教育

Science, Technology and Education

资料整理人员:范　维　　徐晓颖　　余佑玲

18-1 科技活动基本情况
Basic Statistics on Scientific and Technological Activities

项 目	Item	2010	2015	2017	2018	2019	2020
R&D 人员 (人)	**R&D Personels**	**142683**	**220977**	**235263**	**257427**	**285507**	**294524**
R&D 经费内部支出 (万元)	**Inner Expenditures of R&D Funds (10 000 yuan)**	**2637885**	**5617415**	**7006253**	**8220501**	**9578823**	**10052800**
基础研究	Basic Research	102494	230593	279435	305641	432337	455358
应用研究	Practical Research	472497	705635	897664	1081924	1193805	1221727
实验发展	Experiment Development	2062893	4681187	5829155	6832936	7952681	8375715

18-2 科技活动项目、成果与机构情况
Basic Statistics on Scientific and Technical Projects, Achievement and Institutions

项 目	Item	2015	2017	2018	2019	2020
发表科技论文 (篇)	Scientific Research Papers Published (piece)	93190	94556	101559	102385	98356
出版科技专著数 (种)	Scientific and Techincal Books Published (kind)	2827	3022	3085	2828	2629
科技项目(课题)数 (个)	Number of Scientific Projects (unit)	56218	63305	70663	82700	86272
科技项目经费支出 (万元)	Expenses for Scientific Projects (10 000 yuan)	4504527	6560914	7150914	8871831	9054275
科学研究与开发机构数 (个)	Number of Scientific Research Institutions and Development Organizations (unit)	2245	2340	2679	3675	3959
科研机构 R&D 人员数 (人)	R&D Staff (person)	75338	76297	86062	100760	114566
科研机构 R&D 内部支出 (万元)	Inner Expenditures of R&D Funds (10 000 yuan)	2111784	2228424	3702437	4547728	5219225
科研机构年末仪器设备资产原价 (万元)	Original Price of Fixed Assets of Scientific Research Institutions and Organizations at Year-end (10 000 yuan)	2635298	3698655	4163826	5234410	5911531

18-3 政府部门所属科学研究与开发机构科技活动情况

项 目	Item	机构（个）Number of Institutions (unit)	科技活动人员（人）Persons Engaged (person)	大学本科及以上学历 Bachelor's Degrees and Above	#R&D人员 Research and Development Persons	科技活动收入（万元）Revenue (10 000 yuan)	#政府拨款 Government Appropriations
2017 年总计	**Total of 2017**	**196**	**8336**	**6660**	**6925**	**601867**	**405210**
一、自然科学和技术领域	**Natural Science and Technology**	**181**	**7460**	**5872**	**6498**	**572968**	**380729**
县级政府部门属	Department of County	96	725	168	98	15716	5903
市、州级政府部门属	Department of Cities and Prefecture	49	1416	906	604	49557	29462
省政府部门属	Department of Province	38	2881	2525	1700	214987	114533
国务院部门属	Department of State Council	13	3314	3061	4523	321608	255314
#中科院武汉分院属	Chinese Academy of Science Wuhan Branch	7	1772	1653	3547	159915	138045
二、社会、人文科学领域	**Sosiety and Humanity**	**6**	**335**	**289**	**283**	**11362**	**11261**
2018 年总计	**Total of 2018**	**176**	**8747**	**7080**	**7324**	**613235**	**409953**
一、自然科学和技术领域	**Natural Science and Technology**	**163**	**8034**	**6437**	**7064**	**586029**	**386926**
县级政府部门属	Department of County	86	606	151	133	21239	6352
市、州级政府部门属	Department of Cities and Prefecture	38	1357	887	570	48294	31002
省政府部门属	Department of Province	27	2790	2295	1762	196148	107648
国务院部门属	Department of State Council	12	3281	3104	4599	320348	241925
#中科院武汉分院属	Chinese Academy of Science Wuhan Branch	6	1712	1592	3636	168347	141934
二、社会、人文科学领域	**Sosiety and Humanity**	**5**	**307**	**267**	**233**	**13695**	**12611**
2019 年总计	**Total of 2019**	**144**	**9166**	**7715**	**7378**	**586195**	**404084**
一、自然科学和技术领域	**Natural Science and Technology**	**132**	**8404**	**7015**	**7088**	**559699**	**381365**
县级政府部门属	Department of County	58	444	143	85	4661	4518
市、州级政府部门属	Department of Cities and Prefecture	35	1424	1050	588	43696	28822
省政府部门属	Department of Province	27	3194	2764	1973	191070	114526
国务院部门属	Department of State Council	12	3342	3058	4442	320272	233499
#中科院武汉分院属	Chinese Academy of Science Wuhan Branch	6	1792	1595	3402	165982	136781
二、社会、人文科学领域	**Sosiety and Humanity**	**4**	**249**	**223**	**228**	**9515**	**9479**
2020 年总计	**Total of 2020**	**128**	**9160**	**7729**	**7274**	**573845**	**375398**
一、自然科学和技术领域	**Natural Science and Technology**	**117**	**8487**	**7130**	**6962**	**550346**	**355855**
县级政府部门属	Department of County	48	427	152	56	4680	3878
市、州级政府部门属	Department of Cities and Prefecture	32	1256	936	557	43659	31504
省政府部门属	Department of Province	25	3042	2617	1393	177970	109771
国务院部门属	Department of State Council	12	3762	3425	4956	324038	210702
#中科院武汉分院属	Chinese Academy of Science Wuhan Branch	5	2075	1828	3915	186239	145470
二、社会、人文科学领域	**Sosiety and Humanity**	**5**	**322**	**262**	**234**	**9888**	**9888**

Basic Statistics on State-Owned Research and Development Institutions

经费支出（万元） Expenditures (10 000 yuan)	#科技经费支出 Expenditure on Science & Technology	#R&D 经费内部支出 Inner Expenditure of R & D	研究课题数（个） Number of Projects	课题经费投入（万元） Investment on Subject Study (10 000 yuan)	参加课题组（人年） Number of Persons Engaged in Subjects Study (person/year)
557544	**432622**	**252554**	**4372**	**216130**	**6258**
529758	**408102**	**240941**	**4136**	**212735**	**5812**
16101	5943	392	33	708	97
44334	36451	8887	223	4733	675
188790	128464	40141	760	27260	1719
308320	261764	203135	3356	183429	3766
151043	126304	120939	1968	90818	2305
11354	**10501**	**9153**	**101**	**646**	**276**
558237	**457738**	**284470**	**4768**	**231693**	**7056**
532000	**435384**	**275149**	**4620**	**229425**	**6688**
21671	6407	1402	68	2065	188
42862	37172	13274	185	7511	584
176773	133686	58414	833	27668	1974
290693	258120	202059	3534	192181	3942
153315	139524	134301	1994	107938	2400
13749	**11614**	**8785**	**114**	**810**	**175**
597671	**528659**	**333979**	**5086**	**255656**	**6738**
569198	**505384**	**323647**	**4888**	**251776**	**6383**
6821	4571	819	37	1054	90
47031	42114	13009	214	7563	467
199161	164768	72039	898	31141	1830
316183	293751	237780	3739	212018	3996
173397	161080	154309	2179	11834	2525
11166	**8980**	**8384**	**87**	**530**	**174**
601049	**531676**	**325518**	**5412**	**267875**	**6536**
577479	**511470**	**315382**	**5231**	**265785**	**6236**
7406	4969	486	29	1107	80
54145	46402	19199	205	8059	557
187610	150216	49410	834	27686	1384
328318	309882	246288	4163	228933	4214
189451	177582	171295	2462	133261	2659
12983	**10846**	**8484**	**101**	**519**	**112**

18-4 科学情报文献机构情况
Statistics on Scientific Intelligence Literature Organizations

项 目	Item	2000	2005	2010	2015	2017	2018	2019	2020
机构 （个）	**Institutions (unit)**	**14**	**12**	**11**	**9**	**9**	**8**	**8**	**6**
职工总数 （人）	**Total Number of Employees (person)**	**564**	**546**	**553**	**513**	**566**	**429**	**531**	**363**
从事科技活动人员	Persons engaged in Scientific Activities	511	456	512	465	541	406	513	351
#大学本科及以上学历	Bachelor's degrees and Above	337	306	347	386	499	376	477	337
经费收入总额 （万元）	**Funds (10 000 yuan)**	**2629**	**6677**	**8706**	**14573**	**17537**	**13497**	**19384**	**14455**
#政府拨款	Government Appropriations	1679	5210	6009	11840	13221	10416	13240	10180
经费支出总额 （万元）	**Expendtitures (10 000 yuan)**	**2340**	**6778**	**7955**	**12348**	**16432**	**12488**	**17308**	**9406**
#劳务费	Service Charge	970	1179	2668	4210	7988	6103	9351	7945

18-5 高等院校科技活动情况
Statistics on Scientific and Technological Activities of Institutions of Higher Education

项目	Item	2019			2020		
		合计 Total	自然科学和技术领域 Natural Science and Technology	社会、人文科学领域 Society, Humanity and Science	合计 Total	自然科学和技术领域 Natural Science and Technology	社会、人文科学领域 Society, Humanity and Science
科学研究与开发机构数 （个）	Number of Scientific Research and Development Institutions (unit)	846	549	297	900	589	311
科技活动人员数 （人）	Number of Persons Participating in Scientific and Technological Activities (person)	96192	61544	34648	99399	62905	36494
研究与发展经费内部支出 （万元）	Internal Expenditure for Research and Development (10 000 yuan)	1046914	945119	101795	877489	836576	103504
研究课题数 （个）	Number of Research Topics (unit)	65388	40959	24429	65580	41018	24562
项目(课题)经费投入 （万元）	Project (topic) Fund Investment (10 000 yuan)	1005805	932982	72823	1009229	939121	70108
项目(课题)参加人员折合全时当量 （人年）	Full-time Equivalent Project (topic) Participants (man-year)	22305	16234	6071	23272	16743	6510

18-6 大中型工业企业科技活动情况
Statistics on Research and Development Activities of Largeand Medium-Sized Industrial Enterprises

项 目	Item	2010	2015	2017	2018	2019	2020
大中型企业个数 (个)	Large and Medium Enterprises (unit)	1421	2204	2024	1936	1814	1640
有 R&D 活动的企业数 (个)	Number of Enterprises with Scientific Activities (unit)	559	717	833	896	978	960
研究与试验发展人员数 (人)	Persons Engaged in Research and Development (person)	64329	105848	106304	109777	105616	106359
企业办研发机构数 (个)	Number of Research and Development Organizations Opened by Enterprises (unit)	457	534	492	622	727	783
R&D 项目数 (个)	Numbqer of R&D Projects (unit)	4602	4954	6605	6864	8076	8890
全部 R&D 项目经费支出 (万元)	Expenses for Development Projects (10 000 yuan)	1193793	2627715	3405456	3203595	3978954	4081827
研究与发展经费支出 (万元)	Expenditures for Research and Development (10 000 yuan)	1429050	3272348	3412053	3586924	3933177	4186877
新产品开发费支出 (万元)	Expenditures for Developing New Products (10 000 yuan)	1760964	2856350	3337557	3927504	9643198	4861588
技术改造经费支出 (万元)	Expenditures for Technical Innovation (10 000 yuan)	1326521	835034	657675	784592	984980	1147395
技术引进经费支出 (万元)	Expenditures for Technology Introduction (10 000 yuan)	190418	147979	154477	95897	46184	33068
消化吸收经费支出 (万元)	Expenditures for Technology Utilization (10 000 yuan)	29408	16046	13501	11245	763	1048
购买国内技术经费支出 (万元)	Expenditures for Purchasing Domestic Technology (10 000 yuan)	21561	50314	22937	24707	38721	32527

18-7 有科技活动的规模以上工业企业主要分组指标

指 标	Item	有R&D活动企业（个） Number of Enterprises with R&D Activities (unit)	
		2019	2020
总计	**Total**	**4877**	**5649**
一、按登记注册类型分	**Grouped by Type of Registration**		
内资企业	Domestic-funded Enterprises	4655	5390
国有企业	State-owned Enterprises	21	41
集体企业	Collective-owned Enterprises	4	4
股份合作企业	Cooperative Enterprises	2	4
联营企业	Joint Ownership Enterprises		3
有限责任公司	Limited Liability Corporations	1339	1151
股份有限公司	Share-holding Corporations Ltd.	416	353
私营企业	Private Enterprises	2873	3834
其他企业	Other Enterprises		
港、澳、台商投资企业	Enterprises with Funds from Hong Kong, Macao and Taiwan	84	92
合资经营企业(港或澳、台资)	Joint Ventures (Hongkong, Maco or Taiwan Invested Enterprises)	42	45
合作经营企业(港或澳、台资)	Cooperative Ventures (Hongkong, Maco or Taiwan Invested Enterprises)		
港、澳、台商独资经营企业	Enterprises Solely Funded by hongkong, Maco and Taiwan Businessmen	36	36
港、澳、台商投资股份有限公司	Hongkong, Maco and Taiwan Funded Share Holding Co.Ltd.	4	5
其他港澳台投资企业	Other Hongkong, Maco and Taiwan Funded Share Holding Co., Ltd.	2	6
外商投资企业	Foreign-invested Enterprises	138	167
中外合资经营企业	Sino-Foreign Joint Ventures	85	107
中外合作经营企业	Sino-Foreign Contractual Joint Ventures	1	
外资企业	Foreign Funded Enterprises	45	54
外商投资股份有限公司	Foreign Funded Share Holding Co., Ltd.	3	2
其他外商投资企业	Other Enterprises Invested by Foreign Businessmen	4	4
二、按行业分	**Grouped by Sector**		
煤炭开采和洗选业	Coal Mining and Processing		
石油和天然气开采业	Petroleum and Natural Gas Extraction	1	1
黑色金属矿采选业	Ferrous Metals Mining and Processing	11	8
有色金属矿采选业	Non-ferrous Metals Mining and Processing	3	2
非金属矿采选业	Non-metal Minerals Mining and Processing	64	70
开采辅助活动	Mining Auxiliary	2	1
其他采矿业	Other Mining		1
农副食品加工业	Primary Products and Food Processing Industry	319	347

Major Indicators of Industrial Enterprises above Designated Size with Research and Development Activities

有研发机构的企业（个） Number of Enterprises with R&D Units (unit)		R&D 人员合计（人） R&D Personels (person)		R&D 经费支出（万元） Funding for R&D Expenditure (10 000 yuan)		新产品开发经费支出（万元） Funding for New Product Development Expenditures (10 000 yuan)		新产品销售收入（万元） Revenue of New Product Sales (10 000 yuan)	
2019	2020	2019	2020	2019	2020	2019	2020	2019	2020
2012	**2693**	**175724**	**183933**	**5865143**	**6109588**	**6909409**	**7280674**	**97076662**	**95968820**
1905	2572	158762	167055	5200825	5489673	5985985	6381942	83068323	78637597
13	22	2843	4080	106094	190889	117121	168885	936364	1682119
1	2	78	43	4183	2783	2584	156	1182	3920
	2	30	86	509	1240		1649		3356
	1		255		3040		4454		48320
564	559	59915	54409	2210512	2314527	2671060	2624055	32789943	25408122
229	195	31439	31249	1155240	1042448	1290381	1227960	14804894	13329588
1097	1791	64457	76933	1724288	1934746	1904494	2354782	34526729	38162172
1						345		9211	
46	55	5652	5646	160967	226544	230297	299678	3427777	2528351
27	21	4123	3463	105928	67842	150067	100745	2103751	1059599
18	27	1322	1384	38160	33829	59448	62267	1082847	850509
	3	146	343	15193	108790	17025	120318	52405	426858
1	4	61	456	1686	16084	3757	16348	188774	191386
61	66	11310	11232	503351	393371	693128	599054	10580562	14802872
37	40	6423	6382	363942	280910	478262	379021	8045904	8233466
1		45		574		574			
21	24	3887	4005	75156	66233	121149	129710	1210317	5429282
	1	100	580	2152	37224	3817	80832	3406	1037569
2	1	855	265	61527	9004	89325	9492	1320935	102555
1	1	679	48	16533	2773	6842	558	778293	89304
3	2	215	95	3711	1097	1877	653	13338	7252
1	1	198	176	3394	2640	149	3877	96811	101344
29	29	1189	937	50368	36208	13013	9621	225381	152126
1		262	5	2607	76	4229	77		
			23		774				
135	183	6492	5982	200605	158312	226874	231828	6131864	5004054

18-7 续表 continued

指 标	Item	有R&D活动企业（个） Number of Enterprises with R&D Activities (unit)	
		2019	2020
食品制造业	Food Production	119	122
酒、饮料和精制茶制造业	Beverage Production	128	135
烟草制品业	Tabacco Processing	5	5
纺织业	Textile Industry	201	272
纺织服装、服饰业	Textile Wearing Apparel and Accessaries	63	58
皮革、毛皮、羽毛及其制品和制鞋业	Leather, Fur, Feather and Related Products	36	46
木材加工及木、竹、藤、棕、草制品业	Timber Processing and Wood, Bamboo, Rattan, Palm and Sraw Products	58	79
家具制造业	Furniture Manufacturing	31	34
造纸及纸制品业	Papermaking and Paper Products	50	67
印刷和记录媒介复制业	Printing and Record Processing	104	132
文教、工美、体育和娱乐用品制造业	Stationery, Education, Art, Sport and Entertainment Products	72	104
石油加工、炼焦及核燃料加工业	Petroleum Processing, Coking Products and Nuclear Fuel Processing	12	16
化学原料及化学制品制造业	Raw Chemical Material and Chemical Products	411	471
医药制造业	Medical and Pharmaceutical Products	252	279
化学纤维制造业	Chemical Fibers	9	10
橡胶和塑料制品业	Rubber Products and Plastic Products	175	206
非金属矿物制品业	Nonmetal Material Products	421	475
黑色金属冶炼及压延加工业	Smelting and Processing of Ferrous Metals	30	31
有色金属冶炼及压延加工业	Smelting and Processing of Nonferrous Metals	68	70
金属制品业	Metal Products	255	296
通用设备械制造业	Ordinaryly Machinery Manufacturing	302	337
专用设备制造业	Special Purpose Equipment Manufacturing	316	376
汽车制造业	Automobile Manufacturing	561	681
铁路、船舶、航空航天和其他运输设备制造业	Realway, Ship, Aircraft and Other Transport Equipment Manufacturing	66	76
电气机械及器材制造业	Electric Machinery and Equipment	303	339
计算机、通信和其他电子设备制造业	Manufacture of Computers, Communication and Other Electronic Equipment	244	286
仪器仪表制造业	Instruments, Meters Machinery	80	102
其他制造业	Other Manufacturing	21	21
废弃资源和废旧材料回收加工业	Waste Resources and Junk Material Recycled	23	33
金属制品、机械和设备修理业	Repairing of Metal and Mechanical Equipment	11	9
电力、热力的生产和供应业	Electric Power, Steam and Hot Water Production and Supply	33	32
煤气生产和供应业	Gas Production and Supply	5	6
水的生产和供应业	Tap Water Production and Supply	12	13

有研发机构的企业（个）Number of Enterprises with R&D Units (unit)		R&D 人员合计（人）R&D Personels (person)		R&D 经费支出（万元）Funding for R&D Expenditure (10 000 yuan)		新产品开发经费支出（万元）Funding for New Product Development Expenditures (10 000 yuan)		新产品销售收入（万元）Revenue of New Product Sales (10 000 yuan)	
2019	2020	2019	2020	2019	2020	2019	2020	2019	2020
54	70	4078	3749	99318	92212	134988	131259	1662571	1397908
72	90	3174	2709	122231	98315	113177	115452	1144732	1003587
4	3	438	387	11975	15720	23271	14977	416215	1136500
85	118	7764	8558	132130	151622	153856	169597	3823652	5366267
15	24	2069	1633	35565	23875	40674	40496	945645	805731
7	9	869	665	8234	13128	12073	17268	720177	543127
25	34	1424	1228	40280	31119	38687	40077	678039	502490
13	15	648	603	11262	13597	18160	20568	316586	268130
15	25	1810	1824	58718	61847	60835	64382	974580	907583
30	53	2954	2758	72560	66513	82301	74005	1109222	1309287
23	43	2242	2348	40005	50614	52858	66679	959816	1197487
7	10	379	398	52946	66771	52767	21077	968103	928215
184	260	16795	16525	531102	475570	403721	427543	9343121	8298277
131	157	9805	10700	253207	378096	316809	511291	3860736	3750319
3	4	201	400	4214	4510	6241	5131	284284	176487
66	97	4101	4547	111711	128093	138459	159748	2002377	2155627
164	229	9290	11735	286266	266223	327356	371680	4493588	4747476
16	14	3751	3337	315529	294274	448161	391030	3601772	3326770
26	30	2806	2524	78326	91970	63343	66841	3365783	3114988
118	169	6468	6418	166458	187986	228622	228930	3378413	3559548
110	145	8126	8716	207266	217863	250284	249386	3322852	2964739
132	175	8014	9277	187001	228112	269814	306016	2679963	2894100
221	277	25060	26929	980309	860950	1363408	1188618	17030434	17688500
24	38	6572	7277	123418	245070	161801	276619	1233829	1316403
126	158	11122	11858	395216	372826	444802	430281	7769724	6339257
103	128	20001	22023	1068124	1190768	1255882	1424121	11133241	12391982
28	38	2083	2889	49814	77547	71914	101363	669676	724131
5	10	985	937	19750	30747	21297	29970	115514	256119
15	23	886	879	47024	45183	46146	36421	1203445	1155952
4	4	756	786	14322	15698	17120	14457	239061	127067
13	17	1748	1680	57725	104840	32665	35890	250695	177320
1	3	142	109	3062	2340	3732	441	48675	56494
2	7	128	261	2859	3710	1203	2450	84456	26873

18-8 全省高新技术产业发展情况(2020)

Statistics on High and New Technology Industry Development of the Whole Province(2020)

单位:亿元 (100 million yuan)

项 目	Item	全省 the Whole Province	增幅(%) Increase(%)
"四上"高新技术产业增加值	Above Designated Size Added Value of High-tech Industry	8580.82	-1.9
高新制造业增加值	Added Value of High-tech Manufacturing	6163.17	-4.5
高新建筑业增加值	Added Value of High-tech construction	1075.47	9.6
高新服务业增加值	Added Value of High-tech Service	1342.17	0.9
高新制造业产值*	Output Value of High-tech Manufacturing	25383.54	-5.8
高新制造业产品出口交货值*	Export Value of High-tech Manufacturing	24629.41	-5.8
高新制造业产品销售收入*	Revenue of High-tech Manufacturing	1313.23	5.4
"四下"高新技术产业增加值	Below Designated Size Added Value of High-tech Industry	103.32	-1.9

注:带"*"号的指标口径为规模以上高新企业。
Note: Indicators marked with "*" refer to high-tech enterprise above the scale.

18-9 市州高新技术产业发展情况(2020)
Statistics on Development of High and New Technology Industry of Cities and Prefectures(2020)

单位:亿元 (100 million yuan)

市、州	Municipalities and Prefecture	增加值 Value Added	增加值 * Value Added	增速 * Increase(%)
全省合计	**Total of the Province**	**8684.14**	**8580.82**	**-1.9**
武汉市	Wuhan	4088.41	4032.12	-0.2
黄石市	Huangshi	370.21	368.41	-2.1
十堰市	Shiyan	406.12	379.37	-2.0
宜昌市	Yichang	649.61	644.69	-4.0
襄阳市	Xiangyang	1002.05	999.07	-3.3
鄂州市	Ezhou	166.10	165.30	-10.8
荆门市	Jingmen	296.10	294.65	-2.8
孝感市	Xiaogan	324.40	321.90	-5.6
荆州市	Jingzhou	335.98	335.56	-4.3
黄冈市	Huanggang	242.25	241.05	-1.2
咸宁市	Xianning	252.94	251.86	2.8
随州市	Suizhou	169.14	167.60	-5.9
恩施州	Enshi	29.67	29.35	-0.8
仙桃市	Xiantao	130.45	129.82	4.3
潜江市	Qianjiang	126.76	126.26	3.6
天门市	Tianmen	93.79	93.64	-2.9
神农架林区	Shennongjia	0.16	0.16	5.8

注:带“*”号的指标口径为规模以上高新企业。
Note: Indicators with “*” are for high-tech enterprises above the designated size.

18-10 申报登记省、部级以上成果分类及经济效益

Classification and Economic Benefits of Scientific Achievements Applied and Registered above Provincial and Ministry Level

单位:项 (unit)

项 目	Item	2000	2005	2010	2015	2017	2018	2019	2020
成果总类	**Total Calsses of Achievement**	**571**	**717**	**750**	**1933**	**1600**	**1365**	**1580**	**1729**
一、按成果水平分类	**Grouped by Level**								
国际首创/领先	International Innovation/ Leading	19	28	52	130	90	100	108	138
国际先进	Internationl Advanced Technology	97	172	195	373	203	204	199	258
国内首创/领先	Domestic Innovation/ Leading	276	394	362	743	465	291	380	357
国内先进	Domestic Advanced Technology	84	72	69	413	226	140	221	289
其它	Others	18	3	39	216	556	565	672	687
二、按成果类型分类	**Grouped by Type**								
基础理论研究	Basic Theory Research	37	15	15	16	20	40	60	54
应用开发研究	Applicable Development	494	669	717	1875	1540	1300	1384	1623
其它	Others	40	33	18	42	40	25	136	52
三、按成果产业属性分类	**Grouped by Sector Property**								
工业类成果	Industrial Achievements	145	225	226	693	643	374	517	597
农业类成果	Agricultural Achievements	79	129	124	320	218	176	210	243
医学类成果	Medical Achievements	199	291	231	394	144	209	342	220
其他类成果	Others	148	74	169	526	595	606	519	669
四、按成果完成单位分类	**Grouped by Units**								
高等院校完成	Institutions of Higher Education	149	169	137	198	308	453	491	385
研究单位完成	Scientific Research Institutions	92	92	64	99	86	100	120	136
厂矿企业完成	Industrial and Mineral Enterprises	137	176	303	1233	1006	595	854	780
其他单位完成	Others	193	280	246	403	200	217	123	428
五、经济效益 (亿元)	**Economic Benefits (100 million yuan)**								
总收入	Total Income	78.33	199.50		379.48	457.23	257.70	540.87	520.15
本年度节约资金	Capital Saved in This Year	6.33	28.28	36.85	23.19	135.95	11.42	60.66	20.97

18-11 科学技术协会组织与活动
Organizations and Activities of Scientific and Technological Association

项 目	Item	2019	2020
一、机构与人员	**Organizations and Personels**		
1.省级学会 (个)	Provincal Institute (unit)	152	157
会员 (人)	Members (person)	159216	209752
高级(资深)会员 (人)	Senoir Members (person)	35647	28466
外国会员 (人)	Foreign Members (person)	38	10
2.市、州学会数 (个)	City and Prefecture Institute (unit)	347	302
3.省级科协 (个)	Provincal Scientific Assosiations (unit)	1	1
市、州科协 (个)	City and Prefecture Scientific Assosiations (unit)	13	13
县(区)科协 (个)	County (District) Scientific Assosiations (unit)	102	102
二、学术活动省级学会及县以上科协	**Academic Activities Provincial Institutes and Scientific Assosiations above County level**		
国内学术会议 (次)	Domestic Academic Conference (time)	333	282
参加人数 (人次)	Number of Person Participated (person-time)	71829	300868
论文数 (篇)	Number of Scholary Paper (piece)	6940	5038
境内国际学术会议 (次)	Domestic International Academic Conference (time)	34	15
参加人数 (人次)	Number of Person Participated (person-time)	12870	4347
论文数 (篇)	Number of Scholary Paper (piece)	2507	287
三、科普活动省级学会及县以上科协	**Science and Technology Popularization Activities**		
举办科普宣讲活动 (次)	Events of Science Popularization Lectures (time)	4996	10708
宣讲活动受众人数 (人次)	People Participated (person-time)	3712863	11758178
举办实用技术培训 (次)	Technical Training (time)	3864	3849
实用技术培训人数 (人次)	People Participated (person-time)	350765	1048816
播放科技广播、影视节目 (分钟)	Scientific Radio and Video Programs (mimute)	64735	65393
参加活动科技人员 (人次)	People Participated (person-time)	9582	9684
四、青少年科技教育省级学会及县以上科协	**Education in Science and Technology for the Adolescents Provincial Institutes and Scientific Assosiations above County level**		
举办青少年科技竞赛 (项)	Adolescent Technology Competition (unit)	148	107
参加人数 (人次)	Number of Person Participated (person-time)	749579	393868
获奖人数 (人次)	Number of Person Rewarded (person-time)	27710	21867
举办青少年科学营 (次)	Adolescent Technology Campus	42	66
参加人数 (人次)	Number of Person Participated (person-time)	7696	9440
举办青少年科技教育培训 (次)	Adolescent Technology Education Training	769	643
培训人数 (人次)	Number of Person Participated (person-time)	438355	234634
五、科普基础设施建设县以上科协	**Infrastructure Construction of Science Popularization Scientific Assosiations above County Level**		
科技场馆 (个)	Science and Technology Museum (unit)	75	80
建筑面积 (平方米)	Construction Area (square metre)	220902	361149
展厅面积 (平方米)	Exhibition Area (square metre)	109729	227214
全年参观人数 (人次)	Year-round Visitor (person-time)	3665951	1428933
科普活动站 (个)	Science Popularization Station (unit)	2421	2131
科普画廊建筑面积 (平方米)	Science Popularization Gallery Construction Area (square metre)	87836	171710
六、为科技工作者服务省级学会及县以上科协	**Serve for Scientists Provincial Institutes and Scientific Assosiations above County level**		
反映科技工作者建议 (条)	Reported Suggestions of Scientists	522	449
其中:获上级领导批示的建议 (条)	Answered by Leaders	6	112
答复人大政协代表(委员)提案 (件)	Replied Proposal of NPC and CPPCC Representatives(Committees) (piece)	39	37
科学道德与学风建设宣讲活动 (场次)	Preach Ethics of Science	181	228
宣讲活动受众人数 (人次)	Number of Audience (person-time)	10785	27765
技术创新方法培训班 (场次)	Technology Innovation Training Class	121	507
继续教育培训班 (场次)	Continuing Education Class	305	600
继续教育(培训)人次 (人次)	Number of People Completed Courses (person-time)	23268	18479
通过媒体宣传科技工作者 (人)	Propagating Scientific and Technology Workers (person)	3255	3942
表彰奖励科技工作者 (人次)	Rewarded Scientific and Technology Workers (person-time)	1012	1491

18-12 专利受理量、批准量及分布状况
Number of Patent Applications Examination, Approval and Distribution

单位:项 (unit)

项 目	Item	受理量 Number of Patent Applications Examined				批准量 Number of Patent Applications Approved			
		2005	2010	2019	2020	2005	2010	2019	2020
合计	**Total**	**11534**	**31311**	**141411**	**163613**	**3860**	**17362**	**73940**	**110102**
发明	Creations and Inventions	2038	7410	47517	47767	733	2025	14178	17555
实用新型	Utility Models	4835	12792	81220	102936	2238	10431	50159	80229
外观设计	Designs	4661	11109	12674	12910	889	4906	9603	12318
在合计中	**Of This Total**								
个人	Individual	7400	10844	23183		2189	4990	10698	15638
大专院校	Universities and Colleges	1365	3265	21253		574	1972	11897	15661
科研单位	Insitutions of Scientific Research	182	1112	3090		101	532	1681	1694
工矿企业	Industrial and Mineral Enterprises	2305	15856	89863		901	9744	47884	74744
机关团体	Government Agencies and Organizations	283	234	4022		98	124	1780	2365

18-13 按市州分三种专利授权状况(2020)
Three Kinds of Patent Granted by Citiesand Prefectures(2020)

单位:项 (item)

市、州	Municipalities and Prefecture	授权当年累计 Authorization Total of Year	发明 Invention	实用新型 New Type of Practicial Utility	外观设计 Design
全省合计	**Total of the Province**	**110102**	**17555**	**80229**	**12318**
武汉市	Wuhan	58810	14654	39294	4862
黄石市	Huangshi	4031	163	3551	317
十堰市	Shiyan	4063	76	3609	378
宜昌市	Yichang	8245	775	7080	390
襄阳市	Xiangyang	7092	507	5895	690
鄂州市	Ezhou	1285	145	963	177
荆门市	Jingmen	3457	245	2710	502
孝感市	Xiaogan	4263	388	3040	835
荆州市	Jingzhou	5356	240	3919	1197
黄冈市	Huanggang	4741	120	3632	989
咸宁市	Xianning	3665	78	3006	581
随州市	Suizhou	1670	38	1124	508
恩施州	Enshi	1328	71	766	491
仙桃市	Xiantao	801	27	583	191
潜江市	Qianjiang	575	16	508	51
天门市	Tianmen	700	9	533	158
神农架林区	Shennongjia	20	3	16	1

18-14 各类技术合同签定及执行情况

Signing and Implementation of Various Technical Contracts

项 目	Item	合同数(项) Number of Contracts (unit)	合同金额(万元) Value of Contracts (10 000 yuan)
2013	**2013**	**14909**	**4187410**
技术开发合同	Technology Development Contracts	9473	1614052
技术转让合同	Technology Transfer Contracts	574	342631
技术咨询合同	Technology Consultation Contracts	1082	238981
技术服务合同	Technology Service Contracts	3780	1991746
2014	**2014**	**21696**	**6017367**
技术开发合同	Technology Development Contracts	11695	1398146
技术转让合同	Technology Transfer Contracts	518	279765
技术咨询合同	Technology Consultation Contracts	1496	389802
技术服务合同	Technology Service Contracts	7987	3949654
2015	**2015**	**22787**	**8300672**
技术开发合同	Technology Development Contracts	11318	2155738
技术转让合同	Technology Transfer Contracts	547	390390
技术咨询合同	Technology Consultation Contracts	1408	316786
技术服务合同	Technology Service Contracts	9514	5437758
2016	**2016**	**24248**	**9277311**
技术开发合同	Technology Development Contracts	11637	2512842
技术转让合同	Technology Transfer Contracts	696	385274
技术咨询合同	Technology Consultation Contracts	1819	372867
技术服务合同	Technology Service Contracts	10096	6006327
2017	**2017**	**24742**	**10658791**
技术开发合同	Technology Development Contracts	10646	2040680
技术转让合同	Technology Transfer Contracts	871	486457
技术咨询合同	Technology Consultation Contracts	869	614678
技术服务合同	Technology Service Contracts	12356	7516976
2018	**2018**	**28835**	**12371856**
技术开发合同	Technology Development Contracts	10855	2226298
技术转让合同	Technology Transfer Contracts	874	375116
技术咨询合同	Technology Consultation Contracts	1649	1135005
技术服务合同	Technology Service Contracts	15457	8635437
2019	**2019**	**39511**	**14496286**
技术开发合同	Technology Development Contracts	14773	2772441
技术转让合同	Technology Transfer Contracts	1085	543611
技术咨询合同	Technology Consultation Contracts	2190	1278283
技术服务合同	Technology Service Contracts	21463	9901949
2020	**2020**	**39749**	**16869652**
技术开发合同	Technology Development Contracts	14150	3567188
技术转让合同	Technology Transfer Contracts	1008	254230
技术咨询合同	Technology Consultation Contracts	2051	1415045
技术服务合同	Technology Service Contracts	22540	11633189

18-15 全省技术买卖情况(2020)
Purchase and Selling of Technology of the Whole Province (2020)

卖方类别 Type of the Seller / 买方类别 Type of the Buyer		合计 Total		机关法人 Organ Corporations		事业法人 Institutions Corporations		社团法人 Associations Corporations	
		合同数(项) Number of Contracts (unit)	成交额(万元) Contracted Value (10 000 yuan)	合同数(项) Number of Contracts (unit)	成交额(万元) Contracted Value (10 000 yuan)	合同数(项) Number of Contracts (unit)	成交额(万元) Contracted Value (10 000 yuan)	合同数(项) Number of Contracts (unit)	成交额(万元) Contracted Value (10 000 yuan)
总计	**Total**	**39749**	**16869653**	**824**	**490358**	**13536**	**2176075**	**321**	**127052**
机关法人	Departments	8204	4946333	730	445456	2804	1108350	314	123764
事业法人	Institutions	5648	658044	3	247	3930	286630	2	2269
社团法人	Social Groups	240	30553	0	0	168	3730	0	0
企业法人	Corporations	25000	10857662	91	44655	6294	525034	5	1019
自然人	Natural Person	146	39048	0	0	43	1272	0	0
其他组织	Other Organizations	511	338013	0	0	297	251059	0	0

18-15 续表 continued

卖方类别 Type of the Seller / 买方类别 Type of the Buyer		企业法人 Corporations		自然人 Natural Person		其他组织 Other Organizations	
		合同数(项) Number of Contracts (unit)	成交额(万元) Contracted Value (10 000 yuan)	合同数(项) Number of Contracts (unit)	成交额(万元) Contracted Value (10 000 yuan)	合同数(项) Number of Contracts (unit)	成交额(万元) Contracted Value (10 000 yuan)
总计	**Total**	**24892**	**13961819**	**25**	**9520**	**151**	**104828**
机关法人	Departments	4291	3241068	6	1545	59	26149
事业法人	Institutions	1710	368402			3	496
社团法人	Social Groups	72	26822				
企业法人	Corporations	18504	10203611	17	5161	89	78183
自然人	Natural Person	101	34961	2	2815		
其他组织	Other Organizations	214	86954				

18-16 地震观测及地方地震工作情况

Statistics on Earthquake Observation and Local Efforts on Earthquake Works

项 目	Item	2018	2019	2020
职工总数 （人）	Total Number of Staff and Workers (person)	383	384	384
专业技术人员 （人）	Professtional Technical Personel (person)	294	299	299
高级技术人员 （人）	Senior Technical Personel (person)	98	101	101
市州级地震局 （个）	Number of Earthquake Agency (unit)	17	17	17
重点县地震办公室 （个）	Number of Earthquake Offices in Key Counties (unit)	32	32	32
地方地震工作人员 （人）	Local Seismologist (person)	778	611	408
地震观测台(网)人员 （人）	Number of Staff in Earthquake Observation Station (person)	60	58	46
#观测技术人员 （人）	Technical Personel (person)	59	57	45
地震台站 （个）	Earthquake Observation Station (unit)	54	54	54
国家台	National Station	5	6	6
省级台	Provincial Station	49	48	48
GPS 测量 （千米/点）	GPS Measurement (km/point)	100000/200	60000/150	50000/135
流动重力测量 （千米/点）	Flow Gravity Measurement (km/point)	180000/840	80000/660	60000/357

18-17 气象部门基本情况

Basic Conditions of Meteorological Department

项 目	Item	2000	2005	2010	2015	2017	2018	2019	2020
一、气象观测人员总数 （人）	**Total Number of Staff in Meteorological Depaartment (person)**	**333**	**375**	**378**	**446**	**384**	**382**	**376**	**351**
地面观测	Groud Observation	285	320	330	376	315	313	315	296
高空观测	Upper Air Observation	24	18	18	34	28	30	25	18
雷达观测	Radar Observation	24	20	30	36	41	39	36	37
特种观测	Special Observation								
二、气象台站总数 （个）	**Total Number of Meteorological Obervatory (unit)**	**85**	**87**	**87**	**89**	**89**	**89**	**89**	**89**
气象台	Meteorological Obervatory	13	14	14	14	14	14	14	14
气象站	Weather Station	70	71	71	73	73	73	73	73
独立农试站	Independent Agricultural Station	2	2	2	2	2	2	2	2
三、卫星云图接收站点数（个）	**Number of Stations Receiving Satellite Image (unit)**	**11**	**25**	**15**	**17**	**18**	**18**	**18**	**18**
极轨卫星	Polar Orbiting Meteorological Satellite	2	23	5	4	5	5	5	5
同步卫星	Geostationary Satellite	9	7	10	13	13	13	13	13
四、拥有雷达数 （部）	**Number of Radar Owned (unit)**	**11**	**12**	**15**	**14**	**15**	**15**	**15**	**16**
3 厘米	3 cm	2	2	1	1	1	1	1	2
5 厘米	5 cm	2	1	1					
10 厘米	10 cm	3	5	10	10	11	11	11	11
1 波段	1 Wave Band			3	3	3	3	3	3

18-18 质量技术监督检查情况
Statistics on Supervision and Examination of Quality Technology

年份 Year	机构（个） Institutions (unit)	职工人数（人） Number of Staff and Workers (person)	#专业技术人员 Professional Technic Personel	经费收入（万元） Revenue (10 000 yuan)	经费支出（万元） Expenditures (10 000 yuan)	固定资产（万元） Fixed Assets (10 000 yuan)	#仪器设备 Equipment and Devices	计量器具检定台（万套件） Number of Measuring Equipment Tested (10 000 units)	#衡具 Measuring Instrument	#强制检定 Compulsory Test
1980	88	1211	327	308	306	1667	512	60		
1985	107	1668	356	640	515	3234	1402	146	36	
1990	105	3299	1409	3063	2610	7994	3760	136	68	118
1995	167	6275	2121	10095	10374	21213	6327	150	64	140
1996	102	2265	1252	3237	3177	6985	3261	136	61	108
1997	101	2337	1337	3491	3418	6751	3680	150	62	110
1998	106	2479	1439	4 079	4034	6314	3810	126	50	100
1999	105	2531	1446	4 515	4532	6732	3713	120	43	103
2000	104	2790	1478	4 568	4853	8829	5286	150	43	105
2001	91	1632	911	3005	2899	6537	3881	132	33	65
2002	360	9583	4059	36371	34024	39461	9806	165	40	138
2003	403	9137	3960	44450	41317	47323	12114	154	45	118
2004	376	9034	4703	50520	48383	53579	14549	128	23	114
2005	398	9046	3953	59089	56152	62607	19986	120	22	98
2006	398	9050	4094	67864	64078	72440	23840	119	22	110
2007	393	9065	4072	79698	75988	81822	26984	119	19	102
2008	392	9055	3732	93140	89653	94547	27832	109	16	96
2009	395	9077	3718	111477	110965	111627	35047	128	18	107
2010	388	9133	3815	116319	109915	129113	38963	125	17	119
2011	387	8828	3693	134901	135563	150114	44143	142	15	135
2012	385	8997	3645	153332	146310	159772	45440	175	16	155
2013	383	8981	3655	197287	180390	183786	57740	199	15	188
2014	379	8420	3160	191091	177558	234080	64785	202	20	156
2015	409	8297	2996	206214	202262	248957	80114	261	20	232
2016	409	8452	2816	227598	225075	275586	83466	265	17	183
2017	360	7957	2543	266322	272889	392739	115357	323	15	268
2018	35	1829	1298	91850	91850	150937	34847	280	20	241
2019								221	13	180
2020								152		

注：因改革指标统计口径发生变化。
Note: Changes have taken place in the statistical scope of indicators as a result of the reform.

18-19 标准事业基本情况
Basic Statistics on Stand ard Enterprises

项 目	Item	2000	2005	2010	2015	2018	2019	2020
质量监督机构 （个）	Quality Supervision Institution (unit)	86	99	99	99			
制定标准 （项）	Standard Established (unit)	29	36	81	92	103	45	75
修定标准 （项）	Standard Revised (unit)			4	11	7	1	10
废止标准 （项）	Standard Abolished (unit)					196		37
受检产品质量监督 （种）	Number of Products under Quality Supervision (kind)	99			59	68	182	
质量监督检测 （批次）	Quality Supervision Test (batch)	20093	26548	40288	4797	4720	9362	
标准文件馆藏 （万件）	Standard Document Collection (10 000 units)	25	22	30	140	146.63	150.86	32.07
省级产品质量监督抽查 （批次）	Provincial Product Quality Supervision and Spot Inspection (batch)							6891

18-20 档案事业基本情况
Basic Statistics on Archives

指 标	Item	2017	2018	2019	2020
各级各类档案馆数量 （个）	**Number of Institutions (unit)**				
国家综合档案馆	National Comprehensive Archives	115	115	118	118
专门档案馆	National Special Archives	14	8	10	10
部门档案馆	Department Archives	4	6	7	7
各级各类档案馆馆藏	**Number of Collections**				
全宗 （个）	Fonds (unit)	16350	16070	16788	16652
案卷 （万卷）	Archives (10 000 volumes)	1717	1639	1600	1365
以件为保管单位档案 （万件）	Archives (10 000 pieces)	970	1400	1416	1319
照片 （万张）	Photos (10 000 sheets)	152	125	128	
馆藏资料 （万册）	Files (10 000 volumes)	270	190	190	158
国家综合档案馆面积 （万平方米）	**The Area of National Comprehensive Archives (10 000 square meters)**				
总建筑面积	Floor Space	30.0	36.5	43.7	40
库房面积	The Area of Storerooms	10.35	12.20	16.00	16
全省档案专业技术职称人员 （人）	**Full-time Personnel (person)**				
研究馆员	Research Librarian	32	32	36	37
副研究馆员	Associate Research Librarian	178	205	252	299
馆员	Librarian	564	578	615	659
助理馆员	Associate Librarian	418	465	439	501
全省档案馆本年度利用档案	**Utilized Archives**				
利用档案人数 （万人次）	Use of Material (10 000 person-times)	47.70	51.5	42	25
利用档案卷次 （万人次）	Number of Archives Used (10 000 person-times)	101.50	108.00	119.00	92
举办展览 （个）	Display Organized (unit)	311	347	154	136
接待参观 （万人次）	Visitors (10 000 person-times)	43	21	74	13
全省本年编研档案资料	**Materials Edited This Year**				
公开出版种数 （种）	Number of Materials Open Published (kind)	83	68	68	94
公开出版字数 （万字）	Number of Words Open Published (10 000 words)	2297.00	2065.00	2843.00	5077
内部参考种数 （种）	Number of Materials for Inner Reference (kind)	257	125	105	140
内部参考字数 （万字）	Number of Words for Inner Reference (10 000 words)	4028	1831	2302	3180

18-21 各级各类学校数
Number of Schools by Type and Level

单位：所 (unit)

学校分类	Type of Shool	2010	2013	2014	2015	2016	2017	2018	2019	2020
普通高等学校	**Regular Institutions of Higher Education**	**120**	**123**	**123**	**126**	**129**	**128**	**128**	**128**	**129**
#地方院校	Local Schools	112	115	115	118	121	120	120	120	121
中等职业学校	**Secondary Vocation Schools**	**413**	**310**	**301**	**289**	**289**	**289**	**270**	**272**	**263**
普通中学	**Regular Middle School**	**2787**	**2576**	**2552**	**2545**	**2558**	**2573**	**2597**	**2612**	**2650**
#初中	Junior High Schools	2184	2013	2011	2013	2026	2041	2066	2080	2114
城区	Urban	362	509	535	548	582	591	606	622	640
镇区	Township	671	945	955	968	967	978	987	986	993
乡村	Rural	1151	559	521	497	477	472	473	472	481
高中	Senior High School	603	563	541	532	532	532	531	532	536
城区	Urban	243	318	314	311	321	324	326	334	335
镇区	Township	278	212	201	193	188	187	186	180	182
乡村	Rural	82	33	26	28	23	21	19	18	19
小学	**Primary School**	**7749**	**5746**	**5513**	**5398**	**5383**	**5378**	**5396**	**5405**	**5386**
城区	Urban	685	997	1061	1062	1124	1145	1168	1186	1200
镇区	Township	937	1536	1556	1543	1545	1558	1554	1543	1551
乡村	Rural	6127	3213	2896	2793	2714	2675	2674	2676	2635
特殊教育学校	**Special Education School**	**76**	**80**	**83**	**83**	**84**	**84**	**84**	**85**	**88**
幼儿园	**Kindergarten**	**4395**	**6011**	**6491**	**6814**	**7500**	**7825**	**8273**	**8925**	**9265**
技工学校	**School of Technology**	**206**		**131**	**132**	**124**	**146**	**106**	**102**	**105**

18-22 各级各类学校在校学生数
Number of Enrolments of Formal Education by Type and Level

单位：人 (person)

学校分类	Type of Shool	2005	2010	2015	2016	2017	2018	2019	2020
普通高等学校	**Regular Institutions of Higher Education**	**1012665**	**1296920**	**1408738**	**1399948**	**1398805**	**1435937**	**1498070**	**1613706**
#地方院校	Local Schools	824960	1098570	1207217	1200494	1201675	1239161	1300869	1415623
中等职业学校	**Secondary Vocation Schools**	**606014**	**903834**	**364893**	**375637**	**371206**	**369424**	**391910**	**420328**
普通中学	**Regular Middle School**	**4466879**	**3418299**	**2241286**	**2259904**	**2306544**	**2411314**	**2505863**	**2600039**
#初中	Junior High Schools	3172392	2180937	1365319	1414864	1487131	1587795	1653660	1708335
城区	Urban	494739	413930	547028	589002	617505	662668	699973	731536
镇区	Township	750903	848967	625858	646844	683979	728647	750020	773389
乡村	Rural	1926750	918040	192433	179018	185647	196480	203667	203410
高中	Senior High School	1294487	1237362	875967	845040	819413	823519	852203	891704
城区	Urban	541404	427334	512284	509424	498096	499625	522707	548405
镇区	Township	553411	633319	332446	311557	297857	300016	305926	316866
乡村	Rural	199672	176709	31237	24059	23460	23878	23570	26433
小学	**Primary School**	**4291881**	**3655512**	**3358095**	**3461337**	**3545680**	**3665794**	**3764794**	**3808514**
城区	Urban	787812	713491	1202479	1307462	1387044	1485467	1590927	1659866
镇区	Township	593090	974019	1281967	1321295	1357390	1400250	1420425	1428636
乡村	Rural	2910979	1968002	873649	832580	801246	780077	753442	720012
特殊教育学校	**Special Education School**	**9444**	**15349**	**11057**	**11831**	**13953**	**16177**	**28774**	**28871**
幼儿园	**Kindergarten**	**594481**	**1118360**	**1625793**	**1699519**	**1760387**	**1740534**	**1777926**	**1784314**
技工学校	**School of Technology**	**136000**	**229000**	**89400**	**79156**	**77910**	**80570**	**83311**	**91779**

18-23 各级各类学校招生数
Number of Entrants of Formal Education by Type and Level

单位:人 (person)

学校分类	Type of Shool	2005	2010	2015	2016	2017	2018	2019	2020
普通高等学校	**Regular Institutions of Higher Education**	**315560**	**387612**	**391157**	**397623**	**406668**	**426561**	**458777**	**512822**
#地方院校	Local Schools	269042	337621	342310	349234	358168	377924	409947	463575
中等职业学校	**Secondary Vocation Schools**	**273789**	**283610**	**132594**	**132075**	**127224**	**127901**	**144955**	**152287**
普通中学	**Regular Middle School**	**1469777**	**1053418**	**740206**	**782004**	**797433**	**834520**	**866676**	**894322**
#初中	Junior High Schools	1011186	657947	461592	504948	526205	557084	565300	581140
城区	Urban	162324	132571	182684	209080	216945	231237	243404	253596
镇区	Township	241579	251823	213860	232105	242165	256601	253499	259214
乡村	Rural	607283	273553	65048	63763	67095	69246	68397	68330
高中	Senior High School	458591	395471	278614	277056	271228	277436	301376	313182
城区	Urban	187976	138260	161996	166665	165373	167496	184206	191013
镇区	Township	197496	199177	106275	102144	98286	101784	108398	112364
乡村	Rural	73119	58034	10343	8247	7569	8156	8772	9805
小学	**Primary School**	**567411**	**680166**	**625609**	**623202**	**624961**	**672176**	**657842**	**627097**
城区	Urban	113284	126070	217723	233312	247024	279771	291063	286807
镇区	Township	81622	176073	232628	231143	231915	248857	237942	224580
乡村	Rural	372505	378023	175258	158747	146022	143548	128837	115710
特殊教育学校	**Special Education School**	**1038**	**2047**	**2047**	**2413**	**2294**	**2850**	**5549**	**4444**
幼儿园	**Kindergarten**	**396082**	**761044**	**613990**	**575076**	**594869**	**610815**	**568080**	**608799**
技工学校	**School of Technology**	**73000**	**57000**	**34700**	**34694**	**31620**	**32880**	**34316**	**35798**

18-24 各级各类学校毕业生数
Number of Graduates of Formal Education by Type and Level

单位：人 (person)

学校分类	Type of Shool	2000	2005	2010	2015	2017	2018	2019	2020
普通高等学校	**Regular Institutions of Higher Education**	**51932**	**187920**	**331303**	**388621**	**394423**	**374796**	**383037**	**400960**
#地方院校	Local Schools	26461	144529	285599	339709	345217	326982	336345	353372
中等职业学校	**Secondary Vocation Schools**	**125593**	**129436**	**335776**	**125735**	**114889**	**116775**	**116755**	**117794**
普通中学	**Regular Middle School**	**883828**	**1438503**	**1288944**	**778302**	**733571**	**728464**	**773757**	**800784**
#初中	Junior High Schools	718015	1055083	854395	461384	444035	452823	499686	526830
城区	Urban	198402	169257	149922	179771	186696	188206	211418	221319
镇区	Township	61909	239870	326945	213005	201644	208107	227187	239829
乡村	Rural	457704	645956	377528	68608	55695	56510	61081	65682
高中	Senior High School	165813	383420	434549	316918	289536	275641	274071	273954
城区	Urban	98353	161281	147307	183878	175490	167712	168575	169830
镇区	Township	41382	164517	228146	121045	106219	100059	97217	96917
乡村	Rural	26078	57622	59096	11995	7827	7870	8279	7207
小学	**Primary School**	**1160203**	**1020710**	**611620**	**466221**	**524455**	**552516**	**561501**	**579311**
城区	Urban	281706	149766	120208	170042	200923	213495	225046	239918
镇区	Township	84207	134340	160359	180809	205853	217964	218168	224180
乡村	Rural	794290	736604	331053	115370	117679	121057	118287	115213
特殊教育学校	**Special Education School**	**1310**	**1498**	**2261**	**1112**	**1278**	**1515**	**1724**	**2889**
幼儿园	**Kindergarten**				**617733**	**668141**	**698146**	**662895**	**678368**
技工学校	**School of Technology**	**24848**	**45000**		**30000**	**21944**	**21698**	**22878**	**21861**

18-25 各级各类学校教职工数
Number of Faculties at Schools by Type and Level

单位:人 (person)

学校分类	Type of Shool	2000	2005	2010	2015	2017	2018	2019	2020
普通高等学校	**Regular Institutions of Higher Education**	**72265**	**107459**	**123491**	**129118**	**131395**	**129164**	**131228**	**134736**
#地方院校	Local Schools	35120	73079	89205	96039	96612	95510	96865	100584
中等职业学校	**Secondary Vocation Schools**	**28816**	**36658**	**40985**	**27532**	**26595**	**25937**	**25951**	**26002**
普通中学	**Regular Middle School**	**237500**	**273146**	**263055**	**246443**	**244964**	**248406**	**256597**	**263534**
城区	Urban	97054	75581	68468	108438	116058	120037	125912	130366
镇区	Township	28889	78027	107371	106896	102185	101651	103982	106062
乡村	Rural	111557	119538	87216	31109	26721	26718	26703	27106
小学	**Primary Schools**	**299994**	**232888**	**211247**	**197577**	**196951**	**193885**	**197743**	**198871**
城区	Urban	84877	47727	42100	60500	66552	67886	71861	74601
镇区	Township	23515	33532	51059	71355	72747	72017	72568	72265
乡村	Rural	191602	151629	118088	65722	57652	53982	53314	52005
特殊教育学校	**Special Education School**	**1676**	**1679**	**1744**	**1955**	**2043**	**2099**	**2162**	**2216**
幼儿园	**Kindergarten**	**40484**	**33094**	**66202**	**134279**	**165810**	**179255**	**200730**	**209145**
技工学校	**School of Technology**	**13070**	**9934**		**9383**	**8122**	**8214**	**8517**	**8862**

18-26 各级各类学校专任教师数
Number of Full-time Teachers of Schools by Type and Level

单位:人 (person)

学校分类	Type of Shool	2000	2005	2010	2015	2017	2018	2019	2020
普通高等学校	**Regular Institutions of Higher Education**	**30363**	**59009**	**74685**	**83444**	**83507**	**83403**	**85276**	**88750**
#地方院校	Local Schools	15995	43240	57264	65440	64929	64535	66122	69474
中等职业学校	**Secondary Vocation Schools**	**15549**	**24036**	**28476**	**20550**	**20211**	**19891**	**20452**	**20927**
普通中学	**Regular Middle School**	**198486**	**233517**	**227962**	**198342**	**194963**	**195766**	**200037**	**203516**
#初中	Junior High Schools	154543	169084	156836	131325	129034	129756	133135	135046
城区	Urban	49752	31803	30409	46819	49985	51413	54226	56002
镇区	Township	13138	39851	59014	63263	61150	60549	60927	61420
乡村	Rural	91653	97430	67413	21243	17899	17794	17982	17624
高中	Senior High School	43943	64433	71126	67017	65929	66010	66902	68470
城区	Urban	27663	28330	26883	39755	41106	41228	42279	43466
镇区	Township	10336	27235	35091	24716	22851	22829	22822	23108
乡村	Rural	5944	8868	9152	2546	1972	1953	1801	1896
小学	**Primary School**	**274979**	**215693**	**196078**	**200158**	**203304**	**203576**	**208322**	**209808**
城区	Urban	75377	42127	37873	62736	71194	74043	78800	83007
镇区	Township	21459	30351	47480	72318	74630	74912	76379	76438
乡村	Rural	178143	143215	110725	65104	57480	54621	53143	50363
特殊教育学校	**Special Education School**	**1231**	**1317**	**1477**	**1682**	**1765**	**1799**	**1889**	**1950**
幼儿园	**Kindergarten**	**29889**	**20018**	**38494**	**68761**	**84613**	**89995**	**98612**	**102725**
技工学校	**School of Technology**	**6182**	**7064**		**7794**	**6456**	**6421**	**6753**	**7077**

18-27 各级各类学校专任教师学历分类
Statistics on Academic Degree of Full-Time Teachers at Schools by Type and Level

单位：人 (person)

学历分类	Type of School	2016	2017	2018	2019	2020
一、中等职业学校	**Secondary Vocational School**	**20657**	**20211**	**19891**	**20452**	**20927**
高等学校本科毕业及以上	Graduated from Universities and Above	18344	18343	18116	18639	19345
高等学校专科毕业	Graduated from Colleges	2145	1756	1687	1733	1496
高中阶段及以下	Degree Below Senior High School	168	112	88	80	86
二、普通中学	**Regular Secondary Schools**	**195685**	**194963**	**195766**	**200037**	**203516**
高等学校本科毕业及以上	Graduated from Universities and Above	159582	162148	165138	171439	176618
高等学校专科毕业	Graduated from Colleges	35415	32095	29972	28079	26405
中专、高中毕业的	Graduated from Secondary and High Schools	688	720	656	519	485
三、小学	**Primary School**	**202014**	**203304**	**203576**	**208322**	**209808**
中师、高中毕业及以上的	Graduated from Teacher Schools and Degrees Above	201896	203206	203417	208222	209744
四、幼儿园(不包括园长)	**Kindergarten (President is Excluded)**	**78005**	**84613**	**89995**	**98612**	**102725**
中师、高中毕业及以上的	Graduate from Teacher Schools and Degrees Above	75600	82408	87779	96279	100728

18-28 高等学校分类别情况

单位:所、人

学校分类	Type of School	2000				2005			
		学校数 Number of Colleges and Universities	在校生数 Students Enrollment in Schools	招生数 New Enrollment	毕业生数 Graduates	学校数 Number of Colleges and Universities	在校生数 Students Enrollment in Schools	招生数 New Enrollment	毕业生数 Graduates
总计	**Total**	**54**	**346568**	**139666**	**51932**	**85**	**989754**	**306775**	**184706**
综合大学	Comprehensive Universities	6	79303	28489	13871	10	196454	48591	48617
理工院校	Colleges and Universities of Science	11	124501	47724	18603	49	545277	181361	92857
农业院校	Colleges and Universities of Agriculture	2	13111	4311	1775	1	15715	3999	2763
林业院校	Colleges and Universities of Forestry	4	10770	4095	1068	1	1678	1062	121
医药院校	Colleges and Universities of Medicine	7	39694	17186	5950	3	26534	7686	5238
师范院校	Colleges and Universities of Teacher-Training	4	26218	9923	4466	5	52581	15687	12960
语文院校	Chinese Colleges								
财经院校	Colleges and Universities of Finance	1	2482	974	448	6	93524	30319	12771
政法院校	Colleges and Universities of Politics and Law	1	2787	915	515	3	12389	3416	2369
体育院校	Colleges and Universities of Physical Education	2	2255	749	318	1	8837	2735	1154
艺术院校	Colleges and Universities of Art	2	12719	4298	2584	4	8834	4378	814
民族院校	Colleges and Universities of Minority Groups	14	32728	21002	2334	2	27931	7539	5042

Classification of Higher Education Institutions

(unit, person)

2010				2019				2020			
学校数 Number of Colleges and Universities	在校生数 Students Enrollment in Schools	招生数 New Enrollment	毕业生数 Graduates	学校数 Number of Colleges and Universities	在校生数 Students Enrollment in Schools	招生数 New Enrollment	毕业生数 Graduates	学校数 Number of Colleges and Universities	在校生数 Students Enrollment in Schools	招生数 New Enrollment	毕业生数 Graduates
120	**1290243**	**386984**	**327208**	**128**	**1498070**	**458777**	**383037**	**129**	**512822**	**1613706**	**400960**
8	166008	44736	39434	8	172050	44470	39521	8	46499	175991	42194
74	773095	238873	202148	81	909945	294817	239104	81	332615	997550	248772
1	18239	4600	3892	1	18721	4628	4406	1	4719	18907	4381
1	5721	2051	1461	1	10170	4015	2728	1	3794	11100	2800
4	38173	10979	10031	4	40394	10820	9989	5	12302	42253	10478
7	78905	24018	18007	8	108909	32827	30449	8	36003	114340	30244
				1	10750	2888	2271	1	3268	11129	2833
12	123204	37315	30366	11	133603	37819	31175	11	42572	141809	35551
4	11698	2877	4157	4	14750	4978	4121	4	6296	17149	3831
2	14826	4298	2855	3	17196	4530	4063	3	5644	18566	4169
5	26179	8000	6898	4	21881	7130	5433	4	7877	23842	5943
2	34195	9237	7959	2	39701	9855	9777	2	11233	41070	9764

18-29 大学、中专专任教师职称情况
Statistics on Ranks and Titles of Full-Time Teachers at Schools of Various Levels

单位:人 (person)

职 称	Ranks and Titles	2000	2005	2010	2015	2016	2017	2018	2019	2020
普通高等学校专任教师数	**Number of Full-Time Teachers of Regular Higher Education Institutions**	**30363**	**59009**	**74685**	**83444**	**83517**	**83507**	**83403**	**85276**	**88750**
正高级	Senoir	3253	6434	8674	10901	10955	11237	11538	11847	12407
副高级	Associate Senoir	9448	17843	22047	26572	27072	27764	28150	28892	30427
中级	Junior	9847	19169	26077	30983	31186	31009	30650	30727	31335
初级	Primary	5741	10311	13656	9981	9379	8314	7961	7977	8138
未定职级	No Title	2074	5252	4231	5007	4925	5183	5104	5833	6443
中等职业学校专任教师数	**Number of Full-Time Teachers of Specialized Schools**	**15549**	**24036**	**28476**	**20550**	**20657**	**20211**	**19891**	**20452**	**20927**
正高级	Senoir				97	96	75	63	70	71
副高级	Associate Senoir	3523	5152	6441	5262	5170	5109	4601	4691	4622
中级	Junior	7229	11467	12935	9258	9263	8889	9027	8996	9080
初级	Primary	4399	5889	7229	4961	4988	4724	4698	4705	5095
未定职级	No Title	398	1528	1871	972	1140	1414	1502	1990	2059

18-30 各级各类学校校舍建筑面积情况(2020)
Statistics on Floor Space of School Houses under Construction in Schools by Type and Level(2020)

单位:万平方米 (10 000 sq.m)

项 目	Item	学校占地面积 Floor Space	校舍建筑面积 Building Foot Print	其中:教学及辅助用房 Teaching and Assisting Building
普通中学	**Regular Middle School**	**11016.70**	**4866.71**	**1640.40**
城区	Urban	4535.69	2212.22	827.21
镇区	Township	5021.58	2094.61	640.33
乡村	Rural	1459.43	559.87	172.86
其中:初中	Junior High Schools	6963.70	2835.89	996.24
城区	Urban	1982.47	924.03	387.36
镇区	Township	3652.76	1421.99	452.84
乡村	Rural	1328.47	489.87	156.04
其中:高中	Senior High School	4053.01	2030.81	644.16
城区	Urban	2553.23	1288.19	439.85
镇区	Township	1368.82	672.62	187.49
乡村	Rural	130.96	70.00	16.82
小学	**Primary School**	**9529.25**	**3164.00**	**1555.62**
城区	Urban	2008.15	921.43	517.74
镇区	Township	3248.67	1129.02	552.99
乡村	Rural	4272.43	1113.55	484.89
特殊学校	**Special Education School**	**75.14**	**36.76**	**16.66**
城区	Urban	43.10	22.84	10.21
镇区	Township	26.74	12.00	5.56
乡村	Rural	5.29	1.93	0.89

18-31 初中毕业生升入高中和小学毕业生升入初中的升学率
Statistics on Proportion of Middle-School Students Entering High School and Proportion of Primary-School Students Entering Middle School

年 份 Year	初中毕业生升入高中升学率 Proportion of Middle-School Students Entering High-School			小学毕业生升学率 Proportion of Primary-School Students Entering Middle-School		
	初中毕业生数（万人） Number of Middle School Graduates (10 000 persons)	高中招生数（万人） Number of High School Graduates (10 000 persons)	升学率（%） Proportion of Students Entering Schools of Higher Level(%)	小学毕业生数（万人） Number of Primary School Graduates (10 000 persons)	初中招生数（万人） Number of Middle School Graduates (10 000 persons)	升学率（%） Proportion of Students Entering Schools of Higher Level(%)
1965	7.60	3.75	49.40	29.60	24.95	84.30
1975	49.25	31.26	63.50	116.05	110.11	94.90
1978	98.80	43.33	43.90	132.37	119.46	90.30
1980	52.23	25.04	47.70	107.64	88.93	82.60
1985	49.92	19.13	38.30	104.89	69.21	66.00
1990	51.71	16.78	32.50	89.96	66.63	74.10
1995	57.85	19.88	34.40	90.76	80.53	88.70
1996	59.33	19.86	33.50	90.19	83.59	92.70
1997	64.70	21.29	32.90	95.35	89.30	93.70
1998	69.23	24.53	35.40	103.75	96.10	92.60
1999	69.60	27.20	39.10	111.24	101.40	91.20
2000	71.80	31.43	43.80	116.02	109.06	94.00
2001	76.34	35.31	46.30	121.00	113.49	93.80
2002	82.93	42.45	51.20	122.17	120.07	98.30
2003	91.61	39.61	43.20	118.70	117.83	99.30
2004	99.32	42.97	43.30	109.93	109.69	99.80
2005	105.51	45.86	43.50	102.07	101.85	99.80
2006	106.18	45.55	42.90	94.66	97.07	102.60
2007	99.77	43.98	44.10	83.29	87.27	104.80
2008	96.10	43.91	45.70	71.51	77.75	108.70
2009	92.38	42.38	45.90	64.68	69.63	107.70
2010	85.44	39.55	46.30	61.16	65.79	107.60
2011	77.14	36.20	46.90	58.34	61.92	106.10
2012	57.58	32.75	56.90	51.38	51.09	99.40
2013	53.37	31.65	59.30	48.94	48.78	99.70
2014	47.71	29.53	61.90	45.19	45.43	100.50
2015	46.14	27.86	60.39	46.62	46.16	99.01
2016	44.83	27.71	61.81	49.93	50.49	101.13
2017	44.40	27.12	61.08	52.45	52.62	100.33
2018	45.28	27.74	61.27	55.25	55.71	100.83
2019	49.97	30.14	60.31	56.15	56.53	100.68
2020	52.68	31.32	59.45	57.93	58.11	100.32

18-32 小学学龄儿童入学率

Statistics on Proportion of Children at Schooling Age Entering Primary Schools

年 份 Year	学龄儿童数(万人) Number of Children at Schooling Age (10 000 persons)	已入学学龄儿童数(万人) Number of Children Entering School (10 000 persons)	入学率(%) Proportion of Students Entering Schools of Higher Level(%)
1975	629.50	611.00	97.10
1978	616.86	597.73	96.90
1980	594.80	576.86	97.00
1985	496.69	489.38	98.50
1990	485.00	480.32	99.00
1991	556.39	549.35	98.70
1992	571.44	563.44	98.60
1993	574.54	566.84	98.70
1994	599.47	593.88	99.10
1995	637.12	632.34	99.20
1996	661.72	658.38	99.50
1997	681.52	678.95	99.60
1998	685.87	682.53	99.50
1999	669.16	665.88	99.50
2000	641.60	638.57	99.50
2001	585.99	583.29	99.50
2002	538.02	535.98	99.60
2003	490.29	488.68	99.70
2004	440.03	438.66	99.70
2005	397.52	396.11	99.70
2006	363.99	362.14	99.50
2007	345.49	344.77	99.80
2008	340.59	340.08	99.90
2009	343.63	342.74	99.70
2010	350.95	350.82	99.96
2011	362.77	362.74	99.96
2012	317.15	317.06	99.97
2013	320.48	320.41	99.98
2014	315.77	315.72	99.99
2015	330.72	330.69	99.99
2016	340.52	340.51	100.00
2017	349.22	349.22	100.00
2018	360.88	360.88	100.00
2019	370.30	370.30	100.00
2020	373.55	373.55	100.00

18-33 各级各类学校服务的人口及每万人口中在校学生数
Statistics on Number of Population Served by Schools of Various Types and Levels and Number of Students at School per 10 000 Persons

项 目	Item	2000	2005	2010	2015	2016	2017	2018	2019	2020
每一学校服务的人口数（万人）	**Number of Population Served by Each School (10 000 persons)**									
普通高等学校	Regular Institutions of Higher Education	111.63	70.95	47.70	46.44	45.62	46.11	46.23	46.30	44.53
成人高等学校	Adults Higher Education	188.37	354.76	408.86	417.96	420.36	421.57	422.64	423.36	410.36
普通中等专业学校	Specialized Secondary School	29.69	13.80	13.86	20.25	20.36	20.42	21.91	21.79	21.84
普通高中	RegualrHigh-School				11.00	11.06	11.09	11.14	11.14	10.72
普通初中	Regualr Middle-School				2.91	2.90	2.89	2.86	2.85	2.72
小学	Primary School	0.26	0.48	0.74	1.08	1.09	1.10	1.10	1.10	1.07
幼儿园	Kindergarten	1.61	2.58	1.30	0.86	0.78	0.75	0.72	0.66	0.62
每万人口中的学生数（人）	**Number of Students at School per10 000 Persons (person)**									
普通高等学校	Regular Institutions of Higher Education	57.49	167.91	226.58	240.75	258.96	237.01	242.68	252.75	280.89
成人高等学校	Adults Higher Education	35.94	37.05	45.79	40.78	34.64	30.38	33.15	38.73	54.17
普通中等专业学校	Specialized Secondary School	46.22	100.48	157.90	62.36	63.83	62.89	62.43	66.12	73.16
普通高中	RegualrHigh-School				149.70	143.59	138.84	139.18	143.78	155.21
普通初中	Regualr Middle-School				233.33	240.42	251.97	268.34	279.00	297.36
小学	Primary School	1107.77	711.64	638.63	573.89	588.16	600.76	619.54	635.19	662.93
幼儿园	Kindergarten	120.56	98.57	195.38	277.84	288.79	298.27	294.16	299.97	310.59

18-34 各级各类学校每个专任教师负担的学生数
Statistics on Student-Teacher Ratio by Type and Level of School

单位:人 (person)

项 目	Item	2000	2005	2010	2013	2014	2015	2016	2017	2018	2019	2020
普通高等学校	Regular Institutions of Higher Education	11.41	15.86	17.37	17.35	17.14	15.73	15.63	17.52	18.31	18.49	18.43
中等职业学校	Secondary Vocation School	17.92	25.21	31.74	18.23	17.01	17.76	18.18	18.37	18.57	19.16	20.09
普通中学	Regular High School	17.68	19.13	15.00	12.04	11.37	11.30	11.55	11.83	12.32	12.53	12.78
#初中	Junior Middle Schools	18.19	18.76	13.91	10.94	10.30	10.40	10.95	11.53	12.24	12.42	12.65
高中	Senior High School	15.89	20.09	17.40	14.17	13.49	13.07	12.70	12.43	12.48	12.74	13.02
小学	Primary School	24.28	19.90	18.64	16.70	16.12	16.78	17.13	17.44	18.01	18.07	18.15
幼儿园	Kindergarten	24.31	29.70	29.05	25.52	24.41	23.64	21.79	20.81	19.34	18.03	17.37

注:2018年起,教育监测指标口径发生变化。
Note: Since 2018, the scope of educational monitoring indicators has changed.

18-35 各级学校女学生和女教师数

Number of Female Students and Female Teachers at School of Various Types and Levels

单位:万人 (10 000 persons)

项 目	Item	2000	2005	2013	2014	2015	2016	2018	2019	2020
一、女学生数	**Number of Female Students**									
普通高等学校	Regular Institutions of Higher Education	11.93	44.11	69.12	69.04	68.46	68.15	70.81	73.76	78.41
中等专业学校	Specialized Secondary School	14.33	29.14	19.84	17.90	16.96	17.10	16.33	17.10	18.42
普通中学	Regualr High School	155.66	203.98	112.14	104.22	102.39	103.44	111.72	116.34	120.46
小学	Primary School	317.45	194.85	149.88	146.64	153.24	157.50	166.46	171.52	173.72
二、女学生占学生总数%	**Percentage of Female Students in School**									
普通高等学校	Regular Institutions of Higher Education	34.4	43.6	48.6	48.6	48.5	48.6	49.20	49.15	48.5
中等专业学校	Specialized Secondary School	51.4	48.1	48.3	48.0	46.5	45.5	44.20	43.63	43.8
普通中学	Regualr High School	44.4	45.7	45.4	45.4	45.7	45.8	46.30	46.43	46.3
小学	Primary School	47.5	45.4	45.7	45.7	45.6	45.5	45.40	45.56	45.6
三、女教师数	**Number of Female Teachers**									
普通高等学校	Regular Institutions of Higher Education	1.02	2.34	3.59	3.65	3.72	3.77	3.87	4.00	4.22
中等专业学校	Specialized Secondary School	0.60	0.94	0.94	0.92	0.83	0.63	0.67	0.72	0.75
普通中学	Regualr High School	6.26	7.94	8.15	8.21	8.26	8.35	8.83	9.25	9.63
小学	Primary School	12.07	10.32	10.13	10.65	10.06	11.50	12.58	13.32	13.79
四、女教师占教师总数%	**Percentage of Female Teachers in School**									
普通高等学校	Regular Institutions of Higher Education	33.60	39.70	43.90	44.10	44.60	45.10	46.40	46.95	47.50
中等专业学校	Specialized Secondary School	38.50	39.10	41.50	41.80	42.30	43.10	45.20	45.82	46.70
普通中学	Regualr High School	31.50	34.00	39.70	40.70	41.70	42.70	45.10	46.25	47.30
小学	Primary School	43.90	47.90	51.50	53.50	54.50	57.00	61.80	63.94	65.73

18-36 各级各类成人学校在校学生数

Number of Adult Students Enrolled at Schools by Type and Level

单位:万人 (10 000 persons)

各类学校	Item	2000	2005	2010	2015	2016	2017	2018	2019	2020
成人高等学校	**Adult Higher Education**	**21.66**	**22.34**	**26.21**	**23.86**	**20.39**	**17.93**	**19.62**	**22.96**	**31.12**
广播电视大学	Radio and TV Universities	2.78	2.52	0.54	0.35	0.20	0.13	0.11	0.09	0.11
职工大学	Schools of Higher Education for Staff	1.36	0.22	0.04						
管理干部学院	Colleges for Management and Caders	0.90	0.60	0.35	0.00	0.02	0.01	0.02	0.01	
教育学院	Pedagogical College	0.94	0.89	0.37	0.18	0.17	0.17	0.24	0.29	0.34
普通高等学校办函授部、夜大学	Correspondence and Evening College Run by Regualr High Education	15.16	18.11	24.91	23.33	20.00	17.61	19.25	22.55	30.67
成人中等学校	**Secondary Schools for Adults**	**139.75**	**35.90**	**81.77**	**28.16**	**34.71**	**27.41**	**20.65**	**20.06**	
中学	Middle School	0.61	2.42	3.69	3.36	3.37	3.36	3.16	3.16	3.16
技术培训学校	Technical Training Schools	131.86	33.48	78.08	24.80	31.35	24.04	17.50	16.91	16.91

注:成人高等学校学生数是本、专科学生数。
Note: The number of students in Adults Higher Education refers to the number of students in vocational schools.

18-37 研究生基本情况
Basic Conditions about Post-Graduates

单位:人 (person)

项 目	Item	2016	2017	2018	2019	2020
高等学校在校研究生数	**Number of Post-graduates at School in Institutions of Higher Education**	**119676**	**133085**	**145060**	**157673**	**175993**
攻读博士学位研究生	Post-graduate Studying for Doctor's Degree	23088	24284	25213	27450	29596
攻读硕士学位研究生	Post-graduate Studying for Master's Degree	96588	108801	119847	130223	146397
招收研究生数	**New Students Enrollment**	**40014**	**51011**	**51877**	**54139**	**65684**
攻读博士学位研究生	Post-graduate Studying for Doctor's Degree	5023	5366	5982	6473	6897
攻读硕士学位研究生	Post-graduate Studying for Master's Degree	34991	45645	45895	47666	58787
毕业研究生数	**Number of Graduates**	**34838**	**34774**	**36595**	**38790**	**44634**
攻读博士学位研究生	Post-graduate Studying for Doctor's Degree	3669	3888	4294	3958	4375
攻读硕士学位研究生	Post-graduate Studying for Master's Degree	31169	30886	32301	34832	40259
科研单位在学研究生数	**Number of Post-graduates Studying in Research Institutions**	**2443**	**2502**	**2640**	**2705**	**2833**
攻读博士学位研究生	Post-graduate Studying for Doctor's Degree	925	935	979	999	1050
攻读硕士学位研究生	Post-graduate Studying for Master's Degree	1518	1567	1661	1706	1783
招收研究生数	**New Students Enrollment**	**791**	**821**	**871**	**871**	**923**
攻读博士学位研究生	Post-graduate Studying for Doctor's Degree	251	243	250	248	261
攻读硕士学位研究生	Post-graduate Studying for Master's Degree	540	578	621	623	662
毕业研究生数	**Number of Graduates**	**634**	**629**	**607**	**650**	**624**
攻读博士学位研究生	Post-graduate Studying for Doctor's Degree	205	214	199	224	202
攻读硕士学位研究生	Post-graduate Studying for Master's Degree	429	415	408	426	422

主要统计指标解释

科技活动 指在自然科学、农业科学、医药科学、工程与技术科学、人文与社会科学领域(简称科学技术领域)中,与科技知识的产生、发展、传播和应用密切相关的有组织的活动。可分为研究与试验发展(R&D)、研究与试验发展成果应用及相关的科技服务三类活动。该定义是联合国教科文组织考虑成员国特别是发展中国家开展科技统计工作的需要,而对科技活动所作的统计界定。

科技活动人员 指直接从事科技活动、以及专门从事科技活动管理和为科技活动提供直接服务,累计的实际工作时间占全年制度工作时间10%及以上的人员。(1)直接从事科技活动的人员包括:在独立核算的科学研究与技术开发机构、高等学校、各类企业及其他事业单位内设的研究室、实验室、技术开发中心及中试车间(基地)等机构中从事科技活动的研究人员、工程技术人员、技术工人及其它人员;虽不在上述机构工作,但编入科技活动项目(课题)组的人员;科技信息与文献机构中的专业技术人员;从事论文设计的研究生等。(2)专门从事科技活动管理和为科技活动提供直接服务的人员,包括:独立核算的科学研究与技术开发机构、科技信息与文献机构、高等学校、各类企业及其他事业单位主管科技工作的负责人,专门从事科技活动的计划、行政、人事、财务、物资供应、设备维护、图书资料管理等工作的各类人员,但不包括保卫、医疗保健人员、司机、食堂人员、茶炉工、水暖工、清洁工等为科技活动提供间接服务的人员。该指标用来反映投入科技活动人力的规模。

科学家与工程师 指科技活动人员中具有高、中级技术职称(职务)的人员和不具有高、中级技术职称(职务)的大学本科及以上学历人员。该指标用来反映投入科技活动人力的素质。

研究与试验发展(R&D) 指在科学技术领域,为增加知识总量,以及运用这些知识去创造新的应用进行的系统的创造性的活动,包括基础研究、应用研究、试验发展三类活动。国际上通常采用R&D活动的规模和强度指标反映一国的科技实力和核心竞争力。

专业技术人员 指从事专业技术工作和专业技术管理工作的人员,即企事业单位中已经聘任专业技术职务从事专业技术工作和专业技术管理工作的人员,以及未聘任专业技术职务,现在专业技术岗位上工作的人员。包括工程技术人员,农业技术人员,科学研究人员,卫生技术人员,教学人员,经济人员,会计人员,统计人员,翻译人员,图书资料、档案、文博人员,新闻出版人员,律师、公证人员,广播电视播音人员,工艺美术人员,体育人员,艺术人员及企业政治思想工作人员,共十七个专业技术职务类别。用来反映科技人力资源情况。

科技活动经费筹集 指从各种渠道筹集到的计划用于科技活动的经费,包括政府资金、企业资金、事业单位资金、金融机构贷款、国外资金和其他资金等。反映各社会经济主体对促进科技进步所做的努力。

新产品 指采用新技术原理、新设计构思研制、生产的全新产品,或在结构、材质、工艺等某一方面比原有产品有明显改进,从而显著提高了产品性能或扩大了使用功能的产品。既包括政府有关部门认定并在有效期内的新产品,也包括企业自行研制开发,未经政府有关部门认定,从投产之日起一年之内的新产品。用来反映科技产出及对经济增长的直接贡献。

专利 是专利权的简称,是对发明人的发明创造经审查合格后,由专利局依据专利法授予发明人和设计人对该项发明创造享有的专有权。包括发明、实用新型和外观设计。反映拥有自主知识产权的科技和设计成果情况。

发明 指对产品、方法或者其改进所提出的新的技术方案。是国际通行的反映拥有自主知识产权技术的核心指标。

普通高等学校 指按照国家规定的设置标准和审批程序批准举办的,通过全国普通高等学校统一招生考试,招收高中毕业生为主要培养对象,实施高等教育的全日制大学、独立设置的学院和高等专科学校、高等职业学校和其他机构。

大学、独立设置的学院主要实施本科层次以上教育,高等专科学校、高等职业学校实施专科层次教育,其他机构是承担国家普通招生计划任务不计校数的机构。包括普通高等学校分校和批准筹建的普通高等学校等。

成人高等学校 指按照国家规定的设置标准和审批程序批准举办的,通过全国成人高等学校统一招生考试,招收具有高中毕业或同等学历的在职从业人员为主要培养对象,利用函授、业余、脱产等多种形式对其实施高等学历教育的学校。包括职工高等学校、农民高等学校、管理干部学院、教育学院、独立函授学院、广播电视大学、其他机构等。

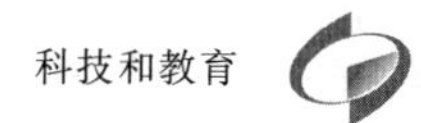

其他机构是承担国家成人招生计划任务不计校数的机构。

小学学龄儿童净入学率 指调查范围内已入小学学习的学龄儿童占校内外学龄儿童总数(包括弱智儿童,不包括盲聋哑儿童)的比重。计算公式为:

$$小学学龄儿童净入学率=\frac{已入学的小学学龄儿童数}{校内外小学学龄儿童总数}\times100\%$$

Explanatory Notes on Main Statistical Indicators

Scientific and Technological Activities (S&T Activities) refer to organized activities which are closely related with the creation, development, dissemination and application of the scientific and technical knowledge in the fields of natural sciences, agricultural science, medical science, engineering and technological science, humanities and social sciences (referred to as scientific and technological fields). S&T activities can be classified in to 3 categories: research and development (R&D) activities, application of R&D results, and related S&T services. This statistical definition is made by UNICHIEF for scientific and technological activities to meet the need of carrying out statistical work in this field for its member countries in particular those developing countries.

Personnel Engaged in S&T Activities refer to personnel directly engaged in S&T activities, in the management of S&T activities, and in providing direct service to S&T activities, who spend over 10% of the total working hours in a year in S&T activities. (1) Personnel directly engaged in S&T activities include researchers, engineers, technicians and other related personnel engaged in S&T activities in independent-accounting R&D institutions, institutions of higher learning, and in research institutes, laboratories, technology development centers and central experiment workshops under enterprises and institutions. Also included are people working in S&T research project teams, professional and technical personnel working in S&T information archiving institutes, and graduate students working on the design of their thesis. (2) Personnel engaged in the management of S&T activities and in providing direct service to S&T activities include senior management people responsible for S&T activities in independent-accounting R&D institutions, S&T information archiving institutes, institutions of higher learning, and in enterprises and institutions where S&T activities are undertaken. Also included are people responsible for the planning, administration, personnel management, financial management, logistics supply, equipment maintenance, information and library management that are related with S&T activities. People providing indirect services are excluded, such as security, medical service, drivers, plumbers, cleaners and those providing catering and related service. This indicator reflects the size of personnel engaged in S&T activities.

Scientists and Engineers refer to persons engaged in S&T activities who have obtained titles of senior and middle level professional positions, and those without such position but have completed university or higher education. This indicator reflects the quality of personnel engaged in S&T activities.

Research and Development (R&D) refers to systematic and creative activities in the field of science and technology aiming at increasing the knowledge and using the knowledge for new application. R&D includes 3 categories of activities: basic research, applied research and experiments and development. The scale and intensity of R&D are widely used internationally to reflect the strength of S&T and the core competitiveness of a country in the world.

Professional and Technical Personnel refer to persons engaged in professional and technical work or in the management of professional and technical activities, i.e., people with professional or technical positions who are engaged in professional and technical work or in the management of professional and technical activities, and people without professional or technical positions but are working on professional or technical posts. They include professionals and technicians working in 17 categories of technical occupations including engineering, agriculture, scientific researches, medical service, teaching, economic research and application, accounting, statistics, translation, libraries, archives, cultural and museum service, journalism and publication, lawyers, notarization service, radio and television broadcasting, handicraft and fine arts, sports, performing art, and political workers in enterprises. This indicator reflects the condition of human resources in S&T.

Funding for S&T Activities refers to funds obtained from various sources for S&T activities, including government funds, self-raised funds by enterprises, self-raised funds by institutions, loans from financial institutions, foreign funds and other funds. This indicator reflects the efforts made by various social economic entities in promoting the development of S&T.

New Products refer to new products produced with new technology and new design, or products that represent noticeable improvement in terms of structure, material, or production process so as to improve significantly the character or function of the older versions. They include new products certified by relevant government agencies within the period of certification, as well as new products designed and produced by enterprises within a year without certification by government agencies. This indictor reflects the direct contribution of S&T output to economic growth.

Patent is an abbreviation for the patent right and refers to the exclusive right of ownership by the inventors or designers for the creation or inventions, given from the patent offices after due process of assessment and approval in accordance with the Patent Law. Patents are granted for inventions, utility models and designs. This indicator reflects the achievements of S&T and design with independent intellectual property.

Inventions refer to the new technical proposals to the products or methods or their modifications. This is universal core indicator reflecting the technologies with independent intellectual property.

Regular Institutions of Higher Learning refer to educational establishments set up according to the government evaluation and approval procedures, enrolling graduates from senior secondary schools and providing higher education courses and training for senior professionals. They include full-time universities, colleges, high professional schools, high professional vocational schools and others.

Universities and colleges are mainly providing undergraduate courses; those high professional schools and high professional vocational schools are mainly providing professional trainings; and others refer to educational establishments, which are responsible for enrolling students but not covered in the total number of schools, including: branch schools of universities and colleges, and universities and colleges that have been proved and prepared to construct.

Institutions of Higher Learning for Adults refer to educational establishments, set up in line with relevant rules approved by the government, enrolling staff and workers with senior secondary school or equivalent education, and providing higher education courses in many forms of correspondence, spare time, or full time for adults. Professionals thus trained receive a qualification equivalent to graduates studying regular courses at regular universities, colleges and professional colleges. Institutions of higher learning for adults include schools of high education for staff and workers, schools of high education for peasants, colleges for management cadres, pedagogical colleges, independent correspondence colleges, Radio and TV universities and other educational establishments. Other educational establishments are responsible for enrolling adult students but not covered in the number of schools.

Enrollment Rate of Primary School Age Children refers to the proportion of school age children enrolled at schools to the total number of school age children both in and outside schools (including retarded children, but excluding blind, deaf and mute children). The formula is:

Enrollment Rate of Primary School-age Children = (Total Primary School-age Children at Schools)/(Total Primary School age Children Both at and Outside Schools) x 100%

19

卫生和社会服务

Public Health and Social Services

资料整理人员:范　维

19-1 卫生机构数
Number of Health Care Institutions

单位：个 (unit)

年 份 Year	总 计 Total	医 院 Hospitals	综合医院 General Hospitals	中医医院 Hosptials Specialized in Traditional Chinese Medicine	专科医院 Specialized Hosptials	基层医疗卫生机构 Basic Medical Institutions	社区卫生服务中心（站） Community Health Service Centers	街道卫生院 Urban Health Centers	乡镇卫生院 Township Health Centers
2006	10052	575	401	82	82		664	55	1140
2007	11093	580	393	83	93		1089	53	1160
2008	10305	593	389	86	106		1115	48	1155
2009	32790	614	409	86	105		1142	48	1134
2010	34269	602	394	87	107		1294	44	1149
2011	35625	608	393	91	111	34509	1278	34	1161
2012	35240	650	414	95	126	34063	1220	34	1165
2013	35631	711	444	98	153	34042	1231	36	1152
2014	36077	771	483	102	169	34503	1175	36	1150
2015	36173	869	532	109	208	34569	1189	29	1140
2016	36261	928	550	115	237	34706	1236	31	1136
2017	36323	976	567	117	261	34742	1173	25	1137
2018	36397	996	561	123	280	34821	1148	21	1139
2019	35479	1034	561	126	311	33893	1149	23	1129
2020	35445	1048	560	123	326	33850	1144	22	1121

注：卫生事业机构数从 2009 年起包含村卫生室数量。
Note: The statistics of health care units, hospital beds and health care professionals started to include the village clinics since 2009.

19-1 续表 continued

单位:个 (unit)

年 份 Year	总 计 Total						
	村卫生室 Village Clinices	门诊部(所) Outpatient Department	专业公共卫生机构 Specialized Public Health Institutions	疾病预防控制中心 Center for Disease Control and Prevention	专科疾病防治院(所/站) Specialized Disease Prevention & Treatment Institution	妇幼保健院(所/站) Women and Children Care Agencies	卫生监督所(中心) Health Inspection Institution (center)
2006		7116		114	116	95	72
2007		7677		113	118	100	83
2008		6871		110	109	99	93
2009	22405	6936		112	87	99	97
2010	24112	6729		115	84	100	98
2011	25204	6832	425	112	83	100	98
2012	24976	6668	438	111	83	100	109
2013	24941	6682	779	113	75	101	102
2014	24919	7223	696	112	76	100	103
2015	24796	7415	577	113	76	103	107
2016	24788	7515	559	115	74	104	109
2017	24633	7774	537	115	73	102	110
2018	24397	8116	504	115	74	103	107
2019	23230	8362	488	112	75	101	106
2020	23199	8364	478	112	73	101	107

19-2 卫生机构人员数
Number of Persons Engaged in Health Care Institutions

单位:万人 (10 000 persons)

年份 Year	总计 Total	卫生技术人员 Medical Technical Personel	执业(助理)医师 Licensed (Assistant) Doctors	执业医师 Licensed Doctors	#注册护士 Pegistertered Nurses	药师(士) Pharmacist	乡村医生和卫生员 Village Doctors and Assistants	每千人口医生数(人) Number of Doctors per 1000 Population (person)
1970	10.30	8.33	4.15		1.83			1.03
1975	15.05	11.85	4.91		2.05			1.11
1980	19.94	15.59	6.32		3.09			1.35
1985	23.58	18.48	7.27		3.77			1.47
1990	26.75	20.92	8.68		5.66			1.62
1991	27.51	21.55	8.79		5.97			1.62
1992	28.24	22.15	9.02		6.25			1.64
1993	28.91	22.46	9.16		6.49			1.64
1994	29.31	22.84	9.38		6.64			1.66
1995	29.55	23.20	9.58		6.83			1.68
1996	29.65	23.47	9.72		7.00			1.67
1997	30.38	23.90	9.96		7.21			1.70
1998	30.31	23.96	10.11		7.29			1.71
1999	30.40	24.05	10.31		7.41			1.74
2000	30.14	23.88	10.30		7.53			1.74
2001	29.48	23.41	10.21		7.51			1.72
2002	25.30	20.59	8.63		6.35			1.43
2003	25.62	20.83	8.72		6.38			1.45
2004	26.06	21.38	8.99		6.62			1.49
2005	26.22	21.50	8.98		6.94			1.49
2006	26.53	21.80	9.01		7.06			1.49
2007	27.80	22.70	9.20	7.65	7.69			1.52
2008	28.48	23.38	9.20	7.70	8.06			1.51
2009	33.71	24.70	9.79	8.22	8.73		3.86	1.59
2010	34.95	25.58	9.95	8.37	9.38	1.77	4.15	1.62
2011	36.52	26.81	10.21	8.53	10.21	1.77	4.41	1.66
2012	38.64	28.87	10.91	9.01	11.57	1.74	4.30	1.89
2013	41.12	30.93	11.72	9.65	12.79	1.77	4.29	1.90
2014	43.82	33.55	12.61	10.39	14.40	1.78	4.22	2.17
2015	47.55	36.76	13.60	11.22	16.51	1.82	4.09	2.32
2016	49.54	38.54	14.24	11.74	17.52	1.85	4.04	2.42
2017	51.04	39.97	14.76	12.23	18.43	1.87	3.96	2.50
2018	52.18	41.08	15.19	12.66	19.08	1.87	3.74	2.57
2019	52.98	41.95	15.50	12.97	19.59	1.87	3.45	2.62
2020	53.87	42.90	16.00	13.44	20.00	1.87	3.27	2.77

注:卫生人员数从2009年起包含村卫生室卫生人员数量。
Note: The statistics of health care units, hospital beds and health care professionals started to include the village clinics since 2009.

19-3 卫生机构床位数
Number of Beds in Health Care Institutions

单位:万张 (10 000 beds)

年份 Year	总计 Total	医院 Hospitals	基层医疗卫生机构 Basic Medical Institutions	乡镇卫生院 Township Health Centers	专业公共卫生机构 Specialized Public Health Institutions	每千人口卫生机构床位数(张) Beds of Medical Institutions Per 1000 Population (bed)
1970	6.14	5.56				1.38
1975	9.90	9.02				2.05
1980	12.59	11.22				2.40
1985	14.70	11.52				2.34
1990	16.34	13.16				2.45
1991	16.52	13.43				2.47
1992	16.62	13.46				2.44
1993	16.30	13.48				2.41
1994	16.13	13.40				2.36
1995	15.78	13.08				2.29
1996	14.42	13.08				2.24
1997	15.30	13.08				2.24
1998	15.09	13.03				2.21
1999	14.90	12.91				2.07
2000	14.96	12.99				2.18
2001	14.62	12.91				2.18
2002	12.72	8.53				2.12
2003	13.59	9.39				2.26
2004	13.78	9.52				2.29
2005	13.96	9.67				2.31
2006	14.24	9.81				2.35
2007	15.06	10.36				2.48
2008	16.73	11.32				2.75
2009	18.72	12.66		4.33		2.82
2010	20.04	13.50		4.64		3.26
2011	22.40	15.20	6.23	5.05	0.96	3.63
2012	25.30	17.38	6.83	5.58	1.09	4.38
2013	28.82	20.05	7.47	6.18	1.32	4.97
2014	31.83	22.20	8.15	6.77	1.48	5.47
2015	34.38	24.66	8.39	6.90	1.57	5.87
2016	36.16	25.73	8.82	7.21	1.61	6.14
2017	37.53	26.95	8.93	7.27	1.65	6.36
2018	39.35	28.15	9.49	7.77	1.71	6.65
2019	40.65	29.12	9.81	8.06	1.71	6.86
2020	41.14	29.66	9.76	8.04	1.72	7.12

19-4 分等级医疗卫生机构情况(2020)
Health Care Institutions by Level(2020)

单位:个 (unit)

项 目	Iem	合计 Total	三级 Thrid-level	二级 Second-level	一级 First-level	其他 Others
医院	**Hospitals**	**1048**	**143**	**361**	**267**	**277**
综合医院	General Hospitals	560	73	166	173	148
中医医院	Hosptials Specialized in Traditional Chinese Medicine	123	23	63	21	16
中西医结合医院	Hospitals of Traditional Chinese Medicine and Western Medicine	24	5	6	9	4
民族医院	Minortiy Hospitals	2		2		
专科医院	Specialized Hosptials	326	42	124	61	99
妇幼保健院	**Women and Children Care Agencies**	**96**	**12**	**82**		**2**
专科疾病防治院	**Specialized Prevention & Treatment Centers**	**12**		**1**	**3**	**8**

19-5 医院业务工作开展情况
Basic Statistics on Hospital Business

项 目	Item	2000	2005	2010	2015	2019	2020
机构数 (个)	Number of Institutions (unit)	507	574	603	869	1034	1048
诊疗总人次数 (万人次)	Number of Clients (10 000 person-times)	4616.20	5452.11	7710.20	12111.16	15063.05	11788.88
#门、急诊人次数 (万人次)	Number of Outpacients and Emergency (10 000 person-times)	4396.10	5107.19	7533.44	11721.98	14617.36	11281.40
出院人数 (万人)	Number of Discharged Patients (10 000 persons)	158.93	219.45	423.28	780.05	993.54	712.66
死亡 (万人)	Dead (10 000 persons)	1.59	2.28	3.13	3.81	4.67	4.93
病死率 (%)	Rate of Death from Illness (%)	1.08	1.04	0.74	0.49	0.47	0.69
病床平均周转次数 (次)	Average times of Beds Usage (time)	18.7	24.0	32.5	34.0	35.5	25.5
病床平均工作日 (日)	Average Day of Beds Usage (day)	218.8	268.2	350.4	337.4	336.1	263.1
病床使用率 (%)	Utilization Rate of Beds (%)	59.94	73.49	96.01	92.44	92.09	72.07
出院者平均住院日 (日)	Average Days for Hospitalization Discharged (day)	11.1	10.7	10.5	9.8	9.3	10.1

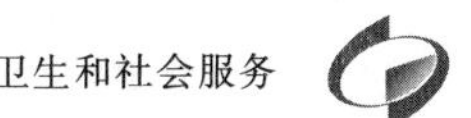

19-6 农村村级卫生组织情况
Statistics on Health Care Institutions at Village Level

项 目	Item	2000	2005	2010	2015	2019	2020
村设置的医疗点数（个）	**Medical care Station Set by Villages (unit)**	**26879**	**21136**	**24057**	**24795**	**23230**	**23199**
#村或集体办	Set by Villages or Collective Set	14666	11207	15395	15495	14452	14373
联合办	Set with Village Doctors	4640	3777	2815	2984	2765	2680
医院设点	Set by Hospital	2403	2410	3348	3559	3410	3912
私人办	Set by Individual	4344	2907	1833	1922	1254	1206
其他	Others	826	835	666	835	1349	1028
乡村医生和卫生员人数（人）	**Number of Village Doctors and Medical Working Personel (person)**	**57511**	**34417**	**41473**	**40897**	**34460**	**32683**
#乡村医生	Village Doctors	44490	33375	40425	38970	32780	31206
卫生员	Medical Working Persone	1301	1042	1048	1927	1680	1477

主要统计指标解释

卫生机构 包括医疗机构、疾病预防控制中心（防疫站）、采供血机构、卫生监督及监测(检验)机构、医学科研和在职培训机构、健康教育所等。

医疗机构 包括医院、社区卫生服务中心(站)、疗养院、卫生院、门诊部、诊所(卫生所、医务室)、妇幼保健院(所、站)、专科疾病防治院(所、站)、急救中心(站)和临床检验中心。医疗机构分为非赢利性医疗机构和赢利性医疗机构。

医院 包括综合医院、中医医院、中西医结合医院、民族医院、各类专科医院和护理院。

卫生技术人员 指卫生机构中医生、护理人员、药剂人员、检验人员等卫生技术人员。

医生 指在医疗、预防保健机构工作且取得《执业医师证书》的执业医师和执业助理医师。

Explanatory Notes on Main Statistical Indicators

Health Care Institutions include medical institutions, disease prevention and control centers (epidemic prevention stations), blood gathering and supplying institutions, health supervision and inspection (check up) institutions, medicinal scientific research and on-job training institutions, health education and so on.

Medical Organizations include hospitals, health service centers (stations) of communities, nursing homes, health centers, clinics, clinics (health stations and infirmaries), maternity and child care agencies (centers and stations), special disease prevention and curing agencies (centers and stations), first aid centers (stations) and clinical inspection centers. Medical organizations are grouped by two types: profit-making and non-profit-making medical organizations.

Hospitals include polyclinics, traditional Chinese medical hospitals, hospitals integrated with traditional Chinese therapeutics and western therapeutics, ethical hospitals, various specialties hospitals and nursing hospitals.

Medical Technical Personnel refers to doctors, assistant nurses, pharmacists, and laboratory technicians working in medical institutions.

Doctors refer to certified physicians and certified assistant physicians with certifications working in medical and health care and prevention agencies.

20

文化和体育

Culture and Sports

资料整理人员:范　维　　谢　涛　　陶　涛

20-1 文化事业机构、人员数
Number of Cultural Institutions and Personnel

单位:个、人 (unit, person)

项 目	Item	2014	2015	2016	2017	2018	2019	2020
艺术业机构	Art Performing Institution	328	340	366	538	550	456	456
#剧团	Troupes	273	282	308	473	489	390	390
#剧场	Theater	52	58	58	65	61	66	66
文物事业机构	Historical Relics Institutions	300	302	310	325	326	336	340
#博物馆	Museums	174	175	183	199	200	213	215
图书馆事业机构	Library Institutions	112	112	112	116	115	116	116
群众文化事业机构	Public Culture Institutions	1390	1399	1402	1406	1406	1405	1405
文化馆	Cultural Centers	121	122	123	125	125	124	124
文化站	Art Center	1269	1277	1279	1281	1281	1281	1281
艺术业人员数	Number of People Engaged in Art Performing	9774	10596	9969	12785	13200	11672	11650
#剧团人员	Staff in Troupes	8520	8999	8699	11464	11853	10857	10911
#剧场人员	Staff in Theater	1241	1597	1270	1321	1347	1085	1090
文物事业人员数	Number of Historical Relics Staffs	4928	5025	5162	5428	5557	5563	5560
#博物馆人员	Number of Staff in Library	3380	3449	3556	3956	4032	4218	4220
图书馆事业人员数	Number of People Engaged in Library	2231	2212	2198	2204	2128	2101	2115
群众文化事业人员数	Number of People Engaged in Public Art	5045	4869	4945	5037	5099	5162	5165
文化馆人员	Number of People in Cultural Centers	2294	2230	2220	2189	2158	2076	2115
文化站人员	Number of People in Art Centers	2751	2639	2725	2848	2941	3086	3085
#乡镇文化站	Township Cultural Stations	2234	2109	2159	2258	2344	2460	2500

20-2 公共图书馆发展情况
Development Statistics on Public Libraries

项 目	Item	2016	2017	2018	2019	2020
机构数 （个）	Number of Library (unit)	112	116	115	116	116
藏书数 （万册）	Total Collections (10 000 volumes)	3318	3597	3910	4221	4559
书架单层总长度 （万米）	Total Length of Bookshelves (10 000 m)	56	55	55	57	57
有效借书证数图书流通情况 （万个）	Valid Library Card Uumber (10 000 units)	167	187	212	220	226
公共图书馆流通人次 （万人次）	Number of Circulation The Public Library Circulation (10 000 person-times)	2082	2388	2577	2646	1350
册次 （万册数）	Volume-time (10 000 volume-times)	1882	2136	2210	2298	2311
为读者服务举办各种活动次数 （次）	Service for Readers Times (time)	4874	5236	4875	5508	3321
参加人数 （万人次）	Number of Readers Involved (10 000 person-times)	233	231	278	290	111
当年新购图书 （万册）	New Books Purchaesd in 2017 (10 000 volume-times)	296	284	359	304	338
图书费 （万元）	Purchase Expenses (10 000 yuan)	7948	8358	8244	8844	8825

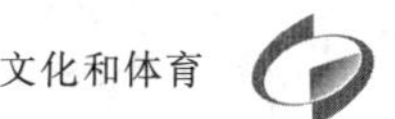

20-3 公共图书馆藏书及分类情况
Statistics on Books and Classification in Public Libraries

单位：万册 (10 000 volumes)

年 份 Year	合 计 Total	#外文 Foreign	#古籍 Ancient	#图书 New Books	其它藏量 Other Reserves
1996	1472	82	97		
1997	1533	81	97		
1998	1599	81	96		
1999	1643	81	96		
2000	1678	82	97		
2001	1709	83	98		
2002	1759	81	99		
2003	1819	83	98		
2004	1867		94		
2005	1923		97		
2006	1981		100		
2007	2037		96		
2008	2106		97		
2009	2181		96		
2010	2361		95		
2011	2410		98	1860	453
2012	2521		98	2008	415
2013	2648		99	2156	393
2014	2822		101	2295	426
2015	3003		101	2462	441
2016	3318		98	2752	468
2017	3597		98	2963	536
2018	3910		97	3259	554
2019	4221		97	3547	577
2020	4559		97	3852	610

20-4 图书、报纸、期刊出版情况
Statistics on Publication of Books, Newspapers and Periodicals

项 目	Item	2000	2005	2010	2015	2017	2018	2019	2020
一、图书出版种数（种）	**Category of Library Books Published (kind)**	**4529**	**6535**	**10464**	**15543**	**13590**	**13419**	**13052**	**13209**
新出版（种）	New Publications (kind)	2443	3739	6328	8932	7404	6852	5847	5692
总印数（千册）	Total Prints (1 000 volume)	288416	345510	275330	262997	229726	268349	317003	295608
总印张（千印张）	Total Number of Paper Printed (1 000 pages)	1552128	2495183	1997639	2250020	1883288	2099493	2359553	2202692
二、期刊出版种数（种）	**Category of Magazines Published (kind)**	**391**	**407**	**407**	**412**	**415**	**415**	**415**	**417**
总印数（千册）	Total Prints (1 000 volume)	220280	196800	300770	251249	143353	118719	104492	70517
总印张（千印张）	Total Number of Paper Printed (1 000 pages)	746145	745526	1482345	1458924	757916	599399	514356	382809
三、报刊出版种数（种）	**Category of Newspapers and Periodicals Published (kind)**	**164**	**193**	**130**	**129**	**129**	**129**	**129**	**129**
总印数（千份）	Total Prints (1 000 copies)	1342282	1956980	1816720	1539203	1064036	899099	732377	571937
总印张（万印张）	Total Number of Paper Printed (10 000 pages)	339434	520833	889514	538040	297345	240632	2058148	1542870

20-5 艺术活动、群众文化活动、图书馆及博物馆活动情况
Statistics on Art Activities, Public Culture Activities, Library and Museum

项　目	Item	2000	2005	2010	2015	2018	2019	2020
艺术表演团体	**Art Performance Troupes**							
演出场次　(万场次)	Number of Performances　(10 000 shows)				3.85	6.69	5.17	3.62
国内演出观众人数 (万人次)	Number of Domestic Audience (10 000 person-times)				2902	4426	6119	3853
艺术表演场馆	**Art Performance Places**							
演(映)出场次 (万场次)	Number of Performances　(10 000 shows)				3.49	6.74	5.20	3.11
观众人次　(万人次)	Number of Audience (10 000 person-times)				288	308	297	115.6
群众文化活动	**Public Culture Activities**							
举办展览个数　(个)	Number of Expo Displayed　(unit)	2785	2653	4276	4399	6309	6332	3554
举办训练班结业人数 (万人次)	Number of Training Activities (10 000 person-times)	9.90	13.00	10.80	97.6	159.3	163.11	83.66
图书馆活动	**Library Activities**							
书刊文献外借人次 (千人次)	Number of Circulation (1 000 person-times)				9918	11429	12212	8562
图书流通册次　(千册)	Number of Circulation　(1 000 volumes)	9485	9267	18462	18164	22103	22975.88	23106
博物馆活动	**Museum Activities**							
基本陈列展览　(个)	Displays Exhibition　(unit)	210	218	686	964	1003	1140	512
参观人数　(千人次)	Visitors　(1 000 person-times)	1819	2194	19212	26239	39225	41100	28567

20-6 文化、文物事业经费支出及基本建设情况
Basic Conditions about Expenditures and Constructionon Culture and Historical Relics

单位：万元 (10 000 yuan)

项 目	Item	2016	2017	2018	2019	2020
文化、文物事业经费支出总计	**Total Expenditures on Culture and Historical Relics**	**571068**	**706865**	**847487**	**1391964.2**	**1418040.9**
文化事业	Culture	416761	515684	663403	1221224	1246616.8
艺术表演团体	Art Performing Groups	74001	93532	103203	112135	120154.5
艺术表演场所	Art Performing Places	10828	22924	26723	20672	21775.8
图书馆	Library	49833	58296	62461	62709	63015.5
群众文化	Public Culture	68180	81421	54823	49354	50114.6
中等专业学校	Secondary Vocation School	22985	21508			
干部训练	Cadre Taining					
其他文化事业	Others	191165	27946	19070	19849	20050.6
文物事业	Historical Relics	154307	191181	184084	170741	171424.1
博物馆	Museum	101517	103765	113859	112266	112305.5
文物事业机构	Institutions of Historical Relics	24814	57771	43886	50445	51123.0
其它文物事业	Others	27976	29645	26339	8029	7995.6
文化、文物基本建设完成投资	Investment in Culture & Historical Relics Cause Construction	45187	76822	30510	16576	16317.2
文化事业	Culture Cause	25945	40955	13206	2297	2350.7
文物事业	Historical Relics Cause	19242	35867	17304	14280	13966.5

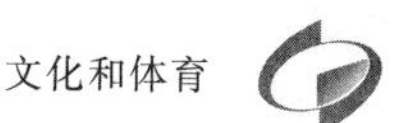

20-7 广播电视从业人员基本情况(2020)
Basic Statistics on Personnel Engaged in Broadcasting and Television(2020)

单位:人 (person)

项 目	Item	全省合计 Total of the Province	省级 Provincial Level	市州级 Municiple and Prefecture Level	县级 County Level
从业人员	**Personel**	**36887**	**22984**	**5314**	**8589**
其中:长期职工	Long-term Staff and Workers	35208	21880	5282	8046
按岗位分:	**Classified by Job Division:**				
管理人员	Management Personel	7004	3370	1235	2399
专业技术人员	Professional Technical Personel	19922	11699	3565	4658
编辑、记者	Editors and Reporters	6376	1953	1854	2569
播音员、主持人	Announcers and Hosts	1010	211	396	403
按学历分:	**Classified by Academic Qualifications:**				
研究生及以上	Graduate and Above	1595	1187	290	118
本科及大专	Undergraduate and Post-secondary	27660	15762	4650	7248
高中及以下	High School and Below	7632	6035	374	1223
按职称分:	**Classified According to Occupation:**				
正高	Senior	233	164	59	10
副高	Vice-senior	1189	637	422	130
中级	Medium	6607	2919	1685	2003
初级及以下	Primary and Below	18689	12349	2606	3734
按年龄分:	**Classified by Age:**				
35岁以下	35 and Below	13013	9007	1593	2413
36岁至50岁	36-50	17457	10574	2606	4277
50岁以上	50 and Above	6417	3403	1115	1899

20-8 广播电视传输覆盖情况
Statistics on Broadcasting and TV Coverage Rating

项 目	Item	2010	2015	2018	2019	2020
广播综合人口覆盖率 (%)	Broadcasting Coverage Rate (%)	98.10	99.08	99.68	99.79	99.86
电视综合人口覆盖率 (%)	TV Coverage Rate (%)	98.11	98.98	99.58	99.70	99.82
有线电视实际用户数 (万户)	Cable Television Users (10 000 household)	894.07	1067.80	1082.77	1071.48	1202.63
中短波发射台 (座)	Medium- and Short-Wave Broadcasting Transmitting Station (set)	26	28	28	26	27
中短波发射机 (部)	Medium- and Short-Wave Transmitter (set)	76	88	89	91	97
中短波发射机功率 (千瓦)	Power of Medium- and Short-Wave Transmitter (kw)	1256	1391	1376	1400	1712
调频电视转播发射台 (座)	FM and Television Transmitting Stations (set)		481	181	404	373
调频发射机 (部)	FM Transmitters (set)	584	484	438	372	302
调频发射机功率 (千瓦)	Power of FM Transmitters (kw)	520.31	623.69	727.65	728.96	921.58
电视发射机 (座)	Television Transmitting Station (set)			739	1397	1185
电视发射机功率 (千瓦)	Power of Television Transmitters (kw)	592.22	598.69	585.12	727.23	662.80
微波线路站数/长度 (座/公里)	Length of Micro-Wave Route Per Station (set/km)	121/2961.05	126/2875.05	73/2158.60	63/2073.90	58/2111.00

注:2017 年起调频发射机台统计口径发生变化。
Note: Since 2017, the Statistical Caliber of FM transmitter has changed.

20-9 广播电视宣传、节目制作和电影活动
Radio and Television Promotion, Program Production and Film Activities

项 目	Item	2005	2010	2018	2019	2020
广播电台 （座）	Broadcasting Station (unit)	11	11	5	1	1
电视台 （座）	TV Station (unit)	12	12	5	1	1
广播电视台 （座）	Radiated TV Station (unit)	71	71	79	82	82
广播节目套数 （套）	Number of Radio Programs (unit)	81	85	94	96	98
广播平均日播音时间 （小时）	Average Broadcasting Hour per Week (h)	1040.40	1225.65	1466.00	1443.00	1603.42
广播节目年制作能力 （万小时）	Annual Capacity of Radio Program Production (10 000 h)	20.59	23.54	24.29	24.67	22.50
电视节目套数 （套）	Number of TV Programs (unit)	113	114	117	116	114
电视平均周播出时间 （万小时）	Average TV Hour per Week (10 000 h)	1.05	1.26	1.38	1.35	1.35
电视节目年制作能力 （万小时）	Annual Capacity of TV Program Production (10 000 h)	7.93	9.48	10.37	8.80	9.27
电视剧制作 （部/集）	Production of TV Series (episode)	11/208	11/314	5/215	2/91	3/130
城市电影活动	Movie of City					
放映场次数 （万场）	Times Projected (10 000 times)			465.10	517.63	159.75
观众人数 （千人次）	Number of the Audience (1 000 person-times)			84620.00	8189.65	2397.29

20-10 分单位类型、分人员类型体育系统从业人员数(2020)
Number of Staff and Workers in Sports Commissions by Unit Type and Personnel Type(2020)

单位:人 (person)

项 目	Item	合计 Total	公务员 Civilian	管理人员 Administrator	专业技术人员 小计 Subtotal	其中:教练员 Coach	其中:科研人员 Scientific Research Personnel	其中:卫生技术人员 Health Technical Personnel	运动员 Athlete	工勤人员 Worker	其他 Others
合计	**Total**	**6208**	**919**	**1284**	**816**	**767**	**25**	**24**	**1166**	**310**	**1713**
体育行政机关	Sports Administrative Authority	1320	919	213	18	18				40	130
运动项目管理部门(优秀运动队)	Sports Management Department	1316		156	188	185		3	947	11	14
本科院校	Undergraduate School	1110		149	43	43			191		727
体育运动学校	Sports School for Athelets	462		76	157	148	9		5	8	216
少年儿童体育学校	Sports School for Kids	559		120	246	244	1	1	17	27	149
体育中学	Middle School for Athelets	38		8	13	13				2	15
训练基地	Training Base	131		74	25	25			6	17	9
体育场馆	Stadium	699		263	82	81		1		180	174
体育科研机构	Sports Science Reaserch Institution	42		6	34		15	19			2
其他事业单位	Other Institution	517		207	10	10				23	277
其它	Others	14		12						2	

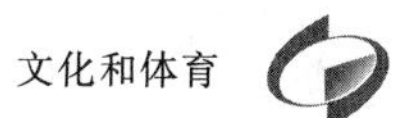

20-11 等级裁判员、运动员情况
Number of Athletes and Referees in Grades

单位:人 (person)

项 目	Item	2000	2005	2010	2014	2015	2016	2017	2018	2019	2020
等级裁判员合计	**Number of Referees in Grades**	**1195**	**787**	**1504**	**1725**	**3021**	**1206**	**1910**	**1625**	**924**	**746**
国际裁判	International Referees							6	6	6	1
国家级裁判	National Referees	29	25	24		4	2	21	39	29	27
一级裁判	First Grade	143	115	352	394	317	176	416	471	288	297
二级裁判	Second Grade	1023	647	1128	1331	2700	1028	1467	1109	601	421
等级运动员合计	**Number of Athletes in Grade**	**418**	**1149**	**1639**	**2111**	**1556**	**2036**	**1987**	**1814**	**1692**	**1218**
国际运动健将	International Master of Sports	6		1	4	4			23	9	2
运动健将	Master of Sports	36	36	21	41	68	5	5	50	111	26
一级运动员	First Grade	10	247	180	359	316	427	382	408	367	366
二级运动员	Second Grade	366	866	1437	1707	1168	1604	1600	1333	1205	824

20-12 体育竞赛成果情况
Statistics on Achievement in Sports Competition

项 目	Item	2000	2005	2010	2015	2017	2018	2019	2020
世界比赛获奖牌数（枚）	**Number of Medals Won in International Games (unit)**	**13**	**5**	**12**	**66**	**116**	**113**	**169**	**32**
金牌	Gold Medal	4	3	2	29	48	60	73	18
银牌	Silver Medal	6	2	3	32	28	27	50	7
铜牌	Bronze Medal	3		7	5	40	26	46	7
亚洲比赛获奖牌数（枚）	**Number of Medals Won in Asia Games (unit)**	**5**	**7**	**13**	**35**	**34**	**51**	**62**	
金牌	Gold Medal	4	5	8	17	18	17	30	
银牌	Silver Medal		2	4	9	10	21	16	
铜牌	Bronze Medal	1		1	9	6	13	16	
全国比赛获前六名（人）	**Top Six Places in National Games (person)**		**155**	**134**	**502**	**651**	**855**	**1266**	**530**
第一名	First Place	35	24	21	75	107	172	230	124
第二名	Second Place	22	23	21	78	123	149	218	92
第三名	Third Place	21	27	17	85	124	167	275	88
第四名	Fourth Place	35	24	23	76	99	125	159	78
第五名	Fifth Place	29	31	30	109	135	153	238	92
第六名	Sixth Place	26	26	22	79	63	89	146	56

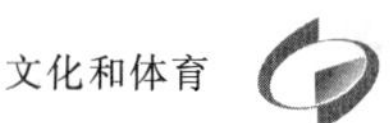

20-13 新建健身场地设施情况(2020)
Situation of New-Built Fitness Facilities(2020)

项 目	Item	合计 Total	村级农民体育健身工程 Town-based Peasant Fitness Project	乡镇体育健身工程 County-based Fitness Project	全民健身路径工程 Citizen Fitness Path Project	全民健身活动中心 Citizen Fitness Center
数量 (个)	Number (unit)	5403	1120	190	3792	23
器材件数 (件)	Number of Instrument (piece)	16538			16538	
场地面积(平方米)	Area (sq. m)	1609794	669352	248150	334969	117927
场地长度 (米)	Length (m)	129400				
投资总额 (万元)	Total Invenstment (10 000 yuan)	46664	6422	7850	5519	14421

20-13 续表 continued

项 目	Item	户外健身场地设施 Outdoor Fitness Facilities					其他场地设施 Other Fitness Facilities
		体育公园 Fitness Park	全民健身广场 Citizen Fitness Square	户外体育营地 Outdoor Fitness Center	社区运动场地 Community-based Fitness Square	健身步道 Fitness Path	
数量 (个)	Number (unit)	5	64	4	68	14	123
器材件数 (件)	Number of Instrument (piece)						
场地面积(平方米)	Area (sq. m)	81318	31734	20000	48266		58078
场地长度 (米)	Length (m)					129400	
投资总额 (万元)	Total Invenstment (10 000 yuan)	2380.00	985.00	500.00	1655.30	5710.00	1221.19

20-14 分市州文化及相关产业“三上”法人单位数(2020)
Number of Legal Persons of Culture and Relavant Industry above Designated by Region(2020)

单位:个 (unit)

地 区	Region	“三上”法人单位数 Legal Persons	规上文化制造业 Cultual Manufacturing	限上文化批发和零售业 Wholesale and Rerail of Culture	规上文化服务业 Services of Culture
全 省	**Province**	**2967**	**925**	**608**	**1434**
武汉市	Wuhan	928	104	108	716
黄石市	Huangshi	73	23	17	33
十堰市	Shiyan	154	24	55	75
宜昌市	Yichang	460	141	97	222
襄阳市	Xiangyang	332	127	104	101
鄂州市	Ezhou	53	24	7	22
荆门市	Jingmen	128	53	39	36
孝感市	Xiaogan	150	101	27	22
荆州市	Jingzhou	112	39	38	35
黄冈市	Huanggang	192	124	28	40
咸宁市	Xianning	166	81	24	61
随州市	Suizhou	48	20	5	23
恩施自治州	Enshi	88	20	40	28
仙桃市	Xiantao	41	20	13	8
潜江市	Qianjiang	15	9	2	4
天门市	Tianmen	23	15	4	4
神农架林区	Shennongjia	4			4

20-15 分市州规模以上文化制造业企业基本情况(2020)
Basic Conditions Cultural Manufacturing Enterprises above Designated Size by Region(2020)

单位:万元 (10 000 yuan)

地 区	Region	企业单位数(个) Number of Enterprises (unit)	年末从业人员(人) Engaged Person at Year-end (person)	资产总计 Total Assets	营业收入 Business Revenue	税金及附加 Taxes and Extra Charges on Business	营业利润 Operating Profit	应交增值税 Value-added Tax Payable
全 省	**Province**	**925**	**143422**	**13668253.5**	**16351527.2**	**129746.5**	**967023.6**	**314305.2**
武汉市	Wuhan	104	15723	3010103.4	2110938.6	8521.7	116299.2	50530.0
黄石市	Huangshi	23	4714	184359.6	118720.6	751.0	7826.4	2022.2
十堰市	Shiyan	24	2071	231482.0	168148.9	2567.1	22280.9	5975.7
宜昌市	Yichang	141	29800	2456056.7	2537531.9	18430.8	161143.2	73513.7
襄阳市	Xiangyang	127	17634	1460542.9	3638652.0	28407.6	269795.9	81440.6
鄂州市	Ezhou	24	2184	174734.4	490113.3	2731.7	36740.1	6618.7
荆门市	Jingmen	53	7607	923345.5	1192734.7	9856.6	47628.8	11572.6
孝感市	Xiaogan	101	15640	1187117.2	2177012.6	29984.7	96660.4	20774.1
荆州市	Jingzhou	39	6136	1228496.7	716789.5	2766.7	19723.7	13310.6
黄冈市	Huanggang	124	17942	1069120.1	893956.8	8847.9	53690.7	21121.3
咸宁市	Xianning	81	9115	783387.0	953236.4	4853.2	36524.4	6259.0
随州市	Suizhou	20	3647	208976.7	379440.3	2930.1	36459.1	6429.0
恩施自治州	Enshi	20	1268	43683.6	69823.0	613.0	1417.2	1050.7
仙桃市	Xiantao	20	3536	319337.8	319230.0	2471.1	19684.5	8231.1
潜江市	Qianjiang	9	1264	177924.6	172285.4	4720.2	12968.3	2148.5
天门市	Tianmen	15	5141	209585.3	412913.2	1293.1	28180.8	3307.4
神农架林区	Shennongjia							

20-16 分市州限额以上文化批发和零售企业基本情况(2020)
Basic Conditions of Enterprises of Wholesale and Retail of Culture above Designated Size by Region(2020)

单位:万元 (10 000 yuan)

地 区	Region	企业单位数(个) Number of Enterprises (unit)	年末从业人员(人) Engaged Person at Year-end (person)	资产总计 Total Assets	营业收入 Business Revenue	税金及附加 Taxes and Extra Charges on Business	营业利润 Operating Profit	应交增值税 Value-added Tax Payable
全 省	**Province**	**608**	**22277**	**3058985.8**	**3518364.1**	**20883.5**	**153279.1**	**52035.5**
武汉市	Wuhan	108	8303	2152567.7	1735915.6	4920.8	49612.2	18113.1
黄石市	Huangshi	17	274	17276.2	24772.8	92.9	248.5	337.8
十堰市	Shiyan	55	1152	59283.6	83952.5	859.8	3963.6	2804.3
宜昌市	Yichang	97	2652	217658.0	440314.8	3946.9	25883.1	8662.2
襄阳市	Xiangyang	104	2473	115196.8	391613.4	5135.5	38636.9	4522.0
鄂州市	Ezhou	7	263	25123.9	62309.8	55.7	-81.4	372.8
荆门市	Jingmen	39	648	30352.3	139840.8	1135.1	11193.1	3874.6
孝感市	Xiaogan	27	2278	92824.9	128035.3	628.7	3548.2	1544.4
荆州市	Jingzhou	38	792	46205.1	125321.9	1377.1	3311.2	1683.6
黄冈市	Huanggang	28	776	42575.8	75211.3	265.0	810.6	1026.2
咸宁市	Xianning	24	529	130489.6	126845.8	684.4	7806.1	6868.3
随州市	Suizhou	5	144	2364.8	6856.7	167.3	433.8	100.6
恩施自治州	Enshi	40	1318	73910.4	97531.1	863.7	-682.0	778.1
仙桃市	Xiantao	13	345	23818.3	36474.1	472.6	7296.0	859.2
潜江市	Qianjiang	2	174	16893.9	20829.7	110.3	-322.1	124.3
天门市	Tianmen	4	156	12444.5	22538.5	167.7	1621.3	364.0
神农架林区	Shennongjia							

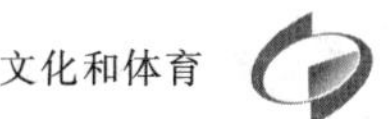

20-17 分市州规模以上文化服务业企业基本情况(2020)
Basic Conditions of Enterprises of Services of Culture above Designated by Region(2020)

单位:万元 (10 000 yuan)

地 区	Region	企业单位数(个) Number of Enterprises (unit)	年末从业人员(人) Engaged Person at Year-end (person)	资产总计 Total Assets	营业收入 Business Revenue	税金及附加 Taxes and Extra Charges on Business	营业利润 Operating Profit	应交增值税 Value-added Tax Payable
全 省	**Province**	**1434**	**200323**	**40138984.1**	**18093504.3**	**171782.9**	**1258573.4**	**354886.7**
武汉市	Wuhan	716	156980	31088098.8	16519775.8	153574.6	1176528.1	314703.7
黄石市	Huangshi	33	1801	203493.4	54588.3	213.7	-3757.3	1429.5
十堰市	Shiyan	75	3941	441776.1	105639.8	1434.5	7966.4	3159.2
宜昌市	Yichang	222	14403	2357453.2	525003.2	6188.6	74575.3	17901.4
襄阳市	Xiangyang	101	4623	542536.4	270644.7	2726.4	27738.9	5618.4
鄂州市	Ezhou	22	876	229032.8	27991.6	438.6	-8589.1	433.5
荆门市	Jingmen	36	2303	3078194.0	113911.0	4369.6	-5388.7	597.0
孝感市	Xiaogan	22	1087	146665.1	33609.0	135.4	-1957.1	1130.8
荆州市	Jingzhou	35	4240	191546.9	150938.9	595.7	7411.3	3927.1
黄冈市	Huanggang	40	2215	602548.7	26519.5	526.4	-2993.0	776.3
咸宁市	Xianning	61	2176	283555.6	66968.5	595.3	6502.8	1680.4
随州市	Suizhou	23	1117	250466.7	38750.1	115.5	-4480.4	180.9
恩施自治州	Enshi	28	2122	456177.0	109918.0	717.7	-10760.5	2164.6
仙桃市	Xiantao	8	1705	60343.6	36723.7	99.0	12141.4	957.3
潜江市	Qianjiang	4	103	3967.7	2901.8	5.1	-192.3	24.7
天门市	Tianmen	4	127	8476.9	6311.6	28.9	1480.3	126.3
神农架林区	Shennongjia	4	504	194651.2	3308.8	17.9	-17652.7	75.6

主要统计指标解释

文化事业机构 指从事专业文化工作和为专业文化工作服务的独立建制的单位。不包括这些单位另外举办独立核算的其他机构和各部门的业余文化组织。该指标主要反映文化事业机构发展规模水平。

艺术表演团体 指从事戏曲、音乐、舞蹈、杂技等专业艺术表演,有独立帐户的单位,不包括半工半艺、半农半艺和民间职业剧团。该指标主要反映全国专业艺术表演团体发展规模水平。

艺术表演观众人数(人次) 指售票、包场演出或民族地区免费演出的艺术表演观众人次数,不包括彩排审查和内部观摩演出的观看人次数。该指标主要反映全国观看专业艺术表演团体演出的效益规模。

等级运动员 是指经考核正式批准授予运动员称号的运动员,等级称号由高到低依次为国际级运动健将、运动健将、一级运动员、二级运动员、三级运动员。

广播节目综合人口覆盖率 指根据国家广电总局制定的《广播电视人口覆盖率统计技术标准和方法》进行统计调查的,在对象区能接收到由中央、省、地区或县通过无线、有线或卫星等技术方式传播的各级广播节目的人口数占全国总人口数的百分比。

电视节目综合人口覆盖率 指根据国家广电总局制定的《广播电视人口覆盖率统计技术标准和方法》进行统计调查的,在对象区能接收到由中央、省、地区或县通过无线、有线或卫星等技术方式传播的各级电视节目的人口数占全国总人口数的百分比。

Explanatory Notes on Main Statistical Indicators

Cultural Institutions refer to units, which have their own organizational system and independent accounting system and specialize in or serve cultural development. They exclude other establishments run by these cultural institutions and amateur cultural groups established by various departments. This indicator reflects the development of cultural units.

Art Troupe refers to the troupe which is engaged in drama, opera, music, dance, acrobatics or other art performance, opens independent accounts with banks and has self-supporting accounting system; excluding the troupes which are engaged partly in industrial or agricultural activities, partly in art performance and the professional troupes organized by the people. This indicator reflects the development of national professional art troupes.

Number of Audience at Art Performance refers to the number of attendants at commercial shows, completely booked shows or free shows given in minority national areas, and does not include the number of spectators at rehearsals for examination and internal shows for study.

Certified Grade Athletes refer to those who are awarded the title of athletes through assessment. The titles rank from high to low as: international level athletes, national level athletes, first grade athletes, second grade athletes and third grade athletes.

Radio Coverage of Population refers to the percentage of population, which can receive central, provincial, city, prefecture, and county radio programs relayed by wireless, cable, satellite and other technical means, in the surveying area, to national total population, according to Statistical Standard and Method on Television and Radio Coverage of Population established by the State Administration of Broadcasting, Film and Television.

Television Coverage of Population refers to the percentage of population, which can receive central, provincial, city, prefecture, and county television programs relayed by wireless, cable, satellite and other technical means, in the surveying area, to national total population, according to Statistical Standard and Method on Television and Radio Coverage of Population established by the State Administration of Broadcasting, Film and Television.

21

公共管理及其他

Public Management and Other

资料整理人员:范　维

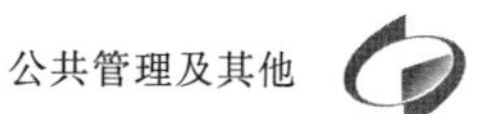

21-1 工会组织情况
Basic Statistics on Labor Union

年 份 Year	工会基层组织数（个） Number of Grassroot Labor Union Organizations (unit)	全省已建工会的基层单位职工与会员人数（万人）Number of Grassroot Staff and Workers and Members of Established Labor Union in the Province(10 000 persons)				工会专职工作人员人数（万人） Number of Fulltime Workers in Labor Union (10 000 persons)
		职工人数 Number of Staff and Workers	#女职工 Women Workers	会员人数 Number of Members	#女会员 Women Members	
1975	18872	280.22	83.18	174.72	56.24	0.87
1980	22802	387.95	139.20	299.41	94.91	1.04
1985	25286	484.68	192.32	404.58	156.62	2.76
1990	33990	559.00	227.00	498.00	198.00	3.40
1995	28461	564.34	230.90	511.11	207.49	1.81
1996	28459	584.30	238.16	527.09	213.08	2.88
1997	20151	472.60	192.65	419.72	168.89	2.68
1998	17488	445.80	183.90	400.90	163.90	2.30
1999	18976	442.97	178.21	396.90	155.03	3.18
2000	45251	532.31	197.81	475.57	176.87	2.45
2001	111309	728.94	218.68	660.82	198.25	2.45
2004	50391	755.90	276.69	721.46	262.74	2.95
2005	54893	856.07	298.78	771.95	279.94	3.09
2006	61627	904.15	314.67	856.95	296.39	3.76
2007	69886	1004.92	358.44	972.30	345.64	3.94
2008	79048	1099.78	382.72	1073.22	377.43	4.48
2009	83436	1160.45	418.82	1127.68	411.12	4.75
2010	88647	1220.52	437.50	1184.88	429.00	5.80
2011	107995	1319.08	462.18	1267.28	453.11	6.10
2012	120561	1336.09	491.49	1292.06	481.87	6.44
2013	130513	1348.45	494.94	1312.16	487.57	6.36
2014	130326	1325.35	495.91	1285.13	487.36	6.67
2015	130118	1355.78	505.27	1301.52	490.43	6.61
2016	131582	1385.96	515.29	1338.23	503.98	6.62
2017	132619	1395.86	516.85	1351.90	506.90	6.62
2018	133850	1384.92	517.48	1343.47	508.34	4.55
2019	131588	1394.14	521.80	1346.14	509.47	4.71
2020	116848	1246.00	469.28	1190.77	454.36	3.56

注：因文革期间工会统计中断，表中1975年数据根据年平均增长值推算。

Note: The data in 1975 were calculated by the average growth rate because Labor Union statistics had been suspended in the period of "The Great Cultural Revolution".

21-2 基层政权和村(居)委会情况
Basic Statistics on Grassroots Regime and Village Committees

单位:个 (unit)

年 份 Year	镇 Township	乡 Villages	街道办事处 Regional Office	居委会个数 Number of Committees	村委会个数 Number of Village Committees
1986	859	3700	178	3257	32796
1987	836	1257	186	3394	32738
1988	828	1260	215	3483	32354
1989	840	1143	298	3545	32094
1990	849	1123	293	3573	32703
1991	849	1121	307	3709	32595
1992	852	1117	297	3830	32716
1993	857	1097	214	3921	32674
1994	864	1092	218	3998	32636
1995	865	1038	236	4110	32547
1996	823	567	252	4170	32486
1997	840	552	252	4287	32393
1998	847	543	253	4364	32293
1999	850	488	271	4425	32187
2000	860	466	283	3619	32001
2001	735	228	250	3468	31191
2002	738	224	272	3265	27667
2003	735	224	273	3351	27127
2004	738	224	274	3356	26470
2005	733	217	277	3465	29534
2006	737	210	277	3545	25828
2007	734	210	279	3653	25722
2008	735	207	285	3794	25551
2009	740	204	283	3882	25517
2010	741	199	290	3983	25763
2011	742	194	297	4051	25643
2012	746	188	298	4032	25575
2013	757	175	300	4208	25452
2014	761	170	302	4187	25448
2015	761	168	304	4294	25109
2016	759	168	307	4390	25064
2017	761	165	308	4401	24970
2018	762	163	310	4528	23392
2019	760	162	327	4631	22653
2020	761	161	329	4808	22665

注:本表数据来源于湖北省民政厅。
Note: The data in this table come from the Department of Civil Affairs of Hubei Province.

21-3 提供住宿的社会服务床位数
Beds of Social Welfare Institutions with Accommodations

单位:万张 (10 000 beds)

年 份 Year	床位数 Number of Beds	#养老 The Aged	#儿童 Child	#其他 Other
2012	25.4	23.7	0.7	0.6
2013	25.2	23.4	0.7	0.6
2014	27.7	23.3	0.8	0.7
2015	24.3	22.5	0.5	0.8
2016	25.7	23.9	0.5	0.8
2017	25.4	23.6	0.4	0.8
2018	23.6	22.4	0.4	0.6
2019	26.6	25.5	0.4	0.7
2020	29.0	28.0	0.4	0.4

注:2018年社会服务床位数不含优抚(军休)床位数。
Note: The number of social service beds in 2018 does not include the number of special care (military rest) beds.

21-4 社会救助情况
Statistics on Social Assistance

单位:万人 (10 000 persons)

年 份 Year	城市居民最低生活保障人数 Number of Urban Residents Receiving Minimum Living Allowance	农村居民最低生活保障人数 Number of Rural Residents Receiving Minimum Living Allowance	城镇特困人员救助供养人数 Urban Households Livelihood Guaranteed in Five Aspects	农村特困人员救助供养人数 Rural Households Livelihood Guaranteed in Five Aspects
2012	129.5	230.7		
2013	125.9	235.7		
2014	107.1	221.6		
2015	84.6	159.5		
2016	55.3	138.2		
2017	45.9	137.9		
2018	37.8	133.8	0.8	24.8
2019	31.8	139.3	1.0	24.3
2020	30.7	144.6	1.0	24.0

21-5 社会保险基本情况
Basic Conditions about Social Insurance

年 份 Year	失业保险 Unemployment Insurance		城镇职工基本养老保险 Basic Endowment Insurance for Urban and Rural Employees		工伤保险年末参保人数（万人） Participants at Year-end (10 000 persons)	年末参加生育保险人数（万人） Number of People Participated in Maternity Insurance at Year-end (10 000 persons)	基本医疗保险 Basic medical insurance	
	年末参保人数（万人） Participants at Year-end (10 000 persons)	全年发放失业保险金（亿元） Unemployed Relief Released (100 million yuan)	年末参保职工人数（万人） Participants at Year-end (10 000 persons)	年末参保离退休人数（万人） Retirees (10 000 persons)			年末职工参保人数（万人） Urban Residents Participanting in Insurance at Year-end (10 000 persons)	年末城乡居民参保人数（万人） Rural Residents Participanting in Insurance at Year-end (10 000 persons)
1996	392.9	0.4	353.2		177.6	137.8		
1997	381.2	0.5	355.8		188.5	165.5		
1998	378.2	0.5	413.1	107.4	190.0	168.8		
1999	517.6	0.6	455.3	122.4	183.8	189.0		
2000	459.6	1.6	465.6	130.4	185.0	191.3		
2001	420.8	3.2	474.4	136.6	182.3	182.1		
2002	416.1	5.4	532.7	154.5	183.2	182.7		
2003	390.1	5.6	554.5	167.5	189.2	182.1		
2004	391.3	4.0	586.1	194.7	187.2	179.9		
2005	391.5	4.0	597.6	206.4	230.3	175.9		
2006	395.5	3.7	630.2	220.5	275.5	194.5		
2007	405.4	3.8	651.4	235.3	328.0	225.0		
2008	422.6	3.6	671.7	252.4	350.7	315.4		
2009	437.0	3.6	701.9	273.7	396.5	350.6		
2010	464.5	3.9	749.1	301.3	444.5	388.7	847.8	
2011	496.0	3.7	766.0	341.4	467.3	412.9	902.8	
2012	501.4	3.8	801.4	367.3	505.8	444.7	921.2	
2013	511.9	4.2	822.0	396.0	541.0	457.9	922.8	
2014	520.9	5.1	847.0	419.3	576.7	480.6	933.3	
2015	531.2	5.8	874.9	440.6	640.1	500.2	949.4	
2016	542.5	7.7	897.1	457.9	651.1	511.9	961.0	
2017	565.4	7.6	1020.5	526.1	656.6	522.1	1018.9	4606.3
2018	590.3	10.1	1047.5	554.1	675.6	540.0	1054.0	4532.2
2019	618.2	8.8	1100.5	584.3	717.6	577.7	1093.2	4469.4
2020	651.7	11.5	1147.9	596.8	745.8	645.9	1136.9	4446.1

21-6 参加基本养老保险人数
Number of Persons Participated in Basic Endowment Insurance

单位:万人 (10 000 persons)

年 份 Year	合 计 Total	职 工 Number of Employees	企业(含其他) Enterprises (including others)	离退休人员 Number of Retirees	企业(含其他) Enterprises (including others)	城乡居民基本养老保险 Endowment Insurance For Urban and Rural Residents
1996	353.2	353.2	353.2			
1997	355.8	355.8	355.8			
1998	520.5	413.1	413.1	107.4	107.4	
1999	577.7	455.3	455.3	122.4	122.4	
2000	596.0	465.6	465.6	130.4	130.4	
2001	611.0	474.4	474.4	136.6	136.6	
2002	687.2	532.7	481.5	154.5	147.2	
2003	722.0	554.5	501.1	167.5	158.6	
2004	780.8	586.1	530.6	194.7	184.5	
2005	804.0	597.6	539.8	206.4	195.1	
2006	850.7	630.2	570.0	220.5	207.5	
2007	886.7	651.4	602.6	235.3	223.0	
2008	924.1	671.7	628.7	252.4	238.7	
2009	975.6	701.9	660.5	273.7	259.2	
2010	1050.4	749.1	690.9	301.3	258.3	
2011	1107.4	766.0	725.5	341.4	325.6	
2012	1168.7	801.4	757.8	367.3	351.2	
2013	1217.9	822.0	779.1	396.0	379.7	
2014	1266.2	847.0	802.5	419.3	402.1	
2015	1315.5	874.9	830.7	440.6	422.9	
2016	1355.0	897.1	853.8	457.9	439.5	
2017	3806.7	1020.5	907.5	526.1	471.1	2260.1
2018	3884.2	1047.5	918.9	554.1	484.3	2282.5
2019	4029.7	1100.5	970.9	584.3	498.9	2344.9
2020	4315.7	1147.9	1015.3	596.8	513.1	2571.0

注:2017年起,基本养老保险参保人数包括参加城乡居民基本养老保险人数。

Note: starting from 2017, the number of participants in basic old-age insurance shall include the number of urban and rural residents participating in Basic old-age insurance.

21-7 婚姻登记和离婚情况
Statistics on Marriage Registrationand Divorce

年 份 Year	准予登记结婚(对) Marriage Registeration Granted(couple)	初婚(人) First Marriage (person)	再婚(人) Digamist (person)	离婚(对) Divorce (couple)	离婚率(‰) Rate of Divorce (‰)
1986	402315	785319	19311	6322	0.25
1987	417552	809808	25296	6660	0.26
1988	362654	698447	26861	7389	0.29
1989	413460	801171	25749	9203	0.35
1990	408688	790477	26899	9477	0.35
1991	424708	820092	29324	9584	0.35
1992	463279	897899	28659	10793	0.39
1993	425276	822044	28508	11937	0.43
1994	457324	884817	29831	12910	0.46
1995	482063	930832	33294	13340	0.46
1996	442532	851577	33487	14590	0.50
1997	426460	820615	32305	21260	0.72
1998	399900	763163	36637	24711	0.84
1999	376961	716175	37747	19519	0.66
2000	353781	673294	34268	21255	0.71
2001	335421	632188	38654	22077	0.74
2002	321517	605055	37979	24003	0.80
2003	329256	614244	44268	29375	0.98
2004	381472	710633	52311	46369	1.54
2005	394093	717495	70691	53394	1.77
2006	445672	822294	69050	57682	1.91
2007	485278	896768	73788	65876	2.17
2008	542251	1025496	59006	76003	2.49
2009	565400	1058851	71949	81133	2.84
2010	570810	1068715	72905	89549	3.11
2011	626912	1169771	84053	98874	3.18
2012	615861	1155365	76357	109862	3.81
2013	645767	1201344	90190	127604	4.40
2014	621946	1182271	61621	133723	4.60
2015	572954	1079852	66056	144684	4.90
2016	513823	971991	55655	160236	5.40
2017	472102	853124	91080	175815	5.96
2018	437777	749195	126359	177022	5.98
2019	389339	631495	147183	188388	6.36
2020	315349	499049	131649	172719	6.36

21-8 残疾人基本情况
Basic Statistics on Disabled Persons

项　目	Item	2019	2020
康复	**Rehabilitation**		
视力残疾康复服务人数（人）	Rehabilitation of Persons with Visual Disability (person)	55195	50474
听力语言残疾康复服务人数（人）	Rehabilitation of Persons with Hearing and Speech Disability (person)	29729	29862
肢体残疾康复服务人数（人）	Rehabilitation of Persons with Physical Disability (person)	200865	198727
智力残疾康复服务人数（人）	Rehabilitation of Persons with Intellectual Disability (person)	35877	35538
精神病防治康复服务人数（人）	Rehabilitation Institutions for the Disabled (unit)	95743	100803
残疾人康复机构（个）	Assistive Appliance Service Organization (unit)	202	237
辅助器具服务机构（个）		122	115
教育	**Education**		
特殊教育普通高中在校生（人）	Students at Special Education Senior High Schools (person)	325	692
高等院校录取残疾考生（人）	Disabled Students Admitted to Higher Education Institutions (person)	453	469
就业			
当年新增残疾人就业人数（人）	Number of New Invalids Employed in the Year (person)	18197	12744
社会保障	**Social Security**		
残疾居民参加城乡社会养老保险（人）	Disabled Residents in Urban and Rural Social Endowment Insurance (person)	1319113	1243830
扶贫	**Poverty Alleviation**		
培训残疾人（人）	Trained Persons with Disabilities (person)	25422	23158
维权	**Rights Protection**		
残疾人法律援助工作站（个）	Legal aid Workstation for Persons with Disabilities (unit)	71	76
残疾人法律救助工作站办理的案件（件）	Barrier Free Home Renovation for Poor PWDs (case)	92	41
残疾人机动轮椅车燃油补贴（人）	Fuel Subsidy for Motor Wheelchairs of PWDs (person)	20713	7505
组织建设	**Organization Development**		
残疾人专职委员（人）	Full-time Commissioner for Persons with Disabilities (person)	18598	12422
残疾人人口库持证残疾人（万人）	PWDs with Disability Certificate in the PWD Database (10 000 persons)	157.6	164.3

21-9 刑事案件发、破案情况
Statistics on Occurrenceand Clearing Up of Criminal Cases

指 标	Item	2000	2005	2010	2015	2016	2017	2018	2019	2020
刑事案件立案总数（件）	Number of Criminal Cases Occurred (case)	114866	147004	221735	299522	275707	233670	210296	198736	192201
刑事案件破案总数（件）	Number of Criminal Cases Cleared (case)	72796	71455	76401	77355	69775	83723	65766	66026	49520
刑事案件破案率（%）	Rate of Criminal Cases Cleared (%)	63.4	48.6	34.5	25.8	25.3	35.8	31.3	33.223	25.8

21-10 交通事故与火灾情况
Basic Statistics on Traffic Accidents and Fire Accidents

指 标	Item	2000	2005	2010	2015	2016	2017	2018	2019	2020
交通事故处理发生件数（起）	**Number of Traffic Accidents (case)**	**20148**	**9585**	**6465**	**4627**	**19269**	**16292**	**23540**	**27086**	**26809**
死亡人数（人）	Deaths (person)	3792	2417	1967	1694	6560	5976	5562	5157	4845
受伤人数（人）	Injuries (person)	16492	10555	7684	4638	18111	15791	26300	30950	29677
折合经济损失（万元）	**Losses Converted into Money (10 000 yuan)**	**7041**	**4958**	**3294**	**5176**	**9801**	**10583**	**14542**	**15075**	**15100**
火灾发生数（起）	**Number of Fire Accsidents (case)**	**6780**	**9356**	**9333**	**2121**	**1964**	**12460**	**13578**	**14528**	
死亡人数（人）	Deaths (person)	54	56	17	3	4	16	23	19	
受伤人数（人）	Injuries (person)	106	47	7	3	12	19	7	4	
折合经济损失（万元）	**Losses Converted into Money (10 000 yuan)**	**1754**	**1945**	**3565**	**4142**	**4380**	**8400**	**6807**	**11221**	

注：2017年起，火灾情况统计口径发生变化。
Note: Since 2017, the statistics of fire situation has changed.

21-11 审查批捕、起诉情况
Statistics on Examination, Arrest and Prosecution

项 目		Item		2000	2005	2010	2015	2016	2017	2018	2019	2020
受理批捕件数	（件）	Number of Cases	(case)	20378	19846	9120	28860	28605	31560	33558	36821	21267
受理批捕人数	（人）	Number of People Arrested	(person)	31245	29427	13391	38400	38587	42891	48246	53372	30954
批准逮捕	（人）	Number of Arrests Granted	(person)	25114	27063	12081	32400	31332	34254	37966	43163	24936
不批捕人数	（人）	Number of Non-Arrest	(person)	4329	1522	1001	5388	6588	7955	9445	9566	5900
受理审查起诉件数	（件）	Number of Cases Received	(case)	17660	21966	10028	42337	43596	50365	50368	59672	47062
受理审查起诉人数	（人）	Number of Prosecution Accepted	(person)	25416	33410	15280	57002	58036	67253	69446	83574	64196
起诉人数	（人）	Prosecutor	(person)	22396	26926	11600	46609	48207	50726	53682	67464	54557
不起诉人数	（人）	Non-prosecutor	(person)	1019	982	329	2235	2369	3082	3924	4893	6380

21-12 律师、公证、调解工作基本情况
Basic Statistics on Lawyers, Notarization and Mediation

项 目	Item	2005	2010	2015	2016	2017	2018	2019	2020
一、律师工作	**Lawyers**								
律师事务所 (个)	Number of Lawyer Office (unit)	387	466	665	717	806	852	901	963
专职律师	Number of Full-Time Lawyer	3722	5869	9419	10314	11388	12258	13324	13540
兼职律师	Number of Part-Time Lawyer	165	252	363	376	363	381	408	418
担任法律顾问 (家)	Number of Units with Legal Advisors (unit)	9565	12059	34772	55269	24059	20850	27685	32764
民事案件诉讼代理 (件)	Agent of Civil Cases (case)	27079	45403	79913	81013	101474	107078	129117	150098
刑事诉讼辩护及代理 (件)	Defender and Agent of Criminal Cases (case)	11341	17724	19076	20457	16440	22934	37597	42147
非诉讼法律事务 (件)	Agent of Non-Litigious Legal Affairs (case)	34674	37521	26276	21731	20130	15144	24980	30210
咨询和代书 (万人次)	Consultation and Representation (10 000 person-times)				16.40	12.60	6.80	7.10	6.81
二、公证工作	**Notarization**								
公证机构 (个)	Number of Notary Offices (unit)	118	116	117	117	112	108	109	109
#公证员	Notaries	455	353	424	449	429	386	377	407
公证员助理	Assistant Notaries	62	167	254	256	239	299	329	388
办理公证文件 (万件)	Number of Domestic Notarized Document (10 000 cases)	31.04	32.65	42.04	47.00	48.20	38.30	38.11	28.28
涉外公证 (件)	Foreign Notarized Documents (case)	65498	79723	113143	112384	106257	83172	94889	44749
三、人民调解工作	**People´s Mediation**								
人民调解委员会 (万个)	Number of People´s Mediation Committees (10 000 units)	3.70	3.62	3.37	3.32	3.30	3.10	3.00	3.11
调解人员 (万人)	Number of Mediators (10 000 persons)	17.20	20.43	14.73	14.28	14.10	11.70	11.90	11.70
调解纠纷总数 (万件)	Number of Disputes Mediated (10 000 cases)	21.62	22.85	32.15	31.03	33.20	31.40	30.30	29.63
调解成功总数 (万件)	Number of Successful Mediation (10 000 cases)	21.13	22.14	31.44	30.46	32.60	30.90	29.70	28.99

21-13 公证文书分类情况
Related Notarial Documents by Type

单位：件 (case)

分 类	Item	2019	2020
合计	**Total**	**381123**	**282817**
出生、生存、死亡	Births、Survival、Death	11939	5630
学历、经历、职称、身份	Academic Degree、Personal Experience、Title、Identity	9949	5857
收养子女、亲属关系、婚姻状况	Children Adoption、Kinship、Marital Status	17441	6999
继承权	Rights of Inheritance	63251	68647
遗嘱	Testament	2697	1844
委托书	Trust Deed	78358	60959
公司章程	Chapter of Company	48	6
副本与原本相符	Confirmation of Copy and Photo-offset Copies to Originals	55333	31604
证书(执照)	Operation Document	20577	10861
声明书	Declaration	22229	20373
合同(协议)	Contract(Agreement)	21481	17895
受、未受刑事处分	Criminal Record & Uncriminal Record	12642	7309
其他	Others	65178	44833

21-14 履行法律监督情况
Supervision on Law Enforcement

单位:人、件 (person, case)

项 目	Item	2000	2005	2010	2015	2016	2017	2018	2019	2020
监督公安机关立案件数	Number of Cases Registered by Public Security	247	554	1088	1412	1107	2109	2909	1332	1774
监督追捕人数	Number of Criminals Hunted under Supervision	300	204	903	1985	1830	2572	3688	2405	1347
监督追诉人数	Number of People Being Prosecuted	61	78	1130	1484	1359	1927	2003	1607	1547
刑事抗诉件数	Number of Cases Against Crimnal Prosecutions	192	123	119	433	467	505	501	346	504
监督刑罚执行纠错人次	Person-times of Error Correction of Execution of Punishment	3546	51	499	3700	3440	1869	2385	2097	3188
民事行政监督抗诉件数	Number of Counterappeal Civil Cases	894	514	432	155	114	94	80	78	67

21-15 调解民间纠纷分类
Civil Disputes Mediation by Type

项 目	Item	调解纠纷(件) Number of Disputes Mediated (case)				各种纠纷所占比重(%) Proportion (%)			
		2017	2018	2019	2020	2017	2018	2019	2020
合计	**Total**	**84051**	**92094**	**109192**	**93958**	**100**	**100**	**100**	**100**
婚姻	Marriage	19924	20049	20119	17328	23.7	21.8	18.4	18.4
继承	Rights of Inheritance	813	844	877	779	1.0	0.9	0.8	0.8
房地产开发	Real Estate Development	15	51	15	7	0.0	0.1	0.0	0.0
运输合同	Transportation Contracts	385	296	614	444	0.5	0.3	0.6	0.5
买卖合同	Selling and Purchasing Contracts	6096	6539	8798	7831	7.3	7.1	8.1	8.3
借款合同	Loans Contracts	18012	22359	27192	23478	21.4	24.3	24.9	25.0
劳动争议	Labor Disputes	3169	3523	4417	3795	3.8	3.8	4.1	4.0
人格权	Personal Rights	1112	1158	1247	959	1.3	1.3	1.1	1.0
所有权	Right of Ownership	172	207	212	212	0.2	0.2	0.2	0.2
其他	Others	34353	37068	45701	39125	40.9	40.3	41.9	41.6

21-16 人民法院审理一审案件情况
Statistics on First Instance Cases in People´s Court

单位:件 (case)

年 份 Year	收案 Cases Received	刑事 Criminal Cases	民商事 Civil Cases	海事海商 Maritime	行政 Administration
1985	63079	12709	40660	26	
1990	227618	29086	166960		568
1995	257312	21391	174908	456	4359
1998	252403	17763	171025	606	6368
1999	238715	19598	151191	647	6247
2000	228804	19204	146838	618	6754
2001	251003	21741	222702	745	6560
2002	211464	19548	188163	525	3753
2003	193780	18943	171282	488	3555
2004	172889	18833	150682	592	3374
2005	155478	19672	132585	745	3221
2006	156885	19914	133584	606	3387
2007	161728	21719	137328	459	2681
2008	165099	22364	140072	746	2663
2009	173032	23481	147319	710	2232
2010	179631	22963	154299	781	2369
2011	280572	25074	249792	1458	5706
2012	395414	31489	354789	1501	9136
2013	422427	31621	387593	1914	3213
2014	344515	33931	306601	1951	3983
2015	316619	37034	272384	2022	7201
2016	326240	37309	281705	2212	7226
2017	375458	40309	327020	2245	8129
2018	431278	41332	380752	1813	9194
2019	484877	48702	426876	1608	9299
2020	418208	40325	370690	821	7193

注:一审案件指人民法院按照诉讼级别管辖按第一审程序审理的案件。
Note: First instance cases refer to cases in the first instance process in People´s Court.

21-17 人民法院刑事一审案件收结案情况

Statistics on End of First Instance Cases in People´s Court of Criminal Lawsuits

单位:件 (case)

项 目	Item	收案 Cases Received				结案 Cases Closed			
		2017	2018	2019	2020	2017	2018	2019	2020
合计	**Total**	**39641**	**41332**	**48702**	**40325**	**40309**	**41104**	**48233**	**40244**
危害公共安全罪	Offences Against Public Security	10814	12349	16565	16360	10913	12369	16544	16318
破坏社会主义市场经济秩序罪	Offences Against Socialism Market Economy Order	1556	1683	1909	1582	1579	1668	1800	1575
侵害公民人身权利民主权利罪	Offences Against Citizens´ Personal and Democratic Rights	6077	5889	5891	5046	6312	5862	5868	4965
侵犯财产罪	Offences Against Properties	10624	9851	10329	7348	10773	9806	10225	7299
妨害社会管理秩序罪	Offences Against Social Management of Order	9182	10452	13162	9238	9309	10214	12943	9294
危害国防利益罪	Offences Against National Defense	12	12	27	25	12	13	26	24
贪污贿赂罪	Offences On Corruption and Bribery	1164	931	679	601	1218	951	691	636
渎职罪	Offences On Dereliction of Duty	208	163	138	124	192	219	133	132
其他	Others	4	2	2	1	1	2	3	1
合计中含自诉案件	Private Prosecution Among the Total	230	436	385	229		345	317	184

21-18 人民法院刑事案件中青少年犯罪情况
Statistics on Juvenile Delinquency in People´s Court of Criminal Lawsuits

单位:人 (person)

年份 Year	刑事犯罪总数 Total Number of Criminal Cases	青少年犯罪(不满25周岁) Juvenile Delinquency (Under the age of 25)	不满18周岁 Juvenile Age under 18	已满18周岁不满25周岁 Age 18-25	青少年罪犯刑事罪犯率% Percentage of Juvenile Delinquency in Criminal Cases %
1999	20534	6836	1302	5534	33.3
2000	20076	5922	1279	4643	29.5
2001	22911	6597	1774	4823	28.8
2002	20868	5669	1901	3768	27.2
2003	20908	6207	2328	3879	29.7
2004	20429	5838	2633	3205	28.6
2005	21669	6283	2939	3344	29.0
2006	22876	6933	2945	3988	30.3
2007	17368	7459	3131	4328	43.0
2008	26682	6810	3030	3780	25.5
2009	28507	7700	2930	4770	27.0
2010	27928	7058	2287	4771	25.3
2011	29280	7263	2229	5034	24.8
2012	35419	7327	2050	5277	20.7
2013	33871	5398	1365	4033	15.9
2014	34599	4721	1170	3551	13.6
2015	43918	6011	1084	4927	13.7
2016	40797	4731	668	4063	11.6
2017	41654	5028	852	4176	12.1
2018	46356	6084	654	5430	13.1
2019	61572	7393	821	6572	12.0
2020	55275	6143	649	5494	11.1

21-19 人民法院民事一审案件收结案情况(2020)
Statistics on end of First Instance Cases in People´s Court of Civil Lawsuits (2020)

单位:件 (case)

项 目	Item	收案 Cases Received	结案 Cases Ended	调解 Mediated	判决 Judgement	驳回 Cases Rejected	撤诉 Cases Withdraw	其他 Others
合计	**Total**	**370690**	**374738**	**89729**	**176231**	**11066**	**92444**	**5268**
婚姻家庭	Marriage	52776	53139	17041	23978	627	10936	557
继承	Rights of Inheritance	1867	1839	630	794	64	328	23
知识产权	Intelligence Property Rights	4497	6321	543	1869	29	3847	33
房地产开发	Real Estate Development	81	99	6	55	8	28	2
运输合同	Transportation Contracts	1386	1475	434	674	28	282	57
买卖合同	Selling and Purchasing Contracts	25029	25464	7596	10137	736	6621	374
借款合同	Loans Contracts	90347	90298	23001	46187	3239	17102	769
劳动争议	Labor Disputes	12060	12412	3139	6238	457	2091	487
海事海商	Martial Commerce	821	1112	159	660	12	277	4
人格权	Personal Right	4091	4122	895	2343	75	784	25
特别程序	Special Procedure	1961	1935	8	1221	154	541	11
破产	Bankruptcy	640	627	8	285	54	212	68
所有权及与其相关合同	Rights of Ownership and Relevant Contracts	913	967	203	407	70	271	16
其他	Others	174221	174928	36066	81383	5513	49124	2842

注:结案中含上年旧存。
Note: The statistics of ended cases include statistics of last year.

21-20 人民法院行政一审案件收结案情况(2020)
Statistics on end of First Instance Cases in People´s Court of Administration (2020)

单位:件 (case)

项 目	Item	收案 Cases Received	结案 Cases Ended	驳回起诉 Rejected	准予撤诉 Withdraw	其他 Others
合计	**Total**	**7193**	**7208**	**1775**	**1507**	**3926**
土地	Land	395	389	109	91	189
公安	Public Security	522	515	100	113	302
城建	City Construction	1020	963	276	190	497
交通运输	Transportation	60	51	9	15	27
工商	Industry and Commerce	108	102	16	29	57
环保	Environment	39	38	3	8	27
林业	Forestry	61	62	6	16	40
税务	Taxes	31	26	17	4	5
卫生	Sanitary and Hygiene	38	38	8	7	23
其他	Others	4919	5024	1231	1034	2759

注:结案中含上年旧存。
Note: The statistics of ended cases include statistics of last year.

主要统计指标解释

基本养老保险

1.(参保)职工人数:指报告期末按照国家法律、法规和有关政策规定参加基本养老保险并在社保经办机构已建立缴费记录档案的职工人数,包括中断缴费但未终止养老保险关系的职工人数,不包括只登记未建立缴费记录档案的人数。

2.(参保)离退休人员人数:指报告期末参加基本养老保险的离休、退休和退职人员的人数。

3.基本养老保险基金收入:指根据国家有关规定,由纳入基本养老保险范围的缴费单位和个人按国家规定的缴费基数和缴费比例缴纳的养老保险基金,以及通过其他方式取得的形成基金来源的收入。包括单位和职工个人缴纳的基本养老保险费、基本养老保险基金利息收入、上级补助收入、下级上解收入、转移收入、财政补贴和其他收入。

4.基本养老保险基金支出:指按照国家政策规定的开支范围和开支标准从养老保险基金中支付给参加基本养老保险的离休、通休、退职人员个人的养老金、丧葬抚恤补助,以及由于保险关系转移、上下级之间调剂资金等原因而发生的支出。包括离休金、退休金、退职金、各种补贴、医疗费、死亡丧葬补助费、抚恤救济费、社会保险经办机构管理费、补助下级支出、上解上级支出、转移支出、其他支出等。

5.基本养老保险基金累计结余:指截止报告期末基本养老保险基金收支相抵后的累计余额。

离休、退休、退职人员 指正式办理了离休、退休、退职手续,并享受相应的离休、退休、退职待遇的人员。

基本医疗保险

1.参保人数:指报告期末按国家有关规定参加基本医疗保险的人数。包括参加保险的职工人数和退休人员人数。

2.基金收入:指根据国家有关规定,由纳入基本医疗保险范围的缴费单位和个人,按国家规定的缴费基数和缴费比例缴纳的基金,以及通过其他方式取得的形成基金来源的款项,包括:单位缴纳的社会统筹基金收入、个人缴纳的个人账户基金收入、财政补贴收入、利息收入、其他收入。

3.基金支出:指按照国家政策规定的开支范围和开支标准从社会统筹基金中支付给参加基本医疗保险的职工和退休人员的医疗保险待遇支出,和从个人帐户基金中支付给参加基本医疗保险的职工和退休人员的医疗费用支出,以及其他支出。包括:住院医疗费用支出、门急诊医疗费用支出、个人账户基金支出、其他支出。

4.基金累计结余:指截止报告期末基本医疗保险的社会统筹和个人帐户基金累计结余金额。包括银行存款、财政专户、债券投资和其他。

失业保险

1.参保人数:指报告期末按照国家法律、法规和有关政策规定参加了失业保险的城镇企业事业单位的职工及地方政府规定参加失业保险的其他人员的人数。

2.失业保险基金收入:指按照规定从企业、事业及其他单位筹集的失业保险费及其他并入失业保险基金收入的总额。包括单位和个人缴纳的失业保险费、失业保险基金利息收入、上级补助收入、下级上解收入、转移收入、财政补贴和其他收入。

3.失业保险基金支出:指报告期内为保障失业人员和下岗职工基本生活、促进其再就业等支出的基金总额。包括失业救济金、医疗费、死亡丧葬补助费、抚恤救济费、转业训练费支出、失业保险经办机构管理费、补助下级支出、上解上级支出、转移支出和其他支出。

4.基金累计结余:指截止报告期末失业保险基金收支相抵后的累计余额。

工伤保险

1.参加保险人数:指报告期末依据国家有关规定参加工伤保险的职工人数。

2.享受保险待遇人数:指劳动者因工负伤致残、死亡或因患职业病致残,根据有关规定享受工伤保险待遇职工或供养直系亲属人数。包括伤残人数、职业病人数、因工死亡人数、供养直系亲属人数。

3.基金收入:指根据国家有关规定,由参加工伤保险的单位按国家规定的缴费基数和缴费比例缴纳的工伤保险基金,以及通过其他形式取得的形成基金来源的款项。包括:单位缴纳的社会统筹基金收入、财政补贴收入、利息收入、其他收入。

4.基金支出:指按照国家政策规定的开支范围和开支标准从工伤保险基金中支付给参加工伤保险的人员及供养直系亲属工伤保险待遇支出及其他支出。包括工伤医疗费、伤残补助金、工亡补助金、护理费、丧葬补助费、工伤预防费用、职业康复费用和其他支出。

5.基金累计结余:指截止报告期末工伤保险基金累计结

余金额。包括银行存款、财政专户、债券投资和其他。

生育保险

1.参保人数:指报告期末依据有关规定参加生育保险的职工人数。

2.基金收入:指根据国家有关规定,由参加生育保险的单位按照国家规定的缴费基数和缴费比例缴纳的生育保险基金,以及通过其他方式取得的形成基金来源的款项,包括:单位缴纳的基金收入、利息收入和其他收入。

3.基金支出:指按照国家政策规定的开支范围和开支标准,从生育保险基金中支付给参加生育保险的职工,因妊娠、分娩和计划生育手术而享受的待遇及其他支出。包括:生育津贴、医疗费用支出及其他支出。

4.基金累计结余:指截止报告期末生育保险基金累计结余金额。包括银行存款、财政专户、债券投资和其他。

离休、退休、退职人员保险福利费用 指离休、退休、退职人员实际得到的生活费用总额,包括从社会保险经办机构和单位得到的费用。

1.离休金:指按规定支付给离休人员的生活费用。

2.退休金:指按规定支付给退休人员的生活费用。

3.退职生活费:指按规定支付给退职人员的生活费用。

4.医疗卫生费:指单位直接支付给离休、退休、退职人员的医疗费、住院费以及住院伙食补助等费用。

5.其他:指离休金、退休金、退职生活费和医疗卫生费以外的其他保险福利费用,如丧葬抚恤救济费、生活补贴、物价补贴、冬季取暖补贴等。

律师 指依法取得律师执业证书,担任法律顾问,民事(刑事、行政)案件代理人、刑事案件辩护人、办理非诉讼业务,解答法律询问,代写法律事务文书等,为社会提供法律服务的人员。

公证人员 指在公证处工作的人员总称,包括公证处主任、副主任、公证员、公证员助理(助理公证员)和其他从事辅助性工作的人员。

公证文书 指公证处根据当事人申请,依照事实和法律,按照法定程序制作的,具有法律效力的司法证明文书。根据公证书用途和使用地,公证书分为国内公证书、国内经济公证书、涉外民事公证书、涉外经济公证书四类。

调解员 指在人民调解委员会担负调解民间纠纷工作的人员,包括调解委员会的委员和调解小组的调解员。该指标主要反映从事人民调解工作的人员数量。

调解民间纠纷 指调解委员会按照法律规定,根据自愿原则,用说服教育的方法调解民间发生的有关民事权利和义务争执的件数,包括调解成功数和调解未成功数。该指标主要反映人民调解委员会的工作量。

立案 指人民检察院对受理的报案、控告、举报或自首及自行发现的犯罪线索、犯罪嫌疑人进行初步调查后,认为存在职务犯罪事实和应追究刑事责任,并决定作为刑事案件进行侦查的诉讼活动,是追究犯罪的开始。该指标主要反映人民检察院依法将职务犯罪线索作为刑事案件进行侦查的诉讼活动。

大案 指贪污、贿赂案数额在5万元以上,挪用公款案数额在10万元以上,集体私分、巨额财产来源不明、隐瞒境外存款案数额在50万元以上以及按照《人民检察院直接受理的渎职、侵权重、特大案件标准(试行)》认定的案件。该指标主要反映人民检察院立案查办的职务犯罪案件中经济损失大、社会危害严重的案件。

要案 指县、处级以上干部的犯罪案件。该指标主要反映国家工作人员中县、处级以上干部因职务犯罪被人民检察院依法立案侦查的情况。

决定逮捕 指人民检察院对直接受理、自行侦查的案件,认为需要逮捕犯罪嫌疑人时,依据法律做出的逮捕决定。该指标主要反映人民检察院对直接受理的案件行使决定逮捕权的情况。

批准逮捕 指人民检察院对公安机关、国家安全机关、监狱管理机关提出逮捕的犯罪嫌疑人进行审查,根据事实,依法做出逮捕决定。该指标主要反映人民检察院对提请逮捕机关提请逮捕犯罪嫌疑人进行审查后依法做出批准逮捕决定的情况。

决定起诉 指人民检察院对公安机关、国家安全机关、监狱管理机关和检察机关内设机构反贪污贿赂部门等移送起诉的案件进行审查,根据事实,做出提起公诉的案件。该指标主要反映人民检察院对各种刑事案件向人民法院提起公诉的情况。

申诉 指经检察机关信访部门审查处理后,移送到检察机关申诉部门的申诉案件,包括不服检察机关处理决定和不服法院刑事判决和裁定的申诉的案件。

受理劳动争议案件数 指劳动争议仲裁委员会根据国家有关规定,对劳动争议当事人的申请予以审查,符合受理条件而正式立案、准备处理的劳动争议案件数。

Explanatory Notes on Main Statistical Indicators

Basic Medical Care Insurance:

1. Number of people participating in the insurance programme refers to people participating in the basic medical care insurance programme according to related regulations by the end of reference period, including number of staff and workers and retirees participating in this insurance programme.

2. Revenue of insurance programme refer to payments made by employers and individuals participating in medical care insurance programs in accordance with the basis and proportion stipulated in state regulations, and income from other sources that become source of medical insurance fund, including income of social comprehensive funds paid by employers, income from individual accounts, government financial subsidies, interest income and other income.

3. Expenses of insurance programme refer to payment made from social comprehensive funds to those retired and resigned people covered in basic medical care insurance within the scope and standards of expenditure according to related national policies, and medical care payment made from individual accounts to staff and workers and retirees, and other expenses, including medical expenses of hospital inpatients, medical expenses for outpatients and emergency patients, payment from individual accounts and other expenditure.

4. Balance of basic medical care insurance refer to the balance of medical care insurance of social comprehensive funds and individual accounts at the end of the reference period, including bank savings, special fiscal accounts, investment in bonds and others.

Unemployment Insurance

1. Number of people covered refers to staff and workers in urban enterprises or institutions who have participated in unemployment insurance programme in line relevant policies and regulations, and other people who have participated according to local government regulations, by the end of reference period.

2. Revenue of unemployment insurance refer to payments made by employers and individuals participating in unemployment insurance programme in accordance with relevant regulations and other income contributed to this programme, including unemployment insurance premium made by employers and individuals, interest income, subsidies from higher level agencies, income as transfer from subordinate agencies, transferred income, government financial subsidies and other income.

3. Expenses of unemployment insurance refer to total expenses during the reference period to guarantee the basic livelihood of unemployed people and laid–off staff and workers and to encourage their re–employment. Included are unemployment relief, medical fees, funeral subsidies, compensation pension, training expenses, management fees for unemployment insurance agencies, subsidies to lower level agencies, expenses as transfer to higher level agencies, transferred expenditure and other expenditure.

4. Balance of unemployment insurance refer to the balance of unemployment revenue deducting unemployment expenses at the end of the reference period.

Work Injury Insurance

1. Number of people covered refers to staff and workers who have participated in work injury insurance programme in line with relevant national regulations.

2. Number of beneficiaries refers to staff and workers and their direct dependents who can, in line with relevant regulations, benefit from work injury insurance, as a result of work injury leading to disability or death of the staff/worker, or occupational disease leading to disability. Included in this category are number of injured and disabled people, number of people with occupational diseases, number of deaths at work places, and number of direct dependents.

3. Revenue of work injury insurance refer to payments made by employers participating in work injury insurance programs in accordance with the basis and proportion stipulated in state regulations, and income from other sources that become source of work injury insurance fund, including income of social comprehensive funds paid by employers, government financial subsidies, interest income and other income.

4. Expenses of work injury insurance refer to payments made from work injury insurance funds to those who participated in the work injury insurance programme and their direct depen-

dents within the scope and standards of expenditure according to related national policies, and other expenditure, including medical fees for work injury, injury and disability subsidies, death subsidies, nursing fees, funeral subsidies, injury prevention fees, rehabilitation fees for occupational diseases and other expenditure.

5. Balance of work injury insurance refer to the balance of the work injury funds at the end of the reference period, including bank savings, special fiscal account, investment in bonds and others.

Maternity Insurance

1. Number of people covered refers to staff and workers who have participated in maternity insurance programme according to relevant regulation at the end of the reporting period.

2. Revenue of maternity insurance refers to payments made by employers participating in maternity insurance programs in accordance with the basis and proportion stipulated in state regulations, and income from other sources that become source of maternity insurance fund, including income of funds paid by employers, interest income and other income.

3. Expenses of maternity insurance refer to payments made from maternity insurance funds to staff and workers who participated in maternity insurance programme within the scope and standards of expenditure according to related national policies, expenses paid for pregnancy, child delivery or surgeries related to family planning, and other expenditure, including allowance for child bearing, medical fees and other expenditure.

4. Balance of the maternity insurance refers to the balance of the maternity insurance funds at the end of reference period, including bank savings, special fiscal account, investment in funds and others.

Insurance and Welfare Funds for Retirees refer to the total payment for living expenses actually received by retirees, including payment received from social insurance management agencies and units.

1. Pensions for retired veteran cadres refer to living expenses paid to retired veteran cadres according to related regulations.

2. Pensions for retirement refer to living expenses paid to retired staff and workers according to related regulations.

3. Living allowances for resigned staff and workers refer to living expenses paid to resigned staff and workers according to related regulation.

4. Medical care expenses refer to medical fees, hospitalization cost and per diem subsidies during hospitalizations paid by employers directly to retirees.

5. Others refer to insurance and welfare payments other than the above-mentioned payments, including funeral subsidies, living allowances, price subsidies and heating subsidies during winter.

Lawyers are certified legal workers according to law, and who are employed by legal counseling firms to act as legal advisers, agents in criminal or civil lawsuits, or defenders in criminal lawsuits, or to handle non-litigious legal affairs, to advise on matters of law or to write legal papers for others, and provide service to the public.

Notary Personnel refers to people working for notary offices including: directors, deputy director, notaries, assistant notaries, and other people providing assistance.

Notary Documents refer to the judicatory notary documents drawn up by the request of the party and are in accordance with facts and laws and following certain legal proceedings. According to usage and locality, the notary documents are divided into following 4 types: domestic notary documents, domestic economic notary documents, foreign-related civil notary documents and foreign-related economic notary documents.

Mediators refer to workers on peoples mediation committees responsible for mediating in civil disputes and cases of slight infraction of the law. They include members of the mediation committees and mediators of mediation groups. This indicator reflects the number of people engaged in meditation.

Mediation of Civil Disputes refers to number of cases made by mediation committees in mediating in civil disputes concerning civil rights and duties through persuasion and education in accordance with the provisions of law on a voluntary basis, so as to solve disputes by helping the parties involved come to an agreement and understanding, including those unsuccessful ones. This indicator reflects the workload of the mediation committees.

Acceptance of Case refers to the decision made by the people's procuratorate office on reported cases, prosecution, impeachment, surrender, self-found criminal clues or suspects after initial investigation to confirm the act of crime and to start legal proceedings of the case as criminal case.

Large Cases refer to cases involving a corruption or bribery of over 50,000 yuan, or a misappropriation of over 100,000 yuan. Cases of collectively illegal possession of public funds, unstated sources of large properties, or disguised overseas savings deposits involving 500,000 yuan, or a case that has been defined by the "Standard on Serious and Large Cases of Misconduct and Tortious that Directly Accepted by People's Procurators Office (trial)". This indicator mainly reflects number of accepted cases of job-related criminals that caused serious economic losses or extremely harmful to the society.

Key Cases refer to cases committed by government officials with a ranking of division director or county administrator. This indicator mainly reflects the recorded and spied on cases by the people's procurators offices toward government official with a ranking of division director or county administrator.

Decision on Arrest refers to decision made by people's procurators office, in accordance with laws, to arrest the suspect(s) in the cases that are accepted and to be investigated by procurators office. This indicator mainly reflects the implementation of the decision on arrest by people's procurators office.

Approval for Arrest refers to the decision made by people's procurators office, in accordance with laws and relevant facts, to approve the arrest of the suspect (s) that is proposed by the public security departments, state security departments or authority of prisons. This indicator reflects approved arrests made by people's procurators office that are proposed by related departments.

Decision on Prosecution refers to the decision made by people's procurators office, in accordance with laws and relevant facts, to institute proceedings to the people's court against the suspect (s) of criminal cases handed over by the public security departments, state security departments or authority of prisons, or by the anti-corruption departments within the procurators office. This indicator reflects the condition of the prosecutions made by people's procurators office toward the people's court.

Appeals refer to cases transferred to the appeal departments of procurator's offices after initial review by departments dealing with complaint letters and calls of the public. Included are appeals against decisions made by procurator's offices and appeals against court rules and verdicts.

Number of Labor Dispute Cases Accepted refers to the number of cases of labor dispute submitted that, after being reviewed by the labor dispute arbitration committees in line with the relevant national regulations, are accepted and registered for treatment.

Basic Pension Insurance

1.Number of staff and workers covered refer to staff and workers participating in basic pension insurance programme in line with national laws, regulations and related policies by the end of reference period, who have already had payment records in social security management agencies, including those who interrupt payment without terminating the insurance programme. Those who have registered in the programme with no payment records are not included.

2. Number of retirees participating in basic pension insurance programme refer to number of retirees participating in basic pension insurance programme by the end of reference period.

3. Revenue of basic pension insurance refer to payments made by employers and individuals participating in pension insurance programs in accordance with the basis and proportion stipulated in state regulations, and income from other sources that become source of pension insurance fund, including the premium paid by employers and staff and works, interest income, subsidies from higher level agencies, income as transfer from subordinate agencies, transferred income, government financial subsidies and other income.

4. Expenses of basic pension insurance refer to payment made to those retired and resigned people covered in pension insurance program in terms of pension or compensation within the scope and standards of expenditure according to related national policies, and expenditure occurred due to shift of the insurance relationship or adjustment of funds among agencies, including pension for resigned people, pension for retired people, pension for people quitting jobs, various subsidies, medical fees, funeral subsidies, compensation pension, management fees for social security agencies, expenses on subsidies to lower subordinates, expenses as transfer to agencies at higher level, transferred expenditure and other expenditure.

5. Balance of basic pension insurance refers to the balance of basic pension insurance at the end of the reference period after deducting expenses from revenue.

Retired or Resigned Personnel refers to people who have formally completed formalities for their retirement or quitting work and enjoy the corresponding retirement treatments.

22

长江经济带国民经济和社会发展主要指标

Main Indicators of National Economic and Social Development by Yangtze River Economic Zone

资料整理人员：文　静

22-1 长江经济带国民经济和社会发展主要指标(2018 年)
Main Indicators of National Economic and Social Development by Yangtze River Economic Zone (2018)

指　标		Item		全国总计 National Total	长江经济带 Yangtze River Economic Zone	占全国比重(%) As Percentage of National Total
总人口(年末)	(万人)	Population at Year-end	(10 000 persons)	139538.0	59873.0	42.9
国内(地区)生产总值	(亿元)	Gross Domestic Product	(100 million yuan)	900309.5	402985.2	44.1
第一产业		Primary Industry		64734.0	27822.9	43.0
第二产业		Secondary Industry		366000.9	166486.2	44.2
第三产业		Tertiary Industry		469574.6	208676.1	44.1
地方一般公共预算收入	(亿元)	General Public Budget Revenue	(100 million yuan)	97903.4	43823.9	44.8
地方一般公共预算支出	(亿元)	General Public Budget Expenditure	(100 million yuan)	188196.3	80969.1	43.0
社会消费品零售总额	(亿元)	Total Retail Sales of Consumer Goods	(100 million yuan)	380986.9	161574.1	42.9
货物进出口总额	(亿元)	Total Value of Imports and Exports	(100 million yuan)	305008.1	133828.7	43.9
出口		Exports		164127.8	76017.0	46.3
进口		Imports		140880.3	57811.7	41.0
主要农产品产量		Output of Major Farm Products				
谷物	(万吨)	Cereal	(10 000 tons)	61003.6	21714.0	35.6
棉花	(万吨)	Cotton	(10 000 tons)	610.3	42.9	7.0
油料	(万吨)	Oil-bearing Crops	(10 000 tons)	3433.4	1531.8	44.6
主要工业产品产量		Output of Major Industrial Products				
原煤	(亿吨)	Coal	(100 million tons)	36.8	3.9	10.7
天然气	(亿立方米)	Natural Gas	(100 million cu.m)	1602.7	466.1	29.1
水泥	(万吨)	Cement	(10 000 tons)	220770.7	114858.4	52.0
粗钢	(万吨)	Crude Steel	(10 000 tons)	92800.9	29683.5	32.0
钢材	(万吨)	Rolled Steel	(10 000 tons)	110551.7	35549.0	32.2
汽车	(万辆)	Motor Vehicles	(10 000 sets)	2781.9	1234.7	44.4
发电量	(亿千瓦小时)	Electricity	(100 million kwh)	71117.7	27491.1	38.7
铁路营业里程	(公里)	Length of Railways in Operation	(km)	131651.3	39043.9	29.7
公路里程	(公里)	Length of Highways	(km)	4846531.7	2117275.0	43.7
#高速公路		Expressway		142593.2	55690.5	39.1
客运量	(万人)	Passenger Traffic	(10 000 persons)	1732646.6	857563.9	49.5
货运量	(万吨)	Freight Traffic	(10 000 tons)	5152731.6	2183615.2	43.1
邮政业务总量	(亿元)	Business Volume of Postal Services	(100 million yuan)	12345.2	5920.7	48.0
电信业务总量	(亿元)	Business Volume of Postal Services	(100 million yuan)	65633.9	28252.4	43.1
普通高等学校数	(个)	Number of Regular Institutions of Higher Education	(unit)	2663.0	1147.0	43.1
本专科在校学生数	(万人)	Graduates of Undergraduates and College Students	(10 000 persons)	2831.0	1208.2	42.7
医院数	(个)	Number of Hospitals	(unit)	33009.0	13635.0	41.3
执业(助理)医师	(万人)	Licensed (Assistant) Doctors	(10 000 persons)	360.7	150.5	41.7
医院床位数	(万张)	Number of Beds of Medical Institutions	(10 000 beds)	652.0	287.4	44.1

注:长江经济带:包括上海、江苏、浙江、安徽、江西、湖北、湖南、重庆、四川、贵州、云南。
Note: Yangtze River Economic Zone includes: Shanghai, Jiangsu, Zhejiang, Anhui, Jiangxi, Hubei, Hunan, Chongqing, Sichuan, Guizhou, Yunnan.

22-2 长江经济带国民经济和社会发展主要指标(2019年)
Main Indicators of National Economic and Social Development by Yangtze River Economic Zone (2019)

指 标	Item	全国总计 National Total	长江经济带 Yangtze River Economic Zone	占全国比重(%) As Percentage of National Total
总人口(年末) (万人)	Population at Year-end (10 000 persons)	140005.0	60205.8	42.9
国内(地区)生产总值 (亿元)	Gross Domestic Product (100 million yuan)	990865.1	457805.2	46.5
第一产业	Primary Industry	70466.7	30603.7	43.4
第二产业	Secondary Industry	386165.3	182341.8	47.3
第三产业	Tertiary Industry	534233.1	244859.7	46.2
地方一般公共预算收入(亿元)	General Public Budget Revenue (100 million yuan)	101080.6	45128.6	44.6
地方一般公共预算支出(亿元)	General Public Budget Expenditure (100 million yuan)	203743.2	88504.2	43.4
社会消费品零售总额 (亿元)	Total Retail Sales of Consumer Goods (100 million yuan)	408017.2	198801.4	48.7
货物进出口总额 (亿元)	Total Value of Imports and Exports (100 million yuan)	315627.3	139828.7	44.3
出口	Exports	172373.6	80124.3	46.5
进口	Imports	143253.7	59704.4	41.7
主要农产品产量	Output of Major Farm Products			
谷物 (万吨)	Cereal (10 000 tons)	61369.7	21543.7	35.1
棉花 (万吨)	Cotton (10 000 tons)	588.9	37.4	6.3
油料 (万吨)	Oil-bearing Crops (10 000 tons)	3493.0	1560.4	44.7
主要工业产品产量	Output of Major Industrial Products			
原煤 (亿吨)	Coal (100 million tons)	38.5	3.7	9.7
天然气 (亿立方米)	Natural Gas (100 million cu.m)	1761.7	541.4	30.7
水泥 (万吨)	Cement (10 000 tons)	234430.6	120915.7	51.6
粗钢 (万吨)	Crude Steel (10 000 tons)	99541.9	32911.1	33.1
钢材 (万吨)	Rolled Steel (10 000 tons)	120456.9	39130.6	32.5
汽车 (万辆)	Motor Vehicles (10 000 sets)	2567.7	1089.7	42.4
发电量 (亿千瓦小时)	Electricity (100 million kwh)	75034.3	28713.3	38.3
铁路营业里程 (公里)	Length of Railways in Operation (km)	139926.4	42795.2	30.6
公路里程 (公里)	Length of Highways (km)	5012495.8	2230326.0	44.5
#高速公路	Expressway	149571.2	58801.3	39.3
客运量 (万人)	Passenger Traffic (10 000 persons)	1760435.7	828795.9	48.9
货运量 (万吨)	Freight Traffic (10 000 tons)	4713624.4	2066338.9	44.7
邮政业务总量 (亿元)	Business Volume of Postal Services (100 million yuan)	16229.6	7634.3	47.0
电信业务总量 (亿元)	Business Volume of Postal Services (100 million yuan)	106810.7	46795.6	43.9
普通高等学校数 (个)	Number of Regular Institutions of Higher Education (unit)	2688.0	1159.0	43.1
本专科在校学生数 (万人)	Graduates of Undergraduates and College Students (10 000 persons)	3031.5	1288.6	42.5
医院数 (个)	Number of Hospitals (unit)	34354.0	14365.0	41.8
执业(助理)医师 (万人)	Licensed (Assistant) Doctors (10 000 persons)	386.7	162.3	42.0
医院床位数 (万张)	Number of Beds of Medical Institutions (10 000 beds)	686.7	304.6	44.4

注:长江经济带:包括上海、江苏、浙江、安徽、江西、湖北、湖南、重庆、四川、贵州、云南。
Note: Yangtze River Economic Zone includes: Shanghai, Jiangsu, Zhejiang, Anhui, Jiangxi, Hubei, Hunan, Chongqing, Sichuan, Guizhou, Yunnan.

22-3 长江经济带国民经济和社会发展主要指标(2020 年)
Main Indicators of National Economic and Social Development by Yangtze River Economic Zone (2020)

指 标		Item		全国总计 National Total	长江经济带 Yangtze River Economic Zone	占全国比重(%) As Percentage of National Total
总人口(年末)	(万人)	Population at Year-end	(10 000 persons)	141178.0	60610.0	42.9
国内(地区)生产总值	(亿元)	Gross Domestic Product	(100 million yuan)	1015986.2	471580.0	46.6
第一产业		Primary Industry		77754.1	34106.8	43.9
第二产业		Secondary Industry		384255.3	182709.4	47.5
第三产业		Tertiary Industry		553976.8	254763.7	46.3
地方一般公共预算收入	(亿元)	General Public Budget Revenue	(100 million yuan)	100123.8	44853.3	44.8
地方一般公共预算支出	(亿元)	General Public Budget Expenditure	(100 million yuan)	210492.5	91637.2	43.5
社会消费品零售总额	(亿元)	Total Retail Sales of Consumer Goods	(100 million yuan)	391980.6	192835.4	49.2
货物进出口总额	(亿元)	Total Value of Imports and Exports	(100 million yuan)	321556.9	149544.2	46.5
出口		Exports		179326.4	89232.0	49.8
进口		Imports		142230.6	60312.2	42.4
主要农产品产量		Output of Major Farm Products				
棉花	(万吨)	Cotton	(10 000 tons)	591.0	29.6	5.0
油料	(万吨)	Oil-bearing Crops	(10 000 tons)	3586.4	1642.6	45.8
主要工业产品产量		Output of Major Industrial Products				
原煤	(亿吨)	Coal	(100 million tons)	39.0	3.4	8.8
天然气	(亿立方米)	Natural Gas	(100 million cu.m)	1925.0	571.0	29.7
水泥	(万吨)	Cement	(10 000 tons)	239483.7	119029.8	49.7
粗钢	(万吨)	Crude Steel	(10 000 tons)	106476.7	34077.3	32.0
钢材	(万吨)	Rolled Steel	(10 000 tons)	132489.2	41900.3	31.6
汽车	(万辆)	Motor Vehicles	(10 000 sets)	2532.5	1078.9	42.6
发电量	(亿千瓦小时)	Electricity	(100 million kwh)	77790.6	29437.2	37.8
客运量	(万人)	Passenger Traffic	(10 000 persons)	966541.7	472411.0	48.9
货运量	(万吨)	Freight Traffic	(10 000 tons)	4735565.8	2108365.2	44.5

注:1.长江经济带:包括上海、江苏、浙江、安徽、江西、湖北、湖南、重庆、四川、贵州、云南。
2.以上数据来源于《中国统计摘要 2021》,其中部分指标由长江经济带发展统计监测协调领导小组办公室收集,最终数据以《中国统计年鉴 2021》为准。

Note: a)Yangtze River Economic Zone includes: Shanghai, Jiangsu, Zhejiang, Anhui, Jiangxi, Hubei, Hunan, Chongqing, Sichuan, Guizhou, Yunnan.
b)The data in this table come from *China Statistical Abstract-2021*, and parts of the indicators are collected by Development Statistical Monitoring Leading Group Office of Yangtze River Economic Zone. Final statistics in *China Statistical Yearbook-2021* shall be the standard data.

23

县域经济主要指标

Main Economic Indicators of Counties

资料整理人员:王静敏　　周　真

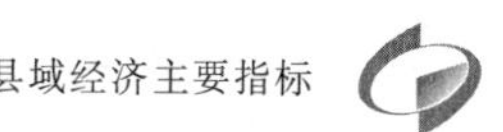

23-1 县域经济主要指标(2020)
Main Economic Indicators of Counties (2020)

指标名称	Item	地区生产总值(亿元) Gross Regional Product (100 million yuan)
蔡甸区	Caidian District	371.34
江夏区	Jiangxia District	842.04
黄陂区	Huangpi District	1013.28
新洲区	Xinzhou District	888.57
阳新县	Yangxin County	281.82
大冶市	Daye City	647.18
郧阳区	Yun County	167.99
郧西县	Yunxi County	95.15
竹山县	Zhushan County	117.12
竹溪县	Zhuxi County	87.68
房县	Fang County	120.46
丹江口市	Danjiangkou City	270.07
夷陵区	Yiling District	531.66
远安县	Yuanan County	174.44
兴山县	Xingshan County	123.98
秭归县	Zigui County	157.55
长阳县	Changyang Tujia A.C.	156.44
五峰县	Wufeng Tujia A.C.	80.76
宜都市	Yidu City	643.02
当阳市	Dangyang City	493.35
枝江市	Zhijiang City	564.00
襄州区	Xiangzhou District	728.22
南漳县	Nanzhang County	293.35
谷城县	Gucheng County	385.86
保康县	Baokang County	132.94
老河口市	Laohekou City	342.44
枣阳市	Zaoyang City	654.98
宜城市	Yicheng City	355.79
梁子湖区	Liangzihu District	82.76
华容区	Huarong District	372.02
鄂城区	Echeng District	550.46
东宝区	Dongbao District	385.49
京山市	Jingshan City	403.12
沙洋县	Shayang County	316.80
钟祥市	Zhongxiang City	526.54
孝南区	Xiaonan District	413.09
孝昌县	Xiaochang County	137.90
大悟县	Dawu County	171.34
云梦县	Yunmeng County	199.57

23-1 续表 1 continued

指标名称	Item	地区生产总值(亿元) Gross Regional Product (100 million yuan)
应城市	Yingcheng City	380.53
安陆市	Anlu City	245.44
汉川市	Hanchuan City	645.66
荆州区	Jingzhou District	341.21
江陵县	Jiangling County	109.05
公安县	Gongan County	311.12
监利市	Jianli County	288.75
石首市	Shishou City	208.86
洪湖市	Honghu City	286.81
松滋市	Songci City	330.46
黄州区	Huangzhou District	241.10
团风县	Tuanfeng County	107.77
红安县	Hongan County	197.93
罗田县	Luotian County	145.59
英山县	Yingshan County	107.16
浠水县	Xishui County	236.03
蕲春县	Qichun County	247.64
黄梅县	Huangmei County	235.38
麻城市	Macheng City	340.35
武穴市	Wuxue City	310.60
咸安区	Xian′an District	361.45
嘉鱼县	Jiayu County	275.39
通城县	Tongcheng County	162.27
崇阳县	Chongyang County	148.60
通山县	Tongshan County	133.57
赤壁市	Chibi City	443.39
曾都区	Zengdu District	501.70
随　县	Sui Country	257.68
广水市	Guangshui City	337.34
恩施市	Enshi City	356.99
利川市	Lichuan City	199.15
建始县	Jianshi County	116.43
巴东县	Badong County	125.28
宣恩县	Xuanen County	79.73
咸丰县	Xianfeng County	93.14
来凤县	Laifeng County	82.08
鹤峰县	Hefeng County	64.91
仙桃市	Xiantiao City	827.91
潜江市	Qianjiang City	765.23
天门市	Tianmen City	617.49

23-1 续表 2 continued

指标名称	Item	固定资产投资增速(%) Growth Rate of Fixed Asset Investment(%)	社会消费品零售总额(亿元) Total Retail Sales of Consumer Goods (100 million yuan)	地方一般公共预算收入(万元) General Public Budget Revenue of Local Governments (10 000 yuan)
蔡甸区	Caidian District	-5.2	138.35	347931
江夏区	Jiangxia District	-14.6	306.13	671227
黄陂区	Huangpi District	-5.9	552.38	513784
新洲区	Xinzhou District	-6.0	531.00	456394
阳新县	Yangxin County	-18.6	138.35	153366
大冶市	Daye City	-18.3	297.88	347130
郧阳区	Yun County	-10.5	113.91	80737
郧西县	Yunxi County	-10.3	87.31	39131
竹山县	Zhushan County	-13.3	77.07	50490
竹溪县	Zhuxi County	-13.3	59.83	39743
房县	Fang County	-22.0	85.67	59862
丹江口市	Danjiangkou City	-57.3	85.72	93735
夷陵区	Yiling District	-16.0	159.66	188174
远安县	Yuanan County	-27.7	52.58	50291
兴山县	Xingshan County	-0.1	37.27	44322
秭归县	Zigui County	-55.6	66.77	40666
长阳县	Changyang Tujia A.C.	-16.2	60.92	39592
五峰县	Wufeng Tujia A.C.	4.6	32.23	18844
宜都市	Yidu City	-24.2	127.87	153768
当阳市	Dangyang City	-15.0	144.33	85784
枝江市	Zhijiang City	-14.8	157.39	109346
襄州区	Xiangzhou District	-18.9	226.65	240503
南漳县	Nanzhang County	-25.3	119.20	74586
谷城县	Gucheng County	-20.2	131.55	85354
保康县	Baokang County	-20.6	59.29	53689
老河口市	Laohekou City	-20.2	133.97	92555
枣阳市	Zaoyang City	-20.3	220.58	164916
宜城市	Yicheng City	-19.7	119.55	87780
梁子湖区	Liangzihu District	-36.9	21.17	39931
华容区	Huarong District	-25.1	165.81	57532
鄂城区	Echeng District	-6.2	139.59	141464
东宝区	Dongbao District	-13.4	220.00	147282
京山市	Jingshan City	-18.7	154.50	128585
沙洋县	Shayang County	-21.0	106.50	64422
钟祥市	Zhongxiang City	-28.4	207.80	139262
孝南区	Xiaonan District	-14.1	194.80	171208
孝昌县	Xiaochang County	-21.9	85.07	76246
大悟县	Dawu County	-22.0	93.75	84325
云梦县	Yunmeng County	-22.0	117.46	98160

23-1 续表 3 continued

指标名称	Item	固定资产投资增速(%) Growth Rate of Fixed Asset Investment(%)	社会消费品零售总额(亿元) Total Retail Sales of Consumer Goods (100 million yuan)	地方一般公共预算收入(万元) General Public Budget Revenue of Local Governments (10 000 yuan)
应城市	Yingcheng City	-20.5	153.97	114774
安陆市	Anlu City	-29.6	117.71	81969
汉川市	Hanchuan City	-21.9	218.48	213798
荆州区	Jingzhou District	-7.2	205.94	138864
江陵县	Jiangling County	-47.7	42.90	37578
公安县	Gongan County	-32.4	164.33	88902
监利市	Jianli County	-30.9	170.50	71696
石首市	Shishou City	-32.4	115.76	61308
洪湖市	Honghu City	-9.8	155.13	83129
松滋市	Songci City	-11.7	141.58	128728
黄州区	Huangzhou District	-25.0	156.21	46866
团风县	Tuanfeng County	-19.0	39.00	46972
红安县	Hongan County	-17.6	86.15	108393
罗田县	Luotian County	-31.3	95.58	53596
英山县	Yingshan County	-19.5	44.67	43895
浠水县	Xishui County	-19.4	145.43	75069
蕲春县	Qichun County	-18.1	140.16	105483
黄梅县	Huangmei County	-19.2	142.04	83169
麻城市	Macheng City	-24.9	152.07	160019
武穴市	Wuxue City	-20.8	148.83	144065
咸安区	Xian′an District	-19.7	150.73	159667
嘉鱼县	Jiayu County	-18.7	79.79	101218
通城县	Tongcheng County	-20.3	83.31	62542
崇阳县	Chongyang County	-23.5	78.38	62430
通山县	Tongshan County	-29.4	66.57	46445
赤壁市	Chibi City	-21.9	145.25	148699
曾都区	Zengdu District	-29.5	308.50	111498
随　县	Sui Country	-17.8	77.73	51234
广水市	Guangshui City	-18.5	133.30	113092
恩施市	Enshi City	-22.1	163.82	165892
利川市	Lichuan City	-17.1	93.37	89870
建始县	Jianshi County	-39.5	62.11	50593
巴东县	Badong County	-18.1	63.24	48261
宣恩县	Xuanen County	-11.7	47.17	31310
咸丰县	Xianfeng County	-24.1	49.54	28821
来凤县	Laifeng County	-15.2	44.52	30447
鹤峰县	Hefeng County	-24.8	38.82	20006
仙桃市	Xiantiao City	-37.2	381.93	326834
潜江市	Qianjiang City	-23.3	248.90	220314
天门市	Tianmen City	-26.8	289.76	146706

23-1 续表 4 continued

指标名称	Item	外贸出口（亿元）Total Exports (100 million yuan)	城镇常住居民人均可支配收入(元) Per Capita Disposable Income of Urban Households (yuan)	农村常住居民人均可支配收入(元) Per Capita Disposable Income of Rural Households(yuan)
蔡甸区	Caidian District	43.85	37359	22371
江夏区	Jiangxia District	15.28	37382	23602
黄陂区	Huangpi District	188.15	38673	22662
新洲区	Xinzhou District	42.71	34856	21488
阳新县	Yangxin County	7.56	29205	13397
大冶市	Daye City	36.27	41829	21553
郧阳区	Yun County	6.46	29818	11786
郧西县	Yunxi County	7.48	28346	11421
竹山县	Zhushan County	6.94	28659	11504
竹溪县	Zhuxi County	1.90	28331	11342
房县	Fang County	5.52	29746	11498
丹江口市	Danjiangkou City	2.16	31221	13078
夷陵区	Yiling District	3.52	39475	22725
远安县	Yuanan County	9.87	35275	21127
兴山县	Xingshan County	37.11	30536	13952
秭归县	Zigui County	9.44	29601	11932
长阳县	Changyang Tujia A.C.	3.77	30563	11986
五峰县	Wufeng Tujia A.C.	1.98	28172	11735
宜都市	Yidu City	23.16	39923	23276
当阳市	Dangyang City	2.80	37151	23224
枝江市	Zhijiang City	21.67	36064	23544
襄州区	Xiangzhou District	37.95	35503	20290
南漳县	Nanzhang County	26.26	34874	17360
谷城县	Gucheng County	21.19	36409	17850
保康县	Baokang County	10.32	31408	13106
老河口市	Laohekou City	19.70	38075	19895
枣阳市	Zaoyang City	13.80	39431	19625
宜城市	Yicheng City	19.60	35184	19711
梁子湖区	Liangzihu District	0.16	26874	14553
华容区	Huarong District	5.92	31437	19951
鄂城区	Echeng District	5.01	36779	20149
东宝区	Dongbao District	7.23	38555	20694
京山市	Jingshan City	8.35	34808	19952
沙洋县	Shayang County	5.42	34584	20123
钟祥市	Zhongxiang City	3.88	34823	20510
孝南区	Xiaonan District	8.08	37872	19719
孝昌县	Xiaochang County	4.76	30734	12096
大悟县	Dawu County	4.93	31014	12423
云梦县	Yunmeng County	21.07	36175	20044

23-1 续表 5 continued

指标名称	Item	外贸出口（亿元）Total Exports (100 million yuan)	城镇常住居民人均可支配收入(元) Per Capita Disposable Income of Urban Households (yuan)	农村常住居民人均可支配收入(元) Per Capita Disposable Income of Rural Households(yuan)
应城市	Yingcheng City	5.85	36723	20416
安陆市	Anlu City	7.91	34973	17131
汉川市	Hanchuan City	32.59	36180	19829
荆州区	Jingzhou District	5.41	38508	20905
江陵县	Jiangling County	1.46	30813	17016
公安县	Gongan County	10.79	33569	19711
监利市	Jianli County	5.97	30810	18101
石首市	Shishou City	5.27	32205	18674
洪湖市	Honghu City	4.70	32655	18529
松滋市	Songci City	12.58	32972	19006
黄州区	Huangzhou District	5.74	35242	17786
团风县	Tuanfeng County	1.40	28063	13740
红安县	Hongan County	1.04	28518	12671
罗田县	Luotian County	3.70	28296	12208
英山县	Yingshan County	1.37	27306	13024
浠水县	Xishui County	3.95	30193	15345
蕲春县	Qichun County	5.32	30046	15144
黄梅县	Huangmei County	8.62	31502	16449
麻城市	Macheng City	4.91	31868	14276
武穴市	Wuxue City	23.16	33560	17126
咸安区	Xian´an District	6.63	36585	17904
嘉鱼县	Jiayu County	4.85	32333	18540
通城县	Tongcheng County	7.53	30834	16218
崇阳县	Chongyang County	6.63	29143	15939
通山县	Tongshan County	3.59	26910	12530
赤壁市	Chibi City	20.46	33586	18347
曾都区	Zengdu District	24.27	33487	18748
随　县	Sui Country	25.85	27993	17782
广水市	Guangshui City	4.39	30475	17439
恩施市	Enshi City	1.06	33696	12327
利川市	Lichuan City	1.00	30892	11791
建始县	Jianshi County	0.20	29229	11806
巴东县	Badong County	0.80	29600	11747
宣恩县	Xuanen County	0.89	28825	11684
咸丰县	Xianfeng County	0.78	29162	11720
来凤县	Laifeng County	0.03	29715	11639
鹤峰县	Hefeng County	1.71	29297	12480
仙桃市	Xiantiao City	225.50	35750	20647
潜江市	Qianjiang City	22.10	33623	18948
天门市	Tianmen City	10.10	31308	18356

23-1 续表 6 continued

指标名称	Item	农业总产值（亿元）Total Value of Agricultural Output (100 million yuan)	粮食产量（万吨）Output of Grain (10 000 tons)	油料产量（万吨）Output of Oil-bearing Crops (10 000 tons)	猪肉产量（万吨）Pork of Meat (10 000 tons)
蔡甸区	Caidian District	83.21	11.49	0.96	1.06
江夏区	Jiangxia District	179.13	20.01	2.96	4.09
黄陂区	Huangpi District	217.50	31.57	5.63	1.75
新洲区	Xinzhou District	147.52	22.71	4.01	1.34
汉南区	Hannan District	26.67	1.40	0.04	0.36
阳新县	Yangxin County	107.02	26.29	5.72	2.73
大冶市	Daye City	89.35	24.61	5.82	2.32
郧阳区	Yun County	57.58	20.28	2.35	3.64
郧西县	Yunxi County	44.04	12.17	1.97	1.00
竹山县	Zhushan County	55.89	14.90	5.32	0.88
竹溪县	Zhuxi County	44.83	14.87	2.90	1.08
房县	Fang County	63.43	10.76	2.48	1.21
丹江口市	Danjiangkou City	60.34	9.11	1.33	1.04
夷陵区	Yiling District	127.57	20.26	2.78	3.72
远安县	Yuanan County	38.93	8.00	1.50	1.80
兴山县	Xingshan County	26.90	5.24	0.92	1.89
秭归县	Zigui County	53.94	8.35	1.74	3.50
长阳县	Changyang Tujia A.C.	79.16	10.65	1.38	3.92
五峰县	Wufeng Tujia A.C.	42.86	9.45	0.37	1.91
宜都市	Yidu City	92.91	9.71	2.19	3.16
当阳市	Dangyang City	160.06	46.27	6.26	3.57
枝江市	Zhijiang City	160.08	31.77	4.66	3.99
襄州区	Xiangzhou District	194.71	126.57	13.27	3.41
南漳县	Nanzhang County	102.44	43.92	1.66	4.29
谷城县	Gucheng County	81.96	26.96	1.98	3.85
保康县	Baokang County	47.85	13.48	1.58	2.10
老河口市	Laohekou City	107.61	35.09	1.76	5.65
枣阳市	Zaoyang City	187.13	126.29	7.18	3.96
宜城市	Yicheng City	111.69	66.21	7.04	4.54
梁子湖区	Liangzihu District	55.76	8.68	1.47	
华容区	Huarong District	47.98	7.52	1.55	
鄂城区	Echeng District	68.02	8.35	1.32	
东宝区	Dongbao District	40.00	18.34	2.88	
京山市	Jingshan County	118.68	65.05	5.18	4.45
沙洋县	Shayang County	123.69	77.95	13.13	4.00
钟祥市	Zhongxiang City	144.72	95.45	10.60	6.60
孝南区	Xiaonan District	71.01	23.83	3.93	1.13
孝昌县	Xiaochang County	71.06	25.33	4.92	1.83
大悟县	Dawu County	76.66	28.72	6.07	1.62
云梦县	Yunmeng County	73.85	24.35	2.59	1.67
应城市	Yingcheng City	99.54	34.59	3.03	1.81
安陆市	Anlu City	75.51	43.79	2.52	3.54

23-1 续表 7 continued

指标名称	Item	农业总产值（亿元）Total Value of Agricultural Output (100 million yuan)	粮食产量（万吨）Output of Grain (10 000 tons)	油料产量（万吨）Output of Oil-bearing Crops (10 000 tons)	猪肉产量（万吨）Pork of Meat (10 000 tons)
汉川市	Hanchuan City	142.15	52.11	3.57	3.01
荆州区	Jingzhou District	85.23	28.42	3.18	1.74
江陵县	Jiangling County	52.63	50.74	5.75	1.40
公安县	Gongan County	124.07	87.55	10.69	1.59
监利市	Jianli County	188.47	126.12	13.77	2.45
石首市	Shishou City	83.33	29.92	4.23	2.40
洪湖市	Honghu City	155.14	63.82	8.14	1.72
松滋市	Songci City	82.86	50.90	3.93	4.74
黄州区	Huangzhou District	27.07	3.14	0.55	0.24
团风县	Tuanfeng County	31.24	10.98	1.44	0.38
红安县	Hongan County	48.30	17.93	8.50	2.15
罗田县	Luotian County	54.74	25.84	3.59	0.74
英山县	Yingshan County	62.18	10.54	1.74	0.70
浠水县	Xishui County	122.99	41.09	7.16	2.85
蕲春县	Qichun County	100.06	45.18	5.54	2.59
黄梅县	Huangmei County	104.75	45.64	7.50	2.78
麻城市	Macheng City	118.29	36.10	10.32	3.52
武穴市	Wuxue City	103.52	32.65	6.66	4.07
咸安区	Xian′an District	62.98	22.11	5.66	2.48
嘉鱼县	Jiayu County	84.22	17.61	1.74	0.45
通城县	Tongcheng County	53.28	16.46	2.22	2.87
崇阳县	Chongyang County	55.63	21.47	2.80	2.83
通山县	Tongshan County	47.66	11.63	1.58	1.46
赤壁市	Chibi City	84.85	27.55	4.81	0.90
曾都区	Zengdu District	67.72	26.43	1.39	2.91
随县	Sui Country	136.37	81.93	3.29	3.86
广水市	Guangshui City	110.37	37.81	5.61	3.84
恩施市	Enshi City	63.09	20.56	2.09	4.91
利川市	Lichuan City	74.21	31.34	1.49	3.37
建始县	Jianshi County	47.99	20.42	1.76	3.36
巴东县	Badong County	46.79	20.10	2.53	3.44
宣恩县	Xuanen County	38.82	11.77	0.69	2.49
咸丰县	Xianfeng County	40.68	19.82	1.87	2.51
来凤县	Laifeng County	31.13	13.06	0.98	1.01
鹤峰县	Hefeng County	27.87	7.05	0.51	1.03
仙桃市	Xiantiao City	164.21	69.74	13.21	2.82
潜江市	Qianjiang City	147.30	59.00	4.19	2.87
天门市	Tianmen City	159.78	80.06	12.49	2.73

注：1.粮食产量和猪肉产量数据由国家统计局湖北调查总队提供；
2.国家统计局湖北调查总队未提供鄂州市所辖梁子湖区、华容区、鄂城区猪肉产量数据；
3.国家统计局湖北调查总队未提供荆门市所辖东宝区、掇刀区猪肉产量数据。

Note: a)The data on grain and pork production was provided by Survey Office of National Bureau of Statistics in Hubei.
b)Survery Office of National Bureau of Statistics in Hubei did not provide the data on pork production in Liangzihu District, Huarong District and Echeng District under the jurisdiction of Ezhou City.
c)Survery Office of National Bureau of Statistics in Hubei did not provide the data on pork production in Dongbao District and Duodao District under the jurisdiction of Jingmen City.

附录

全国分省主要指标

Major Indicators by Region

附录 1-1 分地区行政区划
Divisions of Administrative Areas by Regions

单位：个 (unit)

省级区划名称	Provinces, Autonomous Regions and Municipalities	地级 Number of Regions at Prefecture Level	# 地级市 Cities at Prefecture Level	县级 Number of Regions at County Level	# 市辖区 Districts under the Jurisdiction of Cities	# 县级市 Cities at County Level	# 县 Counties	# 自治县 Autponomous Counties
全 国	**National Total**	**333**	**293**	**2844**	**973**	**388**	**1312**	**117**
北 京	Beijing			16	16			
天 津	Tianjin			16	16			
河 北	Hebei	11	11	167	49	21	91	6
山 西	Shanxi	11	11	117	26	11	80	
内蒙古	Inner Mongolia	12	9	103	23	11	17	
辽 宁	Liaoning	14	14	100	59	16	17	8
吉 林	Jilin	9	8	60	21	20	16	3
黑龙江	Heilongjiang	13	12	121	54	21	45	1
上 海	Shanghai			16	16			
江 苏	Jiangsu	13	13	95	55	21	19	
浙 江	Zhejiang	11	11	90	37	20	32	1
安 徽	Anhui	16	16	104	45	9	50	
福 建	Fujian	9	9	85	29	12	44	
江 西	Jiangxi	11	11	100	27	12	61	
山 东	Shangdong	16	16	136	58	26	52	
河 南	Henan	17	17	158	53	22	83	
湖 北	**Hubei**	**13**	**12**	**103**	**39**	**26**	**35**	**2**
湖 南	Hunan	14	13	122	36	18	61	7
广 东	Guangdong	21	21	122	65	20	34	3
广 西	Guangxi	14	14	111	41	9	49	12
海 南	Hainan	4	4	25	10	5	4	6
重 庆	Chongqing			38	26		8	4
四 川	Sichuan	21	18	183	55	18	106	4
贵 州	Guizhou	9	6	88	16	9	51	11
云 南	Yunnan	16	8	129	17	17	66	29
西 藏	Tibet	7	6	74	8		66	
陕 西	Shaanxi	10	10	107	30	6	71	
甘 肃	Gansu	14	12	86	17	5	57	7
青 海	Qinghai	8	2	44	7	5	25	7
宁 夏	Ningxia	5	5	22	9	2	11	
新 疆	Xinjiang	14	4	106	13	26	61	6
香港特别行政区	Hong Kong Special Administrative Region							
澳门特别行政区	Macao Special Administrative Region							
台湾省	Taiwan							

注：附录数据来自《中国统计摘要 2021》。
Note: Date of the Appendix comes from China Statistical Abstract-2021.

附录 1-1 续表 coutinued

单位：个 (unit)

省级区划名称	Provinces, Autonomous Regions and Municipalities	乡镇级 Number of Regions at Townships Level	# 镇数 towns	# 乡数 Towns	# 街道办事处 Street Communities
全 国	**National Total**	**38741**	**21157**	**8809**	**8773**
北 京	Beijing	343	143	35	165
天 津	Tianjin	250	125	3	122
河 北	Hebei	2254	1230	713	310
山 西	Shanxi	1396	579	610	207
内 蒙 古	Inner Mongolia	1024	508	270	246
辽 宁	Liaoning	1355	640	201	514
吉 林	Jilin	951	426	181	344
黑 龙 江	Heilongjiang	1292	562	340	390
上 海	Shanghai	215	106	2	107
江 苏	Jiangsu	1258	712	31	515
浙 江	Zhejiang	1365	618	259	488
安 徽	Anhui	1501	968	271	262
福 建	Fujian	1107	658	264	185
江 西	Jiangxi	1566	830	568	168
山 东	Shangdong	1822	1072	57	693
河 南	Henan	2453	1181	610	662
湖 北	**Hubei**	**1251**	**761**	**161**	**329**
湖 南	Hunan	1940	1133	392	415
广 东	Guangdong	1611	1116	11	484
广 西	Guangxi	1251	806	312	133
海 南	Hainan	218	175	21	22
重 庆	Chongqing	1031	621	171	239
四 川	Sichuan	3230	1978	793	459
贵 州	Guizhou	1509	833	315	361
云 南	Yunnan	1410	678	540	192
西 藏	Tibet	697	142	534	21
陕 西	Shaanxi	1313	973	17	323
甘 肃	Gansu	1356	892	337	127
青 海	Qinghai	403	144	222	37
宁 夏	Ningxia	241	103	90	48
新 疆	Xinjiang	1128	444	478	205
香港特别行政区	Hong Kong Special Administrative Region				
澳门特别行政区	Macao Special Administrative Region				
台 湾 省	Taiwan				

注：乡镇级总数包含河北省、新疆维吾尔族自治区的各一个区公所。

Note: The total number of township level including one district public of Hubei Province and Xinjiang Uygur Autonomous region respectively.

附录 1-2 分地区按三次产业分法人单位数(2019)

Number of Legal Entities by Three Strata of Industry and Region(2019)

单位:个 (unit)

地 区	Region	法人单位数 Corporate Units	第一产业 Primary Industry	第二产业 Secondary Industry	第三产业 Tertiary Industry
全 国	**National Total**	**25280211**	**1642773**	**5063303**	**18574135**
北 京	Beijing	913369	6648	56711	850010
天 津	Tianjin	321740	11851	62330	247559
河 北	Hebei	1318321	104011	334209	880101
山 西	Shanxi	633960	89111	88670	456179
内蒙古	Inner Mongolia	381670	53421	58227	270022
辽 宁	Liaoning	621156	42302	128162	450692
吉 林	Jilin	212073	23952	33891	154230
黑龙江	Heilongjiang	295952	46100	42623	207229
上 海	Shanghai	482353	5118	70022	407213
江 苏	Jiangsu	2327217	39449	684277	1603491
浙 江	Zhejiang	1905578	45729	527013	1332836
安 徽	Anhui	946508	91691	193725	661092
福 建	Fujian	941297	46383	187183	707731
江 西	Jiangxi	570196	64092	113782	392322
山 东	Shangdong	2309367	100155	544613	1664599
河 南	Henan	1418818	122388	231246	1065184
湖 北	**Hubei**	**1006945**	**57579**	**182723**	**766643**
湖 南	Hunan	672298	56616	103722	511960
广 东	Guangdong	3349156	38120	747589	2563447
广 西	Guangxi	641503	75901	80676	484926
海 南	Hainan	125542	11343	15579	98620
重 庆	Chongqing	591369	74990	78274	438105
四 川	Sichuan	867477	87763	126869	652845
贵 州	Guizhou	471151	102105	77164	291882
云 南	Yunnan	571421	85592	77360	408469
西 藏	Tibet	49191	2498	12128	34565
陕 西	Shaanxi	587005	48581	107214	431210
甘 肃	Gansu	266600	53275	28921	184404
青 海	Qinghai	98516	18227	12473	67816
宁 夏	Ningxia	113259	17361	16403	79495
新 疆	Xinjiang	269203	20421	39524	209258

附录 1-3　分地区按行业分法人单位数(2019)
Number of Legal Entities by Sector and Region(2019)

单位:个　(unit)

地　区	Region	法　人单位数 Corporate Units	#农、林、牧、渔业 Agriculture, Forestry, Animal Husbandry, Fishery	#采矿业 Mining Industry	#制造业 Manufacturing	#电力、热力、燃气及水的生产和供应业 Electricity, Gas and Water Production and Supply	#建筑业 Construction	批发和零售业 Wholesale and Retail Trades
全国总计	**National Total**	**25280211**	**1879887**	**70983**	**3463346**	**113649**	**1458539**	**7155907**
北　京	Beijing	913369	7105	57	23574	1146	33309	259365
天　津	Tianjin	321740	12403	82	41870	875	20734	84886
河　北	Hebei	1318321	114610	4942	226936	5700	98615	374542
山　西	Shanxi	633960	95968	6018	38137	5377	40990	172364
内蒙古	Inner Mongolia	381670	60533	4036	23942	3111	28011	93920
辽　宁	Liaoning	621156	50804	3478	87039	3045	36509	169425
吉　林	Jilin	212073	32629	924	20501	1588	11267	46743
黑龙江	Heilongjiang	295952	50726	1641	25649	2209	13719	66672
上　海	Shanghai	482353	5384	6	52507	221	18472	142793
江　苏	Jiangsu	2327217	52735	338	524675	5061	158896	678171
浙　江	Zhejiang	1905578	48826	856	454683	5678	68111	613479
安　徽	Anhui	946508	108730	1231	116544	5551	71766	252193
福　建	Fujian	941297	51198	1569	135044	6424	45254	317460
江　西	Jiangxi	570196	70862	3006	69191	7415	34744	137446
山　东	Shangdong	2309367	125306	2558	354725	6939	185133	728784
河　南	Henan	1418818	156664	3314	140757	4965	83586	415436
湖　北	**Hubei**	**1006945**	**72337**	**2711**	**100948**	**5593**	**74766**	**276174**
湖　南	Hunan	672298	77090	3575	63104	6798	30989	150912
广　东	Guangdong	3349156	45448	2643	613236	10171	126537	1043904
广　西	Guangxi	641503	83239	3257	44771	3399	29992	165974
海　南	Hainan	125542	12295	182	3949	460	11196	25360
重　庆	Chongqing	591369	78687	1292	53772	2231	21728	174491
四　川	Sichuan	867477	93884	3474	67442	5869	51219	192114
贵　州	Guizhou	471151	103737	4280	47820	2181	23307	97150
云　南	Yunnan	571421	91192	5413	36016	3006	33365	151415
西　藏	Tibet	49191	2830	307	3761	284	7856	7132
陕　西	Shaanxi	587005	54499	4414	42745	3287	59942	149543
甘　肃	Gansu	266600	56833	1133	13165	1513	13480	52004
青　海	Qinghai	98516	18722	473	5057	789	6265	18736
宁　夏	Ningxia	113259	18486	705	8846	629	6477	29111
新　疆	Xinjiang	269203	26125	3068	22940	2134	12304	68208

附录 1-3 续表 1 continued

单位：个 (unit)

地区	Region	法人单位数 Corporate Units					
		# 交通运输、仓储和邮政业 Traffic, Transport, Storage and Postal Industry	# 住宿和餐饮业 Accommodation and Catering Services	# 信息传输、软件和信息技术服务业 Information Transmission, Software and Computer Services	金融业 Financial Intermediation	# 房地产业 Real Estate	# 租赁和商务服务业 Leasing and Business Services
全国总计	**National Total**	**629631**	**449277**	**1047408**	**131744**	**811663**	**2825375**
北京	Beijing	17848	32208	68633	6933	25072	169189
天津	Tianjin	14184	5114	17960	5070	11520	41627
河北	Hebei	32938	15905	42292	4099	46774	109466
山西	Shanxi	16849	10083	25146	2456	20042	55653
内蒙古	Inner Mongolia	11892	4436	9627	1712	13222	35876
辽宁	Liaoning	21331	8368	27372	3445	22162	61673
吉林	Jilin	5959	2439	5987	1280	7282	16725
黑龙江	Heilongjiang	9175	2502	9855	1410	9318	23561
上海	Shanghai	17939	19858	25212	9069	22070	76930
江苏	Jiangsu	65083	28194	98224	6012	67293	229748
浙江	Zhejiang	39002	27954	80752	15777	54133	190757
安徽	Anhui	25554	17297	34281	3243	28027	99194
福建	Fujian	19663	14732	46518	3773	21837	99758
江西	Jiangxi	18704	7384	19117	1670	15933	58559
山东	Shangdong	66140	34177	81022	8141	62011	232002
河南	Henan	26723	21297	56383	2723	47074	129595
湖北	**Hubei**	**25439**	**18322**	**50017**	**2804**	**34986**	**113372**
湖南	Hunan	13531	11407	24214	1928	21082	64185
广东	Guangdong	77590	55598	172828	29733	124439	535456
广西	Guangxi	15801	10205	23516	2781	26062	81127
海南	Hainan	2560	3260	6401	657	12254	18049
重庆	Chongqing	12578	24797	23871	1906	17884	64823
四川	Sichuan	19283	17323	32672	3361	26831	95519
贵州	Guizhou	8270	17206	9345	1501	12923	39758
云南	Yunnan	12164	14549	16934	2841	17669	53986
西藏	Tibet	676	1130	1060	321	637	5558
陕西	Shaanxi	13360	11363	20883	2369	20600	57780
甘肃	Gansu	4510	5350	3732	1232	6852	18415
青海	Qinghai	1776	2251	2214	348	2926	11285
宁夏	Ningxia	3515	1692	2773	792	2869	11277
新疆	Xinjiang	9594	2876	8567	2357	9879	24472

附录 1-3 续表 2 continued

单位:个 (unit)

地区	Region	法人单位数 Corporate Units						
		#科学研究和技术服务 Research and Technical Service	#水利、环境和公共设施管理业 Water, Environment and Public Facilities Management	#居民服务、修理和其他服务业 Resident Services、Repair and Other Services	#教育 Education	#卫生和社会工作 Health and Social Work	#文化、体育和娱乐业 Culture, Sports and Entertainment	#公共管理、社会保障和社会组织 Public Management、Social Security and Social Organization
全国总计	**National Total**	**1390741**	**172856**	**522903**	**698893**	**279155**	**585224**	**1593030**
北京	Beijing	136076	6986	33407	19869	6362	49183	17047
天津	Tianjin	28778	1927	7658	6275	2326	7684	10767
河北	Hebei	59330	9419	22727	28723	10867	24147	86289
山西	Shanxi	27128	6184	13381	17383	7382	15417	58002
内蒙古	Inner Mongolia	16136	3937	7678	12405	5138	8314	37744
辽宁	Liaoning	29061	3601	11873	19436	11182	11952	39400
吉林	Jilin	9169	1637	4066	8276	4302	3922	27377
黑龙江	Heilongjiang	15290	2366	4540	11980	6160	6322	32857
上海	Shanghai	31658	2458	17401	9082	4895	12802	13596
江苏	Jiangsu	157330	13891	44363	39883	30846	44902	81572
浙江	Zhejiang	78935	10103	33452	46240	14637	42742	79461
安徽	Anhui	44132	7114	21340	25780	11490	21037	52004
福建	Fujian	40404	6224	17847	22421	6777	25113	59281
江西	Jiangxi	19027	3608	9237	19511	8166	11180	55436
山东	Shangdong	119160	14663	39141	52077	20243	43350	133795
河南	Henan	77074	11120	24305	60178	20560	33538	103526
湖北	**Hubei**	**62116**	**9743**	**20763**	**27838**	**12768**	**24354**	**71894**
湖南	Hunan	45174	6644	12702	31653	11804	23584	71922
广东	Guangdong	199286	12416	65169	72214	18401	63415	80672
广西	Guangxi	32566	6432	13569	28171	6148	12679	51814
海南	Hainan	6085	1163	3713	5306	1296	3807	7549
重庆	Chongqing	21783	4142	16836	17374	6750	16681	29743
四川	Sichuan	43156	6492	19588	34768	16899	25914	111669
贵州	Guizhou	11837	3613	14726	16440	5621	9162	42274
云南	Yunnan	23728	4831	14557	16398	6005	14523	52829
西藏	Tibet	1423	203	669	1035	573	984	12752
陕西	Shaanxi	28029	5864	13689	20272	11412	13420	53534
甘肃	Gansu	7134	1626	5176	12519	3881	5553	52492
青海	Qinghai	3951	1192	1880	2370	1480	1865	14936
宁夏	Ningxia	3360	824	2370	3667	967	2085	12814
新疆	Xinjiang	12425	2433	5080	9349	3817	5593	37982

附录 1-4 分地区年末常住人口
Population at Year-end by Regions

单位:万人 (10 000 persons)

地 区	Region	2013	2014	2015	2016	2017	2018	2019	2020
全 国	**National Total**	**136726**	**137646**	**138326**	**139232**	**140011**	**140541**	**141008**	**141178**
北 京	Beijing	2125	2171	2188	2195	2194	2192	2190	2189
天 津	Tianjin	1410	1429	1439	1443	1410	1383	1385	1387
河 北	Hebei	7288	7323	7345	7375	7409	7426	7447	7461
山 西	Shanxi	3535	3528	3519	3514	3510	3502	3497	3492
内蒙古	Inner Mongolia	2455	2449	2440	2436	2433	2422	2415	2405
辽 宁	Liaoning	4365	4358	4338	4327	4312	4291	4277	4259
吉 林	Jilin	2668	2642	2613	2567	2526	2484	2448	2407
黑龙江	Heilongjiang	3666	3608	3529	3463	3399	3327	3255	3185
上 海	Shanghai	2448	2467	2458	2467	2466	2475	2481	2487
江 苏	Jiangsu	8192	8281	8315	8381	8423	8446	8469	8475
浙 江	Zhejiang	5784	5890	5985	6072	6170	6273	6375	6457
安 徽	Anhui	5988	5997	6011	6033	6057	6076	6092	6103
福 建	Fujian	3885	3945	3984	4016	4065	4104	4137	4154
江 西	Jiangxi	4476	4480	4485	4496	4511	4513	4516	4519
山 东	Shangdong	9746	9808	9866	9973	10033	10077	10106	10153
河 南	Henan	9573	9645	9701	9778	9829	9864	9901	9937
湖 北	**Hubei**	**5798**	**5816**	**5850**	**5885**	**5904**	**5917**	**5927**	**5775**
湖 南	Hunan	6600	6611	6615	6625	6633	6635	6640	6644
广 东	Guangdong	11270	11489	11678	11908	12141	12348	12489	12601
广 西	Guangxi	4731	4770	4811	4857	4907	4947	4982	5013
海 南	Hainan	920	936	945	957	972	982	995	1008
重 庆	Chongqing	3011	3043	3070	3110	3144	3163	3188	3205
四 川	Sichuan	8109	8139	8196	8251	8289	8321	8351	8367
贵 州	Guizhou	3632	3677	3708	3758	3803	3822	3848	3856
云 南	Yunnan	4641	4653	4663	4677	4693	4703	4714	4721
西 藏	Tibet	317	325	330	340	349	354	361	365
陕 西	Shaanxi	3804	3827	3846	3874	3904	3931	3944	3953
甘 肃	Gansu	2537	2531	2523	2520	2522	2515	2509	2502
青 海	Qinghai	571	576	577	582	586	587	590	592
宁 夏	Ningxia	666	678	684	695	705	710	717	720
新 疆	Xinjiang	2285	2325	2385	2428	2480	2520	2559	2585

注:本表 2011-2019 年数据根据第七次全国人口普查数据修订,2020 年数据为普查时点(2020 年 11 月 1 日零时)数。全国数据包括中国人民解放军现役军人数,但不包括香港、澳洲特别行政区和台湾地区数据;分省数据中未包括中国人民解放军现役军人数。

Note: The data in this table for 2011-2019 are revised based on the data of the seventh national population census. The data for 2020 are data as of the time for the census (0:00 on November 1, 2020). The national data include the number of persons in active military service of the Chinese People's Liberation Army, but exclude the data of Hong Kong Special Administrative Region, Macau Special Administrative Region and Taiwan Region; the data by province do not include the number of persons in active military service of the Chinese People's Liberation Army.

附录 1-5 分地区年末城镇人口比重
Proportion of Urban Populations at Year-end by Region

单位:% (%)

地 区	Region	2011	2012	2013	2014	2015	2016	2017	2018	2019	2020
全 国	**National Total**	**51.83**	**53.10**	**54.49**	**55.75**	**57.33**	**58.84**	**60.24**	**61.50**	**62.71**	**63.89**
北 京	Beijing	86.20	86.29	86.39	86.50	86.71	86.76	86.93	87.09	87.35	87.55
天 津	Tianjin	80.43	81.55	82.29	82.55	82.88	83.27	83.57	83.95	84.31	84.70
河 北	Hebei	45.59	46.60	48.02	49.36	51.67	53.87	55.74	57.33	58.77	60.07
山 西	Shanxi	49.79	51.32	52.88	54.30	55.87	57.27	58.59	59.85	61.29	62.53
内蒙古	Inner Mongolia	57.04	58.42	59.82	60.97	62.09	63.40	64.60	65.51	66.46	67.48
辽 宁	Liaoning	64.05	65.65	66.45	67.05	68.05	68.87	69.49	70.26	71.21	72.14
吉 林	Jilin	53.40	54.54	55.74	56.81	57.64	58.75	59.71	60.85	61.63	62.64
黑龙江	Heilongjiang	56.49	56.88	58.04	59.22	60.47	61.09	61.90	63.46	64.62	65.61
上 海	Shanghai	89.30	89.30	89.60	89.30	88.53	89.00	89.10	89.13	89.22	89.30
江 苏	Jiangsu	62.01	63.01	64.39	65.70	67.49	68.93	70.18	71.19	72.47	73.44
浙 江	Zhejiang	62.29	62.91	63.94	64.96	66.32	67.72	68.91	70.02	71.58	72.17
安 徽	Anhui	44.80	46.30	47.87	49.31	50.97	52.62	54.29	55.65	57.02	58.33
福 建	Fujian	58.11	59.32	60.80	61.99	63.22	64.39	65.78	66.98	67.87	68.75
江 西	Jiangxi	45.75	47.39	49.04	50.55	52.30	53.99	55.70	57.34	59.07	60.44
山 东	Shangdong	50.86	52.03	53.46	54.77	56.97	59.13	60.79	61.46	61.86	63.05
河 南	Henan	40.47	41.99	43.60	45.05	47.02	48.78	50.56	52.24	54.01	55.43
湖 北	**Hubei**	**51.78**	**53.23**	**54.51**	**55.73**	**57.18**	**58.57**	**59.88**	**61.00**	**61.83**	**62.89**
湖 南	Hunan	44.97	46.22	47.63	48.98	50.79	52.70	54.62	56.09	57.45	58.76
广 东	Guangdong	66.57	67.15	68.09	68.62	69.51	70.15	70.74	71.81	72.65	74.15
广 西	Guangxi	41.90	43.48	45.11	46.54	47.99	49.24	50.59	51.82	52.98	54.20
海 南	Hainan	50.34	51.02	52.28	53.30	54.91	56.70	58.04	59.13	59.37	60.27
重 庆	Chongqing	54.98	56.64	58.29	59.74	61.47	63.33	65.00	66.61	68.24	69.46
四 川	Sichuan	41.85	43.35	44.96	46.51	48.27	50.00	51.78	53.50	55.36	56.73
贵 州	Guizhou	35.03	36.30	37.89	40.24	42.96	45.56	47.76	49.54	51.48	53.15
云 南	Yunnan	36.57	38.47	39.99	41.21	42.93	44.64	46.29	47.44	48.67	50.05
西 藏	Tibet	22.81	22.87	23.93	26.23	28.87	31.57	33.38	33.80	34.51	35.73
陕 西	Shaanxi	47.35	49.71	51.57	53.01	54.74	56.39	58.07	59.65	61.28	62.66
甘 肃	Gansu	37.25	38.78	40.50	42.28	44.24	46.07	48.12	49.69	50.70	52.23
青 海	Qinghai	46.53	47.85	49.29	50.84	51.67	53.55	55.45	57.27	58.78	60.08
宁 夏	Ningxia	50.20	51.15	52.84	54.82	56.98	58.74	60.95	62.15	63.63	64.96
新 疆	Xinjiang	43.73	44.22	44.94	46.79	48.78	50.42	51.90	54.01	55.51	56.53

注:本表 2011-2019 年数据根据第七次全国人口普查数据修订,2020 年数据为普查时点(2020 年 11 月 1 日零时)数。

Note: The data in this table for 2011-2019 are revised based on the data of the seventh national population census. The data for 2020 are data as of the time for the population census (0:00 on November 1, 2020).

附录 1-6 地区生产总值(2020)
Gross Regional Product (2020)

地区	Region	地区生产总值(亿元) Gross Regional Product (100 million yuan)	三次产业增加值 Value-Added by Three Strata of Industry 第一产业(亿元) Primary Industry (100 million yuan)	第二产业(亿元) Secondary Industry (100 million yuan)	第三产业(亿元) Tertiary Industry (100 million yuan)	地区生产总值指数(上年=100) Indices of Gross Regional Product (preceding year=100)	人均地区生产总值(元) Per Capita Gross Regional Product (yuan)	人均地区生产总值指数(上年=100) Indices of Per Capita Gross Regional Product (preceding year=100)
北京	Beijing	36102.6	107.6	5716.4	30278.6	101.2	164889	101.2
天津	Tianjin	14083.7	210.2	4804.1	9069.5	101.5	101614	101.3
河北	Hebei	36206.9	3880.1	13597.2	18729.5	103.9	48564	103.6
山西	Shanxi	17651.9	946.7	7675.4	9029.8	103.6	50528	103.7
内蒙古	Inner Mongolia	17359.8	2025.1	6868.0	8466.7	100.2	72062	100.5
辽宁	Liaoning	25115.0	2284.6	9400.9	13429.4	100.6	58872	101.1
吉林	Jilin	12311.3	1553.0	4326.2	6432.1	102.4	50800	104.1
黑龙江	Heilongjiang	13698.5	3438.3	3483.5	6776.7	101.0	42635	103.4
上海	Shanghai	38700.6	103.6	10289.5	28307.5	101.7	155768	101.4
江苏	Jiangsu	102719.0	4536.7	44226.4	53955.8	103.7	121231	103.5
浙江	Zhejiang	64613.3	2169.2	26413.0	36031.2	103.6	100620	102.0
安徽	Anhui	38680.6	3184.7	15671.7	19824.3	103.9	63426	103.6
福建	Fujian	43903.9	2732.3	20328.8	20842.8	103.3	105818	102.5
江西	Jiangxi	25691.5	2241.6	11084.8	12365.1	103.8	56871	103.8
山东	Shandong	73129.0	5363.8	28612.2	39153.0	103.6	72151	103.1
河南	Henan	54997.1	5353.7	22875.3	26768.0	101.3	55435	100.9
湖北	**Hubei**	**43443.5**	**4131.9**	**17023.9**	**22287.6**	**95.0**	**74440**	**96.4**
湖南	Hunan	41781.5	4240.4	15937.7	21603.4	103.8	62900	103.7
广东	Guangdong	110760.9	4770.0	43450.2	62540.8	102.3	88210	101.1
广西	Guangxi	22156.7	3555.8	7108.5	11492.4	103.7	44309	102.9
海南	Hainan	5532.4	1136.0	1055.3	3341.2	103.5	55131	102.0
重庆	Chongqing	25002.8	1803.3	9992.2	13207.3	103.9	78170	103.1
四川	Sichuan	48598.8	5556.6	17571.1	25471.1	103.8	58126	103.4
贵州	Guizhou	17826.6	2539.9	6211.6	9075.1	104.5	46267	104.0
云南	Yunnan	24521.9	3598.9	8287.5	12635.5	104.0	51975	103.7
西藏	Tibet	1902.7	150.6	798.3	953.8	107.8	52345	106.1
陕西	Shaanxi	26181.9	2267.5	11362.6	12551.7	102.2	66292	101.9
甘肃	Gansu	9016.7	1198.1	2852.0	4966.5	103.9	35995	104.2
青海	Qinghai	3005.9	334.3	1143.6	1528.1	101.5	50819	101.0
宁夏	Ningxia	3920.5	338.0	1609.0	1973.6	103.9	54528	103.1
新疆	Xinjiang	13797.6	1981.3	4744.5	7071.8	103.4	53593	102.0

注:1.表中数据为初步核算数。
2.本表绝对数按当年价格计算,指数按不变价格计算。

Note: a)Data in this table are preliminary data.
b)Level data in this table are calculated at current prices while indices at constant prices.

附录 1-7 分地区居民消费价格指数
Consumer Price Index by Region

(上年=100) (Preceding year = 100)

地 区	Region	2013	2014	2015	2016	2017	2018	2019	2020
全 国	**National Total**	**102.6**	**102.0**	**101.4**	**102.0**	**101.6**	**102.1**	**102.9**	**102.5**
北 京	Beijing	103.3	101.6	101.8	101.4	101.9	102.5	102.3	101.7
天 津	Tianjin	103.1	101.9	101.7	102.1	102.1	102.0	102.7	102.0
河 北	Hebei	103.0	101.7	100.9	101.5	101.7	102.4	103.0	102.1
山 西	Shanxi	103.1	101.7	100.6	101.1	101.1	101.8	102.7	102.9
内蒙古	Inner Mongolia	103.2	101.6	101.1	101.2	101.7	101.8	102.4	101.9
辽 宁	Liaoning	102.4	101.7	101.4	101.6	101.4	102.5	102.4	102.4
吉 林	Jilin	102.9	102.0	101.7	101.6	101.6	102.1	103.0	102.3
黑龙江	Heilongjiang	102.2	101.5	101.1	101.5	101.3	102.0	102.8	102.3
上 海	Shanghai	102.3	102.7	102.4	103.2	101.7	101.6	102.5	101.7
江 苏	Jiangsu	102.3	102.2	101.7	102.3	101.7	102.3	103.1	102.5
浙 江	Zhejiang	102.3	102.1	101.4	101.9	102.1	102.3	102.9	102.3
安 徽	Anhui	102.4	101.6	101.3	101.8	101.2	102.0	102.7	102.7
福 建	Fujian	102.5	102.0	101.7	101.7	101.2	101.5	102.6	102.2
江 西	Jiangxi	102.5	102.3	101.5	102.0	102.0	102.1	102.9	102.6
山 东	Shangdong	102.2	101.9	101.2	102.1	101.5	102.5	103.2	102.8
河 南	Henan	102.9	101.9	101.3	101.9	101.4	102.3	103.0	102.8
湖 北	**Hubei**	**102.8**	**102.0**	**101.5**	**102.2**	**101.5**	**101.9**	**103.1**	**102.7**
湖 南	Hunan	102.5	101.9	101.4	101.9	101.4	102.0	102.9	102.3
广 东	Guangdong	102.5	102.3	101.5	102.3	101.5	102.2	103.4	102.6
广 西	Guangxi	102.2	102.1	101.5	101.6	101.6	102.3	103.7	102.8
海 南	Hainan	102.8	102.4	101.0	102.8	102.8	102.5	103.4	102.3
重 庆	Chongqing	102.7	101.8	101.3	101.8	101.0	102.0	102.7	102.3
四 川	Sichuan	102.8	101.6	101.5	101.9	101.4	101.7	103.2	103.2
贵 州	Guizhou	102.5	102.4	101.8	101.4	100.9	101.8	102.4	102.6
云 南	Yunnan	103.1	102.4	101.9	101.5	100.9	101.6	102.5	103.6
西 藏	Tibet	103.6	102.9	102.0	102.5	101.6	101.7	102.3	102.2
陕 西	Shaanxi	103.0	101.6	101.0	101.3	101.6	102.1	102.9	102.5
甘 肃	Gansu	103.2	102.1	101.6	101.3	101.4	102.0	102.3	102.0
青 海	Qinghai	103.9	102.8	102.6	101.8	101.5	102.5	102.5	102.6
宁 夏	Ningxia	103.4	101.9	101.1	101.5	101.6	102.3	102.1	101.5
新 疆	Xinjiang	103.9	102.1	100.6	101.4	102.2	102.0	101.9	101.5

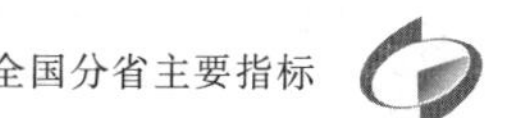

附录 1-8 分地区全体居民人均可支配收入与消费支出
Per Capita Disposable Income and Consumption Expenditure of Urban and Rural Households by Region

单位:元 (yuan)

地 区	Region	可支配收入 Disposable Income		消费支出 Expenses on Consumption	
		2019	2020	2019	2020
全国总计	**National Total**	**30732.8**	**32188.8**	**21558.9**	**21209.9**
北 京	Beijing	67755.9	69433.5	43038.3	38903.3
天 津	Tianjin	42404.1	43854.1	31853.6	28461.4
河 北	Hebei	25664.7	27135.9	17987.2	18037.0
山 西	Shanxi	23828.5	25213.7	15862.6	15732.7
内蒙古	Inner Mongolia	30555.0	31497.3	20743.4	19794.5
辽 宁	Liaoning	31819.7	32738.3	22202.8	20672.1
吉 林	Jilin	24562.9	25751.0	18075.4	17317.7
黑龙江	Heilongjiang	24253.6	24902.0	18111.5	17056.4
上 海	Shanghai	69441.6	72232.4	45605.1	42536.3
江 苏	Jiangsu	41399.7	43390.4	26697.3	26225.1
浙 江	Zhejiang	49898.8	52397.4	32025.8	31294.7
安 徽	Anhui	26415.1	28103.2	19137.4	18877.3
福 建	Fujian	35616.1	37202.4	25314.3	25125.8
江 西	Jiangxi	26262.4	28016.5	17650.5	17955.3
山 东	Shangdong	31597.0	32885.7	20427.5	20940.1
河 南	Henan	23902.7	24810.1	16331.8	16142.6
湖 北	**Hubei**	**28319.5**	**27880.6**	**21567.0**	**19245.9**
湖 南	Hunan	27679.7	29379.9	20478.9	20997.6
广 东	Guangdong	39014.3	41028.6	28994.7	28491.9
广 西	Guangxi	23328.2	24562.3	16418.3	16356.8
海 南	Hainan	26679.5	27904.1	19554.9	18971.6
重 庆	Chongqing	28920.4	30823.9	20773.9	21678.1
四 川	Sichuan	24703.1	26522.1	19338.3	19783.4
贵 州	Guizhou	20397.4	21795.4	14780.0	14873.8
云 南	Yunnan	22082.4	23294.9	15779.8	16792.4
西 藏	Tibet	19501.3	21744.1	13029.2	13224.8
陕 西	Shaanxi	24666.3	26226.0	17464.9	17417.6
甘 肃	Gansu	19139.0	20335.1	15879.1	16174.9
青 海	Qinghai	22617.7	24037.4	17544.8	18284.2
宁 夏	Ningxia	24411.9	25734.9	18296.8	17505.8
新 疆	Xinjiang	23103.4	23844.7	17396.6	16512.1

附录 1-9 分地区城镇居民人均可支配收入与消费支出
Per Capita Disposable Income and Consumption Expenditure of Urban Households by Region

单位:元 (yuan)

地 区	Region	可支配收入 Disposable Income		消费支出 Expenses on Consumption	
		2019	2020	2019	2020
全国总计	**National Total**	**42358.8**	**43833.8**	**28063.4**	**27007.4**
北 京	Beijing	73848.5	75601.5	46358.2	41726.3
天 津	Tianjin	46118.9	47658.5	34810.7	30894.7
河 北	Hebei	35737.7	37285.7	23483.1	23167.4
山 西	Shanxi	33262.4	34792.7	21159.0	20331.9
内 蒙 古	Inner Mongolia	40782.5	41353.1	25382.5	23887.7
辽 宁	Liaoning	39777.2	40375.9	27355.0	24849.1
吉 林	Jilin	32299.2	33395.7	23394.3	21623.2
黑 龙 江	Heilongjiang	30944.6	31114.7	22164.9	20397.3
上 海	Shanghai	73615.3	76437.3	48271.6	44839.3
江 苏	Jiangsu	51056.1	53101.7	31329.1	30882.2
浙 江	Zhejiang	60182.3	62699.3	37507.9	36196.9
安 徽	Anhui	37540.0	39442.1	23781.5	22682.7
福 建	Fujian	45620.5	47160.3	30945.5	30486.5
江 西	Jiangxi	36545.9	38555.8	22714.3	22134.3
山 东	Shangdong	42329.2	43726.3	26731.5	27291.1
河 南	Henan	34201.0	34750.3	21971.6	20644.9
湖 北	**Hubei**	**37601.4**	**36705.7**	**26421.8**	**22885.5**
湖 南	Hunan	39841.9	41697.5	26924.0	26796.4
广 东	Guangdong	48117.6	50257.0	34424.1	33511.3
广 西	Guangxi	34744.9	35859.3	21590.9	20906.5
海 南	Hainan	36016.7	37097.0	25316.7	23559.9
重 庆	Chongqing	37938.6	40006.2	25785.5	26464.4
四 川	Sichuan	36153.7	38253.1	25367.4	25133.2
贵 州	Guizhou	34404.2	36096.2	21402.4	20587.0
云 南	Yunnan	36237.7	37499.5	23454.9	24569.4
西 藏	Tibet	37410.0	41156.4	25636.7	24927.4
陕 西	Shaanxi	36098.2	37868.2	23514.3	22866.4
甘 肃	Gansu	32323.4	33821.8	24453.9	24614.6
青 海	Qinghai	33830.3	35505.8	23799.2	24315.2
宁 夏	Ningxia	34328.5	35719.6	24161.0	22379.1
新 疆	Xinjiang	34663.7	34838.4	25594.2	22951.8

附录 1-10 分地区农村居民人均可支配收入与消费支出
Per Capita Disposable Income and Consumption Expenditure of Rural Households by Region

单位:元 (yuan)

地 区	Region	可支配收入 Disposable Income		消费支出 Expenses on Consumption	
		2019	2020	2019	2020
全国总计	**National Total**	**16020.7**	**17131.5**	**13327.7**	**13713.4**
北 京	Beijing	28928.4	30125.7	21881.0	20912.7
天 津	Tianjin	24804.1	25690.6	17843.3	16844.1
河 北	Hebei	15373.1	16467.0	12372.0	12644.2
山 西	Shanxi	12902.4	13878.0	9728.4	10290.1
内蒙古	Inner Mongolia	15282.8	16566.9	13816.0	13593.7
辽 宁	Liaoning	16108.3	17450.3	12030.2	12311.2
吉 林	Jilin	14936.0	16067.0	11456.6	11863.6
黑龙江	Heilongjiang	14982.1	16168.4	12494.9	12360.0
上 海	Shanghai	33195.2	34911.3	22448.9	22095.5
江 苏	Jiangsu	22675.4	24198.5	17715.9	17021.7
浙 江	Zhejiang	29875.8	31930.5	21351.7	21555.4
安 徽	Anhui	15416.0	16620.2	14545.8	15023.5
福 建	Fujian	19568.4	20880.3	16281.4	16338.9
江 西	Jiangxi	15796.3	16980.8	12496.7	13579.4
山 东	Shangdong	17775.5	18753.2	12308.9	12660.4
河 南	Henan	15163.7	16107.9	11546.0	12201.1
湖 北	**Hubei**	**16390.9**	**16305.9**	**15328.0**	**14472.5**
湖 南	Hunan	15394.8	16584.6	13968.8	14974.0
广 东	Guangdong	18818.4	20143.4	16949.4	17132.3
广 西	Guangxi	13675.7	14814.9	12045.0	12431.1
海 南	Hainan	15113.1	16278.8	12417.5	13169.3
重 庆	Chongqing	15133.3	16361.4	13112.1	14139.5
四 川	Sichuan	14670.1	15929.1	14055.6	14952.6
贵 州	Guizhou	10756.3	11642.3	10221.7	10817.6
云 南	Yunnan	11902.4	12841.9	10260.2	11069.5
西 藏	Tibet	12951.0	14598.4	8417.9	8917.1
陕 西	Shaanxi	12325.7	13316.5	10934.7	11375.7
甘 肃	Gansu	9628.9	10344.3	9694.0	9922.9
青 海	Qinghai	11499.4	12342.5	11343.1	12134.2
宁 夏	Ningxia	12858.4	13889.4	11464.6	11724.3
新 疆	Xinjiang	13121.7	14056.1	10318.4	10778.2

附录 1-11 分地区一般公共预算收入
General Public Budget Revenue by Region

单位:亿元 (100 million yuan)

地 区	Region	2015	2016	2017	2018	2019	2020
地方总计	**Region Total**	**83002.0**	**87239.4**	**91469.4**	**97903.4**	**101080.6**	**100123.8**
北 京	Beijing	4723.9	5081.3	5430.8	5785.9	5817.1	5483.9
天 津	Tianjin	2667.1	2723.5	2310.4	2106.2	2410.4	1923.1
河 北	Hebei	2649.2	2849.9	3233.8	3513.9	3739.0	3826.4
山 西	Shanxi	1642.4	1557.0	1867.0	2292.7	2347.7	2296.5
内 蒙 古	Inner Mongolia	1964.5	2016.4	1703.2	1857.6	2059.7	2051.3
辽 宁	Liaoning	2127.4	2200.5	2392.8	2616.1	2652.4	2655.5
吉 林	Jilin	1229.4	1263.8	1210.9	1240.9	1116.9	1085.0
黑 龙 江	Heilongjiang	1165.9	1148.4	1243.3	1282.6	1262.8	1152.5
上 海	Shanghai	5519.5	6406.1	6642.3	7108.1	7165.1	7046.3
江 苏	Jiangsu	8028.6	8121.2	8171.5	8630.2	8802.4	9059.0
浙 江	Zhejiang	4809.9	5302.0	5804.4	6598.2	7048.6	7248.0
安 徽	Anhui	2454.3	2672.8	2812.4	3048.7	3182.7	3216.0
福 建	Fujian	2544.2	2654.8	2809.0	3007.4	3052.9	3079.0
江 西	Jiangxi	2165.7	2151.5	2247.1	2373.0	2487.4	2507.5
山 东	Shangdong	5529.3	5860.2	6098.6	6485.4	6526.7	6559.9
河 南	Henan	3016.1	3153.5	3407.2	3766.0	4041.9	4155.2
湖 北	**Hubei**	**3005.5**	**3102.1**	**3248.3**	**3307.1**	**3388.6**	**2511.5**
湖 南	Hunan	2515.4	2697.9	2757.8	2860.8	3007.1	3008.7
广 东	Guangdong	9366.8	10390.4	11320.3	12105.3	12654.5	12922.0
广 西	Guangxi	1515.2	1556.3	1615.1	1681.4	1811.9	1716.9
海 南	Hainan	627.7	637.5	674.1	752.7	814.1	816.1
重 庆	Chongqing	2154.8	2227.9	2252.4	2265.5	2134.9	2094.8
四 川	Sichuan	3355.4	3388.9	3578.0	3911.0	4070.8	4258.0
贵 州	Guizhou	1503.4	1561.3	1613.8	1726.9	1767.5	1786.8
云 南	Yunnan	1808.1	1812.3	1886.2	1994.3	2073.6	2116.7
西 藏	Tibet	137.1	156.0	185.8	230.4	222.0	221.0
陕 西	Shaanxi	2060.0	1834.0	2006.7	2243.1	2287.9	2257.2
甘 肃	Gansu	743.9	787.0	815.7	871.1	850.5	874.5
青 海	Qinghai	267.1	238.5	246.2	272.9	282.2	298.0
宁 夏	Ningxia	373.4	387.7	417.6	436.5	423.6	419.4
新 疆	Xinjiang	1330.9	1299.0	1466.5	1531.4	1577.6	1477.2

附录 1-12 分地区一般公共预算支出
General Public Expenditure by Region

单位:亿元 (100 million yuan)

地 区	Region	2015	2016	2017	2018	2019	2020
地方总计	**Region Total**	**150335.6**	**160351.4**	**173228.3**	**188196.3**	**203743.2**	**210492.5**
北 京	Beijing	5737.7	6406.8	6824.5	7471.4	7408.2	7116.2
天 津	Tianjin	3232.4	3699.4	3282.5	3103.2	3555.7	3150.6
河 北	Hebei	5632.2	6049.5	6639.2	7726.2	8309.0	9021.7
山 西	Shanxi	3423.0	3428.9	3756.4	4283.9	4710.8	5111.0
内蒙古	Inner Mongolia	4253.0	4512.7	4529.9	4831.5	5100.9	5268.2
辽 宁	Liaoning	4481.6	4577.5	4879.4	5337.7	5745.1	6002.0
吉 林	Jilin	3217.1	3586.1	3725.7	3789.6	3933.4	4127.2
黑龙江	Heilongjiang	4020.7	4227.3	4641.1	4676.8	5011.6	5449.4
上 海	Shanghai	6191.6	6918.9	7547.6	8351.5	8179.3	8102.1
江 苏	Jiangsu	9687.6	9982.0	10621.0	11657.4	12573.6	13682.5
浙 江	Zhejiang	6646.0	6974.3	7530.3	8629.5	10053.0	10081.9
安 徽	Anhui	5239.0	5523.0	6203.8	6572.1	7392.2	7471.0
福 建	Fujian	4001.6	4275.4	4684.2	4832.7	5077.9	5214.6
江 西	Jiangxi	4412.5	4617.4	5111.5	5667.5	6386.8	6666.1
山 东	Shangdong	8250.0	8755.2	9258.4	10101.0	10739.8	11231.2
河 南	Henan	6799.4	7453.7	8215.5	9217.7	10163.9	10382.8
湖 北	**Hubei**	**6132.8**	**6423.0**	**6801.3**	**7258.3**	**7970.2**	**8439.0**
湖 南	Hunan	5728.7	6339.2	6869.4	7479.6	8034.4	8402.7
广 东	Guangdong	12827.8	13446.1	15037.5	15729.3	17297.9	17484.7
广 西	Guangxi	4065.5	4441.7	4908.6	5310.7	5851.0	6155.4
海 南	Hainan	1239.4	1376.5	1444.0	1691.3	1858.6	1973.9
重 庆	Chongqing	3792.0	4001.8	4336.3	4540.9	4847.7	4893.9
四 川	Sichuan	7497.5	8008.9	8694.8	9707.5	10348.2	11200.7
贵 州	Guizhou	3939.5	4262.4	4612.5	5029.7	5948.7	5723.3
云 南	Yunnan	4712.8	5018.9	5713.0	6075.0	6770.1	6974.0
西 藏	Tibet	1381.5	1588.0	1681.9	1970.7	2187.7	2207.8
陕 西	Shaanxi	4376.1	4389.4	4833.2	5302.4	5718.5	5933.8
甘 肃	Gansu	2958.3	3150.0	3304.4	3772.2	3951.6	4154.9
青 海	Qinghai	1515.2	1524.8	1530.4	1647.4	1863.7	1933.3
宁 夏	Ningxia	1138.5	1254.5	1372.8	1419.1	1438.3	1483.0
新 疆	Xinjiang	3804.9	4138.3	4637.2	5012.5	5315.5	5453.8

附录 1-13 分地区电力消费量
Electricity Consumption by Region

单位:亿千瓦小时 (100 million kw/h)

地 区	Region	2013	2014	2015	2016	2017	2018	2019	2020
北 京	Beijing	913.1	937.1	952.7	1020.3	1066.9	1142.4	1166.4	1140.0
天 津	Tianjin	774.5	794.4	800.6	807.9	805.6	855.1	878.4	874.6
河 北	Hebei	3251.2	3314.1	3175.7	3264.5	3441.7	3665.7	3856.1	3933.9
山 西	Shanxi	1832.3	1822.6	1737.2	1797.2	1990.6	2160.5	2261.9	2341.7
内蒙古	Inner Mongolia	2181.9	2416.7	2542.9	2605.0	2891.9	3353.4	3653.0	3900.5
辽 宁	Liaoning	2008.5	2038.7	1984.9	2037.4	2135.5	2302.4	2401.5	2423.4
吉 林	Jilin	653.8	667.8	652.0	667.6	703.0	750.6	780.4	805.4
黑龙江	Heilongjiang	845.2	859.4	869.0	896.6	928.6	973.9	995.6	1014.4
上 海	Shanghai	1410.6	1369.0	1405.5	1486.0	1526.8	1566.7	1568.6	1576.0
江 苏	Jiangsu	4956.6	5012.5	5114.7	5458.9	5807.9	6128.3	6264.4	6373.7
浙 江	Zhejiang	3453.1	3506.4	3553.9	3873.2	4192.6	4532.8	4706.2	4829.7
安 徽	Anhui	1528.1	1585.2	1639.8	1795.0	1921.5	2135.1	2300.7	2427.5
福 建	Fujian	1700.7	1855.8	1851.9	1968.6	2112.7	2313.8	2402.3	2483.0
江 西	Jiangxi	947.1	1018.5	1087.3	1182.5	1294.0	1428.8	1535.7	1626.8
山 东	Shangdong	4083.1	4223.5	5117.0	5390.7	5430.2	6083.9	6218.7	6939.8
河 南	Henan	2899.2	2919.6	2879.6	2989.2	3166.2	3417.7	3364.2	3391.9
湖 北	**Hubei**	**1629.8**	**1656.5**	**1665.2**	**1763.1**	**1869.0**	**2071.4**	**2214.3**	**2144.2**
湖 南	Hunan	1423.1	1430.9	1447.6	1495.7	1581.5	1745.2	1864.3	1929.3
广 东	Guangdong	4830.1	5235.2	5310.7	5610.1	5959.0	6323.4	6695.9	6926.1
广 西	Guangxi	1237.7	1308.0	1334.3	1359.6	1444.9	1703.0	1907.3	2025.3
海 南	Hainan	232.0	251.9	272.4	287.3	305.0	326.8	354.9	362.1
重 庆	Chongqing	813.3	867.2	875.4	924.9	996.5	1118.8	1160.3	1186.5
四 川	Sichuan	1949.0	2014.8	1992.4	2101.0	2205.2	2459.5	2635.8	2865.2
贵 州	Guizhou	1126.3	1173.7	1174.2	1241.8	1384.9	1482.1	1540.7	1586.1
云 南	Yunnan	1459.8	1529.4	1438.6	1410.5	1538.1	1679.1	1812.3	2025.7
西 藏	Tibet	30.7	34.0	40.5	49.2	58.2	69.0	77.6	82.5
陕 西	Shaanxi	1152.2	1226.0	1221.7	1357.1	1494.7	1594.2	1912.3	1740.9
甘 肃	Gansu	1073.2	1095.5	1098.7	1065.2	1164.4	1289.5	1288.0	1375.7
青 海	Qinghai	676.3	723.2	658.0	637.5	687.0	738.3	716.5	742.0
宁 夏	Ningxia	811.2	848.8	878.3	886.9	978.3	1064.8	1083.9	1038.2
新 疆	Xinjiang	1539.8	1900.2	2160.3	2316.5	2542.8	2686.5	2867.6	2998.3

注:数据来源于中国电力企业联合会,2020 年为快报数。
Note: Data are from China Electricity Council, the data of 2020 are preliminary statistics.

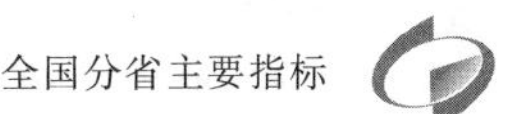

附录 1-14 分地区固定资产投资(不含农户)比上年增长情况
Growth Rate of Total Investment (Excluding Rural Households) over Preceding Year by Region

单位:% (%)

地 区	Region	2018	2019	2020
全国总计	**National Total**	**5.9**	**5.4**	**2.9**
北 京	Beijing	-5.4	-2.5	2.2
天 津	Tianjin	-4.9	13.1	3.0
河 北	Hebei	5.7	6.5	3.2
山 西	Shanxi	5.7	9.3	10.6
内 蒙 古	Inner Mongolia	-28.3	6.7	-1.5
辽 宁	Liaoning	3.9	0.3	2.6
吉 林	Jilin	1.4	-16.2	8.3
黑 龙 江	Heilongjiang	-4.7	6.3	3.6
上 海	Shanghai	5.2	5.1	10.3
江 苏	Jiangsu	5.5	5.1	0.3
浙 江	Zhejiang	7.2	10.0	5.4
安 徽	Anhui	11.8	9.2	5.1
福 建	Fujian	11.5	5.9	-0.4
江 西	Jiangxi	11.1	9.2	8.2
山 东	Shandong	3.8	-8.2	3.6
河 南	Henan	8.1	8.0	4.3
湖 北	**Hubei**	**10.9**	**10.7**	**-18.8**
湖 南	Hunan	10.0	10.1	7.6
广 东	Guangdong	10.7	11.1	7.2
广 西	Guangxi	10.7	9.6	4.2
海 南	Hainan	-12.5	-9.2	8.0
重 庆	Chongqing	7.0	5.6	3.9
四 川	Sichuan	10.2	8.6	2.8
贵 州	Guizhou	15.8	0.9	3.2
云 南	Yunnan	11.6	8.5	7.7
西 藏	Tibet	9.9	-2.2	5.4
陕 西	Shaanxi	10.4	2.5	4.1
甘 肃	Gansu	-3.9	6.6	7.8
青 海	Qinghai	7.3	5.0	-12.2
宁 夏	Ningxia	-18.2	-10.3	4.0
新 疆	Xinjiang	-25.2	2.5	16.2

附录 1-15 分地区房地产开发企业(单位)房屋施工、竣工面积和商品房销售面积
Real Estate Development Enterprises (Units)' Housing Construction, Completion and Sales of Commercial Space Area by Region

单位:万平方米 (10 000 sq.m)

地 区	Region	房屋施工面积 Housing Construction Area		房屋竣工面积 Housing Completed Area		商品房销售面积 Sales of Commercial Area	
		2019	2020	2019	2020	2019	2020
全国总计	**National Total**	**893821**	**926759**	**95942**	**91218**	**171558**	**176086**
北 京	Beijing	12515	13919	1343	1546	939	971
天 津	Tianjin	11453	12035	1656	1634	1479	1307
河 北	Hebei	29853	31408	2680	2367	5283	6028
山 西	Shanxi	19549	21938	2739	1481	2366	2685
内蒙古	Inner Mongolia	15889	15311	951	841	2008	2046
辽 宁	Liaoning	23787	24003	1818	1848	3696	3743
吉 林	Jilin	12404	12341	1222	965	2122	1831
黑龙江	Heilongjiang	11441	11262	1204	1438	1684	1494
上 海	Shanghai	14803	15740	2670	2878	1696	1789
江 苏	Jiangsu	65687	67889	9369	11151	13973	15427
浙 江	Zhejiang	49605	56725	5739	6693	9378	10250
安 徽	Anhui	43591	44975	5674	5101	9229	9534
福 建	Fujian	34140	34557	2882	3804	6456	6607
江 西	Jiangxi	23557	23581	2231	2239	6459	6733
山 东	Shangdong	75767	79792	10179	9326	12727	13272
河 南	Henan	57567	58438	6571	5413	14278	14101
湖 北	**Hubei**	**33825**	**35419**	**2559**	**2647**	**8602**	**6588**
湖 南	Hunan	40045	40757	3975	3964	9104	9437
广 东	Guangdong	86825	91642	9956	7764	13847	14908
广 西	Guangxi	29807	32184	2038	2129	6712	6729
海 南	Hainan	9222	8589	1302	687	829	752
重 庆	Chongqing	27987	27368	5069	3774	6105	6143
四 川	Sichuan	49114	50756	4580	4546	12979	13258
贵 州	Guizhou	27775	26923	955	862	5323	5553
云 南	Yunnan	26314	25801	1844	1638	4835	4857
西 藏	Tibet	764	945	19	28	128	93
陕 西	Shaanxi	27728	28358	1782	1746	4401	4452
甘 肃	Gansu	10977	11328	674	881	1705	1968
青 海	Qinghai	2922	2944	133	154	481	470
宁 夏	Ningxia	5937	5563	1011	772	1010	1095
新 疆	Xinjiang	12970	14268	1117	902	1724	1964

附录 1-16 分地区房地产开发企业(单位)投资和商品房销售额
Investment and Commercial Housing Sales of Real Estate Development Company (Units)

单位:亿元 (100 million yuan)

地区	Region	房地产开发投资额 Real Estate Development Investment		商品房销售额 Commercial Housing Sales		# 住宅 Residential	
		2019	2020	2019	2020	2019	2020
全国总计	**National Total**	**132194.3**	**141442.9**	**159725.1**	**173612.7**	**139440.0**	**154567.0**
北京	Beijing	3838.4	3938.7	3371.0	3656.8	3032.4	3131.3
天津	Tianjin	2727.8	2608.5	2274.1	2113.6	2132.5	2001.0
河北	Hebei	4347.1	4601.1	4138.6	4950.4	3714.6	4597.9
山西	Shanxi	1656.5	1830.4	1631.8	1885.9	1452.4	1753.4
内蒙古	Inner Mongolia	1041.9	1176.5	1243.9	1365.5	1104.1	1242.6
辽宁	Liaoning	2834.0	2978.9	3049.1	3366.3	2814.9	3114.1
吉林	Jilin	1315.5	1460.8	1581.5	1381.5	1373.5	1238.2
黑龙江	Heilongjiang	958.0	982.9	1268.2	1064.2	1070.0	946.1
上海	Shanghai	4231.4	4698.7	5203.8	6047.0	4457.2	5268.8
江苏	Jiangsu	12009.3	13171.3	16259.6	19408.9	14894.8	18027.3
浙江	Zhejiang	10683.0	11413.7	14352.1	17145.0	12723.1	15584.8
安徽	Anhui	6670.5	7042.3	6823.5	7346.1	6126.7	6760.9
福建	Fujian	5673.1	6026.8	6938.8	7497.7	5685.3	6343.3
江西	Jiangxi	2239.1	2378.1	4710.4	5222.8	4038.0	4425.2
山东	Shangdong	8614.9	9450.5	10271.2	11065.6	9287.1	10109.6
河南	Henan	7464.6	7782.3	9010.0	9364.4	8016.9	8402.5
湖北	**Hubei**	**5111.7**	**4888.9**	**7751.8**	**6087.9**	**6903.7**	**5447.3**
湖南	Hunan	4445.5	4880.4	5578.0	5947.1	4721.4	5223.6
广东	Guangdong	15852.2	17312.7	19748.2	22572.5	16758.0	19829.6
广西	Guangxi	3814.4	3845.6	4366.2	4251.5	3913.4	3803.6
海南	Hainan	1336.2	1341.7	1275.8	1232.1	1090.6	1048.9
重庆	Chongqing	4439.3	4352.0	5129.4	5071.3	4457.8	4293.2
四川	Sichuan	6573.2	7315.3	9666.7	10394.3	7869.0	8767.0
贵州	Guizhou	2990.8	3418.7	3183.6	3224.2	2527.4	2760.7
云南	Yunnan	4151.4	4505.2	3846.2	3969.9	3255.8	3452.0
西藏	Tibet	129.6	165.5	96.8	83.9	81.2	72.0
陕西	Shaanxi	3903.6	4404.4	3960.2	4375.3	3359.2	3755.8
甘肃	Gansu	1257.8	1355.6	1019.3	1293.4	907.1	1205.4
青海	Qinghai	406.3	421.3	367.3	383.3	295.6	343.4
宁夏	Ningxia	403.1	433.3	573.9	698.4	498.5	626.3
新疆	Xinjiang	1074.0	1260.9	1034.3	1145.8	877.9	991.1

附录1-17 按收发货人所在地分分地区货物进出口总额(2020)
Total Value of Imports and Exports of Goods by Region and Location of Importers/Exporters (2020)

单位:亿美元 (USD 100 million)

地 区	Region	进出口 Total	出 口 Exports	进 口 Imports
全 国	**National Total**	**46462.6**	**25906.5**	**20556.1**
北 京	Beijing	3350.4	670.1	2680.3
天 津	Tianjin	1059.3	443.6	615.7
河 北	Hebei	637.9	364.6	273.3
山 西	Shanxi	218.7	127.3	91.4
内蒙古	Inner Mongolia	150.7	50.4	100.2
辽 宁	Liaoning	944.6	383.3	561.3
吉 林	Jilin	184.9	42.0	142.9
黑龙江	Heilongjiang	222.0	52.0	169.9
上 海	Shanghai	5031.9	1981.1	3050.8
江 苏	Jiangsu	6427.7	3962.8	2464.9
浙 江	Zhejiang	4879.3	3632.7	1246.7
安 徽	Anhui	780.5	455.8	324.6
福 建	Fujian	2026.7	1224.0	802.6
江 西	Jiangxi	578.2	420.9	157.3
山 东	Shandong	3184.5	1890.4	1294.1
河 南	Henan	969.2	593.0	376.2
湖 北	**Hubei**	**620.8**	**390.6**	**230.2**
湖 南	Hunan	705.3	478.6	226.7
广 东	Guangdong	10236.3	6283.7	3952.6
广 西	Guangxi	702.9	391.9	311.0
海 南	Hainan	135.4	40.1	95.2
重 庆	Chongqing	941.8	605.3	336.5
四 川	Sichuan	1168.0	672.5	495.5
贵 州	Guizhou	79.1	62.3	16.7
云 南	Yunnan	389.5	221.4	168.1
西 藏	Tibet	3.1	1.9	1.2
陕 西	Shaanxi	545.1	278.9	266.2
甘 肃	Gansu	53.9	12.4	41.5
青 海	Qinghai	3.3	1.8	1.5
宁 夏	Ningxia	17.8	12.5	5.3
新 疆	Xinjiang	213.9	158.4	55.5

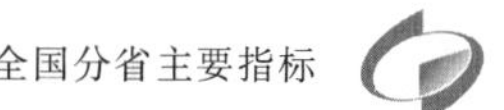

附录 1-18 按境内目的地和货源地分分地区货物进出口总额(2020)

Total Value of Imports and Exports of Goods by Region and Location of Place of Destination or Origin in China (2020)

单位:亿美元 (USD 100 million)

地 区	Region	进出口 Total	出 口 Exports	进 口 Imports
全 国	**National Total**	**46462.6**	**25906.5**	**20556.1**
北 京	Beijing	1148.4	294.9	853.6
天 津	Tianjin	1251.5	405.9	845.6
河 北	Hebei	988.5	500.5	488.0
山 西	Shanxi	219.5	142.2	77.3
内蒙古	Inner Mongolia	201.3	65.2	136.0
辽 宁	Liaoning	1175.4	460.3	715.1
吉 林	Jilin	194.8	46.6	148.2
黑龙江	Heilongjiang	204.8	54.2	150.6
上 海	Shanghai	4786.4	1672.7	3113.7
江 苏	Jiangsu	6840.5	3975.7	2864.8
浙 江	Zhejiang	4648.5	3520.0	1128.5
安 徽	Anhui	746.1	477.8	268.3
福 建	Fujian	1717.5	1109.2	608.3
江 西	Jiangxi	506.1	350.1	156.0
山 东	Shandong	3511.3	1795.4	1715.9
河 南	Henan	1041.0	659.5	381.5
湖 北	**Hubei**	**614.9**	**381.3**	**233.6**
湖 南	Hunan	476.9	306.5	170.4
广 东	Guangdong	12055.2	7561.6	4493.6
广 西	Guangxi	663.5	212.4	451.1
海 南	Hainan	165.6	40.0	125.7
重 庆	Chongqing	840.1	550.3	289.8
四 川	Sichuan	1173.0	658.6	514.5
贵 州	Guizhou	74.8	59.2	15.6
云 南	Yunnan	342.0	170.4	171.6
西 藏	Tibet	2.8	2.5	0.3
陕 西	Shaanxi	512.9	267.4	245.5
甘 肃	Gansu	56.0	18.1	37.9
青 海	Qinghai	3.1	1.8	1.3
宁 夏	Ningxia	29.3	22.4	6.9
新 疆	Xinjiang	270.8	123.5	147.3

附录 1-19 分地区农林牧渔业总产值及增长速度(2020)
Gross Output Value and Growth Rate of Farming, Forestry, Animal Husbandry and Fishery by Region(2020)

地 区	Region	农林牧渔业总产值(亿元) Agriculture, Forestry, Animal Husbandry Fishery (100 million yuan)	# 农业 Agriculture	# 林业 Forestry	# 牧业 Livestock	# 渔业 Fishing	农林牧渔业总产值比上年增长(%) Growth rate over Previous Year (%)
全国总计	**National Total**	**137782.2**	**71748.2**	**5961.6**	**40266.7**	**12775.9**	**3.4**
北 京	Beijing	263.4	107.6	97.7	45.2	4.1	-6.7
天 津	Tianjin	476.4	228.8	15.7	145.5	68.1	1.4
河 北	Hebei	6742.5	3413.3	255.4	2309.7	243.2	3.5
山 西	Shanxi	1935.8	1075.9	137.1	606.3	6.6	5.8
内蒙古	Inner Mongolia	3472.4	1699.0	89.8	1603.4	27.8	1.8
辽 宁	Liaoning	4582.6	2056.8	121.0	1604.7	617.5	3.0
吉 林	Jilin	2976.0	1231.8	71.9	1547.4	41.4	1.8
黑龙江	Heilongjiang	6438.1	4044.1	192.4	1913.0	115.6	2.6
上 海	Shanghai	279.8	138.0	15.2	55.1	51.0	-7.0
江 苏	Jiangsu	7952.6	4102.2	172.8	1315.8	1774.0	2.0
浙 江	Zhejiang	3496.9	1594.0	189.6	472.6	1130.6	1.7
安 徽	Anhui	5680.9	2525.4	387.5	1900.2	542.6	2.7
福 建	Fujian	4901.1	1818.2	390.6	1141.1	1373.1	3.3
江 西	Jiangxi	3820.7	1689.9	367.8	1125.4	473.5	2.7
山 东	Shangdong	10190.6	5168.4	214.2	2571.9	1432.1	3.0
河 南	Henan	9956.3	6244.8	126.7	2855.8	117.6	2.7
湖 北	**Hubei**	**7303.6**	**3492.5**	**245.4**	**1864.8**	**1156.8**	**0.7**
湖 南	Hunan	7512.0	3364.8	428.0	2721.6	477.5	4.1
广 东	Guangdong	7901.9	3769.3	414.3	1778.2	1581.5	4.0
广 西	Guangxi	5913.3	3268.8	437.4	1423.8	508.3	5.0
海 南	Hainan	1821.0	874.8	121.2	357.1	390.8	2.4
重 庆	Chongqing	2749.1	1596.1	126.0	871.9	107.3	5.0
四 川	Sichuan	9216.4	4701.9	379.8	3613.8	287.5	5.6
贵 州	Guizhou	4358.6	2781.8	293.7	1019.0	61.1	6.5
云 南	Yunnan	5920.5	2902.2	429.5	2315.4	104.0	5.8
西 藏	Tibet	233.5	104.0	3.7	119.7	0.1	8.2
陕 西	Shaanxi	4056.6	2807.1	116.9	893.4	30.0	3.5
甘 肃	Gansu	2103.6	1423.8	31.7	495.3	2.0	5.2
青 海	Qinghai	507.1	188.6	11.9	295.1	3.9	4.7
宁 夏	Ningxia	703.1	397.9	10.9	246.6	19.0	3.6
新 疆	Xinjiang	4315.6	2936.3	66.0	1038.1	27.2	4.7

注:本表绝对数按当年价格计算,增速按可比价格计算。总产值包括农林牧渔专业及辅助性活动产值。

Note: Data in value terms in this table are calculated at current prices, while growth rate are calculated at constant prices. Gross output value includes professional and support services for agriculture, forestry, animal husbandry and fishery.

附录 1-20 分地区主要农产品产量(2020)
Output of Major Farm Products by Region(2020)

单位:万吨 (10 000 tons)

地 区	Region	粮 食 Food	棉 花 Cotton	油 料 Oil feed	糖 料 Sugar	蔬 菜 Vegetables	水 果 Fruit
全国总计	**National Total**	**66949.2**	**591.0**	**3586.4**	**12014.0**	**74912.9**	**28692.4**
北 京	Beijing	30.5		0.3		137.9	53.8
天 津	Tianjin	228.2	1.0	0.3		266.5	56.4
河 北	Hebei	3795.9	20.9	119.5	63.7	5198.2	1424.4
山 西	Shanxi	1424.3	0.2	14.3	0.2	861.2	909.8
内蒙古	Inner Mongolia	3664.1		217.3	620.7	1075.1	238.7
辽 宁	Liaoning	2338.8		99.7	9.1	1960.0	851.3
吉 林	Jilin	3803.2		81.4	4.2	464.9	146.6
黑龙江	Heilongjiang	7540.8		12.3	14.1	674.3	170.1
上 海	Shanghai	91.4		0.7	0.2	252.9	43.9
江 苏	Jiangsu	3729.1	1.1	93.0	7.1	5728.1	974.2
浙 江	Zhejiang	605.7	0.7	32.1	46.4	1945.5	755.3
安 徽	Anhui	4019.2	4.1	162.5	11.1	2330.9	741.5
福 建	Fujian	502.3		22.7	27.0	1630.2	764.6
江 西	Jiangxi	2163.9	5.3	122.7	61.2	1642.7	712.8
山 东	Shangdong	5446.8	18.3	290.9		8434.7	2938.9
河 南	Henan	6825.8	1.8	672.6	10.7	7612.4	2563.4
湖 北	**Hubei**	**2727.4**	**10.8**	**344.5**	**28.2**	**4119.4**	**1066.8**
湖 南	Hunan	3015.1	7.4	260.7	34.9	4110.1	1150.8
广 东	Guangdong	1267.6		113.5	1366.8	3706.8	1882.6
广 西	Guangxi	1370.0	0.1	73.9	7412.5	3830.8	2785.7
海 南	Hainan	145.5		7.7	105.8	572.8	495.6
重 庆	Chongqing	1081.4		67.1	8.2	2092.6	514.8
四 川	Sichuan	3527.4	0.2	392.9	37.9	4813.4	1221.3
贵 州	Guizhou	1057.6		103.4	61.5	2990.9	548.1
云 南	Yunnan	1895.9		63.1	1597.2	2507.9	961.6
西 藏	Tibet	102.9		5.1		84.3	2.2
陕 西	Shaanxi	1274.8	0.1	59.1	0.8	1957.7	2070.6
甘 肃	Gansu	1202.2	3.0	61.4	22.4	1478.5	779.0
青 海	Qinghai	107.4		30.2		151.4	2.9
宁 夏	Ningxia	380.5		6.7		566.4	204.5
新 疆	Xinjiang	1583.4	516.1	54.9	462.2	1714.9	1660.4

附录 1-20 续表 continued

单位:万吨 (10 000 tons)

地 区	Region	肉 类 Meat	#猪 肉 Pork	#牛 肉 Beef	#羊 肉 Sheep Meat	奶 类 Dairy
全国总计	**National Total**	**7748.4**	**4113.3**	**672.4**	**492.3**	**3529.6**
北 京	Beijing	3.5	1.4	0.4	0.2	24.2
天 津	Tianjin	29.6	15.4	2.7	0.9	50.1
河 北	Hebei	419.2	226.9	55.6	31.3	488.3
山 西	Shanxi	102.7	62.8	7.4	8.6	117.4
内蒙古	Inner Mongolia	268.0	61.4	66.3	113.0	617.9
辽 宁	Liaoning	378.2	183.5	31.0	6.9	137.1
吉 林	Jilin	237.4	105.0	38.7	5.2	39.3
黑龙江	Heilongjiang	253.2	143.9	48.3	13.4	501.0
上 海	Shanghai	9.3	7.2	0.3	0.2	29.1
江 苏	Jiangsu	268.2	140.7	2.6	6.3	63.0
浙 江	Zhejiang	90.1	54.2	1.4	2.2	18.4
安 徽	Anhui	396.0	183.4	9.9	20.7	37.6
福 建	Fujian	259.4	103.8	2.5	2.3	17.5
江 西	Jiangxi	285.2	180.7	15.2	2.6	9.1
山 东	Shangdong	728.0	271.0	59.7	34.0	241.6
河 南	Henan	544.1	324.8	36.7	28.6	214.7
湖 北	**Hubei**	**307.4**	**203.8**	**15.4**	**8.9**	**13.4**
湖 南	Hunan	455.0	337.7	20.5	16.1	5.6
广 东	Guangdong	401.0	192.4	4.2	1.9	15.2
广 西	Guangxi	380.4	174.1	13.6	3.6	11.2
海 南	Hainan	58.4	20.9	2.3	1.2	0.3
重 庆	Chongqing	161.2	108.8	7.4	6.8	3.2
四 川	Sichuan	597.8	394.8	37.0	27.3	68.0
贵 州	Guizhou	207.9	146.3	23.1	5.0	5.3
云 南	Yunnan	417.4	291.6	40.9	20.8	73.1
西 藏	Tibet	28.3	0.9	21.2	5.7	49.2
陕 西	Shaanxi	107.1	77.7	8.7	9.7	161.5
甘 肃	Gansu	110.2	49.2	24.9	27.6	58.4
青 海	Qinghai	37.0	3.7	19.2	13.3	36.9
宁 夏	Ningxia	33.8	8.0	11.4	11.1	215.3
新 疆	Xinjiang	173.7	37.5	44.0	57.0	206.9

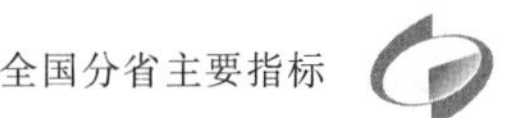

附录 1-21　分地区规模以上工业企业主要经济指标(2020)
Main Indicators of Industrial Enterprises above Designated Size by Region(2020)

单位:亿元 (100 million yuan)

地 区	Region	营业收入 Business Revenue	营业成本 Business Cost	销售费用 Selling Expenses	管理费用 Administrative Expenses	财务费用 Finance Expenses	利润总额 Total Profit
全国总计	**National Total**	**1061433.6**	**890435.0**	**30480.2**	**55318.4**	**11585.9**	**64516.1**
北 京	Beijing	23283.5	19273.9	1214.3	1248.1	261.2	1785.0
天 津	Tianjin	18627.4	15981.6	433.2	873.8	120.7	961.3
河 北	Hebei	42110.1	36729.4	939.1	1562.0	547.2	2038.1
山 西	Shanxi	20673.3	16946.8	619.9	1153.5	704.9	963.8
内蒙古	Inner Mongolia	16640.4	13337.7	450.2	669.9	425.0	1315.1
辽 宁	Liaoning	29215.3	24782.7	731.4	1345.0	432.2	1286.7
吉 林	Jilin	13147.0	10791.4	558.6	717.8	128.2	567.1
黑龙江	Heilongjiang	9825.8	8392.4	290.6	561.6	152.0	279.1
上 海	Shanghai	38595.2	31094.8	1420.2	2850.9	90.6	2810.2
江 苏	Jiangsu	122206.8	102659.6	3673.2	7072.8	968.8	7365.3
浙 江	Zhejiang	77695.4	64378.1	2356.0	4876.3	902.9	5544.6
安 徽	Anhui	37925.9	32268.4	965.7	1849.5	367.7	2294.2
福 建	Fujian	55475.4	47990.5	1268.5	2176.2	390.6	3470.1
江 西	Jiangxi	37909.2	32764.9	733.4	1428.5	272.0	2438.1
山 东	Shandong	84270.4	72890.4	2038.2	3586.9	975.9	4282.9
河 南	Henan	47292.7	41076.3	983.0	1717.7	602.0	2544.7
湖 北	**Hubei**	**40743.5**	**34080.0**	**1195.3**	**2012.3**	**350.2**	**2519.0**
湖 南	Hunan	38339.9	31193.4	1214.0	2650.7	357.1	2032.7
广 东	Guangdong	146856.9	121581.9	5021.4	9985.9	1033.8	9286.9
广 西	Guangxi	17639.6	15309.0	378.3	609.4	202.8	876.0
海 南	Hainan	2089.6	1607.4	116.0	94.3	32.0	132.2
重 庆	Chongqing	22529.6	19172.5	633.3	1121.1	173.1	1318.8
四 川	Sichuan	45250.1	37557.2	1444.1	1941.3	511.5	3197.7
贵 州	Guizhou	8832.3	6417.2	297.1	442.0	196.9	1029.4
云 南	Yunnan	14550.3	11400.8	377.3	589.2	290.8	1005.4
西 藏	Tibet	322.0	250.5	15.0	28.1	9.6	18.9
陕 西	Shaanxi	23435.3	19000.3	576.9	1080.7	347.1	1942.3
甘 肃	Gansu	7290.3	6136.6	131.4	249.9	159.7	284.3
青 海	Qinghai	2421.0	2005.5	45.9	120.3	100.3	93.1
宁 夏	Ningxia	4713.0	3958.3	84.1	200.6	174.9	203.9
新 疆	Xinjiang	11526.3	9405.2	274.6	502.5	304.4	629.1

附录 1-21 续表 continued

单位:亿元 (100 million yuan)

地 区	Region	亏损企业亏损总额 Total Loss of Loss-making Enterprise	流动资产合计 Total Current Assets	应收账款 Accounts Received	存货 Inventory	产成品 Finished Products	资产总计 Total Assets	负债合计 Total Liability
全国总计	**National Total**	**9855.1**	**631504.6**	**164128.6**	**122330.6**	**46018.6**	**1267550.2**	**710582.5**
北 京	Beijing	291.6	21093.8	4517.3	2788.8	1063.0	55276.9	23838.7
天 津	Tianjin	298.7	10487.2	2731.6	2172.2	785.6	21375.9	11623.7
河 北	Hebei	392.8	23688.9	5034.0	4569.3	1626.8	49838.6	30024.8
山 西	Shanxi	521.5	18396.3	3552.8	2182.0	869.4	45287.9	32458.5
内 蒙 古	Inner Mongolia	340.5	10899.6	2281.5	1674.5	559.6	32420.1	19231.2
辽 宁	Liaoning	613.4	20077.9	4282.2	4315.6	1450.2	40050.9	24944.8
吉 林	Jilin	429.5	7386.9	1531.9	1592.4	594.9	17202.5	9049.9
黑 龙 江	Heilongjiang	281.5	7613.3	1605.3	1462.8	441.0	17074.9	10213.4
上 海	Shanghai	346.7	27915.2	7434.5	5277.7	1874.4	47965.7	22934.3
江 苏	Jiangsu	999.7	77201.8	25624.2	15599.0	6228.7	130201.4	68845.0
浙 江	Zhejiang	510.6	53235.9	15757.5	10303.2	4119.8	95438.3	52090.3
安 徽	Anhui	199.6	21575.6	7000.7	4027.8	1616.1	41720.7	23803.2
福 建	Fujian	183.0	21159.9	5065.9	4659.4	1888.9	41501.5	20908.1
江 西	Jiangxi	112.4	14266.7	3630.5	3209.7	1219.7	28392.1	15241.5
山 东	Shangdong	730.9	52936.0	11519.1	10724.3	4451.8	99591.1	62190.8
河 南	Henan	336.1	24499.4	5728.0	4525.1	1611.1	51497.5	29360.3
湖 北	**Hubei**	**327.0**	**20813.6**	**5050.0**	**4090.0**	**1524.1**	**43851.7**	**22859.0**
湖 南	Hunan	213.8	14964.7	4357.9	3220.4	1177.4	31437.0	16168.4
广 东	Guangdong	1018.0	89625.4	25669.5	17992.7	6680.7	149406.7	82985.5
广 西	Guangxi	119.3	10074.9	2321.7	2072.3	805.7	20114.3	12965.1
海 南	Hainan	28.2	1556.8	322.6	227.9	75.1	3438.0	1813.0
重 庆	Chongqing	150.5	11389.0	3620.9	1982.1	758.8	22307.8	12707.7
四 川	Sichuan	217.0	21929.0	5647.3	4244.3	1539.7	50336.2	27646.1
贵 州	Guizhou	158.7	7201.9	1182.9	1343.0	350.0	16315.1	9876.2
云 南	Yunnan	162.3	8503.4	1519.7	2354.9	614.0	22613.9	12689.2
西 藏	Tibet	34.1	476.4	65.8	44.5	17.2	1998.6	992.6
陕 西	Shaanxi	229.8	14626.0	3042.0	2498.9	1038.5	37394.3	20307.6
甘 肃	Gansu	99.5	4273.4	977.6	983.5	266.2	11529.6	6805.2
青 海	Qinghai	100.3	2100.0	487.3	313.9	100.8	6892.4	4679.8
宁 夏	Ningxia	108.5	3344.7	773.7	543.4	209.1	10553.2	6565.3
新 疆	Xinjiang	299.6	8191.3	1792.9	1335.1	460.5	24525.4	14763.5

附录 1-22 分地区主要工业产品产量(2020)
Output of Major Industrial Products by Region(2020)

地 区	Region	原煤（万吨）Raw Coal (10 000 tons)	原油（万吨）Crude Oil (10 000 tons)	天然气（亿立方米）Natural Gas (100 million cu.m)	布（亿米）Cloth (100 million meters)	农用化肥（万吨）Chemical Fertilizers (10 000 tons)	水泥（万吨）Cement (10 000 tons)	生铁（万吨）Pig Iron (10 000 tons)	粗钢（万吨）Crude Steel (10 000 tons)
全国总计	**National Total**	**390157.7**	**19476.9**	**1925.0**	**460.3**	**5496.0**	**239483.7**	**88752.4**	**106476.7**
北 京	Beijing			20.0			286.9		
天 津	Tianjin		3242.2	36.3	0.4	14.8	551.5	2198.9	2171.8
河 北	Hebei	4974.7	543.5	5.6	11.7	212.8	11860.0	22903.8	24977.0
山 西	Shanxi	107905.7		85.9	0.2	400.2	5616.7	6089.1	6637.8
内蒙古	Inner Mongolia	102550.9	13.6	25.5		424.2	3610.9	2380.8	3119.9
辽 宁	Liaoning	3128.8	1049.4	7.4	0.8	35.6	5447.0	7235.2	7609.4
吉 林	Jilin	1040.2	404.4	19.8	0.2	21.9	2232.8	1407.7	1525.6
黑龙江	Heilongjiang	5557.8	3001.0	46.8	0.0	55.3	2409.9	863.1	986.5
上 海	Shanghai		52.0	15.1	1.0	1.0	398.9	1411.3	1575.6
江 苏	Jiangsu	1022.3	152.1	4.2	87.2	200.8	15275.1	10022.9	12108.2
浙 江	Zhejiang				112.8	64.0	13272.9	852.8	1457.0
安 徽	Anhui	11084.4		2.2	7.4	268.0	14189.3	2537.3	3696.7
福 建	Fujian	658.5			77.8	86.2	9718.4	1106.2	2466.5
江 西	Jiangxi	314.5			7.8	23.4	10030.7	2332.1	2682.1
山 东	Shangdong	10944.6	2219.2	5.8	42.1	352.6	15970.4	7523.2	7993.5
河 南	Henan	10647.5	239.9	2.9	14.5	489.2	11767.9	2769.5	3530.2
湖 北	**Hubei**	**40.3**	**53.5**	**1.0**	**42.7**	**490.0**	**9826.6**	**2727.4**	**3557.2**
湖 南	Hunan	1067.8		0.0	1.7	65.1	11043.2	2105.4	2612.9
广 东	Guangdong		1613.1	131.6	20.7	11.3	17165.5	2158.7	3382.3
广 西	Guangxi	413.6	48.8	0.2	0.4	47.7	12129.1	1457.1	3452.2
海 南	Hainan		30.6	1.0		65.3	1838.8		
重 庆	Chongqing	939.4		80.0	1.7	167.2	6524.4	637.8	899.9
四 川	Sichuan	2240.3	7.9	463.3	14.9	359.1	14517.5	2136.8	2792.6
贵 州	Guizhou	12055.3		5.0	0.3	338.9	10820.9	368.6	461.9
云 南	Yunnan	5529.7				224.3	13130.3	1873.3	2233.0
西 藏	Tibet						1085.0		
陕 西	Shaanxi	67973.1	2693.7	527.4	8.2	145.8	6809.8	1232.2	1521.5
甘 肃	Gansu	3859.0	968.7	3.9		24.5	4716.7	782.3	1059.2
青 海	Qinghai	1092.1	228.5	64.0		523.1	1225.8	160.3	193.2
宁 夏	Ningxia	8151.6			0.6	68.2	1979.9	320.0	466.6
新 疆	Xinjiang	26965.7	2914.8	369.8	5.1	315.4	4030.9	1158.3	1306.1

注：因四舍五入原因，各地区数据之和与全国数据不完全一致。

Note: Due to rounding, the sum of regional date and national data are not completely consistent.

附录 1-22 续表 continued

地 区	Region	钢材（万吨） Steel (10 000 tons)	汽车（万辆） Car (10 000 units)	家用电冰箱（万台） Household Refrigerators (10 000 units)	移动通信手持机（万台） Mobile Handset (10 000 units)	微型计算机设备（万台） Micro-computer Equipment (10 000 units)	发电量（亿千瓦小时） Power generation (100 million kilowatt hours)
全国总计	**National Total**	**132489.2**	**2532.5**	**9014.7**	**146961.8**	**37800.4**	**77790.6**
北 京	Beijing	184.4	166.0		9928.5	552.4	457.5
天 津	Tianjin	5724.0	94.6	22.2	6.7	0.0	771.6
河 北	Hebei	31320.1	97.5				3425.1
山 西	Shanxi	6181.4	4.9		2261.4	0.5	3503.5
内蒙古	Inner Mongolia	2883.9	2.9				5811.0
辽 宁	Liaoning	7578.4	74.8	156.9	16.0	46.3	2135.3
吉 林	Jilin	1661.6	265.6				1018.8
黑龙江	Heilongjiang	879.0	7.2		36.8		1137.8
上 海	Shanghai	1879.6	264.7	21.1	3686.6	1799.5	861.7
江 苏	Jiangsu	15004.9	75.2	1265.2	5527.5	5029.5	5217.5
浙 江	Zhejiang	3806.7	90.4	592.7	3704.6	139.2	3531.3
安 徽	Anhui	3607.5	116.1	2437.9	91.3	3097.1	2809.0
福 建	Fujian	3861.6	18.0		2382.8	1493.6	2651.1
江 西	Jiangxi	3093.9	45.2	78.1	5649.1	2188.5	1444.7
山 东	Shangdong	11269.3	115.8	832.4	606.5	0.3	5806.4
河 南	Henan	4233.4	54.5	216.1	13625.3	1.5	2906.1
湖 北	**Hubei**	**3649.1**	**209.3**	**570.1**	**2667.0**	**1720.0**	**3015.8**
湖 南	Hunan	2729.7	39.1		2369.2	184.5	1554.4
广 东	Guangdong	4866.2	313.3	2305.8	61951.1	4621.6	5225.9
广 西	Guangxi	4731.2	174.5	99.4	1504.9	185.1	1970.9
海 南	Hainan		0.1				345.5
重 庆	Chongqing	1310.0	158.0	148.7	13450.5	9130.3	840.5
四 川	Sichuan	3437.2	71.3	111.1	13319.8	7527.0	4182.3
贵 州	Guizhou	741.1	7.5	157.1	1352.9	0.1	2305.4
云 南	Yunnan	2640.7	2.0		574.7	82.6	3674.4
西 藏	Tibet						88.9
陕 西	Shaanxi	2020.0	62.8		1707.7		2379.4
甘 肃	Gansu	1102.6	0.0		51.6		1762.4
青 海	Qinghai	189.1					951.9
宁 夏	Ningxia	482.0	0.0				1882.4
新 疆	Xinjiang	1420.5	0.9		489.2	1.0	4121.9

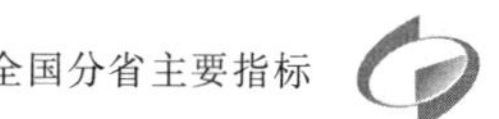

附录 1-23 分地区建筑业总产值和房屋面积(2020)
Total Output Value of Construction and Building Area by Region (2020)

单位:亿元、万平方米 (100 million yuan、10 000 sq.m)

地 区	Region	总产值(亿元) Total Output (100 million yuan)	房屋施工面积(万平方米) Floor Space under Construction (10 000 sq.m)	房屋竣工面积(万平方米) Floor Space Completed (10 000 sq.m)
全国总计	**National Total**	**263947.0**	**1494743.4**	**384819.8**
北 京	Beijing	12905.9	88593.7	9588.1
天 津	Tianjin	4388.2	15234.5	2453.4
河 北	Hebei	5948.1	35081.6	7316.0
山 西	Shanxi	5113.6	19965.8	4944.8
内蒙古	Inner Mongolia	1134.4	7016.7	1411.0
辽 宁	Liaoning	3816.2	16234.9	4021.3
吉 林	Jilin	2005.8	8447.3	2892.8
黑龙江	Heilongjiang	1206.4	3285.4	923.4
上 海	Shanghai	8277.0	53798.6	8150.8
江 苏	Jiangsu	35251.6	267407.7	77802.9
浙 江	Zhejiang	20938.6	180786.2	40742.2
安 徽	Anhui	9365.1	49377.0	14441.8
福 建	Fujian	14117.8	82579.1	18202.3
江 西	Jiangxi	8649.2	34235.5	13911.9
山 东	Shangdong	14947.3	86160.1	21309.6
河 南	Henan	13122.6	65956.9	19412.4
湖 北	**Hubei**	**16136.1**	**85268.2**	**26559.5**
湖 南	Hunan	11863.8	67978.8	21235.3
广 东	Guangdong	18429.7	91890.6	19264.2
广 西	Guangxi	5853.2	28695.3	8295.8
海 南	Hainan	391.4	1823.7	299.5
重 庆	Chongqing	8975.0	38122.6	14050.1
四 川	Sichuan	15612.7	67655.2	22572.8
贵 州	Guizhou	4080.2	17167.5	3951.7
云 南	Yunnan	6724.8	20128.8	6238.4
西 藏	Tibet	294.7	477.2	205.1
陕 西	Shaanxi	8501.1	37555.1	7311.2
甘 肃	Gansu	2049.3	10903.3	2382.8
青 海	Qinghai	512.2	927.6	355.7
宁 夏	Ningxia	641.8	2107.7	757.0
新 疆	Xinjiang	2693.1	9881.0	3816.2

附录 1-24 分地区建筑业主要效益指标(2020 年)
Main Benefit Indicators of Construction by Region (2020)

地区	Region	企业个数(个) Number of Enterprises (unit)	从事建筑业活动的从业人员平均人数(万人) Average number of Employed Persons (10 000 Persons)	按建筑业总产值计算的劳动生产率(元/人) Productivity of Labour (Yuan / person)	人均竣工产值(元/人) Per capita Output Value (Yuan / person)	人均施工面积(平方米/人) Per Capita Floor Space under Construction (M2/person)	人均竣工面积(平方米/人) Per Capita Floor Space Completed (sq.m / person)
全国总计	**National Total**	**116716**	**6241.3**	**422906**	**195724**	**239.5**	**61.7**
北京	Beijing	2503	213.6	604213	236319	414.8	44.9
天津	Tianjin	1931	111.6	393295	110636	136.5	22.0
河北	Hebei	2940	98.5	604025	232615	356.3	74.3
山西	Shanxi	3357	121.3	421446	152710	164.5	40.8
内蒙古	Inner Mongolia	1014	24.0	473094	198647	292.6	58.8
辽宁	Liaoning	5638	79.2	481816	238718	205.0	50.8
吉林	Jilin	2511	37.7	532402	284245	224.2	76.8
黑龙江	Heilongjiang	2237	35.3	341327	132972	93.0	26.1
上海	Shanghai	2365	124.0	667640	320068	433.9	65.7
江苏	Jiangsu	11000	974.0	361942	261644	274.6	79.9
浙江	Zhejiang	8004	581.9	359809	189879	310.7	70.0
安徽	Anhui	5692	204.5	458066	165644	241.5	70.6
福建	Fujian	6772	493.5	286101	122018	167.3	36.9
江西	Jiangxi	3751	177.2	488057	219100	193.2	78.5
山东	Shangdong	8081	305.9	488612	209642	281.6	69.7
河南	Henan	7413	310.0	423340	193260	212.8	62.6
湖北	**Hubei**	**4632**	**214.6**	**752086**	**326161**	**397.4**	**123.8**
湖南	Hunan	3335	303.0	391507	186740	224.3	70.1
广东	Guangdong	7587	372.8	494388	170701	246.5	51.7
广西	Guangxi	1913	145.4	402603	179745	197.4	57.1
海南	Hainan	250	7.9	498607	231236	232.3	38.2
重庆	Chongqing	3335	244.5	367064	153834	155.9	57.5
四川	Sichuan	7067	456.2	342207	146641	148.3	49.5
贵州	Guizhou	1770	93.7	435615	152550	183.3	42.2
云南	Yunnan	3449	187.4	358947	120763	107.4	33.3
西藏	Tibet	402	6.3	469423	163839	76.0	32.7
陕西	Shaanxi	3416	168.7	504020	185777	222.7	43.3
甘肃	Gansu	1827	53.2	384944	142681	204.8	44.8
青海	Qinghai	383	9.8	521494	204704	94.4	36.2
宁夏	Ningxia	654	21.2	302575	150893	99.4	35.7
新疆	Xinjiang	1487	64.6	416649	178444	152.9	59.0

附录 1-25　分地区社会消费品零售总额
Total Retail Sales of Consumer Goods by Region

单位:亿元　　(100 million yuan)

地 区	Region	2015	2016	2017	2018	2019	2020
全国总计	**National Total**	**286587.8**	**315806.2**	**347326.7**	**377783.1**	**408017.2**	**391980.6**
北 京	Beijing	12271.9	13134.9	13933.7	14422.3	15063.7	13716.4
天 津	Tianjin	3963.2	4188.1	4210.4	4231.2	4218.2	3582.9
河 北	Hebei	9367.5	10191.4	11138.5	11973.9	12985.5	12705.0
山 西	Shanxi	5345.1	5699.2	6058.5	6523.3	7030.5	6746.3
内蒙古	Inner Mongolia	4103.5	4415.9	4642.6	4852.3	5051.1	4760.5
辽 宁	Liaoning	8364.8	8597.1	8696.4	9112.8	9670.6	8960.9
吉 林	Jilin	3571.7	3812.9	3992.3	4073.8	4212.9	3824.0
黑龙江	Heilongjiang	4471.0	4794.1	5077.4	5275.0	5603.9	5092.3
上 海	Shanghai	11605.7	12588.2	13699.5	14874.8	15847.6	15932.5
江 苏	Jiangsu	26710.1	29612.5	32818.2	35472.6	37672.5	37086.1
浙 江	Zhejiang	18910.7	20916.7	23121.3	25161.9	27343.8	26629.8
安 徽	Anhui	11190.8	12662.5	14328.8	16156.2	17862.1	18334.0
福 建	Fujian	12273.0	13703.0	15393.9	17178.4	18896.8	18626.5
江 西	Jiangxi	6419.8	7198.5	8118.0	9045.7	10068.1	10371.8
山 东	Shangdong	21550.9	23482.1	25527.9	27480.3	29251.2	29248.0
河 南	Henan	15475.8	17274.5	19289.1	21268.0	23476.1	22502.8
湖 北	**Hubei**	**14847.9**	**16601.9**	**18519.7**	**20598.2**	**22722.3**	**17984.9**
湖 南	Hunan	11241.4	12500.0	13793.7	15134.3	16683.9	16258.1
广 东	Guangdong	30326.8	33303.2	36598.6	39767.1	42951.8	40207.9
广 西	Guangxi	5771.5	6349.8	7038.0	7663.5	8200.9	7831.0
海 南	Hainan	1409.4	1547.3	1729.4	1852.7	1951.1	1974.6
重 庆	Chongqing	7667.6	8728.4	9769.4	10705.2	11631.7	11787.2
四 川	Sichuan	13834.4	15519.7	17404.4	19340.7	21343.0	20824.9
贵 州	Guizhou	4925.2	5651.9	6449.4	7105.0	7468.2	7833.4
云 南	Yunnan	6390.8	7222.7	8194.8	9197.3	10158.2	9792.9
西 藏	Tibet	477.1	539.1	618.8	711.8	773.4	745.8
陕 西	Shaanxi	6859.1	7680.7	8611.2	9510.3	10213.0	9605.9
甘 肃	Gansu	2737.1	2984.2	3206.2	3435.6	3700.3	3632.4
青 海	Qinghai	694.6	769.9	842.9	899.9	948.5	877.3
宁 夏	Ningxia	1039.8	1130.6	1253.7	1330.1	1399.4	1301.4
新 疆	Xinjiang	2769.6	3005.2	3249.8	3429.1	3617.0	3062.5

附录 1-26 分地区网上零售额(2020)
Online Retail Sale by Region(2020)

地 区	Region	网上零售额(亿元) Online Retail Sales (100 million yuan)	比上年增长(%) Growth Rata (%)	其中:实物商品网上零售额(亿元) Online Retail Sales in Goods(100 million yuan)	比上年增长(%) Growth Rate (%)
全国总计	**National Total**	**117601.3**	**10.9**	**97590.3**	**14.8**
北 京	Beijing	9704.3	9.5	7704.4	18.2
天 津	Tianjin	1746.5	-23.6	1510.2	-23.3
河 北	Hebei	2735.8	16.0	2505.3	17.8
山 西	Shanxi	684.1	28.1	430.2	35.5
内蒙古	Inner Mongolia	418.2	12.2	267.0	36.5
辽 宁	Liaoning	1500.1	10.1	1271.1	18.1
吉 林	Jilin	495.3	9.1	325.8	14.3
黑龙江	Heilongjiang	575.8	8.2	417.6	13.4
上 海	Shanghai	11991.9	13.8	10128.9	20.7
江 苏	Jiangsu	10602.4	10.0	9232.6	13.9
浙 江	Zhejiang	17799.9	8.6	14068.1	9.6
安 徽	Anhui	2775.8	20.1	2375.1	24.3
福 建	Fujian	5692.8	18.2	5087.5	18.6
江 西	Jiangxi	1641.7	7.7	1375.3	7.5
山 东	Shangdong	4613.3	13.8	4043.4	17.5
河 南	Henan	2744.4	23.7	2280.3	29.2
湖 北	**Hubei**	**2866.6**	**1.6**	**2448.9**	**4.6**
湖 南	Hunan	1977.3	17.7	1591.1	21.6
广 东	Guangdong	25782.2	10.1	22321.0	11.1
广 西	Guangxi	933.6	23.9	614.8	37.7
海 南	Hainan	394.3	21.5	194.1	91.0
重 庆	Chongqing	1180.3	13.1	869.6	25.8
四 川	Sichuan	3743.1	11.1	3087.7	23.7
贵 州	Guizhou	491.8	18.9	316.8	28.6
云 南	Yunnan	906.5	18.6	618.1	41.0
西 藏	Tibet	116.7	34.6	43.3	62.3
陕 西	Shaanxi	1174.4	15.8	905.4	28.7
甘 肃	Gansu	329.7	21.3	170.5	48.5
青 海	Qinghai	116.2	13.0	35.7	28.4
宁 夏	Ningxia	209.4	10.3	63.2	39.5
新 疆	Xinjiang	309.2	27.6	213.0	35.8

附录 1-27 分地区客运量和旅客周转量(2020)

Passenger Traffic and Turnover Volume of Passenger Traffic by Region(2020)

地 区	Region	客运量（万人） Passenger Traffic (10 000 Persons)	#铁路 Railway	#公路 Highway	#水运 Waterway	旅客周转量（亿人公里） Turnover Volume of Passenger Traffic (100 million passenger-kms)	#铁路 Railway	#公路 Highway	#水运 Waterway
全国总计	**National Total**	**966542**	**220350**	**689425**	**14987**	**19251**	**8266.2**	**4641.0**	**33.0**
北 京	Beijing	30936	6388	24548		114	70.7	43.7	
天 津	Tianjin	10602	2636	7926	40	144	96.0	47.5	0.1
河 北	Hebei	17677	7102	10575		604	520.5	83.1	
山 西	Shanxi	12457	4890	7459	108	226	135.7	90.6	0.0
内蒙古	Inner Mongolia	6522	3298	3224		165	115.5	49.4	
辽 宁	Liaoning	33539	7100	26211	228	432	288.5	141.7	1.6
吉 林	Jilin	15308	3832	11438	38	199	120.9	77.9	0.0
黑龙江	Heilongjiang	12297	4590	7608	99	178	123.3	54.2	0.1
上 海	Shanghai	9234	7605	1332	297	115	69.6	44.5	0.5
江 苏	Jiangsu	85310	16084	67664	1562	943	527.6	414.2	1.3
浙 江	Zhejiang	58075	15854	38861	3360	674	464.7	204.8	4.5
安 徽	Anhui	32366	9479	22776	111	697	529.0	168.2	0.2
福 建	Fujian	23163	7539	14882	742	315	223.2	90.6	0.8
江 西	Jiangxi	41913	8157	33643	113	631	450.3	180.9	0.2
山 东	Shangdong	30757	10457	19475	825	596	433.0	159.3	4.0
河 南	Henan	57909	11415	46322	172	927	612.6	314.2	0.3
湖 北	**Hubei**	**30112**	**8148**	**21731**	**233**	**523**	**390.3**	**131.6**	**1.0**
湖 南	Hunan	56376	11392	44144	840	835	607.9	224.8	1.9
广 东	Guangdong	79351	23060	54946	1345	1191	630.3	556.3	4.3
广 西	Guangxi	34947	7838	26771	338	554	301.6	250.9	1.5
海 南	Hainan	7926	2208	4566	1152	75	36.3	35.6	2.7
重 庆	Chongqing	37205	5232	31450	523	271	128.4	140.6	2.1
四 川	Sichuan	57508	11296	45258	954	560	269.4	289.8	1.0
贵 州	Guizhou	40137	5536	33584	1017	524	225.0	295.8	3.7
云 南	Yunnan	24177	4440	19232	505	264	124.5	138.5	0.7
西 藏	Tibet	825	249	576		27	12.3	14.6	
陕 西	Shaanxi	36798	7044	29581	173	453	303.5	148.8	0.3
甘 肃	Gansu	26686	4153	22478	55	379	237.9	140.8	0.1
青 海	Qinghai	4135	762	3314	59	89	52.1	36.5	0.1
宁 夏	Ningxia	3560	558	2903	99	53	24.2	28.2	0.1
新 疆	Xinjiang	6960	2012	4948		185	141.6	43.4	
不分地区	Not Classified by Region	41778				6311			

注：不分地区合计数为民航完成数。

Note: The total passenger traffic not classified by region refers to that completed by civil aviation.

附录 1-28 分地区货运量和货物周转量(2020)
Freight Traffic and Turnover Volume of Freight Traffic by Region(2020)

地区	Region	货运量(万吨) Freight Traffic (10 000 tons)	#铁路 Railway	#公路 Highway	#水运 Waterway	货物周转量(亿吨公里) Turnover Volume of Freight Traffic (100 million ton-km)	#铁路 Railway	#公路 Highway	#水运 Waterway
全国总计	**National Total**	**4735566**	**445761**	**3426413**	**761630**	**202069**	**30371.8**	**60171.9**	**105834.4**
北京	Beijing	22203	414	21789		1033	767.1	265.7	
天津	Tianjin	52519	11124	32261	9134	2600	518.2	640.1	1442.0
河北	Hebei	247323	30806	211942	4575	13730	4972.0	8103.3	654.7
山西	Shanxi	190232	92002	98206	24	5712	2926.7	2785.0	0.1
内蒙古	Inner Mongolia	170547	61545	109002		4431	2542.7	1888.8	
辽宁	Liaoning	167341	23975	138569	4797	5421	1297.3	2548.3	1575.8
吉林	Jilin	44848	6574	38274		1865	570.2	1294.8	
黑龙江	Heilongjiang	48662	12603	35521	538	1585	839.6	694.0	51.1
上海	Shanghai	138839	494	46051	92294	32795	15.8	684.6	32094.6
江苏	Jiangsu	275209	7118	174624	93467	10890	327.4	3524.5	7038.6
浙江	Zhejiang	300276	4500	189582	106194	12324	231.2	2210.0	9883.1
安徽	Anhui	374503	7735	243529	123239	10242	733.7	3412.2	6095.8
福建	Fujian	140698	4543	91137	45018	9014	180.9	1021.7	7811.7
江西	Jiangxi	157149	4553	141899	10697	4011	497.3	3247.1	266.4
山东	Shangdong	316831	31393	267230	18208	10377	1602.5	6784.4	1990.1
河南	Henan	219939	11157	193632	15150	8833	2159.5	5572.6	1101.1
湖北	**Hubei**	**160422**	**5363**	**114346**	**40713**	**5295**	**915.1**	**1639.9**	**2739.9**
湖南	Hunan	200878	4592	176442	19844	2602	856.4	1350.6	395.3
广东	Guangdong	344439	9510	231170	103759	27211	281.8	2524.2	24404.8
广西	Guangxi	187444	9269	145323	32852	4160	754.2	1486.9	1918.5
海南	Hainan	20670	1135	6853	12682	3683	16.8	41.3	3624.9
重庆	Chongqing	121692	2194	99679	19819	3527	200.9	1055.5	2271.0
四川	Sichuan	171896	7771	157598	6527	2861	951.8	1617.7	291.8
贵州	Guizhou	86444	5801	79412	1231	1265	617.8	609.8	37.5
云南	Yunnan	121058	4919	115620	519	1580	471.0	1101.5	7.2
西藏	Tibet	4091	52	4039		157	39.8	116.7	
陕西	Shaanxi	165260	49056	116057	147	3697	1865.6	1831.1	0.6
甘肃	Gansu	67239	5966	61272	1	2517	1496.4	1020.3	0.0
青海	Qinghai	14291	3456	10835		415	290.3	124.6	
宁夏	Ningxia	42850	8634	34216		698	214.6	483.7	
新疆	Xinjiang	57814	17509	40305		1708	1217.0	491.1	
不分地区	Not Classified by Region	101960			201	5828			137.8

注:不分地区合计中包括管道运输企业、民航运输企业等完成量。货运量和货物周转量的全国总计等于分省数与不分地区数据之和。

Note: The total amount of not classified by region includes pipeline transportation enterprises, civil aviation transportation enterprises and so on. The national total of freight volume and freight turnover volume is equal to the sum of provincial and regional data.

中国统计出版社有限公司最新图书简目

（仅供参考，以实际出版为准）

统计资料

中国统计年鉴	中国统计摘要	中国第三产业统计年鉴
中国第三次全国农业普查综合资料	国际统计年鉴	金砖国家联合统计手册
中国-东盟国家统计手册	中国农村统计年鉴	中国县域统计年鉴
中国农产品价格调查年鉴	中国城市统计年鉴	中国价格统计年鉴
中国贸易外经统计年鉴	中国零售和餐饮连锁企业统计年鉴	中国商品交易市场统计年鉴
大中型批发零售和住宿餐饮企业统计年鉴	中国住户调查年鉴	中国工业统计年鉴
中国环境统计年鉴	中国能源统计年鉴	中国建筑业统计年鉴
中国房地产统计年鉴	中国投资领域统计年鉴	长江经济带发展统计年鉴
中国人口和就业统计年鉴	中国劳动统计年鉴	中国社会统计年鉴
中国科技统计年鉴	中国高技术产业统计年鉴	全国企业创新调查年鉴
中国文化及相关产业统计年鉴	中国妇女儿童状况统计资料	中国青年发展状况统计年鉴
中国基本单位统计年鉴	中国教育统计年鉴	中国教育经费统计年鉴
中国民族统计年鉴	中国残疾人事业统计年鉴	中国电力统计年鉴

省级综合统计年鉴系列

北京 天津 河北 山西 内蒙古 辽宁 吉林 黑龙江 上海 江苏 浙江 安徽 福建 江西 山东 河南 湖北 湖南 广东 广西 海南 重庆 四川 贵州 云南 西藏 陕西 甘肃 青海 宁夏 新疆 新疆生产建设兵团

市(县)级综合统计年鉴系列

滨海新区 石家庄 唐山 邯郸 邢台 保定 承德 沧州 衡水 太原 大同 晋城 晋中 长治 忻州 朔州 临汾 运城 阳泉 吕梁 呼和浩特 包头 鄂尔多斯 赤峰 大连 长春 四平 延吉 延边 哈尔滨 齐齐哈尔 黑龙江垦区 浦东新区 南京 无锡 徐州 常州 苏州 南通 淮安 盐城 扬州 镇江 宿迁 江阴 丹阳 海门 张家港 通州 如东 杭州 宁波 绍兴 台州 温州 金华 嘉兴 湖州 丽水 舟山 合肥 安庆 福州 厦门 漳州 宁德 龙岩 莆田 泉州 三明 南平 思明 南昌 上饶 抚州 赣州 九江 景德镇 宁都 济南 青岛 枣庄 潍坊 聊城 郑州 洛阳 三门峡 南阳 商丘 平顶山 信阳 济源 武汉 宜昌 十堰 荆州 荆门 咸宁 黄冈 长沙 广州 东莞 惠州 深圳 汕尾 珠海 南宁 桂林 柳州 防城港 贵港 梧州 玉林 钦州 海口 三亚 儋州 成都 贵阳 毕节 黔南 昆明 文山 德宏 西安 安康 延安 汉中 渭南 商洛 榆林 银川 兰州 庆阳 乌鲁木齐

调查年鉴系列

天津 内蒙古 上海 河南 湖北 湖南 广西 重庆 四川 云南 甘肃 宁夏 南宁 桂林 贵港 昆明

统计方法应用/实用手册

Python数据分析基础（第二版） 非参数统计（第五版） 现代金融投资统计分析（第四版）

国民经济核算初级教程（第二版） 国民经济核算教程（第五版） 概率统计基础

全国统计专业技术资格考试系列考试用书：统计业务知识（第四版修订版） 统计业务知识学习指导与习题

全国统计专业技术资格考试系列考试用书：统计相关知识（第四版） 统计相关知识学习指导与习题

统计通俗读物/统计科普图书

领导干部统计知识问答（第二版） 统计公文写作及会议办理实用手册 大数据在统计工作中的应用案例汇编

中国国民经济核算知识问答（修订版） 地区生产总值核算国际比较研究 新中国统计制度方法的发展与改革

重点图书

第七次全国人口普查年鉴	第四次全国经济普查地图集	中国经济普查年鉴2018
新编英汉汉英统计大词典	中国国民经济核算体系2016	国民经济行业分类注释
挑大学选专业2020—考研择校指南	挑大学选专业2020—高考志愿填报指南	中华医学统计百科全书

发行部电话：（010）63376907 63376908 63376909 同楫行书店电话：（010）68783171 68783172

地址：北京市丰台区西三环南路甲6号 邮政编码：100073 网址：http://www.zgtjcbs.com